Illustrated Series™

Microsoft® Office 365®
Word 2021

Comprehensive

Cengage

Australia • Brazil • Canada • Mexico • Singapore • United Kingdom • United States

Cengage

Illustrated Series® Collection Microsoft® Office 365® & Word 2021 Comprehensive
Carol Cram

SVP, Product: Erin Joyner

VP, Product: Thais Alencar

Product Director: Mark Santee

Senior Product Manager: Amy Savino

Product Assistant: Ciara Horne

Learning Designer: Zenya Molnar

Content Manager: Grant Davis

Digital Delivery Quality Partner: Jim Vaughey

Developmental Editor: Karen Porter

VP, Product Marketing: Jason Sakos

Director, Product Marketing: Danaë April

Executive Product Marketing Manager: Jill Staut

IP Analyst: Ann Hoffman

IP Project Manager: Ilakkiya Jayagopi

Production Service: Lumina Datamatics, Inc.

Designer: Erin Griffin

Cover Image Source: 4khz/Getty Images 472623756

Mac Users: If you're working through this product using a Mac, some of the steps may vary. Additional information for Mac users is included with the Data files for this product.

Disclaimer: This text is intended for instructional purposes only; data is fictional and does not belong to any real persons or companies.

Disclaimer: The material in this text was written using Microsoft Windows 10 and Office 365 Professional Plus and was Quality Assurance tested before the publication date. As Microsoft continually updates the Windows 10 operating system and Office 365, your software experience may vary slightly from what is presented in the printed text.

For product information and technology assistance, contact us at **Cengage Customer & Sales Support, 1-800-354-9706 or support.cengage.com.**

For permission to use material from this text or product, submit all requests online at **www.copyright.com.**

Library of Congress Control Number: 2022904921

Student Edition ISBN: 978-0-357-67516-8
Looseleaf ISBN: 978-0-357-67517-5*
*Looseleaf available as part of a digital bundle

Cengage
200 Pier 4 Boulevard
Boston, MA 02210
USA

Cengage is a leading provider of customized learning solutions with employees residing in nearly 40 different countries and sales in more than 125 countries around the world. Find your local representative at **www.cengage.com.**

To learn more about Cengage platforms and services, register or access your online learning solution, or purchase materials for your course, visit **www.cengage.com.**

Notice to the Reader

Publisher does not warrant or guarantee any of the products described herein or perform any independent analysis in connection with any of the product information contained herein. Publisher does not assume, and expressly disclaims, any obligation to obtain and include information other than that provided to it by the manufacturer. The reader is expressly warned to consider and adopt all safety precautions that might be indicated by the activities described herein and to avoid all potential hazards. By following the instructions contained herein, the reader willingly assumes all risks in connection with such instructions. The publisher makes no representations or warranties of any kind, including but not limited to, the warranties of fitness for particular purpose or merchantability, nor are any such representations implied with respect to the material set forth herein, and the publisher takes no responsibility with respect to such material. The publisher shall not be liable for any special, consequential, or exemplary damages resulting, in whole or part, from the readers' use of, or reliance upon, this material.

Printed in the United States of America
Print Number: 01 Print Year: 2022

Brief Contents

Getting to Know Microsoft Office Versions OFF-1

Using SAM Projects and Textbook Projects SAM-1

Word 2021

Module 1: Creating Documents with Word .... WD 1-1

Module 2: Editing and Formatting Documents .... WD 2-1

Module 3: Formatting Text and Graphics .... WD 3-1

Module 4: Formatting Tables and Documents .... WD 4-1

Module 5: Working with Styles, Themes, and Building Blocks .... WD 5-1

Module 6: Merging Word Documents .... WD 6-1

Module 7: Illustrating Documents with Graphics .... WD 7-1

Module 8: Integrating with Other Programs and Collaborating .... WD 8-1

Module 9: Developing Multi-Page Documents .... WD 9-1

Module 10: Building Forms .... WD 10-1

Module 11: Automating and Customizing Word .... WD 11-1

Index .... Index 1

Contents

Getting to Know Microsoft Office Versions OFF-1

Using SAM Projects and Textbook Projects SAM-1

Word 2021

Module 1: Creating Documents with Word .... WD 1-1

Understand Word Processing Software .... WD 1-2
Planning a document
Explore the Word Window .... WD 1-4
Start a Document .... WD 1-6
Save a Document .... WD 1-8
Using keyboard shortcuts
Select Text .... WD 1-10
Format Text Using the Mini Toolbar and the Ribbon .... WD 1-12
View and Navigate a Document .... WD 1-14
Using Word document views
Cut and Paste Text .... WD 1-16
Highlighting text in a document
Using the Undo, Redo, and Repeat commands
Copy and Paste Text .... WD 1-18
Splitting the document window to copy and move items in a long document
Copying and moving items between documents
Format with Fonts .... WD 1-20
Applying shadows and other text effects to text
Set Document Margins .... WD 1-22
Changing orientation, margin settings, and paper size
Add Bullets and Numbering .... WD 1-24
Insert a Graphic .... WD 1-26
Enhancing pictures with styles and effects
Apply a Theme .... WD 1-28
Practice .... WD 1-30

Module 2: Editing and Formatting Documents .... WD 2-1

Insert Comments .... WD 2-2
Insert Comments (Continued) .... WD 2-4
Inking comments in Word
Find and Replace Text .... WD 2-6
Navigating a document using the Navigation pane and the Go to command
Check Spelling and Grammar .... WD 2-8
Searching for information
Inserting text with AutoCorrect

Research Information ..... WD 2-10
Reading a document aloud using Word
Using a add-ins for Word
Change Line Spacing and Indents ..... WD 2-12
Apply Styles to Text ..... WD 2-14
Changing the Style set
Insert Page Numbers and Page Breaks ..... WD 2-16
Add Headers and Footers ..... WD 2-18
Add Footnotes and Endnotes ..... WD 2-20
Insert Citations ..... WD 2-22
Create a Bibliography ..... WD 2-24
Finding and citing sources with the Word Researcher
Inspect a Document ..... WD 2-26
Practice ..... WD 2-28

Module 3: Formatting Text and Graphics ..... WD 3-1
Use the Format Painter ..... WD 3-2
Clearing formatting from text
Work with Tabs ..... WD 3-4
Add Borders and Shading ..... WD 3-6
Underlining text
Insert a Table ..... WD 3-8
Insert and Delete Rows and Columns ..... WD 3-10
Apply a Table Style ..... WD 3-12
Insert Online Pictures ..... WD 3-14
Size and Scale a Graphic ..... WD 3-16
Draw and Format Shapes ..... WD 3-18
Correcting pictures, changing colors, and applying artistic effects
Adding alt text and checking documents for accessibility issues
Draw and Format Shapes (Continued) ..... WD 3-20
Enhancing graphic objects with styles and effects
Arrange Graphic Objects ..... WD 3-22
Creating an illustration in a drawing canvas
Create SmartArt Graphics ..... WD 3-24
Practice ..... WD 3-26

Module 4: Formatting Tables and Documents ..... WD 4-1
Modify Character Spacing ..... WD 4-2
Researching job roles and job skills with the Resume Assistant
Work with Indents ..... WD 4-4
Creating multilevel lists
Insert a Section Break ..... WD 4-6
Using sections to vary the layout of a document
Insert a Section Break (Continued) ..... WD 4-8
Adding a custom header or footer to the gallery
Modify a Table ..... WD 4-10
Copying and moving rows and columns

Modify Rows and Columns....WD 4-12
Setting advanced table properties
Sort Table Data....WD 4-14
Sorting lists and paragraphs
Split and Merge Cells....WD 4-16
Changing cell margins
Using tables to lay out a page
Perform Calculations in Tables....WD 4-18
Working with formulas
Modify Table Style Options....WD 4-20
Customize a Table Format....WD 4-22
Drawing a table
Insert a Cover Page....WD 4-24
Practice....WD 4-26

Module 5: Working with Styles, Themes, and Building Blocks....WD 5-1
Add Hyperlinks....WD 5-2
Sharing documents from Word and checking compatibility
Modify Page Margins....WD 5-4
Changing vertical alignment
Create Paragraph Styles....WD 5-6
Saving a document as a webpage
Format with Themes....WD 5-8
Changing the style set
Changing the default theme
Customize a Theme....WD 5-10
Insert Quick Parts....WD 5-12
Creating customized bullet characters
Create Building Blocks....WD 5-14
Inserting icons in a document
Create Building Blocks (continued)....WD 5-16
Renaming a building block and editing other properties
Insert Building Blocks....WD 5-18
Use a Document Template....WD 5-20
Work with PDF Files in Word....WD 5-22
Opening non-native files directly in Word
Practice....WD 5-24

Module 6: Merging Word Documents....WD 6-1
Understand Mail Merge....WD 6-2
Create a Main Document....WD 6-4
Using a mail merge template
Design a Data Source....WD 6-6
Merging with an Outlook data source
Enter and Edit Records....WD 6-8
Add Merge Fields....WD 6-10
Matching fields
Work with Merge Rules....WD 6-12
Merge Data....WD 6-14
Opening Merge Files

Create Labels .... WD 6-16
Printing individual envelopes and labels
Sort and Filter Records .... WD 6-18
Inserting individual merge fields
Practice .... WD 6-20

Module 7: Illustrating Documents with Graphics .... WD 7-1
Use the Office Clipboard .... WD 7-2
Use the Office Clipboard (Continued) .... WD 7-4
Create Sections and Columns .... WD 7-6
Changing page layout settings for a section
Create SmartArt Graphics .... WD 7-8
Inserting a picture into a SmartArt shape
Modify SmartArt Graphics .... WD 7-10
Crop and Rotate a Picture .... WD 7-12
Position a Graphic .... WD 7-14
Position a Graphic (Continued) .... WD 7-16
Inserting and Editing 3D Models
Create WordArt .... WD 7-18
Create a Text Box .... WD 7-20
Linking text boxes
Insert a Word File .... WD 7-22
Configuring line numbers
Inserting online videos and online pictures in a document
Practice .... WD 7-24

Module 8: Integrating with Other Programs and Collaborating .... WD 8-1
Embed an Excel File .... WD 8-2
Understanding Object Linking and Embedding
Insert Objects .... WD 8-4
Publishing a blog directly from Word
Link an Excel Chart .... WD 8-6
Using the Object dialog box to create a linked file
Link a PowerPoint Slide .... WD 8-8
Creating a PowerPoint presentation from a Word outline
Manage Document Links .... WD 8-10
Create Charts .... WD 8-12
Format and Edit Charts .... WD 8-14
Track Changes .... WD 8-16
Using Paste and Paste All with tracked changes
Work with Tracked Changes .... WD 8-18
Manage Reviewers .... WD 8-20
Compare Documents .... WD 8-22
Practice .... WD 8-24

Module 9: Developing Multi-Page Documents .... WD 9-1
Build a Document in Outline View .... WD 9-2
Work in Outline View .... WD 9-4
Navigate a Document .... WD 9-6
Using bookmarks

Create and Modify Screenshots .... WD 9-8
Create and Modify Screenshots (Continued) .... WD 9-10
Use Advanced Find and Replace Options .... WD 9-12
Add and Modify Captions .... WD 9-14
Table of Authorities
Insert a Table of Contents .... WD 9-16
Mark Text for an Index .... WD 9-18
Generate an Index .... WD 9-20
Insert Footers in Multiple Sections .... WD 9-22
Insert Footers in Multiple Sections (Continued) .... WD 9-24
Using text flow options
Insert Headers in Multiple Sections .... WD 9-26
Understanding headers, footers, and sections
Insert Headers in Multiple Sections (Continued) .... WD 9-28
Finalize a Multi-Page Document .... WD 9-30
Finalize a Multi-Page Document (Continued) .... WD 9-32
Using Advanced Print Options
Work with Equations .... WD 9-34
More equation options
Create Master Documents and Subdocuments .... WD 9-36
Inserting endnotes
Practice .... WD 9-38

Module 10: Building Forms .... WD 10-1
Convert Tables and Text .... WD 10-2
Construct a Form Template .... WD 10-4
Editing a Template
Add Text Content Controls .... WD 10-6
Add Date Picker and Picture Content Controls .... WD 10-8
Add Repeating Section and Check Box Content Controls .... WD 10-10
Add Building Block Content Controls .... WD 10-12
Add Drop-Down Content Controls .... WD 10-14
Insert Legacy Tools Controls .... WD 10-16
Using ActiveX controls
Format and Protect a Form .... WD 10-18
Edit a Form .... WD 10-20
Protecting documents with formatting and editing restrictions
Fill in a Form as a User .... WD 10-22
Practice .... WD 10-24

Module 11: Automating and Customizing Word .... WD 11-1
Manage Pages .... WD 11-2
Edit Pictures .... WD 11-4
Applying 3-D and 3-D Rotation effects to a picture
Use Layering Options .... WD 11-6
Arrange and Compress Graphics .... WD 11-8

Create Character Styles ..... WD 11-10
Identifying paragraph, character, and linked styles
Manage Styles ..... WD 11-12
More ways to manage styles
Plan a Macro ..... WD 11-14
Record Macro Steps ..... WD 11-16
Pausing when recording a macro
Run a Macro ..... WD 11-18
Finding keyboard shortcuts
Edit a Macro in Visual Basic ..... WD 11-20
Creating a Macro in Visual Basic
Customize Word ..... WD 11-22
Copying a Macro to Another Document
Sign a Document Digitally ..... WD 11-24
Customizing the Quick Access toolbar
Acquiring a Digital ID
Practice ..... WD 11-26

Index ..... Index 1

Illustrated Series™

Microsoft® Office 365®
Word 2021

Comprehensive

Getting to Know Microsoft Office Versions

Cengage is proud to bring you the next edition of Microsoft Office. This edition was designed to provide a robust learning experience that is not dependent upon a specific version of Office.

Microsoft supports several versions of Office:

- **Office 365:** A cloud-based subscription service that delivers Microsoft's most up-to-date, feature-rich, modern productivity tools direct to your device. There are variations of Office 365 for business, educational, and personal use. Office 365 offers extra online storage and cloud-connected features, as well as updates with the latest features, fixes, and security updates.
- **Office 2021:** Microsoft's "on-premises" version of the Office apps, available for both PCs and Macs, offered as a static, one-time purchase and outside of the subscription model.
- **Office Online:** A free, simplified version of Office web applications (Word, Excel, PowerPoint, and OneNote) that facilitates creating and editing files collaboratively.

Office 365 (the subscription model) and Office 2021 (the one-time purchase model) had only slight differences between them at the time this content was developed. Over time, Office 365's cloud interface will continuously update, offering new application features and functions, while Office 2021 will remain static. Therefore, your onscreen experience may differ from what you see in this product. For example, the more advanced features and functionalities covered in this product may not be available in Office Online or may have updated from what you see in Office 2021.

For more information on the differences between Office 365, Office 2021, and Office Online, please visit the Microsoft Support site.

Cengage is committed to providing high-quality learning solutions for you to gain the knowledge and skills that will empower you throughout your educational and professional careers.

Thank you for using our product, and we look forward to exploring the future of Microsoft Office with you!

Using SAM Projects and Textbook Projects

SAM Projects allow you to actively apply the skills you learned live in Microsoft Word, Excel, PowerPoint, or Access. Become a more productive student and use these skills throughout your career.

To complete SAM Textbook Projects, please follow these steps:

SAM Textbook Projects allow you to complete a project as you follow along with the steps in the textbook. As you read the module, look for icons that indicate when you should download your SAM Start file(s) and when to upload the final project file to SAM for grading.

Everything you need to complete this project is provided within SAM. You can launch the eBook directly from SAM, which will allow you to take notes, highlight, and create a custom study guide, or you can use a print textbook or your mobile app. Download IOS or Download Android.

To get started, launch your SAM Project assignment from SAM, MindTap, or a link within your LMS.

Step 1: Download Files

- Click the "Download All" button or the individual links to download your **Start File** and **Support File(s)** (when available). You must use the SAM Start file.
- Click the Instructions link to launch the eBook (or use the print textbook or mobile app).
- Disregard any steps in the textbook that ask you to create a new file or to use a file from a location outside of SAM.
- Look for the SAM Download icon to begin working with your start file.
- Follow the module's step-by-step instructions until you reach the SAM Upload icon .
- Save and close the file.

Step 2: Save Work to SAM

- Ensure you rename your project file to match the Expected File Name.
- Upload your in-progress or completed file to SAM. You can download the file to continue working or submit it for grading in the next step.

Step 3: Submit for Grading

- Upload the completed file to SAM for immediate feedback and to view the available Reports.
    - The **Graded Summary Report** provides a detailed list of project steps, your score, and feedback to aid you in revising and resubmitting the project.
    - The **Study Guide Report** provides your score for each project step and links to the associated training and textbook pages.
- If additional attempts are allowed, use your reports to assist with revising and resubmitting your project.
- To re-submit the project, download the file saved in step 2.
- Edit, save, and close the file, then re-upload and submit it again.

<u>For all other SAM Projects, please follow these steps:</u>

To get started, launch your SAM Project assignment from SAM, MindTap, or a link within your LMS.

Step 1: Download Files

- Click the "Download All" button or the individual links to download your **Instruction File**, **Start File**, and **Support File(s)** (when available). You <u>must</u> use the SAM Start file.
- Open the Instruction file and follow the step-by-step instructions. Ensure you rename your project file to match the Expected File Name (change _1 to _2 at the end of the file name).

Step 2: Save Work to SAM

- Upload your in-progress or completed file to SAM. You can download the file to continue working or submit it for grading in the next step.

Step 3: Submit for Grading

- Upload the completed file to SAM for immediate feedback and to view available Reports.
    - The **Graded Summary Report** provides a detailed list of project steps, your score, and feedback to aid you in revising and resubmitting the project.
    - The **Study Guide Report** provides your score for each project step and links to the associated training and textbook pages.
- If additional attempts are allowed, use your reports to assist with revising and resubmitting your project.
- To re-submit the project, download the file saved in step 2.
- Edit, save, and close the file, then re-upload and submit it again.

For additional tips to successfully complete your SAM Projects, please view our Common Student Errors Infographic.

Creating Documents with Word

CASE You have been hired to work at JCL Talent, Inc., a business support services company that provides employment and recruitment services for employers and job seekers. Shortly after reporting to your new office, Dawn Lapointe, Director of JCL Talent – Technical Careers division, asks you to use Word to create a memo to staff and a tip sheet for job seekers.

Module Objectives

After completing this module, you will be able to:

- Understand word processing software
- Explore the Word window
- Start a document
- Save a document
- Select text
- Format text using the Mini toolbar and the Ribbon
- View and navigate a document
- Cut and paste text
- Copy and paste text
- Format with fonts
- Set document margins
- Add bullets and numbering
- Insert a graphic
- Apply a theme

Files You Will Need

IL_WD_1-1.docx
Support_WD_1-2.jpg
IL_WD_1-3.docx
Support_WD_1-4.jpg
IL_WD_1-5.docx
Support_WD_1-6.jpg

Understand Word Processing Software

Learning Outcomes
- Identify the features of Word
- State the benefits of using a word processing program

A **word processing program** is a software program that includes tools for entering, editing, and formatting text and graphics. Microsoft Word is a powerful word processing program that allows you to create and enhance a wide range of documents quickly and easily. FIGURE 1-1 shows the first page of a report created using Word and illustrates some of the Word features you can use to enhance your documents. The electronic files you create using Word are called **documents**. One of the benefits of using Word is that document files can be stored on a hard disk, flash drive, or other physical storage device, or to OneDrive or another Cloud storage place, making them easy to transport, share, and revise.

CASE *Before beginning your memo, you explore the editing and formatting features available in Word.*

DETAILS

You can use Word to accomplish the following tasks:

- **Type and edit text**
  The Word editing tools make it simple to insert and delete text in a document. You can add text to the middle of an existing paragraph; replace text with other text; undo an editing change; and correct typing, spelling, and grammatical errors with ease.
- **Copy and move text from one location to another**
  Using the more advanced editing features of Word, you can copy or move text from one location and insert it in a different location in a document. You also can copy and move text between documents. This means you don't have to retype text that is already entered in a document.
- **Format text and paragraphs with fonts, colors, and other elements**
  The sophisticated formatting tools in Word allow you to make the text in your documents come alive. You can change the size, style, and color of text; add lines and shading to paragraphs; and enhance lists with bullets and numbers. Creatively formatting text helps to highlight important ideas in your documents.
- **Format and design pages**
  The page-formatting features in Word give you power to design attractive newsletters, create powerful résumés, and produce documents such as research papers, business cards, brochures, and reports. You can change paper size, organize text in columns, and control the layout of text and graphics on each page of a document. For quick results, Word includes preformatted cover pages, pull quotes, and headers and footers, as well as galleries of coordinated text, table, and graphic styles. If you are writing a research paper, Word makes it easy to manage reference sources and create footnotes, endnotes, and bibliographies.
- **Enhance documents with tables, charts, graphics, screenshots, and videos**
  Using the powerful graphics tools in Word, you can spice up your documents with pictures, videos, photographs, screenshots, lines, preset quick shapes, and diagrams. You also can illustrate your documents with tables and charts to help convey your message in a visually interesting way.
- **Use Mail Merge to create form letters and mailing labels**
  The Word Mail Merge feature allows you to send personalized form letters to many different people. You can also use Mail Merge to create mailing labels, directories, email messages, and other types of documents.
- **Share documents securely**
  The security features in Word make it quick and easy to remove comments, tracked changes, and unwanted personal information from your files before you share them with others. You can also add a password or a digital signature to a document and convert a file to a format suitable for publishing on the web.

FIGURE 1-1: A report created using Word

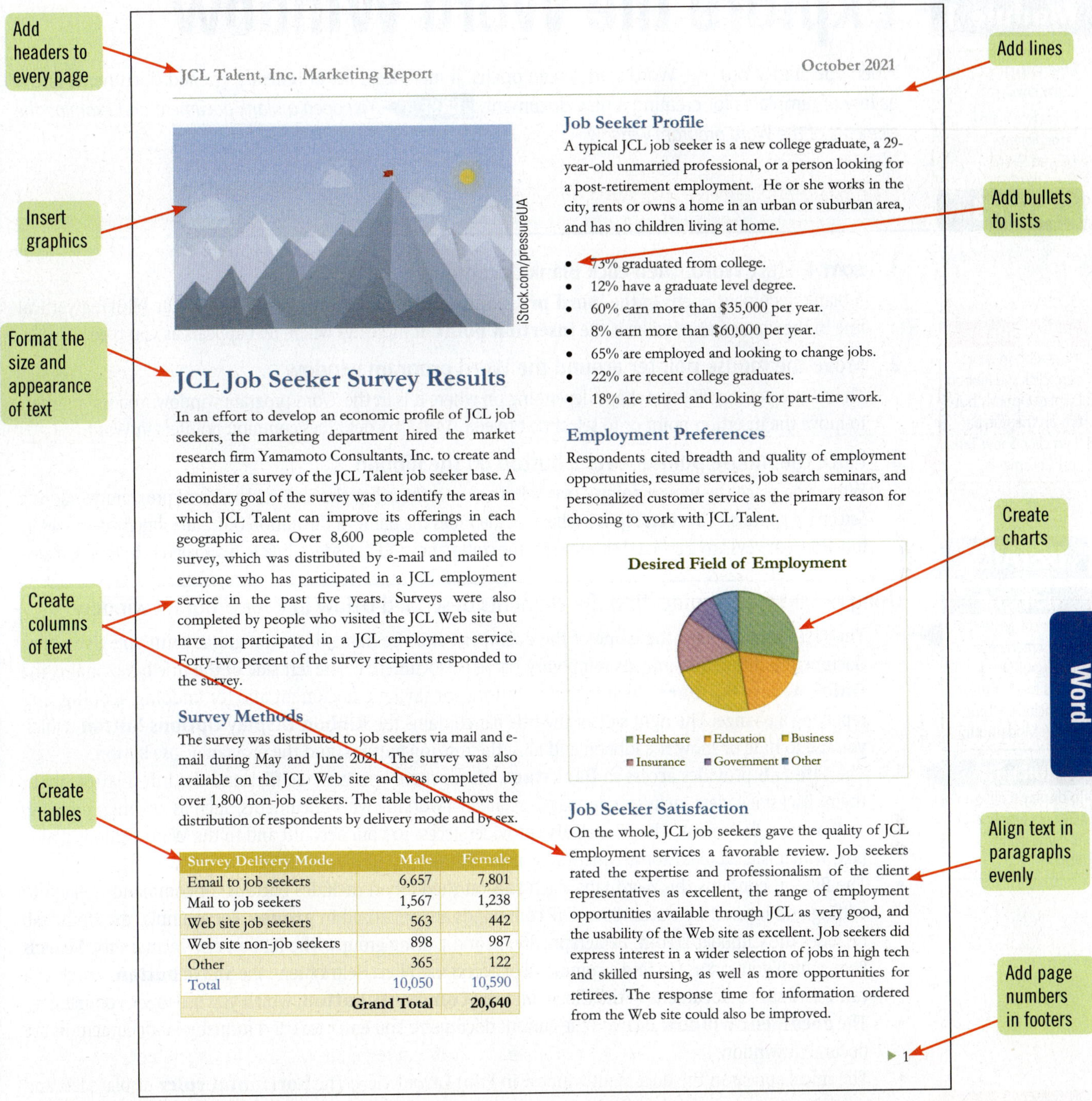

JCL Talent, Inc. Marketing Report October 2021

JCL Job Seeker Survey Results

In an effort to develop an economic profile of JCL job seekers, the marketing department hired the market research firm Yamamoto Consultants, Inc. to create and administer a survey of the JCL Talent job seeker base. A secondary goal of the survey was to identify the areas in which JCL Talent can improve its offerings in each geographic area. Over 8,600 people completed the survey, which was distributed by e-mail and mailed to everyone who has participated in a JCL employment service in the past five years. Surveys were also completed by people who visited the JCL Web site but have not participated in a JCL employment service. Forty-two percent of the survey recipients responded to the survey.

Survey Methods

The survey was distributed to job seekers via mail and e-mail during May and June 2021. The survey was also available on the JCL Web site and was completed by over 1,800 non-job seekers. The table below shows the distribution of respondents by delivery mode and by sex.

Survey Delivery Mode	Male	Female
Email to job seekers	6,657	7,801
Mail to job seekers	1,567	1,238
Web site job seekers	563	442
Web site non-job seekers	898	987
Other	365	122
Total	10,050	10,590
	Grand Total	20,640

Job Seeker Profile

A typical JCL job seeker is a new college graduate, a 29-year-old unmarried professional, or a person looking for a post-retirement employment. He or she works in the city, rents or owns a home in an urban or suburban area, and has no children living at home.

- 73% graduated from college.
- 12% have a graduate level degree.
- 60% earn more than $35,000 per year.
- 8% earn more than $60,000 per year.
- 65% are employed and looking to change jobs.
- 22% are recent college graduates.
- 18% are retired and looking for part-time work.

Employment Preferences

Respondents cited breadth and quality of employment opportunities, resume services, job search seminars, and personalized customer service as the primary reason for choosing to work with JCL Talent.

Job Seeker Satisfaction

On the whole, JCL job seekers gave the quality of JCL employment services a favorable review. Job seekers rated the expertise and professionalism of the client representatives as excellent, the range of employment opportunities available through JCL as very good, and the usability of the Web site as excellent. Job seekers did express interest in a wider selection of jobs in high tech and skilled nursing, as well as more opportunities for retirees. The response time for information ordered from the Web site could also be improved.

1

Planning a document

Before you create a new document, it's a good idea to spend time planning it. Identify the message you want to convey, the audience for your document, and the elements, such as tables or charts, you want to include. You should also think about the tone and look of your document—are you writing a business letter, which should be written in a pleasant, but serious, tone and have a formal appearance, or are you creating a flyer that must be colorful, eye-catching, and fun to read? The purpose and audience for your document determine the appropriate design. Planning the layout and design of a document involves deciding how to organize the text, selecting the fonts to use, identifying the graphics to include, and selecting the formatting elements that will enhance the message and appeal of the document. For longer documents, such as newsletters, it can be useful to sketch the layout and design of each page before you begin.

Explore the Word Window

Learning Outcomes
- Create a blank document
- Open Word

When you start Word, the Word start screen opens. It includes a list of recently opened documents and a gallery of templates for creating a new document. **CASE** *You open a blank document and examine the elements of the Word program window.*

STEPS

1. **sam Start Word, then click Blank document**
   A blank document opens in the **Word program window**, as shown in FIGURE 1-2. The blinking vertical line in the document window is the **insertion point**. It indicates where text appears as you type.
2. **Move the mouse pointer around the Word program window**
   The mouse pointer changes shape depending on where it is in the Word program window. You use pointers to move the insertion point or to select text to edit. TABLE 1-1 describes common pointers in Word.
3. **Place the mouse pointer over a button on the Ribbon**
   When you place the mouse pointer over a button or some other elements of the Word program window, a ScreenTip appears. A **ScreenTip** is a label that identifies the name of the button or feature, briefly describes its function, conveys any keyboard shortcut for the command, and includes a link to associated help topics, if any.

TROUBLE
If the Ribbon is hidden, click the Ribbon Display Options button on the title bar, then click Show Tabs and Commands.

DETAILS

Using FIGURE 1-2 as a guide, find the elements described below in your program window:

- The **title bar** displays the name of the document and the name of the program. Until you give a new document a different name, its temporary name is Document1. The left side of the title bar contains the **Quick Access toolbar**, which includes buttons for saving a document and for undoing, redoing, and repeating a change. The right side of the title bar contains the **Ribbon Display Options button**, which you use to hide or show the Ribbon and tabs, the resizing buttons, and the program Close button.
- The **File tab** provides access to **Backstage view** where you manage files and the information about them. Backstage view includes commands related to working with documents, such as opening, printing, and saving a document. The File tab also provides access to your account and to the Word Options dialog box, which is used to customize the way you use Word.
- The Ribbon contains the Word tabs. Each **tab** on the Ribbon includes buttons for commands related to editing and formatting documents. The commands are organized in **groups**. For example, the Home tab includes the Clipboard, Font, Paragraph, Styles, and Editing groups. The Ribbon also includes the **Search box**, which you can use to find a command or access the Word Help system, the **Share button**, which you can use to save a document to the Cloud, and the **Comments button**, which you use to see comments.
- The **document window** displays the current document. You enter text and format your document in the document window.
- The rulers appear in the document window in Print Layout view. The **horizontal ruler** displays left and right document margins as well as the tab settings and paragraph indents, if any, for the paragraph in which the insertion point is located. The **vertical ruler** displays the top and bottom document margins.
- The vertical and **horizontal scroll bars** are used to display different parts of the document in the document window. The scroll bars include **scroll boxes** and **scroll arrows**, which you use to scroll.
- The **status bar** displays the page number of the current page, the total number of pages and words in the document, and the status of spelling and grammar checking. It also includes the view buttons, the Zoom slider, and the Zoom level button. You can customize the status bar to display other information.
- The **view buttons** on the status bar allow you to display the document in Focus Mode, Read Mode, Print Layout, or Web Layout view. The **Zoom slider** and the **Zoom level button** provide quick ways to enlarge and decrease the size of the document in the document window, making it easy to zoom in on a detail of a document or to view the layout of the document as a whole.

QUICK TIP
If your computer has touchscreen capability, your Quick Access toolbar may also include a Touch/Mouse Mode button.

QUICK TIP
To display a different tab, you simply click its name on the Ribbon.

TROUBLE
Click the View tab, then click the Ruler check box in the Show group to display the rulers if they are not already displayed.

FIGURE 1-2: Elements of the Word program window

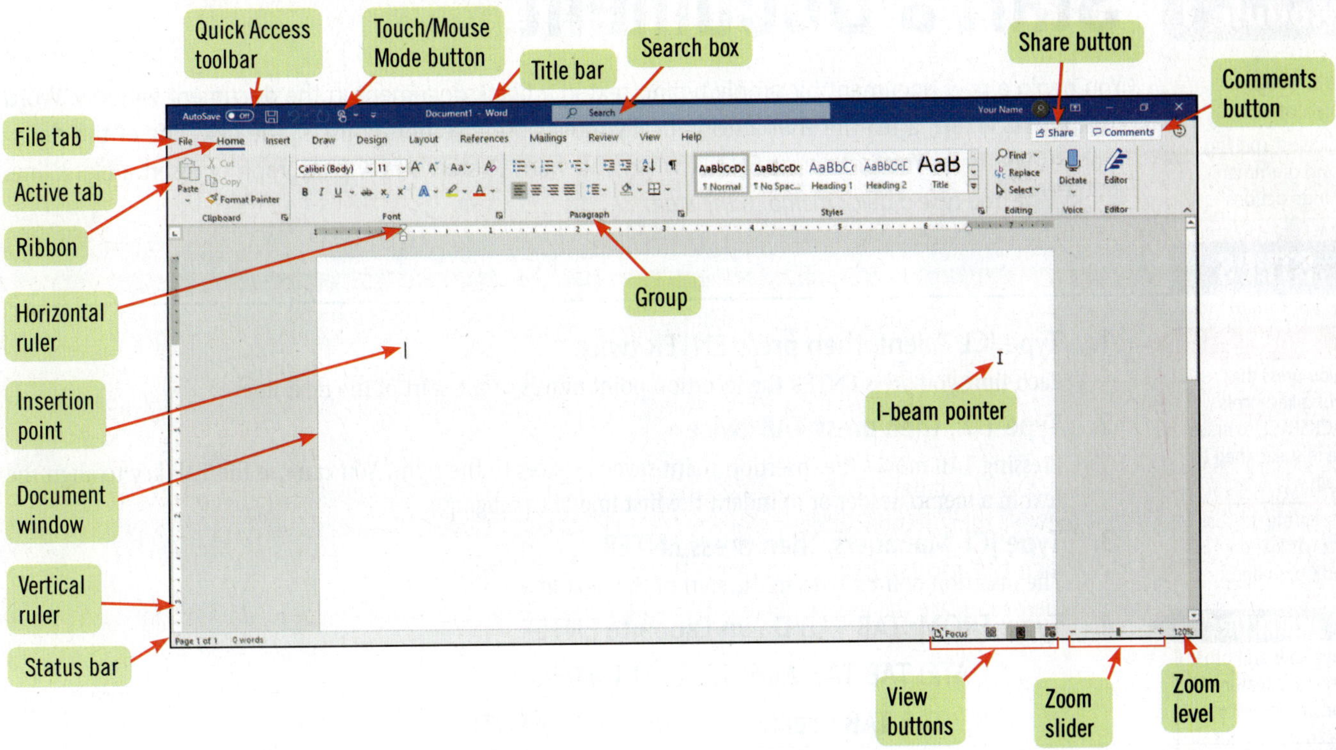

Word

TABLE 1-1: Common mouse pointers in Word

name	pointer	use to
I-beam pointer		Move the insertion point in a document or to select text
Click and Type pointers, including left-align and center-align		Move the insertion point to a blank area of a document in Print Layout or Web Layout view; double-clicking with a Click and Type pointer automatically applies the Paragraph formatting (alignment and indentation) required to position text or a graphic at that location in the document
Selection pointer		Click a button or other element of the Word program window; appears when you point to elements of the Word program window
Right-pointing arrow pointer		Select a line or lines of text; appears when you point to the left edge of a line of text in the document window
Hand pointer		Open a hyperlink; appears when you point to a hyperlink in a task pane or when you press CTRL and point to a hyperlink in a document
Hide white space pointer		Hide the white space in the top and bottom margins of a document in Print Layout view
Show white space pointer		Show the white space in the top and bottom margins of a document in Print Layout view

Start a Document

Learning Outcomes
- Correct spelling and grammar
- Undo actions

You begin a new document by simply typing text in a blank document in the document window. Word uses **word wrap**, a feature that automatically moves the insertion point to the next line of the document as you type. You only press ENTER when you want to start a new paragraph or insert a blank line.

CASE *You type a quick memo to the staff.*

STEPS

TROUBLE
If you press the wrong key, press BACKSPACE to erase the mistake, then try again.

QUICK TIP
Wavy lines and other automatic feature markers appear on screen but do not print.

TROUBLE
To reverse an AutoCorrect adjustment, immediately click the Undo button on the Quick Access toolbar.

QUICK TIP
If you want uniform spacing between lines and paragraphs, apply the No Spacing style to the document by clicking the No Spacing button in the Styles group on the Home tab before you begin to type. Alternatively, select the text and then click the No Spacing button.

1. **Type JCL Talent, then press ENTER twice**
   Each time you press ENTER the insertion point moves to the start of the next line.
2. **Type TO:, then press TAB twice**
   Pressing TAB moves the insertion point several spaces to the right. You can use the TAB key to align the text in a memo header or to indent the first line of a paragraph.
3. **Type JCL Managers, then press ENTER**
   The insertion point moves to the start of the next line.
4. **Type: FROM: TAB TAB Dawn Lapointe ENTER**
   DATE: TAB TAB April 12, 2021 ENTER
   RE: TAB TAB Creative Meeting ENTER ENTER
   Red wavy or blue double lines may appear under the words you typed, indicating a possible spelling or grammar error. Spelling and grammar checking is one of the many automatic features you will encounter as you type. TABLE 1-2 describes several automatic features. You can correct any typing errors you make later.
5. **Type The next creative staff meeting will be held on the 18th of April at 3 p.m. in the conference room on the ground floor., then press SPACEBAR**
   As you type, notice that the insertion point moves automatically to the next line of the document. You also might notice that Word automatically changed "18th" to "18th" in the memo. This feature is called **AutoCorrect**. AutoCorrect automatically makes typographical adjustments and detects and adjusts typing errors, certain misspelled words (such as "taht" for "that"), and incorrect capitalization as you type.
6. **Type Heading the agenda will be the accessibility design of our new Recruitment Tips webpage. The page is scheduled for September.**
   When you type the first few characters of "September," the Word AutoComplete feature displays the complete word in a ScreenTip. **AutoComplete** suggests text to insert quickly into your documents. You can ignore AutoComplete for now. Your memo should resemble FIGURE 1-3.
7. **Press ENTER, then type Anna Jocharz has been hired to draft content. A preliminary content outline is attached. Prior to the meeting, please review the web content accessibility guidelines recommended by the World Wide Web Consortium.**
   When you press ENTER and type the new paragraph, notice that Word adds more space between the paragraphs than it does between the lines in each paragraph. This is part of the default style for paragraphs in Word, called the **Normal style**.
8. **Position the I pointer after for (but before the space) in the last sentence of the first paragraph, then click to move the insertion point after for**
9. **Press BACKSPACE three times, then type to launch in**
   Pressing BACKSPACE removes the character before the insertion point.
10. **Move the insertion point before staff in the first sentence, then press DELETE six times to remove the word "staff" and the space after it**
    Pressing DELETE removes the character after the insertion point. FIGURE 1-4 shows the revised memo.

FIGURE 1-3: Memo text in the document window

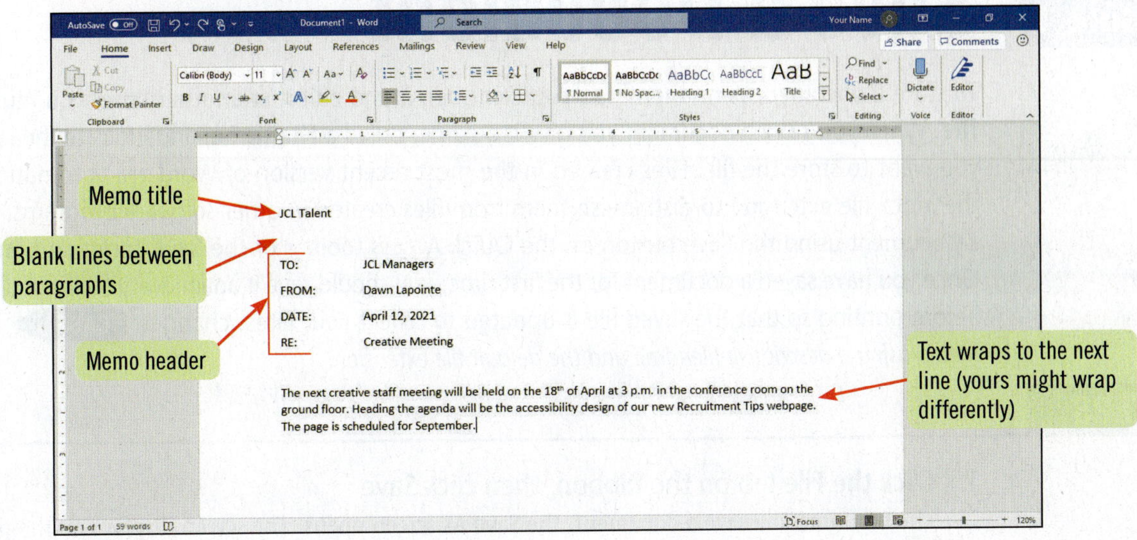

FIGURE 1-4: Edited memo text

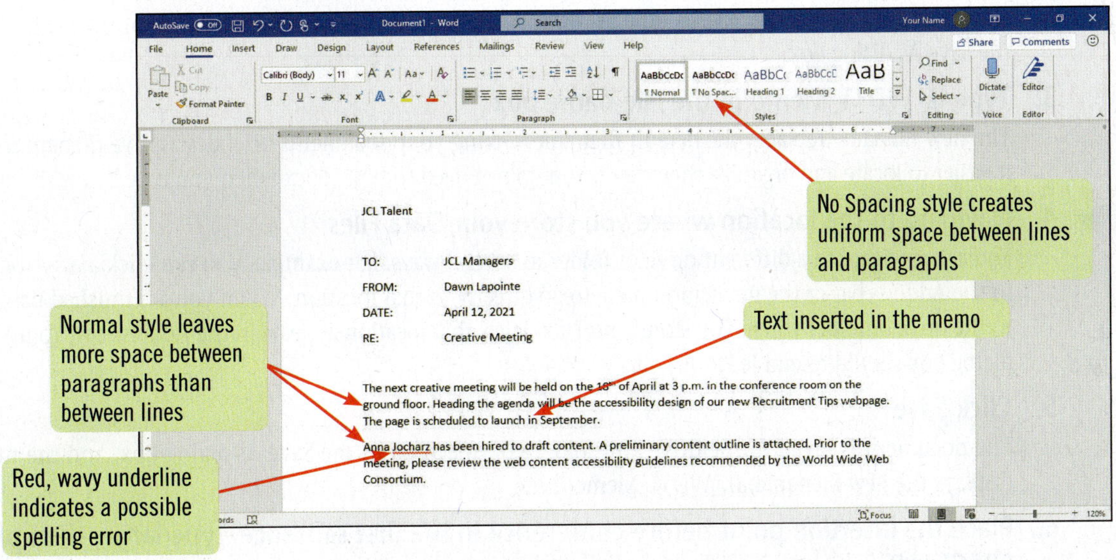

TABLE 1-2: Automatic features that appear as you type in Word

feature	what appears	to use
AutoComplete	A ScreenTip suggesting text to insert appears as you type	Press ENTER to insert the text suggested by the ScreenTip; continue typing to reject the suggestion
AutoCorrect	A small blue box appears when you place the pointer over text corrected by AutoCorrect; an AutoCorrect Options button appears when you point to the blue box	Word automatically corrects typos, minor spelling errors, and capitalization, and adds typographical symbols (such as © and ™) as you type; to reverse an AutoCorrect adjustment, click the AutoCorrect Options arrow, then click the option that will undo the action
Spelling and Grammar	A red wavy line under a word indicates a possible misspelling or a repeated word; a blue double line under text indicates a possible grammar error	Right-click red- or blue-underlined text to display a shortcut menu of correction options; click a correction option to accept it and remove the colored underline, or click Ignore to leave the text as is

Save a Document

Learning Outcome
- Save a document

To store a document permanently so you can open it and edit it at another time, you must save it as a **file**. When you **save** a document you give it a name, called a **filename**, and indicate the location where you want to store the file. Files created in the most recent version of Word are automatically assigned the .docx file extension to distinguish them from files created in other software programs. You can save a document using the Save button on the Quick Access toolbar or the Save command on the File tab. Once you have saved a document for the first time, you should save it again every few minutes and always before printing so that the saved file is updated to reflect your latest changes. **CASE** *You save your memo using a descriptive filename and the default file extension.*

STEPS

1. **Click the File tab on the Ribbon, then click Save**

   The first time you save a document, the Save As screen opens. The screen displays all the places you can save a file to, including OneDrive, your PC (identified as This PC), or a different location.

2. **Click Browse in the Save As screen**

   The Save As dialog box opens, similar to **FIGURE 1-5**. The default filename, JCL Talent, appears in the File name box. The default filename is based on the first few words of the document. The default file type, Word Document, appears in the Save as type list box. **TABLE 1-3** describes the functions of some of the buttons in the Save As dialog box.

3. **Type IL_WD_1_Memo in the File name box**

   The new filename replaces the default filename. Giving your documents brief descriptive filenames makes it easier to locate and organize them later. You do not need to type .docx when you type a new filename.

4. **Navigate to the location where you store your Data Files**

   You can navigate to a different drive or folder in several ways. For example, you can click a drive or folder in the Address bar or the navigation pane to go directly to that location. When you are finished navigating to the drive or folder where you store your Data Files, that location appears in the Address bar. Your Save As dialog box should resemble **FIGURE 1-6**.

5. **Click Save**

   The document is saved to the drive and folder you specified in the Save As dialog box, and the title bar displays the new filename, IL_WD_1_Memo.docx.

6. **Place the insertion point before conference in the first sentence, type large, then press SPACEBAR**

   You can continue to work on a document after you have saved it with a new filename.

7. **Click the Save button on the Quick Access toolbar**

   Your change to the memo is saved. After you save a document for the first time, you must continue to save the changes you make to the document.

TROUBLE
If you don't see the extension .docx as part of the filename, the setting in Windows to display file extensions is not active.

QUICK TIP
You can also double-click a drive or folder in the folder window to change the active location.

QUICK TIP
You also can press CTRL+S to save a document.

Using keyboard shortcuts

A **shortcut key** is a function key, such as F1, or a combination of keys, such as CTRL+S, that you press to perform a command. For example, instead of using the Cut, Copy, and Paste commands on the Ribbon or the Mini toolbar, you can use the **keyboard shortcuts** CTRL+X to cut text, CTRL+C to copy text, and CTRL+V to paste text. You can also press CTRL+S to save changes to a document instead of clicking the Save button on the Quick Access toolbar or clicking Save on the File tab. Becoming skilled at using keyboard shortcuts can help you quickly accomplish many of the tasks you perform in Word. If a keyboard shortcut is available for a command, then it is listed in the ScreenTip for that command.

FIGURE 1-5: Save As dialog box

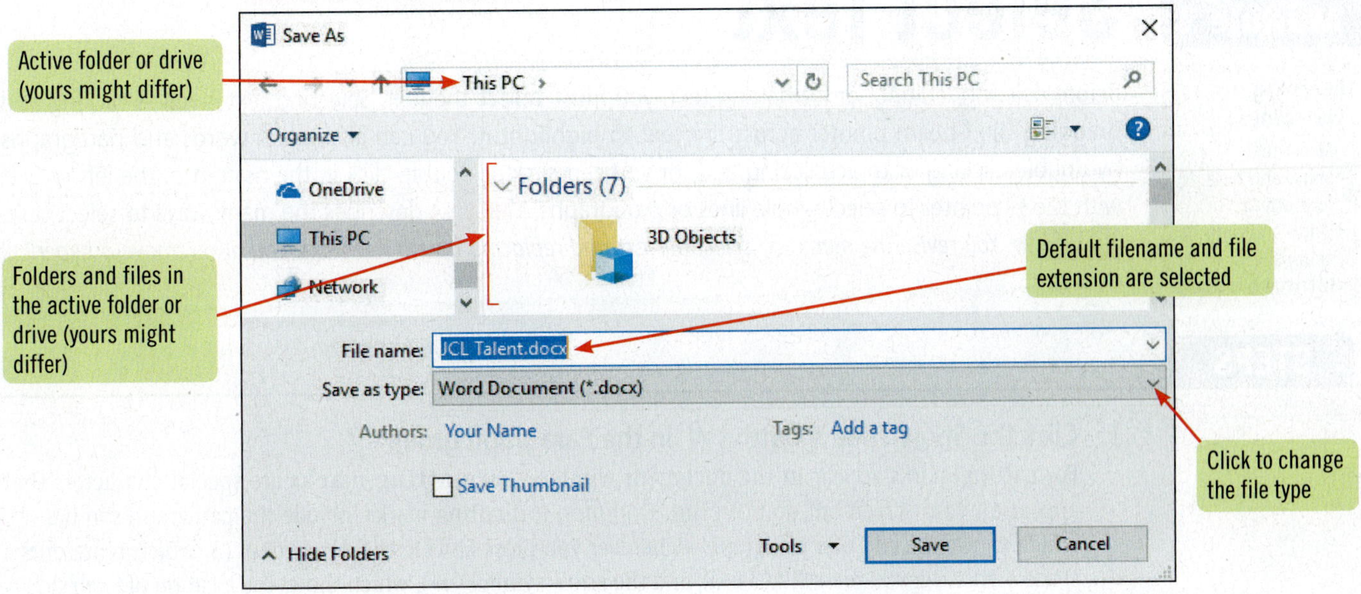

FIGURE 1-6: File to be saved to the Module 1 folder

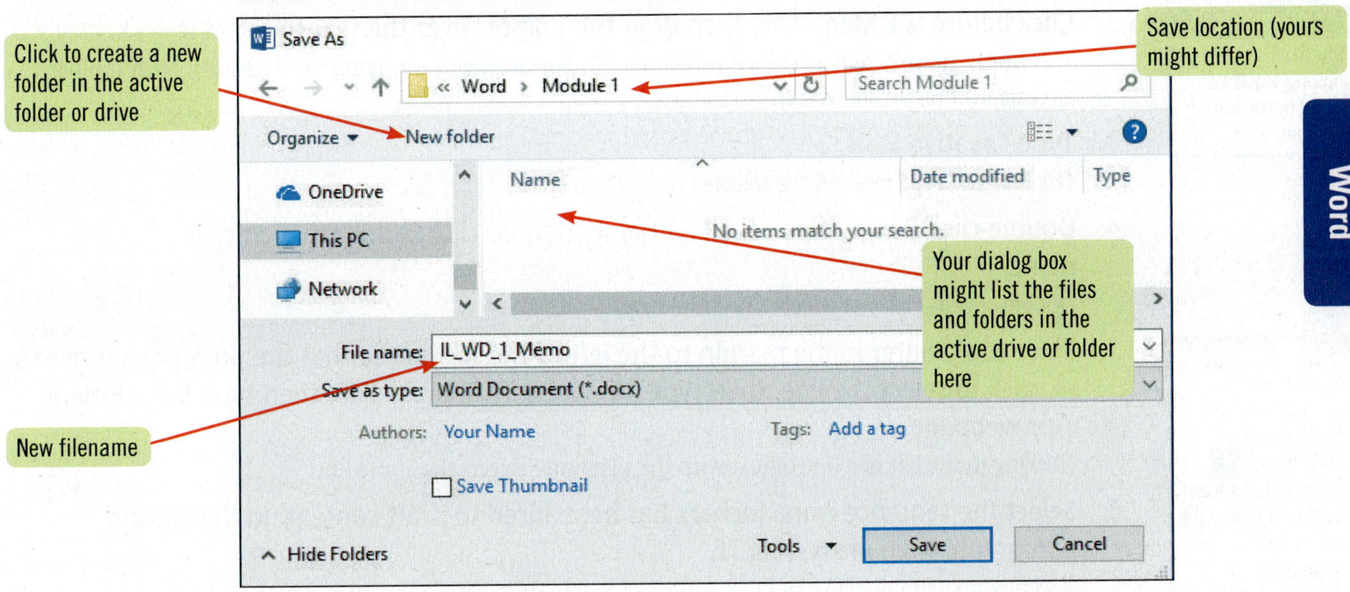

Word

TABLE 1-3: Save As dialog box buttons

button	use to
Back	Navigate back to the last location shown in the Address bar
Forward	Navigate to the location that was previously shown in the Address bar
Up to	Navigate to the location above the current location in the folder hierarchy
Organize	Open a menu of commands related to organizing the selected file or folder, including Cut, Copy, Delete, Rename, and Properties
New folder	Create a new folder in the current folder or drive
Change your view	Change the way folder and file information is shown in the folder window in the Save As dialog box; click the Change your view button to toggle between views, or click the arrow to open a menu of view options

Select Text

Learning Outcomes
- Select text
- Show and hide formatting
- Undo and redo actions
- Manage hyperlinks

Before deleting, editing, or formatting text, you must **select** the text. Selecting text involves clicking and dragging the I-beam pointer across the text to highlight it. You can also select words and paragraphs by double-clicking or triple-clicking text, or you can click or double-click in the margin to the left of text with the pointer to select whole lines or paragraphs. TABLE 1-4 describes the many ways to select text.

CASE *You revise the memo by selecting text and replacing it with new text. You also remove a hyperlink from text.*

STEPS

1. **Click the Show/Hide ¶ button in the Paragraph group**
   Formatting marks appear in the document window. **Formatting marks** are special characters that appear on your screen but do not print. Common formatting marks include the paragraph symbol (¶), which shows the end of a paragraph—wherever you press ENTER; the dot symbol (.), which represents a space—wherever you press SPACEBAR; and the arrow symbol (→), which shows the location of a tab stop—wherever you press TAB. Working with formatting marks turned on can help you to select, edit, and format text with precision.

QUICK TIP You deselect text by clicking anywhere in the document window.

2. **Click before JCL Managers, then drag the pointer over the text to select it**
   The words are selected, as shown in FIGURE 1-7. For now, you can ignore the floating Mini toolbar that appears over text when you first select it.
3. **Type Creative Staff**
   The text you type replaces the selected text.
4. **Double-click Dawn, type your first name, double-click Lapointe, then type your last name**
   Double-clicking a word selects the entire word.

TROUBLE If you delete text by mistake, immediately click the Undo button on the Quick Access toolbar to restore the deleted text to the document.

5. **Place the pointer in the margin to the left of the RE: line so that the pointer changes to , click to select the line, then type RE:, press TAB, press TAB, then type Recruitment Tips webpage**
   Clicking to the left of a line of text with the pointer selects the entire line.
6. **Select the sentence Anna Jocharz has been hired to draft content. in the second paragraph, then press DELETE**
   Selecting text and pressing DELETE removes the text from the document.
7. **Click after the period at the end of the second paragraph, press SPACEBAR, then type See www.w3.org for more information.**
   When you press SPACEBAR after typing the web address, Word automatically formats the web address as a hyperlink. A **hyperlink** is text that when clicked opens a webpage in a browser window. Text that is formatted as a hyperlink appears as colored, underlined text. You want to remove the hyperlink formatting.
8. **Right-click www.w3.org, then click Remove Hyperlink**
   Removing a hyperlink removes the link, but the text remains.

QUICK TIP Always save before and after editing text.

9. **Click ¶, then click the Save button on the Quick Access toolbar**
   Formatting marks are turned off, and your changes to the memo are saved. The Show/Hide ¶ button is a **toggle button**, which means you can use it to turn formatting marks on and off. The edited memo is shown in FIGURE 1-8.

FIGURE 1-7: Text selected in the memo

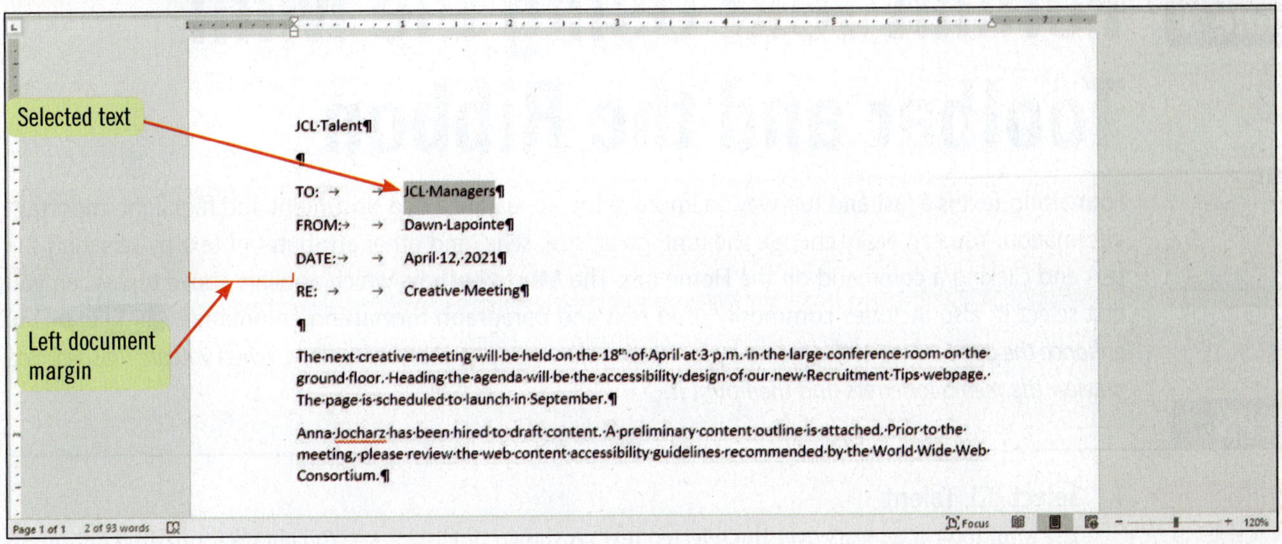

FIGURE 1-8: Edited memo with replacement text

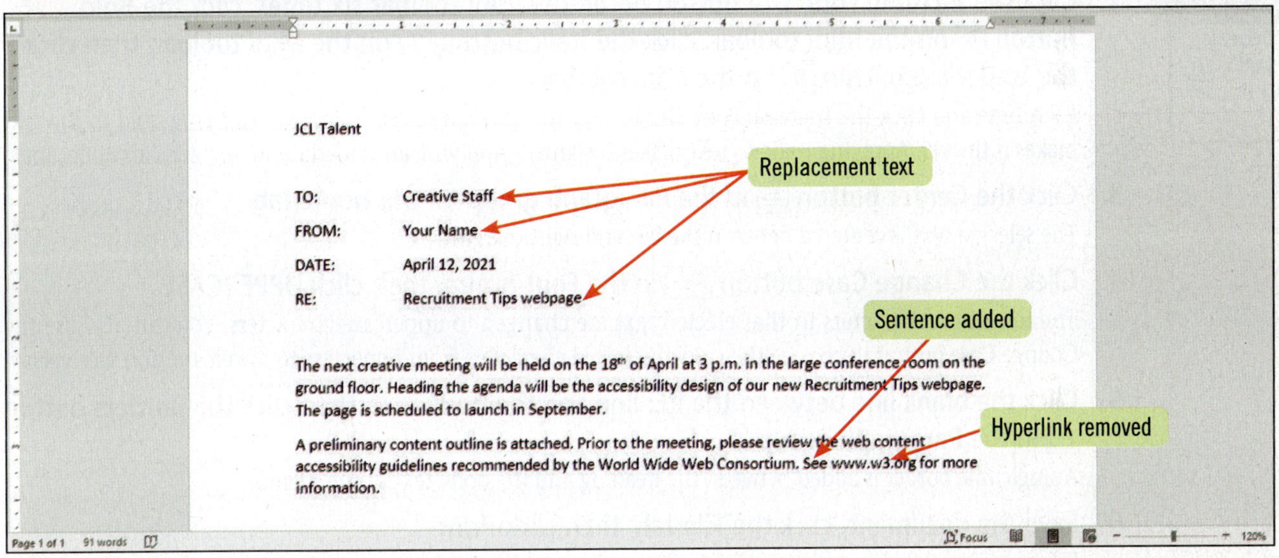

TABLE 1-4: Methods for selecting text

to select	use the pointer to
Any amount of text	Drag over the text
A word	Double-click the word
A line of text	Move the pointer to the left of the line, then click
A sentence	Press and hold CTRL, then click the sentence
A paragraph	Triple-click the paragraph or double-click with the pointer to the left of the paragraph
A large block of text	Click at the beginning of the selection, press and hold SHIFT, then click at the end of the selection
Multiple nonconsecutive selections	Select the first selection, then press and hold CTRL as you select each additional selection
An entire document	Triple-click with the pointer to the left of any text; press CTRL+A; or click the Select button in the Editing group on the Home tab, and then click Select All

Word

Format Text Using the Mini Toolbar and the Ribbon

Learning Outcomes
- Modify text formatting
- Print a document
- Modify print settings
- Close a document

Formatting text is a fast and fun way to improve the appearance of a document and highlight important information. You can easily change the font, color, size, style, and other attributes of text by selecting the text and clicking a command on the Home tab. The **Mini toolbar**, which appears above text when you first select it, also includes commonly used text and paragraph formatting commands. **CASE** *You enhance the appearance of the memo by formatting the text using the Mini toolbar. When you are finished, you preview the memo for errors and then print it.*

STEPS

TROUBLE
If the Mini toolbar disappears, right-click the selection to display it again.

QUICK TIP
Click the Decrease Font Size button to decrease the font size.

1. **Select JCL Talent**
   The Mini toolbar appears over the selected text, as shown in FIGURE 1-9. You click a formatting option on the Mini toolbar to apply it to the selected text. TABLE 1-5 describes the function of the buttons on the Mini toolbar. The buttons on the Mini toolbar are also available on the Ribbon.
2. **Click the Increase Font Size button on the Mini toolbar six times, click the Bold button on the Mini toolbar, click the Italic button on the Mini toolbar, then click the Underline button on the Mini toolbar**
   Each time you click the Increase Font Size button the selected text is enlarged. Applying bold to the text makes it thicker. Applying italic to text makes it slanted. Applying an underline to text adds an underline.
3. **Click the Center button in the Paragraph group on the Home tab**
   The selected text is centered between the left and right margins.
4. **Click the Change Case button in the Font group, then click UPPERCASE**
   The lowercase characters in the selected text are changed to uppercase characters. You can also use the Change Case button to change the case of selected characters from uppercase to lowercase, and vice versa.
5. **Click the blank line between the RE: line and the body text, then click the Borders button in the Paragraph group**
   A single line border is added between the heading and the body text in the memo.
6. **Save the document, click the File tab, then click Print**
   Information related to printing the document appears on the Print screen in Backstage view. Options for printing the document appear on the left side of the Print screen and a preview of the document as it will look when printed appears on the right side, as shown in FIGURE 1-10. Before you print a document, it's a good habit to examine it closely so you can identify and correct any problems.
7. **Click the Zoom In button on the status bar five times, then proofread your document carefully for errors**
   The document is enlarged in print preview. If you notice errors in your document, you need to correct them before you print. To do this, press ESC or click the Back button in Backstage view, correct any mistakes, save your changes, click the File tab, and then click the Print command again to be ready to print the document.
8. **Click the Print button on the Print screen**
   A copy of the memo prints using the default print settings. To change the current printer, change the number of copies to print, select which pages of a document to print, or modify another print setting, you simply change the appropriate setting on the Print screen before clicking the Print button.
9. **sam Click the File tab, then click Close**
   The document closes, but the Word program window remains open.

FIGURE 1-9: Mini toolbar

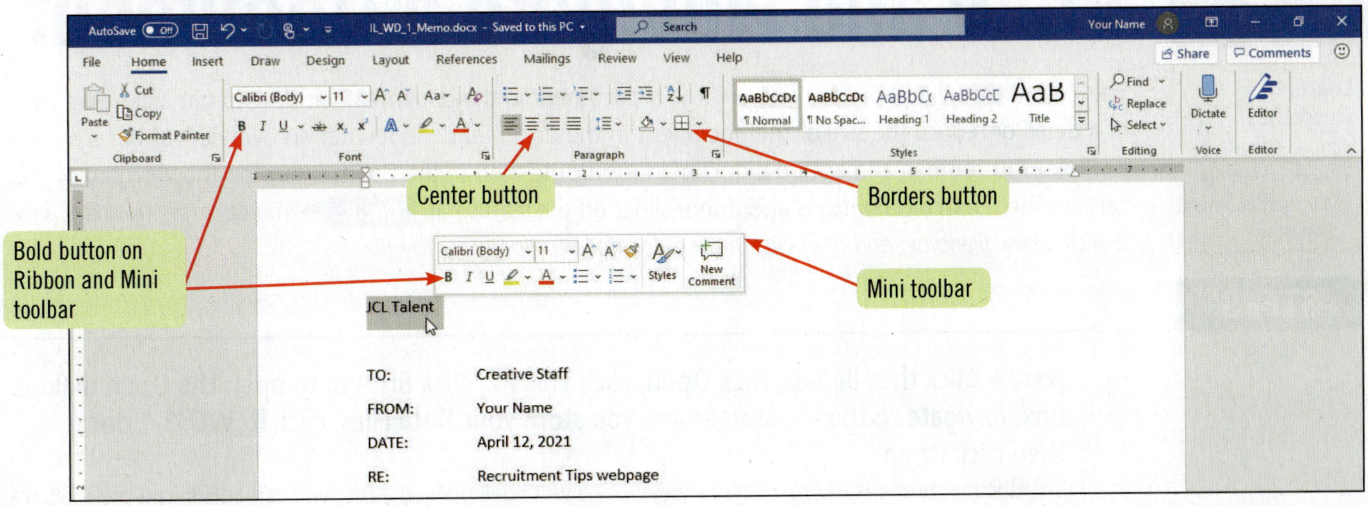

FIGURE 1-10: Preview of the completed memo

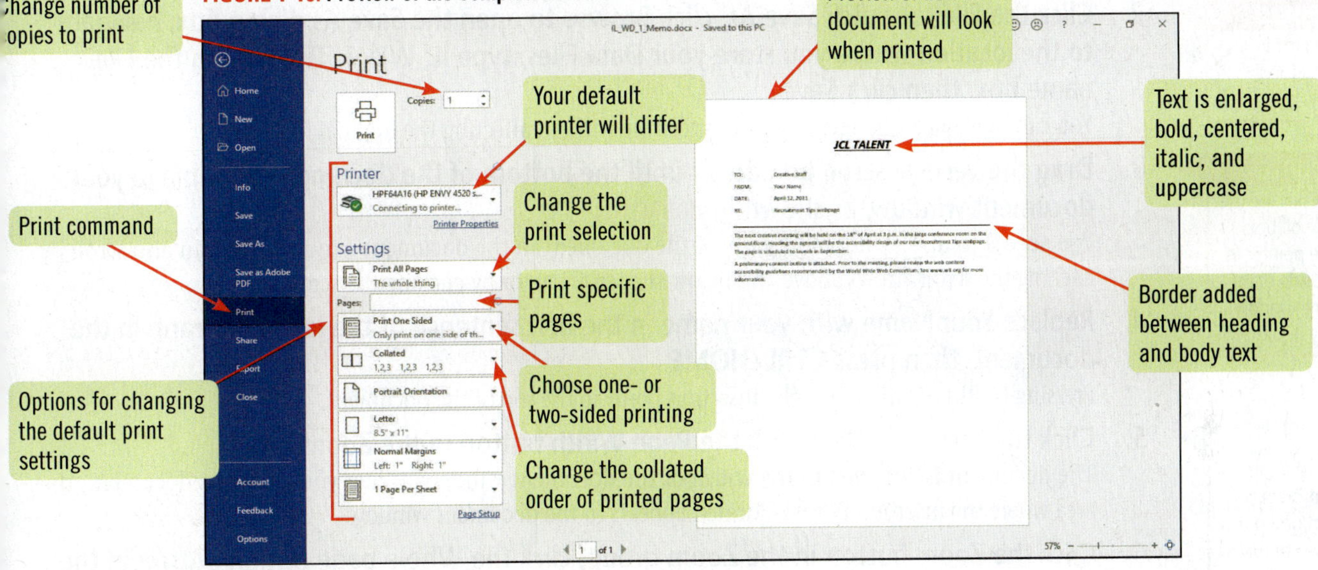

TABLE 1-5: Buttons on the Mini toolbar

button	use to	button	use to
Calibri (Body)	Change the font of text	B	Apply bold to text
11	Change the font size of text	I	Apply italic to text
A	Make text larger	U	Apply an underline to text
A	Make text smaller		Apply colored highlighting to text
	Copy the formats applied to selected text to other text	A	Change the color of text
	Apply a style to text		Apply bullets to paragraphs
	Insert a new comment		Apply numbering to paragraphs

Word

Word
Module 1

View and Navigate a Document

Learning Outcomes
- Open documents
- Zoom in and out
- Manage document properties

The Zoom feature in Word lets you enlarge a document in the document window to get a close-up view of a detail or reduce the size of the document in the document window for an overview of the layout as a whole. You zoom in and out on a document using the tools in the Zoom group on the View tab or you can use the Zoom level buttons and Zoom slider on the status bar. **CASE** *You open the tip sheet, save it with a new filename, and then customize a document property for the file.*

STEPS

TROUBLE
Click the Enable Editing button if necessary.

TROUBLE
If you do not see the vertical scroll box, move the pointer to the right side of the document window to display it.

QUICK TIP
Click the Multiple Pages button in the Zoom group to display two or more pages of a multi-page document in the document window.

1. **sam Click the File tab, click Open, click This PC, click Browse to open the Open dialog box, navigate to the location where you store your Data Files, click IL_WD_1-1.docx, then click Open**
   The document opens in Print Layout view. Once you have opened a file, you can edit it and use the Save or the Save As command to save your changes. You use the **Save** command when you want to save the changes you make to a file, overwriting the stored file. You use the **Save As** command when you want to leave the original file intact and create a duplicate file with a different filename, file extension, or location.
2. **Click the File tab, click Save As, click Browse to open the Save As dialog box, navigate to the location where you store your Data Files, type IL_WD_1_TipSheet in the File name box, then click Save**
   You can now make changes to the tip sheet file without affecting the original file.
3. **Drag the vertical scroll box down until the bottom of the document is visible in your document window, as shown in FIGURE 1-11**
   You **scroll** to display different parts of the document in the document window. You can also scroll by clicking the scroll arrows above and below the scroll bar, or by clicking the scroll bar.
4. **Replace Your Name with your name in the first sentence of the last paragraph in the document, then press CTRL+HOME**
   Pressing CTRL+HOME moves the insertion point to the top of the document.
5. **Click the View tab, then click the Page Width button in the Zoom group**
   The document is enlarged to the width of the document window. When you enlarge a document, the area where the insertion point is located appears in the document window.
6. **Click the Zoom button in the Zoom group, click the Whole page option button in the Zoom dialog box, then click OK to view the entire document**
   You use the Zoom dialog box to select a zoom level for displaying the document in the document window.
7. **Move the Zoom slider on the status bar to the right until the Zoom percentage is approximately 200%, then click the Zoom Out button [−] until the zoom level is 120%**
   Dragging the Zoom slider enlarges or reduces a document in the document window. You can also click the Zoom Out and Zoom In buttons to change the zoom level.
8. **Click the File tab, then click Info**
   The right side of the Info screen in Backstage view shows the document properties for the file. **Document properties** are user-defined details about a file that describe its contents and origin, including the name of the author, the title of the document, and keywords that you can assign to help organize and search your files.
9. **Click the Add a title box in the Properties section of the Info screen, type Tips, then click outside the box**
   The new Title property for the document appears in Backstage view as shown in as shown in FIGURE 1-12
10. **Click Back button to return to the Home tab, then save your changes**
    The document appears at 120% zoom in Print Layout view.

FIGURE 1-11: Zoom slider

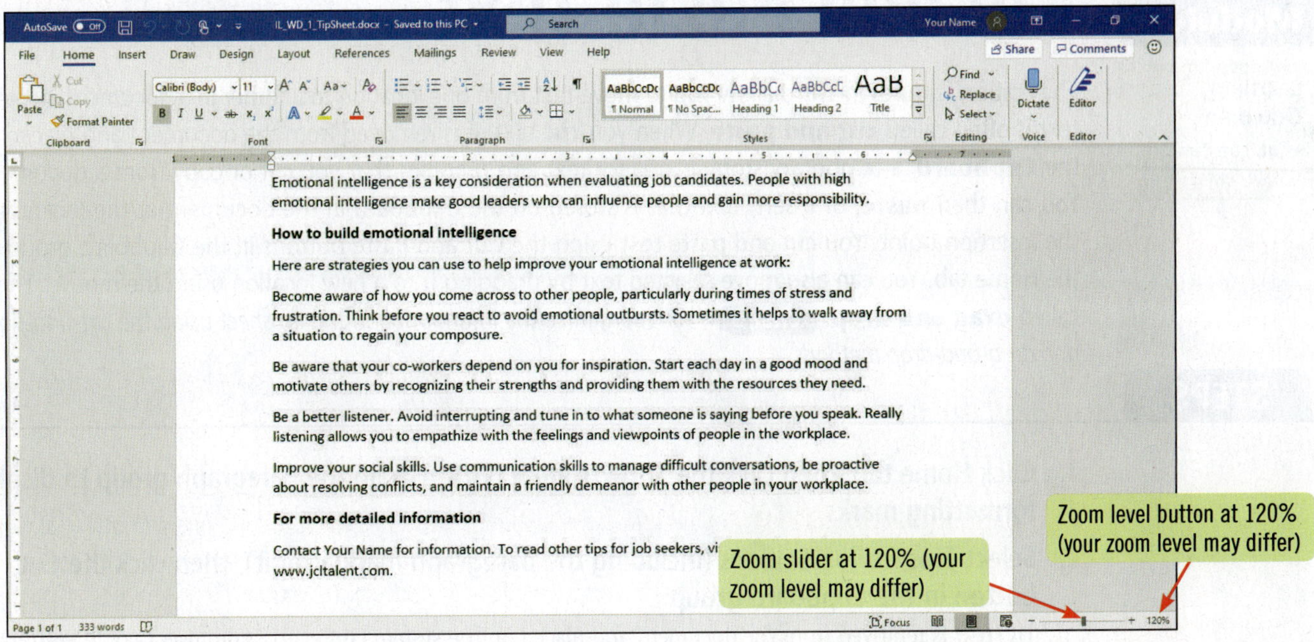

FIGURE 1-12: Document properties in Backstage view

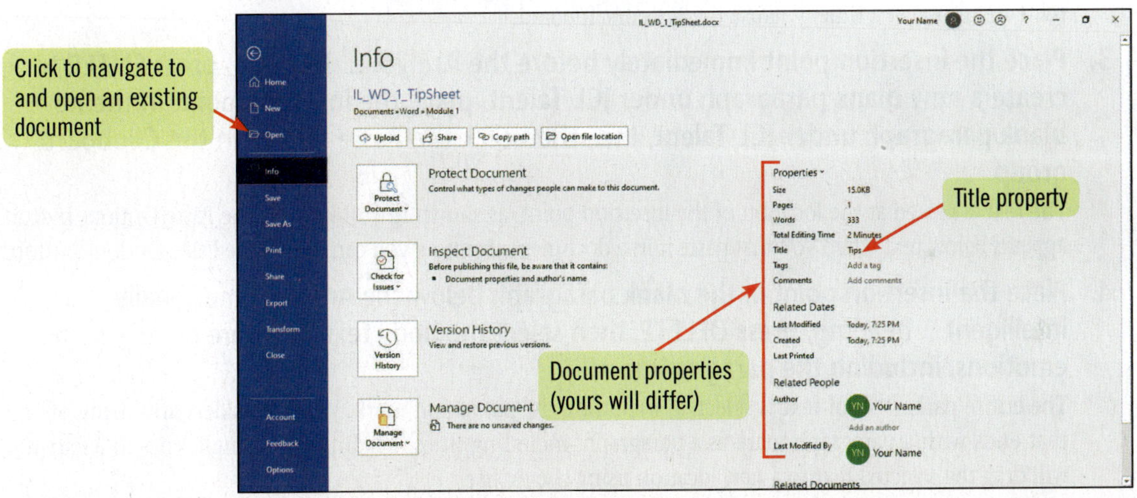

Using Word document views

Document views are different ways of displaying a document in the document window. Each Word view provides features that are useful for working on different types of documents. The default view, **Print Layout view,** displays a document as it will look on a printed page. Print Layout view is helpful for formatting text and pages, including adjusting document margins, creating columns of text, inserting graphics, and formatting headers and footers. Also useful is **Read Mode view,** which displays document text so that it is easy to read on screen. Other Word views are helpful for performing specialized tasks. **Web Layout view** allows you to format webpages or documents that will be viewed on a computer screen. In Web Layout view, a document appears just as it will when viewed with a web browser. Outline view is useful for editing and formatting longer documents that include multiple headings. **Outline view** allows you to reorganize text by moving the headings. Finally, **Draft view**, shows a simplified layout of a document, without margins, headers and footers, or graphics. When you want to quickly type and edit text, it's often easiest to work in Draft view. You switch between views by clicking the view buttons on the status bar or by using the commands on the View tab. Changing views does not affect how the printed document will appear. It simply changes the way you view the document in the document window.

Word
Module 1

Cut and Paste Text

Learning Outcome
- Cut, copy, and paste text

The editing features in Word allow you to move text from one location to another in a document. Moving text is often called **cut and paste**. When you **cut** text, it is removed from the document and placed on the **Clipboard**, a temporary storage area for text and graphics that you cut or copy from a document. You can then **paste**, or insert, text that is stored on the Clipboard in the document at the location of the insertion point. You cut and paste text using the Cut and Paste buttons in the Clipboard group on the Home tab. You can also move selected text by dragging it to a new location using the mouse. This is called **drag and drop**. CASE *You reorganize the information in the tip sheet using the cut-and-paste and drag-and-drop methods.*

STEPS

QUICK TIP
As you drag, the pointer changes to ⬚, and a black vertical line, which is the insertion point, moves with the pointer.

QUICK TIP
If you make a mistake, click the Undo button on the Quick Access toolbar, then try again.

1. **Click Home tab, then click the Show/Hide ¶ button ¶ in the Paragraph group to display formatting marks**
2. **Select Tips for Job Seekers (including the paragraph mark after it), then click the Cut button in the Clipboard group**

   The text is removed from the document and placed on the system clipboard. Word uses two different clipboards: the system **clipboard**, which holds just one item and is not visible, and the **Office Clipboard** (the Clipboard), which holds up to 24 items and can be displayed. When you cut-and-paste or copy-and-paste items one at a time, you use the system clipboard.
3. **Place the insertion point immediately before the Are you... heading, press ENTER to create a new blank paragraph under JCL Talent, place the insertion point in the new blank paragraph under JCL Talent, Inc., then click the Paste button in the Clipboard group**

   The text is pasted at the location of the insertion point, as shown in FIGURE 1-13. The Paste Options button appears below text when you first paste it in a document. For now you can ignore the Paste Options button.
4. **Place the insertion point in the blank paragraph below the Are you emotionally intelligent... heading, press DELETE, then select the body text Be aware of your own emotions, including the paragraph mark**

   The entire paragraph of text is selected, including the paragraph mark. Word considers any string of text that ends with a paragraph mark as a paragraph, including titles, headings, and single lines in a list. You will drag the selected text to a new location using the mouse.
5. **Press and hold the mouse button over the selected text, then drag the pointer's vertical line to the beginning of the Control how you express... paragraph, as shown in FIGURE 1-14**

   You drag the insertion point to where you want the text to be inserted when you release the mouse button.
6. **Release the mouse button, click to deselect the text, then save your changes**

   The selected text is moved to the location of the insertion point. Text is not placed on the Clipboard when you drag and drop it.

Highlighting text in a document

The Highlight tool allows you to mark and find important text in a document. **Highlighting** is transparent color that is applied to text using the Highlight pointer. To highlight text, click the Text Highlight Color arrow in the Font group on the Home tab, select a color, then use the I-beam part of the pointer to select the text you want to highlight. Click to turn off the Highlight pointer. To remove highlighting, select the highlighted text, click then click No Color. Highlighting prints, but it is used most effectively when a document is viewed on screen.

FIGURE 1-13: Moved text with Paste Options button

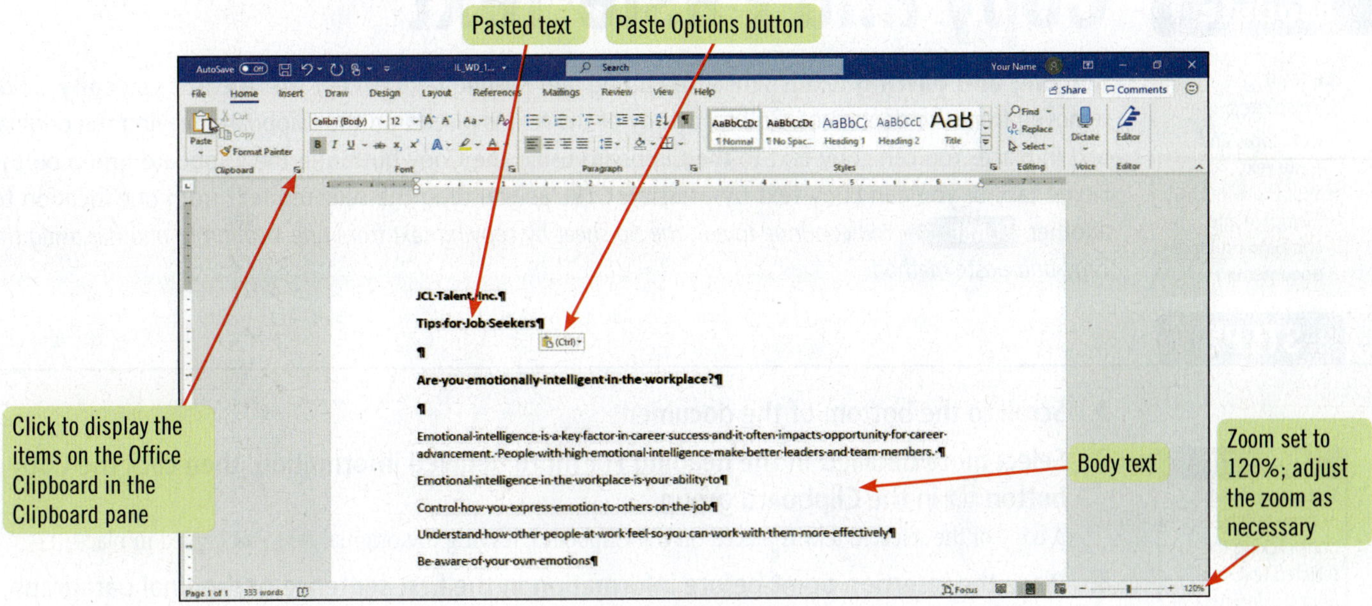

FIGURE 1-14: Dragging and dropping text in a new location

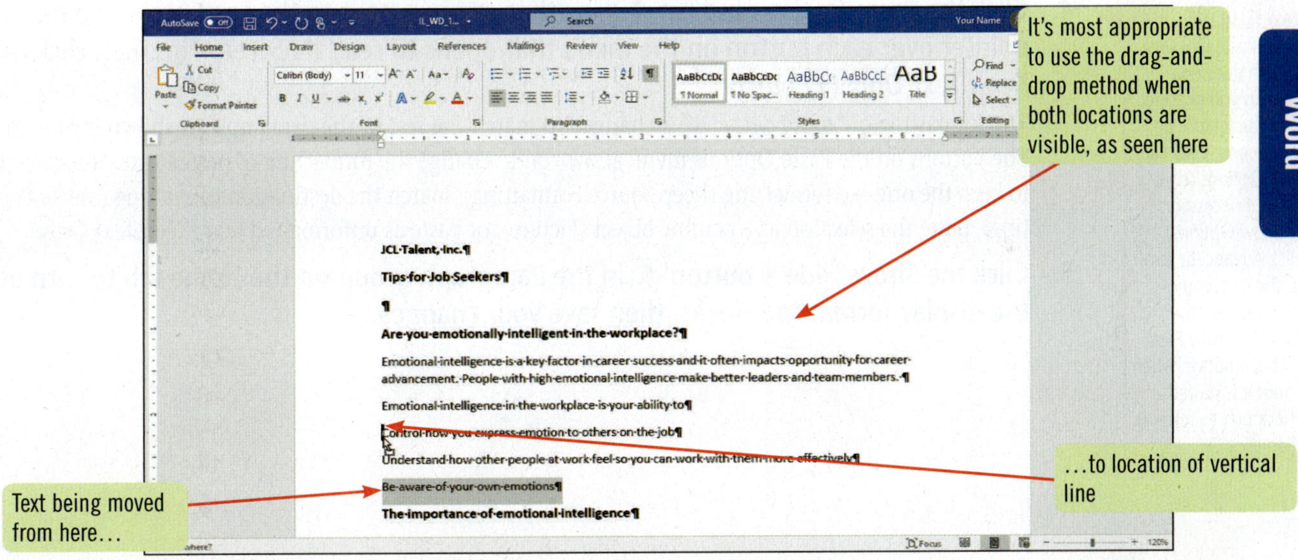

Word

Using the Undo, Redo, and Repeat commands

Word remembers the editing and formatting changes you make so that you can easily reverse or repeat them. You can reverse the last action you took by clicking the Undo button on the Quick Access toolbar, or you can undo a series of actions by clicking the Undo arrow and selecting the action you want to reverse. When you undo an action using the Undo arrow, you also undo all the actions above it in the list—that is, all actions that were performed after the action you selected. Similarly, you can keep the change you just reversed by using the Redo button on the Quick Access toolbar. The Redo button appears only immediately after clicking the Undo button to undo a change.

If you want to repeat an action you just completed, you can use the Repeat button on the Quick Access toolbar. For example, if you just typed "thank you," clicking inserts "thank you" at the location of the insertion point. If you just applied bold, clicking applies bold to the currently selected text. You also can repeat the last action you took by pressing F4.

Copy and Paste Text

Learning Outcomes
- Cut, copy, and paste text
- Split the window
- Compare and combine multiple documents

Copying and pasting text is similar to cutting and pasting text, except that the text you **copy** is not removed from the document. Rather, a copy of the text is placed on the Clipboard, leaving the original text in place. You can copy text to the Clipboard using the Copy button in the Clipboard group on the Home tab, or you can copy text by pressing CTRL as you drag the selected text from one location to another. **CASE** *You continue to edit the tip sheet by copying text from one location to another using the copy-and-paste method.*

STEPS

1. **Scroll to the bottom of the document**
2. **Select more detailed in the heading For more detailed information, then click the Copy button in the Clipboard group**

   A copy of the selected text is placed on the Clipboard, leaving the original text you copied in place.
3. **Place the insertion point before information in the first sentence of the final paragraph, then click the Paste button**

   The text "more detailed" is inserted in the final paragraph, as shown in FIGURE 1-15. Notice that the pasted text is formatted differently than the paragraph in which it was inserted.
4. **Click the Paste Options button (Ctrl) that appears next to the text, move the mouse pointer over each button on the menu that opens to read its ScreenTip, then click the Keep Text Only (T) button**

   The formatting of "more detailed" is changed to match the rest of the paragraph, as shown in FIGURE 1-16. The buttons on the Paste Options menu allow you to change the formatting of pasted text. You can choose to keep the original formatting (Keep Source Formatting), match the destination formatting (Merge Formatting), paste the selection as a graphic object (Picture), or paste as unformatted text (Keep Text Only).
5. **Click the Show/Hide ¶ button in the Paragraph group on the Home tab to turn off the display formatting marks, then save your changes**

QUICK TIP

You can also cut or copy text by right-clicking the selected text, and then clicking the Cut or Copy command on the menu that opens.

TROUBLE

If the Paste Options button does not appear, you need to turn the feature on in Options. Click File, click Options (click More if necessary to show Options), click Advanced, scroll to the Cut, copy, and paste section, click the Show Paste Options button when content is pasted check box to select it, then click OK.

Splitting the document window to copy and move items in a long document

If you want to copy or move items between parts of a long document, it can be useful to split the document window into two panes. This allows you to display the item you want to copy or move in one pane and the destination for the item in the other pane. To split a window, click the Split button in the Window group on the View tab, and then drag the horizontal split bar that appears to the location where you want to split the window. Once the document window is split into two panes, you can use the scroll bars in each pane to display different parts of the document. To copy or move an item from one pane to another, you can use the Cut, Copy, and Paste commands, or you can drag the item between the panes. When you are finished editing the document, double-click the split bar to restore the window to a single pane, or click the Remove Split button in the Window group on the View tab.

FIGURE 1-15: Text pasted in document

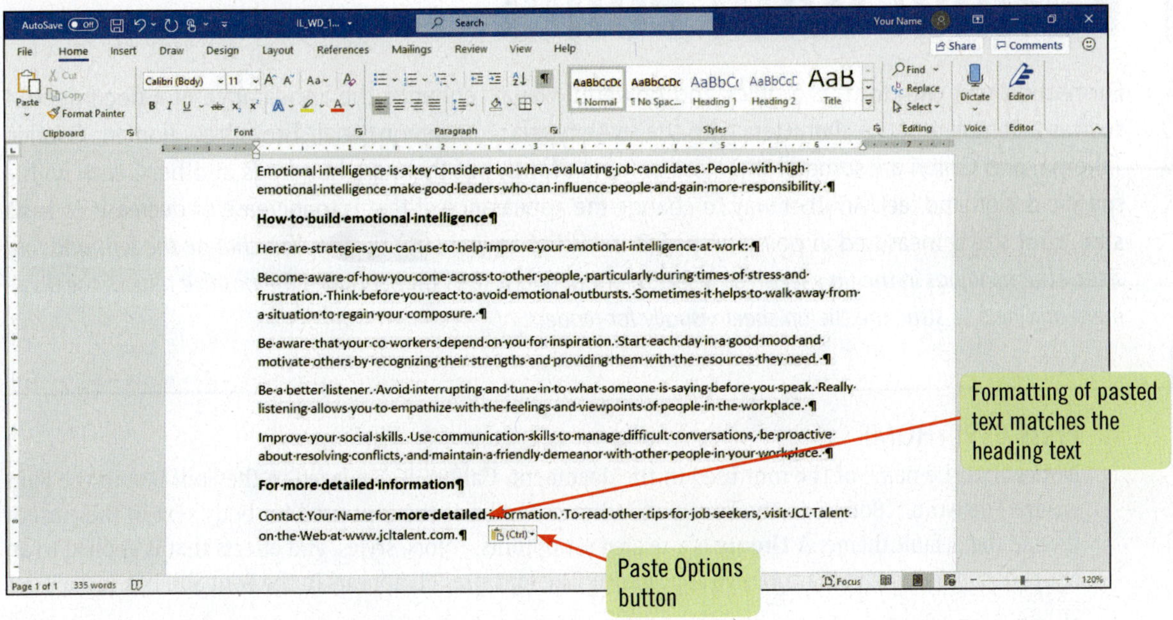

FIGURE 1-16: Copied text in document

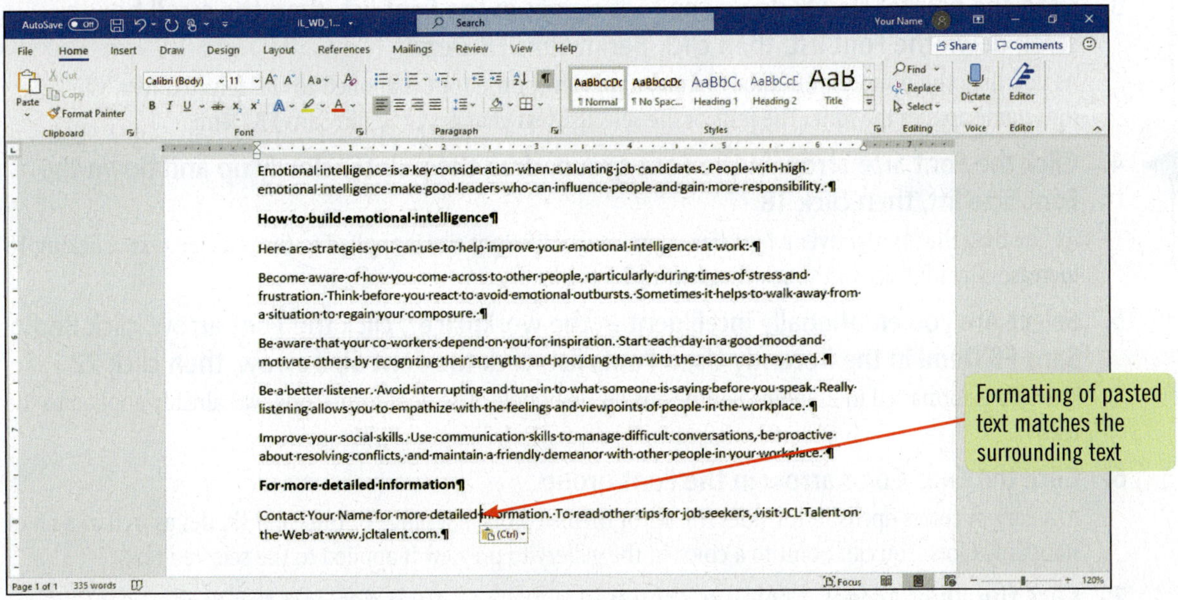

Copying and moving items between documents

You can also use the Clipboard to copy and move items between documents. To do this, open both documents and the Clipboard pane. With multiple documents open, copy or cut an item from one document and then switch to the other document and paste the item. To switch between open documents, point to the Word icon on the taskbar, and then click the document you want to appear in the document window. You can also display more than one document at the same time by clicking the Arrange All button or the View Side by Side button in the Window group on the View tab.

Format with Fonts

Learning Outcome
- Modify text formatting

Formatting text with fonts is a quick and powerful way to enhance the appearance of a document. A **font** is a complete set of characters with the same typeface or design. Arial, Times New Roman, Courier, Tahoma, and Calibri are some of the more common fonts, but there are hundreds of others, each with a specific design and feel. Another way to change the appearance of text is to increase or decrease its **font size**. Font size is measured in points. A **point** is 1/72 of an inch. **CASE** *You change the font and font size of the headings in the tip sheet. You select a font and font sizes that enhance the positive tone of the document and help to structure the tip sheet visually for readers.*

STEPS

1. **Press CTRL+HOME**

   Notice that the name of the font used in the document, Calibri, is displayed in the Font box in the Font group. The word "(Body)" in the Font box indicates Calibri is the font used for body text in the current theme, the default theme. A **theme** is a related set of fonts, colors, styles, and effects that is applied to an entire document to give it a cohesive appearance. The font size, 11, appears in the Font Size box in the Font group.

> **QUICK TIP**
> There are two types of fonts: **serif fonts** have a small stroke, called a serif, at the ends of characters; **sans serif fonts** do not have a serif.

2. **Select Tips for Job Seekers, then click the Font arrow in the Font group**

   The Font list, which shows the fonts available on your computer, opens as shown in FIGURE 1-17. The font names are formatted in the font. Font names can appear in more than one location on the Font list.

3. **Drag the pointer slowly down the font names in the Font list, drag the scroll box to scroll down the Font list, then click Berlin Sans FB Demi**

   As you drag the pointer over a font name, a preview of the font is applied to the selected text. Clicking a font name applies the font. The font of the selected text changes to Berlin Sans FB Demi.

> **QUICK TIP**
> You can also type a font size in the Font Size box.

4. **Click the Font Size arrow in the Font group, drag the pointer slowly up and down the Font Size list, then click 18**

   As you drag the pointer over a font size, a preview of the font size is applied to the selected text. Clicking 18 increases the font size of the selected text to 18 points.

5. **Select Are you emotionally intelligent in the workplace?, click the Font arrow, click Berlin Sans FB Demi in the Recently Used Fonts list, click the Font Size arrow, then click 22**

   The title is formatted in 22-point Berlin Sans FB Demi bold. The bold formatting was already applied to the text.

6. **Click the Font Color arrow in the Font group**

   A gallery of colors opens. It includes the set of theme colors in a range of tints and shades as well as a set of standard colors. You can point to a color in the gallery to preview it applied to the selected text.

7. **Click the Blue, Accent 1 color as shown in FIGURE 1-18, then deselect the text**

   The color of the title text changes to blue. The active color on the Font Color button also changes to blue.

> **TROUBLE**
> If the Mini toolbar closes, select the text again.

8. **Scroll down, select the heading The importance of emotional intelligence, then, using the Mini toolbar, click the Font arrow, click Berlin Sans FB Demi, click the Font Size arrow, click 14, click A, then deselect the text**

   The heading is formatted in 14-point Berlin Sans FB Demi bold with a blue color.

9. **Repeat Step 8 to apply 14-point Berlin Sans FB Demi blue to the How to build emotional intelligence and For more detailed information headings, press CTRL+HOME, then save your changes**

   Compare your document to FIGURE 1-19.

FIGURE 1-17: Font list

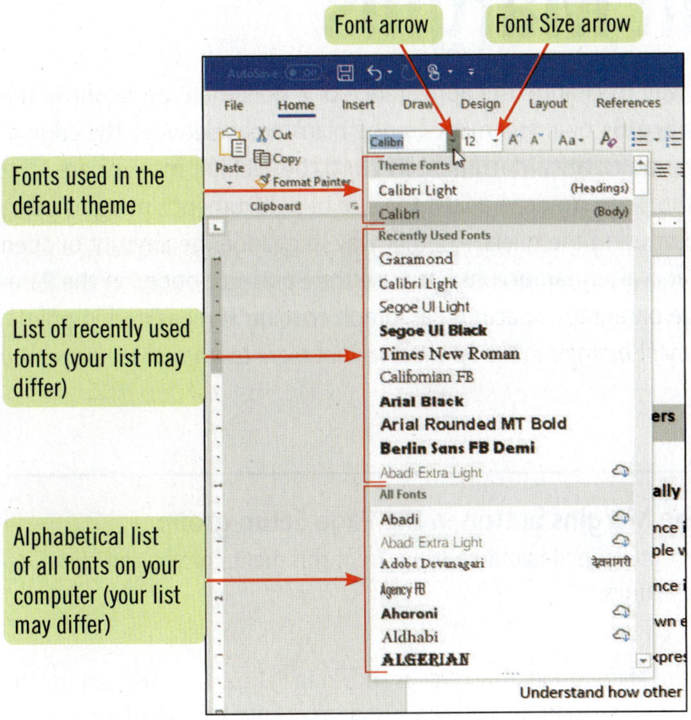

FIGURE 1-18: Font Color Palette

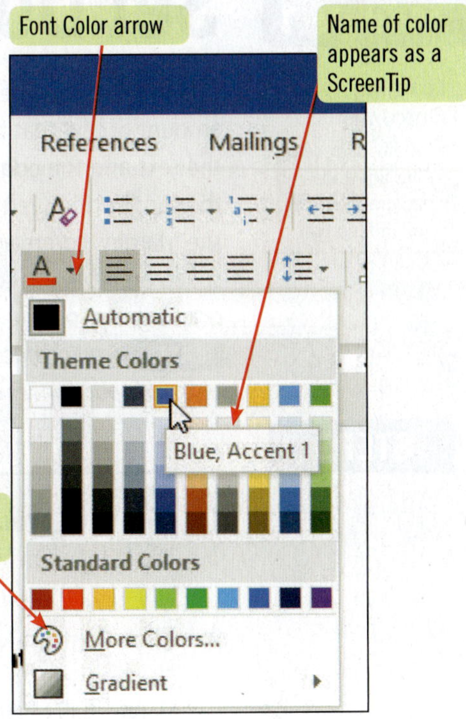

FIGURE 1-19: Document formatted with fonts

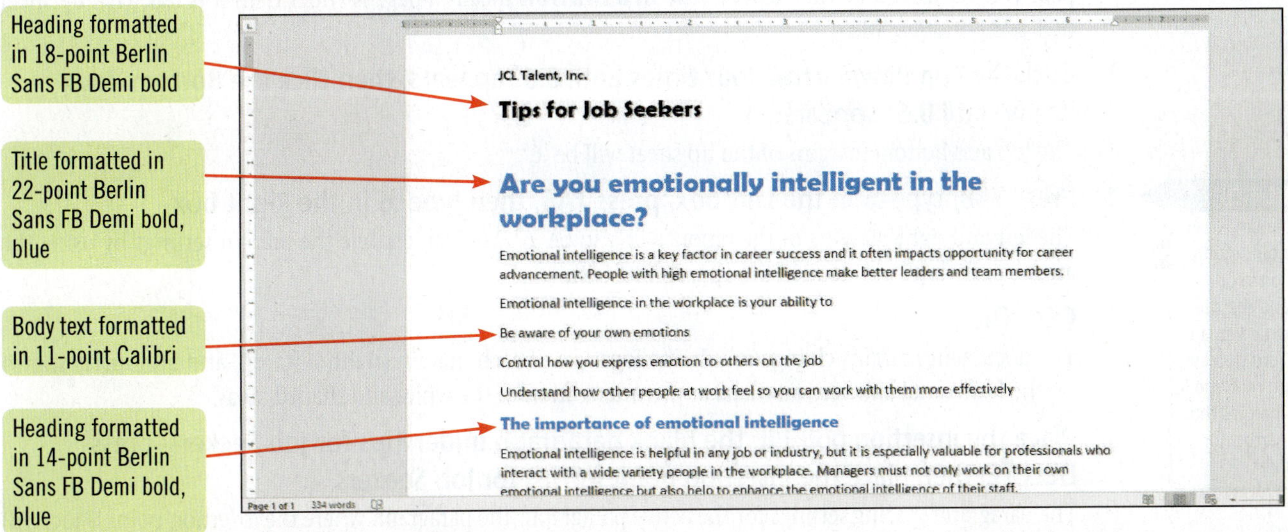

Applying shadows and other text effects to text

The Word Text Effects and Typography feature allows you to add visual appeal to your documents by adding special text effects to text, including outlines, shadows, reflections, and glows. The feature also includes a gallery of preformatted combined text effect styles, called **WordArt**, that you can apply to your text to format it quickly and easily. To apply a WordArt style to text, simply select the text, click the Text Effects and Typography button in the Font group on the Home tab, and select a WordArt style from the gallery. To apply an individual text effect style, such as a shadow, outline, reflection, or glow, select the text, click the Text Effects and Typography button, point to the type of text effect you want to apply, and then select a style from the gallery that opens. Experiment with combining text effect styles to give your text a striking appearance.

If you are unhappy with the way text is formatted, you can use the Clear All Formatting command to return the text to the default format settings—11-point Calibri. Select the text, then click the Clear All Formatting button in the Font group on the Home tab.

Word **Module 1**

Set Document Margins

Learning Outcomes
- Modify page setup
- Alter line and paragraph spacing and indentation

Changing a document's margins is one way to change the appearance of a document and control the amount of text that fits on a page. The **margins** of a document are the blank areas between the edge of the text and the edge of the page. When you create a document in Word, the default margins are 1" at the top, bottom, left, and right sides of the page. You can adjust the size of a document's margins using the Margins command on the Layout tab or using the rulers. Another way to change the amount of open space on a page is to add space before and after paragraphs. You use the Spacing options in the Paragraph group on the Layout tab to change paragraph spacing. Paragraph spacing is measured in points. **CASE** *You reduce the size of the document margins in the tip sheet so that more text fits on the page. You also add space under a paragraph.*

STEPS

1. **Click the Layout tab, then click the Margins button in the Page Setup group**
   The Margins menu opens. You can select predefined margin settings from this menu, or you can click Custom Margins to create different margin settings.
2. **Click Custom Margins**
   The Page Setup dialog box opens with the Margins tab displayed, as shown in **FIGURE 1-20**. You can use the Margins tab to change the top, bottom, left, or right document margin; to change the orientation of the pages from portrait to landscape; and to alter other page layout settings. **Portrait orientation** means a page is taller than it is wide; **landscape orientation** means a page is wider than it is tall. This tip sheet uses portrait orientation.
3. **Click the Top down arrow four times until 0.6" appears, then click the Bottom down arrow until 0.6" appears**
   The top and bottom margins of the tip sheet will be .6".
4. **Press TAB, type .6 in the Left box, press TAB, then type .6 in the Right box**
   The left and right margins of the report will also be .6". You can change the margin settings by using the arrows or by typing a value in the appropriate box.
5. **Click OK**
   The document margins change to .6". The location of each margin (right, left, top, and bottom) is shown on the horizontal and vertical rulers at the intersection of the white and shaded areas.
6. **Place the insertion point in the blank paragraph under Tips for Job Seekers, press DELETE, then place the insertion point in Tips for Job Seekers**
   The paragraph spacing settings for the active paragraph (the paragraph where the insertion point is located) are shown in the Before and After text boxes in the Paragraph group on the Layout tab.
7. **Click the Before up arrow in the Spacing section in the Paragraph group once until 6 pt appears, then click the After up arrow in the Spacing section in the Paragraph group four times until 30 pt appears**
   Six points of space are added before the Tips for Job Seekers paragraph, and 30 points of space are added after, as shown in **FIGURE 1-21**.

QUICK TIP
The minimum allowable margin settings depend on your printer and the size of the paper you are using. Word displays a warning message if you set margins that are too narrow for your printer.

FIGURE 1-20: Margins tab in Page Setup dialog box

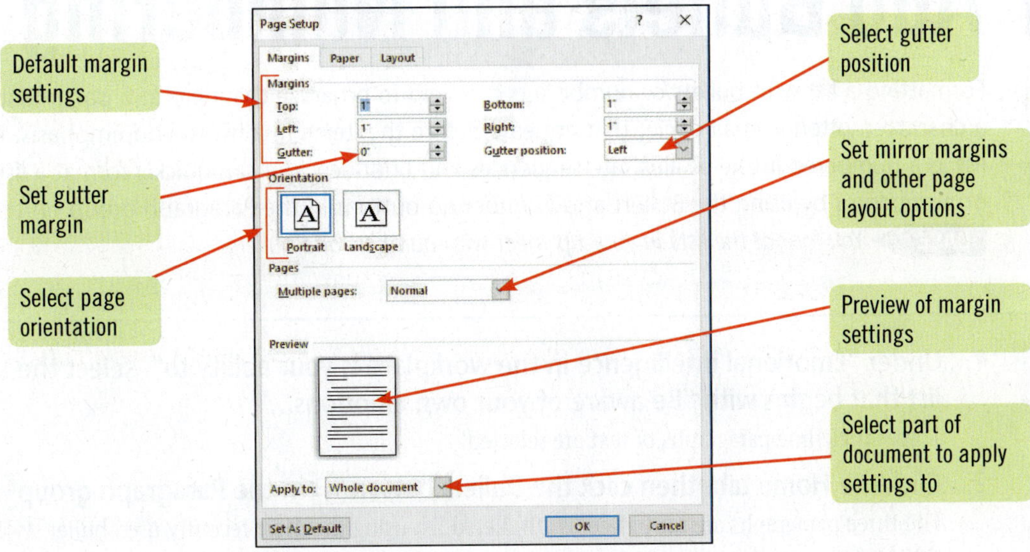

FIGURE 1-21: Info sheet with smaller margins and space after a paragraph

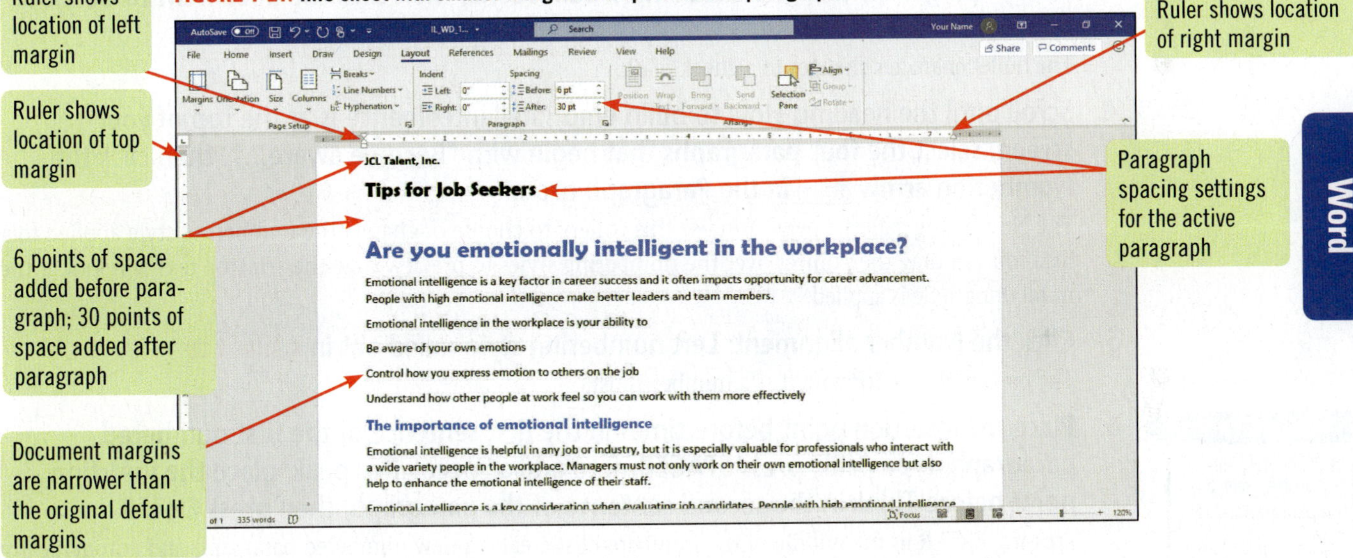

Changing orientation, margin settings, and paper size

By default, the documents you create in Word use an 8 ½" × 11" paper size in portrait orientation with the default margin settings. You can change the orientation, margin settings, and paper size to common settings using the Orientation, Margins, and Size buttons in the Page Setup group on the Layout tab. You can also adjust these settings and others in the Page Setup dialog box. For example, to change the layout of multiple pages, use the Multiple pages arrow on the Margins tab to create pages that use mirror margins, that include two pages per sheet of paper, or that are formatted using a book fold. **Mirror margins** are used in a document with facing pages, such as a magazine, where the margins on the left page of the document are a mirror image of the margins on the right page. Documents with mirror margins have inside and outside margins, rather than right and left margins. Another type of margin is a gutter margin, which is used in documents that are bound, such as books. A gutter adds extra space to the left, top, or inside margin to allow for the binding. Add a gutter to a document by adjusting the setting in the Gutter position box on the Margins tab. To change the size of the paper used, use the Paper size arrow on the Paper tab to select a standard paper size, or enter custom measurements in the Width and Height boxes.

Word

Word
Module 1

Add Bullets and Numbering

Learning Outcome
• Create numbered and bulleted lists

Formatting a list with bullets or numbering can help to organize the ideas in a document. A **bullet** is a character, often a small circle, that appears before the items in a list to add emphasis. Formatting a list as a numbered list helps illustrate sequences and priorities. You can quickly format a list with bullets or numbering by using the Bullets and Numbering buttons in the Paragraph group on the Home tab.

CASE *You format the lists in your tip sheet with numbers and bullets.*

STEPS

1. **Under "Emotional intelligence in the workplace is your ability to", select the three-line list that begins with "Be aware of your own emotions..."**
   Three single-line paragraphs of text are selected.
2. **Click the Home tab, then click the Bullets button in the Paragraph group**
   The three paragraphs are formatted as a bulleted list using the most recently used bullet style as shown in FIGURE 1-22.
3. **Click a bullet in the list to select all the bullets, click the Bullets arrow in the Paragraph group, click the check mark bullet style, then click the document to deselect the text**
   The bullet character changes to a check mark.
4. **Scroll until the heading How to build emotional intelligence is at the top of your screen, select the four paragraphs that begin with "Become aware...", then click the Numbering arrow in the Paragraph group**
   The Numbering gallery opens. You use this gallery to choose or change the numbering style applied to a list. You can drag the pointer over the numbering styles to preview how the selected text will look if the numbering style is applied.
5. **Click the Number alignment: Left numbering style called out in FIGURE 1-23**
   The paragraphs are formatted as a numbered list.
6. **Place the insertion point before times in the first sentence of the first numbered paragraph, type peak, press SPACEBAR to add a space after peak, place the insertion point before Think in the second sentence of the paragraph, then press ENTER**
   Pressing ENTER in the middle of the numbered list creates a new numbered paragraph and automatically renumbers the remainder of the list. Similarly, if you delete a paragraph from a numbered list, Word automatically renumbers the remaining paragraphs.
7. **Click 1 in the list**
   Clicking a number in a list selects all the numbers, as shown in FIGURE 1-24.
8. **Click the Bold button in the Font group, then save your changes**
   The numbers are all formatted in bold. Notice that the formatting of the items in the list does not change when you change the formatting of the numbers. You can also use this technique to change the formatting of bullets in a bulleted list.

QUICK TIP
To remove a bullet or number, select the paragraph(s), then click or .

FIGURE 1-22: Bullets applied to list

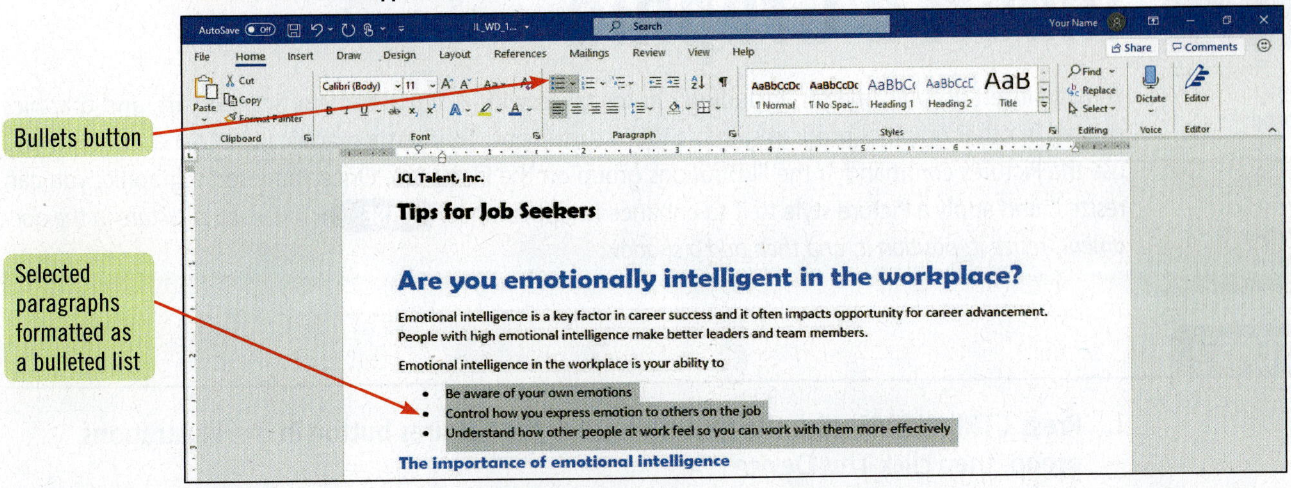

FIGURE 1-23: Numbering gallery

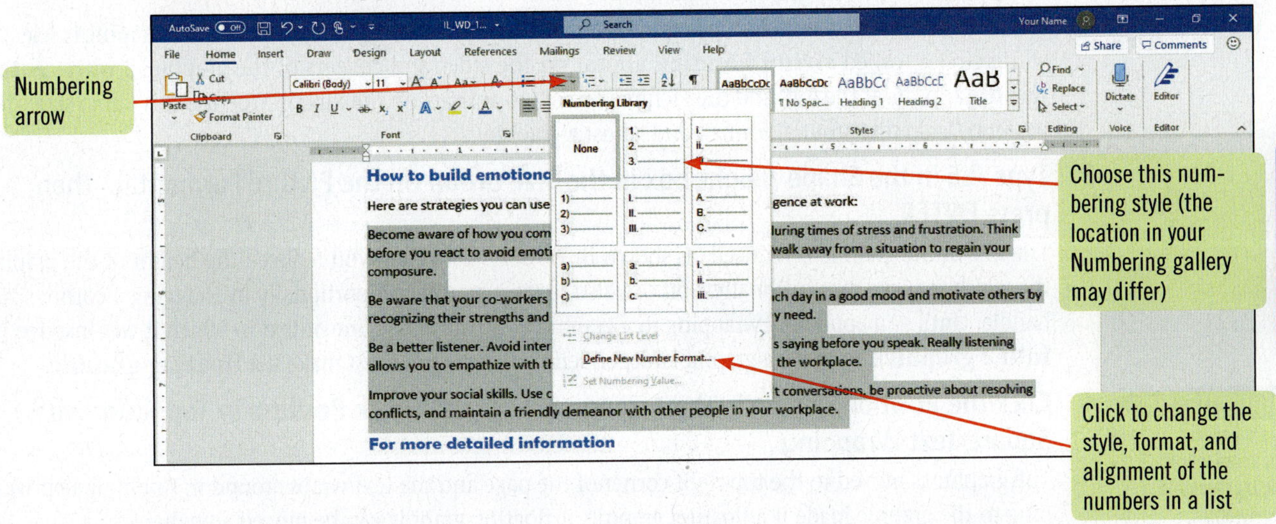

FIGURE 1-24: Numbered list

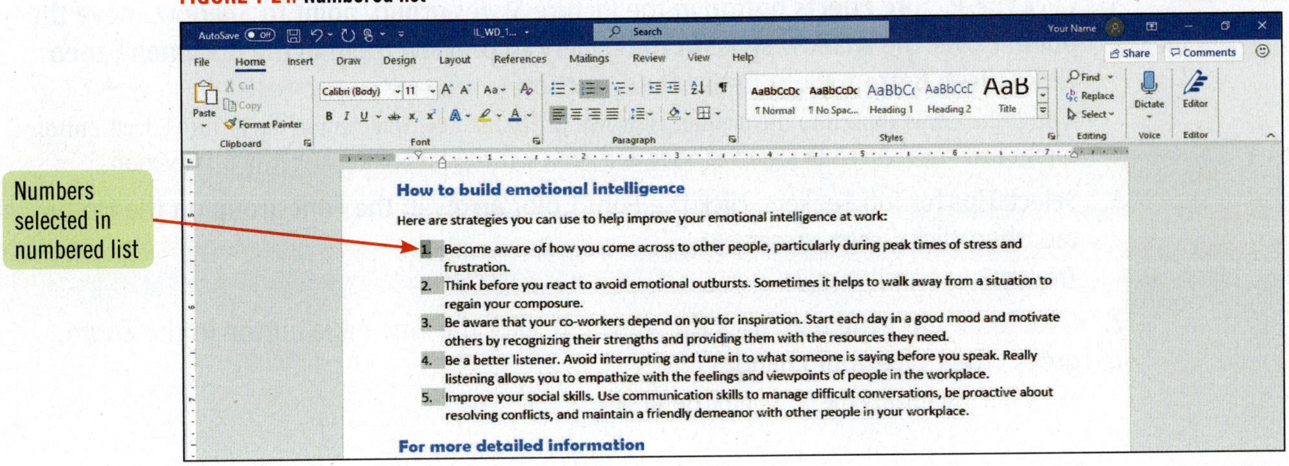

Word
Module 1

Insert a Graphic

Learning Outcomes
- Insert pictures
- Apply artistic and picture effects
- Apply styles to objects
- Format objects

You can insert graphic images, including photos taken with a digital camera, scanned art, and graphics created in other graphics programs, into a Word document. To insert a graphic file into a document, you use the Pictures command in the Illustrations group on the Insert tab. Once you insert a graphic, you can resize it and apply a Picture style to it to enhance its appearance. **CASE** *You insert a picture in the document, resize it, position it, and then add a shadow.*

STEPS

1. **Press CTRL+HOME, click the Insert tab, click the Pictures button in the Illustrations group, then click This Device**

   The Insert Picture dialog box opens. You use this dialog box to locate and insert graphic files. Most graphic files are **bitmap graphics**, which are often saved with a .bmp, .png, .jpg, .tif, or .gif file extension.

2. **Navigate to the location where you store your Data Files, click the file Support_WD_1-2.jpg, then click Insert**

   The picture is inserted as an inline graphic at the location of the insertion point. When a graphic is selected, white circles, called **sizing handles**, appear on the sides and corners of the graphic, a white **rotate handle** appears at the top, and the Picture Format tab appears on the Ribbon. You use this tab to size, crop, position, wrap text around, format, and adjust a graphic.

3. **Type 2.5 in the Shape Height box in the Size group on the Picture Format tab, then press ENTER**

   The size of the graphic is reduced, as shown in FIGURE 1-25. When you reduced the height of the graphic, the width reduced proportionally. You can also resize a graphic proportionally by dragging a corner sizing handle. Until you apply text wrapping to a graphic, it is part of the line of text in which it was inserted (an **inline graphic**). To move a graphic independently of text, you must make it a **floating graphic**.

> **QUICK TIP**
> Change a floating graphic to an inline graphic by changing the text-wrapping style to In Line with Text.

4. **Click the Position button in the Arrange group, then click Position in Top Right with Square Text Wrapping**

   The graphic is moved to the top-right corner of the page and the text wraps around it. Applying text wrapping to the graphic made it a floating graphic. A floating graphic can be moved anywhere on a page. You can also move a floating graphic to a new location by dragging it using the mouse.

5. **Click the Picture Effects button in the Picture Styles group, point to Shadow, move the pointer over the shadow styles in the gallery to preview them in the document, then click Offset: Bottom Right in the Outer section**

   A drop shadow is applied to the picture, as shown in FIGURE 1-26. You can use the Picture Effects button to apply other visual effects to a graphic, such as a glow, soft edge, reflection, bevel, or 3-D rotation.

6. **Select Tips for Job Seekers, click the Font Color arrow in the Font group on the Home tab, then click Green, Accent 6**

   The text is formatted in green.

7. **Click to deselect the text, click the View tab, click the One Page button in the Zoom group, then save your changes**

   Next, you will finalize the look of the tip sheet.

FIGURE 1-25: Inline graphic in document

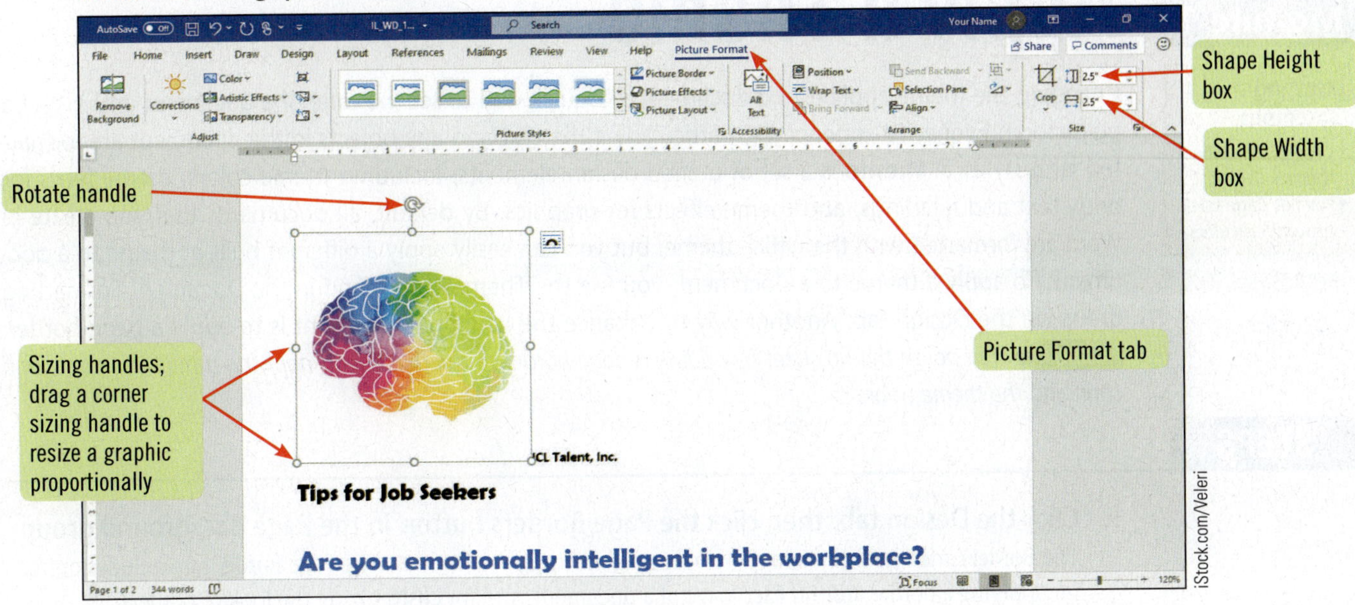

FIGURE 1-26: Floating graphic with shadow effect applied

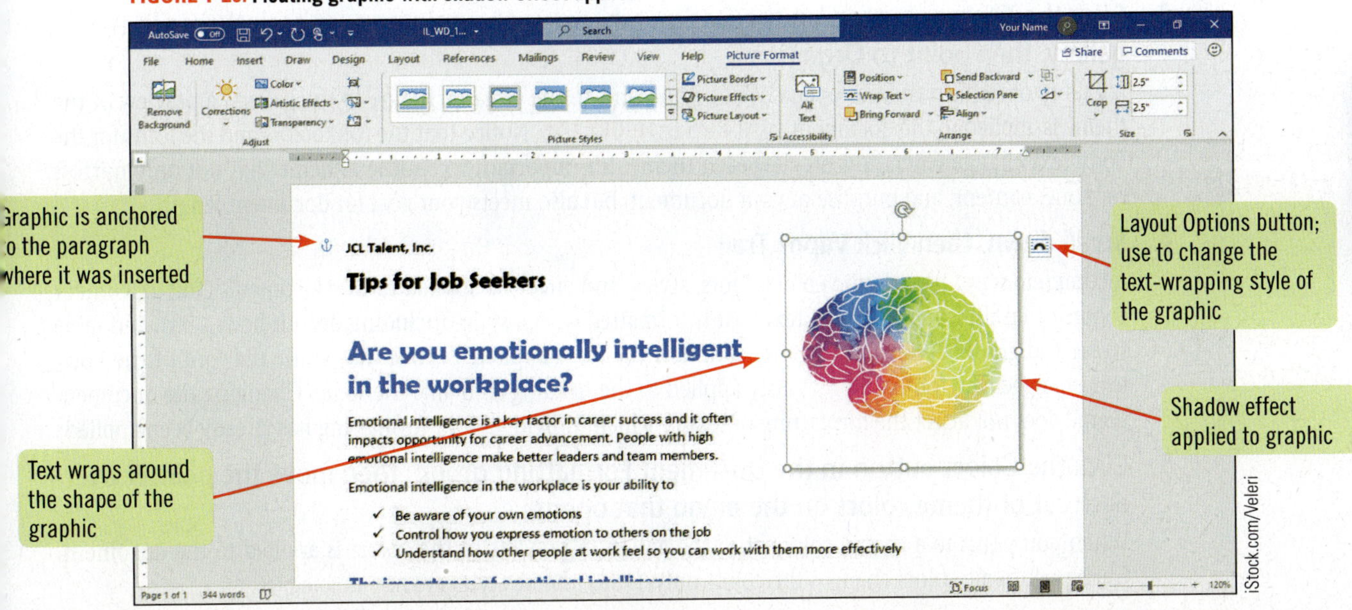

Word

Enhancing pictures with styles and effects

A fun way to give a document personality and flair is to apply a style or an effect to a picture. To apply a style, select the picture and then choose from the style options in the Styles group on the Picture Format tab. Styles include a preset mixture of effects, such as shading, borders, shadows, and other settings. The Effects command in the Styles group on the Picture Format tab gives you the power to apply a customized variety of effects to an object, including a shadow, bevel, glow, reflection, soft edge, or 3-D rotation. To apply an effect, select the object, click the Picture Effects arrow, point to the type of effect you want to apply, and then select from the options in the gallery that opens. To further customize an effect, click the Options command for that type of effect at the bottom of the gallery to open the Format Picture pane. The best way to learn about styles and effects is to experiment by applying them to a picture and seeing what works. To return a picture to its original settings, click the Reset Picture button in the Adjust group on the Picture Format tab.

Word
Module 1

Apply a Theme

Learning Outcomes
- Change document themes
- Format page background elements

Changing the theme applied to a document is a quick way to set the tone of a document and give it a polished and cohesive appearance, particularly if the text and any objects in the document are formatted with styles. A **theme** is a set of unified design elements, including theme colors, theme fonts for body text and headings, and theme effects for graphics. By default, all documents that you create in Word are formatted with the Office theme, but you can easily apply a different built-in theme to a document. To apply a theme to a document, you use the Themes command in the Document Formatting group on the Design tab. Another way to enhance the look of a document is to apply a page border. **CASE** *You polish the tip sheet by adding a page border to the document, applying a built-in theme, and changing the theme colors.*

STEPS

1. **Click the Design tab, then click the Page Borders button in the Page Background group**
   The Borders and Shading dialog box opens, as shown in FIGURE 1-27. The Page Border tab includes options for applying a border around each page of a document, and for customizing the look of borders.
2. **Click the Box button on the Page Border tab, then click OK**
   A single line page border is added to the document.
3. **Click the Themes button on the Design tab, move the pointer over each theme in the gallery, then point to Organic**
   A gallery of built-in themes opens. When you point to the Organic theme in the gallery, a preview of the theme is applied to the document, as shown in FIGURE 1-28. Notice that the font colors and the fonts for the body text change when you preview each theme. It's important to choose a theme that not only mirrors the tone, content, and purpose of your document, but also meets your goal for document length.
4. **Scroll down, then click Vapor Trail**
   A complete set of new theme colors, fonts, styles, and effects is applied to the document. Only document content that uses theme colors, text that is formatted with a style (including default body text), and table styles and graphic effects change when a new theme is applied. Notice that while the font of the body text changed, the font you previously applied to the headings remains the same. Changing the document theme does not affect the formatting of text to which individual font formatting has already been applied.
5. **Click the Colors button in the Document Formatting group, then move the pointer over each set of theme colors on the menu that opens**
   When you point to a theme color set in the gallery, a preview of the colors is applied to the document. Changing theme colors changes the colors only. Other theme styles are not affected.
6. **Click Blue**
   The Blue theme colors are applied to the document, as shown in FIGURE 1-29.
7. **sam Save the document, submit the document to your instructor, close the file, then exit Word**

FIGURE 1-27: Page Border tab in Borders and Shading dialog box

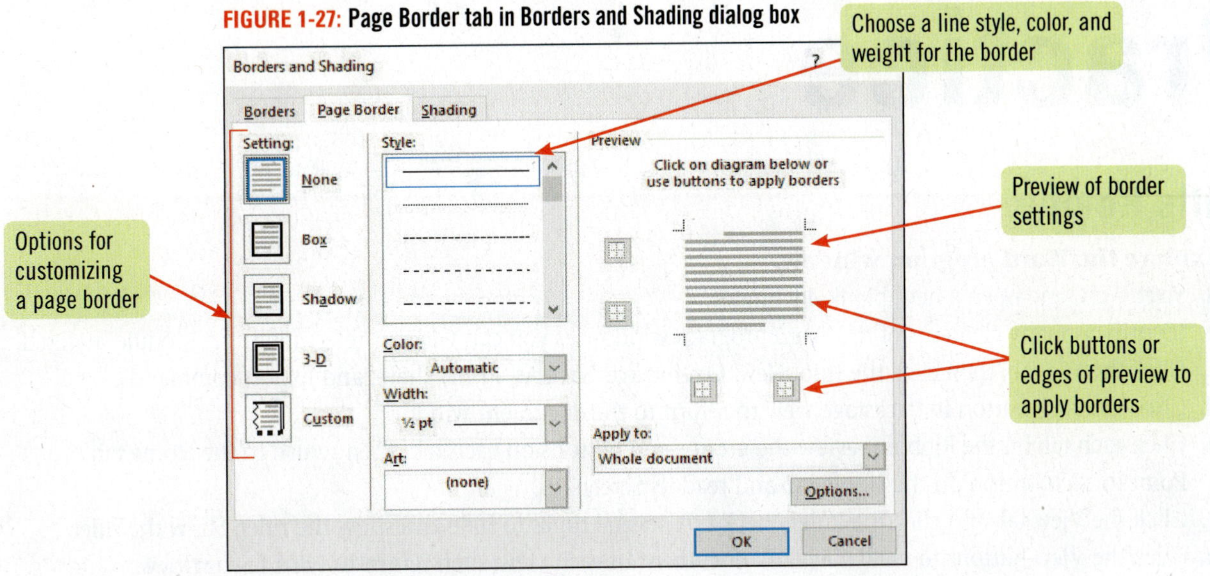

FIGURE 1-28: Organic theme previewed in document

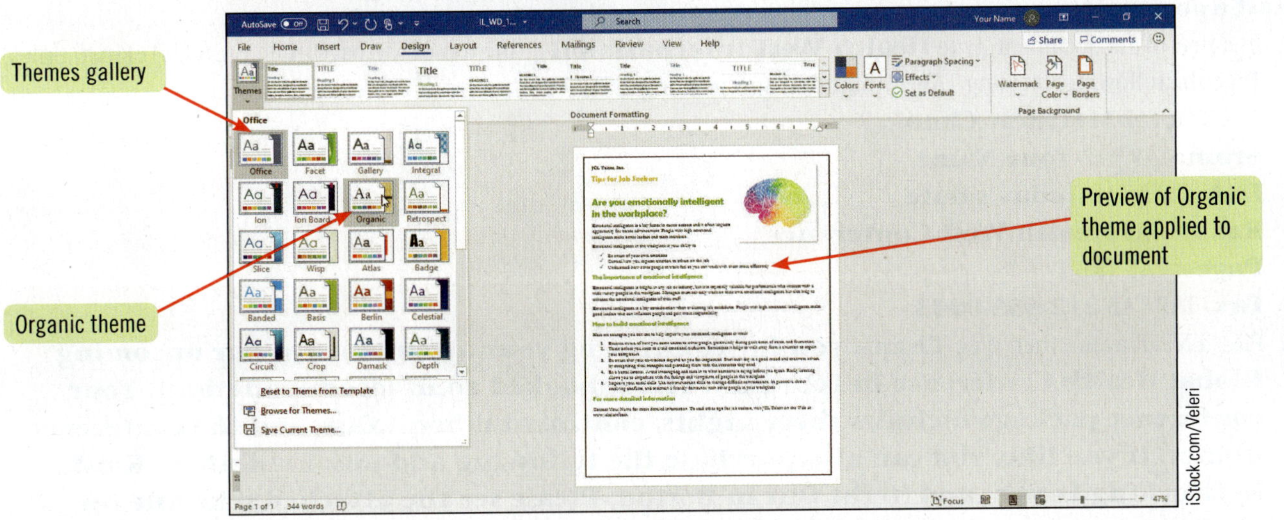

FIGURE 1-29: Vapor Trail theme and Blue theme colors applied to document

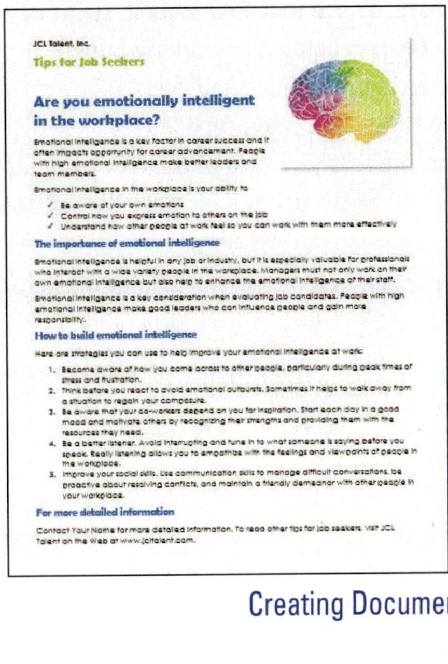
JCL Talent, Inc.

Tips for Job Seekers

Are you emotionally intelligent in the workplace?

Emotional intelligence is a key factor in career success and it often impacts opportunity for career advancement. People with high emotional intelligence make better leaders and team members.

Emotional intelligence in the workplace is your ability to

- ✓ Be aware of your own emotions
- ✓ Control how you express emotion to others on the job
- ✓ Understand how other people at work feel so you can work with them more effectively

The importance of emotional intelligence

Emotional intelligence is helpful in any job or industry, but it is especially valuable for professionals who interact with a wide variety people in the workplace. Managers must not only work on their own emotional intelligence but also help to enhance the emotional intelligence of their staff.

Emotional intelligence is a key consideration when evaluating job candidates. People with high emotional intelligence make good leaders who can influence people and gain more responsibility.

How to build emotional intelligence

Here are strategies you can use to help improve your emotional intelligence at work:

1. Become aware of how you come across to other people, particularly during peak times of stress and frustration.
2. Think before you react to avoid emotional outbursts. Sometimes it helps to walk away from a situation to regain your composure.
3. Be aware that your co-workers depend on you for inspiration. Start each day in a good mood and motivate others by recognizing their strengths and providing them with the resources they need.
4. Be a better listener. Avoid interrupting and tune in to what someone is saying before you speak. Really listening allows you to empathize with the feelings and viewpoints of people in the workplace.
5. Improve your social skills. Use communication skills to manage difficult conversations, be proactive about resolving conflicts, and maintain a friendly demeanor with other people in your workplace.

For more detailed information

Contact Your Name for more detailed information. To read other tips for job seekers, visit JCL Talent on the Web at www.jcltalent.com.

iStock.com/Veleri

Practice

Skills Review

1. **Explore the Word program window.**
   a. Start Word and open a new, blank document.
   b. Identify as many elements of the Word program window as you can without referring to the module material.
   c. Click the File tab, then click the Info, New, Open, Save, Save As, Print, Share, and Export commands.
   d. Click the Back button in Backstage view to return to the document window.
   e. Click each tab on the Ribbon, review the groups and buttons on each tab, then return to the Home tab.
   f. Point to each button on the Home tab and read its ScreenTip.
   g. Click the View tab and click the Ruler check box several times to hide and show the ruler. Show the ruler.
   h. Click the View buttons to view the blank document in each view, then return to Print Layout view.
   i. Use the Zoom slider to zoom all the way in and all the way out on the document, then return to 120%.
2. **Start a document.**
   a. In a new blank document, type **Health West International** at the top of the page, then press ENTER two times.
   b. Type the following, pressing TAB as indicated and pressing ENTER at the end of each line:
      To: TAB TAB **Matthew Chao**
      From: TAB TAB **Your Name**
      Date: TAB TAB **Today's date**
      Re: TAB TAB **Health West Conference**
      Pages: TAB TAB **1**
      Fax: TAB TAB **212-555-0043**
   c. Press ENTER again, then type **Thank you for confirming your attendance at our upcoming Global Health Conference in February. I have booked your accommodations. Your conference package includes three nights, continental breakfast, and the conference dinner. If you like, you can also purchase the following add-ons: Exhibitor's Kiosk, Networking Lunch, and Night Out in Boston. Please see the attached schedule for conference dates and details.**
   d. Press ENTER, then type **To make a payment, please call me at 617-555-0156 or visit our website at www.healthwest5.com. Payment must be received in full by the 3rd of October to hold your room. We look forward to seeing you!**
   e. Insert **Fireside Chat Social Hour,** before Networking Lunch.
   f. Insert **Insurance** before Conference in the first sentence.
   g. Use BACKSPACE to delete 1 in the Pages: line, then type **2**.
   h. Use DELETE to delete upcoming in the first sentence of the first paragraph.
3. **Save a document.**
   a. Click the File tab, then click Save.
   b. Save the document as **IL_WD_1_ChaoFax** with the default file extension to the location where you store your Data Files.
   c. After your name, type a comma, press SPACEBAR, then type **Conference Manager**.
   d. Save the document.
4. **Select text.**
   a. Turn on formatting marks.
   b. Select the Re: line, then type **Re:** TAB TAB **Global Health Insurance Conference**

Skills Review (continued)

c. Select three in the third sentence, then type **two**.

d. Select 3rd of October in the second sentence of the last paragraph, type **15th of November**, select room, then type **reservation**.

e. Delete the sentence We look forward to seeing you!

f. Turn off the display of formatting marks, then save the document.

5. Format text using the Mini toolbar.

a. Select Health West International, click the Increase Font Size button on the Mini toolbar eight times, apply bold, then click the Decrease Font Size button on the Mini toolbar twice.

b. Center Health West International on the page.

c. Change the case of Health West International to uppercase.

d. Apply a bottom border under Health West International.

e. Apply bold to the following words in the fax heading: To:, From:, Date:, Re:, Pages:, and Fax:.

f. Apply yellow highlighting to 15th of November.

g. Use the Undo, Redo, and Repeat buttons to undo the highlighting, redo the highlighting, undo, repeat, then undo the highlighting again.

h. Remove the hyperlink from the website address, then underline 15th of November.

i. Italicize the last sentence of the first paragraph.

j. Read the document using the Read Mode view.

k. Return to Print Layout view, zoom in on the document, then proofread the fax.

l. Correct any typing errors in your document, then save the document. Compare your document to FIGURE 1-30.

m. Preview the document in Print Preview, identify each printing option available to you on the Print screen in Backstage view, then print the document only if required to do so by your instructor.

n. Return to Print Layout view, save, submit the fax per your instructor's directions, then close the document.

FIGURE 1-30

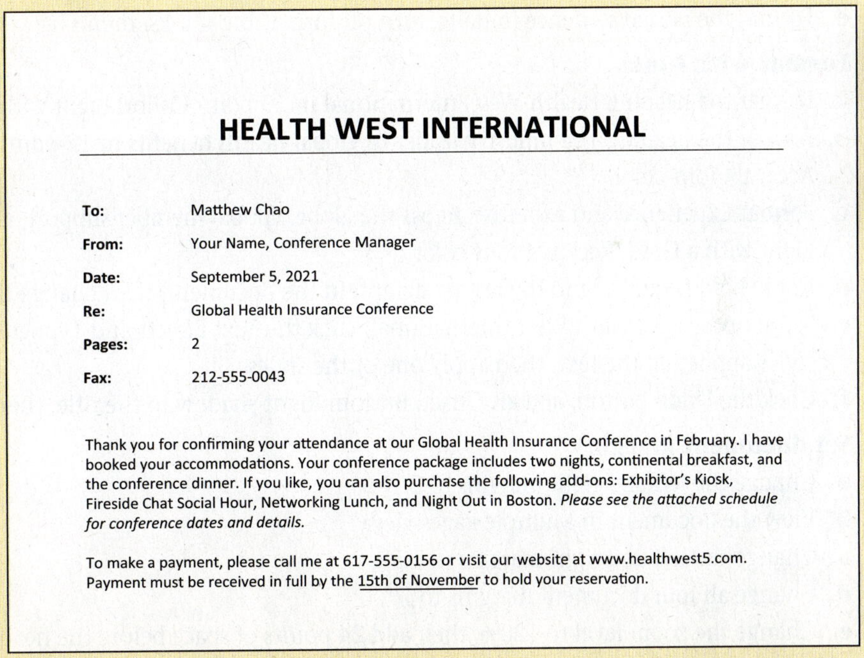

HEALTH WEST INTERNATIONAL

To:	Matthew Chao
From:	Your Name, Conference Manager
Date:	September 5, 2021
Re:	Global Health Insurance Conference
Pages:	2
Fax:	212-555-0043

Thank you for confirming your attendance at our Global Health Insurance Conference in February. I have booked your accommodations. Your conference package includes two nights, continental breakfast, and the conference dinner. If you like, you can also purchase the following add-ons: Exhibitor's Kiosk, Fireside Chat Social Hour, Networking Lunch, and Night Out in Boston. *Please see the attached schedule for conference dates and details.*

To make a payment, please call me at 617-555-0156 or visit our website at www.healthwest5.com. Payment must be received in full by the 15th of November to hold your reservation.

6. View and navigate a document.

a. Open the file IL_WD_1-3.docx from the location where you store your Data Files, then save it as **IL_WD_1_HealthWest** in the File name box.

b. Switch to Page Width view, then scroll through the document to get a feel for its contents.

c. Use the Zoom dialog box to view the Whole Page.

d. Use the Zoom slider to set the Zoom percentage at approximately 100%.

e. Read the document using the Read Mode view. (*Hint*: Press ESC to leave Read Mode view.)

Skills Review (continued)

- **f.** Return to Print Layout view, zoom in, scroll to the bottom of the document, then replace Your Name with your name in the final sentence.
- **g.** Add the Title property **Global** to the document properties in the file, return to Print Layout view, change the zoom level to 120%, then save your changes.

7. Cut and paste text.

- **a.** Turn on the display of formatting marks.
- **b.** Select the first body paragraph that begins We aim… (including the paragraph mark after it), cut it to the clipboard, then paste the paragraph before the heading Experience and expertise across the globe.
- **c.** Delete the heading The Health West International Difference.
- **d.** In the list of locations, move the Middle East paragraph after the Europe paragraph.
- **e.** Move the United States paragraph after the Greater China paragraph.
- **f.** Move the Southeast Asia paragraph before the United States paragraph.
- **g.** Move the Greater China paragraph after the Europe paragraph, then save your changes.

8. Copy and paste text.

- **a.** Scroll to the bottom of the document, then remove the hyperlink in the final paragraph.
- **b.** Select the sentence Get an online quote at www.healthwest5.com., then copy the sentence to the clipboard.
- **c.** Scroll to the top of the page, add a blank paragraph under the Health West International heading, then paste the sentence at the location of the blank paragraph.
- **d.** Use the Paste Options button to Keep Source formatting.
- **e.** Format the pasted sentence in italic, turn off formatting marks, then save your changes.

9. Format with fonts.

- **a.** Format the heading Health West International in 20-point Calibri Light with a Blue, Accent 1 font color.
- **b.** Format the heading The industry leader in global health benefits in 12-point Calibri Light with a Gold, Accent 4 font color.
- **c.** Format Experience and expertise across the globe, Global member support, and Clinical expertise in 12-point Calibri Light with a Gold, Accent 4 font color.
- **d.** Apply bold formatting to the last paragraph in the document, then change the font color to Blue, Accent 1.
- **e.** Scroll up, select Health West International, click the Text Effects and Typography arrow, preview several WordArt styles applied to the text, then apply one of the styles.
- **f.** Click the Undo button, add an Offset: Bottom Right shadow to the title, then save your changes.

10. Set document margins.

- **a.** Change the left and right margins to 2".
- **b.** View the document in Multiple Pages view.
- **c.** Change the left and right margins to 1.5".
- **d.** Change all four document margins to .7".
- **e.** Change the zoom level to 120%, then add 24 points of space before the heading The industry leader in global health benefits.
- **f.** Save your changes.

11. Add bullets and numbering.

- **a.** Select the five-line list of locations that begins with Europe and ends with United States, then format it as a bulleted list using the circle bullet symbol.
- **b.** Change the font color of the bullets to Blue, Accent 1.
- **c.** Press and hold CTRL to select the headings Experience and expertise across the globe, Global member support, and Clinical expertise, then apply numbering.
- **d.** Click 1 in the list, then change the font color of the numbers to Blue, Accent 1.
- **e.** Save your changes.

Skills Review (continued)

12. Insert a graphic.

a. Click in the first body paragraph to move the insertion point to the top of the document, then open the Insert Picture dialog box.

b. Navigate to the location where you store Data Files, then insert the file **Support_ WD_1-4.jpg**.

c. Change the height of the graphic to 1.2 using the Shape Height box in the Size group on the Picture Format tab.

d. Use the Position command to wrap text around the graphic and position it in the Top Left with Square Text Wrapping.

e. Apply the Double Frame, Black picture style to the graphic.

f. Click the Reset Picture arrow in the Adjust Group on the Picture Format tab, reset the picture, then apply the Simple Frame, White picture style.

g. Change the font size of Health West International to 28 point.

h. Click before The industry leader in global health benefits heading, press ENTER, change the font size of the heading to 18 point, then save your changes.

13. Apply a theme.

a. Change the view to One Page, click the Design tab, click the Page Borders button, then apply a single line box border to the page.

b. Use the Themes feature, preview several different themes applied to the document. Apply a theme, zoom in and out on the document to evaluate its suitability, then apply another theme, zoom in and out, and so forth.

c. Apply the View theme.

d. Change all four document margins to .6" to better fit the text on the page.

e. Zoom in on the bottom of the document, then add 24 points of space above the last paragraph.

f. Change the theme colors to Red.

g. Zoom in on the top of the document, then change the font color of the Get an online quote... paragraph to Brown, Accent 5.

h. Change the font color of the four light brown headings to Orange, Accent 3. Compare your document to **FIGURE 1-31**.

i. Save your changes, preview the document, submit it per your instructor's directions, then close the document and exit Word.

FIGURE 1-31

Health West International

Get an online quote at www.healthwest5.com.

The industry leader in global health benefits

Our award-winning global health insurance business provides health benefits to more than one million members worldwide. We are world leaders in providing health care benefits with a seventy-five year track record of excellence and expertise. In addition, we have developed world-class health systems for governments, businesses, and health providers around the world. By delivering comprehensive health benefits worldwide, we are committed to helping create a stronger, healthier global community.

More than 1,500 dedicated Health West employees can be found in our global locations, including

- Europe (Madrid, London, and Berlin)
- Greater China (Shanghai and Hong Kong)
- Middle East (Dubai, Cairo, and Abu Dhabi)
- Southeast Asia (Singapore, Manila, and Jakarta)
- United States (Hartford and nationally)

We aim to be the global leader in delivering world-class health solutions. Our goals are to make quality health care more accessible to empower people to live healthier lives. Our strengths include

1. **Experience and expertise across the globe**

With nearly a century of experience in health care, we've specialized in international health benefits insurance for more than 55 years. Our global footprint reaches wherever our members travel. Our prestigious awards include "Best International Health Insurance Provider" and "International Health Insurer of the Year."

2. **Global member support**

Our professional Member Service representatives are trained to assist you, 24 hours a day, 365 days a year. We can help locate health care services wherever you are, arrange for reimbursement in more than 180 currencies, and answer your questions about claims, benefit levels, and coverage—in ten languages with the ability to communicate in more than 160 languages through interpretation services.

3. **Clinical expertise**

You can depend on our clinical knowledge and experience for help with pre-trip planning, which is especially important if you have a chronic health condition. We can also coordinate medical care, obtain prescription medications and medical devices, and handle medical emergency or evacuation services.

Looking for international health insurance? Get an online quote at www.healthwest5.com. For more information, contact Your Name at 860-555-0035.

Independent Challenge 1

You work at the Riverwalk Medical Clinic, a large outpatient medical facility staffed by family physicians, specialists, nurses, and other allied health professionals. Your boss has drafted an information sheet to help seasonal allergy sufferers and asks you to edit and format it so that it is eye catching and attractive.

a. Open the file IL_WD_1-5.docx from the drive and folder where you store your Data Files, save it as **IL_WD_1_AllergyInfo**, then read the document to get a feel for the content. FIGURE 1-32 shows how you will format the info sheet.

b. Show the rulers in your document window if they are not already visible.

c. Accept or ignore all suggested spelling and grammar changes in the document.

d. Insert the Riverwalk Medical Clinic logo file Support_WD_1-6.jpg at the top of the document. Change the height of the logo to 1", then position the logo in the bottom right with square text wrapping. (*Hint*: Zoom in and out on the document as necessary. If an anchor symbol appears in the margin, you can ignore it.)

e. Center the first two lines of text in the document.

f. Change the font of Riverwalk Medical Clinic to Arial Black. Change the font size to 18 point. Change the font color to Orange, Accent 2. Apply an Offset: Bottom Right shadow text effect.

g. Format Advice for Seasonal Allergy Sufferers in 28-point Arial Black with a Blue, Accent 1 font color. Apply an Offset: Bottom Right shadow text effect.

FIGURE 1-32

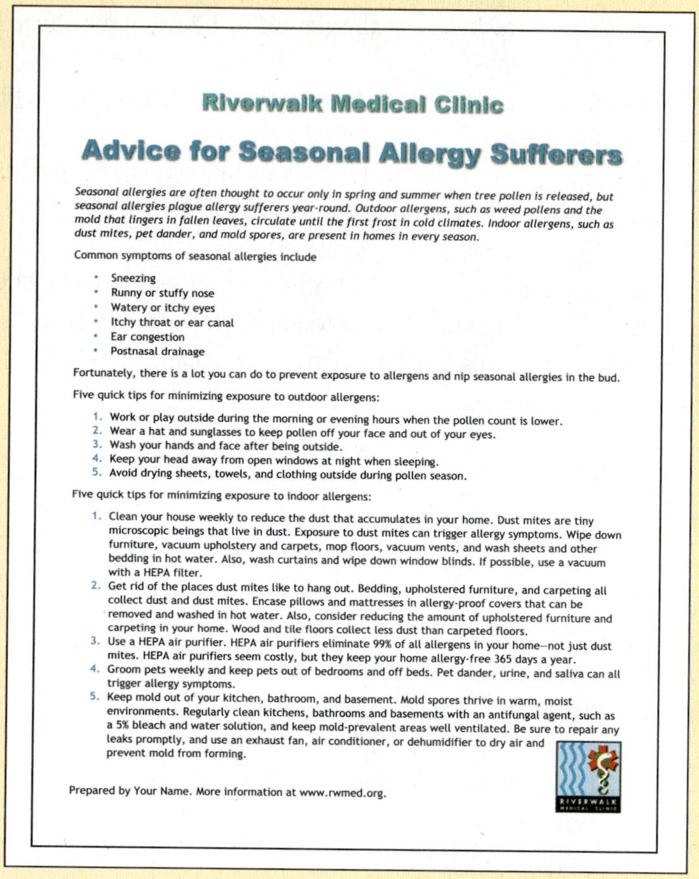
Riverwalk Medical Clinic

Advice for Seasonal Allergy Sufferers

Seasonal allergies are often thought to occur only in spring and summer when tree pollen is released, but seasonal allergies plague allergy sufferers year-round. Outdoor allergens, such as weed pollens and the mold that lingers in fallen leaves, circulate until the first frost in cold climates. Indoor allergens, such as dust mites, pet dander, and mold spores, are present in homes in every season.

Common symptoms of seasonal allergies include

- Sneezing
- Runny or stuffy nose
- Watery or itchy eyes
- Itchy throat or ear canal
- Ear congestion
- Postnasal drainage

Fortunately, there is a lot you can do to prevent exposure to allergens and nip seasonal allergies in the bud.

Five quick tips for minimizing exposure to outdoor allergens:

1. Work or play outside during the morning or evening hours when the pollen count is lower.
2. Wear a hat and sunglasses to keep pollen off your face and out of your eyes.
3. Wash your hands and face after being outside.
4. Keep your head away from open windows at night when sleeping.
5. Avoid drying sheets, towels, and clothing outside during pollen season.

Five quick tips for minimizing exposure to indoor allergens:

1. Clean your house weekly to reduce the dust that accumulates in your home. Dust mites are tiny microscopic beings that live in dust. Exposure to dust mites can trigger allergy symptoms. Wipe down furniture, vacuum upholstery and carpets, mop floors, vacuum vents, and wash sheets and other bedding in hot water. Also, wash curtains and wipe down window blinds. If possible, use a vacuum with a HEPA filter.
2. Get rid of the places dust mites like to hang out. Bedding, upholstered furniture, and carpeting all collect dust and dust mites. Encase pillows and mattresses in allergy-proof covers that can be removed and washed in hot water. Also, consider reducing the amount of upholstered furniture and carpeting in your home. Wood and tile floors collect less dust than carpeted floors.
3. Use a HEPA air purifier. HEPA air purifiers eliminate 99% of all allergens in your home—not just dust mites. HEPA air purifiers seem costly, but they keep your home allergy-free 365 days a year.
4. Groom pets weekly and keep pets out of bedrooms and off beds. Pet dander, urine, and saliva can all trigger allergy symptoms.
5. Keep mold out of your kitchen, bathroom, and basement. Mold spores thrive in warm, moist environments. Regularly clean kitchens, bathrooms and basements with an antifungal agent, such as a 5% bleach and water solution, and keep mold-prevalent areas well ventilated. Be sure to repair any leaks promptly, and use an exhaust fan, air conditioner, or dehumidifier to dry air and prevent mold from forming.

Prepared by Your Name. More information at www.rwmed.org.

RIVERWALK MEDICAL CLINIC

h. Apply italic to the first body paragraph.

i. Change all four document margins to .5", then reduce the font size of Advice for Seasonal Allergy Sufferers by 2 points.

j. Format the six-line list of common symptoms (beginning with Sneezing) as a bulleted list, then apply the Blue, Accent 1 font color to the bullets.

k. Format the five-line list of tips for minimizing exposure to outdoor allergens (beginning with Work or play outside) as a numbered list. (*Hint*: If you make a mistake, click the Undo button and try again.)

l. Format the five-paragraph list of tips for minimizing exposure to indoor allergens, beginning with Clean your house weekly, as a numbered list.

m. Apply bold to the numbers in each numbered list, and change the font color of the numbers to Blue, Accent 1.

n. In the second numbered list, select paragraph 2, cut it, place the insertion point before Groom in the new paragraph 3, then paste the text.

o. Change the document theme to Facet, then change the theme colors to Blue Green.

p. Add a Shadow page border to the document.

q. Increase the font size of **Riverwalk Medical Clinic** to 22, then add 12 points of space after **Advice for Seasonal Allergy Sufferers**.

r. Zoom in on the bottom of the document. Replace Your Name in the final line with your name, remove the hyperlink from www.rwmed.org, and add 24 points of space before the final line paragraph.

s. Zoom out, examine the document carefully for formatting errors, and make any necessary adjustments so that all the text fits on one page.

t. Save the document, submit it per your instructor's directions, then close the file and exit Word.

Independent Challenge 2

Yesterday you interviewed for a job as the administrative assistant in the Business Department at Jericho College. You spoke with several people at the college, including Sonia Alvarado, director of human resources, whose business card is shown in FIGURE 1-33. You need to write a follow-up letter to Ms. Alvarado, thanking her for the interview and expressing your interest in the college and the position. She also asked you to send her some samples of your work as evidence of your Word skills.

a. Start Word and save a new blank document as **IL_WD_1_AlvaradoLetter** to the location where you store your Data Files.

b. Begin the letter by clicking the No Spacing button in the Styles group. You use this button to apply the No Spacing style to the document so that your document does not include extra space between paragraphs.

c. Type a personal letterhead for the letter that includes your name, address, telephone number, email address, and webpage or LinkedIn address, if you have one. Remove any hyperlinks. Accept or undo any automatic corrections. (*Note: Format the letterhead after you finish typing the letter.*)

d. Four lines below the bottom of the letterhead, type today's date.

e. Four lines below the date, type the inside address, referring to FIGURE 1-33 for the information. Include the recipient's title, college name, and full mailing address.

FIGURE 1-33

f. Two lines below the inside address, type **Dear Ms. Alvarado:** for the salutation.

g. Two lines below the salutation, type the body of the letter, leaving a blank space between each paragraph, according to the following guidelines:
   - In the first paragraph, thank her for the interview. Then restate your interest in the position and express your desire to work for the college. Add any specific details you think will enhance the power of your letter.
   - In the second paragraph, note that you are enclosing three samples of your work, and explain something about the samples you are enclosing.
   - Type a short final paragraph.

h. Two lines below the last body paragraph, type a closing, then four lines below the closing, type the signature block. Be sure to include your name in the signature block.

i. Two lines below the signature block, type an enclosure notation. (*Hint*: An enclosure notation usually includes the word "Enclosures" or the abbreviation "Enc." followed by the number of enclosures in parentheses.)

j. Edit your letter for clarity and precision. Move sentences if necessary, replace words with more precise words, and correct any spelling or grammar errors.

k. Change the font of the letter to a serif font, such as Times New Roman, Garamond, or something similar. Adjust the font size so the letter can be read easily.

l. Format the letterhead using fonts, font colors, text effects, borders, themes, paragraph spacing, paragraph alignment, change case, and other formatting features. Be sure the design of your letterhead reflects your personality and is suitable for a professional document.

m. Change the Title document property to **Letter**.

n. Save your changes, preview the letter, submit it per your instructor's directions, then close the document and exit Word.

Visual Workshop

Create the letter shown in **FIGURE 1-34**. Before beginning to type, click the No Spacing button in the Styles group on the Home tab. Type the letter before formatting the letterhead and applying the theme. To format the letterhead, change the font size of the first line of text to 40 point and apply the Gradient Fill: Blue, Accent color 5, Reflection WordArt style. Change the font color of the address line to Blue, Accent 5. Add the bottom border to the letterhead. When the letterhead is formatted, change the font size of the body text to 12 point, apply the Organic theme, then change the font color of the letterhead text to Green, Accent 1. Save the document as **IL_WD_1_SakuraDoksa** to the location where you store your Data Files, submit the letter to your instructor, then close the document and exit Word.

FIGURE 1-34

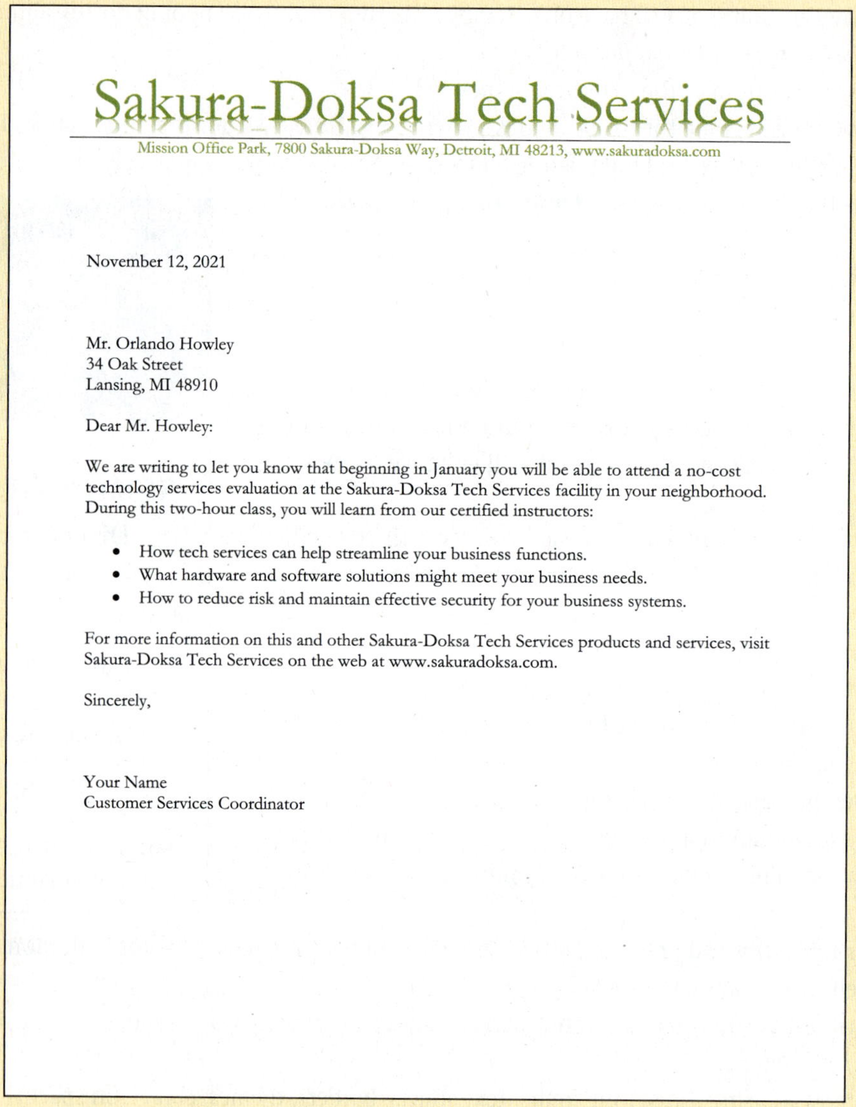

Sakura-Doksa Tech Services

Mission Office Park, 7800 Sakura-Doksa Way, Detroit, MI 48213, www.sakuradoksa.com

November 12, 2021

Mr. Orlando Howley
34 Oak Street
Lansing, MI 48910

Dear Mr. Howley:

We are writing to let you know that beginning in January you will be able to attend a no-cost technology services evaluation at the Sakura-Doksa Tech Services facility in your neighborhood. During this two-hour class, you will learn from our certified instructors:

- How tech services can help streamline your business functions.
- What hardware and software solutions might meet your business needs.
- How to reduce risk and maintain effective security for your business systems.

For more information on this and other Sakura-Doksa Tech Services products and services, visit Sakura-Doksa Tech Services on the web at www.sakuradoksa.com.

Sincerely,

Your Name
Customer Services Coordinator

Editing and Formatting Documents

CASE You have been asked to edit and format a research report on job growth in the tech sector. After editing the report and applying styles to format the text, you plan to add page numbers, a header, footnotes, and a bibliography to the report. Finally, before distributing the report file electronically, you will strip the file of private information.

Module Objectives

After completing this module, you will be able to:

- Insert comments
- Find and replace text
- Check spelling and grammar
- Research information
- Change line spacing and indents
- Apply styles to text
- Insert page numbers and page breaks
- Add headers and footers
- Add footnotes and endnotes
- Insert citations
- Create a bibliography
- Inspect a document

Files You Will Need

IL_WD_2-1.docx
IL_WD_2-2.docx
IL_WD_2-3.docx
IL_WD_2-4.docx

Word
Module 2

Insert Comments

Learning Outcome
- Add comments

You can collaborate on documents with colleagues in different ways. One way is to insert comments into a document when you want to ask questions or provide information to other reviewers. A **comment** is text that appears to the right of your document in Print Layout view. Shading appears in the document at the point where you inserted the comment. A comment icon may appear to the right of the commented text. Each reviewer is assigned a unique color automatically, which is applied to the background of the reviewer's initials. **CASE** *Your colleague, Dawn Lapointe, read the draft of the report and inserted comments. You open the report to review and respond to Dawn's comments. You add and edit comments.*

STEPS

QUICK TIP
When you click the reviewer's initials, a person card for the reviewer appears; use this to communicate quickly with reviewers.

TROUBLE
If you don't see the Reply box, click the Reply button, type your reply, then click anywhere in the document text.

1. **sam Start Word, open the file IL_WD_2-1.docx from the location where you store your Data Files, save it as IL_WD_2_TechJobs, change the zoom level to 100%, then click the Review tab**
   Simple Markup is the default option in the Display for Review box in the Tracking group on the Review tab. A different markup option may be selected if another user was working on the computer before you. With this option, comments appear along the right side of the page. If you see comment icons and no comment wording, then click a comment icon to read the comment. If you want to see all comments, click the Show Comments button in the Comments group.
2. **Click the Display for Review arrow in the Tracking group, then click All Markup**
   In the second body paragraph, the text "job" is shaded in a color, indicating the text is associated with the comment.
3. **Select the word Sector in the title (the first line), then click the New Comment button in the Comments group**
   The word "Sector" is shaded, and space for a comment appears to the right of the document. Your name or the name assigned to your computer appears. To navigate between comments in a long document, use the Next and Previous buttons in the Comments group.
4. **Type This title is approved by the web team., then click the Post comment button or, if a Post comment button does not appear in your comment, click anywhere in the document text**
   Your comment appears as shown in **FIGURE 2-1**.
5. **Click Dawn's first comment (starts with "This is..."), click the Reply box in the comment, type I am compiling a list., then click the Post reply button**
   Your response appears indented under the original comment.

FIGURE 2-1: New comment in document

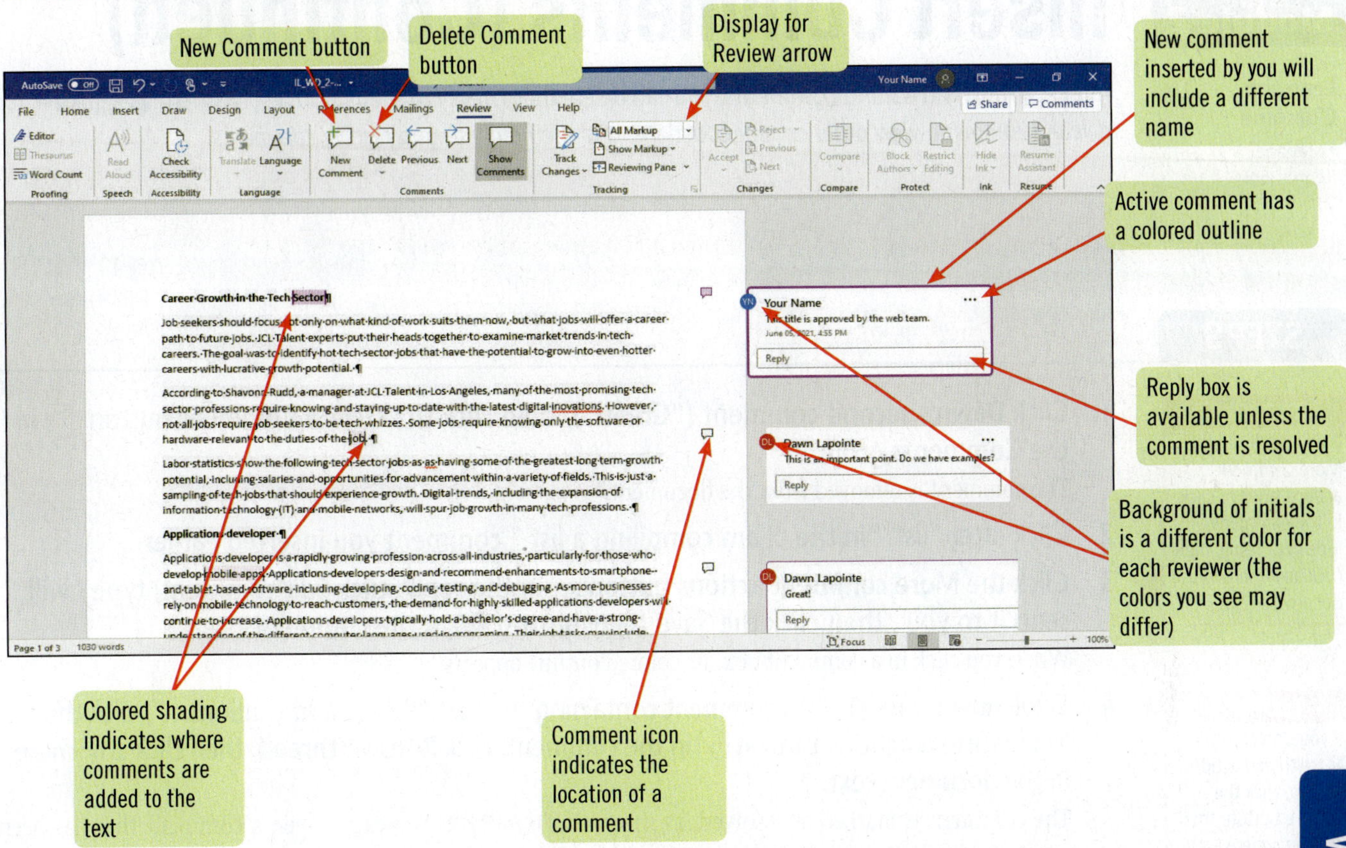

Word

Insert Comments (Continued)

Learning Outcome
- Manage comments

After inserting and editing comments, you can delete them, reply to them, and resolve them. **CASE** *You delete a comment, view other comment actions, and then reply to and resolve comments.*

STEPS

TROUBLE
If you don't see the More comment actions button, click in the comment, type your reply, then click anywhere in the document text.

TROUBLE
If you don't see the More thread actions button, click the Resolve button, then click anywhere in the document text.

QUICK TIP
To delete all comments in a document, click the Delete Comment arrow, then click Delete All Comments in Document.

1. **Click Dawn's second comment ("Great!"), then click the Delete Comment button in the Comments group**
   The comment is removed from the document.
2. **Click after "list." in the "I am compiling a list." comment you inserted earlier**
3. **Click the More comment actions button ··· in the reply, click Edit comment, type I will send it to you., then click the Save reply button in the comment**
   When you click in a comment box, its colored outline appears.
4. **Scroll down, click Dawn's comment containing the text "Please add citations…", click the More thread actions button ··· in the comment, click Resolve thread, then click anywhere in the document text**
   The comment is marked as resolved, as shown in **FIGURE 2-2**. You can reopen a comment that has been marked as resolved by clicking the comment icon or the comment itself and then clicking the Reopen button in the comment.
5. **Click All Markup in the Tracking group, click No Markup, then save your changes**
   Selecting No Markup hides the comments. Hiding the comments does not remove them from the document. It simply hides them from view on the screen. You will keep the comments hidden while you format the document.

FIGURE 2-2: Resolved comment in document

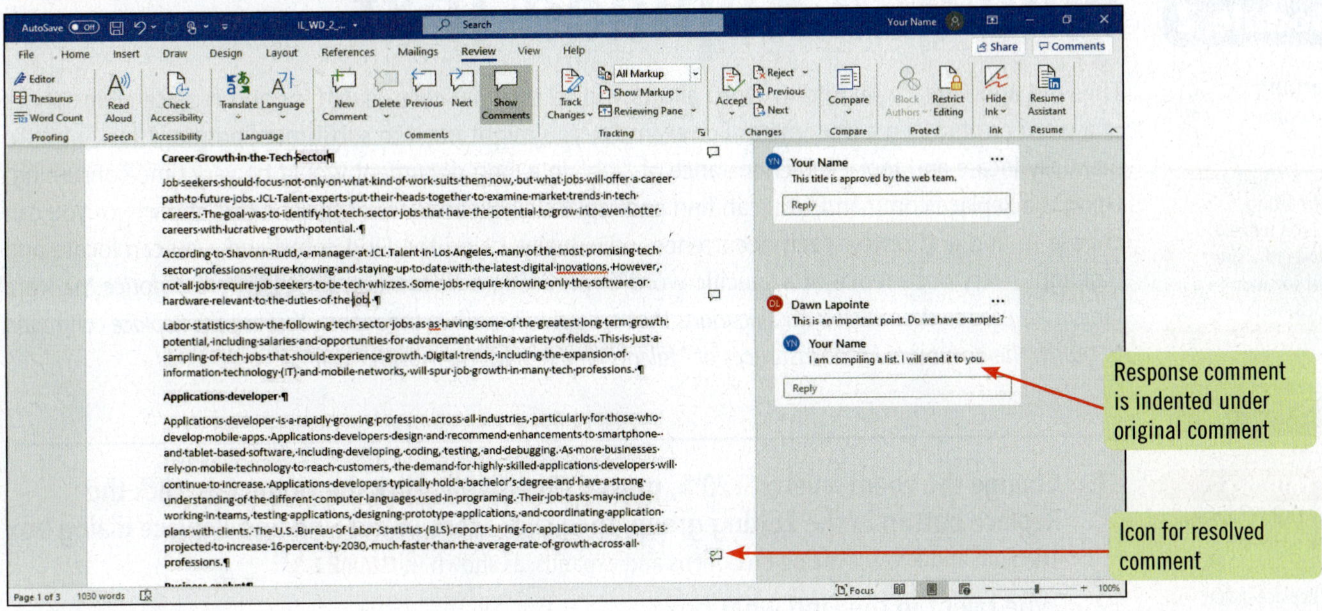

Inking comments in Word

If you are working in Touch mode on a touch-enabled device, you can draw or write comments using your finger, a digital pen, or a mouse. The type of inking features available to you will depend on your device. To begin, click the Draw tab on the Ribbon, click a pen in the Drawing Tools group to create an ink comment, and then use your finger, stylus, or mouse to draw or write in the document. On some devices, you can change the color and type of pen stroke to use for inking by using the Pen button in the Drawing Tools group. You can hide inked comments using the Hide Ink button in the Ink group on the Review tab. When you are finished inking a comment, click anywhere in the document. If you are on a touch-enabled device and want to switch your device to Touch mode and use the full range of inking features available in Word, you can add the Touch/Mouse Mode button to the Quick Access toolbar by clicking the Customize Quick Access Toolbar button on the Quick Access toolbar, and then clicking Touch/Mouse Mode. To use Touch mode, click the Touch/Mouse Mode button, and then click Touch.

Word

Find and Replace Text

Learning Outcomes
- Find and replace text and formatting
- Search for text
- Move to a specific location in a document

The Find and Replace feature in Word allows you to automatically search for and replace all instances of a word or phrase in a document. For example, you might need to substitute "position" for "job". To manually locate and replace each instance of "job" in a long document would be very time-consuming. Using the Replace command, you can find and replace all occurrences of specific text at once, or you can choose to find and review each occurrence individually. Using the Find command, you can locate and highlight every occurrence of a specific word or phrase in a document. **CASE** *You notice the word "talent" is used to describe job qualifications that are actually skills in the report. You use the Replace command to search the document for all instances of "talent" and replace them with "skill".*

STEPS

TROUBLE
If any Search Options check boxes are selected in your Find and Replace dialog box, deselect them. If Format appears under the Find what or Replace with box, click in the box, then click the No Formatting button.

QUICK TIP
To find, review, and replace each occurrence individually, click Find Next.

1. **Change the zoom level to 120%, press CTRL+HOME, click the Home tab, click the Replace button in the Editing group, then click More in the Find and Replace dialog box**
   The Find and Replace dialog box opens and expands, as shown in **FIGURE 2-3**.
2. **Type talent in the Find what box**
   The text "talent" is the text that will be replaced.
3. **Press TAB, then type skill in the Replace with box**
   The text "skill" will replace the text "talent".
4. **Click the Match case check box in the Search Options section to select it**
   Selecting the Match case check box tells Word to find only exact matches for the uppercase and lowercase characters you entered in the Find what text box. You want to replace all instances of "talent" in the body text of the report. You do not want to replace "Talent" in the proper name "JCL Talent".
5. **Click Replace All**
   Clicking Replace All changes all occurrences of "talent" to "skill" in the press release. A message box reports eight replacements were made.
6. **Click OK to close the message box, then click Close in the Find and Replace dialog box**
   Word replaced "talent" with "skill" in eight locations but did not replace "Talent" in the company name. To find or replace text that is formatted a certain way, click the Find arrow in the Editing group, click Advanced Find, click Format in the Find and Replace dialog box, and then select the appropriate format options. To find or replace special characters such as em dashes and paragraph marks, click Special in the Find and Replace dialog box.
7. **Click the Find button in the Editing group**
   Clicking the Find button opens the Navigation pane, which is used to browse a longer document by headings, by pages, or by specific text. The Find command allows you to quickly locate all instances of text in a document. You use it to verify that Word did not replace "Talent" in JCL Talent.
8. **Type Talent in the search box in the Navigation pane**
   The word "Talent" is highlighted and selected in the document, as shown in **FIGURE 2-4**.
9. **Click the Close button in the Navigation pane**
   The highlighting is removed from the text when you close the Navigation pane.
10. **Press CTRL+HOME, then save the document**

FIGURE 2-3: Find and Replace dialog box

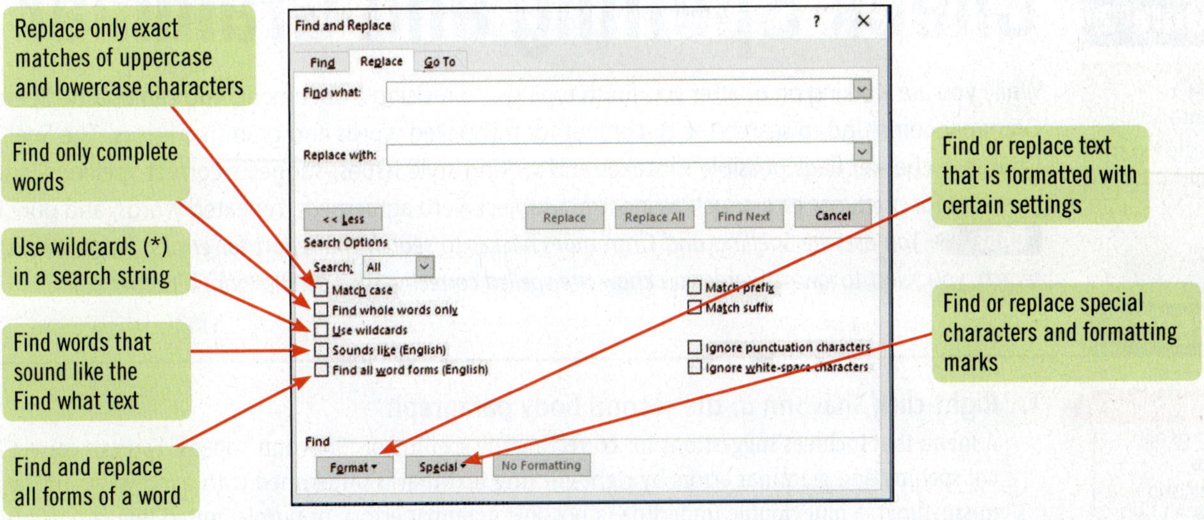

FIGURE 2-4: Found text highlighted in document

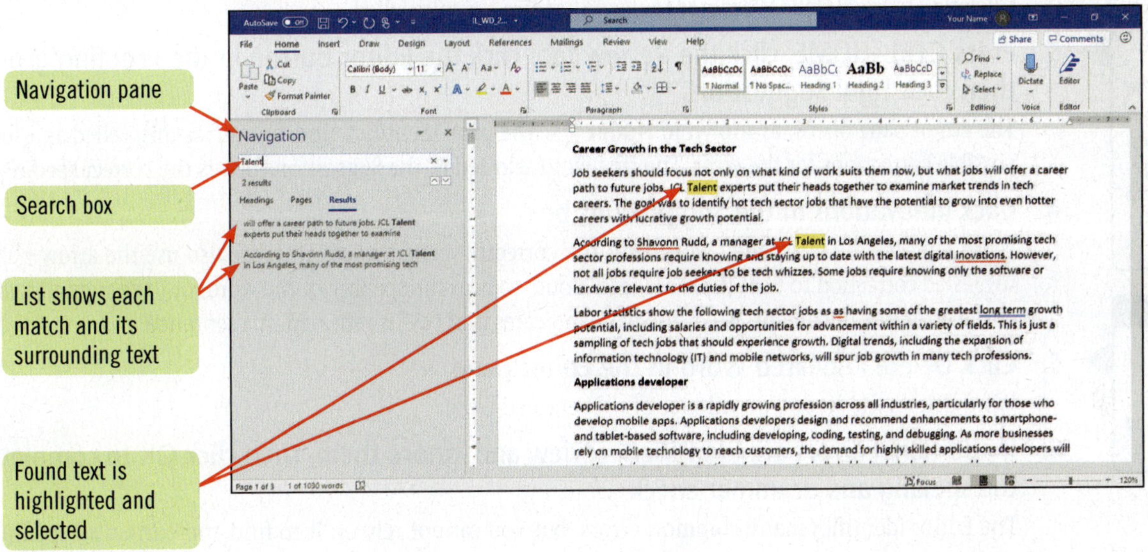

Navigating a document using the Navigation pane and the Go to command

Rather than scrolling to move to a different place in a longer document, you can use the Navigation pane to quickly move the insertion point to a specific page, a specific heading, or specific text. One way to open the Navigation pane is by clicking the Page number button on the status bar, then clicking the link in the Navigation pane for the type of item, headings or pages, you want to use to navigate the document.

To move to a specific page, section, line, table, graphic, or other item in a document, you use the Go To tab in the Find and Replace dialog box. On the Go To tab in the Find and Replace dialog box, select the type of item you want to find in the Go to what list, enter the relevant information about that item, and then click Next to move the insertion point to the item.

Word Module 2

Check Spelling and Grammar

Learning Outcome
- Check spelling and grammar

While you are working on or after you finish typing and revising a document, you can use the Spelling and Grammar command to search the document for misspelled words and grammar errors. The Spelling and Grammar checker flags possible mistakes and writing style issues, suggests correct spellings, and offers remedies for grammar errors such as incorrect subject–verb agreement, repeated words, and punctuation. **CASE** *You use the Spelling and Grammar checker to search the report for errors. Before beginning the search, you select to ignore words you know are spelled correctly, such as Shavonn, a proper noun.*

STEPS

TROUBLE
If Shavonn is not flagged as misspelled, skip to Step 3.

QUICK TIP
To change the language used by the Word proofing tools, click the Language button in the Language group on the Review tab, click Set Proofing Language, select the language you prefer in the dialog box that opens, then click OK.

QUICK TIP
To add a word to the Dictionary so it is not flagged as misspelled, click Add to Dictionary.

1. **Right-click Shavonn in the second body paragraph**
   A menu that includes suggestions for correcting the spelling of "Shavonn" opens. You can correct individual spelling and grammar errors by right-clicking text that is underlined with a red wavy line (a possible misspelling), a blue double underline (a possible grammar error), or purple dotted line (a possible writing style issue), and then selecting a correction. Although "Shavonn" is not in the Word dictionary, it is a proper name that is spelled correctly in the document.
2. **Click Ignore All**
   Clicking Ignore All tells Word not to flag "Shavonn" as misspelled.
3. **Press CTRL+HOME, click the Review tab, click the Editor button in the Proofing group, then click Total Suggestions**
   The Editor pane opens, as shown in **FIGURE 2-5**. The pane identifies "inovations" as misspelled and suggests possible corrections for the error. The first word selected in the Suggestions box is the correct spelling.
4. **Click innovations in the Suggestions box**
   Word replaces the misspelled word with the correctly spelled word. You can also use the arrow next to a suggested correction to hear the word read aloud, to hear the spelling of the word, or to change all instances of the error in a document. Next, the pane indicates that "as" is repeated in a sentence.
5. **Click Delete Repeated Word in the Editor pane**
   Word deletes the second occurrence of the repeated word.
6. **If additional errors are identified, review and ignore them, then click OK to complete the spelling and grammar check**
   The Editor identifies many common errors, but you cannot rely on it to find and correct all spelling and grammar errors in your documents, or to always suggest a valid correction. Always proofread your documents carefully.
7. **Click the Close button in the Editor pane, press CTRL+HOME, then save the document**

Searching for information

The Search feature on the References tab gives you quick access to information about document text, including definitions, images, and other material from online sources. For example, you might use Search to see the definition of a word used in a document or to hear the word pronounced. To use Search, select the text you want to look up in your document, right-click it, then click Search. You can also select text, then click the Search button in the Research group on the References tab. The Search pane opens and displays images and web links related to the selected text. Click the More button to display only pictures, web information, or help articles.

FIGURE 2-5: Editor pane

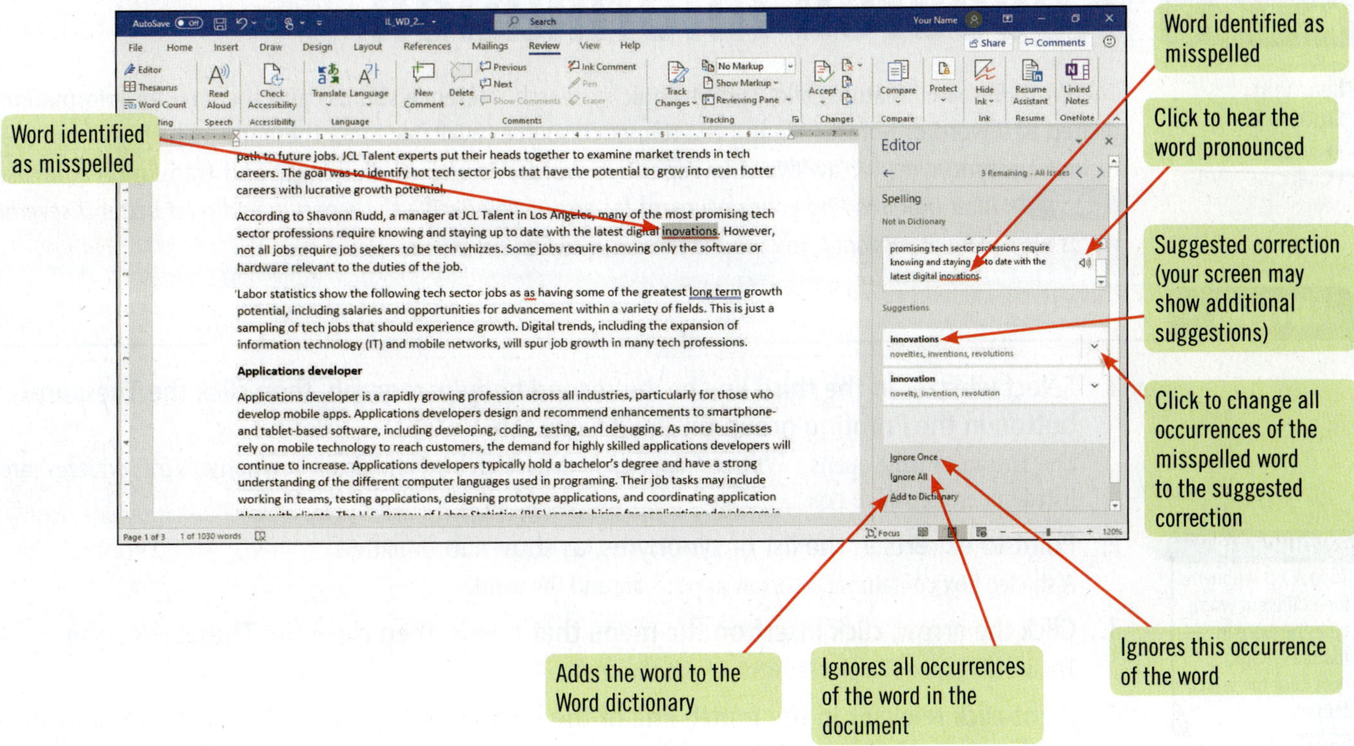

Inserting text with AutoCorrect

As you type, AutoCorrect automatically corrects many commonly misspelled words. By creating your own AutoCorrect entries, you can set Word to insert text that you type often, such as your name or contact information, or to correct words you misspell frequently. For example, you could create an AutoCorrect entry so that the name "Mary T. Watson" is automatically inserted whenever you type "mtw" followed by a space. You create AutoCorrect entries and customize other AutoCorrect and AutoFormat options using the AutoCorrect dialog box. To open the AutoCorrect dialog box, click the File tab, click Options, click Proofing in the Word Options dialog box that opens, and then click AutoCorrect Options. On the AutoCorrect tab in the AutoCorrect dialog box, type the text you want to be corrected automatically in the Replace box (such as "mtw"), type the text you want to be inserted in its place automatically in the With box (such as "Mary T. Watson"), and then click Add. The AutoCorrect entry is added to the list. Click OK to close the AutoCorrect dialog box, and then click OK to close the Word Options dialog box. Word inserts an AutoCorrect entry in a document when you press SPACEBAR or a punctuation mark after typing the text you want Word to correct. For example, Word inserts "Mary T. Watson" when you type "mtw" followed by a space. If you want to remove an AutoCorrect entry you created, simply open the AutoCorrect dialog box, select the AutoCorrect entry you want to remove in the list, click Delete, click OK, and then click OK to close the Word Options dialog box.

Word
Module 2

Research Information

Learning Outcomes
- Find synonyms
- Check the word count

The Word Research features allow you to quickly search reference sources and the web for information related to a word or phrase. Among the reference sources available are a thesaurus, which you can use to look up synonyms for awkward or repetitive words, as well as dictionary and translation sources. **CASE** *After proofreading your document for errors, you decide the report would read better if several words were more professional. You use the thesaurus to find synonyms.*

STEPS

1. **Select whizzes in the third line of the second body paragraph, then click the Thesaurus button in the Proofing group on the Review tab**

   The Thesaurus pane opens. "Whizzes" appears in the search box, and possible synonyms for "whizzes" are listed under the search box.

2. **Point to experts in the list of synonyms, as shown in FIGURE 2-6**

   A shaded box containing an arrow appears around the word.

3. **Click the arrow, click Insert on the menu that opens, then close the Thesaurus pane**

   The word "experts" replaces "whizzes" in the report.

4. **Right-click relevant in the fourth line of the second body paragraph, point to Synonyms on the menu that opens, then click pertinent**

   The word "pertinent" replaces "relevant" in the report.

5. **Select the three paragraphs of body text under the "Career Growth..." title, then click the Word Count button in the Proofing group**

   The Word Count dialog box opens, as shown in FIGURE 2-7. The dialog box lists the number of pages, words, characters, paragraphs, and lines included in the selected text. Notice that the status bar also displays the number of words included in the selected text and the total number of words in the entire document. If you want to view the page, character, paragraph, and line count for the entire document, make sure nothing is selected in your document, and then click Word Count in the Proofing group.

6. **Click Close, then save the document**

QUICK TIP
To look up synonyms for a different word, type the word in the search box, then click the search button.

Reading a document aloud using Word

The Word Read Aloud feature reads a document aloud for you. Reading a document aloud can help you hear grammar errors, discover missing words, or notice other writing issues you might not notice when proofreading a document on screen. As Word reads the document aloud, each word is highlighted on the screen as it is pronounced. To read a document aloud using Word, move the insertion point to the beginning of the document, then click the Read Aloud button in the Speech group on the Review tab. A toolbar of playback controls opens at the top of the document window and Word begins to read aloud. You can use the Settings button on the playback controls to change the reading speed or the reading voice. The Previous, Next, Pause, and Play buttons allow you to pause and resume the reading, or to navigate through the document paragraph by paragraph. When you are finished reading the document aloud using Word, click the Stop button on the playback controls.

FIGURE 2-6: Thesaurus pane

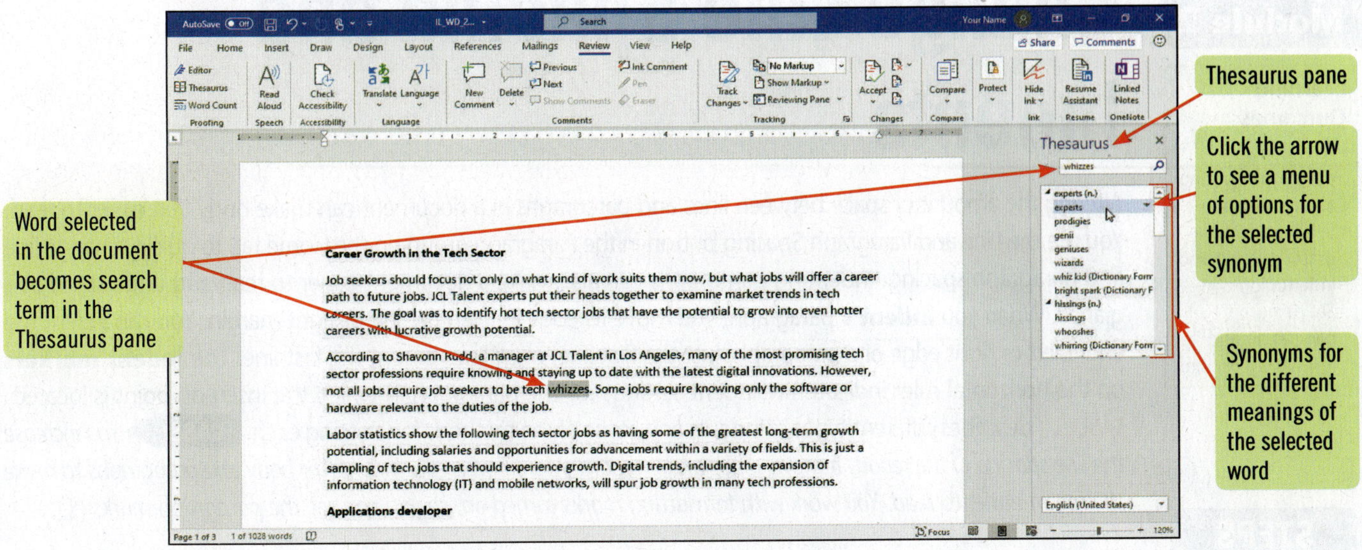

FIGURE 2-7: Word Count dialog box

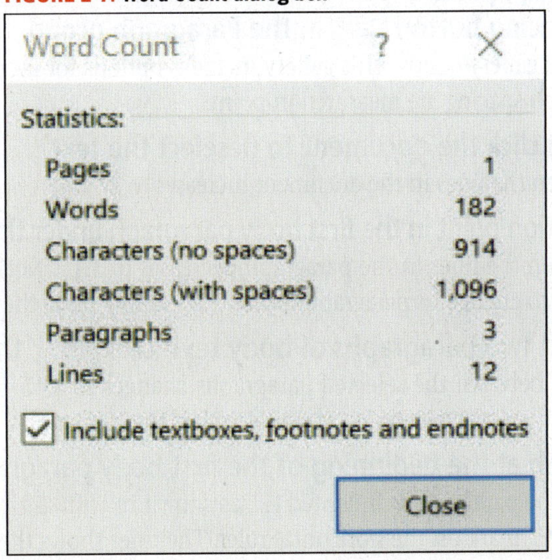

Using a add-ins for Word

Add-ins are small programs embedded in Word that allow you to access information on the web without having to leave Word. For example, you can look up something on Wikipedia, insert an online map in one of your documents, or access dictionaries and other reference sources, all from within Word using an add-in. To find and install an add-in, click the Get Add-ins button in the Add-ins group on the Insert tab to open the Office Add-ins gallery. The Store tab in the Office Add-ins gallery includes a searchable list of the add-ins available to you, which you can also browse by category. Some add-ins are free, and some require purchase.

To install an add-in, click the Add button next to it on the Store tab. To use an add-in after you have installed it, click the My Add-ins button on the Insert tab to open the Office Add-ins gallery with the My Add-ins tab displayed. Select the Add-in you want to use on this tab, and then click Add. A new button for the add-in may be added to your ribbon. When you no longer need an add-in you have installed, you can remove it by right-clicking the add-in on the My Add-in tab in the Office Add-ins gallery, and then clicking Remove.

Change Line Spacing and Indents

Learning Outcomes
- Alter line and paragraph spacing and indentation
- Set line and paragraph spacing and indentation
- Set paragraph pagination and formatting options

Altering the amount of space between lines and paragraphs in a document can make body text easier to read. You use the Line and Paragraph Spacing button in the Paragraph group on the Home tab to quickly change line and paragraph spacing. Indenting paragraphs can also make a document easier to read and understand at a glance. When you **indent** a paragraph, you move its edge in from the left or right margin. You can indent the entire left or right edge of a paragraph, just the first line, or all lines except the first line. The **indent markers** on the horizontal ruler indicate the indent settings for the paragraph in which the insertion point is located. TABLE 2-1 describes different types of indents and some of the methods for creating each. **CASE** *You increase the line spacing of the report, remove space under a paragraph, and create indents for body text paragraphs to make the report easier to read. You work with formatting marks turned on, so you can see the paragraph marks (¶).*

STEPS

1. **Press CTRL+HOME, click the Home tab, click the Show/Hide ¶ button [¶] in the Paragraph group, press CTRL+A to select the entire document, then click the Line and Paragraph Spacing button [line spacing icon] in the Paragraph group**
   The Line Spacing gallery opens. This gallery includes options for increasing the space between lines. Both line and paragraph spacing are measured in points.
2. **Click 2.0, then click the document to deselect the text**
   The space between the lines in the document increases to 2.
3. **Place the insertion point in the first body paragraph under the title, click [line spacing icon] then click 1.15**
   The space between the lines in the paragraph decreases to 1.15. Notice that you do not need to select an entire paragraph to change its paragraph formatting; simply place the insertion point in the paragraph.
4. **Select the next two paragraphs of body text, click [line spacing icon], then click 1.15**
   The line spacing between the selected paragraphs changes to 1.15. To change the paragraph-formatting features of more than one paragraph, you must select the paragraphs.
5. **Click before Job at the beginning of the first body paragraph, then press TAB**
   The first line of the paragraph is indented ½", as shown in FIGURE 2-8. Notice the First Line Indent marker is located at the ½" mark on the horizontal ruler. The ruler shows the indent settings for the paragraph in which the insertion point is located. Pressing TAB is a quick way to indent the first line of a paragraph ½".
6. **Place the insertion point in the second body paragraph, then drag the First Line Indent marker [▽] right to the ½" mark on the horizontal ruler**
   FIGURE 2-9 shows the First Line Indent marker being dragged. The first line of the second body paragraph is indented 1/2". Dragging the First Line Indent marker indents only the first line of a paragraph.
7. **Place the insertion point in the third body paragraph, then drag the Hanging Indent marker [△] right to the ½" mark on the ruler**
   Take care to drag the Hanging Indent marker and not the Left Indent marker. FIGURE 2-10 shows the Hanging Indent marker being dragged. The lines under the first line of the third body paragraph are indented ½". Dragging the Hanging Indent marker indents the subsequent lines of a paragraph more than the first line.
8. **Place the insertion point in the first body paragraph, click [line spacing icon], click Remove Space After Paragraph, then save your changes**
   The space between the first and second body paragraphs is eliminated. Using the Line and Paragraph Spacing button is a quick way to add or remove space between paragraphs. You can also change the paragraph spacing settings for the active paragraph using the Spacing Before and After boxes in the Paragraph group on the Layout tab.

QUICK TIP
Word recognizes any string of text that ends with a paragraph mark as a paragraph, including titles, headings, and single lines in a list.

QUICK TIP
If the rulers are not displayed, click the View tab, then click the Ruler check box.

TROUBLE
Take care to drag only the First Line Indent marker. If you make a mistake, click the Undo button [undo icon], then try again.

FIGURE 2-8: First line indent

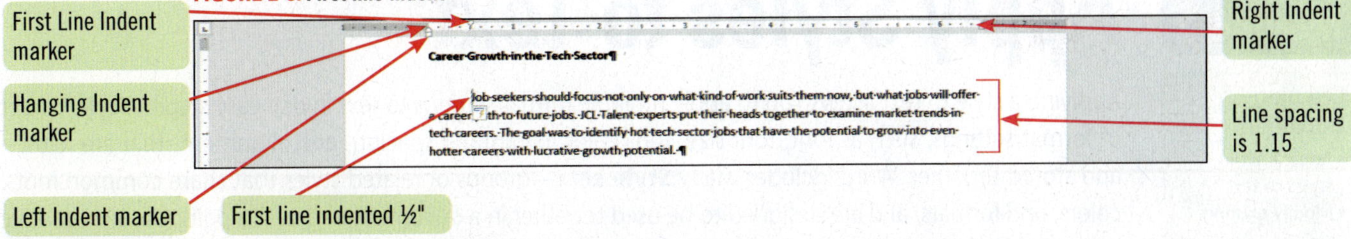

FIGURE 2-9: Dragging the First Line Indent marker

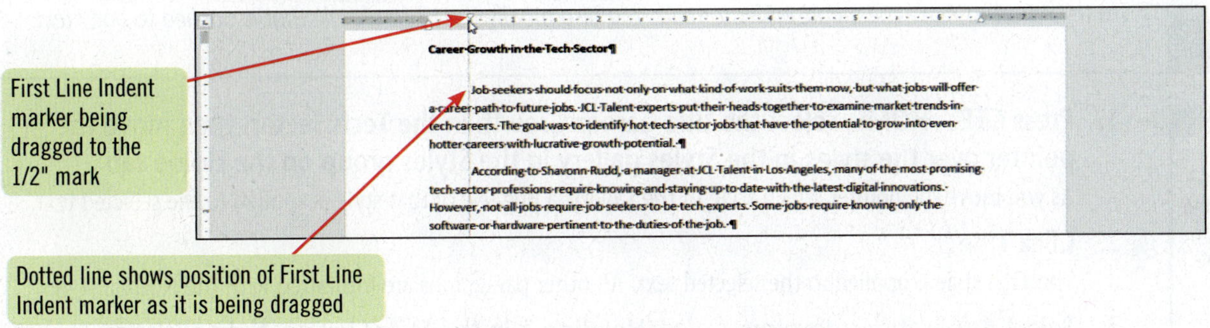

FIGURE 2-10: Dragging the Hanging Indent marker

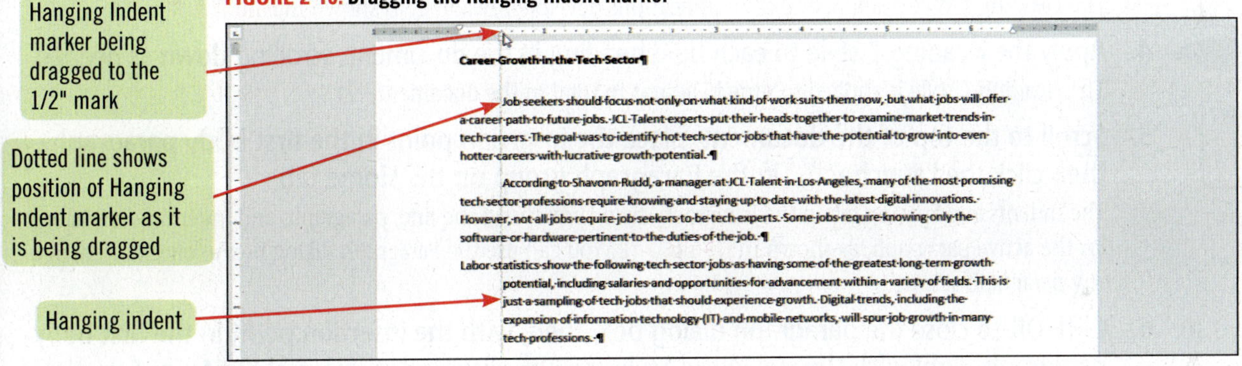

TABLE 2-1: Types of indents

indent type: description	to create
Left indent: left edge of a paragraph is moved in from the left margin	Drag the Left Indent marker ▭ on the ruler to the right to the position where you want the left edge of the paragraph to align; when you drag the left indent marker, all the indent markers move as one
Right indent: right edge of a paragraph is moved in from the right margin	Drag the Right Indent marker △ on the ruler to the left to the position where you want the right edge of the paragraph to align
First line indent: first line of a paragraph is indented more than the subsequent lines	Drag the First Line Indent marker ▽ on the ruler to the right to the position where you want the first line of the paragraph to begin; or activate the First Line Indent marker ▽ in the tab indicator, and then click the ruler at the position where you want the first line of the paragraph to begin
Hanging indent: subsequent lines of a paragraph are indented more than the first line	Drag the Hanging Indent marker △ on the ruler to the right to the position where you want the hanging indent to begin; or activate the Hanging Indent marker △ in the tab indicator, and then click the ruler at the position where you want the second and remaining lines of the paragraph to begin; when you drag the hanging indent marker, the left indent marker moves with it
Negative indent (or Outdent): left edge of a paragraph is moved to the left of the left margin	Drag the Left Indent marker ▭ on the ruler left to the position where you want the negative indent to begin; when you drag the left indent marker, all markers move as one

Word

Word
Module 2

Apply Styles to Text

Learning Outcomes
- Apply built-in styles to text
- Modify existing styles

Applying a style to text allows you to apply multiple format settings to text in one easy step. A **style** is a set of format settings, such as font, font size, font color, paragraph spacing, and alignment, that are named and stored together. Word includes many **Style sets**—groups of related styles that share common fonts, colors, and formats, and are designed to be used together in a document to give it a polished and cohesive look. Each Style set includes styles for a title, subtitle, several heading levels, body text, and other text elements. By default, all text is formatted using the Normal style. **CASE** *You apply title and heading styles to the report to make the report easier to read. You also modify the Normal style that is applied to body text.*

STEPS

QUICK TIP
To change the active Style set, click the Design tab, click the More button in the Document Formatting group, then select a different style set.

1. **Press CTRL+HOME, select the title Career Growth in the Tech Sector, then move the pointer over the styles in the Styles gallery in the Styles group on the Home tab**
   As you move the pointer over a style in the gallery, a preview of that style is applied to the selected text.
2. **Click Title**
   The Title style is applied to the selected text. All other paragraphs are formatted with the Normal style.
3. **Select Applications developer, click Heading 1 in the Styles group, then click the heading to deselect the text**
   The Heading 1 style is applied to the Applications developer heading, as shown in **FIGURE 2-11**.

QUICK TIP
The body text paragraphs are formatted with the Normal style.

4. **Apply the Heading 1 style to each bold heading in the document, scrolling down as needed**
   The Heading 1 style is applied to nine headings in total in the document.
5. **Scroll to the top of the document, place the insertion point in the first body paragraph, then click the Launcher in the Paragraph group on the Home tab**
   The Indents and Spacing tab in the Paragraph dialog box shows the line, paragraph, and indentation settings for the active paragraph, as shown in **FIGURE 2-12**. You can use the Paragraph dialog box to check or change any paragraph setting.
6. **Click OK to close the paragraph dialog box, then, with the insertion point in the first body paragraph, right-click Normal in the Styles group, click Update Normal to Match Selection**
   The format of each paragraph formatted with the Normal style in the document is changed to match the first body paragraph. The title and headings are indented now, too because the Heading 1 and Title styles are based on the Normal style. When the Normal style changed, the styles based on the Normal style changed, too.

TROUBLE
If you apply the wrong style, click the Undo button on the Quick Access toolbar, then right-click the style name in the Styles group again.

7. **Right-click Heading 1 in the Styles group, click Modify, click the Style based on arrow in the Modify Style dialog box, click (no style), then click OK**
   The Heading 1 style is now based on no style and the indent is removed from the headings in the document. You can use the Modify Style dialog box to change any format setting in a style.
8. **Right-click Title in the Styles group, click Modify, click the Style based on arrow in the Modify Style dialog box, click (no style), then click OK**
   The Title style is now based on no style and the indent is removed from the title in the document.
9. **Select the Career Growth... title, click the Increase Font Size button in the Font group, click the Font Color arrow, click Blue, Accent 1, Darker 25%, click the Line and Paragraph Spacing button in the Paragraph group, click Add Space After Paragraph, deselect the title, then save your changes**
   The font size of the title is increased, the font color changes to dark blue, and extra space is added after the title paragraph, as shown in **FIGURE 2-13**. You can modify the format of text to which a style has been applied without changing the style itself.

FIGURE 2-11: Styles applied to the report

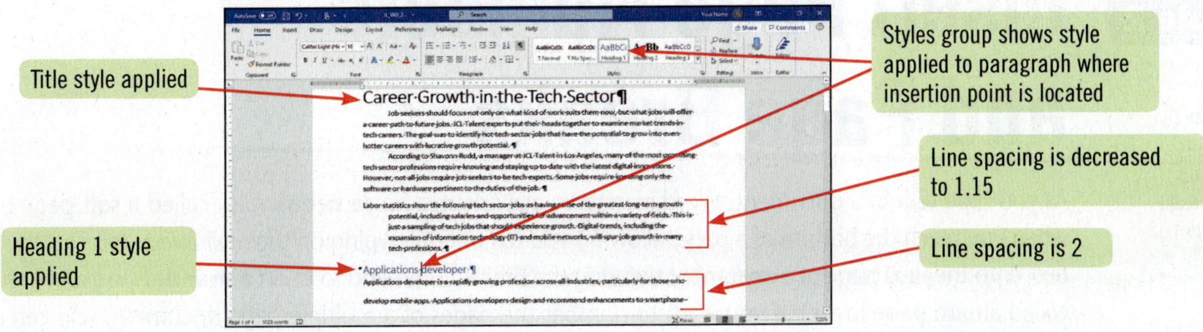

FIGURE 2-12: Indents and Spacing tab in Paragraph dialog box

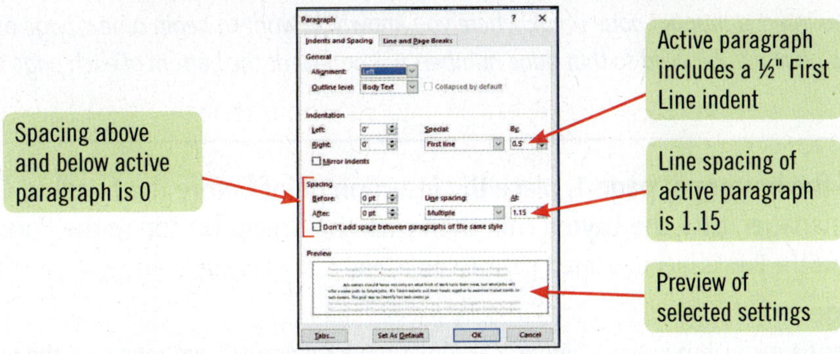

FIGURE 2-13: Modified styles applied to the document

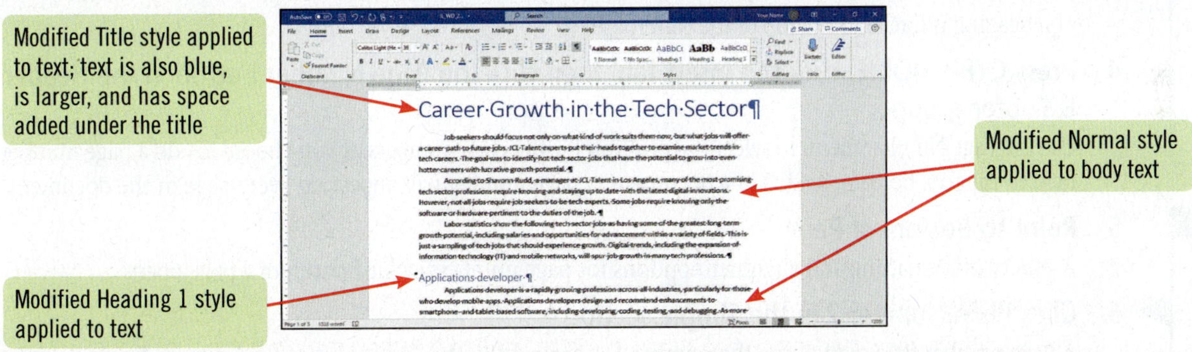

Changing the Style set

Changing the Style set applied to a document is a quick way to give a document a different look and design. Style sets include font and paragraph settings for headings and body text. When you change the Style set, a complete set of new fonts and colors is applied to the entire document. All the body text and all the headings that have been formatted with a style change to the format settings for the active Style set. To change the Style set, you click one of the Style sets available in the Document Formatting group on the Design tab. You can also change the color scheme or font used in the active Style set by clicking the Colors or Fonts buttons in the Document Formatting group and then selecting from the available color schemes or font options.

You can also save a group of font and paragraph settings as a new Style set. To do this, click the More button in the Document Formatting group, and then click Save as a New Style Set. If you want to return a document to its original Style set, click the More button, and then click Reset to the Default Style Set.

Insert Page Numbers and Page Breaks

Learning Outcomes
- Insert page, section, and column breaks
- Insert page numbers

As you type text in a document, Word inserts an **automatic page break** (also called a soft page break) when you reach the bottom of a page, allowing you to continue typing on the next page. You can also force text onto the next page of a document by using the Breaks command to insert a **manual page break** (also called a hard page break). If you want to number the pages of a multiple-page document, you can insert a page number field to add a page number to each page. A **field** is a code that serves as a placeholder for data that changes in a document, such as a page number or the current date. When you use the Page Number button on the Insert tab to add page numbers to a document, you insert the page number field at the top, bottom, or side of any page, and Word automatically numbers all the pages in the document for you.

CASE *You insert a manual page break where you know you want to begin a new page of the report, and then you add a page number field so that page numbers will appear at the bottom of each page in the document.*

STEPS

> **QUICK TIP**
> Pressing CTRL+ENTER is a fast way to insert a manual page break.

1. **Scroll to the bottom of page 1, place the insertion point before the heading Customer service manager, click the Layout tab, then click the Breaks button in the Page Setup group**

   You also use the Breaks menu to insert page, column, and text-wrapping breaks. See TABLE 2-2.

2. **Click Page**

   Word inserts a manual page break before "Customer service manager" and moves all the text following the page break to the beginning of the next page, as shown in FIGURE 2-14.

> **QUICK TIP**
> To delete a page break, select it and then press DELETE. Page breaks are only visible when formatting marks are turned on.

3. **Scroll down, place the insertion point before the heading Intelligence analyst on page 2, press and hold CTRL, then press ENTER**

   The heading is forced to the top of the third page.

4. **Press CTRL+HOME, click the Insert tab, then click the Page Number button in the Header & Footer group**

   Use the Page Number menu to select the position for the page numbers. If you choose to add a page number field to the top, bottom, or side of a document, a page number will appear on every page in the document.

> **QUICK TIP**
> To change the location or formatting of page numbers, click the Page Number button, point to a page number location, then select a format from the gallery.

5. **Point to Bottom of Page**

   A gallery of formatting and alignment options for page numbers at the bottom of a page opens.

6. **Click Plain Number 2 in the Simple section**

   A page number field containing the number 1 is centered in the Footer area at the bottom of page 1 of the document, as shown in FIGURE 2-15. The document text is gray, or dimmed, because the Footer area is open. Text that is inserted in a Footer area appears at the bottom of every page in a document.

7. **Double-click the document text**

   The page number is now dimmed because it is located in the Footer area, which is no longer the active area. When the document is printed, the page numbers appear as normal text.

> **QUICK TIP**
> To remove page numbers from a document, click the Page Number button, then click Remove Page Numbers.

8. **Press CTRL+HOME, click the View tab, click the Multiple Pages button in the Zoom group, then save the document**

   Word numbered each page of the report automatically, and each page number is centered at the bottom of the page, as shown in FIGURE 2-16.

FIGURE 2-14: Manual page break in document

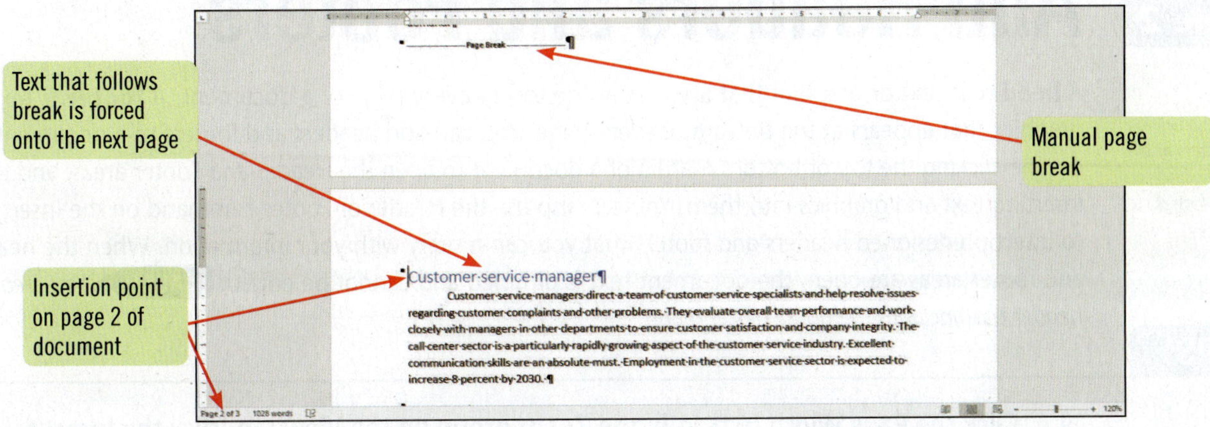

FIGURE 2-15: Page number in document

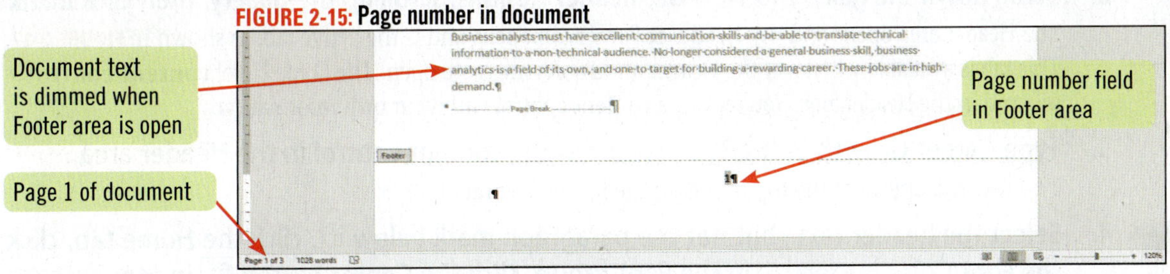

FIGURE 2-16: Pages 1, 2, and 3

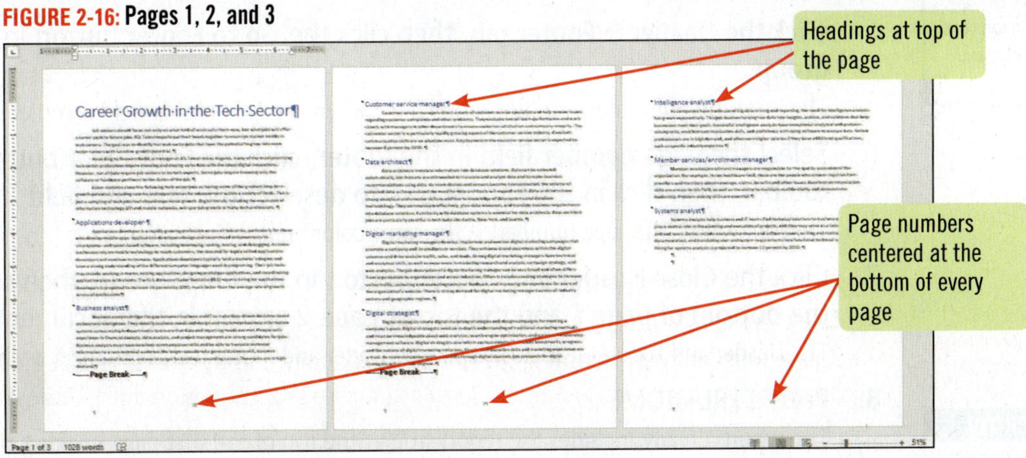

TABLE 2-2: Types of breaks

break	function
Page	Forces the text following the break to begin at the top of the next page
Column	Forces the text following the break to begin at the top of the next column
Text Wrapping	Forces the text following the break to begin at the beginning of the next line

Add Headers and Footers

Learning Outcomes
- Insert headers and footers
- Manage headers and footers

A **header** is text or graphics that appears at the top of every page of a document. A **footer** is text or graphics that appears at the bottom of every page. You can add headers and footers to a document by double-clicking the top or bottom margin of a document to open the Header and Footer areas, and then inserting text and graphics into them. You can also use the Header or Footer command on the Insert tab to insert predesigned headers and footers that you can modify with your information. When the header and footer areas are open, the document text is dimmed and cannot be edited. CASE *You create a header that includes the name of the report.*

STEPS

1. **Click the Page Width button in the Zoom group on the View tab, click the Insert tab, then click the Header button in the Header & Footer group**
   A gallery of built-in header designs opens.
2. **Scroll down the gallery to view the header designs, scroll up the gallery, then click Blank**
   The Header area opens and the Header & Footer tab opens and is the active tab, as shown in FIGURE 2-17. This tab is available whenever the Header and Footer areas are open. The [Type Here] **content control** is selected in the Header area. You replace a content control with your own information.
3. **Type Career Growth in the Tech Sector in the content control in the Header area**
   This text will appear at the top of every page in the document.

QUICK TIP
You can also use the Insert Alignment Tab button in the Position group on the Header & Footer tab to left-, center-, and right-align text in the Header and Footer areas.

4. **Select the header text (but not the paragraph mark below it), click the Home tab, click the Font Color button in the Font group, click the Center button in the Paragraph group, click the Borders button, then click in the Header area to deselect the text**
   The text is the same blue used in the document and is centered in the Header area with a bottom border.
5. **Click the Header & Footer tab, then click the Go to Footer button in the Navigation group**
   The insertion point moves to the Footer area, where a page number field is centered in the Footer area.
6. **Select the page number field in the footer, click the Font Color button on the Mini toolbar, then click in the Footer area to deselect the text and field**
   The footer text (the page number) is the same color blue as the headings.
7. **Click the Close Header and Footer button in the Close group, then scroll down until the bottom of page 1 and the top of page 2 appear in the document window**
   The Header and Footer areas close, and the header and footer text is dimmed, as shown in FIGURE 2-18.
8. **Press CTRL+HOME**
   The report already includes the report title at the top of the first page, making the header information redundant.

QUICK TIP
To remove headers or footers from a document, click the Header or Footer button, and then click Remove Header or Remove Footer.

9. **Position the pointer over the header text at the top of page 1, double-click the header to open the Header area, click the Different First Page check box in the Options group on the Header and Footer tab, then click the Close Header and Footer button**
   The header and footer text is removed from the Header and Footer areas on the first page.
10. **Click Show/Hide ¶ button in the Paragraph group on the Home tab, click the View tab, click the Multiple Pages button in the Zoom group, then save your changes**
    The headers and footers and all the pages in the document are shown in FIGURE 2-19.

FIGURE 2-17: Header area

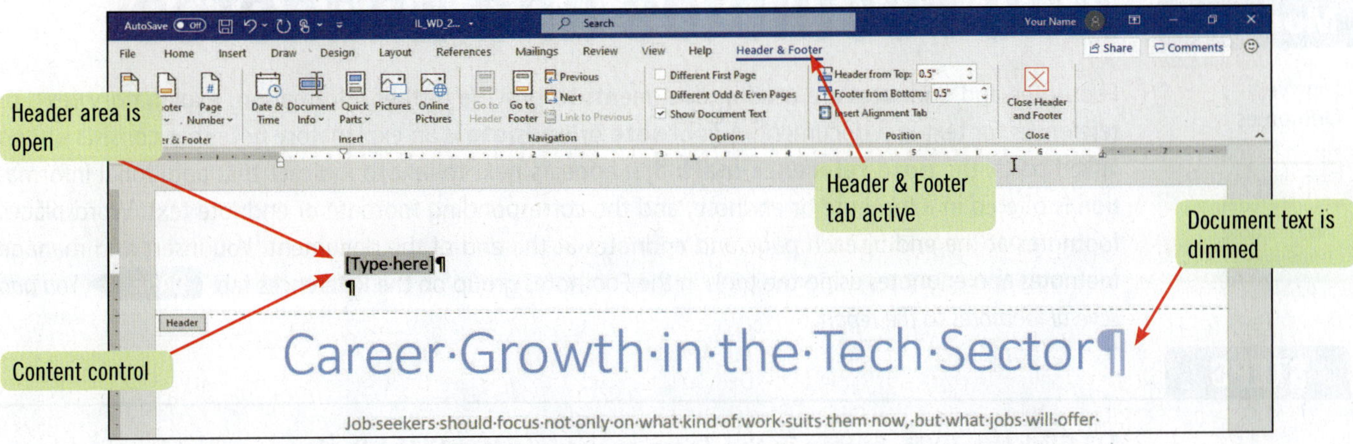

FIGURE 2-18: Header and footer in document

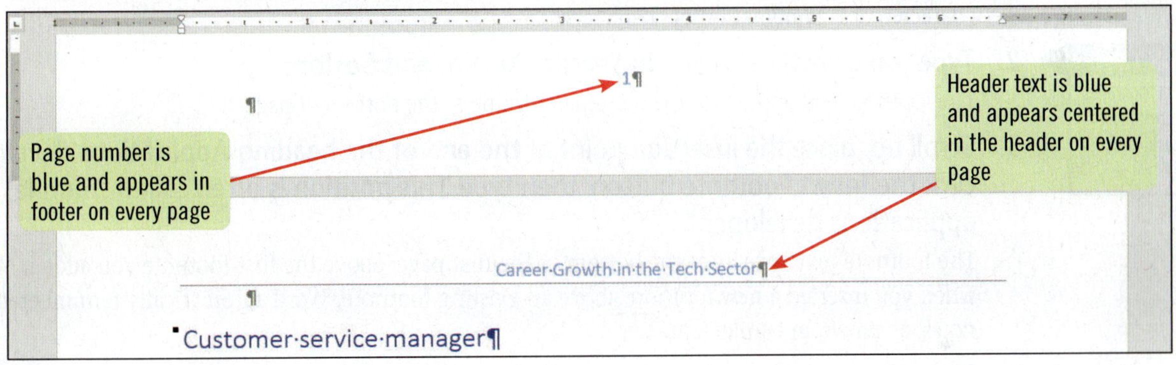

FIGURE 2-19: Header and footer on pages 2 and 3

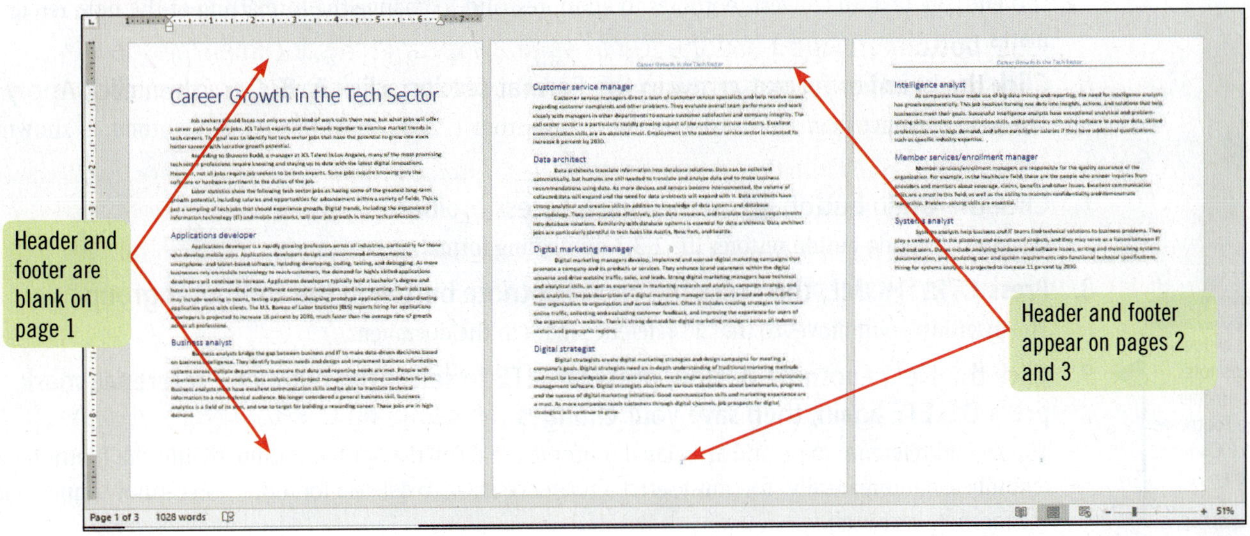

Word

Add Footnotes and Endnotes

Learning Outcomes
- Insert footnotes and endnotes
- Modify footnote and endnote properties

Footnotes and endnotes are used in documents to provide further information, explanatory text, or references for text in a document. A **footnote** or **endnote** is an explanatory note that consists of two linked parts: the **note reference mark** that appears next to text to indicate that additional information is offered in a footnote or endnote, and the corresponding footnote or endnote text. Word places footnotes at the end of each page and endnotes at the end of the document. You insert and manage footnotes and endnotes using the tools in the Footnotes group on the References tab. CASE *You add several footnotes to the report.*

STEPS

1. **Click the 100% button in the Zoom group, scroll until the Business analyst heading is at the top of your screen, place the insertion point at the end of the last body paragraph (after "demand."), click the References tab, then click the Insert Footnote button in the Footnotes group**

   A note reference mark, in this case a superscript 1, appears after "demand.", and the insertion point moves below a separator line at the bottom of the page. A note reference mark can be a number, a symbol, a character, or a combination of characters.

2. **Type Job growth is strong in Seattle, Austin, and Boston.**

   The footnote text appears below the separator line at the bottom of page 1.

> **QUICK TIP**
> To delete a footnote, select the note reference mark, then press DELETE.

3. **Scroll up, place the insertion point at the end of the heading Applications developer, click the Insert Footnote button, then type This position is often called "mobile applications developer."**

   The footnote text appears at the bottom of the first page, above the first footnote you added. Notice that when you inserted a new footnote above an existing footnote, Word automatically renumbered the footnotes, as shown in FIGURE 2-20.

4. **Place the insertion point at the end of the paragraph under the Applications developer heading, click the Insert Footnote button, then type Many hold a master's degree.**

   The footnote text appears between the text for footnotes 1 and 3 at the bottom of the page.

5. **Click the Launcher in the Footnotes group**

   The Footnote and Endnote dialog box opens. You can use this dialog box to change the location of footnote and endnote text, to convert footnotes to endnotes, and to change the formatting of the note reference marks.

6. **Click the Number format arrow in the Format section, click A, B, C,..., then click Apply**

   The note reference marks in the document change from 1, 2, 3 format to an A, B, C format, as shown in FIGURE 2-21.

7. **Click the Undo button on the Quick Access toolbar**

   Clicking the Undo button restores the 1,2,3 numbering format.

8. **Press CTRL+HOME, then click the Next Footnote button in the Footnotes group**

   The insertion point moves to the "1" reference mark in the document.

> **QUICK TIP**
> To convert all footnotes to endnotes, click the Launcher in the Footnotes group, click Convert, click OK, then click Close.

9. **Click the Next Footnote button, press DELETE to select the number 2 reference mark, press DELETE again, then save your changes**

   The second reference mark and associated footnote are deleted from the document and the footnotes are renumbered automatically. You must select a reference mark to delete a footnote; you cannot simply delete the footnote text itself.

FIGURE 2-20: Renumbered footnotes in the document

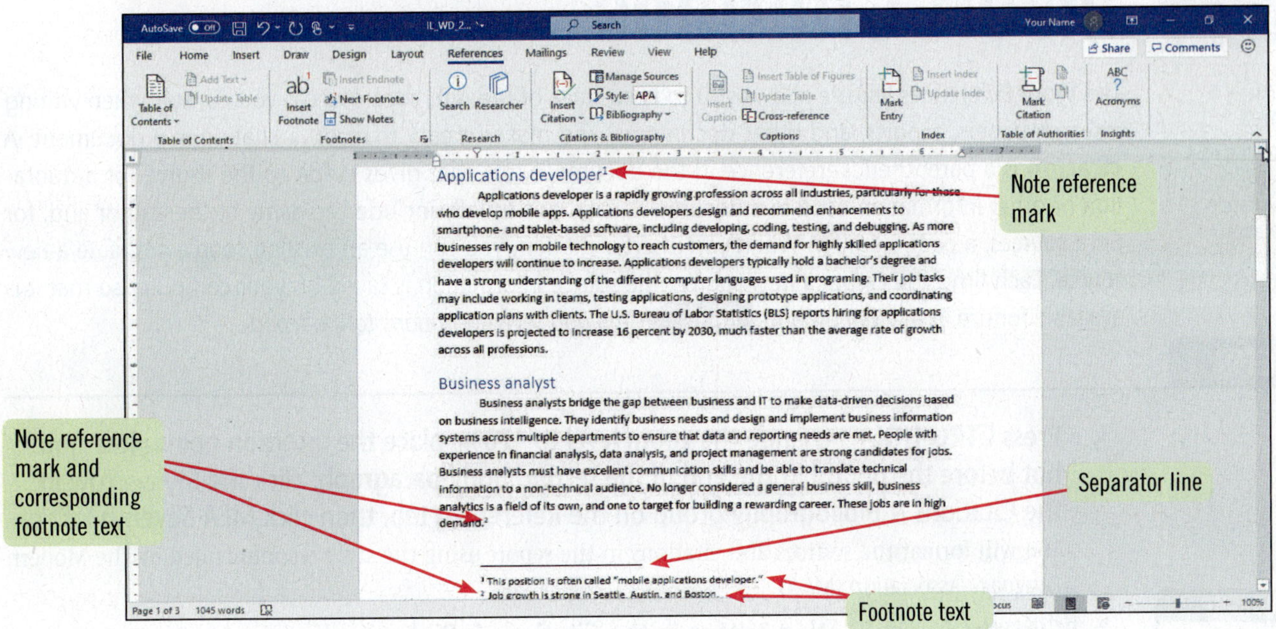

FIGURE 2-21: Note reference marks in new format

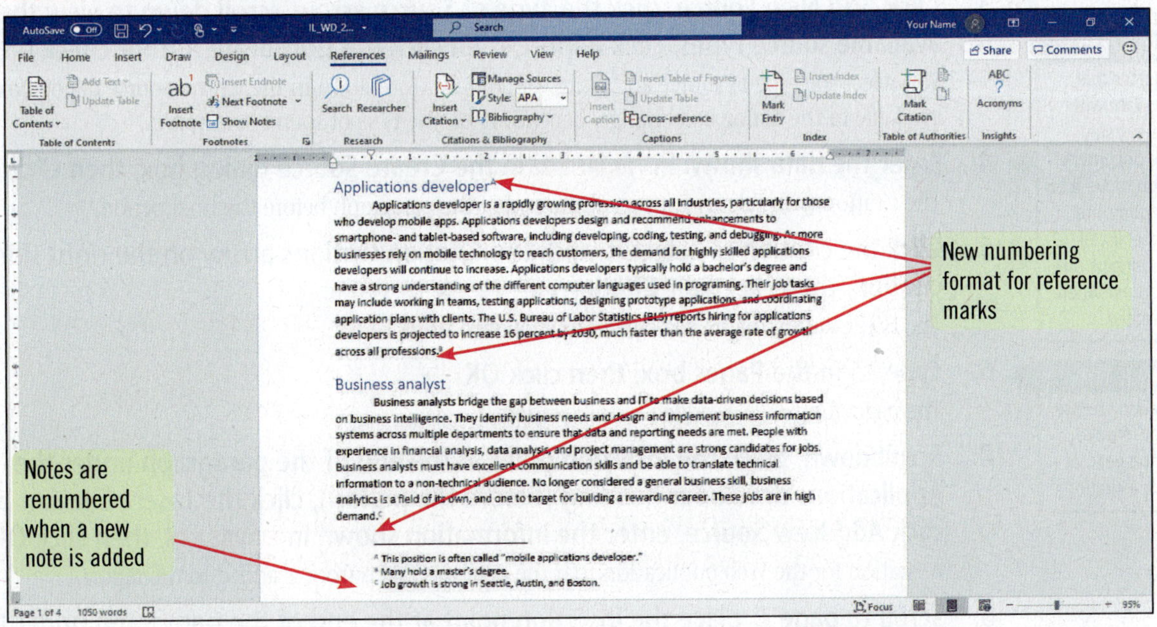

Word

Word
Module 2

Insert Citations

Learning Outcomes
- Add a source to a document
- Insert a citation
- Edit a citation

The Word References feature allows you to keep track of the reference sources you consult when writing research papers, reports, and other documents, and makes it easy to insert a citation in a document. A **citation** is a parenthetical reference in the document text that gives credit to the source for a quotation or other information used in a document. Citations usually include the name of the author and, for print sources, a page number. When you insert a citation, you can use an existing source or create a new source. Each time you create a new source, the source information is saved on your computer so that it is available for use in any document. **CASE** *You add several citations to the report.*

STEPS

1. **Press CTRL+HOME, change the zoom level to 120%, place the insertion point after "job" but before the period at the end of the second body paragraph, click the Style arrow in the Citations & Bibliography group on the References tab, then click MLA Seventh Edition**
   You will format the sources and citations in the report using the style recommended by the Modern Language Association (MLA).
2. **Click the Insert Citation button in the Citations & Bibliography group**
   A list of the sources (one) already used in the file opens. You can choose to cite this source, create a new source, or add a placeholder for a source. When you add a new citation to a document, the source is added to the list of master sources stored on the computer. The new source is also associated with the document.
3. **Click Add New Source, click the Type of Source arrow, scroll down to view the available source types, click Report, then click the Corporate Author check box**
   You select the type of source and enter the source information in the Create Source dialog box. The fields available in the dialog box change, depending on the type of source selected.
4. **Enter the data shown in FIGURE 2-22 in the Create Source dialog box, then click OK**
   The citation (JCL Talent) appears at the end of the paragraph before the final period.
5. **Click the citation to select it, click the Citation Options arrow on the right side of the citation, then click Edit Citation**
   The Edit Citation dialog box opens, as shown in FIGURE 2-23.
6. **Type 15 in the Pages box, then click OK**
   The page number 15 is added to the citation.
7. **Scroll down, place the insertion point at the end of the paragraph under the Applications developer heading (before the period), click the Insert Citation button, click Add New Source, enter the information shown in FIGURE 2-24, then click OK**
   A citation for the Web publication that the data was taken from is added to the report.
8. **Scroll to page 2, place the insertion point at the end of the paragraph under the Customer service manager heading (before the period) click the Insert Citation button, then click U.S. Bureau of Labor Statistics in the list of sources**
   The citation (U.S. Bureau of Labor Statistics) appears at the end of the paragraph.
9. **Press CTRL+END, then repeat Step 8 to insert a U.S. Bureau of Labor Statistics citation at the end of the last paragraph in the document**
10. **Scroll up to page 2, place the insertion point at the end of the paragraph under the Data architect heading (before the period) click the Insert Citation button, click Add New Placeholder, type NYT, click OK, then save your changes**
    You added a citation placeholder for a source that you still need to add to the document.

QUICK TIP
When you create a new source for a document, it appears automatically in the bibliography when you generate it.

QUICK TIP
Only sources that you associate with a document stay with the document when you move it to another computer. The master list of sources remains on the computer where it was created.

QUICK TIP
You can also choose to add or remove the author, year, or title from a citation.

FIGURE 2-22: Creating a report source

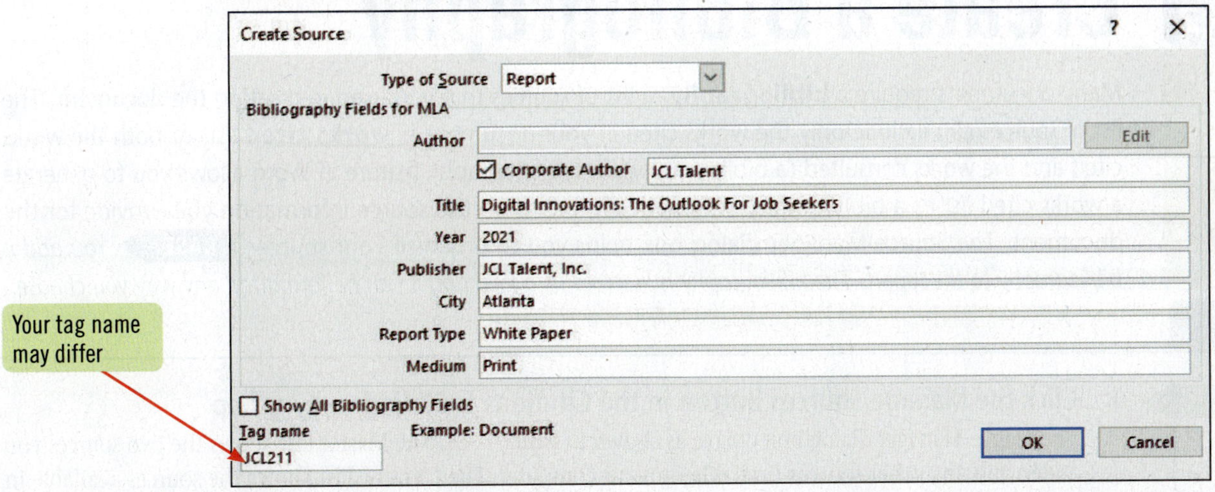

FIGURE 2-23: Edit Citation dialog box

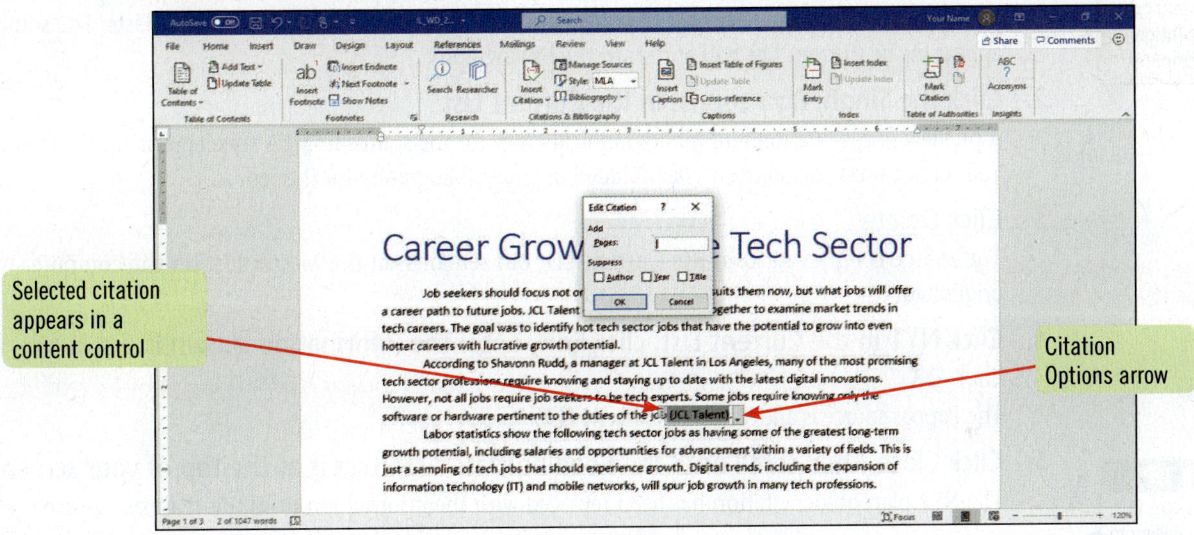

FIGURE 2-24: Adding a Web publication source

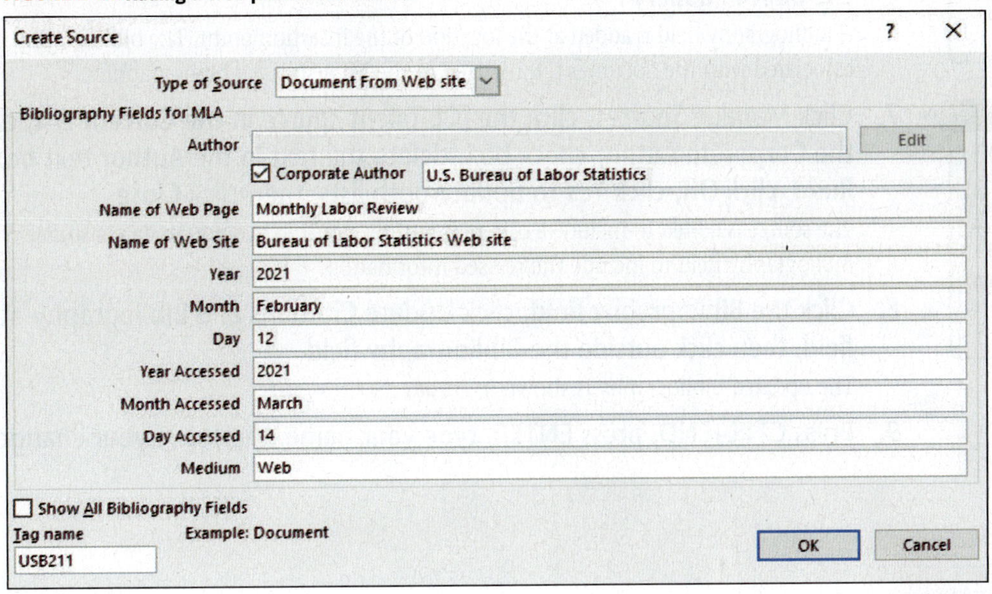

Word
Module 2

Create a Bibliography

Learning Outcomes
- Add and delete sources
- Edit a source
- Insert a bibliography field

Many documents require a **bibliography**, a list of sources that you used in creating the document. The list of sources can include only the works cited in your document (a **works cited** list) or both the works cited and the works consulted (a bibliography). The Bibliography feature in Word allows you to generate a works cited list or a bibliography automatically, based on the source information you provide for the document. The Source Manager dialog box helps you to organize your sources. CASE *You add a bibliography to the report. The bibliography is inserted as a field and it can be formatted any way you choose.*

STEPS

QUICK TIP
You must copy sources from the Master List to the Current List for the sources to be available when you open the document on another computer.

1. **Click the Manage Sources button in the Citations & Bibliography group**
   The Source Manager dialog box opens, as shown in FIGURE 2-25. The Master List shows the two sources you added and any other sources available on your computer. The Current List shows the sources available in the current document, as well as the NYT placeholder you added. A check mark next to a source indicates the source is cited in the document. You use the tools in the Source Manager dialog box to add, edit, and delete sources from the lists, and to copy sources between the Master and Current Lists. The sources that appear in the Current List will appear in the bibliography.

2. **Click the Singh, Riya source in the Current List**
   A preview of the citation and bibliographical entry for the source in MLA style appears in the Preview box. You do not want this source to be included in your bibliography for the report.

3. **Click Delete**
   The source is removed from the Current List but remains on the Master List on the computer where it originated.

4. **Click NYT in the Current List, click Edit, enter the information shown in FIGURE 2-26, then click OK**
   The Pappas source is added to the Current List.

QUICK TIP
Click References in the Built-in gallery to insert a References list. Click Works Cited in the Built-in gallery to insert a Works Cited list.

5. **Click Close, then scroll until the heading Data Architect is at the top of your screen**
   The NYT placeholder citation has been replaced with the information from the "Pappas" source.

6. **Press CTRL+END to move the insertion point to the end of the document, click the Bibliography button in the Citations & Bibliography group, then click Bibliography in the Built-in gallery**
   A Bibliography field is added at the location of the insertion point. The bibliography includes all the sources associated with the document, formatted in the MLA style for bibliographies.

QUICK TIP
To change the style used for citations and the bibliography, click the Style arrow in the Citations & Bibliography group, then select a different style.

7. **Click Manage Sources, click the JCL Talent source in the Current List, click Edit, deselect the Corporate Author check box, delete the text in the Author text box, type Shavonn Rudd, click OK, click Yes to update both lists, then click Close**
   The source is edited to include a different author name. When you update a source, you need to update the Bibliography field to include the revised information.

8. **Click the Bibliography field, click Update Citations and Bibliography at the top of the field, then click outside the Bibliography field**
   The updated Bibliography is shown in FIGURE 2-27.

9. **Press CTRL+END, press ENTER, type your name, then save your changes**

FIGURE 2-25: Source Manager dialog box

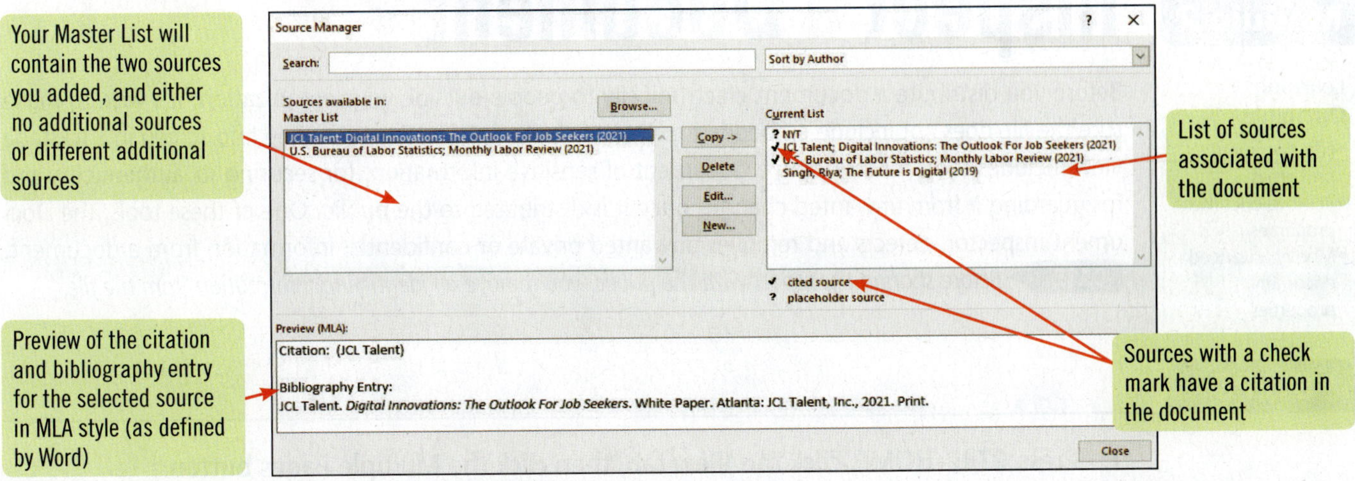

FIGURE 2-26: Adding a periodical source

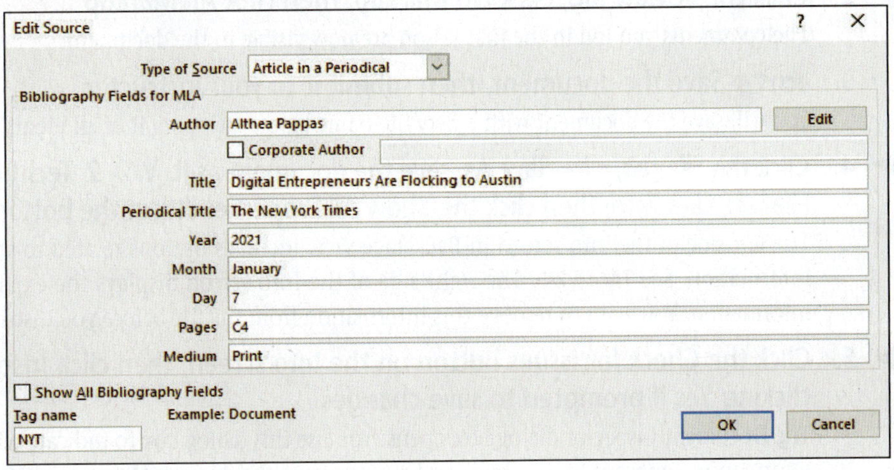

FIGURE 2-27: Bibliography field in document

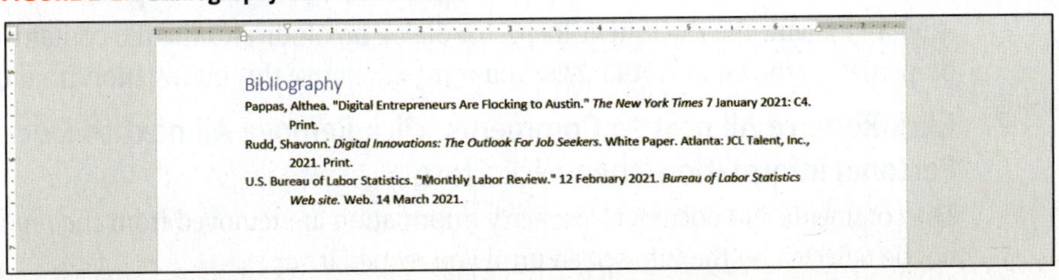

Finding and citing sources with the Word Researcher

The Word Researcher tool helps you find citable sources, quotations, images, and other material for a research paper. Using Researcher, you can search for journal articles and websites that relate to a topic, add information from those sources into a document, automatically create a citation for the source, and automatically create and update a bibliography—all without having to manually enter the source information. To begin, click the Researcher button in the Research group on the References tab to open the Researcher pane. Type a keyword for your topic in the search box, press ENTER, and then explore the list of sources related to your topic. When you find a source that is useful to you, you can select text (or an image) from it and add the selection to your document, choosing to add text only or to add the text and a citation. When you add a citation, Word automatically creates a bibliography that is updated each time you add additional material to the document. To avoid plagiarism, be sure to paraphrase text that is not a quote, and always include citations giving credit for any content that is not your original work. Also, always verify that the bibliographies you create using Word are formatted in the most up-to-date MLA, APA, Chicago, or other style.

Inspect a Document

Learning Outcomes
- Edit document properties
- Remove document properties
- Modify advanced document properties

Before you distribute a document electronically to people outside your organization, it's wise to make sure the file does not include embedded private or confidential information. The Info screen in Backstage view includes tools for stripping a document of sensitive information, for securing its authenticity, and for guarding it from unwanted changes once it is distributed to the public. One of these tools, the Document Inspector, detects and removes unwanted private or confidential information from a document.

CASE *Before sharing the report with the public, you remove all identifying information from the file.*

STEPS

1. **Press CTRL+HOME, click the View tab, then click the Multiple Pages button**
   The completed document is shown in FIGURE 2-28.
2. **Click the Review tab, click No Markup, then click All Markup**
   The comments you hid in the first lesson are now visible in the document.
3. **sam Save the document, then submit it to your instructor**
   You will save the document with a new file name before stripping it of all identifying information.
4. **Click the File tab, click Save As, save the document as IL_WD_2_TechJobs_Inspected, click the File tab, click Info, then click the Show All Properties link at the bottom of the Info screen**
   The left side of the Info screen in Backstage view includes options related to stripping the file of private information. See TABLE 2-3. The right side of the Info screen displays the expanded document property information. You want to remove this information from the file before you distribute it electronically.
5. **Click the Check for Issues button on the Info screen, then click Inspect Document, clicking Yes if prompted to save changes**
   The Document Inspector dialog box opens. You use this dialog box to indicate which private or identifying information you want to search for and remove from the document.
6. **Make sure all the check boxes are selected, then click Inspect**
   After a moment, the Document Inspector dialog box indicates the file contains comments and document properties, as shown in FIGURE 2-29. You want to remove this information from the file.
7. **Click Remove All next to Comments, click Remove All next to Document Properties and Personal Information, then click Close**
   The comments and document property information are removed from the report file, but the change will not be reflected on the Info screen until you reopen it.
8. **Click the Back button on the Info screen, save your changes to the document, click the File tab, then click Info**
   The comments have been removed from the file. The Info screen shows the document properties have been removed from the file.
9. **Submit the document to your instructor, close the file, then exit Word**

QUICK TIP
To recover unsaved changes to a file, click Manage Document on the Info screen, then click Recover Unsaved Documents.

QUICK TIP
A document property, such as author name, might appear automatically in a content control in a document. Stripping a file of document properties does not remove information from a content control.

FIGURE 2-28: Formatted document

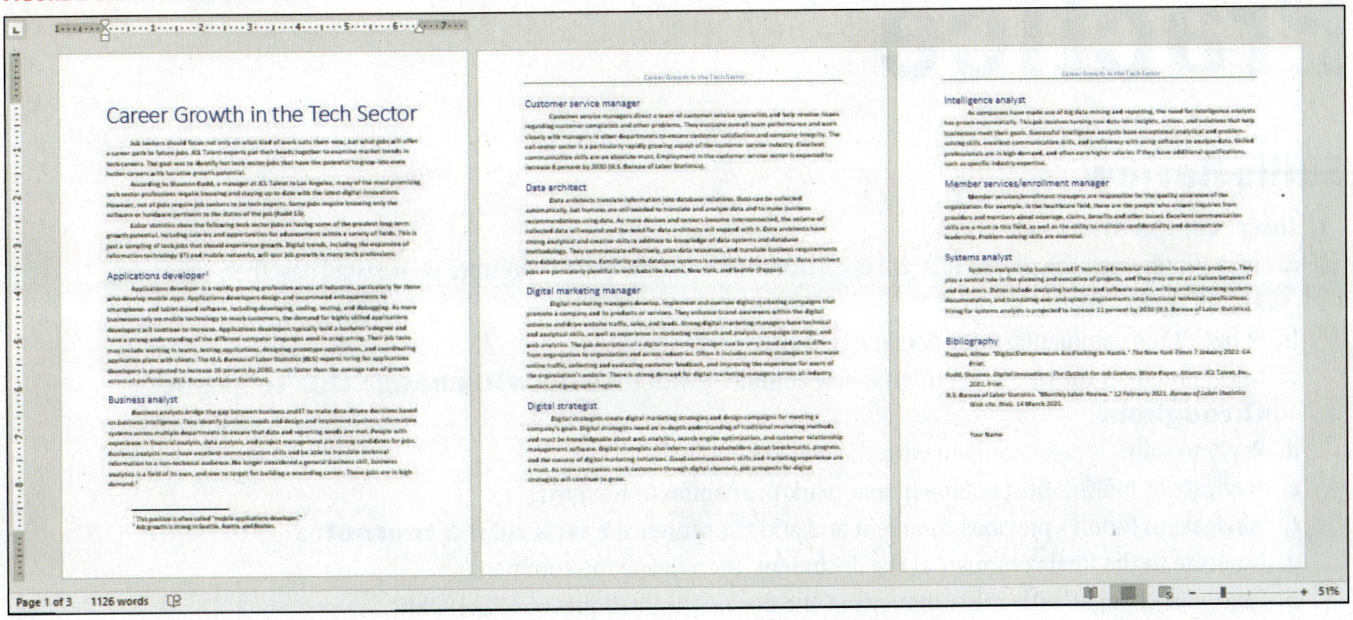

FIGURE 2-29: Results after inspecting document

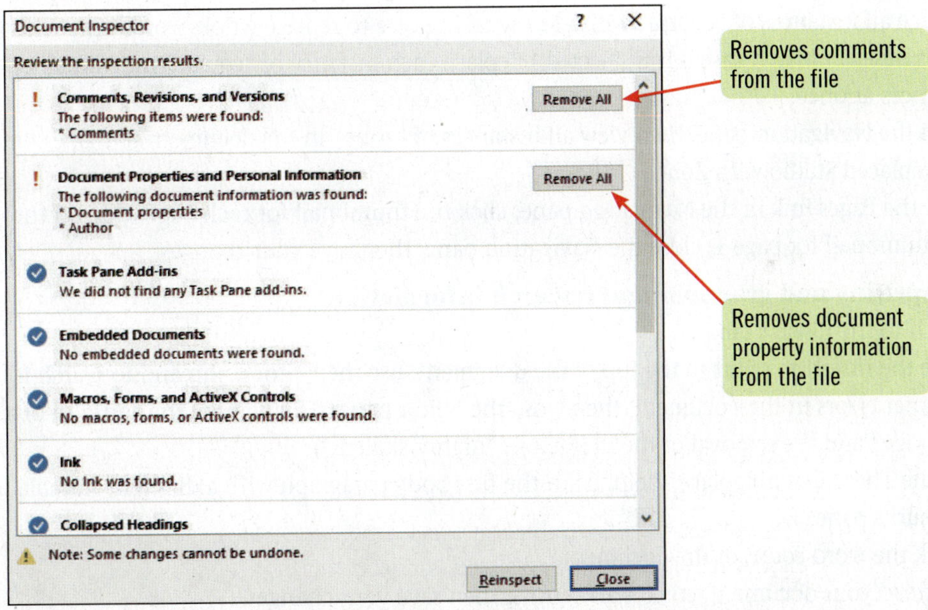

TABLE 2-3: Options on the Info screen

option	use to
Protect Document	Mark a document as final so that it is read-only and cannot be edited; encrypt a document so that a password is required to open it; restrict what kinds of changes can be made to a document and by whom; restrict access to editing, copying, and printing a document and add a digital signature to a document to verify its integrity
Check for Issues	Detect and remove unwanted information from a document, including document properties and comments; check for content that people with disabilities might find difficult to read; and check the document for features that are not supported by previous versions of Microsoft Word
Manage Document	Browse and recover draft versions of unsaved files

Word

Practice

Skills Review

1. **Insert comments.**
   a. Start Word, open the file IL_WD_2-2.docx from the location where you store your Data Files, then save it as **IL_WD_2_Zone**.
   b. Show all the comments in the document, if necessary.
   c. Select Studio in the title, then insert a new comment with the text **I will change this to "Zone" throughout.**
   d. Reply to Judith's first comment with the text **OK.**
   e. Navigate to Judith's next comment and mark the comment resolved.
   f. Navigate to Judith's previous comment and add the sentence **I will add a footnote.**
   g. Navigate to the final comment in the document, then delete the comment.
   h. Save your changes, hide the comments in the document, then press CTRL+HOME.
2. **Find and replace text.**
   a. Using the Replace command, replace all instances of "2017" with **2019**.
   b. Replace all instances of "Studio" with **Zone**, taking care to match the case when you perform the replace.
   c. Replace all instances of "course" with **class,** taking care to replace whole words only when you perform the replace. (*Hint*: Deselect Match case if it is selected.) Replace each instance of "course" individually rather than replacing all instances at once.
   d. Open the Navigation pane, then view all instances of "zone" in the document to make sure no errors occurred when you replaced Studio with Zone.
   e. Click the Pages link in the Navigation pane, click the thumbnail for each page to scroll through the document, click the thumbnail for page 1, close the Navigation pane, then save your changes.
3. **Check spelling and grammar and research information.**
   a. Switch to the Review tab.
   b. Move the insertion point to the top of the document, use the Editor command to search for and correct spelling and grammar errors in the document, then close the Editor pane. (*Hint*: Ignore the addition of a question mark following "massage" and the removal of the hyphen in "highly-skilled.")
   c. Use the Thesaurus to replace "helpful" in the first body paragraph with a different suitable word, then close the Thesaurus pane.
   d. Check the word count of the document.
   e. Proofread your document, correct any errors, then save your changes.
4. **Change line spacing and indents.**
   a. Change the line spacing of the entire document to 1.5.
   b. Change the line spacing of the first body paragraph to 1.15.
   c. Indent the first line of the first body paragraph .3". (*Hint*: Use the Paragraph dialog box.)
   d. Remove the paragraph space under the first body paragraph, then save your changes.
5. **Apply styles to text.**
   a. Apply the Title style to the title "The Global Fitness Zone".
   b. Apply the Subtitle style to the subtitle "A Health, Fitness, and Rehabilitation Facility".
   c. Apply the Heading 1 style to each red heading in the document.
   d. Apply the Heading 2 style to each green heading in the document.
   e. With the insertion point in the first body paragraph, update the Normal style to match the first body paragraph.

Skills Review (continued)

f. Modify the Title style to be based on no style.
g. Modify the Subtitle, Heading 1, and Heading 2 styles to be based on no style.
h. Change the theme of the document to Gallery. (*Hint*: Use the Design tab.)
i. Select the title, change the font size to 36, change the font color to Red, Accent 1, Darker 25%, then apply bold.
j. Select the subtitle, change the font size to 14, then add 24 points of space after the paragraph.
k. Select the heading "Welcome…", add 6 points of space after the paragraph, then update the Heading 1 style to match the selection
l. Select the heading "Benefits of Exercise", add 6 points of space before the paragraph, and 3 points of space after the paragraph, then update the Heading 2 style to match the selection.
m. Scroll to the bottom of page 1, click the first item in the bulleted list, add 6 points of space before the paragraph, then save your changes.

6. Insert page numbers and page breaks.

a. Scroll to the bottom of page 2, then insert a manual page break before the heading "Facilities and Services".
b. Insert page numbers in the document at the bottom of the page. Select the Accent Bar 1 page number style from the gallery.
c. Close the Footer area, scroll through the document to view the page number on each page.
d. Turn on formatting marks, delete the manual page break at the bottom of page 2, then save your changes to the document.

7. Add headers and footers.

a. Double-click the Footer area, then use the Go to Header button to move the insertion point to the Header area.
b. Click the Header button, scroll down the gallery of built-in header designs, then select the Filigree header.
c. Click the Document title content control in the header, then type **The Global Fitness Zone**.
d. Replace the text in the Author content control with your name, press END to move the insertion point out of the content control, then press SPACEBAR. (*Note*: If your name does not appear in the header, right-click the Author content control, click Remove Content Control, then type your name in the header.)
e. Close headers and footers, then scroll to view the header and footer on each page.
f. Open headers and footers, select the text in the Header area, including the paragraph mark after your name, change the alignment of the selected text to left, then remove the first line indent. (*Hint*: You can drag the indent marker on the ruler or use the Paragraph dialog box to remove the first line indent.)
g. Remove the header and footer from the first page of the document, close headers and footers, then save your changes.

8. Add footnotes and endnotes.

a. Press CTRL+HOME, scroll down, place the insertion point at the end of the first body paragraph, insert a footnote, then type **Active people live longer and feel better!**
b. Place the insertion point at the end of the first paragraph under the Getting Started heading, insert a footnote, then type **Each day is 1,440 minutes. We help you set aside 30 of them for physical activity.**
c. Place the insertion point at the end of the Getting Started heading, insert a footnote, type **Always consult a physician before beginning an exercise program.**
d. Change the number format of the footnotes to *, †, ‡, then save your changes.

9. Insert citations.

a. Place the insertion point at the end of the second paragraph under the Benefits of Exercise heading (after "down from 52% in 2019" but before the period), then be sure the style for citations and bibliography is set to MLA Seventh Edition.
b. Insert a citation, add a new source, enter the source information shown in the Create Source dialog box in FIGURE 2-30, then click OK.

Word

Skills Review (continued)

- **c.** Place the insertion point at the end of the second paragraph under the Getting Started heading, insert a citation, then select Shree, Maxine from the list of sources.
- **d.** Edit the citation to include the page number **22**.
- **e.** Scroll to page 2, place the insertion point at the end of the "Be a morning exerciser" paragraph in the bulleted list, but before the ending period, insert a citation for WebMD, then save your changes.

FIGURE 2-30

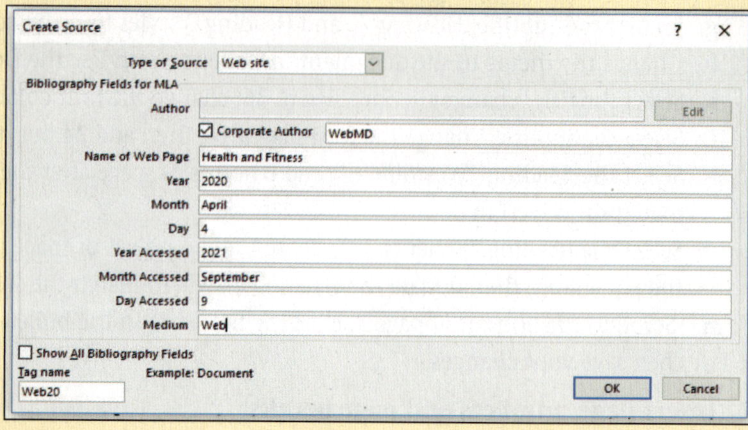

10. Create a bibliography.

- **a.** Press CTRL+END, then insert a bibliography labeled **Works Cited**.
- **b.** Open the Source Manager dialog box.
- **c.** Delete the National Heart/Lung Health Institute source from the Current list.
- **d.** Select the source Health, National Institute of: … in the Current List, click Edit, click the Corporate Author check box, edit the entry so it reads **National Institute of Health**, click OK, then click Close.
- **e.** Update the bibliography field.
- **f.** With the bibliography field selected, click the Bibliographies button above the Bibliography field, then select References.
- **g.** Click the Bibliographies button again, select Bibliography, then save your changes. Pages 1 and 3 of the formatted document are shown in FIGURE 2-31.
- **h.** Save your changes to the document, then submit it to your instructor without closing the document.

FIGURE 2-31

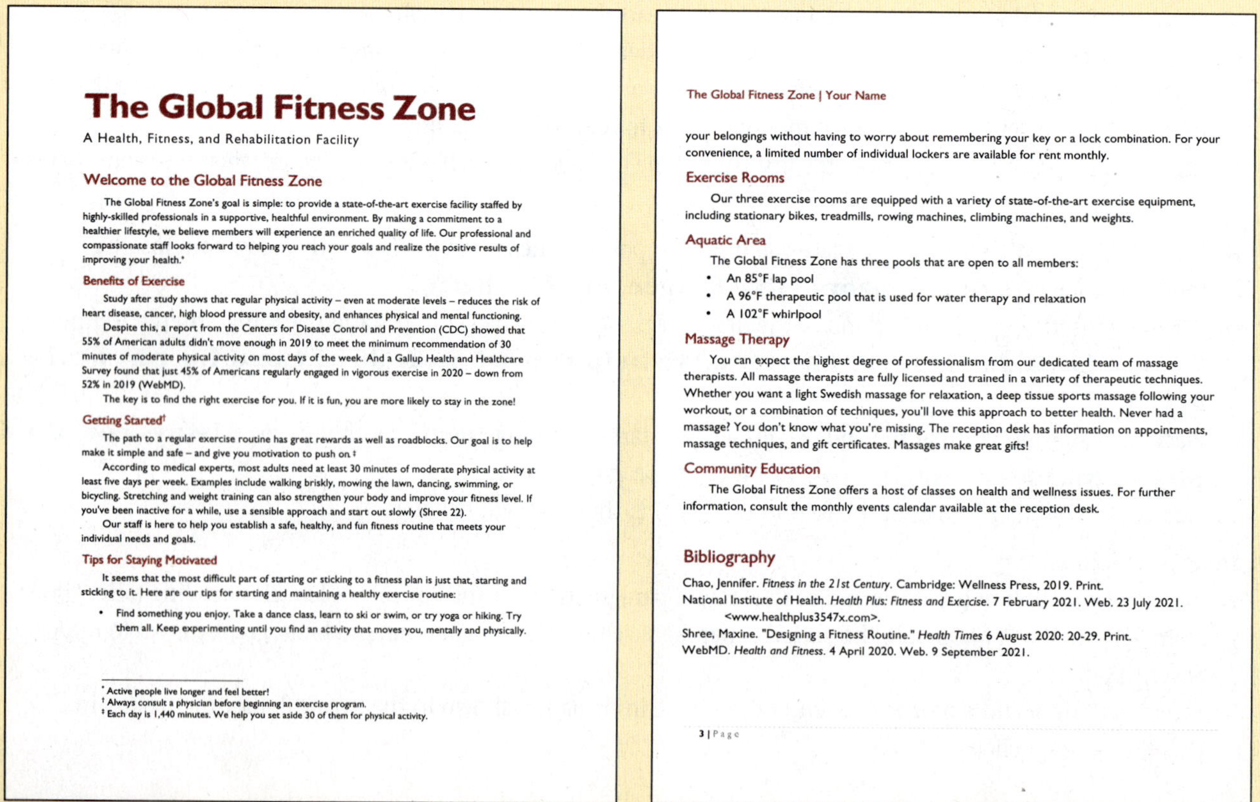

The Global Fitness Zone

A Health, Fitness, and Rehabilitation Facility

Welcome to the Global Fitness Zone

The Global Fitness Zone's goal is simple: to provide a state-of-the-art exercise facility staffed by highly-skilled professionals in a supportive, healthful environment. By making a commitment to a healthier lifestyle, we believe members will experience an enriched quality of life. Our professional and compassionate staff looks forward to helping you reach your goals and realize the positive results of improving your health.*

Benefits of Exercise

Study after study shows that regular physical activity – even at moderate levels – reduces the risk of heart disease, cancer, high blood pressure and obesity, and enhances physical and mental functioning.

Despite this, a report from the Centers for Disease Control and Prevention (CDC) showed that 55% of American adults didn't move enough in 2019 to meet the minimum recommendation of 30 minutes of moderate physical activity on most days of the week. And a Gallup Health and Healthcare Survey found that just 45% of Americans regularly engaged in vigorous exercise in 2020 – down from 52% in 2019 (WebMD).

The key is to find the right exercise for you. If it is fun, you are more likely to stay in the zone!

Getting Started†

The path to a regular exercise routine has great rewards as well as roadblocks. Our goal is to help make it simple and safe – and give you motivation to push on.‡

According to medical experts, most adults need at least 30 minutes of moderate physical activity at least five days per week. Examples include walking briskly, mowing the lawn, dancing, swimming, or bicycling. Stretching and weight training can also strengthen your body and improve your fitness level. If you've been inactive for a while, use a sensible approach and start out slowly (Shree 22).

Our staff is here to help you establish a safe, healthy, and fun fitness routine that meets your individual needs and goals.

Tips for Staying Motivated

It seems that the most difficult part of starting or sticking to a fitness plan is just that, starting and sticking to it. Here are our tips for starting and maintaining a healthy exercise routine:

- Find something you enjoy. Take a dance class, learn to ski or swim, or try yoga or hiking. Try them all. Keep experimenting until you find an activity that moves you, mentally and physically.

* Active people live longer and feel better!
† Always consult a physician before beginning an exercise program.
‡ Each day is 1,440 minutes. We help you set aside 30 of them for physical activity.

The Global Fitness Zone | Your Name

your belongings without having to worry about remembering your key or a lock combination. For your convenience, a limited number of individual lockers are available for rent monthly.

Exercise Rooms

Our three exercise rooms are equipped with a variety of state-of-the-art exercise equipment, including stationary bikes, treadmills, rowing machines, climbing machines, and weights.

Aquatic Area

The Global Fitness Zone has three pools that are open to all members:

- An 85°F lap pool
- A 96°F therapeutic pool that is used for water therapy and relaxation
- A 102°F whirlpool

Massage Therapy

You can expect the highest degree of professionalism from our dedicated team of massage therapists. All massage therapists are fully licensed and trained in a variety of therapeutic techniques. Whether you want a light Swedish massage for relaxation, a deep tissue sports massage following your workout, or a combination of techniques, you'll love this approach to better health. Never had a massage? You don't know what you're missing. The reception desk has information on appointments, massage techniques, and gift certificates. Massages make great gifts!

Community Education

The Global Fitness Zone offers a host of classes on health and wellness issues. For further information, consult the monthly events calendar available at the reception desk.

Bibliography

Chao, Jennifer. *Fitness in the 21st Century*. Cambridge: Wellness Press, 2019. Print.
National Institute of Health. *Health Plus: Fitness and Exercise*. 7 February 2021. Web. 23 July 2021. <www.healthplus3547x.com>.
Shree, Maxine. "Designing a Fitness Routine." *Health Times* 6 August 2020: 20-29. Print.
WebMD. *Health and Fitness*. 4 April 2020. Web. 9 September 2021.

3 | Page

Skills Review (continued)

11. Inspect a document.

- **a.** Save a copy of the document as **IL_WD_2_Zone_Inspected** to the drive and folder where you store your Data Files.
- **b.** Open the Navigation pane, click the Headings link, click the headings listed in the Navigation pane to scroll through the document, then close the Navigation pane.
- **c.** Use the Go To command to move the insertion point to the top of page 1.
- **d.** Use the Find and Replace dialog box to find all em dashes in the document, but do not replace the em dashes. (*Hint*: Scroll through the document using the Find Next button.)
- **e.** Use the Find and Replace dialog box to find text formatted with the Heading 2 style, but do not replace the text.
- **f.** Select a word in the document, look it up using the Search button on the References tab, then close the Search pane.
- **g.** Show the comments in the document, then, using the Review tab, delete all the comments in the document.
- **h.** Use the Check for Issues command to run the Document Inspector.
- **i.** Remove all document property and personal information data from the document, then save your changes.
- **j.** Submit a copy of the document to your instructor, close the document, then exit Word.

Independent Challenge 1

The Riverwalk Medical Clinic publishes a variety of newsletters and information reports related to health and wellness for patients. Your colleague has drafted a newsletter about staying healthy while traveling and forwarded the file to you. The file includes comments with instructions for finalizing the document. You need to add citations and footnotes and format the newsletter for distribution to patients.

- **a.** Start Word, open the file IL_WD_2-3.docx from the drive and folder where you store your Data Files, save it as **IL_WD_2_Newsletter**, then read the document to get a feel for its contents.
- **b.** Show the comments in the document, scroll through the comments, reply to or resolve each comment, add a comment, then delete all comments from the document.
- **c.** Format the newsletter using styles. Apply the Title style to the orange text, the Heading 1 style to the blue text, and the Heading 2 style to the green text. (You will format the masthead after formatting the body of the document.)
- **d.** Apply a theme to the document. Choose a theme that suits the purpose and audience for the document. You can change the theme colors or style set if you wish.
- **e.** Change the font size of the title so that the title fits on one line.
- **f.** Modify the Heading 1 and Heading 2 styles so that the font, font size, font color, and paragraph spacing of the headings gives the newsletter an attractive and cohesive look.
- **g.** Using styles, format the first three lines of the document as a masthead for the newsletter. The masthead for this document should be attractive, but should not compete with the title of the document for attention. After applying styles, apply other formats, such as font size, font color, text effects, paragraph alignment, and borders to customize the look of the masthead.
- **h.** Add a header to the document using the Filigree header style. Type **Riverwalk Medical Clinic** in the Document title content control, then type your name in the Author content control. (*Hint*: If the Author content control shows different text, replace that text with your name.)
- **i.** Add a page number to the bottom of each page using the page number style of your choice.
- **j.** Remove headers and footers from the first page of the document.
- **k.** Use the Find command or the Navigation pane to find the text specified in the table below, then add a footnote at each location, using the footnote text specified in the table.

Independent Challenge 1 (continued)

Find text	Footnote text
behavior and health of the traveler	**Behavior is a critical factor. For example, going outdoors in a malaria-endemic area could result in becoming infected.**
public health	**It is best to consult a travel medicine specialist.**
tweezers	**Pack these items in checked luggage.**
Sunscreen	**SPF 15 or greater.**

l. Change the Citations and Bibliography style to MLA Seventh Edition. Use the Find command or the Navigation pane to find the text specified in the table below, then add a citation at each location, using the source specified in the table. Some citations include a page number. Remember to insert the citation before the period at the end of a sentence.

Find text	Citation source	Citation page number
people travel	World Tourism Organization	15
consequences	World Health Organization	
Source:	Johnson, Margaret	50
prevalent in sub-Saharan Africa	Centers for Disease Control and Prevention	
pregnancy	Clinton, Edmund	92

m. Press CTRL+END, then add a bibliography to the newsletter.

n. Check the document for spelling and grammar errors, then use the thesaurus to replace a word with a synonym.

o. View the document in Multiple pages view, then make any formatting adjustments necessary so that the document flows smoothly between pages and is easy to read. **FIGURE 2-32** shows a sample first page of the newsletter.

p. Save the document, submit a copy to your instructor, close the document, then exit Word.

FIGURE 2-32

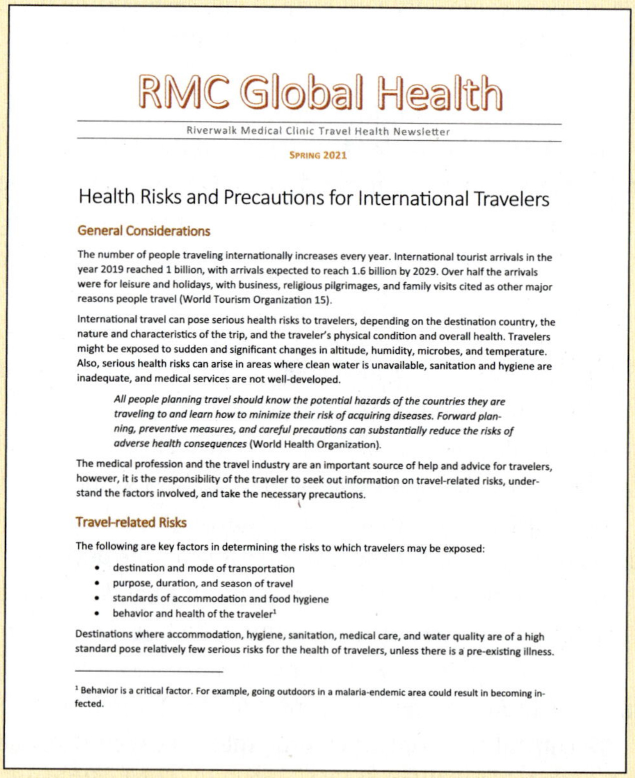

RMC Global Health

Riverwalk Medical Clinic Travel Health Newsletter

SPRING 2021

Health Risks and Precautions for International Travelers

General Considerations

The number of people traveling internationally increases every year. International tourist arrivals in the year 2019 reached 1 billion, with arrivals expected to reach 1.6 billion by 2029. Over half the arrivals were for leisure and holidays, with business, religious pilgrimages, and family visits cited as other major reasons people travel (World Tourism Organization 15).

International travel can pose serious health risks to travelers, depending on the destination country, the nature and characteristics of the trip, and the traveler's physical condition and overall health. Travelers might be exposed to sudden and significant changes in altitude, humidity, microbes, and temperature. Also, serious health risks can arise in areas where clean water is unavailable, sanitation and hygiene are inadequate, and medical services are not well-developed.

All people planning travel should know the potential hazards of the countries they are traveling to and learn how to minimize their risk of acquiring diseases. Forward planning, preventive measures, and careful precautions can substantially reduce the risks of adverse health consequences (World Health Organization).

The medical profession and the travel industry are an important source of help and advice for travelers, however, it is the responsibility of the traveler to seek out information on travel-related risks, understand the factors involved, and take the necessary precautions.

Travel-related Risks

The following are key factors in determining the risks to which travelers may be exposed:

- destination and mode of transportation
- purpose, duration, and season of travel
- standards of accommodation and food hygiene
- behavior and health of the traveler[1]

Destinations where accommodation, hygiene, sanitation, medical care, and water quality are of a high standard pose relatively few serious risks for the health of travelers, unless there is a pre-existing illness.

[1] Behavior is a critical factor. For example, going outdoors in a malaria-endemic area could result in becoming infected.

Independent Challenge 2

As an administrative assistant at a community college, you frequently format the research papers written by the members of your department. The format recommended by the *MLA Handbook for Writers of Research Papers*, a style guide that includes information on preparing, writing, and formatting research papers, is the standard format used by many schools, colleges, and universities. In this independent challenge, you will research the MLA guidelines for formatting a research paper and use the guidelines you find to format the pages of a research report.

a. Use your favorite search engine to search the web for information on the MLA guidelines for formatting a research report. Use the keywords **MLA Style** and **research paper format** to conduct your search.

b. Look for information on the proper formatting for the following aspects of a research paper: paper size, margins, title page or first page of the report, line spacing, paragraph indentation, and page numbers. Also find information on proper formatting for citations and a works cited page. Print the information you find.

c. Start Word, open the file IL_WD_2-4.docx from the drive and folder where you store your Data Files, then save it as **IL_WD_2_Research**. Using the information you learned, format this document as a research report.

d. Correct spelling and grammar errors in the document. If possible, add "stormwater" to the Word dictionary.

e. Adjust the margins, set the line spacing, and add page numbers to the document in the format recommended by the MLA. Use **Stormwater Management: A Case Study** as the title for your sample report, use your name as the author name, and use the name of the course you are enrolled in currently as well as the instructor's name for that course. Make sure to format the title page exactly as the MLA style dictates.

f. Format the remaining text as the body of the research report. Indent the first line of each paragraph rather than use quadruple spacing between paragraphs.

g. Create five sources and insert five citations in the document—including at least one journal article and one website. If possible, use the Researcher tool to add sources and citations. FIGURE 2-33 shows the Researcher pane with sample sources. You can also make up sources. (*Note*: For this practice document, you are allowed to make up sources. Never make up sources for real research papers.)

h. Add two citation placeholders to the document.

i. Create a works cited page, following MLA style. If necessary, edit the format of the citations and works cited page to conform to MLA format.

j. Save the document, submit a copy to your instructor, close the document, then exit Word.

FIGURE 2-33

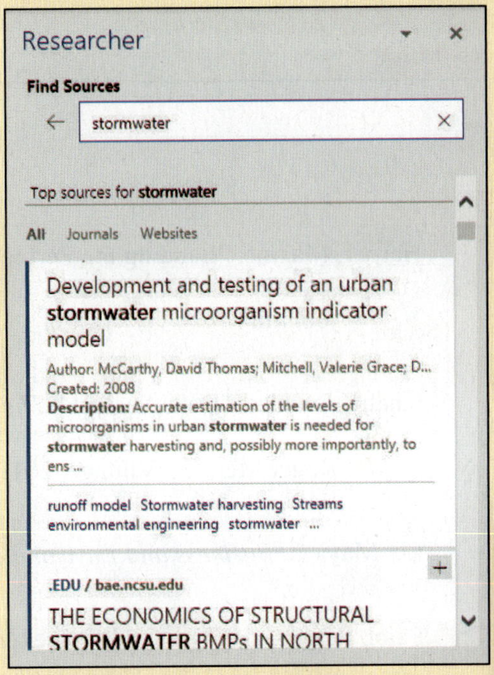

Visual Workshop

Use a blank document to create the Works Cited page shown in **FIGURE 2-34**, then save the document as **IL_WD_2_WorksCited**. Use 12-point Times New Roman for the text, double-space the lines in the document, and apply a hanging indent to the paragraphs in the list. Format "Works Cited" with the Heading 1 style and center the heading at the top of the document. Add your name and a page number to the header, then format the header text in 12-point Times New Roman. Correct spelling and grammar errors, remove the document property information from the file, then submit a copy to your instructor.

FIGURE 2-34

Works Cited

Harper, Maxine. "Landing the Perfect Job." *eHow,* www.ehow.com/landing-32980-the-perfect-job.html.

Khatri, Jamaica. "Data Analyst." *The Vintage Book of Contemporary Professions,* edited by Roger Mendez, Vintage, 2019, pp. 204-07.

Lu, Maya C. *Business and Environmentalism.* Reed Publishers, 2020.

Patel, Simon. "10 Tips for Job Seekers." *Working: Business Careers for the Digital World,* 20 Aug. 2020, example.com/article/working. Accessed 14 June 2021.

Formatting Text and Graphics

CASE You have been asked to finalize a report on the activities of the Technology department that will be distributed to other departments at JCL Talent. After formatting the headings in the report, you use tabs and create tables to organize the information so that it is easy to understand. Finally, you illustrate the report with images, shapes, and SmartArt.

Module Objectives

After completing this module, you will be able to:

- Use the Format Painter
- Work with tabs
- Add borders and shading
- Insert a table
- Insert and delete rows and columns
- Apply a table style
- Insert online pictures
- Size and scale a graphic
- Draw and format shapes
- Arrange graphic objects
- Create SmartArt graphics

Files You Will Need

IL_WD_3-1.docx
IL_WD_3-2.docx
IL_WD_3-3.docx
IL_WD_3-4.docx
IL_WD_3-5.docx

Use the Format Painter

Learning Outcomes
- Apply formatting using the Format Painter
- Clear formatting
- Insert special characters

You can dramatically change the appearance of text by applying different font styles, font effects, and character-spacing effects. When you are satisfied with the formatting of specific text, you can quickly apply the same formats to other text in the document using the Format Painter. The **Format Painter** is a powerful Word feature that allows you to copy all the format settings applied to selected text to other text that you want to format the same way. **CASE** *You enhance the appearance of the text in the report on the activities of the Technology department by applying different font styles and text effects. You also insert the date and a copyright symbol in the document.*

STEPS

1. **sam Start Word, open the file IL_WD_3-1.docx from the location where you store your Data Files, save it as IL_WD_3_Update, then drag the Zoom slider to 100**
2. **Select the title Update: JCL Technical Careers Division, click the Text Effects and Typography button in the Font group on the Home tab, click the Fill: Blue; Accent color 1; Shadow style (the second WordArt style in the first row), click the Font Size arrow, click 24, click the Font Color arrow, then click Green, Accent 6, Darker 25%**
   The title is formatted in 24-point WordArt style, green.
3. **Select the heading Career Connections Webinar Series to display the Mini toolbar, click the Font Size arrow, click 14, click the Bold button B, click the Italic button I, click the Font Color arrow, click the Blue, Accent 1, Darker 25% color in the theme colors, then deselect the text**
   The heading is formatted in 14-point bold, italic, and blue.
4. **Select Career Connections Webinar Series, then click the Format Painter button in the Clipboard group on the Home tab**
   The pointer changes to the Format Painter pointer.
5. **Scroll down, drag the Format Painter pointer to select the heading Social Media Advertising Campaign, then deselect the text**
   The heading is formatted in 14-point bold, italic, and blue, as shown in **FIGURE 3-1**.
6. **Select Social Media Advertising Campaign again, then double-click the Format Painter button**
   Double-clicking the Format Painter button allows the Format Painter to remain active until you turn it off. By keeping the Format Painter active, you can apply formatting to multiple items.
7. **Scroll down, select the headings Upcoming Conferences and Technical Careers Division Personnel, then click the Format Painter button to turn off the Format Painter**
   The headings are formatted in 14-point bold, italic, and blue.
8. **Press CTRL+END, type Prepared by, press SPACEBAR and type your name followed by a comma, press SPACEBAR, click the Insert tab, then click the Insert Date and Time button in the Text group**
   The Date and Time dialog box opens with available formats for inserting the date and time.
9. **Select the third format in the list, click OK to insert the current date at the insertion point, press ENTER, then click the Symbol button in the Symbols group**
   A gallery of commonly used symbols opens similar to the one in **FIGURE 3-2**. You may see a different selection of symbols depending on which symbols you insert most frequently. You can insert a symbol from this gallery or click More Symbols to open a larger gallery of symbols.
10. **Click the copyright symbol © in the gallery, press SPACEBAR, type JCL Talent, click the Home tab, press CTRL+HOME, then save your changes**
    The copyright symbol is inserted before JCL Talent.

QUICK TIP
To change the WordArt style currently applied to text, select the text, click the Text Effects and Typography button, then select a different WordArt style from the gallery.

TROUBLE
Move the pointer over the document text to see the Format Painter pointer.

QUICK TIP
You can also press ESC to turn off the Format Painter.

QUICK TIP
You can also click in the left margin to select the heading text.

QUICK TIP
To insert the date as a field that is updated automatically, select the Update automatically check box.

TROUBLE
If you do not see the copyright symbol, click More Symbols, select the code in the Character code box, type 00A9, click Insert, then click Close.

FIGURE 3-1: Formats copied and applied using the Format Painter

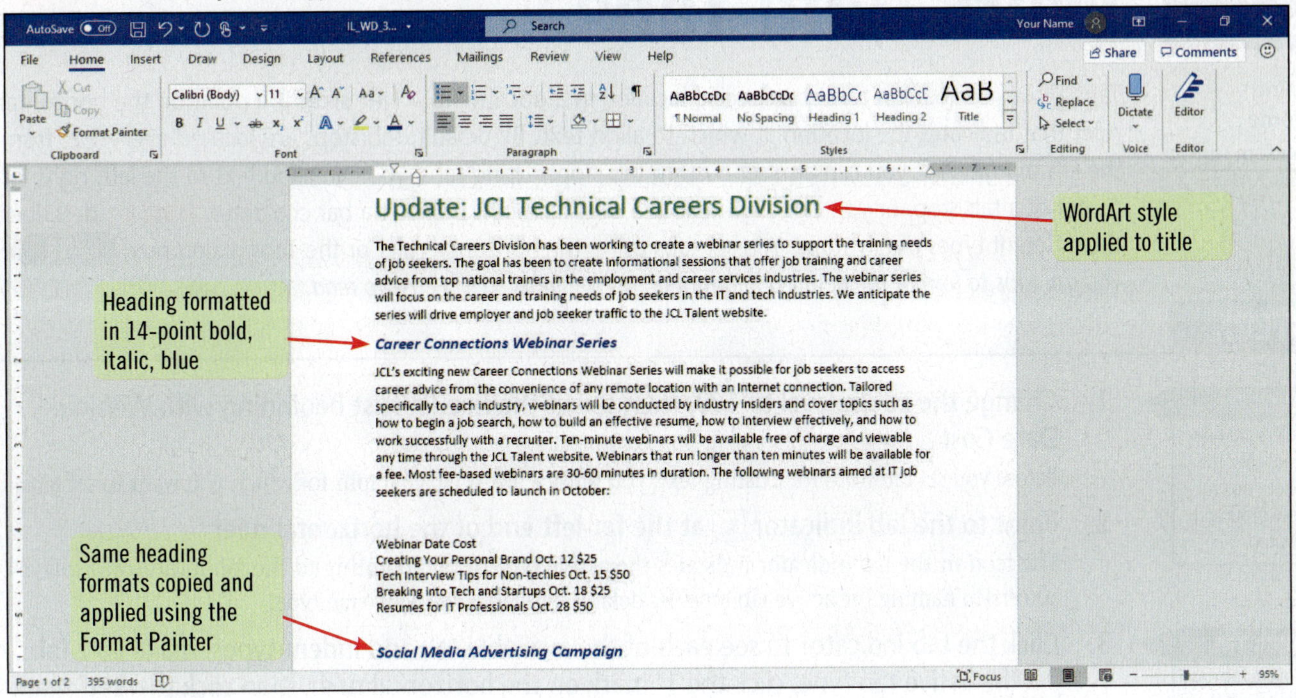

FIGURE 3-2: Symbol gallery

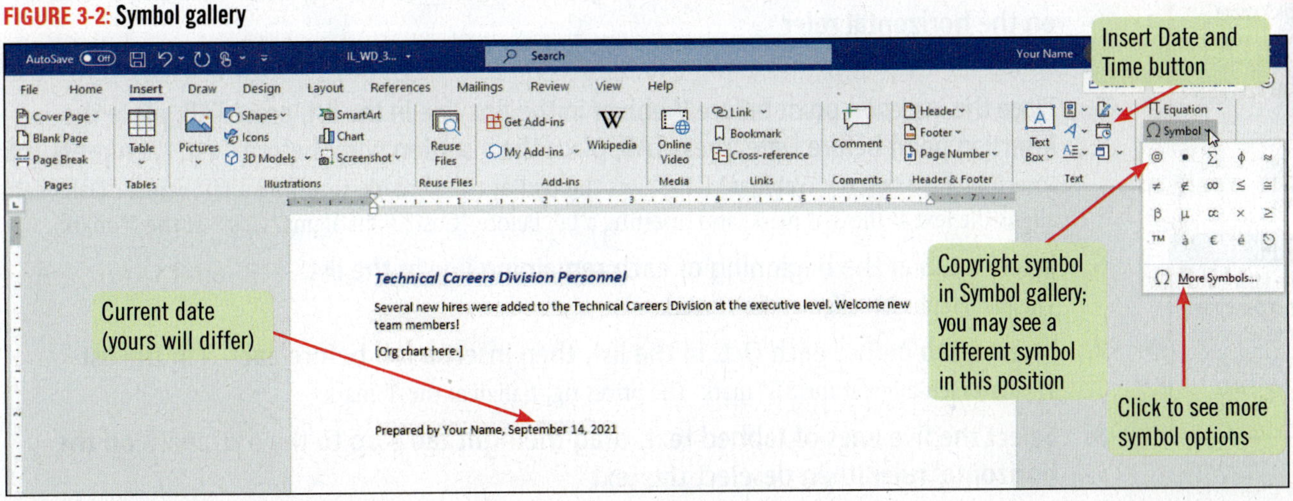

Clearing formatting from text

If you are unhappy with the way text is formatted, you can use the Clear All Formatting command to return the text to the default format settings. The default format includes font and paragraph formatting: text is formatted in 11-point Calibri, and paragraphs are left-aligned with 1.08 point line spacing, 8 points of space after, and no indents. To clear formatting from text and return it to the default format, select the text you want to clear, and then click the Clear All Formatting button in the Font group on the Home tab. If you prefer to return the text to the default font and remove all paragraph formatting, making the text 11-point Calibri, left-aligned, single spaced, with no paragraph spacing or indents, select the text and then click the No Spacing button in the Styles group on the Home tab.

Word
Module 3

Work with Tabs

Learning Outcome
- Set and use tab stops

Tabs allow you to align text at a specific location in a document. A **tab stop** is a point on the horizontal ruler that indicates the location at which to align text. By default, tab stops are located every 1/2" from the left margin, but you can also set custom tab stops. Using tabs, you can align text to the left, right, or center of a tab stop, or you can align text at a decimal point or insert a bar character. TABLE 3-1 describes the different types of tab stops. You set tabs using the horizontal ruler or the Tabs dialog box. CASE *You use tabs to format the detailed information on webinars so it is easy to read.*

STEPS

QUICK TIP
If the rulers are not displayed, click the Ruler check box in the Show group on the View tab.

QUICK TIP
To remove a tab stop, drag it off the ruler.

TROUBLE
If you click more than twice, keep clicking until the Right Tab icon again appears.

QUICK TIP
Place the insertion point in a paragraph to see the tab stops for that paragraph on the horizontal ruler.

QUICK TIP
Double-click a tab stop on the ruler to open the Tabs dialog box.

1. **Change the zoom level to 120, then select the five-line list beginning with Webinar Date Cost**
   Before you set tab stops for existing text, you must select the paragraphs for which you want to set tabs.
2. **Point to the tab indicator at the far-left end of the horizontal ruler**
   The icon in the tab indicator indicates the active type of tab; pointing to the tab indicator displays a ScreenTip naming the active tab type. By default, left tab is the active tab type.
3. **Click the tab indicator to see each of the available tab and indent types, make Left Tab the active tab type, click the 1" mark on the horizontal ruler, then click the 3¾" mark on the horizontal ruler**
   Clicking the horizontal ruler inserts a tab stop of the active type for the selected paragraph or paragraphs. A left tab stop is inserted at the 1" mark and the 3¾" mark.
4. **Click the tab indicator twice so the Right Tab icon is active, then click the 5" mark on the horizontal ruler**
   A right tab stop is inserted at the 5" mark on the horizontal ruler, as shown in FIGURE 3-3.
5. **Place the insertion point before Webinar in the first line in the list, press TAB, place the insertion point before Date, press TAB, place the insertion point before Cost, then press TAB**
   Inserting a tab before "Webinar" left-aligns the text at the 1" mark, inserting a tab before "Date" left-aligns the text at the 3¾" mark, and inserting a tab before "Cost" right-aligns "Cost" at the 5" mark.
6. **Insert a tab at the beginning of each remaining line in the list**
   The paragraphs left-align at the 1" mark.
7. **Insert a tab before each Oct. in the list, then insert a tab before each $ in the list**
   The dates left-align at the 3¾" mark. The prices right-align at the 5" mark.
8. **Select the five lines of tabbed text, drag the right tab stop to the 5½" mark on the horizontal ruler, then deselect the text**
   Dragging the tab stop moves it to a new location. The prices right-align at the 5½" mark.
9. **Select the last four lines of tabbed text, click the Launcher in the Paragraph group, then click Tabs at the bottom of the Paragraph dialog box**
   The Tabs dialog box opens, as shown in FIGURE 3-4. You can use the Tabs dialog box to set tab stops, change the position or alignment of existing tab stops, clear tab stops, and apply tab leaders to tabs. **Tab leaders** are lines that appear in front of tabbed text.
10. **Click 3.75" in the Tab stop position list box, click the 2 option button in the Leader section, click Set, click 5.5" in the Tab stop position list box, click the 2 option button in the Leader section, click Set, click OK, deselect the text, then save your changes**
    A dotted tab leader is added before each 3.75" and 5.5" tab stop in the last four lines of tabbed text, as shown in FIGURE 3-5.

FIGURE 3-3: Left and right tab stops on the horizontal ruler

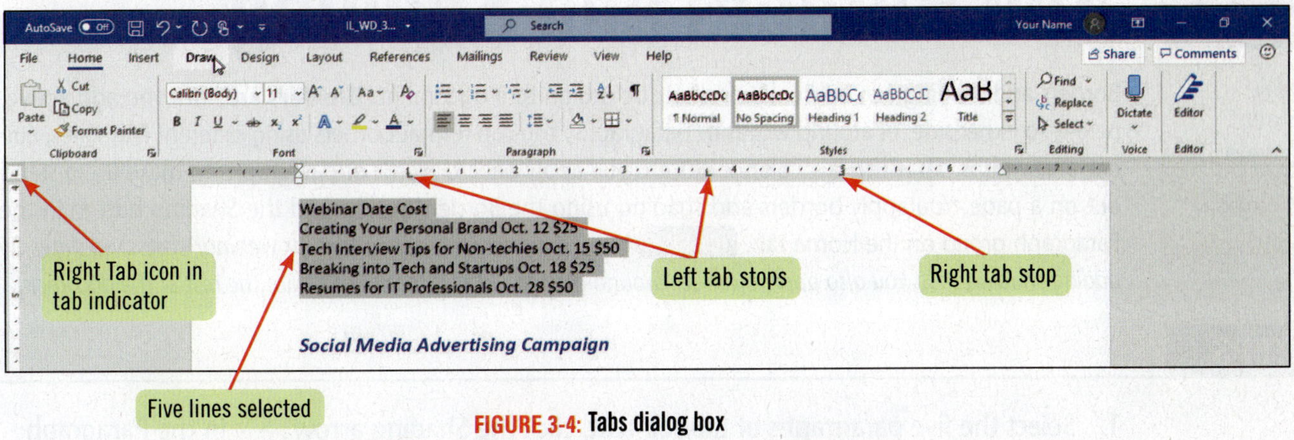

FIGURE 3-4: Tabs dialog box

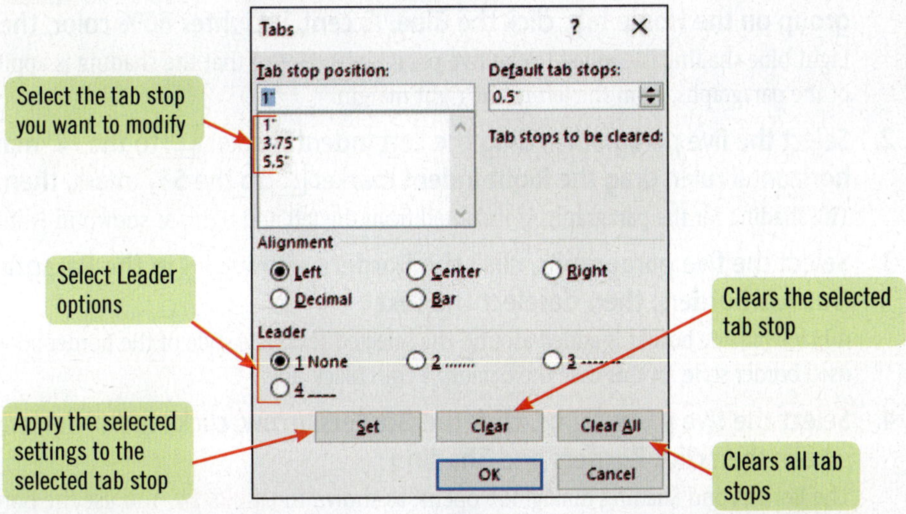

FIGURE 3-5: Tab leaders

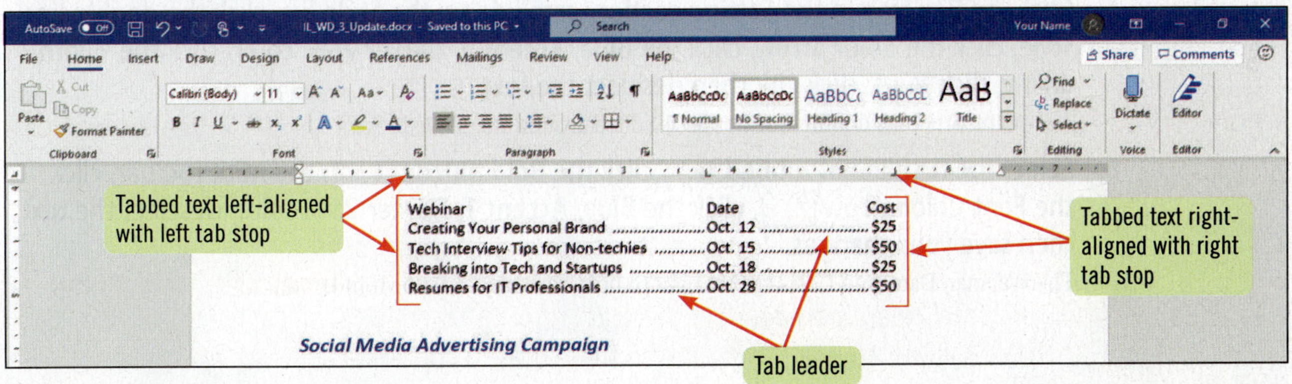

TABLE 3-1: Types of tabs

tab	use to
Left tab	Set the start position of text so that text runs to the right of the tab stop as you type
Center tab	Set the center align position of text so that text stays centered on the tab stop as you type
Right tab	Set the right or end position of text so that text moves to the left of the tab stop as you type
Decimal tab	Set the position of the decimal point so that numbers align around the decimal point as you type
Bar tab	Insert a vertical bar at the tab position

Word
Module 3

Add Borders and Shading

Learning Outcomes
- Apply shading to text
- Apply borders to text

Borders and shading can add color and artistic design to a document. **Borders** are lines you add above, below, to either side, or around words or paragraphs. You can format borders using different line styles, colors, and widths. **Shading** is a color or pattern you apply behind words or paragraphs to make them stand out on a page. You apply borders and shading using the Borders button and the Shading button in the Paragraph group on the Home tab. **CASE** *You enhance the tabbed text for webinar costs and dates by adding shading to it. You also apply a border around the tabbed text to set it off from the rest of the document.*

STEPS

1. **Select the five paragraphs of tabbed text, click the Shading arrow in the Paragraph group on the Home tab, click the Blue, Accent 1, Lighter 80% color, then deselect the text**
   Light blue shading is applied to the five paragraphs. Notice that the shading is applied to the entire width of the paragraphs, from the left to the right margin.
2. **Select the five paragraphs, drag the Left Indent marker to the ¾" mark on the horizontal ruler, drag the Right Indent marker to the 5¾" mark, then deselect the text**
   The shading for the paragraphs is indented from the left and right, as shown in FIGURE 3-6.
3. **Select the five paragraphs, click the Borders arrow in the Paragraph group, click Outside Borders, then deselect the text**
   A black outside border is added around the selected text. The style of the border added is the most recently used border style, in this case the default, a thin black line.
4. **Select the five paragraphs, click the Borders arrow, click No Border, click the Borders arrow, then click Borders and Shading**
   The Borders and Shading dialog box opens, as shown in FIGURE 3-7. You use the Borders tab to change the border style, color, and width, and to add boxes and lines to words or paragraphs.
5. **Click the Box icon in the Setting section, scroll down the Style list, click the double-line style, click the Color arrow, click the Blue, Accent 1, Darker 25% color, click the Width arrow, click ¾ pt, click OK, then deselect the text**
   A ¾-point dark blue double-line border is added around the tabbed text.
6. **Select the first line of tabbed text, click the Bold button on the Mini toolbar, click the Font Color arrow, click the Blue, Accent 1, Darker 25% color, deselect the text, then save your changes**
   The Webinar, Date, and Cost text changes to bold dark blue, as shown in FIGURE 3-8.

Underlining text

Another way to call attention to text and to enhance the appearance of a document is to apply an underline style to words you want to highlight. The Underline arrow in the Font group displays straight, dotted, wavy, dashed, and mixed underline styles, along with a gallery of colors to choose from. To apply an underline to text, select it, click the Underline arrow, and then select an underline style from the list. For a wider variety of underline styles, click More Underlines in the list, and then select an underline style in the Font dialog box. You can change the color of an underline at any time by selecting the underlined text, clicking the Underline arrow, pointing to Underline Color, and then choosing from the options in the color gallery. If you want to remove an underline from text, select the underlined text, and then click the Underline button.

FIGURE 3-6: Shading applied to the tabbed text

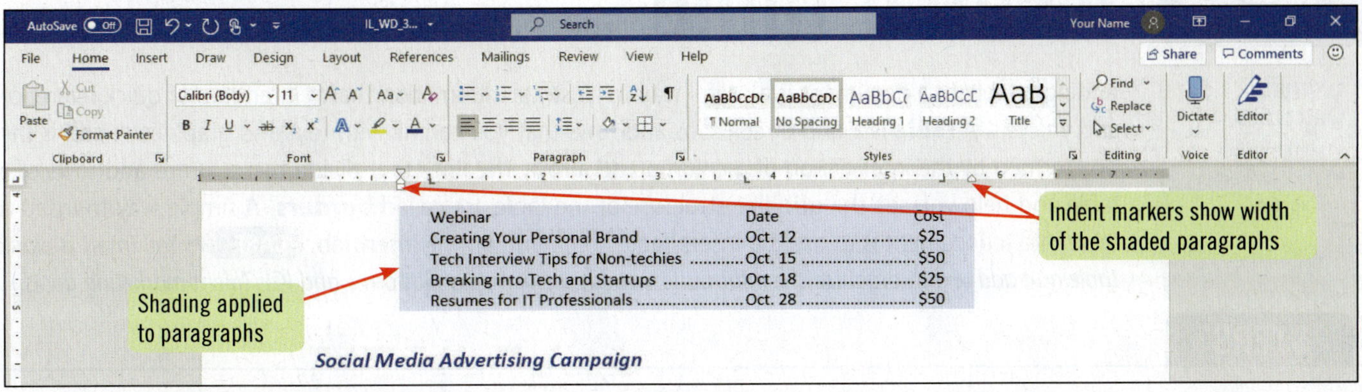

FIGURE 3-7: Borders tab in Borders and Shading dialog box

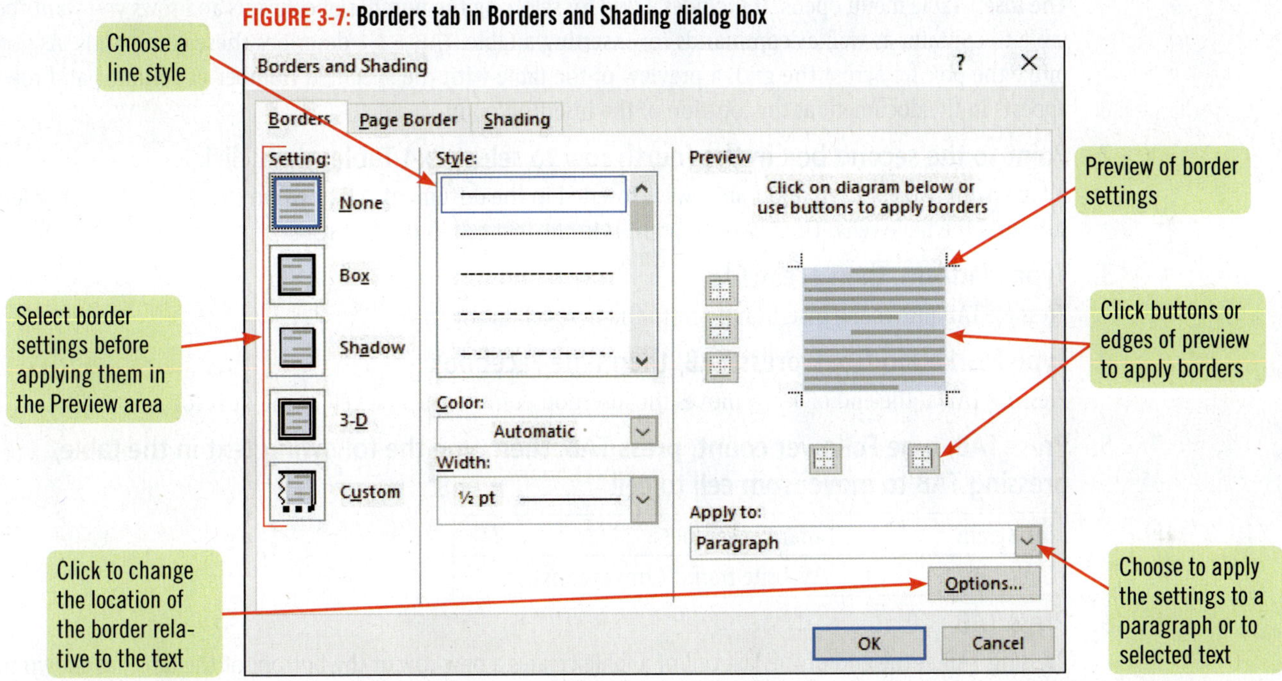

FIGURE 3-8: Borders and shading applied to the document

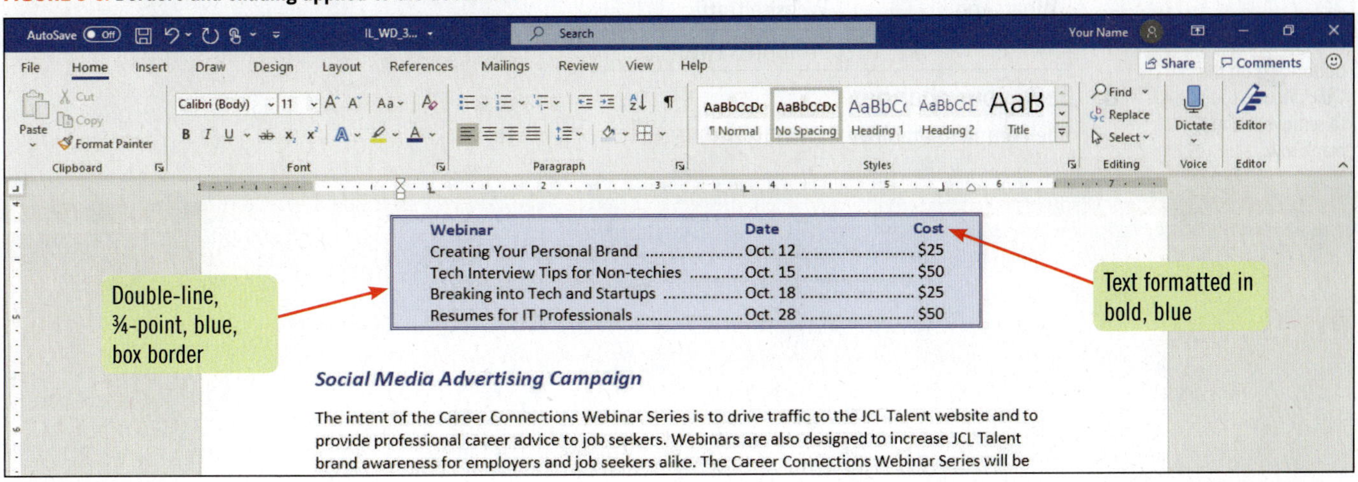

Word Module 3

Insert a Table

Learning Outcomes
- Insert a table
- Select and enter table data

Adding a table to a document is a useful way to illustrate information that is intended for quick reference and analysis. A **table** is a grid of columns and rows that you can fill with text and graphics. A **cell** is the box formed by the intersection of a column and a row. The lines that divide the columns and rows of a table and help you see the grid-like structure of the table are called **borders**. A simple way to insert a table into a document is to use the Insert Table command on the Insert tab. CASE *You insert a blank table and add text to organize the information about social media platforms and JCL Talent marketing goals.*

STEPS

1. **Scroll down, place the insertion point in the blank paragraph above the Upcoming Conferences heading, click the Insert tab, then click the Table button in the Tables group**
   The Insert Table menu opens. It includes a grid for selecting the number of columns and rows you want the table to contain, as well as commands for inserting a table. TABLE 3-2 describes these commands. As you move the pointer across the grid, a preview of the table with the specified number of columns and rows appears in the document at the location of the insertion point.
2. **Point to the second box in the fourth row to select 2x4 Table, then click**
   A table with two columns and four rows is inserted in the document, as shown in FIGURE 3-9. Black borders surround the table cells. The insertion point is in the first cell in the first row.
3. **Type Platform, then press TAB**
   Pressing TAB moves the insertion point to the next cell in the row.
4. **Type Marketing Goal, press TAB, then type Facebook**
   Pressing TAB at the end of a row moves the insertion point to the first cell in the next row.
5. **Press TAB, type Follower count, press TAB, then type the following text in the table, pressing TAB to move from cell to cell**

Instagram	Brand awareness
LinkedIn	Website traffic/Conversions

6. **Press TAB**
   Pressing TAB at the end of the last cell of a table creates a new row at the bottom of the table, as shown in FIGURE 3-10. The insertion point is located in the first cell in the new row.
7. **Type the following, pressing TAB to move from cell to cell and to create a new row**

WhatsApp	Website traffic
Twitter	Promoted tweets

8. **Save your changes**
   The completed table is shown in FIGURE 3-11.

TROUBLE
If you pressed TAB after the last row, click the Undo button on the Quick Access toolbar to remove the new blank row.

FIGURE 3-9: Blank table

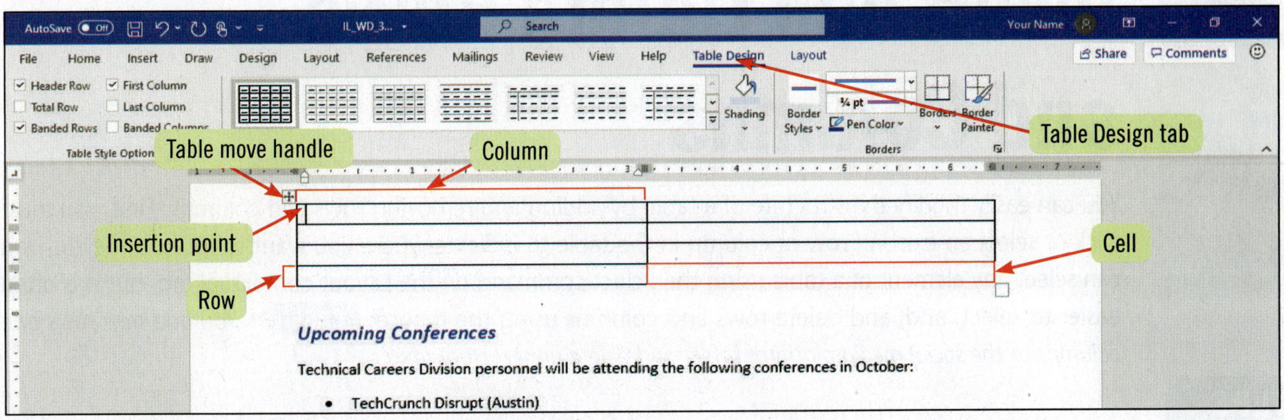

FIGURE 3-10: New row in table

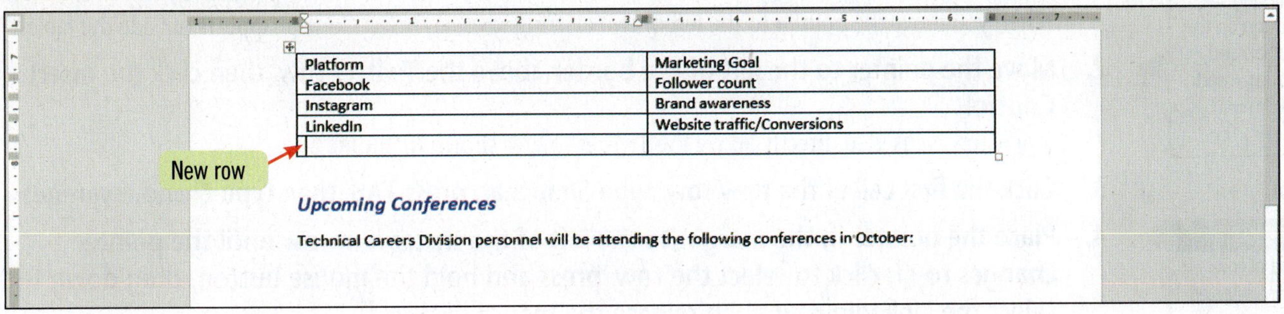

FIGURE 3-11: Text in the table

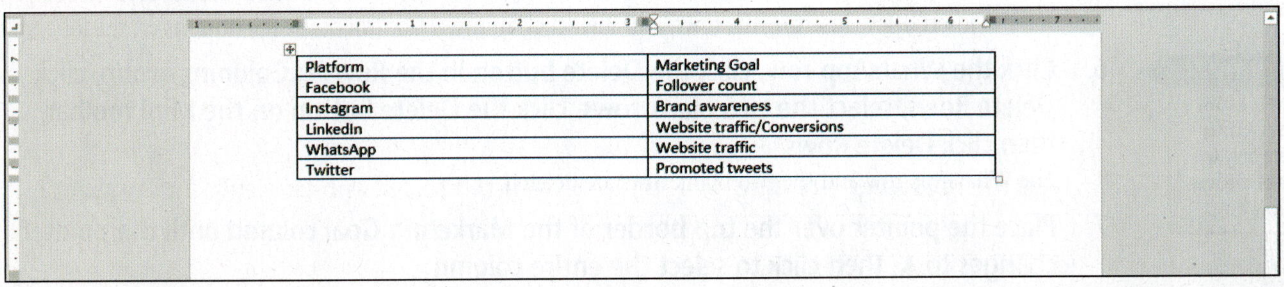

TABLE 3-2: Table menu commands

command	use to
Insert Table	Create a table with any number of columns and rows and select an AutoFit behavior
Draw Table	Create a complex table by drawing the table columns and rows
Convert Text to Table	Convert text that is separated by tabs, commas, or another separator character into a table
Excel Spreadsheet	Insert a blank Excel worksheet into the document as an embedded object
Quick Tables	Insert a preformatted table template and replace the placeholder data with your own data

Insert and Delete Rows and Columns

Learning Outcome
- Insert and delete rows and columns

You can easily modify the structure of a table by adding and removing rows and columns. First, you must click or select an existing row or column in the table to indicate where you want to insert or delete. You can select any element of a table using the Select command on the Layout contextual tab, but it is often easier to select, add, and delete rows and columns using the mouse. **CASE** *You add new rows and columns to the social media platform table, and delete unnecessary rows.*

STEPS

QUICK TIP
You can also insert a row by right-clicking a row, clicking the Insert button on the Mini toolbar, and then clicking Insert Above or Insert Below.

QUICK TIP
If the end of row mark is not selected, you have selected only the text in the row, not the row itself.

QUICK TIP
If you select a row and press DELETE, you delete only the contents of the row, not the row itself.

QUICK TIP
To select a cell, place the pointer near the left border of the cell, then click.

QUICK TIP
You can use the arrow keys or press TAB to move the insertion point from cell to cell.

1. **Click the Home tab, click the Show/Hide ¶ button ¶ in the Paragraph group to display formatting marks, then move the pointer up and down the left edge of the table**
   An end of cell mark appears at the end of each cell, and an end of row mark appears at the end of each row. When you move the pointer to the left of two existing rows, an Insert Control appears outside the table.
2. **Move the pointer to the left of the border above the Twitter row, then click the Insert Control**
   A new row is inserted directly above the Twitter row, as shown in FIGURE 3-12.
3. **Click the first cell of the new row, type Snapchat, press TAB, then type Brand awareness**
4. **Place the pointer in the margin to the left of the Instagram row until the pointer changes to ↗, click to select the row, press and hold the mouse button, drag down to select the LinkedIn row, then release the mouse button**
   The Instagram and LinkedIn rows are selected, including the end of row marks.
5. **Click the Layout contextual tab, then click the Insert Below button in the Rows & Columns group**
   Two new rows are added below the selected rows. To insert multiple rows, you select the number of rows you want to insert before inserting the rows, and then click an Insert Control or use the buttons on the Ribbon.
6. **Click the WhatsApp row, click the Delete button in the Rows & Columns group, click Delete Rows, select the two blank rows, click the Delete button on the Mini toolbar, then click Delete Rows**
   The WhatsApp row and the two blank rows are deleted.
7. **Place the pointer over the top border of the Marketing Goal column until the pointer changes to ⬇, then click to select the entire column**
8. **Click the Insert Right button in the Rows & Columns group, then type Cost Basis**
   A new column is inserted to the right of the Marketing Goal column, as shown in FIGURE 3-13.
9. **Place the pointer over the border between the Marketing Goal and Cost Basis columns at the top of the table, click the Insert Control, then type Budget in the first cell of the new column**
   A new column for Budget is added between the Marketing Goal and Cost Basis columns.
10. **Press DOWN ARROW to move the insertion point to the next cell in the Budget column, click the Home tab, click ¶ to turn off the display of formatting marks, enter the text shown in FIGURE 3-14 in each cell in the Budget and Cost Basis columns, then save your changes**
    Compare your table to FIGURE 3-14.

FIGURE 3-12: Inserted row

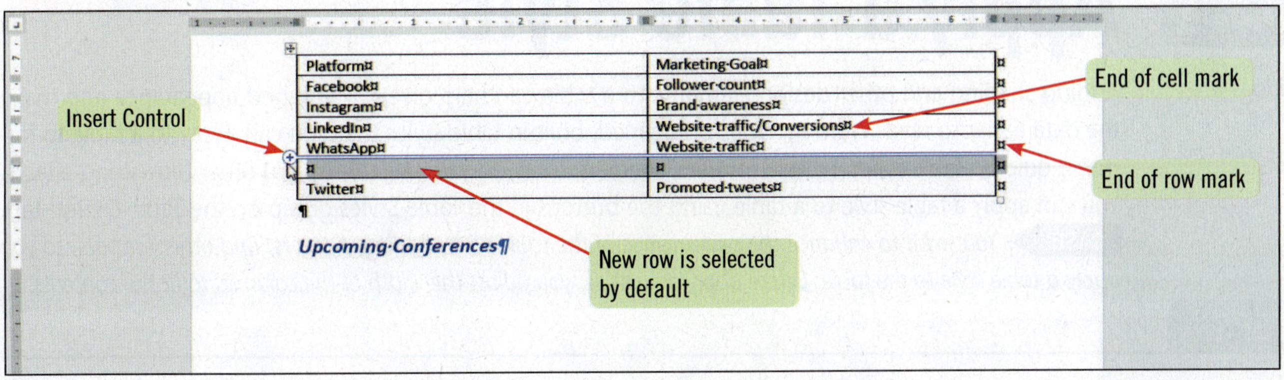

FIGURE 3-13: Inserted column

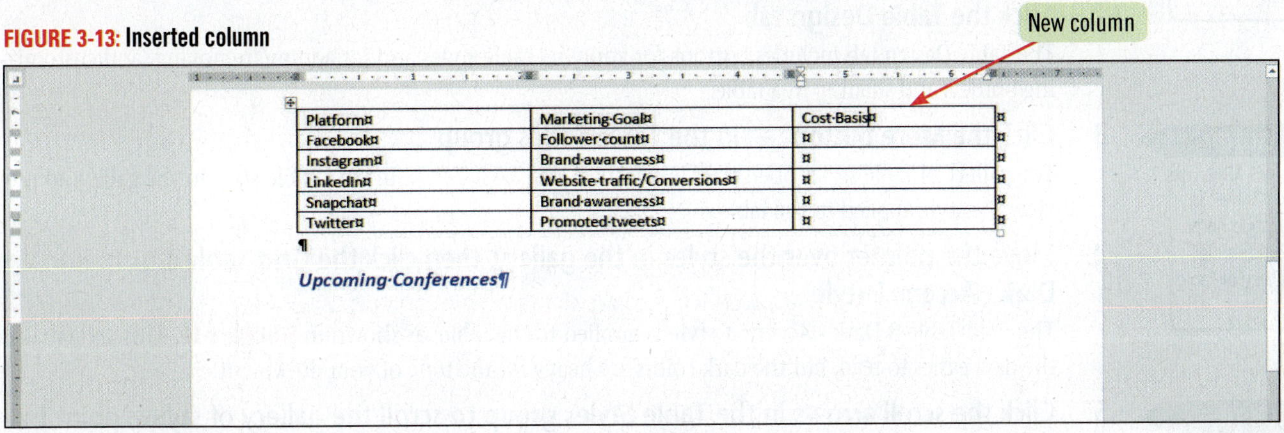

FIGURE 3-14: Text in Budget and Cost Basis columns

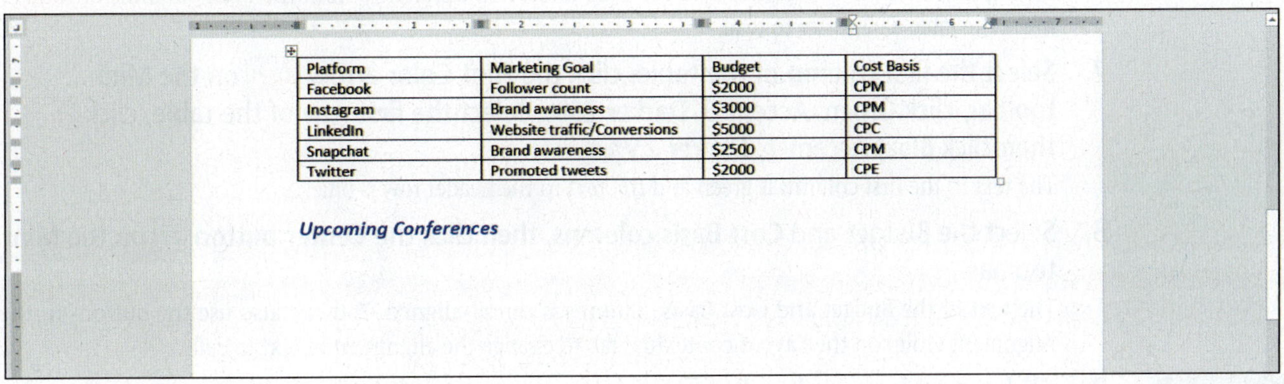

Word

Apply a Table Style

Learning Outcome
- Apply a table style

Adding shading and other design elements to a table can help give it a polished appearance and make the data easier to read. Word includes predefined, built-in table styles that you can apply to a table to format it quickly. Table styles include borders, shading, fonts, alignment, colors, and other formatting effects. You can apply a table style to a table using the buttons in the Table Styles group on the Table Design tab. **CASE** *You want to enhance the appearance of the table with shading, borders, and other formats, so you apply a table style to the table. Before applying a style, you adjust the width of the columns to fit the contents.*

STEPS

QUICK TIP The insertion point must be in the table for the table contextual tabs to be active.

QUICK TIP The number after the word "Table" in the Table style name is the row identifier in the gallery of table styles.

QUICK TIP Click Clear in the gallery of table styles to remove all borders, shading, and other style elements from a table.

QUICK TIP You can also use the Select button in the Table group on the Layout contextual tab to select a table, row, column, or cell.

1. **Click the Layout contextual tab, click the AutoFit button in the Cell Size group, then click AutoFit Contents**

   The width of the table columns is adjusted to fit the text. The Layout contextual tab includes buttons for modifying the structure and size of a table.

2. **Click the Table Design tab**

   The Table Design tab includes buttons for applying table styles and for adding, removing, and customizing borders and shading in a table.

3. **Click the More button in the Table Styles group**

   The gallery of table styles opens, as shown in FIGURE 3-15. You point to a table style in the gallery to preview the style applied to the table.

4. **Move the pointer over the styles in the gallery, then click the Grid Table 5 Dark - Accent 1 style**

   The Grid Table 5 Dark - Accent 1 style is applied to the table, as shown in FIGURE 3-16. This style makes the data easier to read, but the dark colors are heavy for the tone of your document.

5. **Click the scroll arrows in the Table Styles group to scroll the gallery of styles, point to several styles to see each style applied to the table, click the More button in the Table Styles group, then click the Grid Table 2 - Accent 3 style**

   The Grid Table 2 - Accent 3 style is applied to the table. This style makes the table data easier to read.

6. **In the Table Style Options group, click the Banded Rows check box to clear it**

   The shading is removed from alternating rows in the table. When the banded columns or banded rows setting is active, the odd columns or rows are formatted differently from the even columns or rows to make the table data easier to read.

7. **Select the first column of the table, click the Font Color arrow on the Mini toolbar, click Green, Accent 6, Darker 25%, select the first row of the table, click , then click Blue, Accent 1, Darker 25%**

   The text in the first column is green and the text in the header row is blue.

8. **Select the Budget and Cost Basis columns, then click the Center button on the Mini toolbar**

   The text in the Budget and Cost Basis columns is center-aligned. You can also use the buttons in the Alignment group on the Layout contextual tab to change the alignment of text in cells.

9. **Click the table move handle, click the Home tab, click the Center button in the Paragraph group on the Ribbon, then deselect the table**

   Clicking the table move handle selects the entire table. Clicking the Center button with the entire table selected centered the table between the margins, as shown in FIGURE 3-17.

10. **Press CTRL+HOME, then save your changes**

FIGURE 3-15: Gallery of table styles

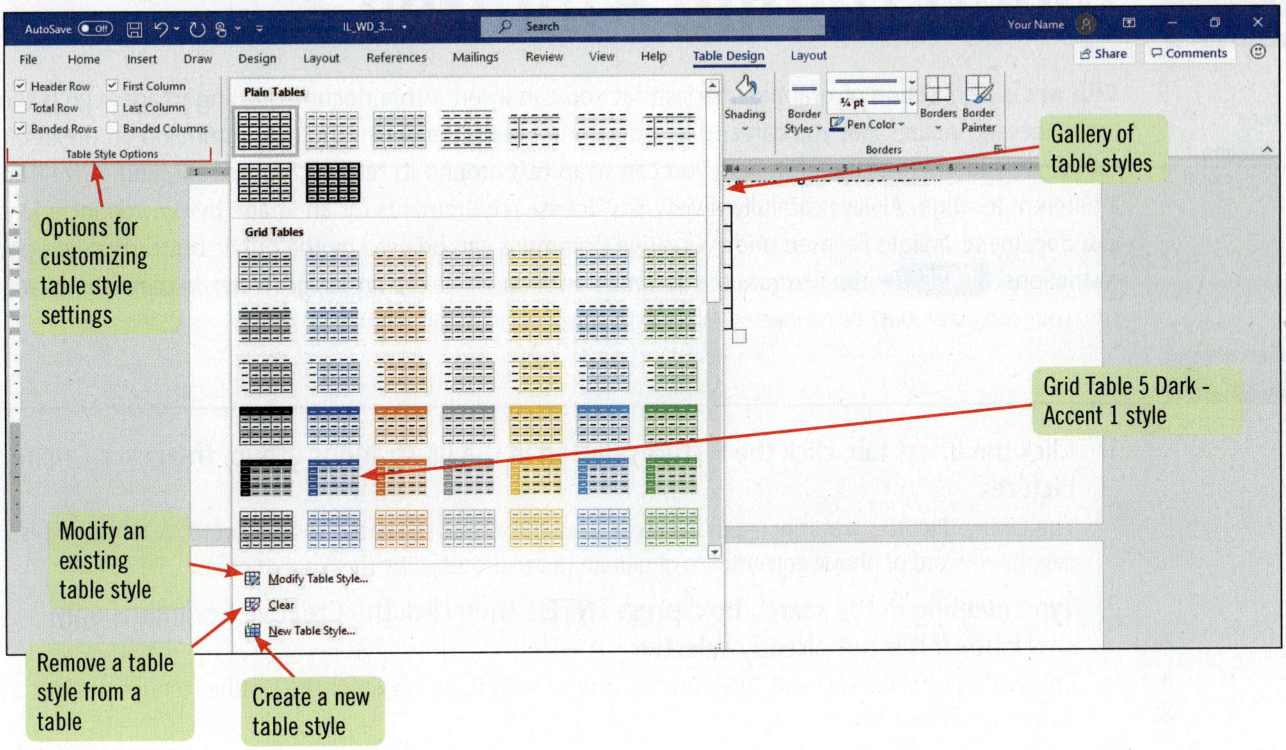

FIGURE 3-16: Grid Table 5 Dark - Accent 1 style applied to table

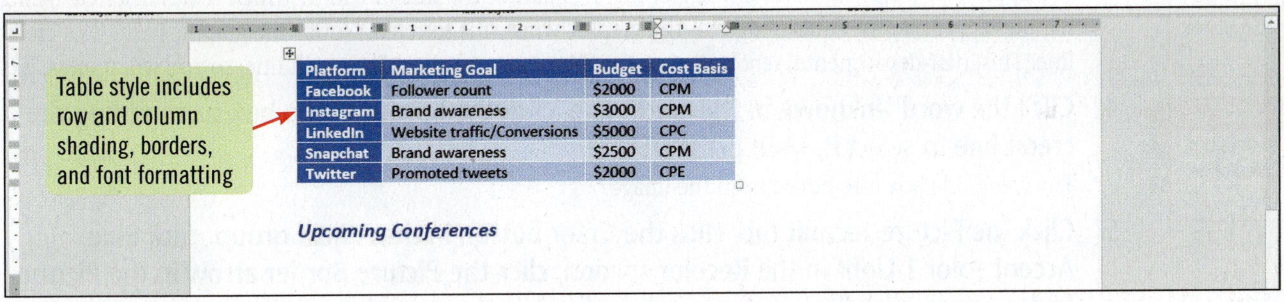

FIGURE 3-17: Completed table

Word

Insert Online Pictures

Learning Outcomes
- Insert pictures
- Wrap text around objects

Clip art is a collection of graphic images that you can insert into a document. Bing image search clip art images are images that you can add to a document using the Online Pictures command on the Insert tab. Once you insert a clip art image, you can wrap text around it, resize it, enhance it, and move it to a different location. Always carefully review any license requirements for an image before you include it in a document. Images licensed under Creative Commons can be used by the public but carry copyright restrictions. **CASE** *You illustrate the document with an online clip art image. Note: To complete this lesson, your computer must be connected to the Internet.*

STEPS

1. **Click the Insert tab, click the Pictures button in the Illustrations group, then click Online Pictures**

   The Online Pictures window opens. You can search for images related to a keyword. A **keyword** is a descriptive word or phrase you enter to obtain an image described by the word or phrase.

2. **Type meeting in the search box, press ENTER, then click the Creative Commons only check box if it is not already selected**

   Images that have the keyword "meeting" associated with them appear in the Online Pictures window, as shown in FIGURE 3-18.

TROUBLE Select a different clip that has square dimensions if the clip shown in FIGURE 3-18 is not available to you.

3. **Click the Filter button, click Clipart, click the clip called out in FIGURE 3-18, then click Insert**

   The clip is inserted as an inline graphic at the location of the insertion point, as shown in FIGURE 3-19. Until you apply text wrapping to an inline graphic, it is part of the line of text in which it was inserted. Sizing handles appear on the square edges of the graphic when it is selected. Notice the graphic includes a credit line. This inter-departmental report does not require that you retain the credit line, so you will remove it.

TROUBLE If your clip does not include a credit line, skip Step 4.

4. **Click the word Unknown in the credit line, click the border of the box surrounding the credit line to select it, then press DELETE**

   The credit line box is removed from the image.

5. **Click the Picture Format tab, click the Color button in the Adjust group, click Blue, Accent color 1 Light in the Recolor section, click the Picture Border arrow in the Picture Styles group, click Blue, Accent 1, then deselect the graphic**

   The color of the image changes from black to blue, and a blue picture border is added. To move a graphic independently of the line of text in which it was inserted, you must make it a floating graphic.

QUICK TIP To position a graphic anywhere on a page, you must apply text wrapping to it even if there is no text on the page.

6. **Click the image to select it, click the Layout Options button on the side of the image, then click the Square button in the With Text Wrapping section**

   Depending upon the size of the graphic, the text wraps around the square sides of the graphic, making the graphic a floating object. Notice the anchor that appears to the left of the graphic. The anchor indicates the floating graphic is **anchored** to the nearest paragraph, so that the graphic moves with the paragraph if the paragraph is moved. The anchor is a nonprinting symbol that appears when an object is selected.

QUICK TIP To position a graphic using precise measurements, click the Position button, click More Layout Options, then adjust the settings on the Position tab in the Layout dialog box.

7. **Position the pointer over the graphic, when the pointer changes to ✥, drag the graphic down, using the green guidelines that appear, so its top is directly under the document title and its left aligns with the left margin, as shown in FIGURE 3-20, then release the mouse button**

   The graphic is positioned below the title on the left side of the page.

8. **Deselect the graphic, then save your changes.**

FIGURE 3-18: Online Pictures window

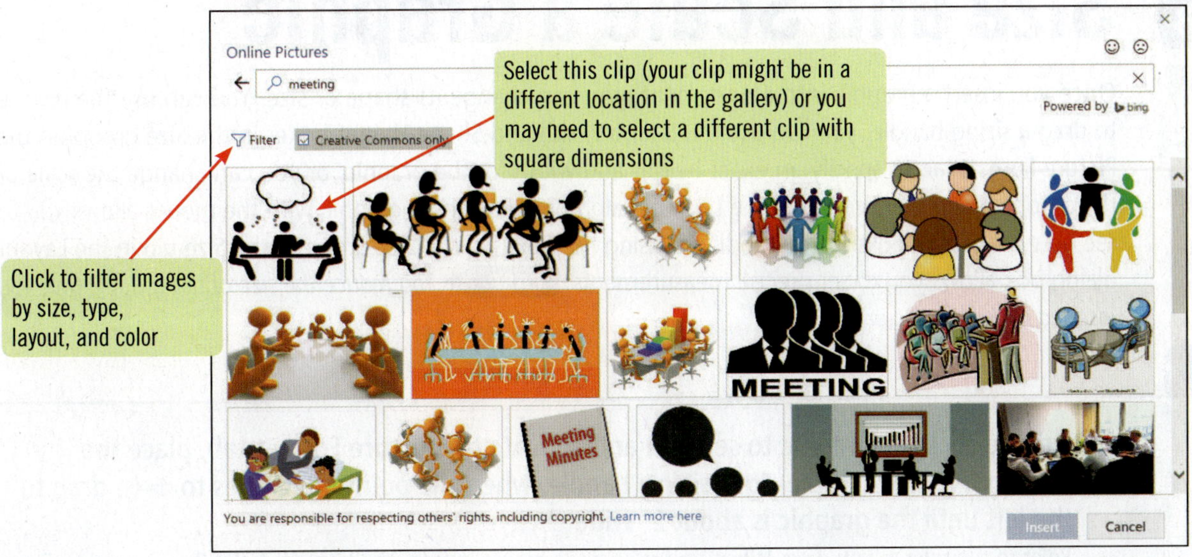

FIGURE 3-19: Inline graphic

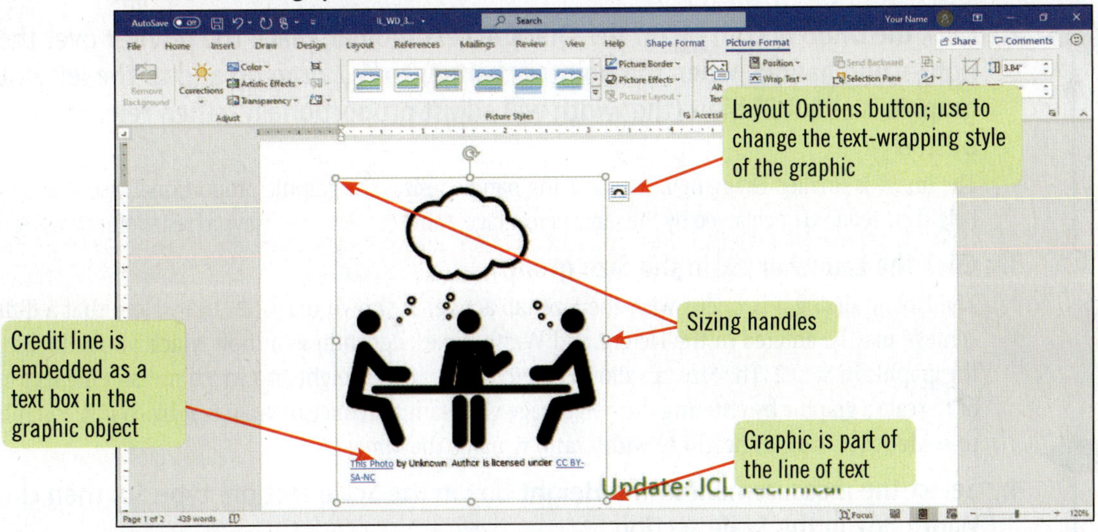

FIGURE 3-20: Graphic being moved to a new location

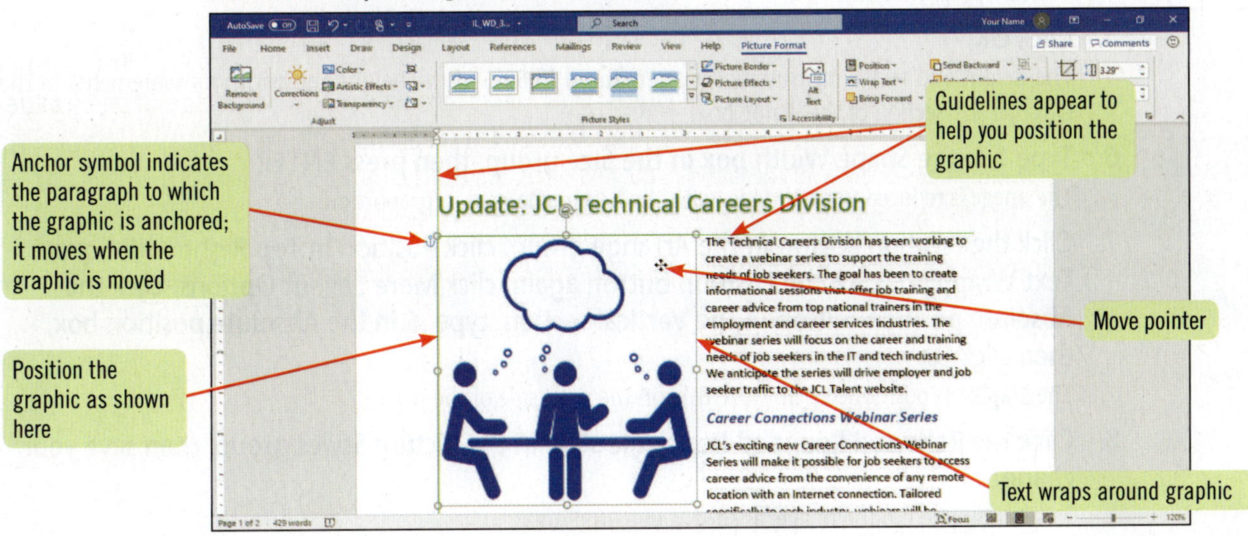

Word
Module 3

Size and Scale a Graphic

Learning Outcomes
- Format objects
- Scale a graphic

Once you insert a graphic into a document, you can change its shape or size. You can use the mouse to drag a sizing handle, you can use the Shape Width and Shape Height boxes in the Size group on the Picture Format tab to specify an exact height and width for the graphic, or you can change the scale of the graphic using the Size tab in the Layout dialog box. Resizing a graphic with the mouse allows you to see how the image looks as you modify it. Using the boxes in the Size group or the Size tab in the Layout dialog box allows you to set precise measurements. **CASE** *You reduce the size of the graphic that you inserted in the JCL document.*

STEPS

1. **Double-click the graphic to select it and activate the Picture Format tab, place the pointer over the middle-right sizing handle, when the pointer changes to ⇔, drag to the left until the graphic is about 2" wide**

   Refer to the ruler as you drag. When you release the mouse button, the image is taller than it is wide. Dragging a side, top, or bottom sizing handle changes only the width or height of a graphic.

2. **Click the Undo button on the Quick Access toolbar, place the pointer over the lower-right sizing handle, when the pointer changes to ⤡, drag up and to the left until the graphic is about 2" high (the width will adjust proportionally), then release the mouse button**

   The image is smaller. Dragging a corner sizing handle resizes the graphic proportionally so that its width and height are reduced or enlarged by the same percentage. TABLE 3-3 describes ways to resize objects using the mouse.

QUICK TIP
As you drag the corner handle, refer to the measurements in the Size group on the Ribbon to best approximate the size of the image.

3. **Click the Launcher in the Size group**

   The Layout dialog box opens with the Size tab active, as shown in FIGURE 3-21. Note that a different percentage may be entered in the Height and Width boxes, depending on how much you reduced the size of the graphic in Step 2. The Size tab allows you to enter precise height and width measurements for a graphic or to scale a graphic by entering the percentage you want to reduce or enlarge it by. When a graphic is sized to **scale** (or scaled), its height to width ratio remains the same.

QUICK TIP
Deselect the Lock aspect ratio check box if you want to change a graphic's proportions.

4. **Select the measurement in the Height box in the Scale section, type 50, then click the Width box in the Scale section**

   The scale of the width changes to 50% and the Absolute measurements in the Height and Width sections decrease proportionally.

5. **Click OK**

   The height and width measurements are reduced to 50% of the height and width measurements in the Original size section of the dialog box.

6. **Type 1 in the Shape Width box in the Size group, then press ENTER**

   The image is reduced to be 1" wide, with the height changed in proportion.

7. **Click the Position button in the Arrange group, click Position in Top Right with Square Text Wrapping, click the Position button again, click More Layout Options, click the Absolute position button in the Vertical section, type .6 in the Absolute position box, then click OK**

   The graphic is positioned below the title on the right side of the page.

8. **Click the Reflected Rounded Rectangle style in the Picture Styles group, then save your changes**

   A style is applied to the image, as shown in FIGURE 3-22.

FIGURE 3-21: Size tab in the Layout dialog box

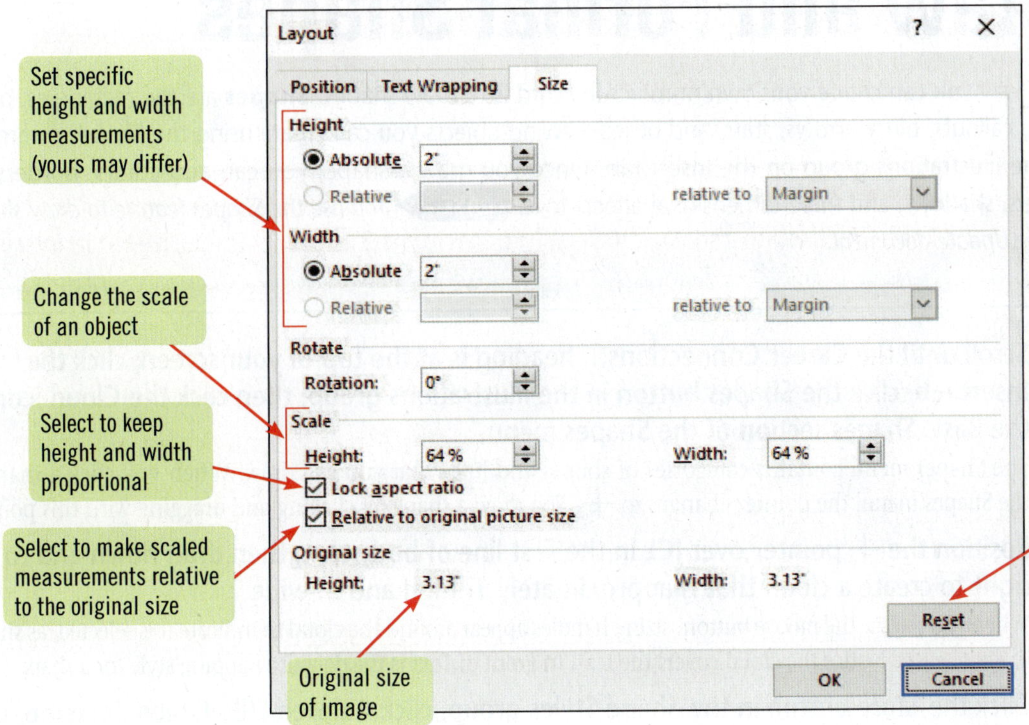

FIGURE 3-22: Style applied to resized image

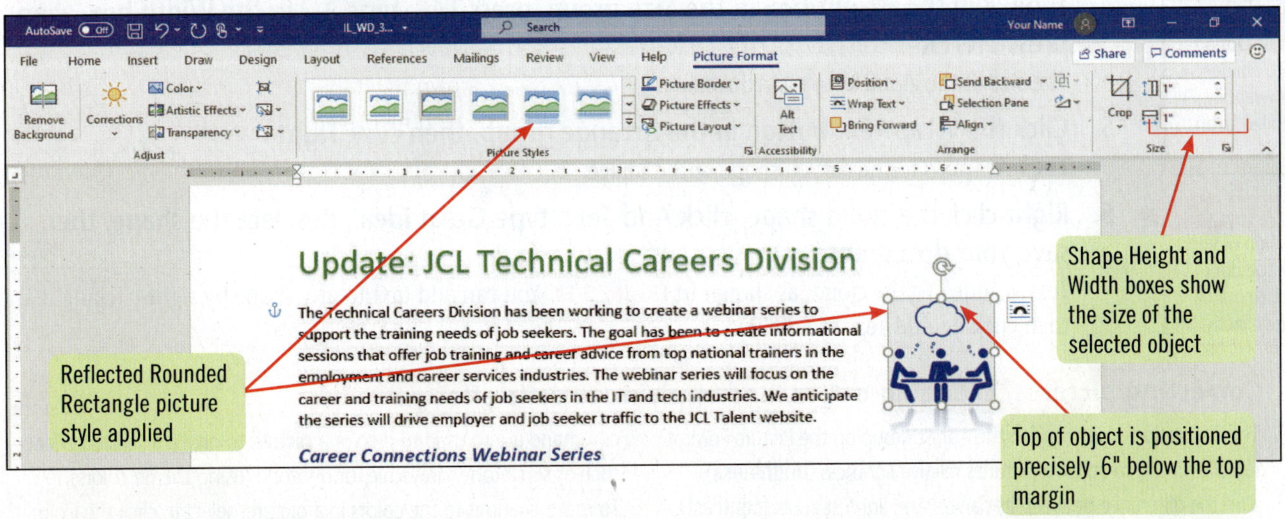

TABLE 3-3: Methods for resizing an object using the mouse

do this	to
Drag a corner sizing handle	Resize a clip art or bitmap graphic and maintain its proportions
Press SHIFT and drag a corner sizing handle	Resize any graphic object and maintain its proportions
Press CTRL and drag a side, top, or bottom sizing handle	Resize any graphic object vertically or horizontally while keeping the center position fixed
Press CTRL and drag a corner sizing handle	Resize any graphic object diagonally while keeping the center position fixed
Press SHIFT+CTRL and drag a corner sizing handle	Resize any graphic object while keeping the center position fixed and maintaining its proportions

Word
Module 3

Draw and Format Shapes

Learning Outcomes
- Insert shapes
- Apply styles to objects

One way you can create your own graphics in Word is to draw shapes. **Shapes** are the rectangles, ovals, lines, callouts, block arrows, stars, and other drawing objects you can create using the Shapes command in the Illustrations group on the Insert tab. Once you draw a shape, you can add colors, borders, fill effects, shadows, and three-dimensional effects to it. **CASE** *You use the Shapes feature to draw shapes in the Update document.*

STEPS

1. **Scroll until the Career Connections... heading is at the top of your screen, click the Insert tab, click the Shapes button in the Illustrations group, then click the Cloud icon in the Basic Shapes section of the Shapes menu**

   The Shapes menu contains categories of shapes and lines that you can draw. When you click a shape in the Shapes menu, the pointer changes to +. You draw a shape by clicking and dragging with this pointer.

2. **Position the + pointer over JCL in the first line of body text, then drag down and to the right to create a cloud that is approximately 1" high and 2" wide**

   When you release the mouse button, sizing handles appear around the cloud to indicate it is selected, as shown in FIGURE 3-23. Notice the cloud covers the text. In Front of Text is the default wrapping style for a shape.

3. **Click the More button in the Shape Styles group, click Colored Fill - Green Accent 6, click the Shape Effects button, point to Preset, then click Preset 5**

   The color of the cloud changes to green and the image is formatted with a bevel and shadow style.

4. **Type .8 in the Height box in the Size group, press TAB, type 1.2 in the Width box, then press ENTER**

   The size of the cloud shape is reduced.

5. **Click the Wrap Text button in the Arrange group, then click Tight**

   The text wraps to the curved shape of the image.

6. **Right-click the cloud shape, click Add Text, type Great idea!, deselect the shape, then save your document**

   Text is added to the cloud, as shown in FIGURE 3-24. You can add text to any shape by right-clicking it and then clicking Add Text or Edit Text.

QUICK TIP
To draw a perfect square or circle, click the Rectangle or Oval shape on the menu, then press SHIFT while you drag with the pointer.

QUICK TIP
You can also use the Layout Options button to change the text wrapping style applied to an object.

TROUBLE
The position of your cloud shape does not need to match the figure exactly.

Correcting pictures, changing colors, and applying artistic effects

The Corrections command in the Adjust group on the Picture Format tab allows you to adjust a picture's relative lightness **(brightness)**, alter the difference between its darkest and lightest areas **(contrast)**, and change the sharpness of an image. To make these adjustments, select the image and then click the Corrections button to open a gallery of preset percentages applied to the selected picture. Point to an option in the gallery to preview it in the document; click an option in the gallery to apply it. You can also fine-tune brightness, contrast, or sharpness by clicking Picture Corrections Options in the Corrections gallery, and then using the sliders in the Picture Corrections section of the Format Picture pane to adjust the percentage.

The Color command in the Adjust group is used to change the vividness and intensity of color in an image **(color saturation)**, and to change the "temperature" of a photo by bringing out the cooler blue tones or the warmer orange tones **(color tone)**. The Color command is also used to recolor a picture to give it a stylized effect, such as sepia tone, grayscale, or duotone (using theme colors). To make changes to the colors in a picture, select it, click the Color button, and then select one of the color modes or variations in the gallery that opens, or click Picture Color Options to fine-tune color settings using the Format Picture pane.

The Artistic Effects command in the Adjust group allows you to make a photo look like a drawing, a painting, a photocopy, a sketch, or some other artistic medium. To experiment with applying an artistic effect, select a photo, click the Artistic Effects button, and then point to each effect to preview it applied to the photo.

After you adjust a picture, you can undo any changes by clicking the Reset Picture arrow in the Adjust group. This command discards all formatting changes made to a picture, including size, cropping, borders, and effects.

FIGURE 3-23: Shape in document

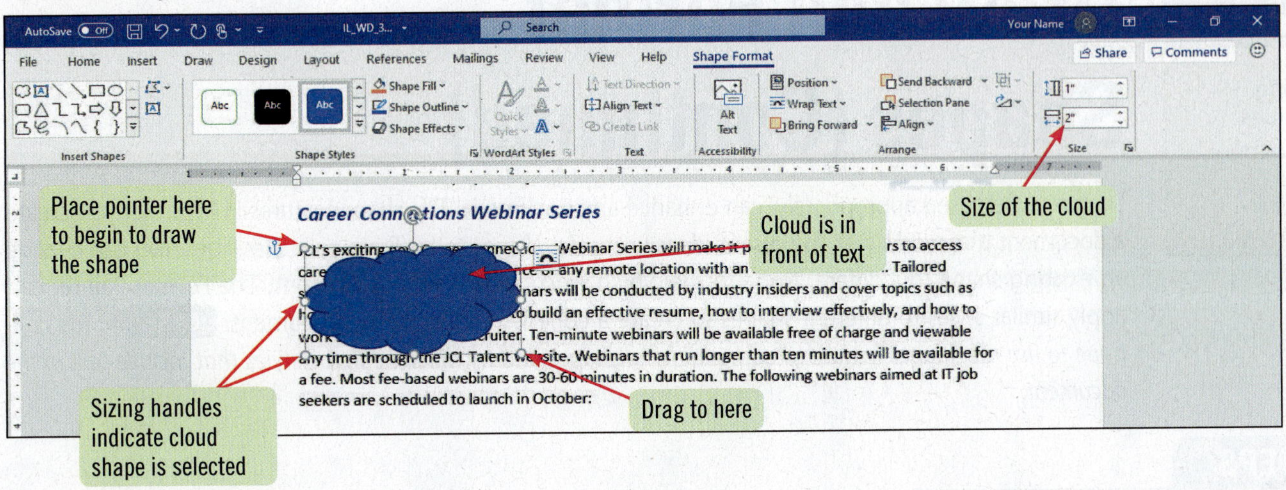

FIGURE 3-24: Text added to shape

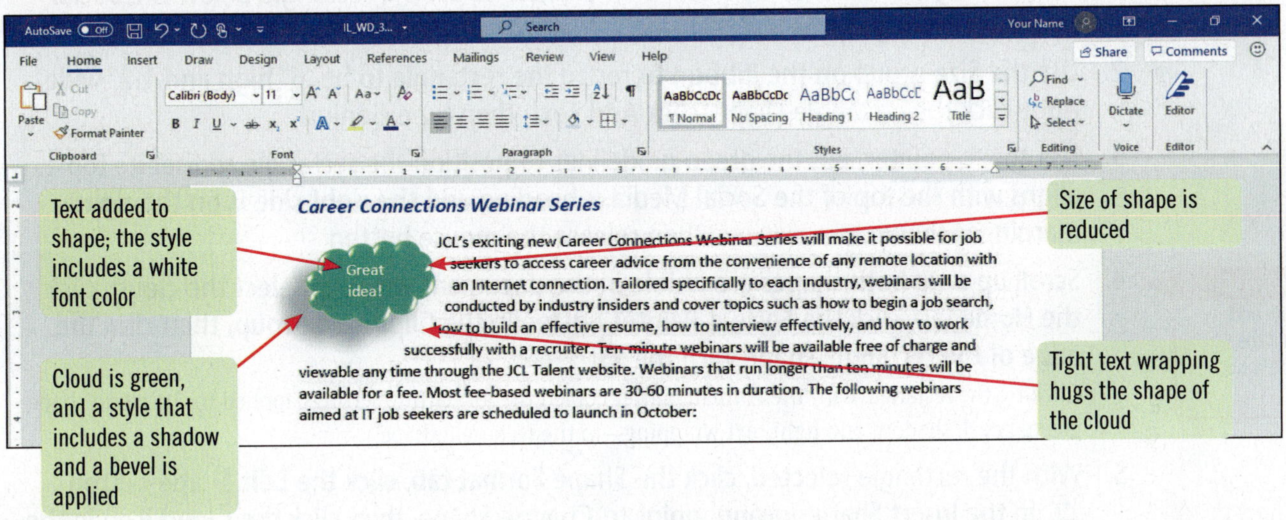

Adding alt text and checking documents for accessibility issues

It's important to design documents so that they are accessible to people of all abilities. The Alt Text command allows you to add a text description of a graphic image to a document so that people who are visually impaired and using a screen reader can access the content of the image. The alt text associated with an image should serve the same purpose and convey the same essential information as the image so that no information or functionality is lost for readers who are visually impaired. To add alt text to an image, select the image, click the Alt Text command in the Accessibility group on the Picture Format tab, and then type the alternative text description in the box on the Alt Text pane. When you are finished, close the Alt Text pane. You can edit alt text at any time by right-clicking an image and then clicking Edit Alt Text.

The Accessibility Checker locates elements of a document that might be a potential problem for readers with disabilities, and it offers suggestions on how to resolve each issue. For example, the Accessibility Checker might flag a graphic that does not include alt text, or it might issue a warning about formatting that makes text hard to read. To check a document for accessibility issues, click the Check Accessibility button in the Accessibility group on the Review tab. The results of the inspection appear in the Accessibility pane.

(Continued)

Draw and Format Shapes (Continued)

Learning Outcomes
- Use the Format Painter
- Change and modify shapes

Shapes, when used appropriately, can enhance any document. The shape features in Word let you create a document that works well to present ideas using visual cues to facilitate your message. You can change an existing shape to a different one to see which works best for the document. The Format Painter can apply similar styles to different shapes to create a cohesive design in the document. **CASE** *You continue to use the Shapes feature to add additional shapes and try different shape styles that include text in the document.*

STEPS

1. **Scroll down until the Social Media... heading is at the top of your screen, click the Insert tab, click the Shapes button in the Illustrations group, click the Rectangle icon in the Rectangles section, then use the + pointer to draw a rectangle below the Social Media... heading**
2. **Use the Size group on the Ribbon to resize the rectangle to be .6" high and 1.2" wide, right-click the rectangle shape, click Add Text, then type Genius!**
3. **Use the pointer and the green guidelines to position the rectangle so that its top aligns with the top of the Social Media... heading and the right side is on the right margin, as shown in FIGURE 3-25, then release the mouse button**
4. **Scroll up until both shapes are visible in the document window, select the cloud, click the Home tab, click the Format Painter button in the Clipboard group, then click the edge of the rectangle shape with the pointer**
   Clicking the rectangle with the Format Painter copied the formatting settings applied to the cloud shape—green, bevel, shadow, and tight text wrapping—to the rectangle shape.
5. **With the rectangle selected, click the Shape Format tab, click the Edit Shape button in the Insert Shapes group, point to Change Shape, then click the Cloud icon in the Basic Shapes section**
   The rectangle changes to a cloud. Notice that changing the object shape does not change the text or the format settings applied to the object.
6. **Select the Great idea! cloud, click the Edit Shape button, point to Change Shape, then click the Thought Bubble: Cloud icon in the Callouts section**
   The cloud changes to a thought bubble cloud.
7. **Position the pointer over the yellow adjustment handle on the thought bubble cloud, drag the handle down and left, similar in FIGURE 3-26, then release the mouse button**
   Dragging the adjustment handle modifies the shape of the thought bubble cloud.
8. **Save your changes**

TROUBLE
Press Undo and try again if the formatting is not applied.

TROUBLE
Do not be concerned if your cloud shape does not match the figure exactly.

FIGURE 3-25: Positioning the rectangle

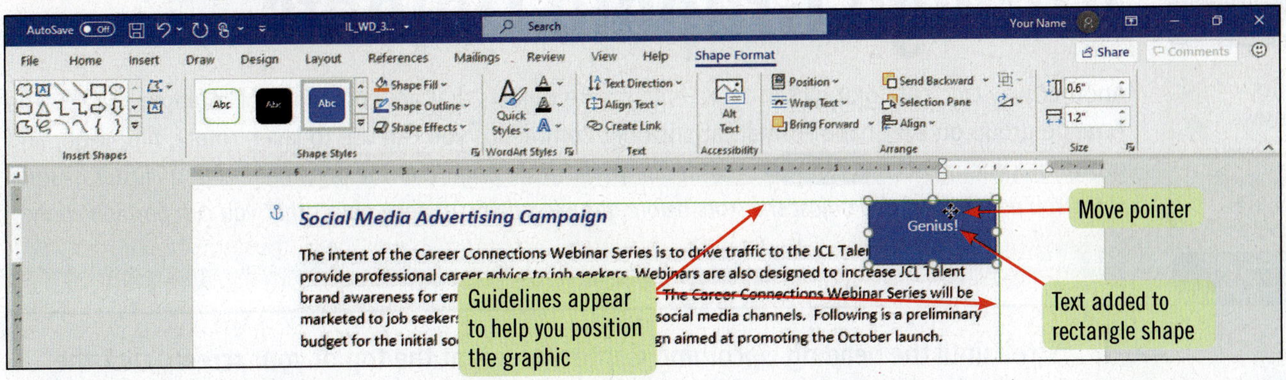

FIGURE 3-26: Cloud shapes in document

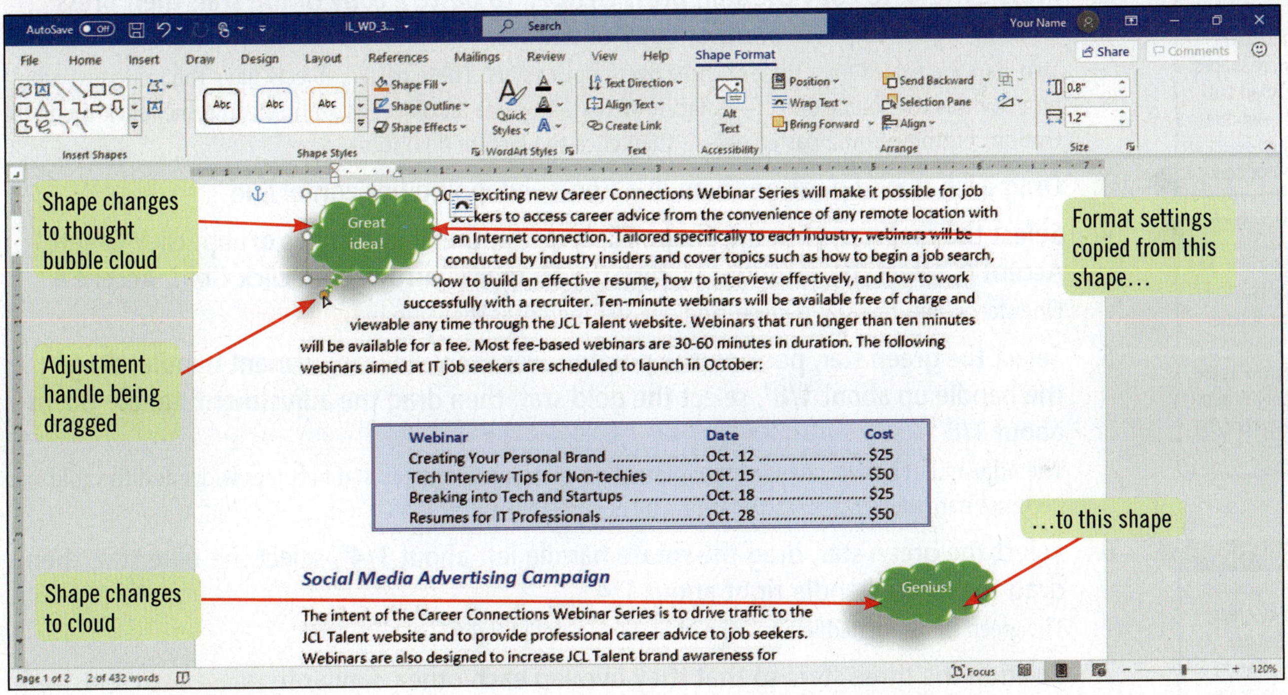

Enhancing graphic objects with styles and effects

Another way to make a document fun and visually appealing for the reader is to apply a style or an effect to a graphic object. To apply a style, select the object and then choose from the style options in the Styles group on the active Format tab for that type of object. Styles include a preset mixture of effects, such as shading, borders, shadows, and other settings. The Effects command in the Styles group on the active Format tab gives you the power to apply a customized variety of effects to an object, including a shadow, bevel, glow, reflection, soft edge, or 3-D rotation. To apply an effect, select the object, click the Effects command for that type of object, point to the type of effect you want to apply, and then select from the options in the gallery that opens. To further customize an effect, click the Options command for that type of effect at the bottom of the gallery to open the Format Shape pane. The best way to learn about styles and effects is to experiment by applying them to an object and seeing what works.

Arrange Graphic Objects

Learning Outcomes
- Format objects
- Arrange objects
- Paste objects

Another way to create graphics in Word is to create objects that are composed of multiple shapes. The Arrange group on the Shape Format tab includes commands you can use to layer, rotate, flip, align, and group graphic objects. **CASE** *You decide to illustrate page 2 of the document with a cluster of small stars. You edit, rotate, and adjust the stars before grouping them into one object that you can position easily.*

STEPS

1. **Scroll until the heading Upcoming Conferences is at the top of your screen, click the Insert tab, click the Shapes button in the Illustrations group, click the Star: 5 Points icon in the Stars and Banners section of the Shapes menu, then click a blank area of page 2**
   A 1" square star shape is inserted in the document.

2. **Press CTRL+C to copy the star, press CTRL+V to paste a copy of the star, then press CTRL+V again to paste another copy of the star**
   Two stars are pasted for a total of three overlapping stars. These pasted objects have the same text wrapping style as the source object—In Front of Text. To paste an object as an inline graphic, click the Paste Options button below a pasted object, then click the Picture (P) option.

3. **Drag each star to position them in a non-overlapping horizontal line**

4. **Select the first star, click the Shape Fill arrow in the Shape Styles group, click Green, Accent 6, select the second star, click the Shape Fill arrow, then click Gold, Accent 4**
   One star is blue, one star is green, and one star is gold, as shown in in FIGURE 3-27.

5. **Select the green star, position the pointer over the yellow adjustment handle, drag the handle up about 1/8", select the gold star, then drag the adjustment handle down about 1/8"**
   The Adjustment handle changed the internal proportions. The green star becomes wider and the gold star becomes narrower.

6. **Select the green star, drag the rotate handle left about 1/4", select the blue star, then drag the rotate handle right about 1/4"**
   The green star is rotated left and the blue star is rotated right.

7. **Position the three stars so that they overlap each other, similar to FIGURE 3-28**
   The stars are stacked in layers. Don't be concerned if the layering of your stars is different.

8. **Select the gold star, click the Bring Forward arrow in the Arrange group, then click Bring to Front**
   The gold star becomes the front layer of the stack of objects. You use the Bring Forward and Send Backward arrows to shift the order of the layers in a stack of graphic objects.

9. **Press and hold CTRL, click the blue star, click the green star so that all three stars are selected, click the Group Objects button in the Arrange group, then click Group**
   The three star objects become a single object with sizing handles around a surrounding border. Any formatting applied will affect all the objects within the grouped object.

10. **Type 1 in the Shape Height box in the Size group, type 1.2 in the Shape Width box, press ENTER, click the Position button in the Arrange group, click Position in Top Right with Square Text Wrapping, deselect the object, then save your changes**
    The size of the grouped object is reduced to 1" high and 1.2" wide, and the object is positioned in the top-right corner of the page, as shown in FIGURE 3-29.

QUICK TIP
To align shapes with each other, select two or more shapes, click the Align button in the Arrange group, then select an alignment option.

QUICK TIP
To change color, line weight, or line style of a shape outline, click the Shape Outline arrow in the Shape Styles group, then select from the options.

QUICK TIP
To rotate a graphic object 90 degrees, click the Rotate Objects button in the Arrange group, then click Rotate Right or Rotate Left.

QUICK TIP
To flip a graphic object, click the Rotate Objects button, then click Flip Vertical or Flip Horizontal.

FIGURE 3-27: Stars with fill color applied

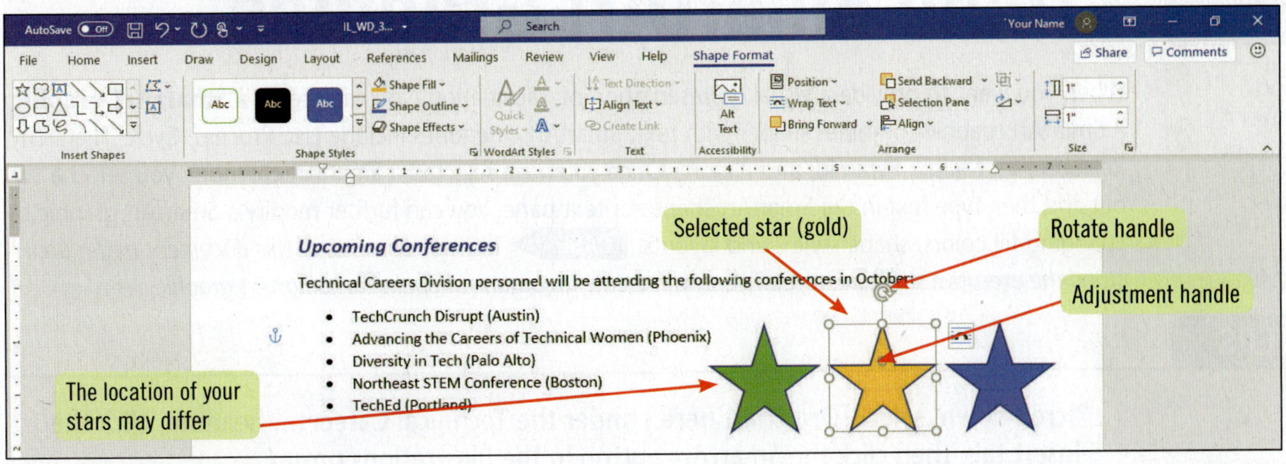

FIGURE 3-28: Stars layered in document

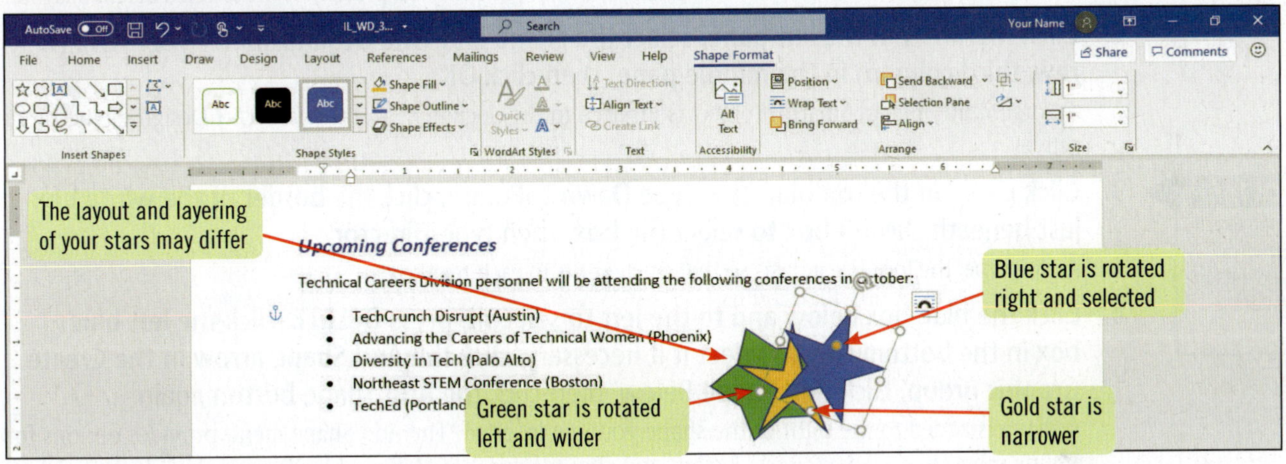

FIGURE 3-29: Grouped and resized object positioned in top corner

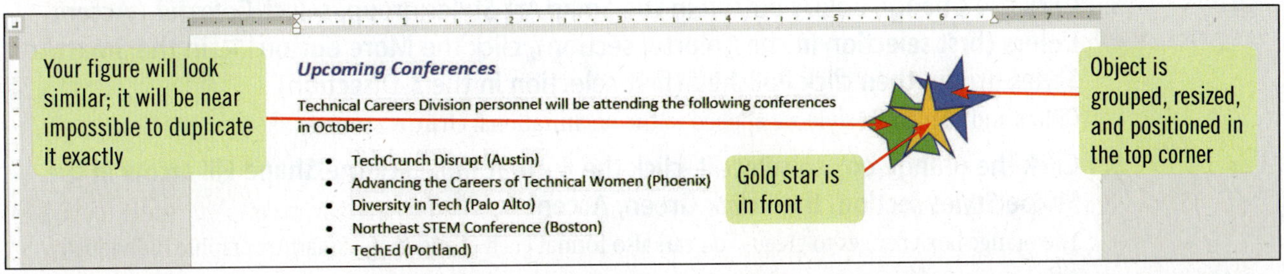

Creating an illustration in a drawing canvas

A **drawing canvas** is a workspace for creating your own graphics. It provides a frame-like boundary between an illustration and the rest of the document so that the illustration can be sized, formatted, and positioned like a single graphic object. If you are creating an illustration that includes multiple shapes, such as a flow chart, it is helpful to create the illustration in a drawing canvas. To draw shapes or lines in a drawing canvas, click the Shapes button in the Illustrations group on the Insert tab, click New Drawing Canvas to open a drawing canvas in the document, and then create and format your illustration in the drawing canvas. When you are finished, right-click the border of the drawing canvas and then click Fit to resize the drawing canvas to fit the illustration. You can then resize the illustration by dragging a border of the drawing canvas. Once you have resized a drawing canvas, you can wrap text around it and position it. By default, a drawing canvas has no border or background so that it is transparent in a document, but you can add fill and borders to it if you wish.

Word
Module 3

Create SmartArt Graphics

Learning Outcomes
- Insert SmartArt
- Customize SmartArt

When you want to provide a visual representation of information, you can create a **SmartArt graphic**. A SmartArt graphic combines shapes with text. SmartArt categories include List, Process, Cycle, Hierarchy, Relationship, Matrix, Pyramid, and Picture. Once you have selected a SmartArt category, you select a layout and then type text in the SmartArt shapes or text pane. You can further modify a SmartArt graphic by changing fill colors, shape styles, and layouts. **CASE** *To help recipients of this document better understand the executive structure at JCL Talent, you create an organizational chart SmartArt graphic.*

STEPS

1. **Scroll down, select [Org chart here.] under the Technical Careers… heading, click the Insert tab, then click the SmartArt button in the Illustrations group**
   The Choose a SmartArt Graphic dialog box opens. You use it to select the category of diagram you want to create and the layout and design for the diagram. The right pane shows a preview of the selected diagram layout.
2. **Click Hierarchy in the left pane, select the Name and Title Organization Chart style (first row, third column) in the middle pane, then click OK**
   An organization chart SmartArt object is inserted in the document and the SmartArt Design tab becomes active.
3. **Click [Text] in the top blue box, type Dawn LaPointe, click the border of the white box just beneath Dawn's box to select the box, then type Director**
   As you type, the font size adjusts so that the text fits in each text box.

   QUICK TIP
   You can type directly in the shapes, or you can use the text pane to enter the text.
4. **Click the blue box below and to the left to select it, press DELETE, click the left blue box in the bottom row to select it if necessary, click the Add Shape arrow in the Create Graphic group, click Add Shape Below, then click the Add Shape button again**
   A shape is added to the right of the shape you just inserted. The Add Shape menu provides options for adding more shapes below, above, before, and after to your SmartArt graphic. You can also add an Assistant shape. New shapes will be added depending upon which box is currently selected in the SmartArt graphic.
5. **Click the Change Colors button in the SmartArt Styles group, select Colorful - Accent Colors (first selection in the Colorful section), click the More button in the SmartArt Styles group, then click Polished (first selection in the 3-D section)**
   Colors and a SmartArt style are applied to the organizational chart.
6. **Click the orange box to select it, click the Format tab, click the Shape Fill arrow in the Shape Styles section, then click Green, Accent 6**
   The orange box changes to green. You can also format each element of a SmartArt graphic individually.
7. **Type the text shown in FIGURE 3-30 in each box the SmartArt graphic, click outside the object to deselect it, then save your changes**
8. **Click the View tab, then click Multiple Pages in the Zoom group**
   The completed document is shown in FIGURE 3-31.
9. **sam Submit the document to your instructor, close the file, then exit Word**

FIGURE 3-30: Organizational chart

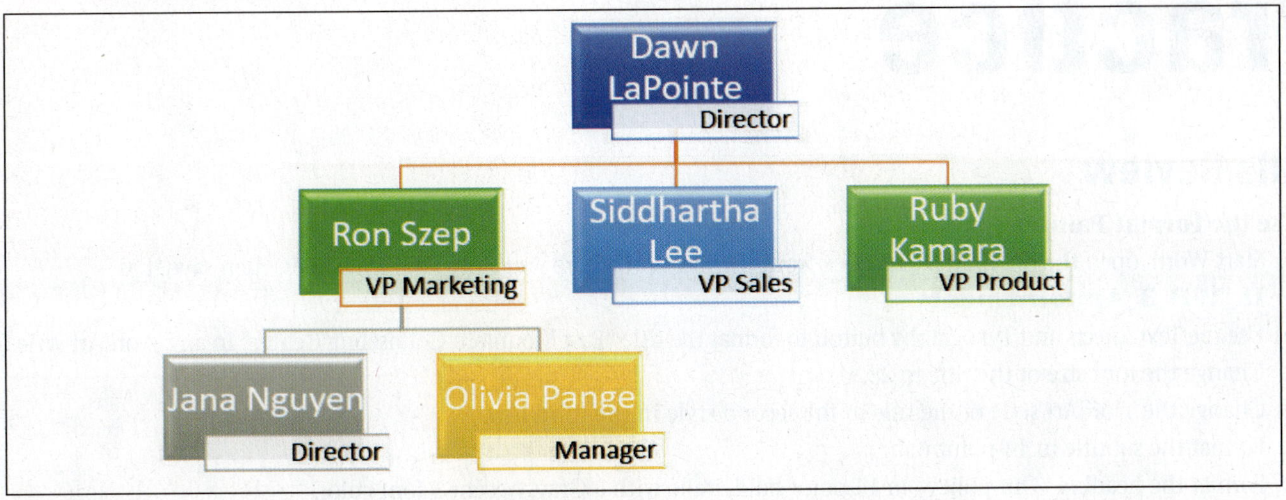

FIGURE 3-31: Completed document

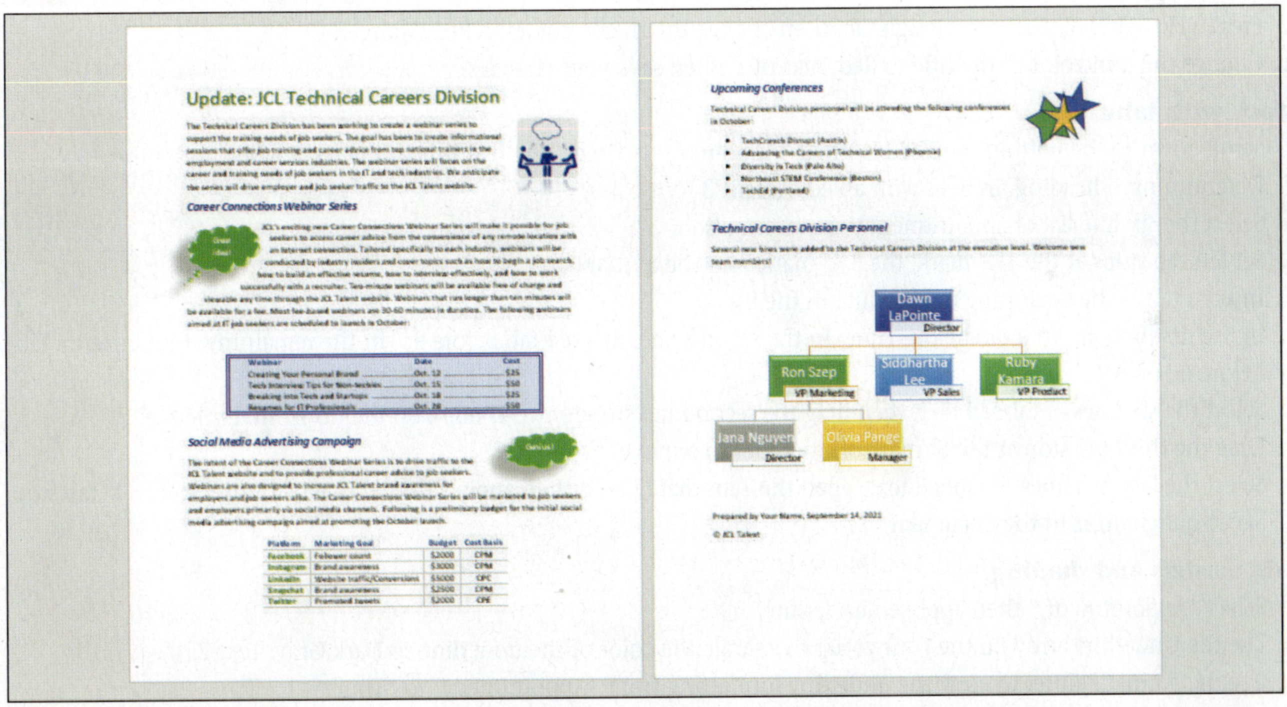

Update: JCL Technical Careers Division

The Technical Careers Division has been working to create a webinar series to support the training needs of job seekers. The goal has been to create informational sessions that offer job training and career advice from top national trainers in the employment and career services industries. The webinar series will focus on the career and training needs of job seekers in the IT and tech industries. We anticipate the series will drive employer and job seeker traffic to the JCL Talent website.

Career Connections Webinar Series

JCL's exciting new Career Connections Webinar Series will make it possible for job seekers to access career advice from the convenience of any remote location with an Internet connection. Tailored specifically to each industry, webinars will be conducted by industry insiders and cover topics such as how to begin a job search, how to build an effective resume, how to interview effectively, and how to work successfully with a recruiter. Ten-minute webinars will be available free of charge and viewable any time through the JCL Talent website. Webinars that run longer than ten minutes will be available for a fee. Most fee-based webinars are 30-60 minutes in duration. The following webinars aimed at IT job seekers are scheduled to launch in October:

Webinar	Date	Cost
Creating Your Personal Brand	Oct. 12	$25
Tech Interview Tips for Non-techies	Oct. 15	$50
Breaking into Tech and Startups	Oct. 18	$25
Resumes for IT Professionals	Oct. 28	$50

Social Media Advertising Campaign

The intent of the Career Connections Webinar Series is to drive traffic to the JCL Talent website and to provide professional career advice to job seekers. Webinars are also designed to increase JCL Talent brand awareness for employers and job seekers alike. The Career Connections Webinar Series will be marketed to job seekers and employers primarily via social media channels. Following is a preliminary budget for the initial social media advertising campaign aimed at promoting the October launch.

Platform	Marketing Goal	Budget	Cost Basis
Facebook	Follower count	$2000	CPM
Instagram	Brand awareness	$3000	CPM
LinkedIn	Website traffic/Conversions	$5000	CPC
Snapchat	Brand awareness	$2500	CPM
Twitter	Promoted tweets	$2000	CPE

Upcoming Conferences

Technical Careers Division personnel will be attending the following conferences in October:

- TechCrunch Disrupt (Austin)
- Advancing the Careers of Technical Women (Phoenix)
- Diversity in Tech (Palo Alto)
- Northeast STEM Conference (Boston)
- TechEd (Portland)

Technical Careers Division Personnel

Several new hires were added to the Technical Careers Division at the executive level. Welcome new team members!

Dawn LaPointe, Director
Ron Szep, VP Marketing
Siddhartha Lee, VP Sales
Ruby Kamara, VP Product
Jana Nguyen, Director
Olivia Pange, Manager

Prepared by Your Name, September 14, 2021

© JCL Talent

Practice

Skills Review

1. **Use the Format Painter.**
   a. Start Word, open the file IL_WD_3-2.docx from the location where you store your Data Files, then save it as **IL_WD_3_Appointments**.
   b. Use the Text Effects and Typography button to format the title "East Mountain Counseling Center" in any WordArt style.
   c. Change the font size of the title to 28.
   d. Change the WordArt style of the title to the second style in the third row.
   e. Format the subtitle in 14-point italic.
   f. Format the heading "Our policy" in 14-point bold, italic with a Gray, Accent 3 font color.
   g. Use the Format Painter to copy the format of the Our policy heading to the following headings: Five-step approach to scheduling appointments, Determining the time required for an appointment, and Processing new clients.
   h. Press CTRL+END to go to the end of the document, type **Last revised**, insert the current date using a format that includes the year as four digits, type **by**, then type your name followed by a period and a space.
   i. Type **East Mountain Counseling is an affiliate of PRG Health.**, then insert a trademark symbol (™) after Health. (*Hint*: The Trademark symbol is character code 2122.)
   j. Press CTRL+HOME, click the Design tab, then change the theme colors to Red Orange.
   k. Change the font color of the title to Red, Accent 3, then save your changes.

2. **Work with tabs.**
   a. Scroll down to the bottom of page 1, format "Appointment Time," the first line in the six-line list under the Determining... heading, in bold with a Red, Accent 3 font color.
   b. Select the six-line list of appointment time information.
   c. Set left tab stops at the 1½" mark, the 3¾" mark, and the 5" mark.
   d. Insert a tab at the beginning of each line in the list.
   e. In the first line, insert a tab before Time. In the second line, insert a tab before 90. In the remaining lines, insert a tab before 60 or 90.
   f. Select the six lines of tabbed text, then drag the second tab stop to the 4" mark on the horizontal ruler.
   g. Drag the third tab stop at the 5" mark off the ruler to remove it.
   h. Select the last five lines of tabbed text, open the Tabs dialog box, then apply a dotted line tab leader to the 4" tab stop.
   i. Save your changes to the document.

3. **Add borders and shading.**
   a. Select "Appointment," then apply an underline.
   b. Use the Underline arrow in the Font group to change the color of the underline to Dark Gray, Text 2.
   c. Use the Format Painter to copy the underline formatting from "Appointment" to "Time."
   d. Click the heading Determining..., add 6 points of space after the paragraph, then open the Borders and Shading dialog box.
   e. Use the Borders tab to apply a ½-point width, Dark Gray, Text 2 colored border below the heading.
   f. Use the Format Painter to apply the same paragraph and border settings to the other headings in the report: Our policy, Five-step approach..., and Processing new clients.
   g. Scroll to the end of the document, click in the Last revised... paragraph, then center the paragraph.
   h. Apply Dark Gray, Text 2, Lighter 80% shading to the paragraph.
   i. Add a ½ -point, dotted line, Dark Gray, Text 2 box border around the paragraph.
   j. Save your changes.

Skills Review (continued)

4. Insert a table.

a. Turn on formatting marks, click in the middle blank paragraph above the Processing new clients heading, then insert a table that contains two columns and three rows.

b. Type the text shown below, pressing TAB to add rows as necessary.

S. Beran	10-2
M. Kurosawa	1-5
C. Foth	2-7
M. Smith	2-4
P. Eriksen	12-6
F. Janda	10-3

c. Save your changes.

5. Insert and delete rows and columns.

a. Insert a row above the S. Beran row, type **Counselor** in the first cell, then type **Availability** in the second cell.

b. Delete the M. Smith row.

c. Insert a column to the left of the Counselor column, then type **Day** in the first cell.

d. Type the days of the work week, begin with Monday and end with Friday, in each empty cell in the new column.

e. Save your changes.

6. Apply a table style.

a. Select the table, then use the AutoFit command to fit the table to the contents.

b. Click the Table Design tab, preview table styles applied to the table, and then apply an appropriate style.

c. Apply the List Table 4 - Accent 3 style to the table, then remove the Banded Rows and First Column table style options.

d. Center the text in the Availability column.

e. Center the table between the margins, then save your changes.

7. Insert online pictures. (*Note:* To complete these steps, your computer must be connected to the Internet.)

a. Press CTRL+HOME, then open the Online Pictures window.

b. Search using Bing Image Search to find images related to the keyword **mountain**. Click the Filter link in the Online Pictures window, select Clipart on the Filter menu to filter the search results, then verify the Creative Commons only check box is selected.

c. Insert the mountain with orange sky image shown in FIGURE 3-32. (*Note:* Select a different image if this one is not available to you. It is best to select an image that is similar in shape to the image shown in FIGURE 3-32.)

d. Scroll down, click Unknown in the credit line, select the box that surrounds the credit line, then delete the credit line box, if necessary.

e. Use the Shape Width box in the Size group on the Picture Format tab to change the width of the image to 3".

f. Use the Position command to position the image in the top right with square text wrapping.

g. Apply a 1-point Black, Text 1 color picture border, then change the color of the image to Gold, Accent color 5 Light.

h. Use the Reset Picture arrow to reset the picture (but not the size).

i. Use the Artistic Effects button to apply the Glow Diffused artistic effect to the image (second row, fourth column).

j. Use the Color button to change the color tone to Temperature: 11200 K.

k. Use the Corrections button to adjust the brightness and contrast to Brightness: 0% (Normal) Contrast: −20%, then save your changes.

FIGURE 3-32

Word

Skills Review (continued)

8. **Size and scale a graphic.**
   a. Resize the image proportionally so that it is about **1"** high and **1.5"** wide.
   b. Drag the image so its top is aligned with the first line of body text and its left side is aligned with the left margin.
   c. Resize the image so that it is precisely **1.18"** high and **1.78"** wide. Deselect the Lock aspect ratio check box, if necessary.
   d. Position the image so its Horizontal absolute position is 0" to the right of the margin and its Vertical absolute position is 1" below the margin.
   e. Add ¼-point Black, Text 1 picture border around the image, then save your changes.
9. **Draw and format shapes.**
   a. Scroll until the Five-step approach… heading is at the top of your screen.
   b. Click the Shapes button, click the Star: 7 Points shape, then click in the numbered list below the Five-step… heading.
   c. Resize the shape to be **1"** high and **1.5"** wide.
   d. Right-click the shape, click Add Text, type **New!**, select the text, then apply bold.
   e. Fill the shape with Intense Effect – Gold, Accent 2, then apply the Preset 1 shape effect.
   f. Change the shape of the object to Explosion: 8 Points (Stars and Banners section).
   g. Apply square text wrapping, then position the shape so it aligns with the right margin and the first line of body text under the Five-step… heading. (*Hint*: Make sure the shape is under the border.)
   h. Draw a rectangle shape over the numbered list, then resize it to **.5"** high and **.8"** wide.
   i. Select the explosion shape, then use the Format Painter to copy the format of the explosion shape to the rectangle shape.
   j. Change the shape of the rectangle to Star: 4 Points.
   k. Position the Star: 4 Points shape to the left of the tabbed text at the bottom of page 1, so that it aligns with the left margin, then save your changes.
10. **Arrange graphic objects.**
    a. Select the Star: 4 Points shape, copy it, then paste two copies.
    b. Drag the two pasted copies of the star shape to a blank area of the page.
    c. Change the fill color of one star to be Red, Accent 3.
    d. Position the two stars so that they overlap each other slightly, then use the Bring Forward arrow to bring the gold star to the front.
    e. Select the two stars, then use the Group arrow to group them into a single object.
    f. Position the grouped object in the bottom right of the page with square text wrapping.
    g. Select the single gold star on the left side of the page, rotate the shape 90 degrees to the left, then save your changes.
11. **Create SmartArt graphics.**
    a. Scroll to the end of the document, click in the middle blank paragraph above the Last revised… shaded paragraph, then click the SmartArt button.
    b. Select Process in the list of SmartArt types, select the Accent Process style, then click OK.
    c. Change the colors of the SmartArt object to the Colorful Range - Accent Colors 5 to 6 style.
    d. Enter text in the SmartArt object so that the process diagram appears as shown in FIGURE 3-33.
    e. Resize the SmartArt object to be **3.2"** high, then save your changes.
    f. Adjust the size or position of objects as needed to so that your document resembles the document shown in the figure. View your document in two-page view and compare it to the document shown in FIGURE 3-34.
    g. Save your changes to the document, submit it to your instructor, close the file, and then exit Word.

FIGURE 3-33

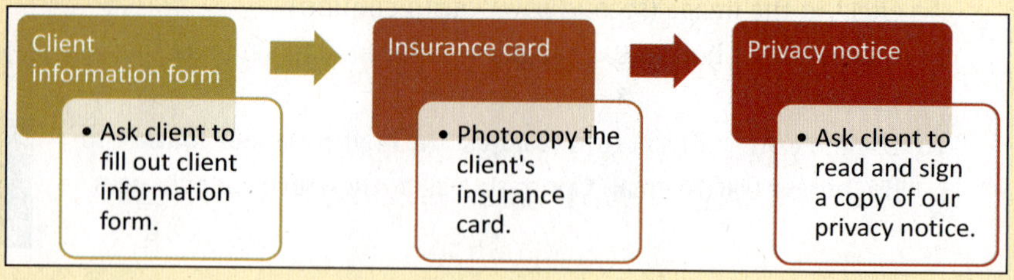

Skills Review (continued)

FIGURE 3-34

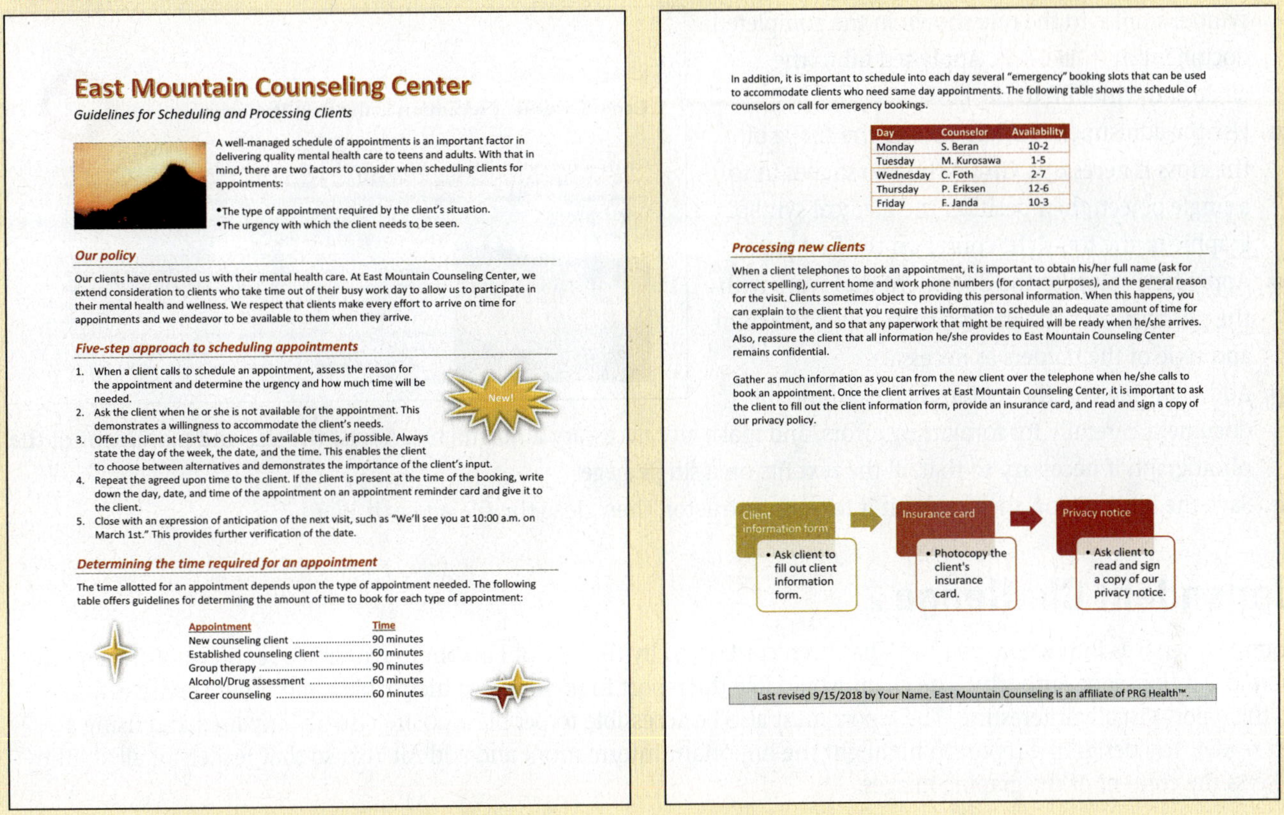

East Mountain Counseling Center

Guidelines for Scheduling and Processing Clients

A well-managed schedule of appointments is an important factor in delivering quality mental health care to teens and adults. With that in mind, there are two factors to consider when scheduling clients for appointments:

- The type of appointment required by the client's situation.
- The urgency with which the client needs to be seen.

Our policy

Our clients have entrusted us with their mental health care. At East Mountain Counseling Center, we extend consideration to clients who take time out of their busy work day to allow us to participate in their mental health and wellness. We respect that clients make every effort to arrive on time for appointments and we endeavor to be available to them when they arrive.

Five-step approach to scheduling appointments

1. When a client calls to schedule an appointment, assess the reason for the appointment and determine the urgency and how much time will be needed.
2. Ask the client when he or she is not available for the appointment. This demonstrates a willingness to accommodate the client's needs.
3. Offer the client at least two choices of available times, if possible. Always state the day of the week, the date, and the time. This enables the client to choose between alternatives and demonstrates the importance of the client's input.
4. Repeat the agreed upon time to the client. If the client is present at the time of the booking, write down the day, date, and time of the appointment on an appointment reminder card and give it to the client.
5. Close with an expression of anticipation of the next visit, such as "We'll see you at 10:00 a.m. on March 1st." This provides further verification of the date.

Determining the time required for an appointment

The time allotted for an appointment depends upon the type of appointment needed. The following table offers guidelines for determining the amount of time to book for each type of appointment:

Appointment	Time
New counseling client	90 minutes
Established counseling client	60 minutes
Group therapy	90 minutes
Alcohol/Drug assessment	60 minutes
Career counseling	60 minutes

In addition, it is important to schedule into each day several "emergency" booking slots that can be used to accommodate clients who need same day appointments. The following table shows the schedule of counselors on call for emergency bookings.

Day	Counselor	Availability
Monday	S. Beran	10-2
Tuesday	M. Kurosawa	1-5
Wednesday	C. Foth	2-7
Thursday	P. Eriksen	12-6
Friday	F. Janda	10-3

Processing new clients

When a client telephones to book an appointment, it is important to obtain his/her full name (ask for correct spelling), current home and work phone numbers (for contact purposes), and the general reason for the visit. Clients sometimes object to providing this personal information. When this happens, you can explain to the client that you require this information to schedule an adequate amount of time for the appointment, and so that any paperwork that might be required will be ready when he/she arrives. Also, reassure the client that all information he/she provides to East Mountain Counseling Center remains confidential.

Gather as much information as you can from the new client over the telephone when he/she calls to book an appointment. Once the client arrives at East Mountain Counseling Center, it is important to ask the client to fill out the client information form, provide an insurance card, and read and sign a copy of our privacy policy.

Last revised 9/15/2018 by Your Name. East Mountain Counseling is an affiliate of PRG Health™.

Independent Challenge 1

The Riverwalk Medical Clinic publishes a variety of helpful tips and information sheets related to health issues. Your colleague has assembled a "Fast Facts" sheet on Lyme disease and has asked you to format it so it highlights the important information regarding the disease. Design and formatting elements will make the document attractive to readers.

a. Start Word, open the file IL_WD_3-3.docx from the drive and folder where you store your Data Files, save it as **IL_WD_3_FastFacts**, then read the document to get a basic understanding of its contents.
b. Select the entire document, then change the font to 11-point Garamond.
c. Change all four document margins to Narrow .5.
d. Change the theme colors to Orange Red. (*Hint*: Use the Theme Colors button on the Design tab.)
e. Change the font size of the first line, "Riverwalk Medical Clinic—Fast Facts", to 14, and apply italic.
f. Change the font size of the second line, the title "Lyme Disease…", to 20.
g. Change the font size of the heading "How ticks spread the disease" to 14, apply bold, then add a single bottom border with the Gray, Text 2 color, and a width of 1/2 pt.
h. Use the Format Painter to copy the format of the "How ticks spread the disease" heading to the following headings in the tip sheet: Tick habitat and distribution, Symptoms and signs, Treatment and prognosis, and Protection from tick bites.
i. Insert an online picture that is a photograph. Select a photograph that is appropriate to the content. (*Hint*: Use the Filter link in the Online Pictures window to filter for photographs.)
j. Remove the credit line box from the image, if necessary.
k. Resize the image proportionally so that it is 2.5" wide, wrap text around the image, then position the photograph to the left of the "How ticks spread the disease" heading. FIGURE 3-35 shows a sample layout.
l. Enhance the photograph with corrections, colors, artistic effects, borders, or styles.

Independent Challenge 1 (continued)

m. Using circle and cross shapes, create a medical symbol similar to the one shown in the completed document in FIGURE 3-35. Apply red fill to the circle and white fill to the cross.

n. Use the adjustment handle to alter the shape of the cross if necessary. Group the two shapes in to a single object, then position the medical symbol graphic in the top-right corner on the first page.

o. Apply font colors to the document that work with the photograph you selected, then adjust the color and style of the borders as necessary.

p. Add your name to the footer, then examine the document carefully for formatting errors, and make any necessary adjustments. Adjust the size and placement of the photograph if necessary so that all the text fits on a single page.

q. Save the information sheet, submit it to your instructor, then close the file and exit Word.

FIGURE 3-35

Riverwalk Medical Clinic—Fast Facts

Lyme Disease: Prevention is the Best Protection

Lyme disease, an inflammatory disease transmitted by the bite of a deer tick, has become a serious public health risk in certain areas of the United States and Canada. Campers, hikers, fishermen, outdoor enthusiasts, and other travelers or residents in endemic areas who have frequent or prolonged exposure to tick habitats during the spring and summer months are at increased risk for Lyme disease.

How ticks spread the disease

The bacterium that causes Lyme disease is spread by the bite of infected Ixodes ticks, commonly known as deer ticks. Ticks can attach to any part of the human body but are most often found in hairy areas such as the scalp, groin, and armpit. In most cases the tick must be attached for at least 48 hours before the bacteria can be transmitted. During the spring and summer months, when people spend more time outdoors, the young (nymphal) ticks are most often responsible for spreading the disease. These ticks are tiny (about the size of the head of a pin) and rarely noticed, making it difficult for people to find and remove an infected tick.

Independent Challenge 2

The business services firm where you work has been contracted by the city of Lincoln to redesign a report published by the Economic Development Authority. The client would like the report to include graphics, tables, and other elements that make the report visually interesting. The report must also be accessible to people who are visually impaired and using a screen reader. You design the report to highlight the important information, and add Alt Text so that readers of all abilities can access the content of the graphic images.

a. Start Word, open the file IL_WD_3-4.docx from the drive and folder where you store your Data Files, then save it as **IL_WD_3_Lincoln**.

b. Read the document to get a basic understanding of the contents, use CTRL+A to select all the text in the document, then clear all formatting from the text.

c. Determine the font and font sizes you will use for the body text, title, subtitle, and headings.

d. Select all the text again, change the style to No Spacing, then apply the font you intend to use for the body text to all the text in the report.

e. Format the title and subtitle using a font, font size, and font color of your choice.

f. Format the heading Mission using a font, font size, and font color of your choice, then, use the Format Painter to copy the formatting of the Mission heading to the Lincoln Advantage and Issues headings.

g. Format the subheading Services using a font, font size, and font color of your choice, then use the Format Painter to copy the formatting of the Services heading to the following headings: Project Finance, Real Estate Development, Business Loans, Technology/Innovation, Arts/Creativity, Geography, and Expected Population Growth.

h. Scroll to the bottom of the document. Above the final paragraph, insert a table with two columns and three rows, then enter the following text.

Years	Population Growth
2020–2040	18%
2040–2060	32% (projected)

i. Autofit the table to the content, apply an appropriate table style to the table, adjust the formatting, then center the table between the margins.

Independent Challenge 2 (continued)

j. Scroll to the top of the document. Using shapes, create a graphic to illustrate the document. The graphic should be composed of two or more shapes. For example, you might draw city buildings, an abstract design, or something else you think will represent the content.

k. Format the shapes with fills, outlines, and effects. Use the adjustment and rotate handles to alter the shapes as necessary.

l. Position the shapes so that they overlap, use the Bring Forward and Send Backward buttons to adjust the layers, then group the shapes into a single object.

m. Resize the grouped object, wrap text around it, and position it in the document.

n. Create a SmartArt graphic similar to FIGURE 3-36. Use the Alternating Hexagons SmartArt style (List group), then format the SmartArt graphic using colors, styles, and effects.

o. Resize the SmartArt graphic and position it in the document.

p. Use the Multiple Pages button to view both pages of the document, then adjust the size and position of the graphics.

q. Select the shapes graphic you created in steps j–m, use the Alt Text button to open the Alt Text pane, then mark the shapes graphic as decorative.

r. Select the SmartArt graphic, then type a description of the SmartArt graphic in the Alt Text pane.

s. Use the Check Accessibility button on the Review tab to check the document for accessibility issues.

t. Add your name to the footer, save your changes to the document, submit it to your instructor, close the file, and then exit Word.

FIGURE 3-36

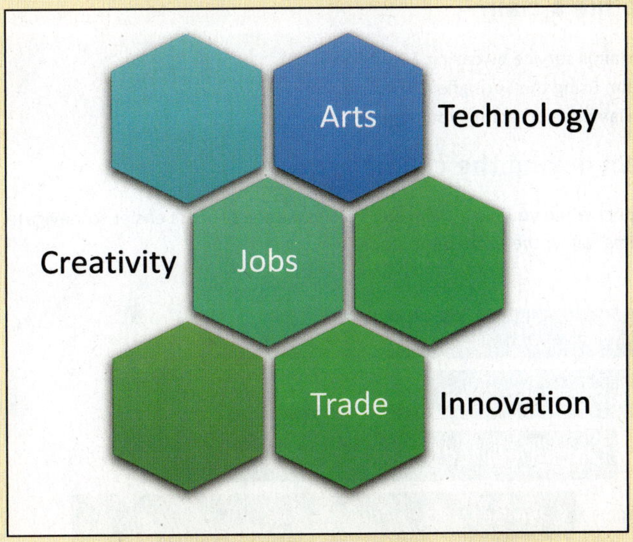

Visual Workshop

Open the file IL_WD_3-5.docx from the location where you store your Data Files, then save the document as **IL_WD_3_ClaimFlyer**. Create the one-page flyer shown in FIGURE 3-37. Use 12-point Calibri for the body text, 36-point Calibri for the title, 16-point Calibri for the subtitle, and 18-point Calibri for the headings. To create the SmartArt graphic object, use the Staggered Process style from the Process group. Add a registered trademark symbol ® after "Springfield" in each instance of "Springfield Mobile app". Add your name to the footer, then submit a copy of the flyer to your instructor.

FIGURE 3-37

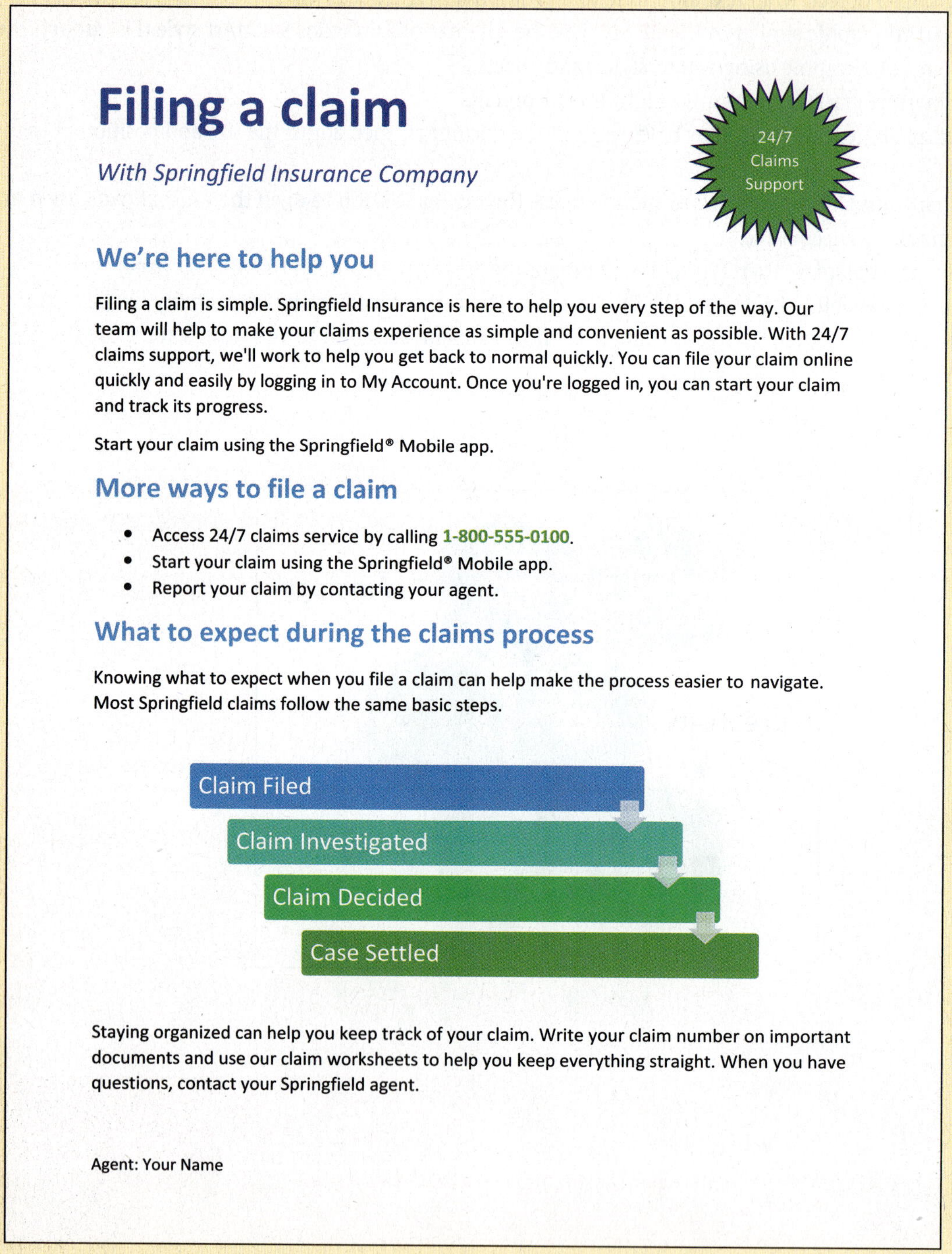

Filing a claim

With Springfield Insurance Company

24/7
Claims
Support

We're here to help you

Filing a claim is simple. Springfield Insurance is here to help you every step of the way. Our team will help to make your claims experience as simple and convenient as possible. With 24/7 claims support, we'll work to help you get back to normal quickly. You can file your claim online quickly and easily by logging in to My Account. Once you're logged in, you can start your claim and track its progress.

Start your claim using the Springfield® Mobile app.

More ways to file a claim

- Access 24/7 claims service by calling 1-800-555-0100.
- Start your claim using the Springfield® Mobile app.
- Report your claim by contacting your agent.

What to expect during the claims process

Knowing what to expect when you file a claim can help make the process easier to navigate. Most Springfield claims follow the same basic steps.

Claim Filed
Claim Investigated
Claim Decided
Case Settled

Staying organized can help you keep track of your claim. Write your claim number on important documents and use our claim worksheets to help you keep everything straight. When you have questions, contact your Springfield agent.

Agent: Your Name

Formatting Tables and Documents

CASE You are preparing a prospectus for an advertising campaign aimed at the New York market. The goal of the ad campaign is to promote JCL Talent to employers and job seekers in the office support industries. You format the budget information in the prospectus as a table, so that it is easy to read and analyze, and then add headers and footers and a cover page to the prospectus.

Module Objectives

After completing this module, you will be able to:

- Modify character spacing
- Work with indents
- Insert a section break
- Modify a table
- Modify rows and columns
- Sort table data
- Split and merge cells
- Perform calculations in tables
- Modify table style options
- Customize a table format
- Insert a cover page

Files You Will Need

IL_WD_4-1.docx
IL_WD_4-2.docx
IL_WD_4-3.docx

Word
Module 4

Modify Character Spacing

Learning Outcome
• Modify text formatting

A powerful way to change the appearance of text is to modify character spacing. **Character spacing** is formatting that changes the scale (or width) of characters, expands or condenses the amount of space between characters, raises or lowers characters relative to the line of text, and adjusts the kerning of characters. **Kerning** is the space between standard combinations of letters. You use the Advanced tab in the Font dialog box to modify character spacing. **CASE** *You enhance the appearance of the headings in the prospectus by modifying the character spacing.*

STEPS

1. **sam Start Word, open the file IL_WD_4-1.docx from the location where you store your Data Files, save it as IL_WD_4_Prospectus, then drag the Zoom slider to 120**
2. **Select the heading Executive Summary, click the Font Size arrow on the Mini toolbar, then click 48**

   The font size of the heading is enlarged to 48.
3. **Click the Launcher in the Font group on the Home tab to open the Font dialog box, click the Small caps check box in the Effects area on the Font tab, then click OK**

   The lowercase characters change to small capital characters. You can use the options on the Font tab to apply other font effects, as well, including Subscript, Superscript, and Strikethrough.
4. **Click the Launcher in the Font group, then click the Advanced tab in the Font dialog box**

   The Advanced tab in the Font dialog box is shown in **FIGURE 4-1**. You use the options on the Advanced tab to change the scale and spacing of characters, or to raise or lower the characters.
5. **Click the Scale arrow, click 80%, click the Spacing arrow, click Expanded, then click OK**

   Decreasing the scale of the characters makes them narrower and gives the text a tall, thin appearance. Expanding the spacing increases the amount of white space between characters.
6. **Click the Font Size arrow 11 in the Font group, click 24, double-click the Format Painter button in the Clipboard group, then move the pointer over the document text to see**

   The font size of the heading changes to 24. The Format Painter is turned on and the pointer changes to .
7. **Scroll down, select the headings Development Timeline and Projected Budget, click the Format Painter button to turn off the Format Painter, press CTRL+HOME, then save your changes**

   The headings are formatted the same; they are 24-point, small caps, character scale of 80%, with character spacing expanded by 1 point, as shown in **FIGURE 4-2**.

FIGURE 4-1: Advanced tab in Font dialog box

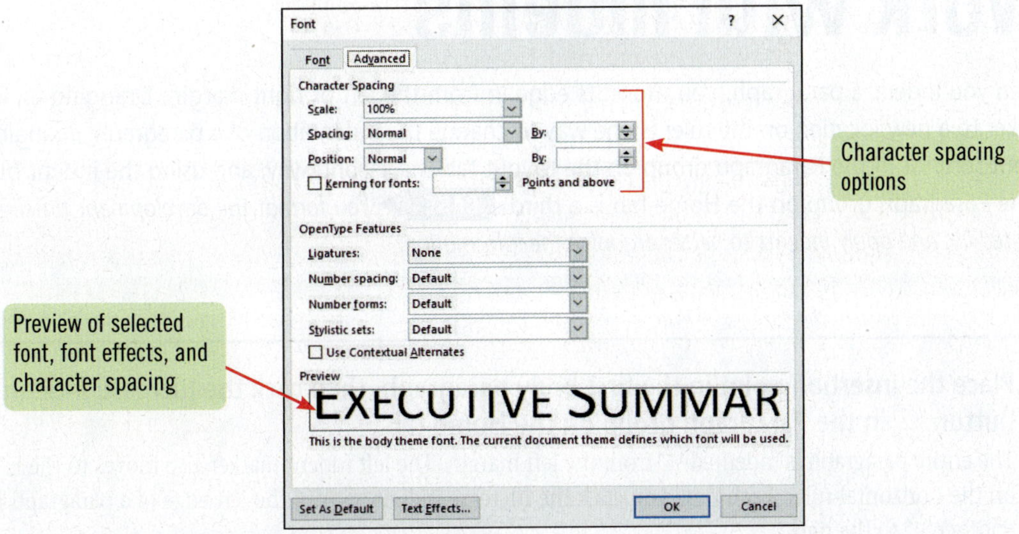

FIGURE 4-2: Font and character spacing effects applied to text

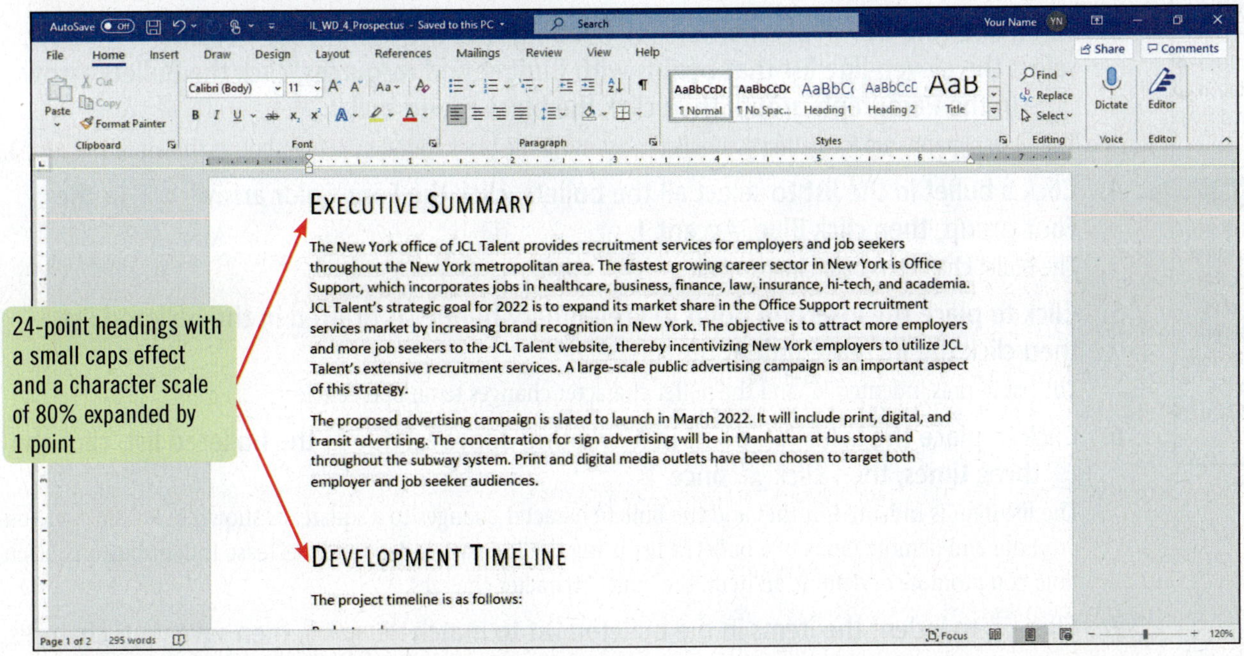

Researching job roles and job skills with the Resume Assistant

The Resume Assistant in Word can help you research job roles and the types of skills they typically require. The Resume Assistant is available when you enable Intelligent Services in your Office installation. To open Resume Assistant, click the Review tab, and then click the Resume Assistant button in the Resume group. In the Resume Assistant pane, type keywords for a job role, such as "medical assistant," and an industry, such as "hospital" or "mental health care," you wish to explore. Descriptions of work experience from the LinkedIn public profiles of users with similar job and industry titles will appear in the Resume Assistant pane. If you want to learn more about the job skills typically related to the role, click the Filter examples by top skills arrow to see the top job skills for the role (as identified by LinkedIn). The descriptions of work experience and top job skills you find using the Resume Assistant might be helpful to you as inspiration for writing descriptions of your own work experience for your résumé. Keep in mind that Resume Assistant is for reference use only. It's important that your résumé be original content that is unique to you.

Word
Module 4

Work with Indents

Learning Outcomes
- Increase and decrease list levels
- Change bullet characters

When you indent a paragraph, you move its edge in from the left or right margin. Dragging an indent marker to a new location on the ruler is one way to change the indentation of a paragraph, changing the indent settings in the Paragraph group on the Layout tab is a second way, and using the indent buttons in the Paragraph group on the Home tab is a third. **CASE** *You format the development timeline as a bulleted list and apply indents to better organize the information.*

STEPS

QUICK TIP
To create a right indent, drag the right indent marker on the horizontal ruler to the left.

QUICK TIP
To create mirror indents, select the Mirror indents check box on the Indents and Spacing tab in the Paragraph dialog box.

QUICK TIP
To use a symbol or a picture for a bullet character, click the Bullets arrow, click Define New Bullet, and then select from the options in the Define New Bullet dialog box.

1. **Place the insertion point in the first body paragraph, then click the Increase Indent button in the Paragraph group on the Home tab**

   The entire paragraph is indented ½" from the left margin. The left indent marker also moves to the ½" mark on the horizontal ruler. Each time you click the Increase Indent button, the left edge of a paragraph moves another ½" to the right.

2. **Click the Decrease Indent button in the Paragraph group**

   The left edge of the paragraph moves ½" to the left, and the indent marker moves back to the left margin.

3. **Scroll until the Development Timeline heading is at the top of your document window, select the eleven-line list that begins with Budget and resources, click the Bullets arrow in the Paragraph group, then click the black round bullet**

   The 11 paragraphs are formatted as a bulleted list using the black round bullet symbol, as shown in FIGURE 4-3.

4. **Click a bullet in the list to select all the bullets, click the Font Color arrow in the Font group, then click Blue, Accent 1**

   The bullet characters all change to blue.

5. **Click to place the insertion point in Preliminary budget is drafted in the bulleted list, then click the Increase Indent button**

   The list item is indented ½" and the bullet character changes to an open circle.

6. **Click to place the insertion point in Marketing approval due in the bulleted list, click the three times, then click once**

   The list item is indented further and the bullet character changes to a square, as shown in FIGURE 4-4. You promote and demote items in a bulleted list using the Increase Indent and Decrease Indent buttons. Each time you promote or demote an item, the bullet character changes.

7. **Click to indent the items in the bulleted list to match FIGURE 4-5, then save your changes**

Creating multilevel lists

You can create lists with hierarchical structures by applying a multilevel list style to a list. To create a multilevel list, also called an outline, begin by applying a multilevel list style using the Multilevel List arrow in the Paragraph group on the Home tab, then type your outline, pressing ENTER after each item. To demote items to a lower level of importance in the outline, place the insertion point in the item, then click the Increase Indent button in the Paragraph group on the Home tab. Each time you indent a paragraph, the item is demoted to a lower level in the outline. Similarly, you can use the Decrease Indent button to promote an item to a higher level in the outline. You can also create a hierarchical structure in any bulleted or numbered list by using and to demote and promote items in the list. To change the multilevel list style applied to a list, select the list, click and then select a new style.

FIGURE 4-3: Bulleted list

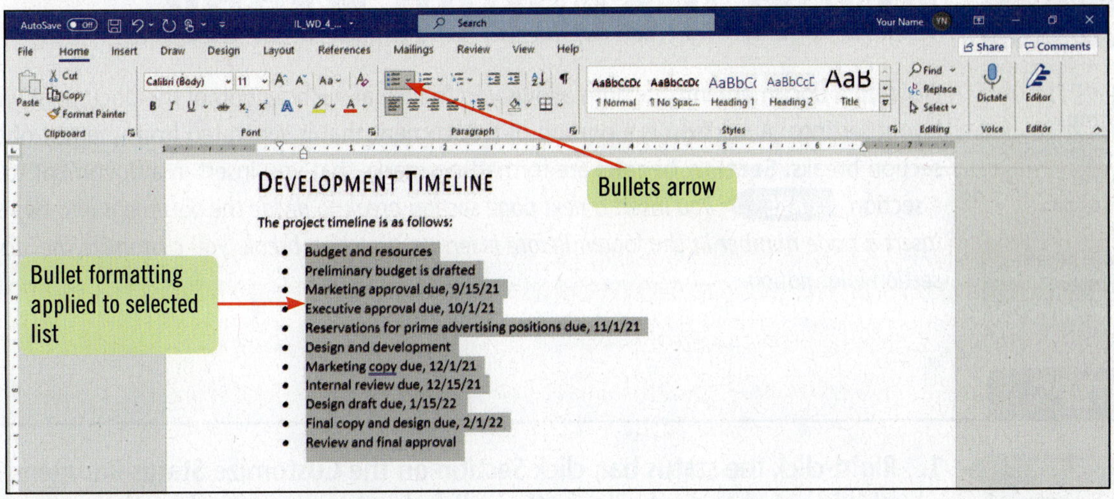

FIGURE 4-4: Demoted items in list

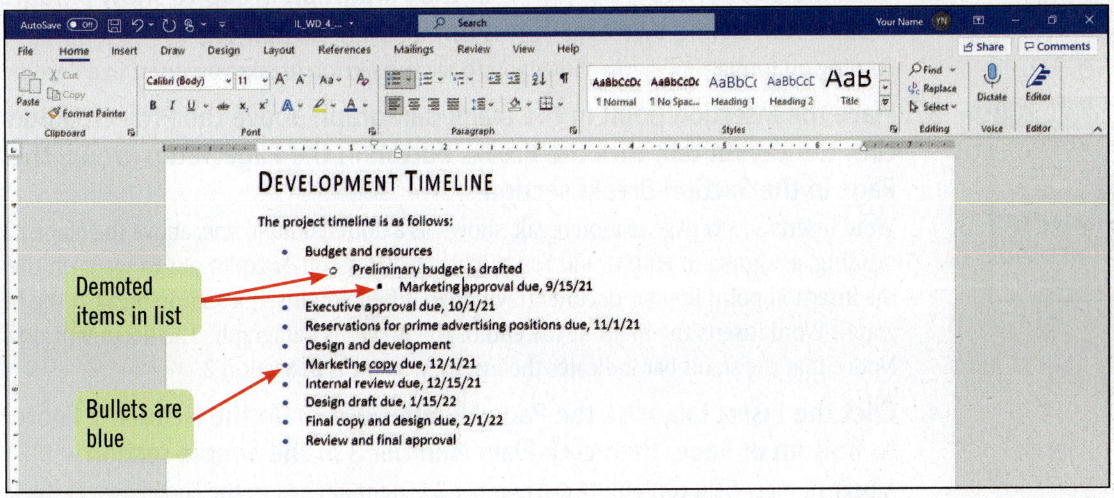

FIGURE 4-5: Multilevel list

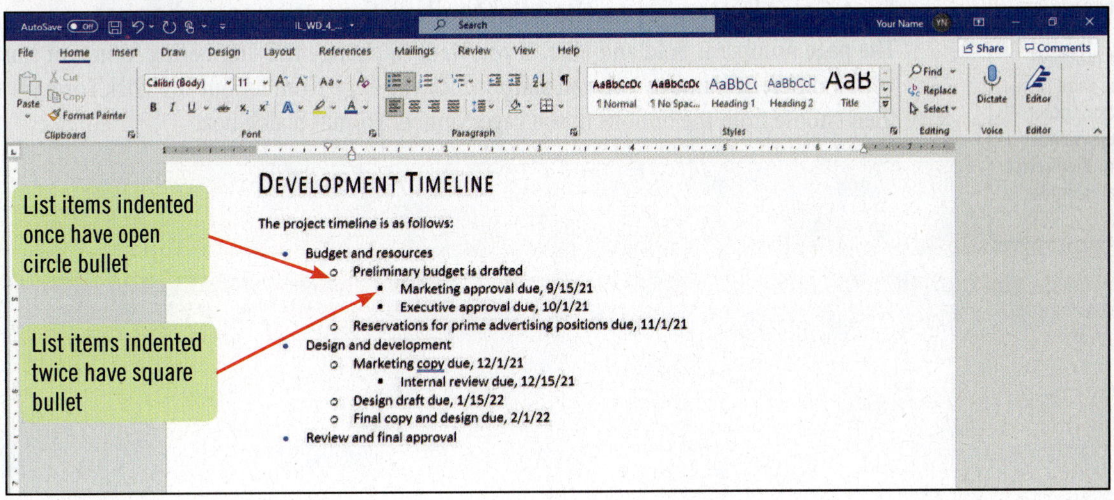

Word

Word
Module 4

Insert a Section Break

Learning Outcomes
- Customize the status bar
- Insert section breaks
- Manage headers and footers

Dividing a document into sections allows you to format each section of the document with different page layout settings. A **section** is a portion of a document that is separated from the rest of the document by section breaks. **Section breaks** are formatting marks that you insert in a document to show the end of a section. **CASE** *You insert a next page section break to divide the document into two sections, and then insert a page number in the footer. Before inserting a section break, you customize the status bar to display section information.*

STEPS

QUICK TIP
Use the Customize Status Bar menu to turn on and off the display of information in the status bar.

1. **Right-click the status bar, click Section on the Customize Status Bar menu that opens (if it is not already checked), then click the document to close the menu**
   The status bar indicates the insertion point is located in Section 1 of the document.

2. **Click the Show/Hide ¶ button ¶ in the Paragraph group to show paragraph marks and hidden formatting symbols (if it is not already turned on)**
   Turning on formatting marks allows you to see the section breaks you insert in a document.

QUICK TIP
To delete a break, click to the left of the break with the selection pointer to select it, then press DELETE.

3. **Place the insertion point in the blank paragraph above the Projected Budget heading, click the Layout tab, click the Breaks button in the Page Setup group, then click Next Page in the Section Breaks section**
   Word inserts a next page section break, shown as a dotted double line, above the blank paragraph above the heading, as shown in **FIGURE 4-6**. You might need to scroll or zoom out to see both the section break and the insertion point in your document window. When you insert a section break at the beginning of a paragraph, Word inserts the break at the end of the previous paragraph. The document now has two sections. Notice that the status bar indicates the insertion point is in Section 2.

4. **Click the Insert tab, click the Page Number button in the Header & Footer group, point to Bottom of Page, then click Plain Number 3 in the Simple section**
   A page number field containing the number 2 is right-aligned in the Footer area at the bottom of page 2 of the document. The document text is dimmed.

QUICK TIP
To change the location or formatting of page numbers, click the Page Number button, point to a page number location, then select a format from the gallery.

5. **Select the page number, click the Bold button B on the Mini toolbar, click the Font Color button A on the Mini toolbar, then save your changes**
   The page number is bold and blue. If you want to change the numbering format or start page numbering with a different number, you can simply click the Page Number button, click Format Page Numbers, and then choose from the options in the Page Number Format dialog box.

FIGURE 4-6: Next Page section break

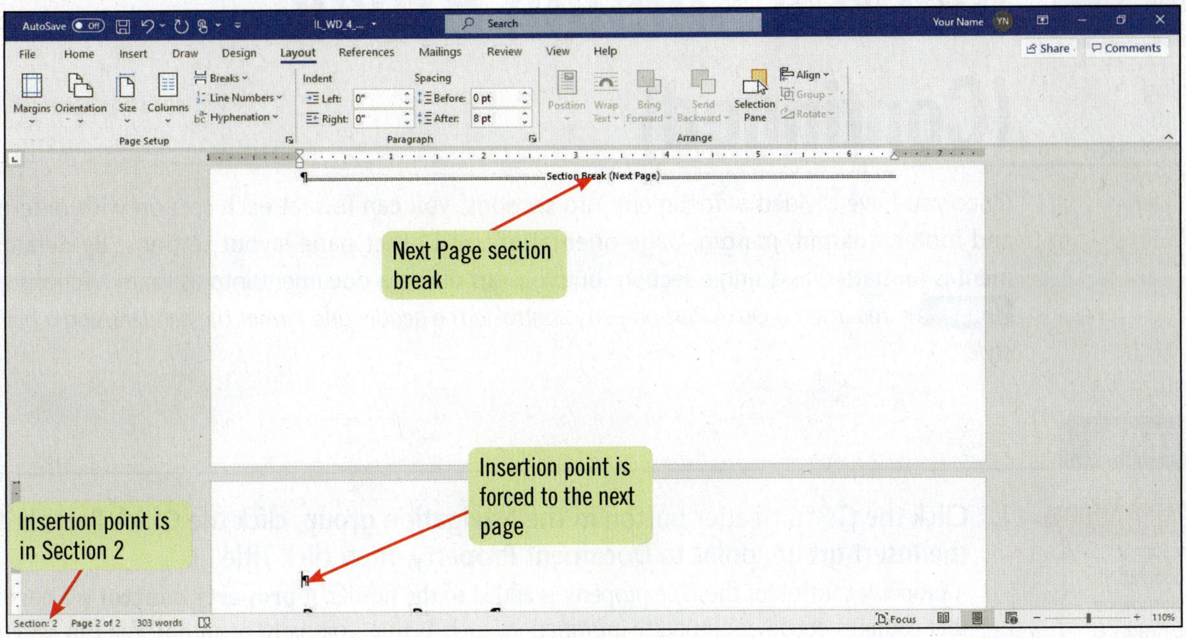

Using sections to vary the layout of a document

Dividing a document into sections allows you to vary the layout of a document. In addition to applying different column settings to sections, you can apply different margins, page orientation, paper size, vertical alignment, header and footer, page numbering, footnotes, endnotes, and other page layout settings. For example, if you are formatting a report that includes a table with many columns, you might want to change the table's page orientation to landscape so that it is easier to read. To do this, you would insert a section break before and after the table to create a section that contains only the table, and then you would change the page orientation of the section that contains the table to landscape. If the table does not fill the page, you could also change the vertical alignment of the table so that it is centered vertically on the page. To do this, use the Vertical alignment arrow on the Layout tab of the Page Setup dialog box.

To check or change the page layout settings for an individual section, place the insertion point in the section, then open the Page Setup dialog box. Select any options you want to change, click the Apply to arrow, click This section, then click OK. When you select This section, the settings are applied to the current section only. When you select This point forward, the settings are applied to the current section and all sections that follow it. If you select Whole document, the settings are applied to all the sections in the document. Use the Apply to arrow in the Columns dialog box or the Footnote and Endnote dialog box to change those settings for a section.

(Continued)

Insert a Section Break (Continued)

Learning Outcomes
- Manage headers and footers
- Insert property controls

Once you have divided a document into sections, you can format each section with different header and footer, column, margin, page orientation, and other page layout settings. By default, a document is formatted as a single section, but you can divide a document into as many sections as you like. **CASE** *You insert a Quick Part property control in the header and format the header using a built-in header style.*

STEPS

TROUBLE
If the Header & Footer contextual tab is not showing, click the Header & Footer tab.

1. **Click the Go to Header button in the Navigation group, click the Quick Parts button in the Insert group, point to Document Property, then click Title**
   A property control for the Title property is added to the header. A **property control** is a content control that contains document property information, such as title, company, or author. You can assign or update a document property by typing directly in a property control or by typing in the Properties boxes on the Info screen.

2. **Type Advertising Campaign Prospectus in the Title property control**
   The document title is added to the header. When you assign or update a document property by typing in a property control, all controls of the same type in the document are updated with the change, as well as the corresponding property field on the Info screen.

QUICK TIP
To remove a header, click in the Header or Footer area, click the Header button in the Header & Footer group, then click Remove Header. To remove a footer, click the Footer button, then click Remove Footer.

3. **Click the Header button in the Header & Footer group, scroll down the gallery, click Integral, then scroll until the bottom of page 1 and the top of page 2 are visible in the document window**
   The header design changes to the Integral design, as shown in FIGURE 4-7. The headers and footers are the same in Section 1 and Section 2. If you wanted to create different headers and footers for different sections, you would need to break the link between sections by clicking the Link to Previous button in the Navigation group. The Link to Previous button is a toggle button that you can use to link and unlink headers and footers between sections in a multi-section document.

4. **Click the Close Header and Footer button in the Close group**
   The header and footer areas close and are dimmed. The body of the document is now active.

5. **Click the Home tab, click the Show/Hide ¶ button ¶, then save your changes**

FIGURE 4-7: Integral header

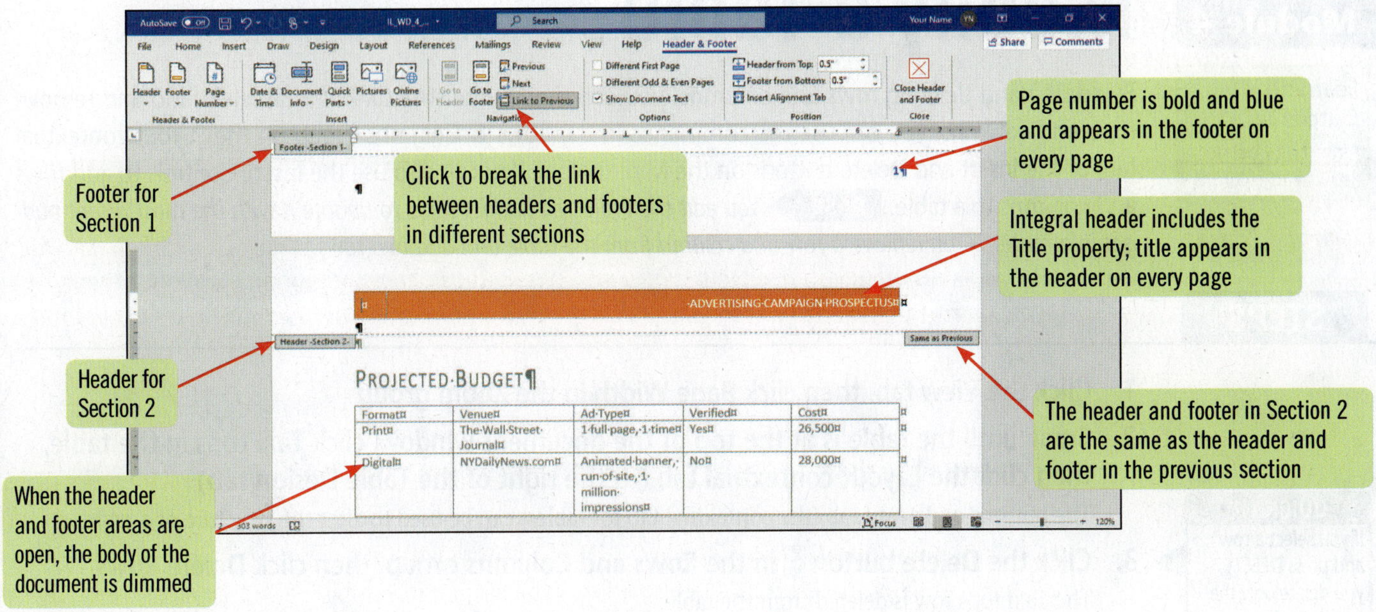

Adding a custom header or footer to the gallery

When you design a header that you want to use again in other documents, you can add it to the Header gallery by saving it as a building block. Building blocks are reusable pieces of formatted content or document parts, including headers and footers, page numbers, and text boxes, that are stored in galleries. **Building blocks** include predesigned content that comes with Word, as well as content that you create and save for future use. For example, you might create a custom header that contains your company name and logo and is formatted using the fonts, border, and colors you use in all company documents.

To add a custom header to the Header gallery, select all the text in the header, including the last paragraph mark, click the Header button, and then click Save Selection to Header Gallery. In the Create New Building Block dialog box that opens, type a unique name for the header in the Name box, click the Gallery arrow and select the appropriate gallery, verify that the Category is General, and then type a brief description of the new header design in the Description box. This description appears in a ScreenTip when you point to the custom header in the gallery. When you are finished, click OK. The new header appears in the Header gallery under the General category.

To remove a custom header from the Header gallery, click the Header button in the Header & Footer group, scroll to the new header, right-click it in the Header gallery, click Organize and Delete, make sure the appropriate building block is selected in the Building Blocks Organizer that opens, click Delete, click Yes, and then click Close. You can follow the same process to add or remove a custom footer to the Footer gallery.

Word
Module 4

Modify a Table

Learning Outcome
- Insert and delete rows and columns

By adding and deleting rows and columns, you can modify the structure of a table. To add and remove rows and columns, you can use the commands in the Rows & Columns group on the Layout contextual tab, or the Insert and Delete buttons on the Mini toolbar. You can also use the Insert Controls to add rows and columns to a table. **CASE** *You edit the Projected Budget table to update it with the most recent budget information. You remove a row and column from the table and add two rows.*

STEPS

1. **Click the View tab, then click Page Width in the Zoom group**
2. **Scroll until the table is at the top of the document window, click Taxi tops in the table, then click the Layout contextual tab (to the right of the Table Design tab)**
   The buttons on Layout tab (the contextual tab for tables) can be used to alter the structure of a table.
3. **Click the Delete button in the Rows and Columns group, then click Delete Rows**
   The Taxi tops row is deleted from the table.
4. **Place the pointer over the Verified column top border until the pointer changes to ⬇, then click**
   The entire Verified column is selected, as shown in FIGURE 4-8.
5. **Click the Delete button on the Mini toolbar, then click Delete Columns**
   The Verified column is deleted from the table.
6. **Place the pointer at the left edge of the table over the border between the NYDailyNews.com and NYPost.com rows to display the Insert Control, then click the Insert Control**
   A new row is added between the NYDailyNews.com and NYPost.com rows.
7. **Click in the first cell in the new row, type Sign, press TAB, type Subway cars, press TAB, type 1000 panels, 2 weeks, press TAB, type 18,000, then save your changes**
   Text is added to the new row, as shown in FIGURE 4-9.

QUICK TIP
If you select a row and press DELETE, you delete only the contents of the row, not the row in the table.

QUICK TIP
To select a cell, place the pointer near the left border of the cell, then click.

Copying and moving rows and columns

You can copy and move rows and columns within a table in the same manner you copy and move text. Select the row or column you want to move, then use the Copy or Cut button to place the selection on the Clipboard. Place the insertion point in the location where you want to insert the row or column, then click the Paste button to paste the selection. Rows are inserted above the row containing the insertion point; columns are inserted to the left of the column containing the insertion point. You can also copy or move columns and rows by selecting them and using the pointer to drag them to a new location in the table. To copy or move an entire table, select the entire table and then use the Cut, Copy, and Paste commands.

FIGURE 4-8: Column is selected

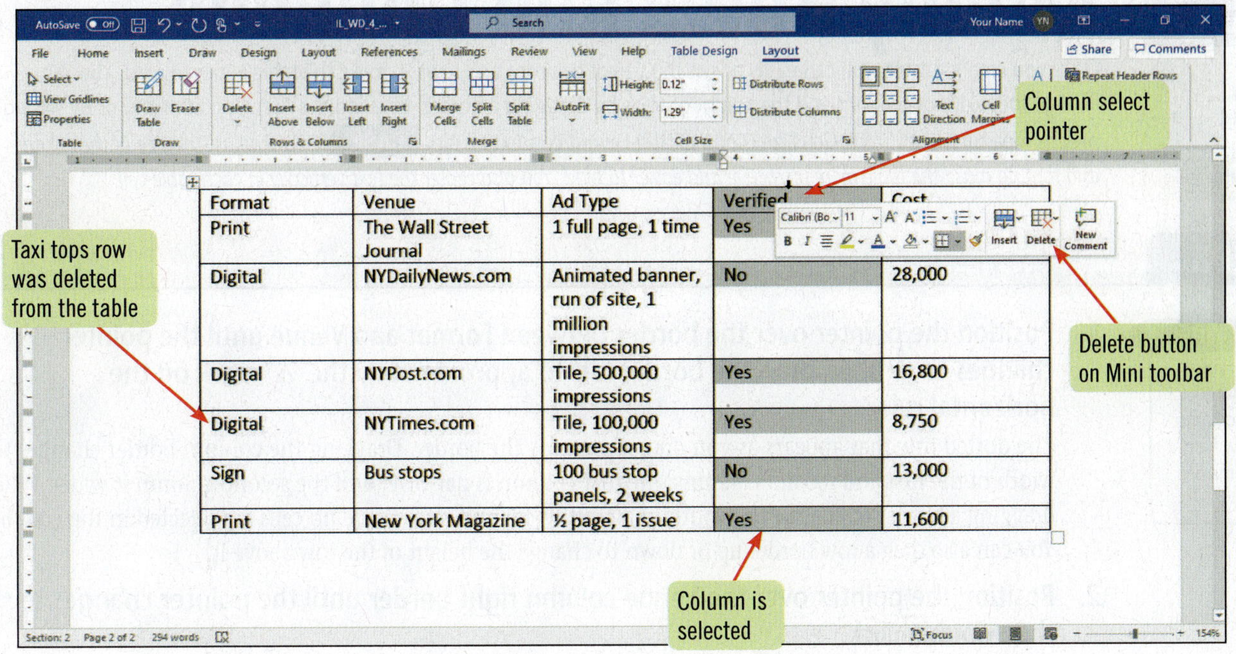

FIGURE 4-9: New row in table

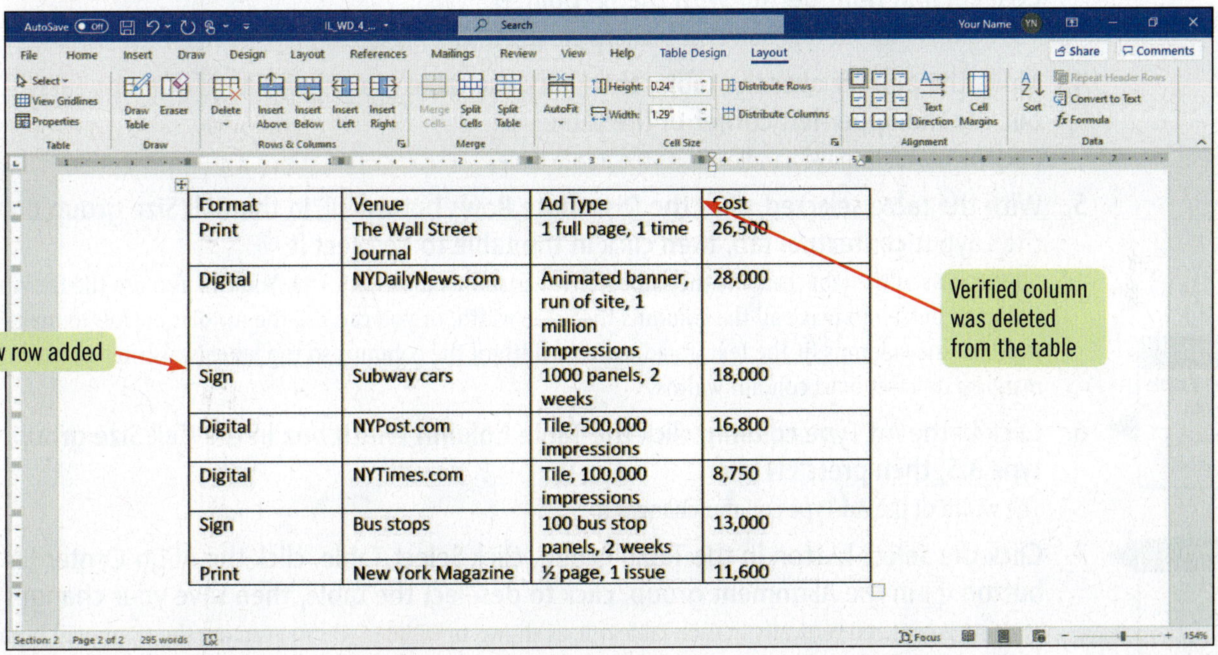

Word

Word
Module 4

Modify Rows and Columns

Learning Outcomes
- Resize columns
- Format table cells

Once you create a table, you can easily adjust the size of columns and rows to make the table easier to read. You can change the width of columns and the height of rows by dragging a border, by using the AutoFit command, or by setting precise measurements in the Cell Size group on the Layout contextual tab. **CASE** *You adjust the size of the columns and rows to make the table more attractive and easier to read. You also center the text vertically in each table cell.*

STEPS

> **QUICK TIP**
> Press ALT as you drag a border to display the column width or row height measurements on the ruler.

1. **Position the pointer over the border between Format and Venue until the pointer changes to ✛ then drag the border left to approximately the ½" mark on the horizontal ruler**

   The dotted line that appears as you drag represents the border. Dragging the column border changes the width of the first and second columns: the first column is narrower and the second column is wider. When dragging a border to change the width of an entire column, make sure no cells are selected in the column. You can also drag a row border up or down to change the height of the row above it.

2. **Position the pointer over the Venue column right border until the pointer changes to ✛ then double-click**

   Double-clicking a column border automatically resizes the column to fit the text.

3. **Double-click the Ad Type column right border with the ✛ pointer, then double-click the Cost column right border with the ✛ pointer**

   The widths of the Ad Type and Cost columns are adjusted.

4. **Move the pointer over the table, then click the table move handle ⊞ that appears outside the upper-left corner of the table**

   Clicking the table move handle selects the entire table.

5. **With the table selected, click the Distribute Rows button in the Cell Size group on the Layout contextual tab, then click in the table to deselect it**

   All the rows in the table become the same height, as shown in **FIGURE 4-10**. You can also use the Distribute Columns button to make all the columns the same width, or you can use the AutoFit button to make the width of the columns fit the text, to adjust the width of the columns so the table is justified between the margins, or to set fixed column widths.

> **QUICK TIP**
> Quickly move a table by dragging the table move handle to a new location.

6. **Click in the Ad Type column, click the Table Column Width box in the Cell Size group, type 3.5, then press ENTER**

   The width of the Ad Type column changes to 3.5".

> **QUICK TIP**
> Quickly center a table on a page by selecting the table and clicking the Center button in the Paragraph group on the Home tab.

7. **Click the Select button in the Table group, click Select Table, click the Align Center Left button in the Alignment group, click to deselect the table, then save your changes**

   The text is centered vertically in each table cell, as shown in **FIGURE 4-11**. You can use the alignment buttons in the Alignment group to change the vertical and horizontal alignment of the text in selected cells or in the entire table.

FIGURE 4-10: Resized columns and rows

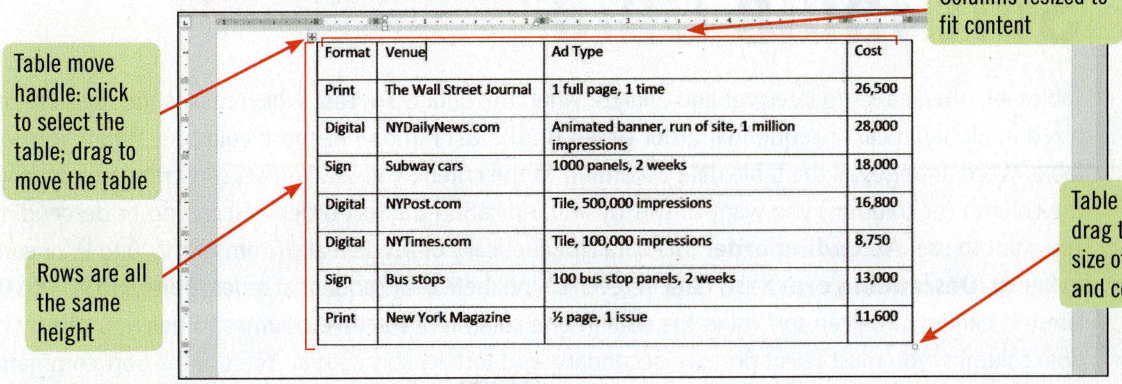

Format	Venue	Ad Type	Cost
Print	The Wall Street Journal	1 full page, 1 time	26,500
Digital	NYDailyNews.com	Animated banner, run of site, 1 million impressions	28,000
Sign	Subway cars	1000 panels, 2 weeks	18,000
Digital	NYPost.com	Tile, 500,000 impressions	16,800
Digital	NYTimes.com	Tile, 100,000 impressions	8,750
Sign	Bus stops	100 bus stop panels, 2 weeks	13,000
Print	New York Magazine	½ page, 1 issue	11,600

FIGURE 4-11: Text centered vertically in cells

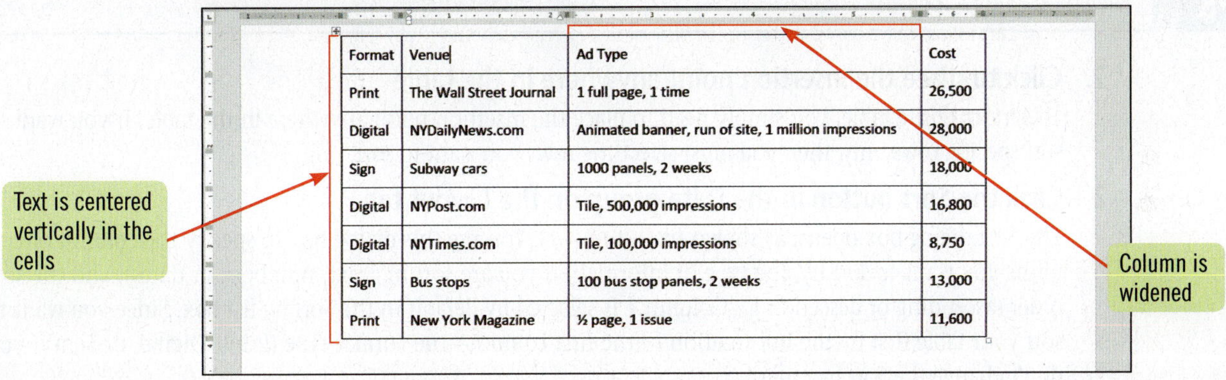

Format	Venue	Ad Type	Cost
Print	The Wall Street Journal	1 full page, 1 time	26,500
Digital	NYDailyNews.com	Animated banner, run of site, 1 million impressions	28,000
Sign	Subway cars	1000 panels, 2 weeks	18,000
Digital	NYPost.com	Tile, 500,000 impressions	16,800
Digital	NYTimes.com	Tile, 100,000 impressions	8,750
Sign	Bus stops	100 bus stop panels, 2 weeks	13,000
Print	New York Magazine	½ page, 1 issue	11,600

Setting advanced table properties

When you want to wrap text around a table, indent a table, or set other advanced table properties, you click the Properties command in the Table group on the Layout tab to open the Table Properties dialog box, shown in **FIGURE 4-12**. Using the Table tab in this dialog box, you can set a precise width for the table, change the horizontal alignment of the table between the margins, indent the table, and set text wrapping options for the table. You can also click Options on the Table tab to open the Table Options dialog box, which you use to customize the table's default cell margins and the spacing between table cells. Alternatively, click Borders and Shading on the Table tab to open the Borders and Shading dialog box, which you can use to create a custom format for the table.

The Row, Column, and Cell tabs in the Table Properties dialog box allow you to set an exact height for rows, to specify an exact width for columns, and to indicate an exact size for individual cells. The Alt Text tab is used to add alternative text for a table, such as a description of its content, so that the table can be understood by a person using a screen reader.

FIGURE 4-12: Table Properties dialog box

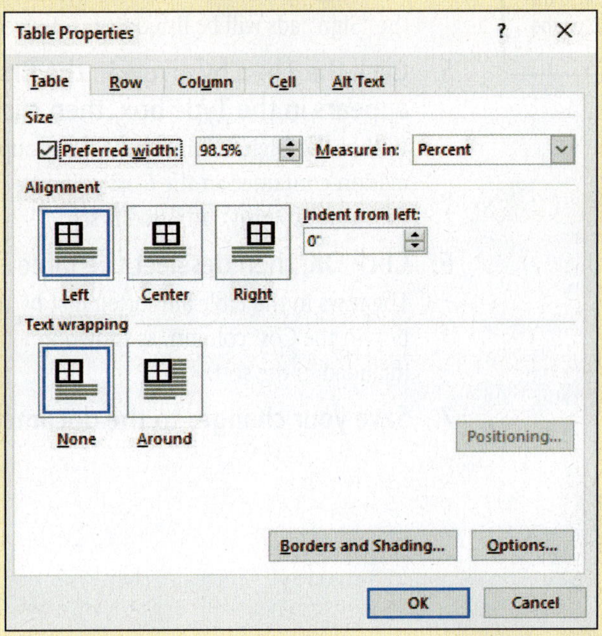

Word

Word
Module 4

Sort Table Data

Learning Outcomes
- Sort table data by one or more criteria
- Sort lists and paragraphs

Tables are often easier to interpret and analyze when the data is **sorted**, which means the rows are organized in alphabetical or sequential order based on the data in one or more columns. When you sort a table, Word arranges all the table data according to the criteria you set. You set sort criteria by specifying the column (or columns) you want to sort by and indicating the sort order—ascending or descending—you want to use. **Ascending order** lists data alphabetically or sequentially (from A to Z, 0 to 9, or earliest to latest). **Descending order** lists data in reverse alphabetical or sequential order (from Z to A, 9 to 0, or latest to earliest). You can sort using the data in one column or multiple columns. When you sort by multiple columns, you must select primary, secondary, and tertiary sort criteria. You use the Sort command in the Data group on the Layout tab to sort a table. CASE *You sort the table so that all ads of the same format type are listed together. You also add secondary sort criteria so that the ads within each format type are listed in descending order by cost.*

STEPS

1. **Click to place the insertion point anywhere in the table**
   To sort an entire table, you simply need to place the insertion point anywhere in the table. If you want to sort specific rows only, then you must select the rows you want to sort.

2. **Click the Sort button in the Data group on the Layout tab**
   The Sort dialog box opens, as shown in FIGURE 4-13. You use this dialog box to specify the column or columns you want to sort by, the type of information you are sorting (text, numbers, or dates), and the sort order (ascending or descending). Column 1 is selected by default in the Sort by list box. Since you want to sort your table first by the information in the first column—the Format type (Print, Digital, or Sign)—you don't change the Sort by criteria.

QUICK TIP
To repeat the header row on every page of a table that spans multiple pages, click the Repeat Header Rows button in the Data group on the Layout tab.

3. **Click the Header row option button in the My list has section to select it**
   The table includes a **header row**, which is the first row of a table that contains the column headings. You must select the Header row option button first when you do not want the header row included in the sort.

4. **Click the Descending option button in the Sort by section**
   The information in the Format column will be sorted in descending—or reverse alphabetical—order, so that the "Sign" ads will be listed first, followed by the "Print" ads, and then the "Digital" ads.

5. **Click the Then by arrow in the first Then by section, click Cost, verify that Number appears in the Type box, then click the Descending option button**
   Within the Digital, Print, and Sign groups, the rows will be sorted by the cost of the ad, which is the information contained in the Cost column. The rows will appear in descending order within each group, with the most expensive ad listed first.

6. **Click OK, then deselect the table**
   The rows in the table are sorted first by the information in the Format column and second by the information in the Cost column, as shown in FIGURE 4-14. The first row of the table, which is the header row, is not included in the sort.

7. **Save your changes to the document**

FIGURE 4-13: Sort dialog box

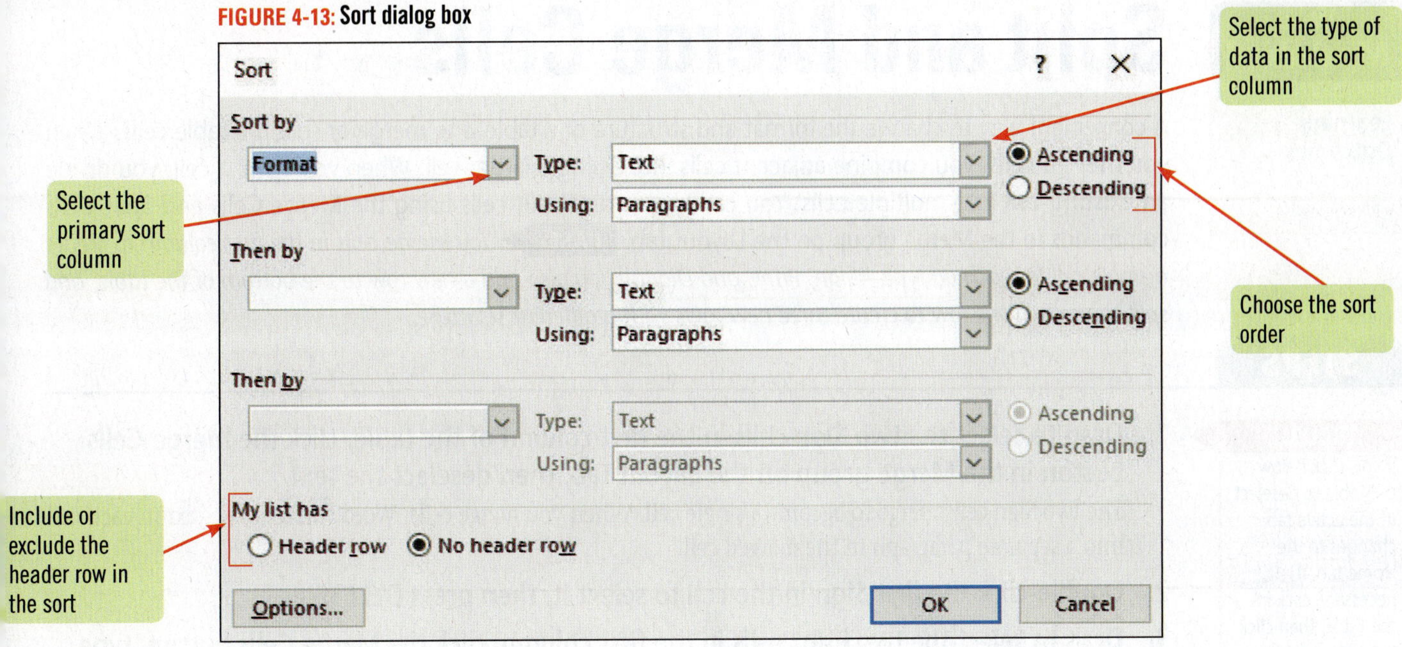

FIGURE 4-14: Sorted table

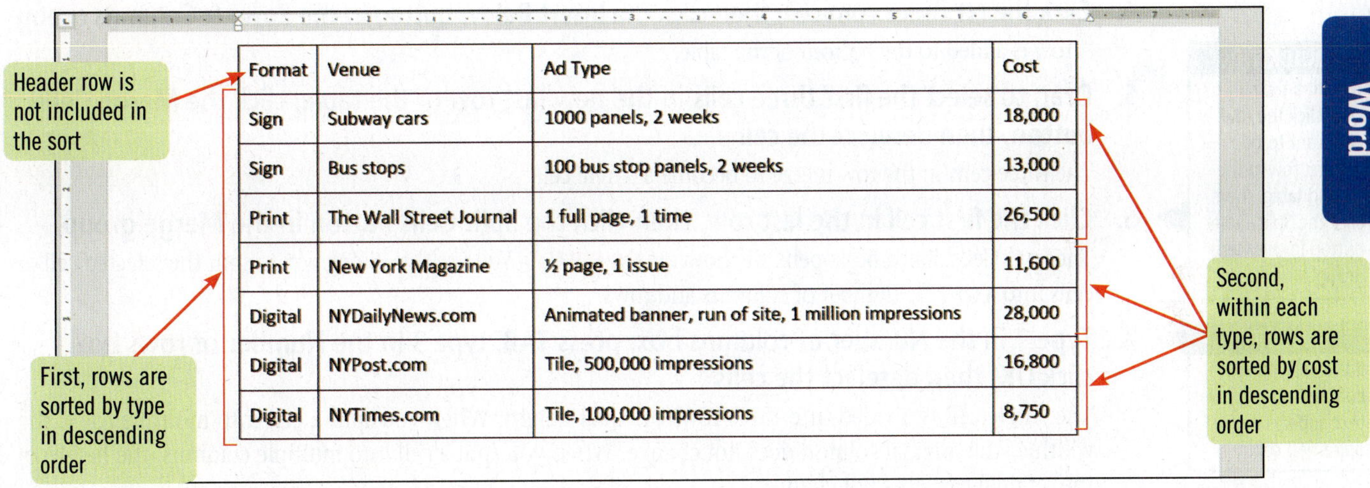

Format	Venue	Ad Type	Cost
Sign	Subway cars	1000 panels, 2 weeks	18,000
Sign	Bus stops	100 bus stop panels, 2 weeks	13,000
Print	The Wall Street Journal	1 full page, 1 time	26,500
Print	New York Magazine	½ page, 1 issue	11,600
Digital	NYDailyNews.com	Animated banner, run of site, 1 million impressions	28,000
Digital	NYPost.com	Tile, 500,000 impressions	16,800
Digital	NYTimes.com	Tile, 100,000 impressions	8,750

Sorting lists and paragraphs

In addition to sorting table data, you can use the Sort command to alphabetize text or sort numerical data. When you want to sort data that is not formatted as a table, such as lists and paragraphs, you use the Sort command in the Paragraph group on the Home tab. To sort lists and paragraphs, select the items you want included in the sort, then click the Sort button. In the Sort Text dialog box, use the Sort by arrow to select the sort by criteria (such as paragraphs or fields), use the Type arrow to select the type of data (text, numbers, or dates), and then click the Ascending or Descending option button to choose a sort order.

When sorting text information in a document, the term "fields" refers to text or numbers that are separated by a character, such as a tab or a comma. For example, you might want to sort a list of names alphabetically. If the names you want to sort are listed in "Last name, First name" order, then last name and first name are each considered a field. You can choose to sort the list in alphabetical order by last name or by first name. Use the Options button in the Sort Text dialog box to specify the character that separates the fields in your lists or paragraphs, along with other sort options.

Word
Module 4

Split and Merge Cells

Learning Outcomes
- Split cells
- Merge cells

A convenient way to change the format and structure of a table is to merge or split the table cells. When you **merge** cells, you combine adjacent cells into a single larger cell. When you **split** a cell, you divide an existing cell into multiple cells. You can merge and split cells using the Merge Cells and Split Cells commands in the Merge group on the Layout tab. CASE *You merge cells in the first column to create a single cell for each ad type—Sign, Print, and Digital. You also add a new row to the bottom of the table, and split the cells in the row to create three new rows with a different structure.*

STEPS

TROUBLE
If you click below the table to deselect it, the active tab changes to the Home tab. If necessary, click in the table, then click the Layout tab to continue with the steps in this lesson.

QUICK TIP
To split a table in two, click the row you want to be the first row in the second table, then click the Split Table button in the Merge group.

QUICK TIP
If the cell you split contains text, all the text appears in the upper-left cell.

1. **Drag to select the two Sign cells in the first column of the table, click the Merge Cells button in the Merge group on the Layout tab, then deselect the text**
   The two Sign cells merge to become a single cell. When you merge cells, Word converts the text in each cell into a separate paragraph in the merged cell.
2. **Double-click the first Sign in the cell to select it, then press DELETE**
3. **Drag to select the two Print cells in the first column, click the Merge Cells button, type Print, drag to select the three Digital cells, click the Merge Cells button, then type Digital**
   The two Sign cells merge to become one cell, the two Print cells merge to become one cell, and the three Digital cells merge to become one cell.
4. **Click the NYTimes.com cell, then click the Insert Below button in the Rows & Columns group**
   A row is added to the bottom of the table.
5. **Drag to select the first three cells in the new last row of the table, click the Merge Cells button, then deselect the cell**
   The three cells in the row merge to become a single cell.
6. **Click the first cell in the last row, then click the Split Cells button in the Merge group**
   The Split Cells dialog box opens, as shown in FIGURE 4-15. You use this dialog box to split the selected cell or cells into a specific number of columns and rows.
7. **Type 1 in the Number of columns box, press TAB, type 3 in the Number of rows box, click OK, then deselect the cells**
   The single cell is divided into three rows of equal height. When you split a cell into multiple rows, the width of the original column does not change. When you split a cell into multiple columns, the height of the original row does not change.
8. **Click the last cell in the Cost column, click the Split Cells button, type 1 in the Number of columns box, press TAB, type 3 in the Number of rows box, click OK, then save your changes**
   The cell is split into three rows, as shown in FIGURE 4-16. The last three rows now have only two columns.

Changing cell margins

By default, table cells have .08" left and right cell margins with no spacing between the cells, but you can adjust these settings for a table using the Cell Margins button in the Alignment group on the Layout tab. First, place the insertion point in the table, and then click the Cell Margins button to open the Table Options dialog box. Enter new settings for the top, bottom, left, and right cell margins in the boxes in the Default cell margins section of the dialog box, or select the Allow spacing between cells check box and then enter a setting in the Cell spacing section to increase the spacing between table cells. You can also deselect the Automatically resize to fit contents check box in the Options section of the dialog box to turn off the setting that causes table cells to widen to fit the text as you type. Any settings you change in the Table Options dialog box are applied to the entire table.

FIGURE 4-15: Split Cells dialog box

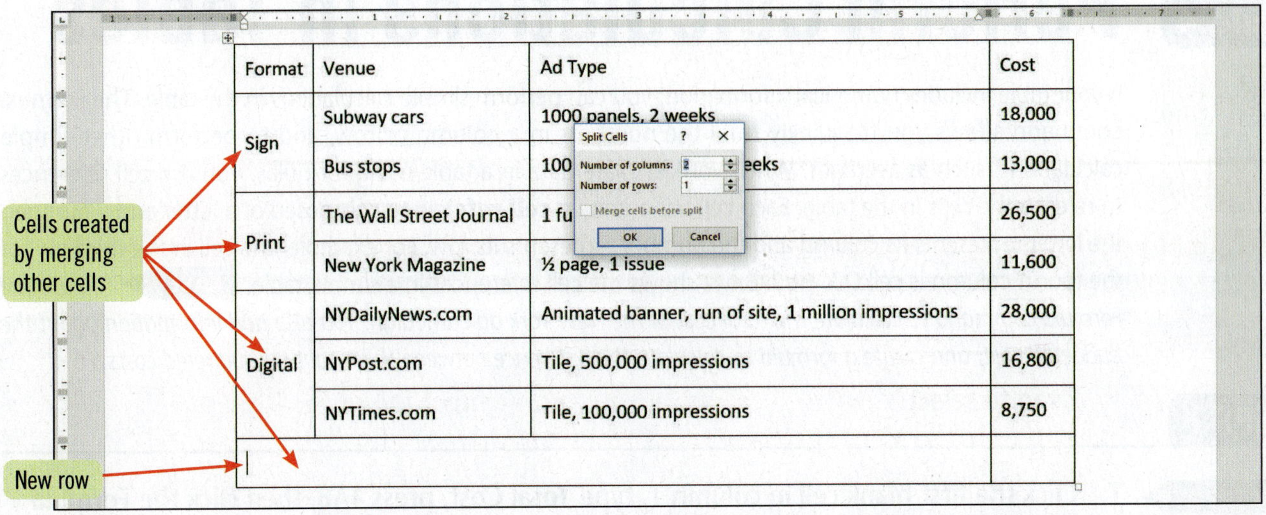

Format	Venue	Ad Type	Cost
Sign	Subway cars	1000 panels, 2 weeks	18,000
	Bus stops	100 … eeks	13,000
Print	The Wall Street Journal	1 fu…	26,500
	New York Magazine	½ page, 1 issue	11,600
Digital	NYDailyNews.com	Animated banner, run of site, 1 million impressions	28,000
	NYPost.com	Tile, 500,000 impressions	16,800
	NYTimes.com	Tile, 100,000 impressions	8,750

FIGURE 4-16: Cells split into three rows

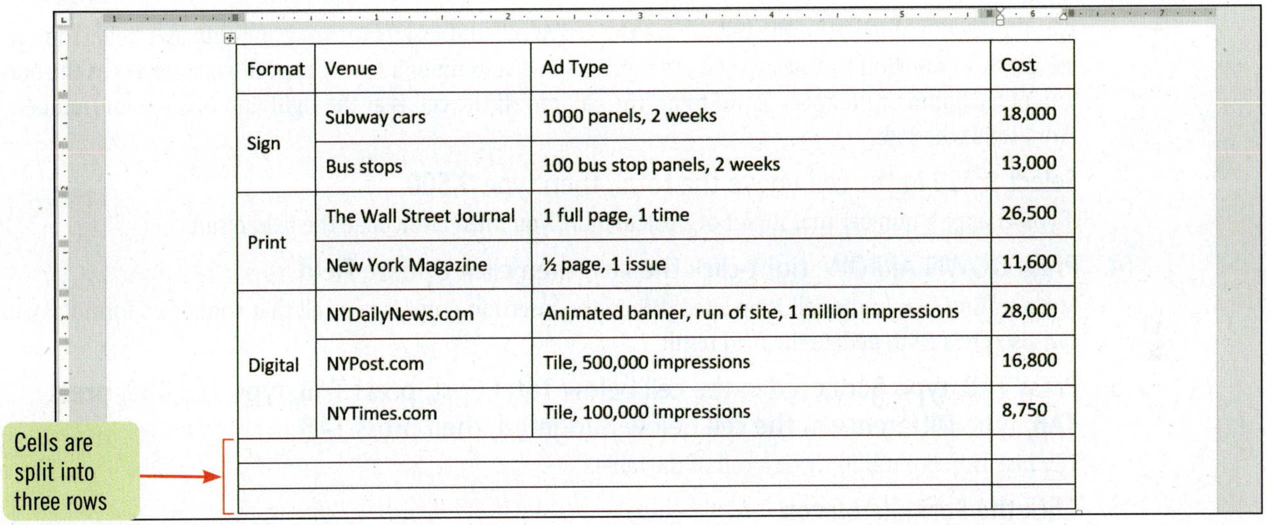

Format	Venue	Ad Type	Cost
Sign	Subway cars	1000 panels, 2 weeks	18,000
	Bus stops	100 bus stop panels, 2 weeks	13,000
Print	The Wall Street Journal	1 full page, 1 time	26,500
	New York Magazine	½ page, 1 issue	11,600
Digital	NYDailyNews.com	Animated banner, run of site, 1 million impressions	28,000
	NYPost.com	Tile, 500,000 impressions	16,800
	NYTimes.com	Tile, 100,000 impressions	8,750

Using tables to lay out a page

Tables are often used to display information for quick reference and analysis, but you can also use tables to structure the layout of a page. You can insert any kind of information in the cell of a table—including graphics, bulleted lists, charts, and other tables (called **nested tables**). For example, you might use a table to lay out a résumé, a newsletter, or a webpage. When you use a table to lay out a page, you generally remove the table borders to hide the table structure from the reader. After you remove borders, it can be helpful to display the table gridlines on screen while you work. **Gridlines** are dotted lines that show the boundaries of cells, but do not print. If your document will be viewed online—for example, if you are planning to email your résumé to potential employers—you should turn off the display of gridlines before you distribute the document so that it looks the same online as it looks when printed. To turn gridlines off or on, click the View Gridlines button in the Table group on the Layout tab.

Perform Calculations in Tables

Learning Outcomes
- Sum numbers in a table
- Update a field
- Insert a formula

If your table includes numerical information, you can perform simple calculations in the table. The Formula command allows you to quickly total the numbers in a column or row, and to perform other simple calculations, such as averages. When you calculate data in a table using formulas, you use cell references to refer to the cells in the table. Each cell has a unique **cell reference** composed of a letter and a number; the letter represents its column and the number represents its row. For example, the cell in the third row of the fourth column is cell D3. **FIGURE 4-17** shows the cell references in a simple table. **CASE** *You use the Formula command to calculate the total cost of the New York ad campaign. You also add information about the budgeted cost, and create a formula to calculate the difference between the total and budgeted costs.*

STEPS

QUICK TIP
You must type a zero in any blank cell in a row or column before using the SUM function.

1. **Click the first blank cell in column 1, type Total Cost, press TAB, then click the Formula button in the Data group on the Layout tab**
   The Formula dialog box opens, as shown in **FIGURE 4-18**. The SUM function appears in the Formula box followed by the reference for the cells to include in the calculation, (ABOVE). The formula =SUM(ABOVE) indicates that Word will sum the numbers in the cells above the active cell.
2. **Click OK**
   Word totals the numbers in the cells above the active cell and inserts the resulting sum as a field. You can use the SUM function to quickly total the numbers in a column or a row. If the cell you select is at the bottom of a column of numbers, Word totals the column. If the cell is at the right end of a row of numbers, Word totals the row.
3. **Select 8,750 in the cell above the total, then type 9,500**
   If you change a number that is part of a calculation, you must recalculate the field result.
4. **Press DOWN ARROW, right-click the cell, then click Update Field**
   The resulting sum in the cell is updated. When the insertion point is in a cell that contains a formula, you can also press F9 to update the field result.
5. **Press TAB, type Budgeted in the cell below Total Cost, press TAB, type 125,000, press TAB, type Difference in the cell below Budgeted, then press TAB**
   The insertion point is in the last cell of the table.
6. **Click the Formula button**
   The Formula dialog box opens. Word proposes to sum the numbers above the active cell, but you want to insert a formula that calculates the difference between the total and budgeted costs. You can type simple custom formulas using a plus sign (+) for addition, a minus sign (–) for subtraction, an asterisk (*) for multiplication, and a slash (/) for division.

QUICK TIP
Cell references are determined by the number of columns in each row, not by the number of columns in the table. Rows 9 and 10 have only two columns: A and B.

7. **Select =SUM(ABOVE) in the Formula box, then type =B9–B10**
   You must type an equal sign (=) to indicate that the text following the equal sign (=) is a formula. You want to subtract the budgeted cost in the second column of row 10 from the total cost in the second column of row 9; therefore, you type a formula to subtract the value in cell B10 from the value in cell B9.
8. **Click OK, then save your changes**
   The difference appears in the cell, as shown in **FIGURE 4-19**.

FIGURE 4-17: Cell references in a table

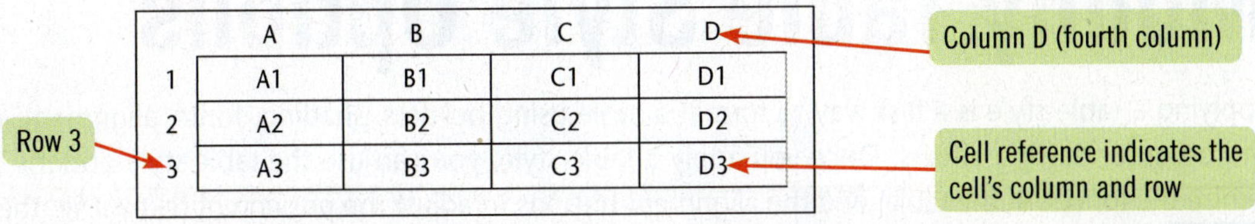

FIGURE 4-18: Formula dialog box

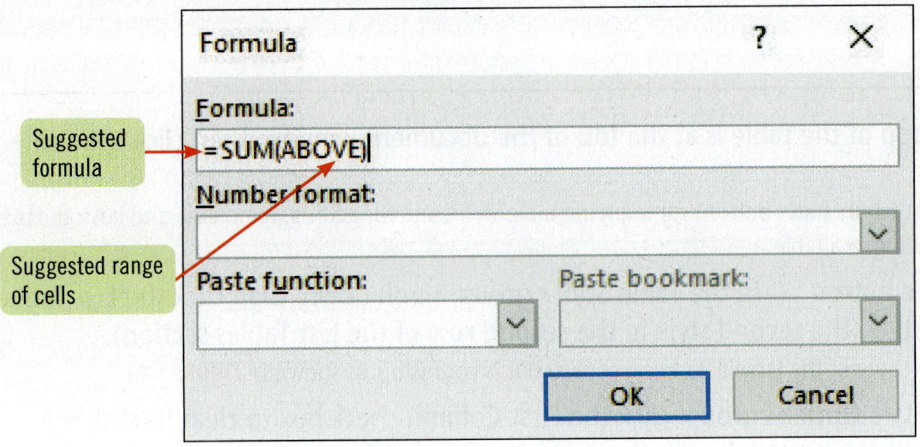

FIGURE 4-19: Difference calculated in table

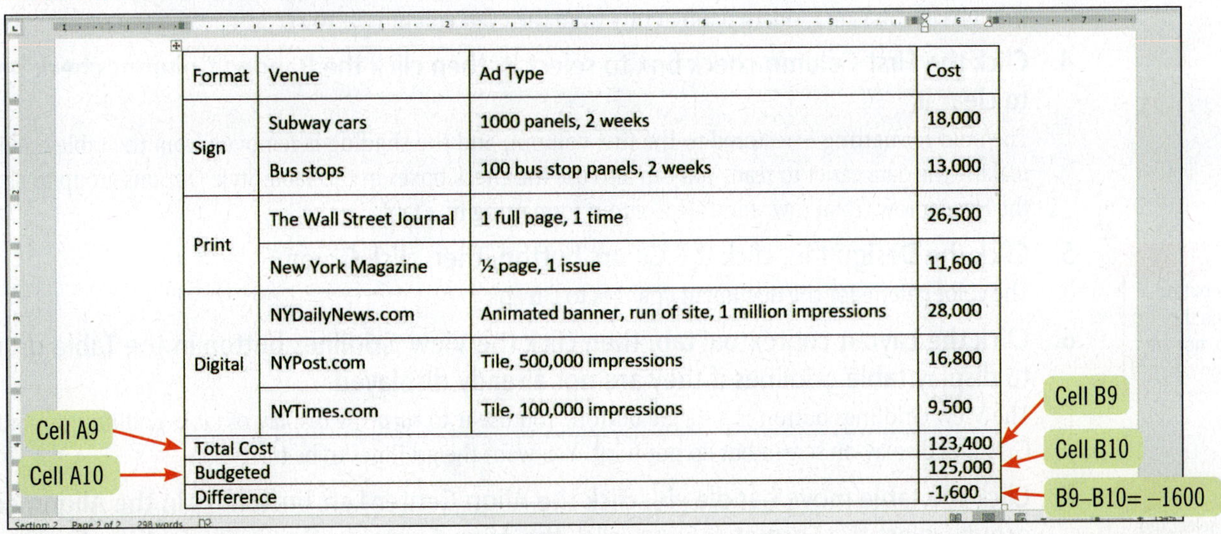

Format	Venue	Ad Type	Cost
Sign	Subway cars	1000 panels, 2 weeks	18,000
	Bus stops	100 bus stop panels, 2 weeks	13,000
Print	The Wall Street Journal	1 full page, 1 time	26,500
	New York Magazine	½ page, 1 issue	11,600
Digital	NYDailyNews.com	Animated banner, run of site, 1 million impressions	28,000
	NYPost.com	Tile, 500,000 impressions	16,800
	NYTimes.com	Tile, 100,000 impressions	9,500
Total Cost			123,400
Budgeted			125,000
Difference			-1,600

Working with formulas

In addition to the SUM function, Word includes formulas for averaging, counting, and rounding data, to name a few. To use a Word formula, delete any text in the Formula box, type =, click the Paste function arrow in the Formula dialog box, select a function, and then insert the cell references of the cells you want to include in the calculation in parentheses after the name of the function. When entering formulas, you must separate cell references by a comma. For example, if you want to average the values in cells A1, B3, and C4, enter the formula =AVERAGE(A1,B3,C4). You must separate cell ranges by a colon. For example, to total the values in cells A1 through A9, enter the formula =SUM(A1:A9). To display the result of a calculation in a particular number format, such as a decimal percentage (0.00%), click the Number format arrow in the Formula dialog box and select a number format. Word inserts the result of a calculation as a field in the selected cell.

Word Module 4

Modify Table Style Options

Learning Outcome
- Format a table
- Align cells in a table

Applying a table style is a fast way to format a table using borders, shading, fonts, alignment, colors, and other formatting effects. Once you apply a table style, you can use the table style options to customize the format of the table, and the alignment buttons to adjust the position of text within the table. **CASE** *You want to enhance the appearance of the table, so you apply a table style to the table, adjust the table style options, and then change the alignment of text in the table cells.*

STEPS

1. **Scroll so the top of the table is at the top of the document window, then click the Table Design tab**

   The Table Design tab includes buttons for applying table styles and for adding, removing, and customizing borders and shading in a table.

QUICK TIP
Click Clear in the gallery of table styles to remove all borders, shading, and other style elements from the table.

2. **Click the More button in the Table Styles group, scroll down, then click the List Table 2 – Accent 1 style (the second style in the second row of the List Tables section)**

   This style makes some of the table data easier to read but is confusing, as shown in **FIGURE 4-20**.

3. **In the Table Style Options group, click the First Column check box to clear it, click the Banded Rows check box to clear it, then click the Banded Columns check box to select it**

   The bold formatting is removed from the first column, the shading is removed from the table rows, and shading is added to the table columns. When the banded columns or banded rows setting is active, the odd columns or rows are formatted differently from the even columns or rows.

4. **Click the First Column check box to select it, then click the Banded Columns check box to clear it**

   The bold formatting is restored to the first column, and the shading is removed from the table columns, making the data easier to read. You can also use the check boxes in the Table Style Options group to change the Header row, Total row, and Last Column formatting in a table.

TROUBLE
The Colors button is located on the Design tab, not the Table Design tab.

5. **Click the Design tab, click the Colors button, then click Green**

   The color palette for the document changes to Green.

6. **Click the Layout contextual tab, then click the View Gridlines button in the Table group to display table gridlines if they are not already displayed**

   The View Gridlines button is a toggle button. You use it to turn the display of table gridlines on and off. Gridlines display on screen but do not print. You want the gridlines to be turned on.

TROUBLE
When you select the Format column, the first column in the last three rows is also selected.

7. **Click the table move handle, click the Align Center Left button in the Alignment group, select the Format column, click the Align Center button, select the Cost column, then click the Align Center Right button**

   First, the data in the table is left-aligned and centered vertically, then the data in the Format column is centered, and finally the data in the Cost column is right-aligned.

QUICK TIP
You can also use the alignment buttons in the Paragraph group on the Home tab to change the alignment of text in a table.

8. **Select the last three rows of the table, click the Bold button B on the Mini toolbar twice, then click the Align Center Right button in the Alignment group on the Layout tab on the Ribbon**

   The text in the last three rows is right-aligned and bold is applied.

9. **Select the first row of the table, click the Center button on the Mini toolbar, click the Font Size arrow on the Mini toolbar, click 12, deselect the row, then save your changes**

   The text in the header row is centered and enlarged, as shown in **FIGURE 4-21**.

FIGURE 4-20: List Table 2 - Accent 1 style applied to table

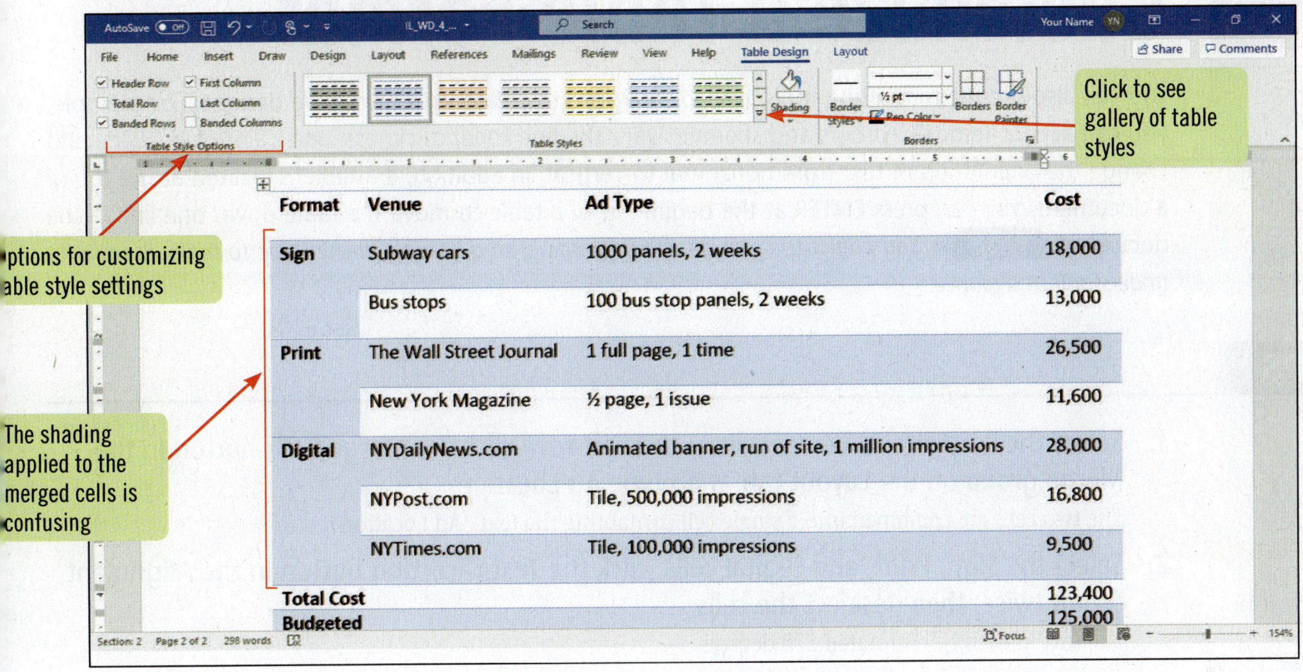

FIGURE 4-21: Table format modified with table style options

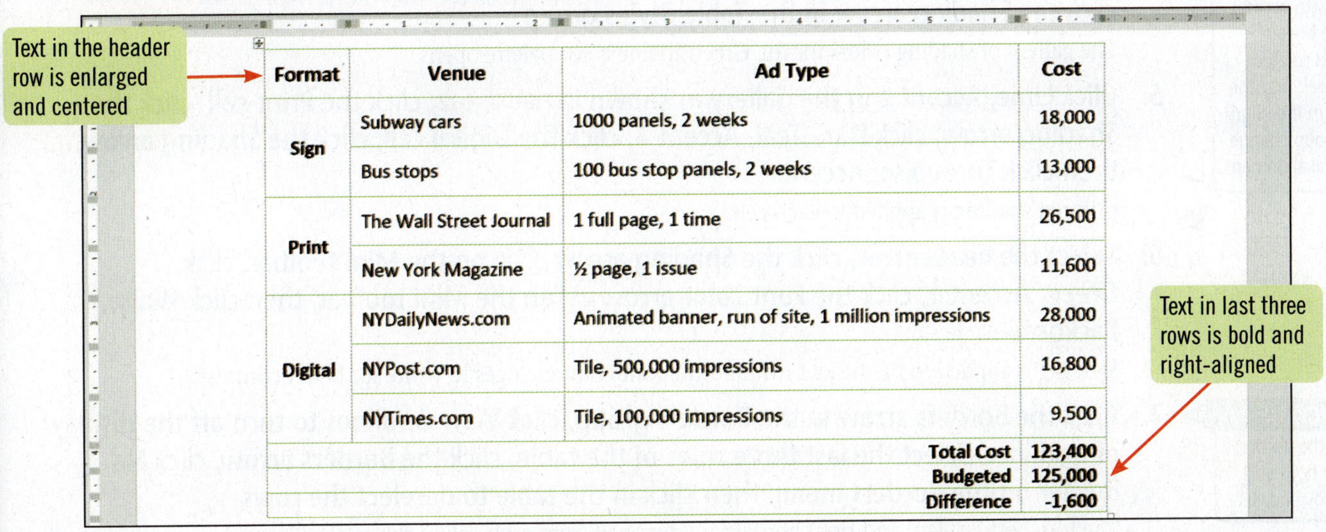

Word
Module 4

Customize a Table Format

Learning Outcomes
- Add shading and borders to a table
- Rotate text

You can also use the formatting tools available in Word to create your own table designs. For example, you can add or remove borders and shading; vary the line style, thickness, and color of borders; and change the orientation of text from horizontal to vertical. In addition, if a table is located at the top of a document, you can press ENTER at the beginning of a table to move the table down one line in the document. **CASE** *You adjust the text direction, shading, and borders in the table to make it easier to understand at a glance.*

STEPS

1. **Select the Format and Venue cells in the first row, click the Merge Cells button in the Merge group on the Layout tab, then type Ad Location**
   The two cells are combined into a single cell containing the text "Ad Location".
2. **Select the Sign, Print, and Digital cells, click the Text Direction button in the Alignment group twice, then deselect the cells**
   The text in each cell is rotated 270 degrees.
3. **Position the pointer over the Sign cell right border until the pointer changes to ⇹, then drag the border left to approximately the ¼" mark on the horizontal ruler**
   The width of the column containing the vertical text narrows.
4. **Click Sign to place the insertion point in the Sign cell, click the Table Design tab, then click the Shading arrow in the Table Styles group**
   The gallery of shading colors for the Green theme color palette opens.
5. **Click Lime, Accent 2 in the gallery as shown in FIGURE 4-22, click the Print cell, click the Shading arrow, click Dark Teal, Accent 4, click the Digital cell, click the Shading arrow, then click Turquoise, Accent 6**
   Colored shading is applied to each cell.
6. **Select the header row, click the Shading arrow on the Mini toolbar, click Green, Accent 1, click the Font color arrow on the Mini toolbar, then click White, Background 1**
   Shading is applied to the header row and the font color changes to white for better contrast.
7. **Click the Borders arrow in the Borders group, click View Gridlines to turn off the display of gridlines, select the last three rows of the table, click the Borders arrow, click No Border on the Borders menu, then click in the table to deselect the rows**
   The top, bottom, left, and right borders are removed from each cell in the selected rows.
8. **Select the Total Cost row, click the Borders arrow, click Top Border, click the 125,000 cell, click the Borders arrow, then click Bottom Border**
   The active border color is black. A black top border is added to the Total Cost row, and a black bottom border is added below 125,000. You can use the buttons in the Borders group to change the active color, line weight, line style, and border style settings before adding a border to a table.
9. **Select the Total Cost row, click the Borders arrow, click Borders and Shading, click the Color arrow, click Green, Accent 1, click the top border in the Preview area, click OK, deselect the row, then save your changes**
   The top border changes to green. The completed table is shown in FIGURE 4-23.

QUICK TIP
In cells with vertical text, the I-beam pointer is rotated 90 degrees, and the buttons in the Alignment group change to vertical alignment.

QUICK TIP
You use the Borders menu to both add and remove borders.

QUICK TIP
To change the color, line weight, line style, or border style of an existing border, adjust the active settings in the Borders group, click the Border Painter button, then click the border with the Border Painter pointer.

FIGURE 4-22: Gallery of shading colors from the Green theme color palette

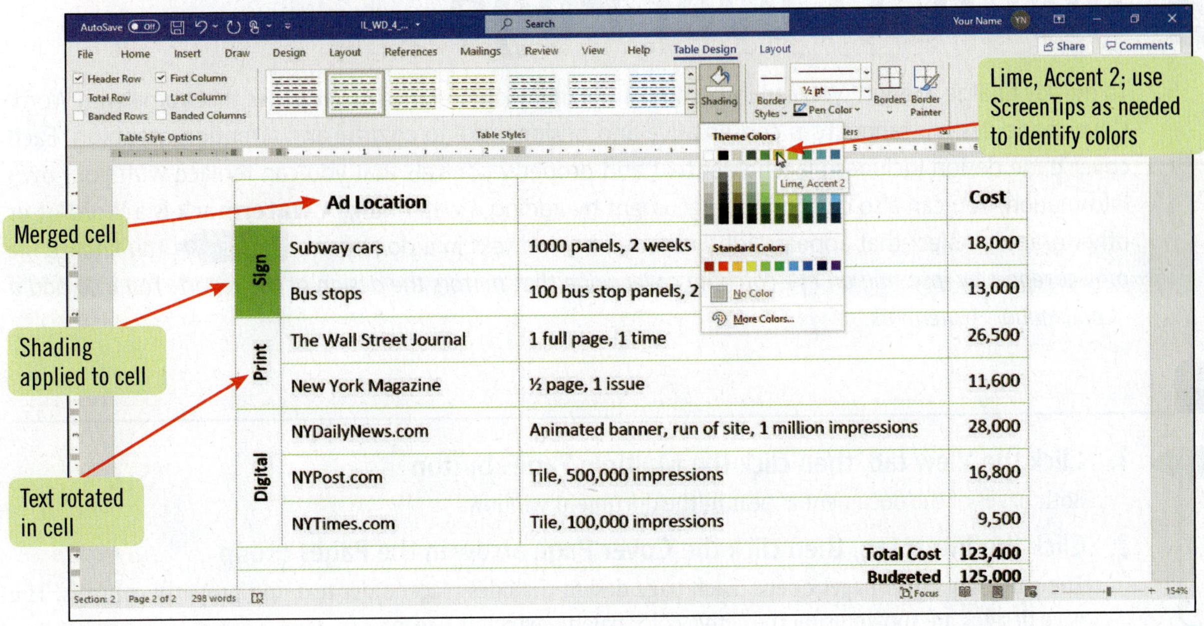

FIGURE 4-23: Completed table

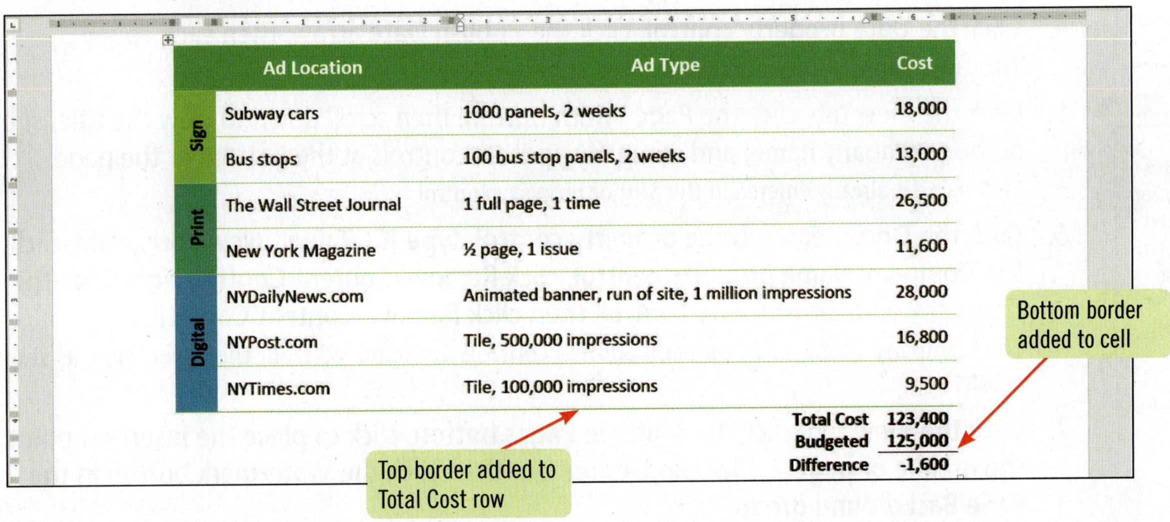

Drawing a table

The Word Draw Table feature allows you to draw table cells exactly where you want them. To draw a table, click the Table button on the Insert tab, and then click Draw Table. If a table is already started, you can click the Draw Table button in the Draw group on the Layout tab to turn on the Draw pointer, and then click and drag to draw a cell. Using the same method, you can draw borders within the cell to create columns and rows, or draw additional cells attached to the first cell. Click the Draw Table button to turn off the draw feature. The borders you draw are added using the active line style, line weight, and pen color settings found in the Borders group on the Table Design tab.

If you want to remove a border from a table, click the Eraser button in the Draw group to activate the Eraser pointer, and then click the border you want to remove. Click the Eraser button to turn off the erase feature. You can use the Draw pointer and the Eraser pointer to change the structure of any table, not just the tables you draw from scratch.

Word Module 4

Insert a Cover Page

Learning Outcomes
- Manage a cover page
- Add a watermark

To quickly finalize a report, you can insert one of the many predesigned cover pages that come with Word. Cover page designs range from conservative and business-like to colorful and attention grabbing. Each cover page design includes placeholder text and property controls that you can replace with your own information. You can also customize a document by adding a watermark. A **watermark** is a WordArt or other graphic object that appears lightly shaded behind text in a document. CASE *You finalize the project report by inserting an eye-catching cover page that mirrors the design of the report. You also add a "Confidential" watermark.*

STEPS

1. **Click the View tab, then click the Multiple Pages button**
   Both pages of the document appear in the document window.
2. **Click the Insert tab, then click the Cover Page arrow in the Pages group**
   The gallery of cover pages opens. Each page design includes placeholder text and property controls. The page designs are shown using the active color palette, which is Green.
3. **Scroll down the gallery, then click Semaphore**
   The Semaphore cover page is added at the beginning of the document. Notice that the document title was added automatically to the Title property control.
4. **Click the Date property control, click the Publish Date arrow, then click Today**
   The date changes to the current date.
5. **Click the View tab, click the Page Width button, then scroll down to view the title, subtitle, author, company name, and company address controls at the bottom of the page**
   Your name is already entered in the Author property control.
6. **Click the Document Subtitle property control, type JCL Talent, New York, right-click the Company Name property control, click Remove Content Control, right-click the Company address property control, then click Remove Content Control**
   The Company Name and Company address controls are removed from the cover page, as shown in FIGURE 4-24.
7. **Click the View tab, click the Multiple Pages button, click to place the insertion point in the middle of page 2, click the Design tab, then click the Watermark button in the Page Background group**
   A gallery of watermarks opens. You can apply one of the preformatted watermarks or create a custom watermark.
8. **Click Confidential 1, then save your changes**
   The word "Confidential" appears lightly shaded behind the text on each page of the document, but not the cover page. The completed document is shown in FIGURE 4-25.
9. **sam Submit the document to your instructor, close the file, then exit Word.**

QUICK TIP
Click the Blank Page button in the Pages group to insert a blank page at the insertion point.

QUICK TIP
To remove a cover page, click the Cover Page arrow, then click Remove Current Cover Page.

TROUBLE
If your name is not entered in the Author property control, right-click the Author control, click Remove Content Control, select the text that remains, then type your name.

QUICK TIP
To remove a watermark, click the Watermark button, then click Remove Watermark.

FIGURE 4-24: Semaphore cover page

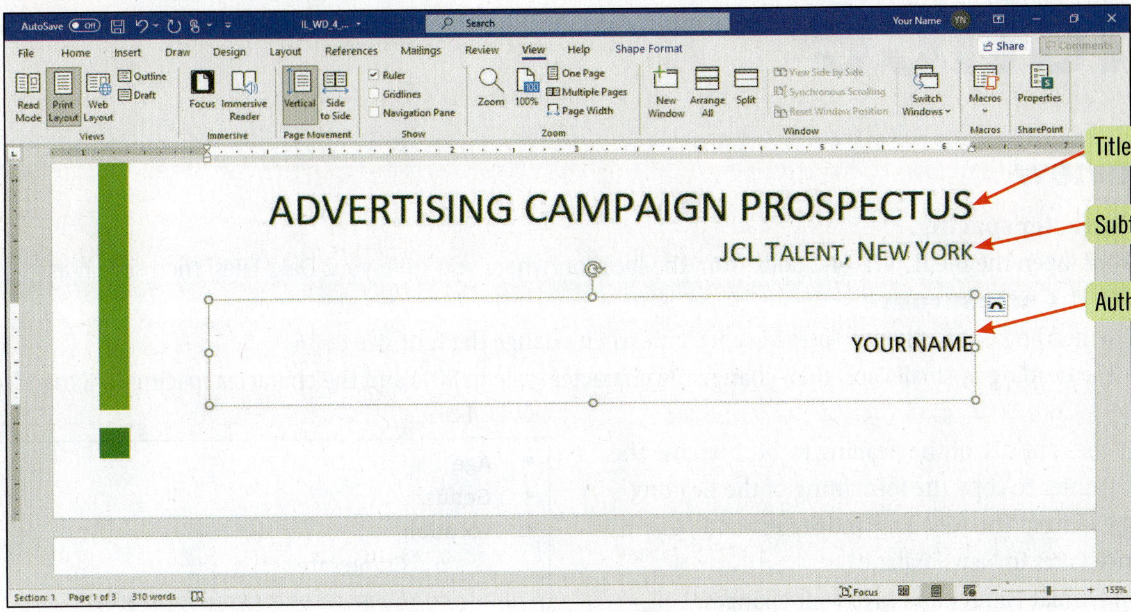

FIGURE 4-25: Completed document

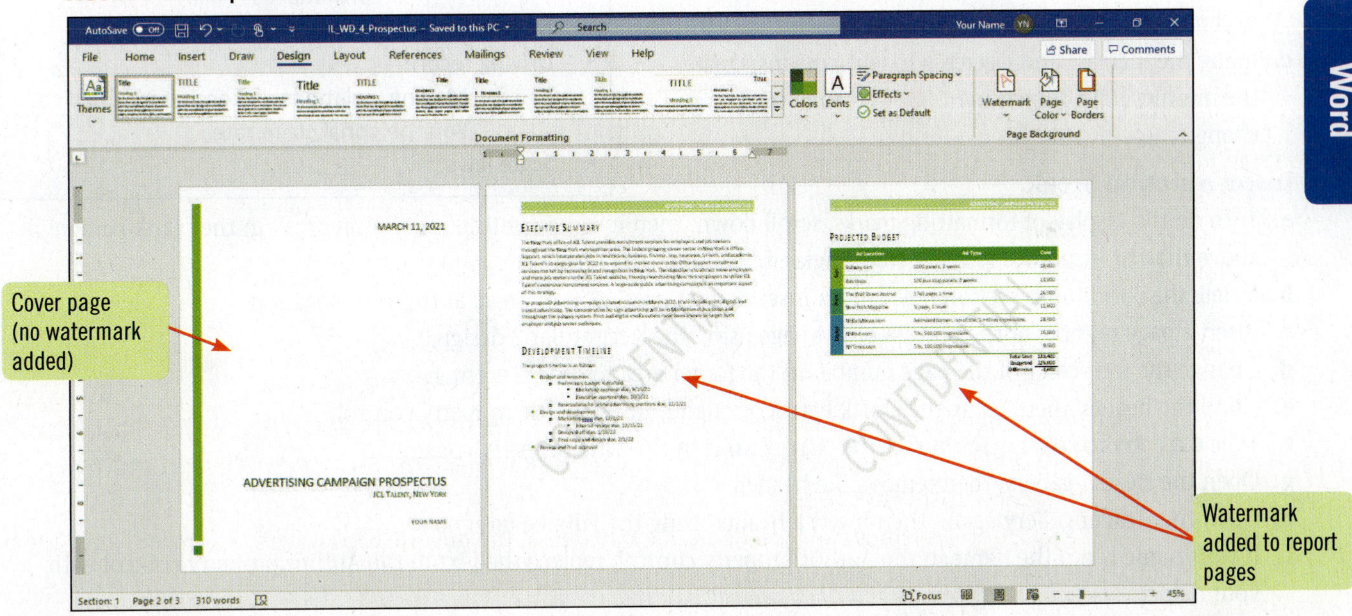

Practice

Skills Review

1. **Modify character spacing.**
   a. Start Word, open the file IL_WD_4-2.docx from the location where you store your Data Files, then save it as **IL_WD_4_CarInsurance**.
   b. Select the heading Car Insurance Rates Vary By State, then change the font size to 36.
   c. Format the heading in small caps, then change the character scale to 80% and the character spacing to Expanded by 1 point.
   d. Change the font size of the heading to 24, then use the Format Painter to copy the formatting of the heading to the headings "The New England States" and "Car Insurance Rates in New England".
   e. Turn off Format Painter and save your changes.
2. **Work with indents.**
   a. Scroll up, select the list that begins with "Age" and ends with "State laws", then apply square bullets to the list.
   b. Change the font color of the bullet characters to Blue, Accent 1.
   c. Using the Increase and Decrease Indent buttons, create the multilevel list shown in FIGURE 4-26, then save your changes.

FIGURE 4-26

- Age
- Gender
- Location
  - Crime rate
  - Claim rates for your local area
  - Percentage of uninsured drivers
  - Weather- and climate-related disaster rate
    - Blizzards, hurricanes, and tornados
    - Wildfires
    - Earthquakes
- Model and year of the car you drive
- Driving record
  - Moving violations and accidents
  - Your personal claim rate
- State laws

3. **Insert a section break.**
   a. Turn on the display of formatting marks, scroll down, then insert a continuous section break in the blank paragraph above the Car Insurance Rates in New England heading.
   b. Delete the continuous section break, then insert a next page section break at the same location.
   c. Insert a page number at the bottom of the page using the Accent Bar 2 design.
   d. Change the font color of the page number in the footer area to Blue, Accent 1.
   e. Go to the header, then, using the Quick Parts command, insert a Title property control.
   f. Type **Car Insurance Rates: New England** in the Title property control.
   g. Open the Header gallery, then remove the header.
   h. Open the Header gallery again, then insert a header using the Filigree design.
   i. If your name is not the name in the Author property control, replace the text in the Author property control with your name.
   j. Close the header area, turn off the display of formatting marks, then save your changes.

Skills Review (continued)

4. **Modify a table.**
   a. Scroll to page 2 to display the table in your document window.
   b. Insert a table row above the Rhode Island row, then type the following text in the new row:

Maine	2506	2038	1176	1199	1116	1163	1189

   c. Delete the New York row, then delete the 65+ column.
   d. Insert a column to the right of the 45F column, type **Nat'l Rank** in the header row, then enter the following numbers in each cell in the column: **39**, **51**, **47**, **5**, **38**, **4**.
   e. Move the Nat'l Rank column to the right of the State column, then save your changes.

5. **Modify rows and columns.**
   a. Double-click the border between the first and second columns to resize the columns.
   b. Drag the border between the second and third columns left to resize the column.
   c. Double-click the right border of the Nat'l Rank, 45M, and 45F columns to resize the columns.
   d. Select the 16M, 16F, 30M, 30F, 45M, and 45F columns, then distribute the columns evenly.
   e. Select rows 2–7, set the row height to exactly .3", then save your changes.

6. **Sort table data.**
   Perform three separate sorts, making sure to select that your list has a header row, as follows:
   a. Sort the table data in descending order by the information in the 45F column, then click OK.
   b. Sort the table data by state in alphabetical order then click OK.
   c. Sort the table data in ascending order by national rank, click OK, then save your changes.

7. **Split and merge cells.**
   a. Insert a row above the header row, then merge the first cell in the new row with the State cell.
   b. Merge the second cell in the new row with the Nat'l Rank cell.
   c. Merge the six remaining blank cells in the first row into a single cell, then type **Average Annual Premium** in the merged cell.
   d. Select the second column (from Nat'l Rank to 51), open the Split Cells dialog box, clear the Merge cells before split check box, then split the cells into two columns.
   e. Type **PD Rank** as the heading for the new column, then enter the following text in the remaining cells in the column: **4**, **8**, **45**, **5**, **27**, and **37**.
   f. Add a new row to the bottom of the table.
   g. Merge the first three cells in the new row, then type **Average Premium** in the merged cell.
   h. AutoFit the content of the table to fit the window, then save your changes.

Skills Review (continued)

8. Perform calculations in tables.

- **a.** Place the insertion point in the last cell in the 16M column.
- **b.** Open the Formula dialog box, delete the text in the Formula box, type **=average(above)**, click the Number format arrow, scroll down, click 0, then click OK.
- **c.** Repeat Step b to insert the average premium in the last cell in the 16F, 30M, 30F, 45M, and 45F columns.
- **d.** Change the value of the 16M premium for Vermont from 1986 to **2500**.
- **e.** Recalculate the average premium for 16M. (*Hint*: Right-click the cell and select Update Field, or use F9.)
- **f.** Type **$** in front of every number in the last row of the table, then save your changes.

9. Modify table style options.

- **a.** Click the Table Design tab, then apply the Grid Table 5 Dark – Accent 1 style to the table.
- **b.** Remove the style from First Column and Banded Rows.
- **c.** Add the Total Row, Last Column, and Banded Columns styles.
- **d.** Add the First Column and Banded Rows styles.
- **e.** Remove all table styles options except the Header Row option.
- **f.** Clear all formatting from the table.
- **g.** Apply the Table Grid Light style (top row) to the table.
- **h.** Apply bold to the 16M, 16F, 30M, 30F, 45M, and 45F column headings, and to the bottom row of the table.
- **i.** Center the table title Car Insurance Rates in New England, then save your changes.

10. Customize a table format.

- **a.** Use the Align Center button in the Alignment group on the Layout tab for the table to center the text in every cell vertically and horizontally.
- **b.** Center right-align the numbers in columns 4–9.
- **c.** Center left-align the state names in column 1, but not the column heading.
- **d.** Center right-align the text in the bottom row. Make sure the text in the header row is still centered.
- **e.** Select all the cells in the header row, including the 16M, 16F, 30M, 30F, 45M, and 45F column headings, apply Blue, Accent 1 shading, then change the font color to White, Background 1.
- **f.** Apply Blue, Accent 1, Lighter 60% shading to the Connecticut, Massachusetts, and Vermont rows.
- **g.** Change the font color of the bottom row to Blue, Accent 1.
- **h.** Add a ½-point white bottom border to the Average Annual Premium cell in the header row, then save your changes. (*Hint*: Click in the cell, then, using the buttons in the Borders group on the Table Design tab, verify that the line style is a single line, verify that the weight is ½ pt, change the pen color to white, click the Border Painter button to turn off the Border Painter, then use the Borders button to apply the bottom border.)

Skills Review (continued)

11. Insert a cover page.

a. Change the view to multiple pages, then insert the Filigree cover page.

b. Remove the Filigree cover page, then insert the Banded cover page.

c. Zoom in on the cover page, verify that the name in the Author property control is your name. If not, remove the property control, select the text that remains, then replace it with your name.

d. Remove the Company Name and Company address controls.

e. Click Title in the Title property control to select the title, change the font size to 48, use the Change Case button to change the case to Capitalize Each Word, then deselect the Title control.

f. Zoom out to see both pages of the document, click page 2, then insert the Confidential 1 watermark.

g. Remove the watermark, insert the Do Not Copy 1 watermark, then save your changes.

h. Compare your document to **FIGURE 4-27**, then make any necessary adjustments.

i. Save your changes, submit a copy to your instructor, close the file, then exit Word.

FIGURE 4-27

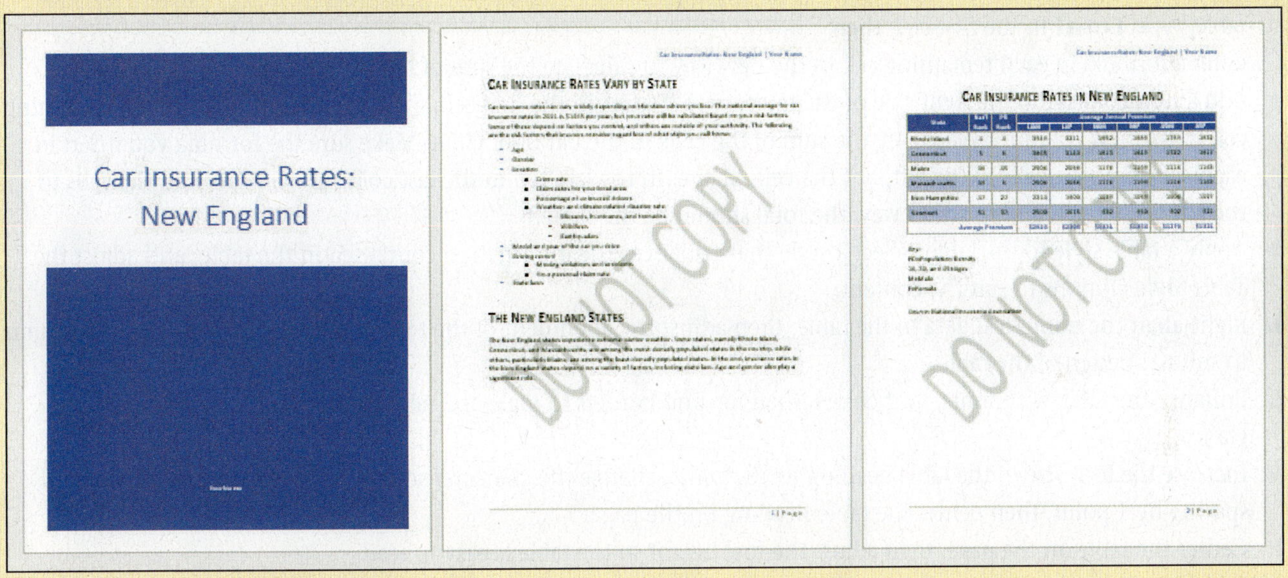

Independent Challenge 1

You work at the Riverwalk Medical Clinic. In preparation for a meeting of the board of directors, you create a summary report that shows quarterly client visits by department for fiscal year 2021. You format the information as a table and prepare the document for presentation to the board.

a. Start Word, then save a new blank document as **IL_WD_4_ClientVisits** to the location where you store your Data Files.

b. Type the table heading **Quarterly Client Visits, Fiscal Year 2021** at the top of the document, then press ENTER.

c. Insert a table with five columns and four rows, then enter the data shown in FIGURE 4-28 into the table, adding rows as necessary. (*Note: Do not format the text or the table at this time.*)

d. Resize the columns to fit the text.

e. Sort the table rows in alphabetical order by Department.

f. Add a new row to the bottom of the table, type **Total** in the first cell, then enter a formula in each remaining cell in the new row to calculate the sum of the cells above it.

FIGURE 4-28

Department	Q1	Q2	Q3	Q4
Mental Health	345	276	421	389
Pediatrics	1168	834	782	1340
Pharmacy	2145	1973	1989	2346
Adult Family Care	867	593	772	1048
Dental	357	298	423	359
Health & Wellness	473	385	381	447
Insurance & Other Support	636	722	578	1245

g. Add a new column to the right side of the table, type **Total** in the first cell, then enter a formula in each remaining cell in the new column to calculate the sum of the cells to the left of it. (*Hint*: Make sure the formula you insert in each cell sums the cells to the left, not the cells above. In the last cell in the last column, you can sum the cells to the left or the cells above; either way, the total should be the same.)

h. Apply a table style to the table. Select a style that enhances the information contained in the table, and adjust the Table Style Options to suit the content.

i. Right-align the numerical data in the table, then adjust the alignment of the text in the header row and first column to suit the design of the table.

j. Enhance the table with fonts, font colors, shading, and borders to make the table attractive and easy to read at a glance.

k. Increase the font size of the table heading to 18 points, change the character scale to 80%, expand the character spacing by 1 point, then center the table heading on the page.

l. Center the table on the page, then adjust the row height so the table is easy to read.

m. Add a header to the document that includes the title property. Type **Riverwalk Medical Clinic** in the Title property control.

n. Add the Ion (Light) cover page to the document. Type **Quarterly Report, Fiscal Year 2021** for the subtitle, add your name as the author, and add the current year for the date.

o. Save your changes, submit the file to your instructor, close the file, then exit Word.

Independent Challenge 2

A well-written and well-formatted résumé gives you an advantage when it comes to getting a job interview. In a winning résumé, the content and format support your career objective and effectively present your background and qualifications. One simple way to create a résumé is to lay out the page using a table. In this exercise you research guidelines for writing and formatting résumés and search for descriptions of job roles that align with your career objective. You then create your own résumé using a table for its layout.

a. Use your favorite search engine to search the web for information on writing and formatting résumés. Use the keywords **resume advice**.

b. Find helpful advice on writing and formatting résumés from at least two websites.

c. Think about the information you want to include in your résumé. The header should include your name, address, telephone number, email address, and other contact information. The body should include your career objective and information on your education, work experience, and skills. You may want to add additional information.

d. Sketch a layout for your résumé using a table as the underlying grid. Include the table rows and columns in your sketch.

e. Start Word, open a new blank document, then save it as **IL_WD_4_Resume** to the location where you store your Data Files.

f. If Intelligent Services is enabled on your system, use the Resume Assistant in Word to research job roles in the industries that interest you. Take note of the top job skills for the job role you would like to have. (*Hint*: Enable Intelligent Services through the Word Options dialog box.)

g. Set appropriate margins, then insert a table to serve as the underlying grid for your résumé. Split and merge cells and adjust the size of the table columns as necessary. **FIGURE 4-29** shows a sample layout for a résumé that uses a table for an underlying structure.

h. Type your résumé in the table cells. Take care to use a professional tone and keep your language to the point.

i. Format your résumé with fonts, bullets, and other formatting features. Adjust the spacing between sections by resizing the table columns and rows.

j. When you are satisfied with the content and format of your résumé, remove the borders from the table, then hide the gridlines if they are visible. You may want to add some borders back to the table to help structure the résumé for readers.

k. Check your résumé for spelling and grammar errors.

l. Save your changes, preview your résumé, submit a copy to your instructor, close the file, then exit Word.

FIGURE 4-29

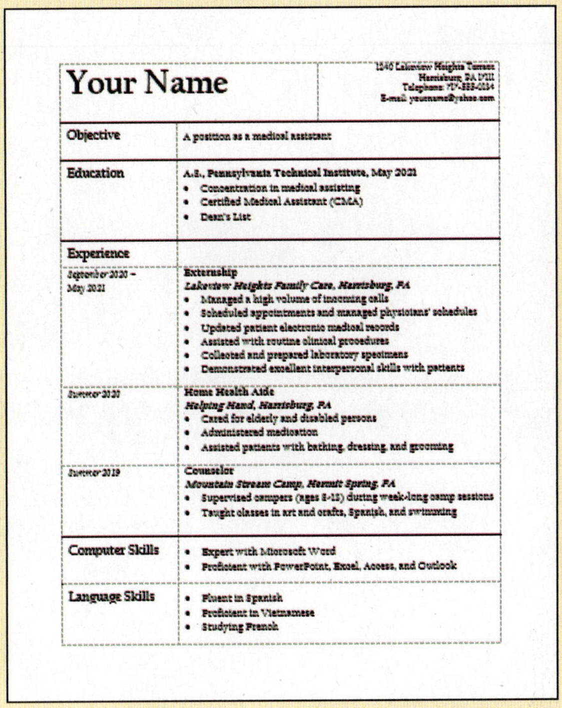
Your Name

E-mail: yourname@yahoo.com

Objective: A position as a medical assistant

Education: A.S., Pennsylvania Technical Institute, May 2021
- Concentration in medical assisting
- Certified Medical Assistant (CMA)
- Dean's List

Experience

September 2020 – May 2021: Externship
Lakeview Heights Family Care, Harrisburg, PA
- Managed a high volume of incoming calls
- Scheduled appointments and managed physicians' schedules
- Updated patient electronic medical records
- Assisted with routine clinical procedures
- Collected and prepared laboratory specimens
- Demonstrated excellent interpersonal skills with patients

Summer 2020: Home Health Aide
Helping Hand, Harrisburg, PA
- Cared for elderly and disabled persons
- Administered medication
- Assisted patients with bathing, dressing, and grooming

Summer 2019: Counselor
Mountain Stream Camp, Hermit Spring, PA
- Supervised campers (ages 8-12) during week-long camp sessions
- Taught classes in art and crafts, Spanish, and swimming

Computer Skills
- Expert with Microsoft Word
- Proficient with PowerPoint, Excel, Access, and Outlook

Language Skills
- Fluent in Spanish
- Proficient in Vietnamese
- Studying French

Word

Visual Workshop

Open the file IL_WD_4-3.docx from the location where you store your Data Files, save it as **IL_WD_4_ProjectedSales**, then format document as shown in **FIGURE 4-30**. The headings are formatted with 80% character scale and character spacing expanded by 0.1 point. The Plain Table 5 table style is applied to the table. The theme colors are Marquee. Add a total row and total column to the table. Sort the table rows by Total in descending order. Use a formula to insert the totals in the Total column and Total row. Type your name in the header, save the document, then submit a copy to your instructor.

FIGURE 4-30

Your Name

The Laghari–Agarwal Group

Projected Sales in Millions, Fiscal Year 2022

	Q1	*Q2*	*Q3*	*Q4*	*Total*
Mumbai	$8.42	$7.81	$9.82	$9.43	**$35.48**
Melbourne	$8.81	$8.51	$6.89	$7.46	**$31.67**
Frankfurt	$8.90	$5.86	$4.95	$9.81	**$29.52**
Dubai	$5.47	$7.44	$5.94	$8.28	**$27.13**
Hong Kong	$5.82	$7.28	$4.77	$8.23	**$26.10**
Mexico City	$6.71	$8.96	$4.68	$4.92	**$25.27**
Seoul	$7.93	$6.83	$3.89	$6.22	**$24.87**
Total	*$52.06*	*$52.69*	*$40.94*	*$54.35*	*$200.04*

Working with Styles, Themes, and Building Blocks

CASE You are preparing a Frequently Asked Questions (FAQ) sheet for JCL Talent. You create a customized style and theme for the FAQ document and then simplify the process of designing the layout of the document by using predesigned building blocks. You save the reusable customized theme and content you created so that you can use easily them again in other JCL Talent documents.

Module Objectives

After completing this module, you will be able to:

- Add hyperlinks
- Modify page margins
- Create paragraph styles
- Format with themes
- Customize a theme
- Insert Quick Parts
- Create building blocks
- Insert building blocks
- Use a document template
- Work with PDF files in Word

Files You Will Need

IL_WD_5-1.docx
IL_WD_5-2.docx
IL_WD_5-3.docx
IL_WD_5-4.docx
IL_WD_5-5.docx
IL_WD_5-6.docx
IL_WD_5-7.docx

Word
Module 5

Add Hyperlinks

Learning Outcomes
- Insert a hyperlink
- Share documents

A **hyperlink** is text or a graphic that, when clicked, "jumps" the viewer to a different location or program. When a document is viewed on screen, hyperlinks allow readers to link (or jump) to a webpage, an email address, a file, or a specific location in a document. When you create a hyperlink in a document, you select the text or graphic you want to use as a hyperlink, and then you specify the location you want to jump to when the hyperlink is clicked. You create a hyperlink using the Link button in the Links group on the Insert tab. Text that is formatted as a hyperlink appears as colored, underlined text. **CASE** *JCL clients will receive the FAQ document by email or view it on the JCL website. To make it easier for these people to access additional information, you add several hyperlinks to the document.*

STEPS

1. **sam Start Word, open the file IL_WD_5-1.docx from the location where you store your Data Files, save it as IL_WD_5_EmployerFAQ, then drag the Zoom slider to 120**
   The document includes FAQ (Frequently Asked Questions), the JCL logo, and a preformatted sidebar. A **sidebar** is a text box that is positioned adjacent to the body of a document and contains auxiliary information.

QUICK TIP
By default, Word automatically creates a hyperlink to an email address or URL when you type an email address or a URL in a document.

2. **Select send us an email in the first body paragraph, click the Insert tab, then click the Link button in the Links group**
   The Insert Hyperlink dialog box opens, as shown in **FIGURE 5-1**. You use this dialog box to specify the location you want to jump to when the hyperlink—in this case, "send us an email"—is clicked.
3. **Click E-mail Address in the Link to section**
   The Insert Hyperlink dialog box changes so you can create a hyperlink to an email address.
4. **Type your email address in the E-mail address box, type Employer Inquiry in the Subject box, then click OK**
   As you type, Word automatically adds mailto: in front of your email address. After you close the dialog box, the hyperlink text—send us an email—is formatted in blue and underlined. Before distributing a document, it's important to test any hyperlinks you added.

TROUBLE
If an email message does not open, close any window that opens and continue with Step 7.

5. **Press and hold CTRL, then click the send us an email hyperlink**
   An email message addressed to you with the subject "Employer Inquiry" opens in the default email program.
6. **Close the email message window, clicking No if you are prompted to save**
   The hyperlink text changed color, indicating the hyperlink has been followed.

QUICK TIP
To remove a hyperlink, right-click it, then click Remove Hyperlink. Removing a hyperlink removes the link, but the text remains.

7. **Scroll down, select Find an office near you in the second paragraph, click the Link button, click Existing File or Web Page in the Link to section of the Insert Hyperlink dialog box, type www.jcltalent.com in the Address box, then click OK**
   As you type the web address, Word automatically adds "http://" in front of "www." The text "Find an office near you" is formatted as a hyperlink to the JCL Talent home page www.jcltalent.com. When clicked, the hyperlink will open the webpage in the default browser window. If you point to a hyperlink in Word, the link to the location appears in a ScreenTip. You can edit ScreenTip text to make it more descriptive.

QUICK TIP
You can also edit the hyperlink destination or the hyperlink text.

8. **Right-click office in the Find an office near you hyperlink, click Edit Hyperlink, click ScreenTip in the Edit Hyperlink dialog box, type Search for JCL Talent locations in the ScreenTip text box, click OK, click OK, save your changes, then point to the Find an office near you hyperlink in the document**
   The ScreenTip you created appears above the Find an office near you hyperlink, as shown in **FIGURE 5-2**.

FIGURE 5-1: Insert Hyperlink dialog box

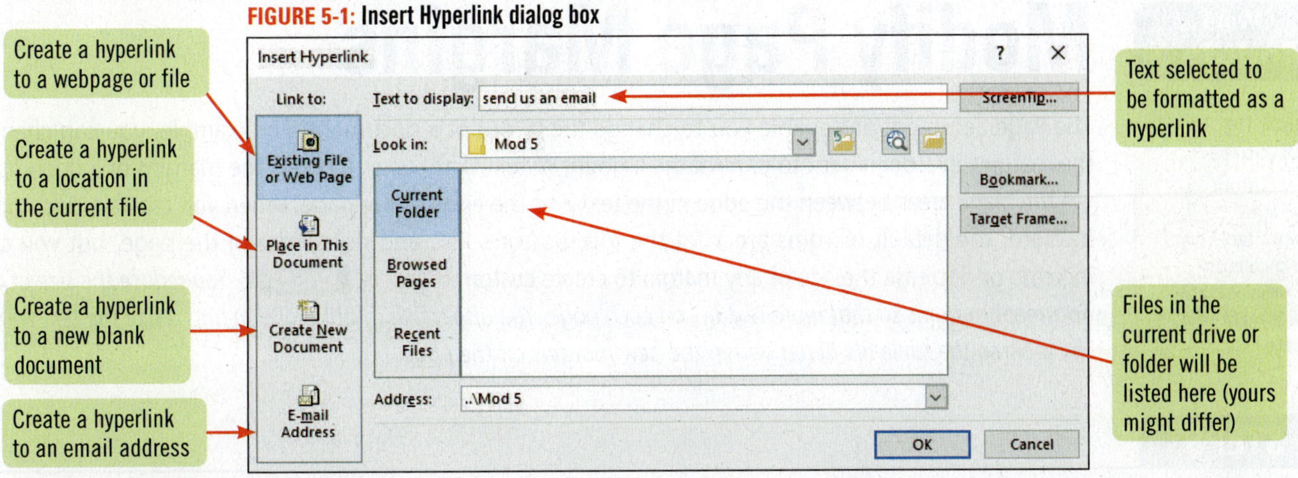

FIGURE 5-2: Hyperlinks in the document

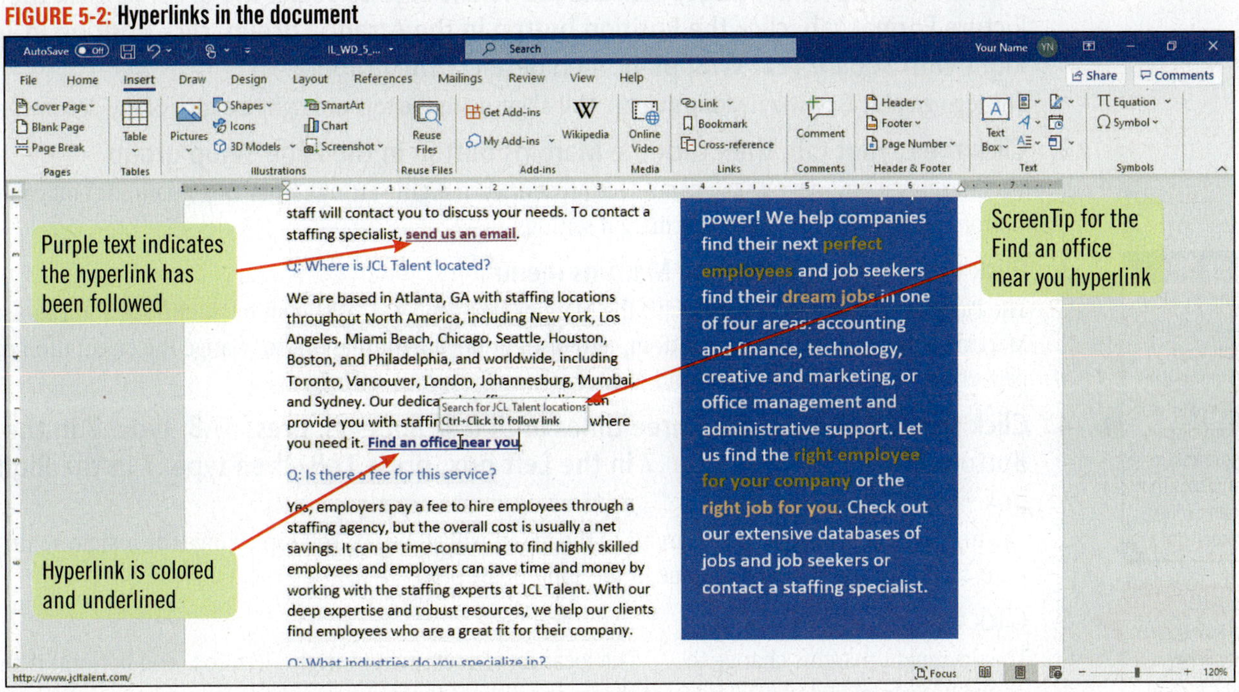

Sharing documents from Word and checking compatibility

Word includes several options for distributing and sharing documents over the Internet directly from within Word, including saving a document to OneDrive for others to view and edit, emailing a document, presenting a document online so others can view it in a web browser, sending an Adobe pdf to others for review, and posting a document to a blog. To share a document, open the file in Word, click the File tab, click Share, then click one of the Share options. You can also use the Share button on the title bar to save a document to an online location.

When you email a document from within Word, the document is sent as an attachment to an email message using your default email program. You can choose to attach the document as a Word file, a .pdf file, or an .xps file, or to send it as an Internet fax. When you click an option, a message window opens that includes the filename of the current file as the message subject and the file as an attachment. Type the email address(es) of the recipient(s) in the To and Cc boxes, type any message you want in the message window, then click Send. The default email program sends a copy of the document to each recipient. Note that faxing a document directly from Word requires registration with a third-party Internet fax service.

Before you share a document with others, it's a good idea to check it for compatibility with previous versions of Word. Click the File tab, click Info, click Check for Issues, click Check Compatibility, select the versions you want to check for in the Microsoft Word Compatibility Checker dialog box, then click OK.

Word
Module 5

Modify Page Margins

Learning Outcomes
- Set custom margins
- Move table rows and columns
- Change vertical alignment of a page

The Page Setup options enable you to change the layout of a document. For example, you can change the margins in a document to control the amount of text that fits on a page. The margins of a document are the blank areas between the edge of the text and the edge of the page. When you create a document in Word, the default margins are 1" at the top, bottom, left, and right sides of the page, but you can increase or decrease the size of any margin to create custom margins. **CASE** *You reduce the size of the document margins so that more text fits on each page. You also move a table column and resize the text within the table so the table fits better within the new margins on the page.*

STEPS

1. **Scroll to the top of the page, click the JCL Talent logo to select the graphic, click the Picture Format tab, click the Position button in the Arrange group, click Position in Top Right with Square Text Wrapping, then deselect the graphic**

   The logo graphic is now a floating graphic that aligns with the top and right margins of the document.

2. **Click the Layout tab, then click the Margins button in the Page Setup group**

   The Margins menu opens. You can select predefined margin settings from this menu, or you can click Custom Margins to create different margin settings.

3. **Click Custom Margins on the Margins menu**

   The Page Setup dialog box opens with the Margins tab displayed, as shown in **FIGURE 5-3**. You can use the Margins tab to change the top, bottom, left, or right document margin, to change the orientation of the pages from portrait to landscape, and to alter other page layout settings.

QUICK TIP
The minimum allowable margin settings depend on your printer and the size of the paper you are using. Word displays a warning message if you set margins that are too narrow for your printer.

4. **Click the Top down arrow three times until 0.7" appears, press TAB, type .7 in the Bottom box, press TAB, type .7 in the Left box, press TAB, then type .7 in the Right box**

   The top, bottom, left, and right margins of the report will all be .7". You can change the margin settings by using the arrows or by typing a value in the appropriate box.

TROUBLE
Click the Ruler check box in the Show group on the View tab to display the rulers if they are not already displayed.

5. **Click OK**

   The document margins change to .7". The location of each margin (right, left, top, and bottom) is shown on the horizontal and vertical rulers at the intersection of the white and shaded areas.

6. **Scroll until the Sample Timesheet table on page 2 is at the top of the document window, then click the Home tab**

QUICK TIP
To copy or move a table row, select the row, click the Copy or Cut button in the Clipboard group, place the insertion point in the location you want to insert the row, then click the Paste button. Use the Paste Options button to determine the formatting of a pasted column or row.

7. **Place the pointer over the top of the second column in the table, click to select the Day column, click the Cut button in the Clipboard group, click in the Date cell, then click the Paste button in the Clipboard group**

   The Day column moves to become the first column in the table.

8. **Click in the table, click the Layout contextual tab for tables, click the AutoFit button in the Cell Size group, click AutoFit Window, click the View tab, click the Multiple Pages button in the Zoom group, then save your changes**

   The table is resized to fit the new margin settings, as shown in **FIGURE 5-4**.

FIGURE 5-3: Margins tab in Page Setup dialog box

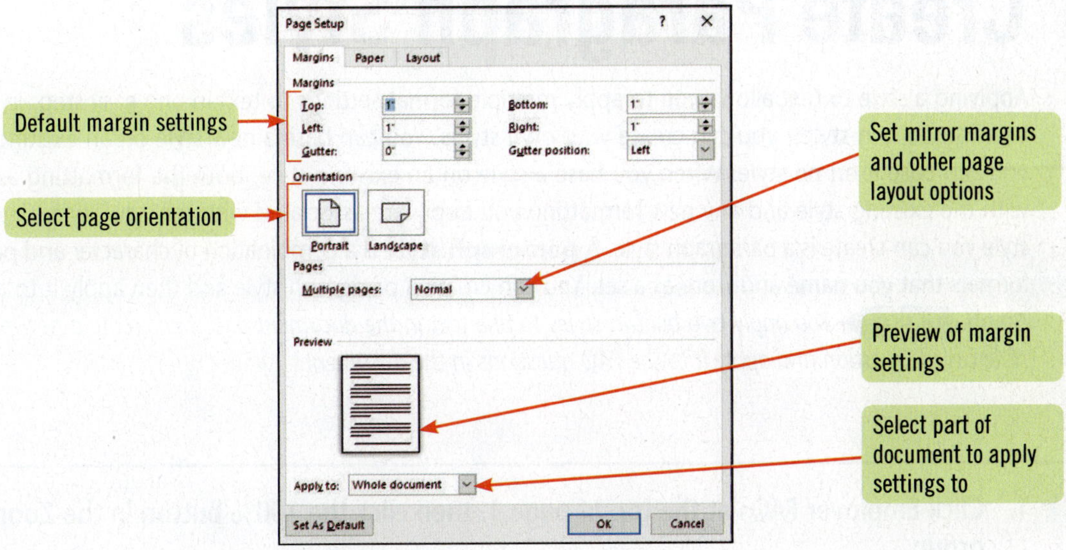

FIGURE 5-4: Document with smaller margins

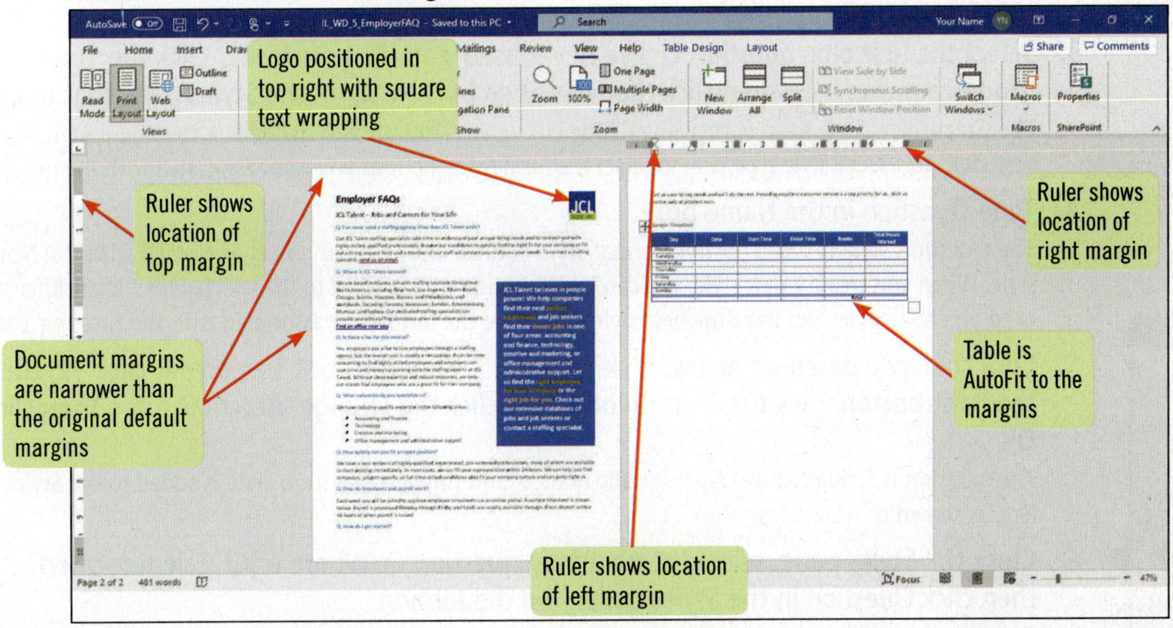

Changing vertical alignment

By default, text is aligned vertically at the top margin of a document, but you can change the vertical alignment of text to align with the bottom margin, to be centered between the top and bottom margins, or to be justified. To change the vertical alignment of text, click the Layout tab in the Page Setup dialog box, click the Vertical alignment arrow, then click the alignment option you want. Using the Apply to arrow on the Layout tab, you can choose to apply the vertical alignment settings to the whole document, to the current section, or to the current section and all sections that follow it. When you are finished, click OK.

Word
Module 5

Create Paragraph Styles

Learning Outcomes
- Create styles
- Resolve style conflicts
- Create web pages

Applying a style to text allows you to apply multiple format settings to text in one easy step. In addition to using built-in styles, you can create your own styles. You can base a new style on an existing style or you can base it on no style. When you base a style on an existing style, both the formatting associated with the existing style and any new formatting you apply are associated with the new style. One type of style you can create is a paragraph style. A **paragraph style** is a combination of character and paragraph formats that you name and store as a set. You can create a paragraph style and then apply it to any paragraph. CASE *You apply two built-in styles to title text in the document and then create a new paragraph style called Question and apply it to the FAQ questions in the document.*

STEPS

1. **Click Employer FAQs at the top of page 1, then click the 100% button in the Zoom group**
2. **Select the title Employer FAQs, click the Home tab, click Title in the Styles group, select the subtitle JCL Talent – Jobs and Careers for Your Life, then click Subtitle in the Styles group**
   The built-in Title and Subtitle styles are applied to the selected text.
3. **Select the first blue question Q: I've never used a staffing agency..., click the Styles group Launcher, then click the New Style button in the Styles pane that opens**
   The Create New Style from Formatting dialog box opens. You use this dialog box to enter a name for the new style, to select a style type, and to select the formatting options you want associated with the new style.
4. **Type Question in the Name box**
   The Question style is based on the Normal style because the selected text is formatted with the Normal style. When you create a new style, you can base it on the style applied to the selected text, to another style, or to no preset style. You want the new style to include the formatting associated with the Heading 1 style.
5. **Click the Style based on arrow, click Heading 1, click the Font Size arrow, click 12, click the Italic button, click the Font Color arrow, click the Orange, Accent 2 color, then click OK**
   The question is formatted in 12-point italic orange, and the new Question style is added to the Styles gallery, as shown in FIGURE 5-5.
6. **Close the Styles pane, select the next blue question Q: Where is JCL Talent located?, then click Question in the Styles gallery on the Ribbon**
   The new Question style is applied to the selected text.
7. **Scroll down and apply the Question style to the remaining five blue questions in the document, then press CTRL+HOME**
   The new Question style is applied to every FAQ question in the document.
8. **Click in the first orange question, then press SHIFT+F1**
   The Reveal Formatting pane opens, as shown in FIGURE 5-6. This pane lists exactly which styles and formats are applied to the character, paragraphs, and section of the selected text.
9. **Click several other paragraphs, notice the format settings in the Reveal Formatting pane for each paragraph, close the Reveal Formatting pane, close all other panes if necessary, then save your changes**

TROUBLE
Don't be concerned if the logo graphic is also selected. The graphic is anchored to the Employer FAQs paragraph.

QUICK TIP
When you paste text or a table to which a style has been applied, use the Paste Options button to determine the formatting of the pasted text or table. To paste with the original style formatting intact, use the Keep Source Formatting option.

QUICK TIP
Another way to open the Reveal Formatting pane is to click the Launcher in the Styles group, click the Style Inspector button in the Styles pane, then click the Reveal Formatting button.

FIGURE 5-5: New style in Styles gallery

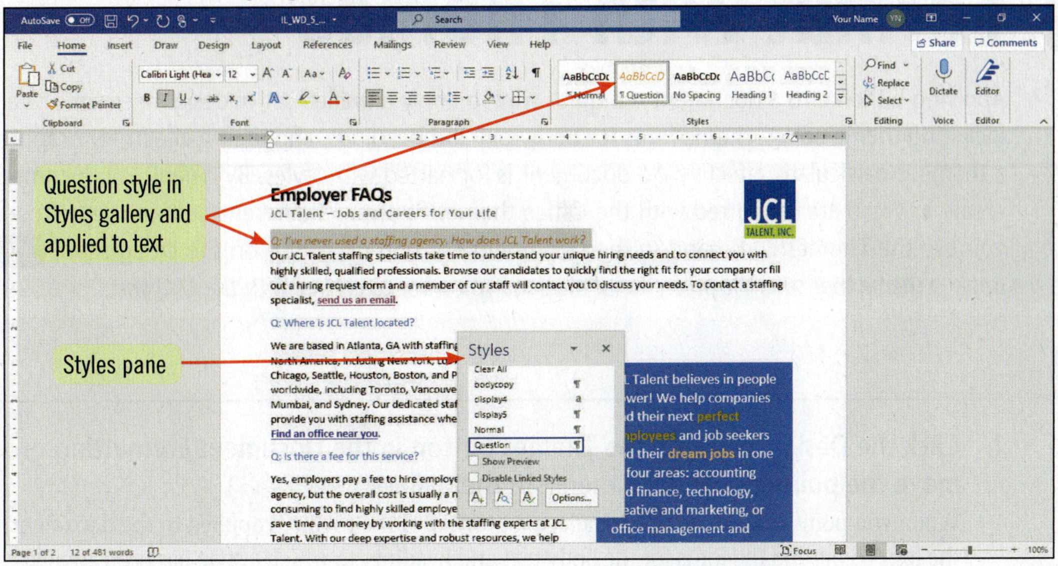

FIGURE 5-6: Reveal Formatting pane

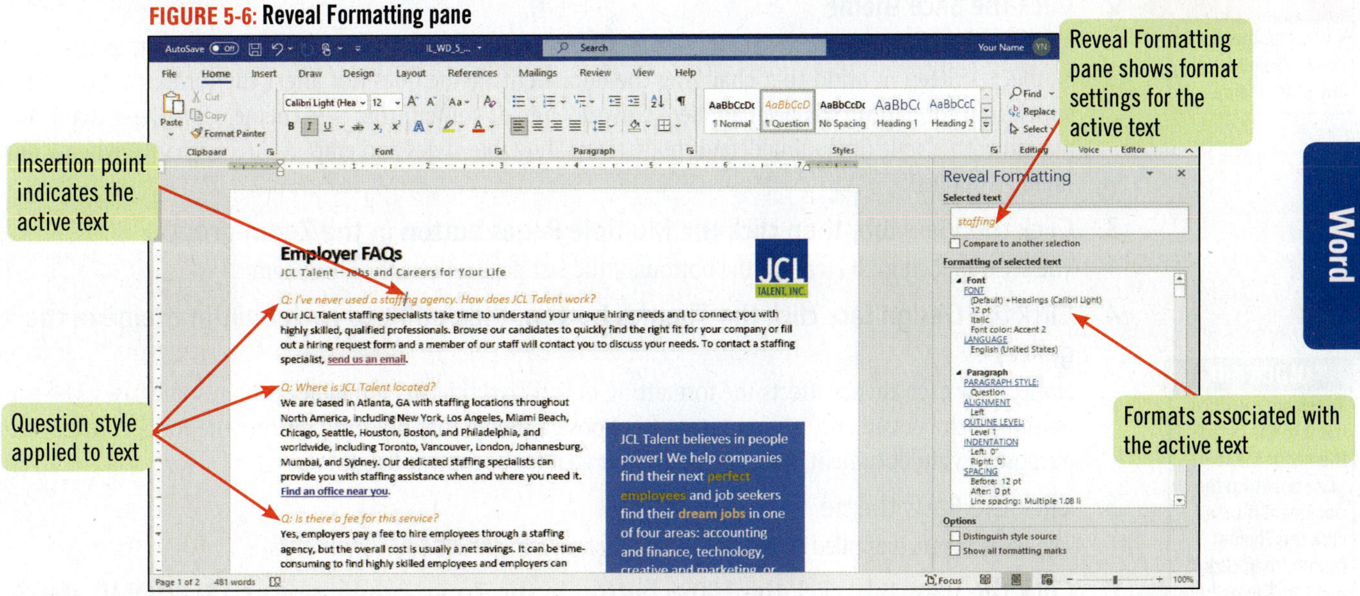

Saving a document as a webpage

Creating a webpage and posting it on the Internet or an intranet is a powerful way to share information with other people. You can design a webpage from scratch in Word, or you can use the Save As command to save an existing document in HTML format so it can be viewed with a browser. When you save an existing document as a webpage, Word converts the content and formatting of the Word file to HTML and displays the webpage in Web Layout view, which shows the webpage as it will appear in a browser. Any formatting that is not supported by web browsers is either converted to similar supported formatting or removed from the webpage.

To save a document as a webpage, open the Save As dialog box, and then select a Web Page format in the Save as type list. You have the option of saving the document in Single File Web Page (.mht or .mhtml) format, or in Web Page or Web Page, Filtered (.htm or .html) format. In a single file webpage, all the elements of the webpage, including the text and graphics, are saved together in a single MIME encapsulated aggregate HTML (MHTML) file, making it simple to publish your webpage or send it via email. By contrast, if you choose to save a webpage as an .htm file, Word automatically creates a supporting folder in the same location as the .htm file. This folder has the same name as the .htm file plus the suffix files, and it houses the supporting files associated with the webpage, such as graphics.

Format with Themes

Learning Outcomes
- Apply a theme
- Change the style set
- Change the default theme

Applying a theme to a document is a quick way to apply a unified set of design elements to a document, including theme colors, theme fonts for body text and headings, and theme effects for graphics. Applying a theme is particularly effective if a document is formatted with styles. By default, all documents that you create in Word are formatted with the Office theme. To apply a different built-in theme to a document, you use the Themes command in the Document Formatting group on the Design tab. **CASE** *You apply a theme that suits the professional message you want to convey with the FAQ sheet.*

STEPS

TROUBLE
If the Slice theme is not available, select any other theme.

QUICK TIP
To restore the document to the default theme for the template on which the document is based, click the Themes button, then click Reset to Theme from Template.

1. **Click the Design tab, click the Themes button in the Document Formatting group, then move the pointer over each theme in the gallery**
   When you point to a theme in the gallery, a preview of the theme is applied to the document. Notice that the font colors and the fonts for the body text and headings to which a style has been applied change when you preview each theme.
2. **Click the Slice theme**
   A complete set of new theme colors, fonts, styles, and effects is applied to the document, as shown in FIGURE 5-7. Keep in mind that changing the document theme does not affect the formatting of text to which font formatting has been applied. Only document content that uses theme colors, text that is formatted with a style (including default body text), and table styles and graphic effects change when a new theme is applied.
3. **Click the View tab, then click the Multiple Pages button in the Zoom group**
   The style applied to the table at the bottom of the last page reflects the Slice theme.
4. **Click the Design tab, click the Themes button, then point to each built-in theme in the gallery**
   Notice how each theme affects the formatting of the text, sidebar, and table, and, in some cases, the pagination of the document. It's important to choose a theme that not only mirrors the tone, content, and purpose of your document, but also meets your goal for document length.
5. **Click the Basis theme**
   The Basis theme is applied to the document as shown in FIGURE 5-8.
6. **Click the View tab, click the 100% button in the Zoom group, press CTRL+HOME, then save your changes**

Changing the style set

Applying a different style set is another quick way to change the look of an entire document. Style sets include font and paragraph settings for headings and body text so that when you apply a new style set to a document, all the body text and all the headings that have been formatted with a style change to the format settings for the active style set. You apply styles to a document using the styles available in the Styles group on the Home tab. You apply a style set using the style sets available in the Document Formatting group on the Design tab.

You can also save a group of font and paragraph settings as a new style set. To do this, click the More button in the Document Formatting group, then click Save as a New Style Set. If you want to return a document to its original style set, click the More button, then click Reset to the Default Style Set.

FIGURE 5-7: Slice theme applied to document

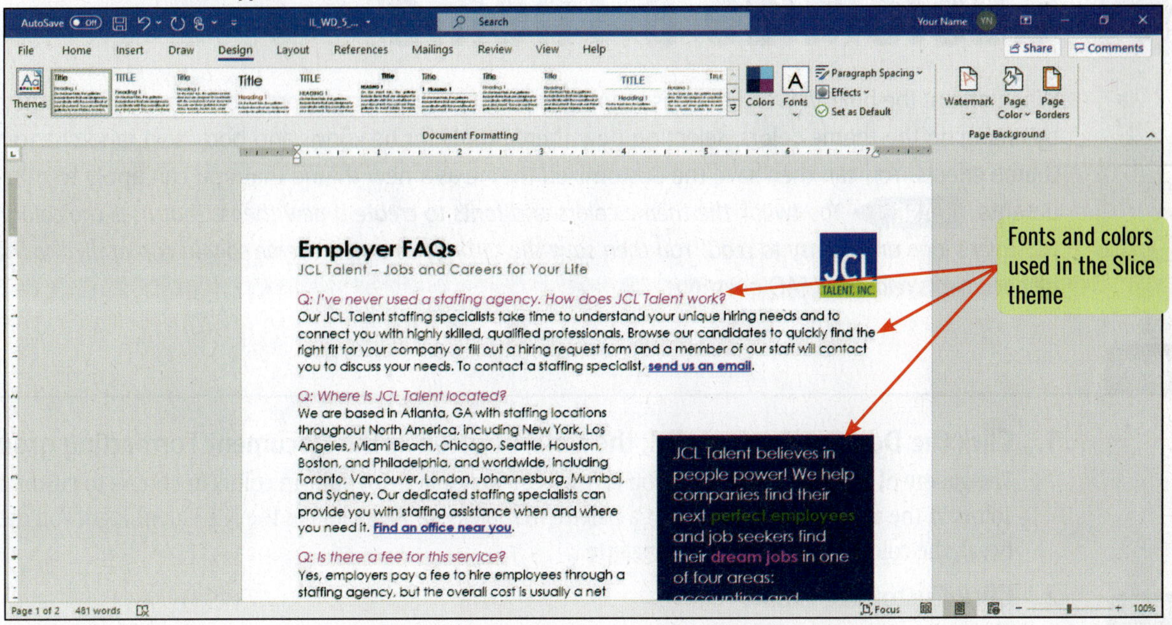

FIGURE 5-8: Basis theme applied to document

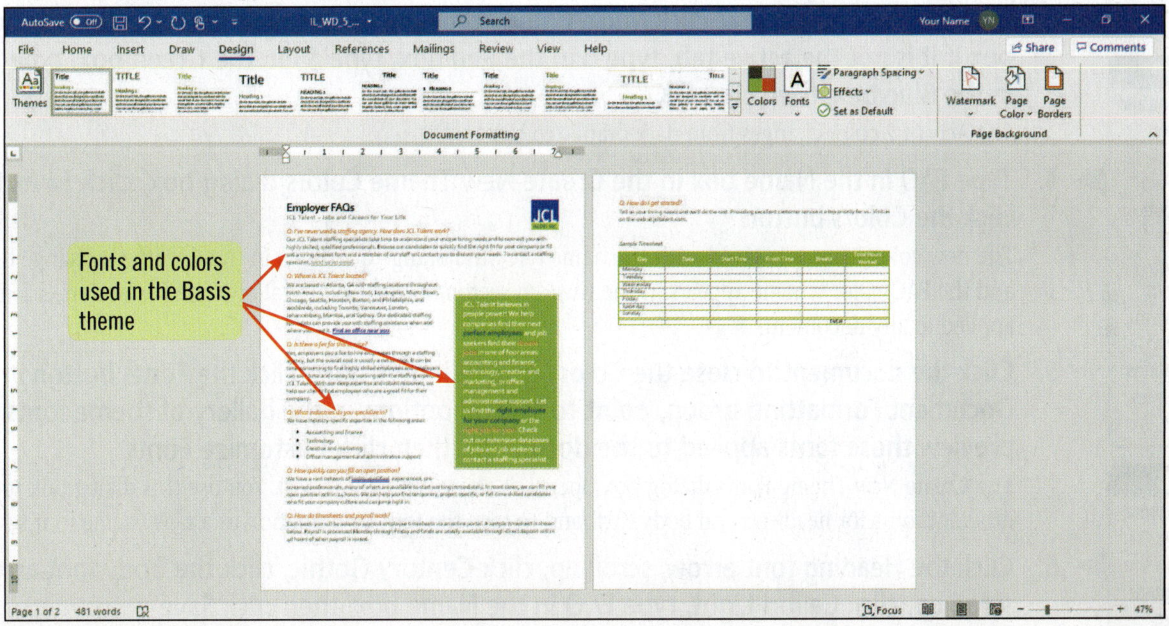

Changing the default theme

By default, all new documents created in Word are formatted with the Office theme, but you can change your settings to use a different theme as the default. To change the default theme to a different built-in theme, press CTRL+N to open a new blank document, click the Themes button in the Document Formatting group on the Design tab, and then click the theme you want to use as the default. If you want to customize the theme before saving it as the new default, use the Colors, Fonts, and Effects buttons in the Document Formatting group to customize the settings for theme colors, fonts, and effects. Alternatively, click the More button in the Document Formatting group then select a new style set to use in the new default theme. When you are satisfied with the settings for the new default theme, click the Set as Default button in the Document Formatting group. The Themes gallery will be updated to reflect your changes.

Word
Module 5

Customize a Theme

Learning Outcomes
- Customize theme colors and fonts
- Save a custom theme

When one of the built-in Word themes is not quite right for your document, you can customize the theme by changing the theme colors, selecting new theme fonts for headings and body text, and changing the theme effects. You can then save the customized theme as a new theme that you can apply to other documents. **CASE** *You tweak the theme colors and fonts to create a new theme that uses the colors of the JCL Talent logo and is easy to read. You then save the settings as a new theme so you can apply the theme to all documents related to FAQ questions.*

STEPS

1. **Click the Design tab, then click the Colors button in the Document Formatting group**
The gallery of theme colors opens. You can select a new palette of built-in colors or choose to customize the colors in the active palette. You want a palette that picks up the colors of the JCL Talent logo. You decide to tweak the colors in the Basis theme palette.

2. **Click Customize Colors**
The Create New Theme Colors dialog box opens and shows the color palette from the Basis theme, as shown in FIGURE 5-9. You use this dialog box to change the colors in the active palette and to save the set of colors you create with a new name.

3. **Click the Accent 2 arrow, click More Colors, click the Custom tab in the Colors dialog box if it is not the active tab, type 0 in the Red box, type 51 in the Green box, type 153 in the Blue box, then click OK**
The Accent 2 color changes from dark orange to blue.

4. **Type FAQ in the Name box in the Create New Theme Colors dialog box, click Save, then click the Colors button**
The new color scheme is saved with the name FAQ, the orange questions in the document change to blue, and the FAQ color scheme appears in the Custom section in the Colors gallery. The FAQ colors can now be applied to any document.

5. **Click the document to close the Colors gallery if necessary, click the Fonts button in the Document Formatting group, point to several options in the gallery of theme fonts to preview those fonts applied to the document, then click Customize Fonts**
The Create New Theme Fonts dialog box opens, as shown in FIGURE 5-10. You use this dialog box to select different fonts for headings and body text, and to save the font combination as a new theme font set.

6. **Click the Heading font arrow, scroll up, click Century Gothic, click the Body font arrow, scroll up, click Calibri Light, type FAQ in the Name box, then click Save**
The font of the headings in the report changes to Century Gothic, the font of the body text changes to Calibri Light, and the FAQ theme font set is added to the Custom section of the Fonts gallery.

7. **Click the Themes button, click Save Current Theme, type FAQ in the File name box in the Save Current Theme dialog box, then click Save**
The FAQ theme colors and FAQ theme fonts are saved together as a new theme called FAQ in the default location for document themes.

8. **Save your changes, then click the Themes button**
The new theme appears in the Custom section of the Themes gallery, as shown in FIGURE 5-11.

QUICK TIP
To remove a custom color palette from the gallery, right-click the palette, then click Delete.

QUICK TIP
To change the line and paragraph spacing applied to a document, click the Paragraph Spacing button in the Document Formatting group, then click a Built-In style or click Custom Paragraph Spacing to enter custom settings in the Manage Styles dialog box.

QUICK TIP
To customize theme effects, click the Effects button in the Document Formatting group, then select an effect from the gallery.

QUICK TIP
To remove a custom theme from the gallery, right-click the theme, then click Delete.

FIGURE 5-9: Create New Theme Colors dialog box

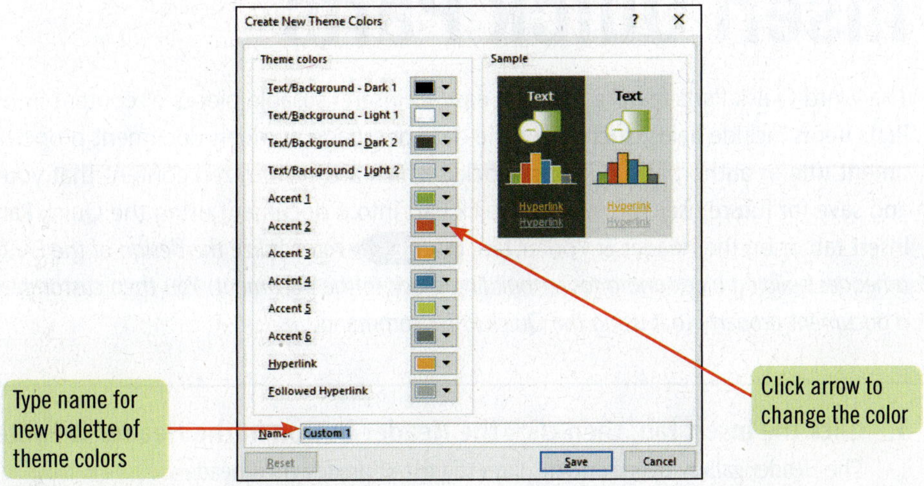

FIGURE 5-10: Create New Theme Fonts dialog box

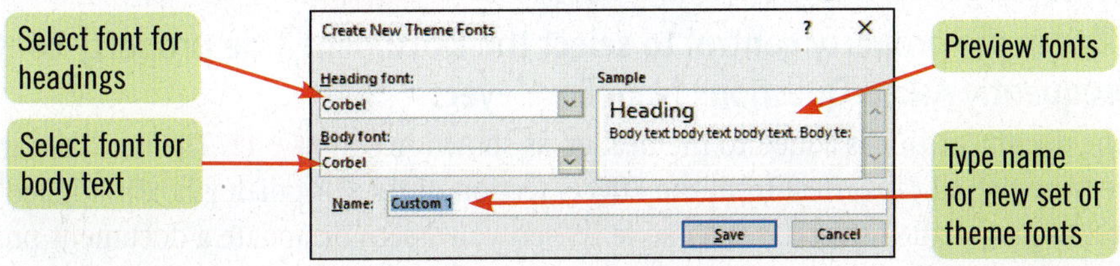

FIGURE 5-11: Custom theme in the Themes gallery

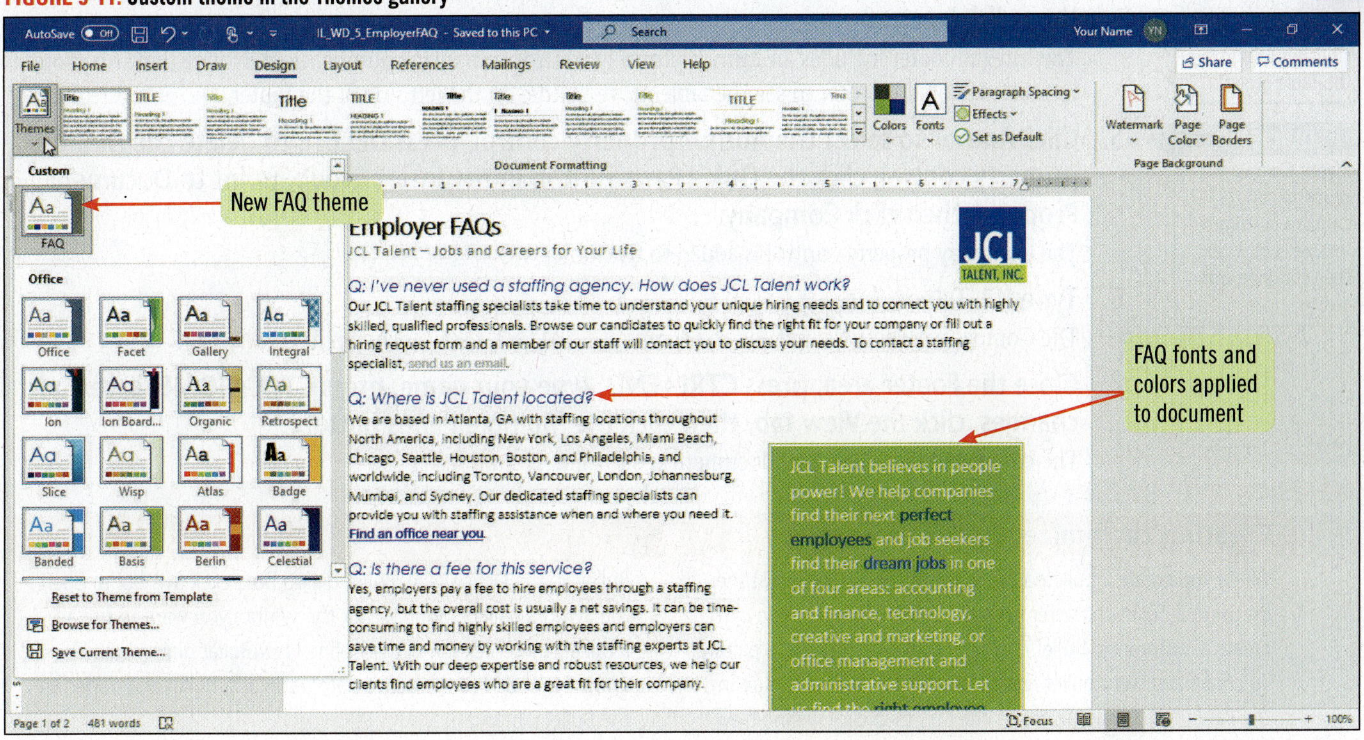

Word

Word
Module 5

Insert Quick Parts

Learning Outcomes
- Insert headers and footers
- Update a document property
- Insert and delete a property control

The Word Quick Parts feature makes it easy to insert reusable pieces of content into a document. Quick Parts items include fields, such as for the date or a page number; document properties, such as the document title or author; and building blocks, which are customized content that you can create, format, and save for future use. You insert a Quick Part into a document using the Quick Parts command on the Insert tab or on the Header & Footer tab. **CASE** *You finalize the design of the FAQ document by adding a header building block and a footer building block to the document. You then customize the footer by adding a document property to it using the Quick Parts command.*

STEPS

QUICK TIP
When you update a document property on the Info screen, the property controls in the document are updated with the new information.

TROUBLE
Zoom in and out on the document as necessary.

QUICK TIP
To turn the table gridlines on and off, click the Layout contextual tab for tables, then click the View Gridlines button in the Table group.

QUICK TIP
If your Company property control contains customized text, select the text, then continue with Step 6.

1. **Click the Insert tab, then click the Header button in the Header & Footer group**
   The Header gallery opens and displays the list of predesigned headers.
2. **Scroll down the Header gallery, then click Integral**
   The Integral header is added to the document and the Header area opens. The Integral header includes a property control for the Document Title. A **property control** is a content control that contains document property information, such as title, company, or author. You can assign or update a document property by typing directly in a property control or by typing in the Properties boxes on the Info screen.
3. **Click in the property control to select the Document Title property control, then type Frequently Asked Questions from Employers**
   The document title is added to the header, as shown in **FIGURE 5-12**. The text appears as all capital letters because the All caps effect from the Effects section of the Font dialog box is applied to the property control as part of the Integral header style. When you assign or update a document property by typing in a property control, all controls of the same type in the document are updated with the change, as well as the corresponding property field on the Info screen.
4. **Click the Footer button in the Header & Footer group, scroll down the Footer gallery, then click Integral**
   The Integral footer includes an Author property control and a page number field. Notice that this footer is formatted as a table; you can see the table move handle on the left side of the footer.
5. **Click Author to select the Author property control, press DELETE to delete the Author property control, click the Quick Parts button in the Insert group, point to Document Property, then click Company**
   The Company property control is added to the footer.
6. **Type JCL Talent, Inc.**
   The Company property is updated to become JCL TALENT, INC., as shown in **FIGURE 5-13**.
7. **Close the Footer area, press CTRL+END, type your name, press CTRL+HOME, save your changes, click the View tab, then click the Multiple Pages button**
   The completed Employer FAQ document is shown in **FIGURE 5-14**.

Creating customized bullet characters

When you create a bulleted list, you can choose to format the list using a bullet character from the Bullet Library, or you can create a customized bullet character using a symbol or a picture. To create a custom bullet character, click the Bullets button in the Paragraph group on the Home tab, then click Define New Bullet. In the Define New Bullet dialog box, click Symbol to open the Symbol gallery, double-click the symbol you want to use as a bullet, then click OK in the Define New Bullet dialog box. The symbol is added to the active paragraph as a bullet and added to the Bullet Library.

FIGURE 5-12: Document Title property control in Integral header

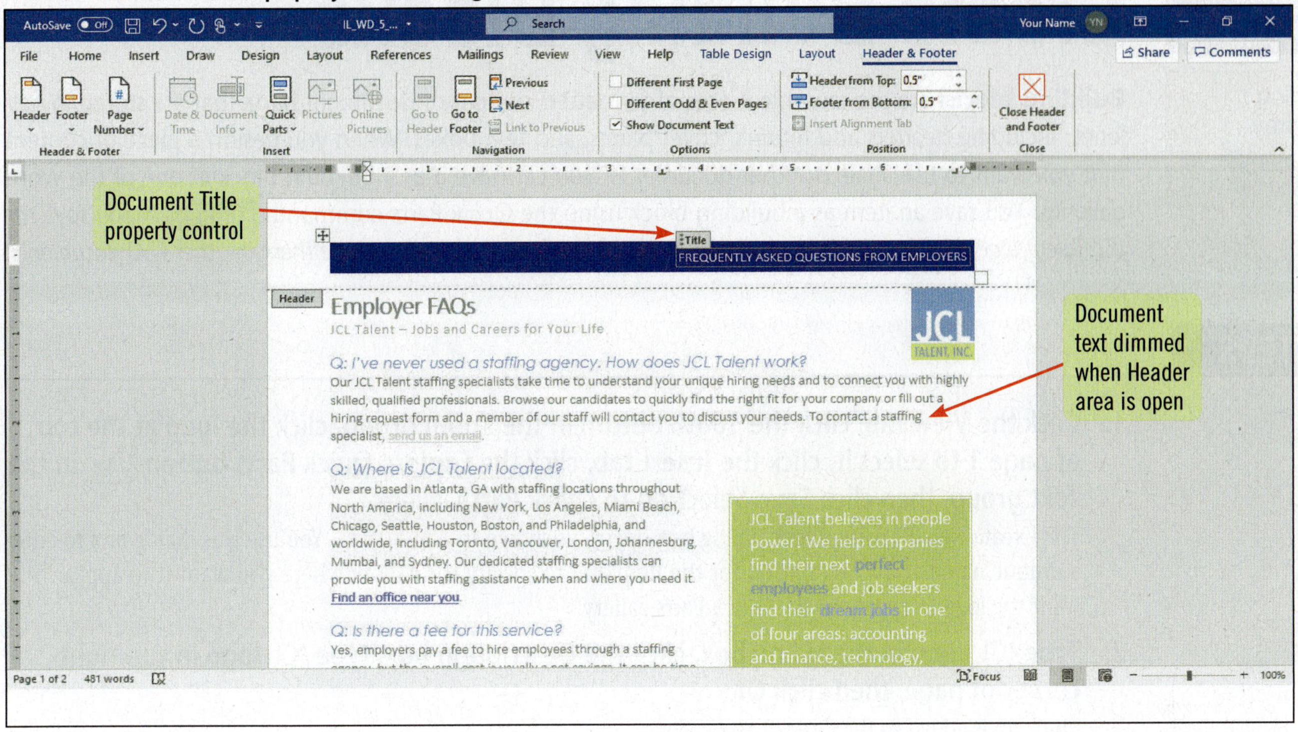

FIGURE 5-13: Company property control in Integral footer

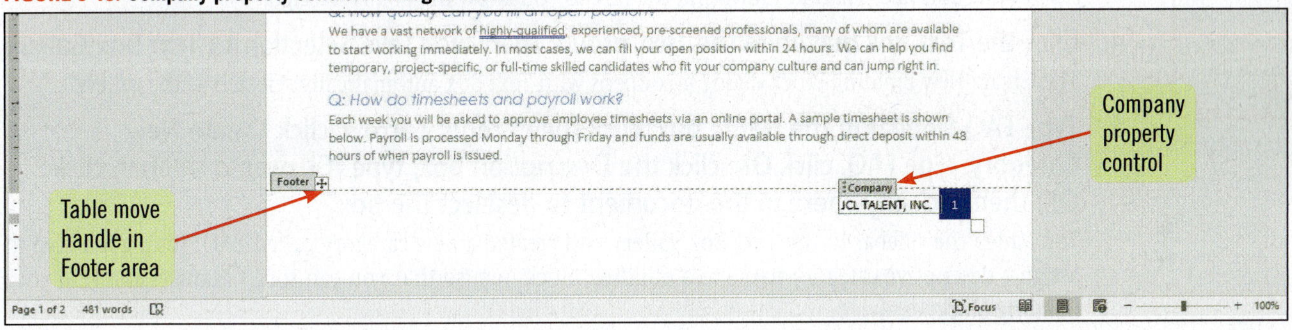

FIGURE 5-14: Completed Employers FAQ document

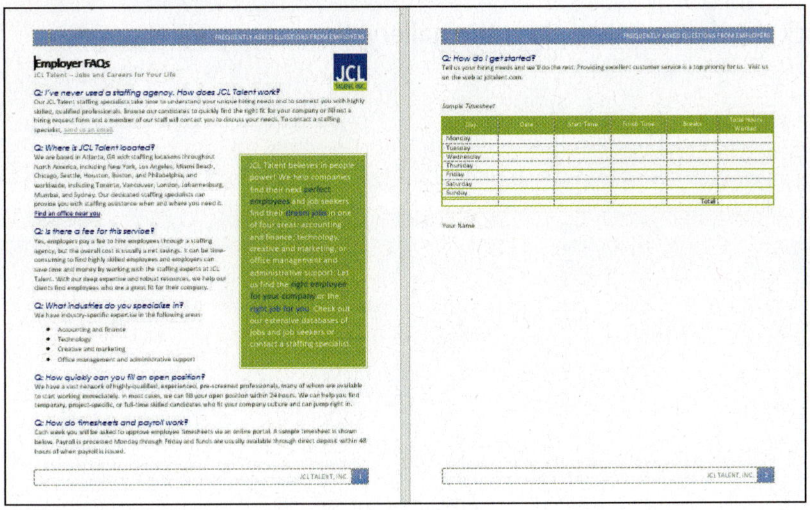

Word Module 5

Create Building Blocks

Learning Outcome
- Save a custom building block

Building blocks are the reusable pieces of formatted content or document parts that are stored in galleries, including headers and footers, cover pages, and text boxes. When you design a piece of content that you want to use again in other documents, you can save it as a building block in one of the Word galleries. You save an item as a building block using the Quick Parts command. **CASE** *You save the JCL Talent logo and the sidebar as building blocks so that you can easily include them in other FAQ documents.*

STEPS

TROUBLE
Take care to click the edge of the text box; do not click any of the text inside the text box.

QUICK TIP
To store paragraph formatting with a building block, make sure to also select the final paragraph mark.

1. **Click the View tab, click the 100% button in the Zoom group, click the logo at the top of page 1 to select it, click the Insert tab, click the Explore Quick Parts button in the Text group, then click Save Selection to Quick Part Gallery**

   The Create New Building Block dialog box opens, as shown in FIGURE 5-15. You use this dialog box to enter a unique name and a description for the item and to specify the gallery where you want it to appear. You want the logo to appear in the Quick Parts gallery.

2. **Type JCL Logo in the Name box, click the Description box, type JCL logo in top-right corner of page, then click OK**

   The logo is added to the Quick Parts gallery.

3. **Click the edge of the green sidebar to select it**

   A solid line and sizing handles surround the box so you know the box is selected.

4. **Click the Text Box button in the Text group, then click Save Selection to Text Box Gallery**

   The Create New Building Block dialog box opens with Text Box automatically selected as the gallery.

5. **Type FAQ Sidebar in the Name box, click the Category arrow, click Create New Category, type FAQ, click OK, click the Description box, type JCL promo sidebar, click OK, then click anywhere in the document to deselect the box**

   You added the sidebar to the Text Box gallery and created a new category called FAQ. It's a good idea to assign a descriptive category name to a building block item so that you can sort, organize, and find your building blocks easily.

6. **Click the Text Box button in the Text group, then scroll to the bottom of the gallery**

   The FAQ Sidebar building block is displayed in the Text Box gallery in the FAQ category, as shown in FIGURE 5-16.

7. **Click the document to close the gallery, then save your changes**

FIGURE 5-15: Create New Building Block dialog box

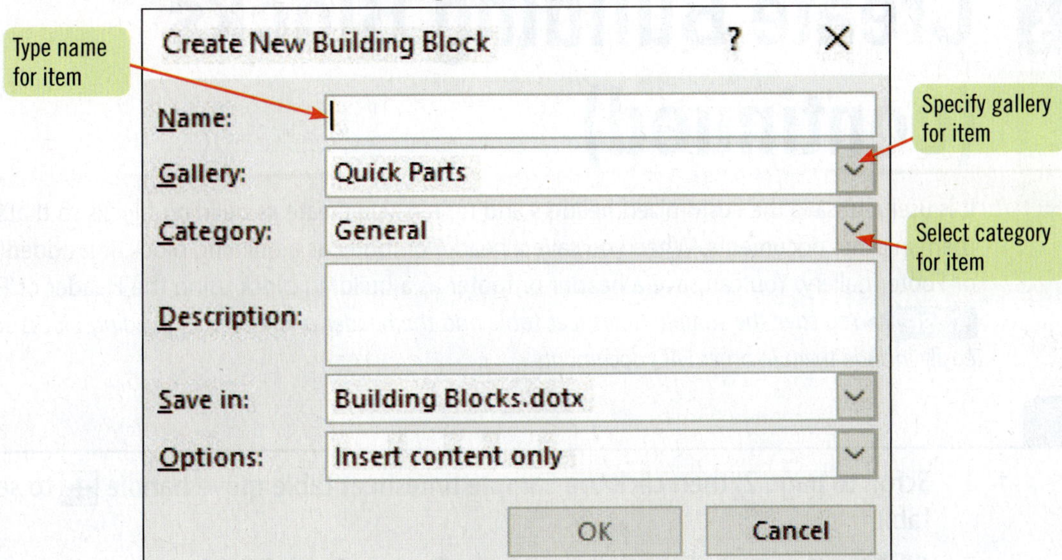

FIGURE 5-16: New building block in Text Box gallery

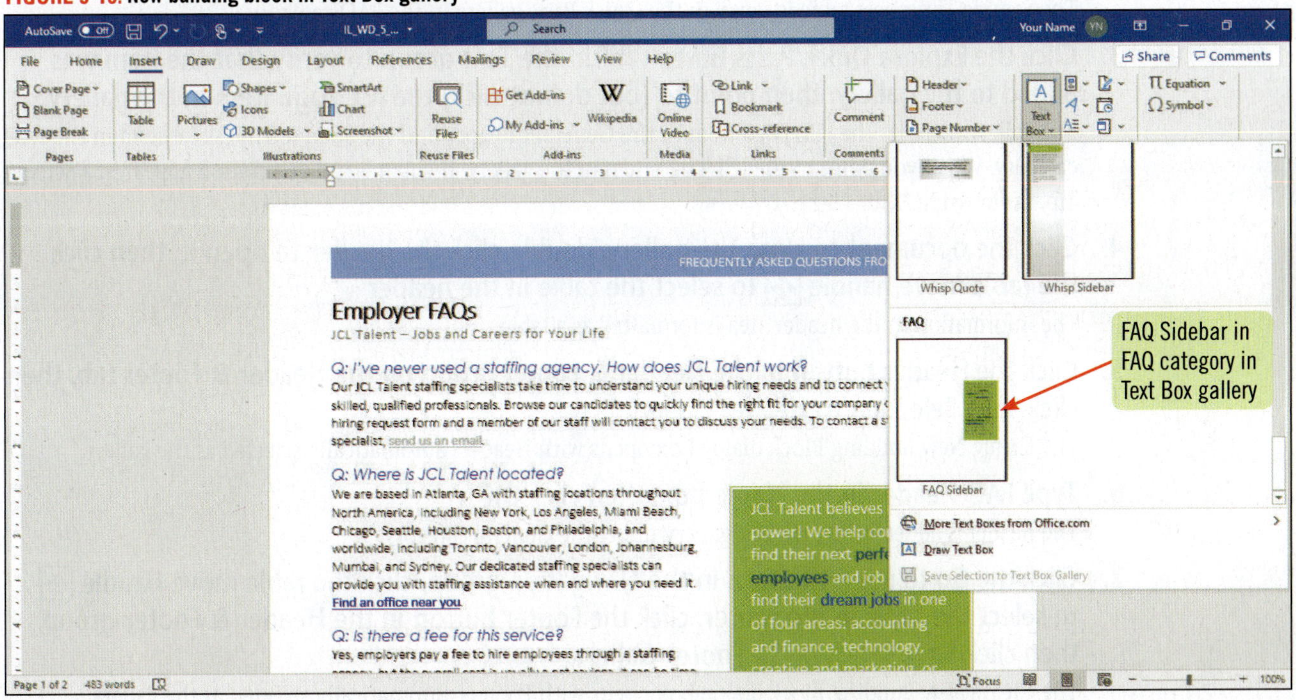

Inserting icons in a document

Word includes hundreds of icon images that you can insert into documents to visually communicate using symbols. To insert an icon in a document, click the Icons button in the Illustrations group on the Insert tab, scroll the gallery of icons in the Insert Icon dialog box, select an icon, then click Insert. The icon is inserted as a graphic object at the location of the insertion point. Like any graphic object, you can use the options on the Graphics Format tab to size, position, and format the icon graphic.

Create Building Blocks (continued)

Learning Outcome
- Save a custom building block

It is useful to save the customized headers and footers you create as building blocks so that you can reuse them in other documents. When you save a header or footer as a building block, it is added to the Header or Footer gallery. You can save a header or footer as a building block using the Header or Footer button. **CASE** *You save the sample timesheet table and the header and footer as building blocks so that you can easily include them in other FAQ documents.*

STEPS

1. **Scroll to page 2, then click the Sample timesheet table move handle ⊞ to select the table**
2. **Click the Insert tab if necessary, click the Explore Quick Parts button in the Text group, click Save Selection to Quick Part Gallery, type Sample Timesheet in the Name box, click the Category arrow, click Create New Category, type FAQ, click OK, then click OK**
   The Sample Timesheet table is saved in the Quick Parts gallery in the FAQ category.
3. **Click the Explore Quick Parts button in the Text group to verify that the item was added to the gallery, then point to (but do not click) the JCL Logo item in the gallery**
   The gallery includes the JCL Logo item in the General category and the Sample Timesheet item in the FAQ category. When you point to the JCL Logo item in the gallery, the name and description appear in a ScreenTip, as shown in FIGURE 5-17.
4. **Click the document to close the gallery, double-click the header to open it, then click the table move handle ⊞ to select the table in the header**
   The information in the header area is formatted as a table.
5. **Click the Header button in the Header & Footer group on the Header & Footer tab, then click Save Selection to Header Gallery**
   The Create New Building Block dialog box opens with Headers automatically selected as the gallery.
6. **Type FAQ Header in the Name box, then click OK**
   The header is added to the Header gallery under the General category.
7. **Click the Go to Footer button in the Navigation group, click the table move handle ⊞ to select the table in the footer, click the Footer button in the Header & Footer group, then click Save Selection to Footer Gallery**
   The Create New Building Block dialog box opens with Footers automatically selected as the gallery.
8. **Type FAQ Footer in the Name box, click OK, then close the Header and Footer**
   The footer is added to the Footer gallery under the General category. You now will be able to insert the building blocks you created into a different FAQ document.
9. **sam Save the document, submit it, then close the document without exiting Word**

FIGURE 5-17: Items in Quick Parts gallery

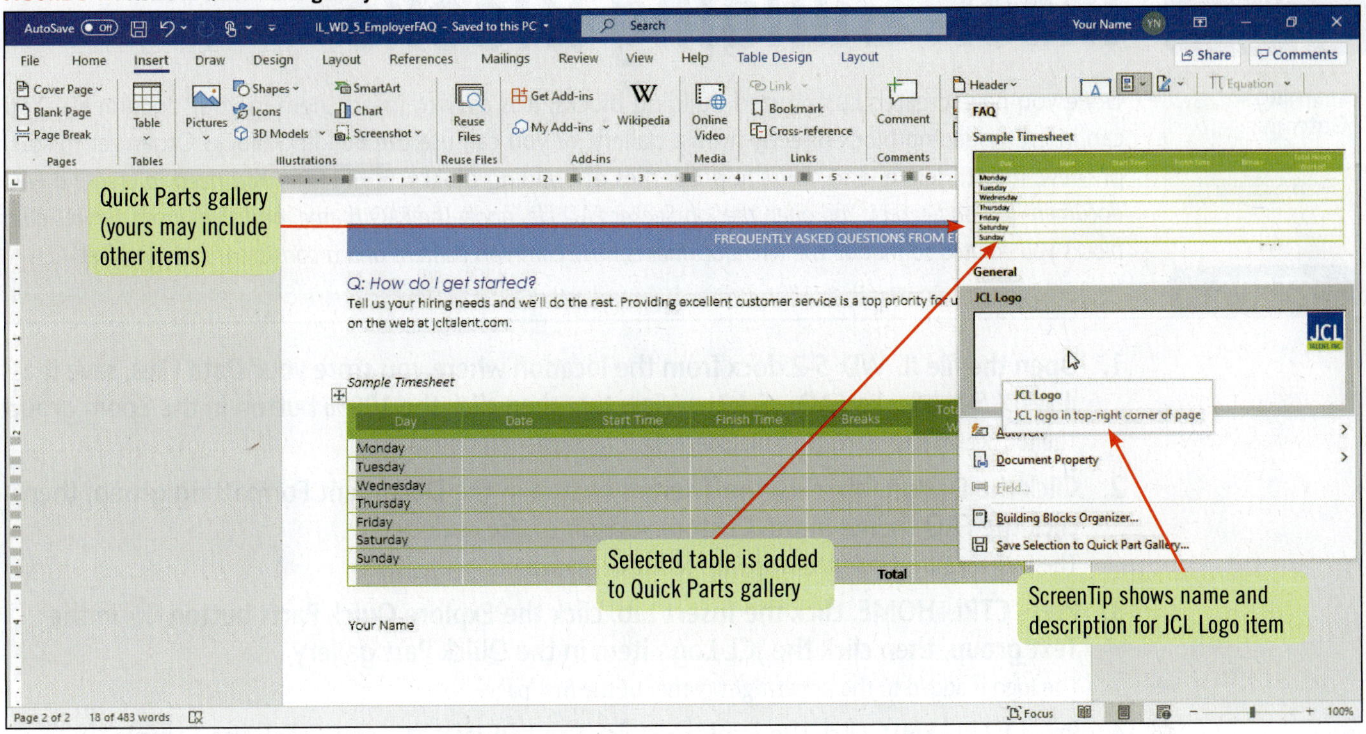

Word

Renaming a building block and editing other properties

You can edit the properties of a building block at any time, including changing its name, gallery location, category, and description. To modify building block properties, simply right-click the item in a gallery, then click Edit Properties. In the Modify Building Block dialog box that opens, edit the item's name or description, or assign it to a new gallery or category. When you are finished, click OK, then click Yes in the warning box that opens. You can also modify the properties of a building block by selecting the item in the Building Blocks Organizer, then clicking Edit Properties.

Insert Building Blocks

Learning Outcome
- Insert a building block

Once you have created customized building blocks, it is easy to insert them in your documents. You can insert a building block directly from a gallery, or you can use the Building Blocks Organizer to sort, preview, insert, delete, and edit the properties of building blocks. **CASE** *You need to create a FAQ document for Job Seekers. You open the Job Seeker FAQ file, apply the FAQ theme, and then insert the building blocks you created so that all the FAQ documents have common content and a consistent look and feel.*

STEPS

1. **Open the file IL_WD_5-2.docx from the location where you store your Data Files, save it as IL_WD_5_JobSeekerFAQ, click the View tab, then click the 100% button in the Zoom group**
   The Job Seeker FAQ document includes text formatted with styles.
2. **Click the Design tab, click the Themes button in the Document Formatting group, then click the FAQ theme in the Custom section of the gallery**
   The FAQ theme you created is applied to the document.
3. **Press CTRL+HOME, click the Insert tab, click the Explore Quick Parts button in the Text group, then click the JCL Logo item in the Quick Part gallery**
   The logo is added to the upper-right corner of the first page.
4. **Press CTRL+END, click the Explore Quick Parts button, then click the Sample Timesheet item in the Quick Part gallery**
   The Sample Timesheet table is added to the end of the document.
5. **Click anywhere on page 1, click the Header button in the Header & Footer group, scroll down the Header gallery, click FAQ Header in the General section, click the Footer button, scroll down the Footer gallery, click FAQ Footer in the General section, then click the Close Header and Footer button**
   The custom header and footer you created are added to pages 1 and 2. The property information that appears in the header and footer, in this case the document title and the company name, are the property information for the current document.
6. **Click the Q: Where is JCL Talent located? paragraph, click the Insert tab, click the Explore Quick Parts button in the Text group, then click Building Blocks Organizer**
   The Building Blocks Organizer opens, as shown in **FIGURE 5-18**. The Building Blocks Organizer includes a complete list of the built-in and customized building blocks from every gallery. You use the Building Blocks Organizer to sort, preview, insert, delete, and edit the properties of building blocks.
7. **Click the Category column heading in the list of building blocks**
   The building blocks are sorted and grouped by category.
8. **Scroll down the list to locate the items in the FAQ category, click the FAQ Sidebar item to select it, then click Insert**
   The FAQ Sidebar is inserted on page 1. The sidebar is anchored to the Q: Where is JCL Talent located paragraph, which is the current position of the insertion point.
9. **With the sidebar selected, click the Shape Format tab, click the Position button in the Arrange group, click Position in Middle Left with Square Text Wrapping, click the View tab, click the Multiple Pages button, press CTRL+END, press ENTER, then type your name**
   The sidebar is moved to the left of the text, and your name is added to the end of the document. The completed Job Seekers FAQ document is shown in **FIGURE 5-19**.
10. **Save your changes, submit the document, then close the file without exiting Word**

QUICK TIP
To edit the content of a building block, insert the item in a document, edit the item, then save the selection to the same Quick Parts gallery using the same name.

QUICK TIP
To delete a building block, select it in the Building Blocks Organizer, then click Delete.

TROUBLE
If you are working on your personal computer and you want to save the building blocks you created, click Save to save the Building Blocks.dotx file.

FIGURE 5-18: Building Blocks Organizer

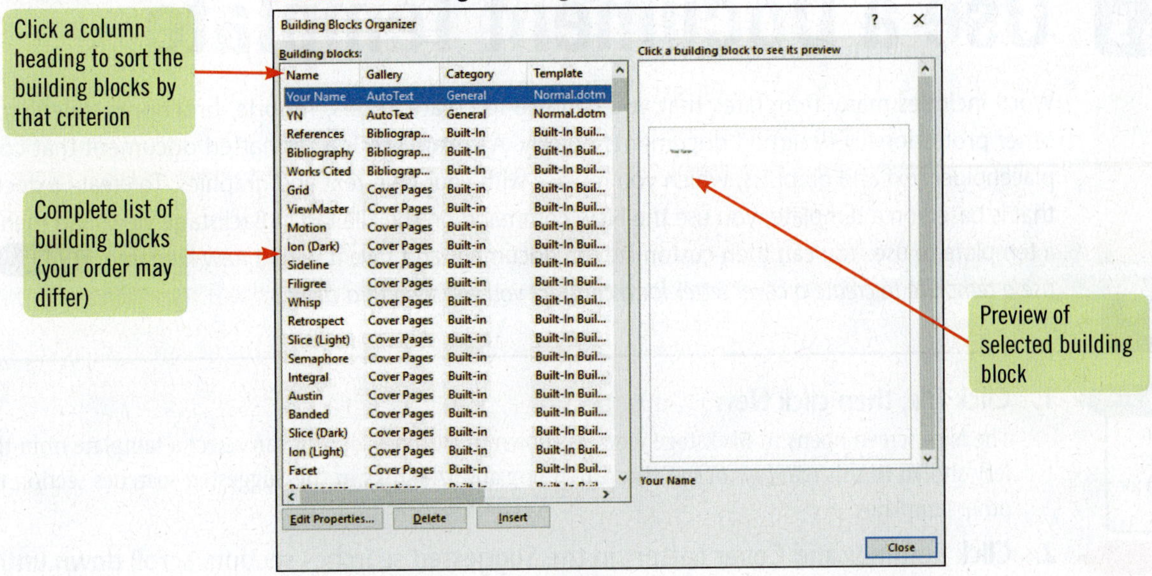

FIGURE 5-19: Completed Job Seekers FAQ document

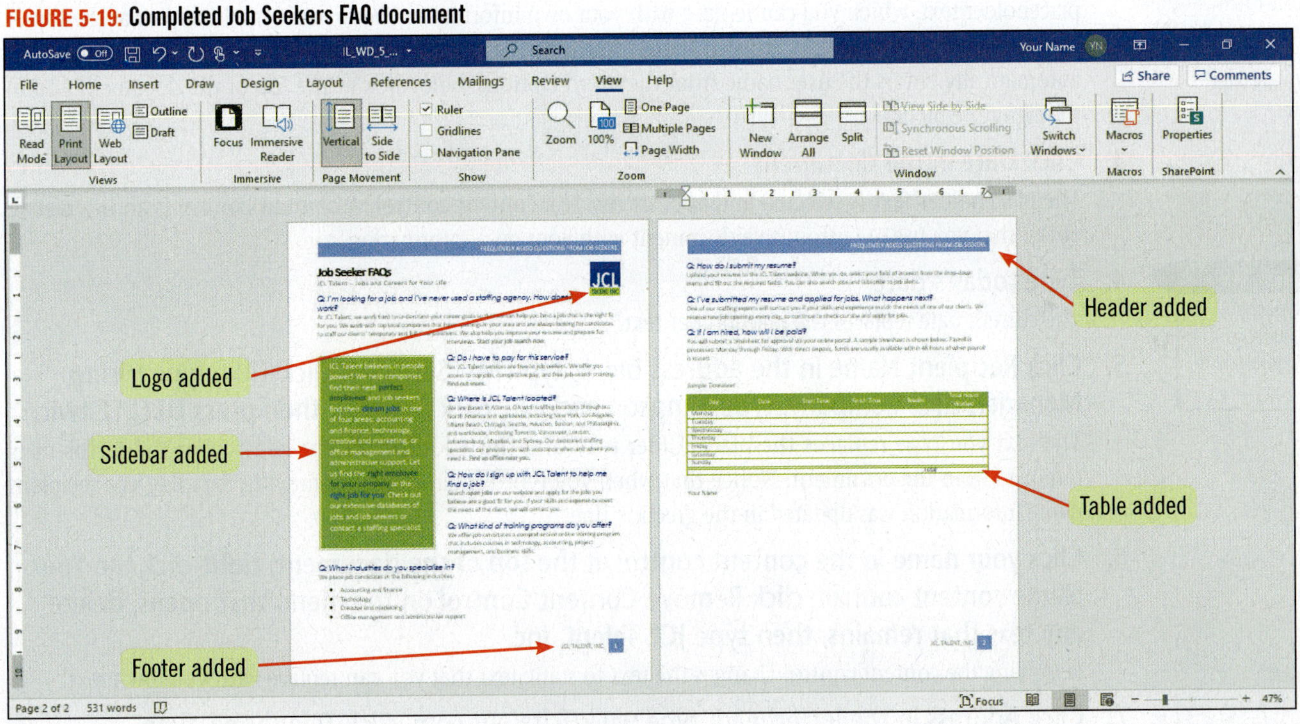

Word Module 5

Use a Document Template

Learning Outcomes
- Customize a template
- Use content controls

Word includes many templates that you can use to create letters, reports, brochures, calendars, and other professionally designed documents quickly. A **template** is a formatted document that contains placeholder text and graphics, which you replace with your own text and graphics. To create a document that is based on a template, you use the New command on the File tab in Backstage view, and then select a template to use. You can then customize the document and save it with a new filename. **CASE** *You use a template to create a cover letter for a contract you will send to a client.*

STEPS

QUICK TIP You must have an active Internet connection to search for templates.

1. **Click File, then click New**

   The New screen opens in Backstage view, as shown in FIGURE 5-20. You can select a template from the gallery shown in this window or use the search box and the links in the Suggested searches section to find other templates.

TROUBLE Templates change over time. If this template is not available, select another Cover Letter template or just read the steps to understand how to work with templates.

2. **Click Resumes and Cover Letters in the Suggested searches section, scroll down until you find the Cover letter (blue) thumbnail on the New screen, click it, preview the template in the preview window that opens, click Create, then change the zoom level to 100%**

   The Cover Letter (blue) template opens as a new document in the document window. It contains placeholder text, which you can replace with your own information. Your name might appear at the top of the document. Don't be concerned if it does not. When a document is created using this template, Word automatically enters the user name from the Word Options dialog box at the top of the document and in the signature block.

3. **Click Date in the document**

   The placeholder text is selected and appears inside a content control. A content control is an interactive object that you use to customize a document with your own information.

QUICK TIP As you type the month, AutoComplete suggests text to insert.

4. **Type today's date**

   The current date replaces the placeholder text.

5. **Click Recipient Name in the address block, type Ms. Sara Bay, click Title, type Hiring Manager, click Company, type Simpson and Co., click Address, then press DELETE twice**

   The text you type replaces the placeholder text, and the Address content control for the recipient is removed from the document. Notice that when you typed the recipient name, Ms. Sara Bay, the recipient name information was updated in the greeting line.

6. **Click your name in the content control at the top of the document, right-click the Your Name content control, click Remove Content Control on the menu that opens, delete any text that remains, then type JCL Talent, Inc.**

   Removing the content control changes the text to static text that you can replace with your own text.

7. **Click Address in the letterhead, type www.jcltalent.com, click Telephone, type 555-555-0789, click Email, then type jcl@jcltalent.com**

8. **Scroll down, select the three paragraphs of placeholder body text, type Enclosed please find a copy of our contract for staffing services. We look forward to working with you., then, if the name in the signature block is not your name, select the text in the content control and type your name**

   The text you type replaces the placeholder text, as shown in FIGURE 5-21.

9. **Save the document as IL_WD_5_ContractLetter to the location where you store your Data Files**

FIGURE 5-20: New screen in Backstage view

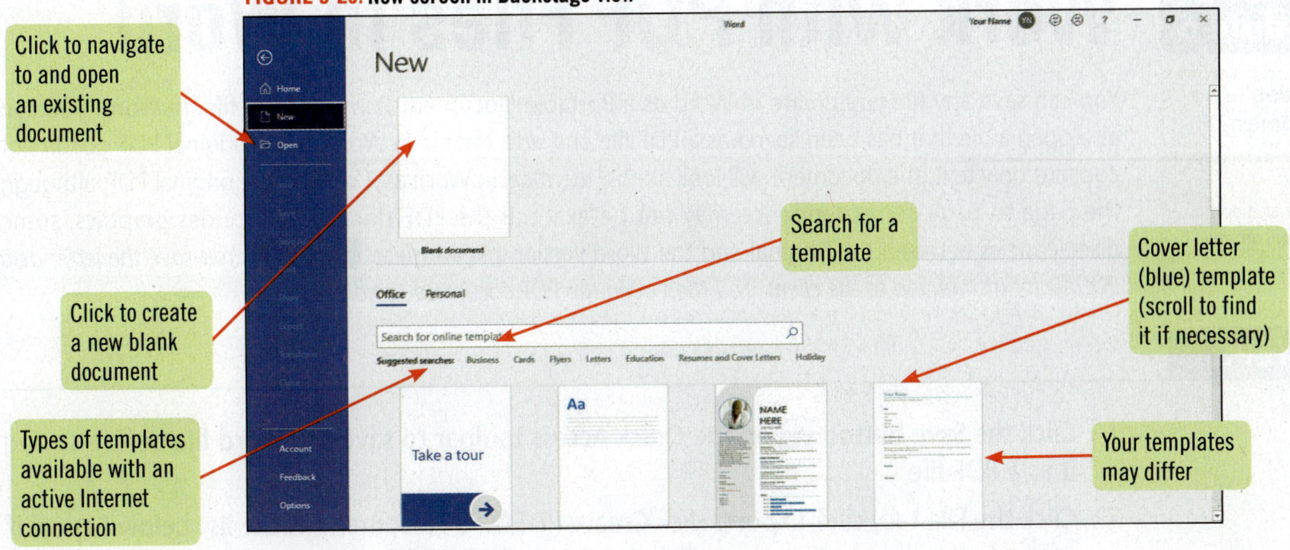

FIGURE 5-21: Document created using the Cover Letter (blue) template

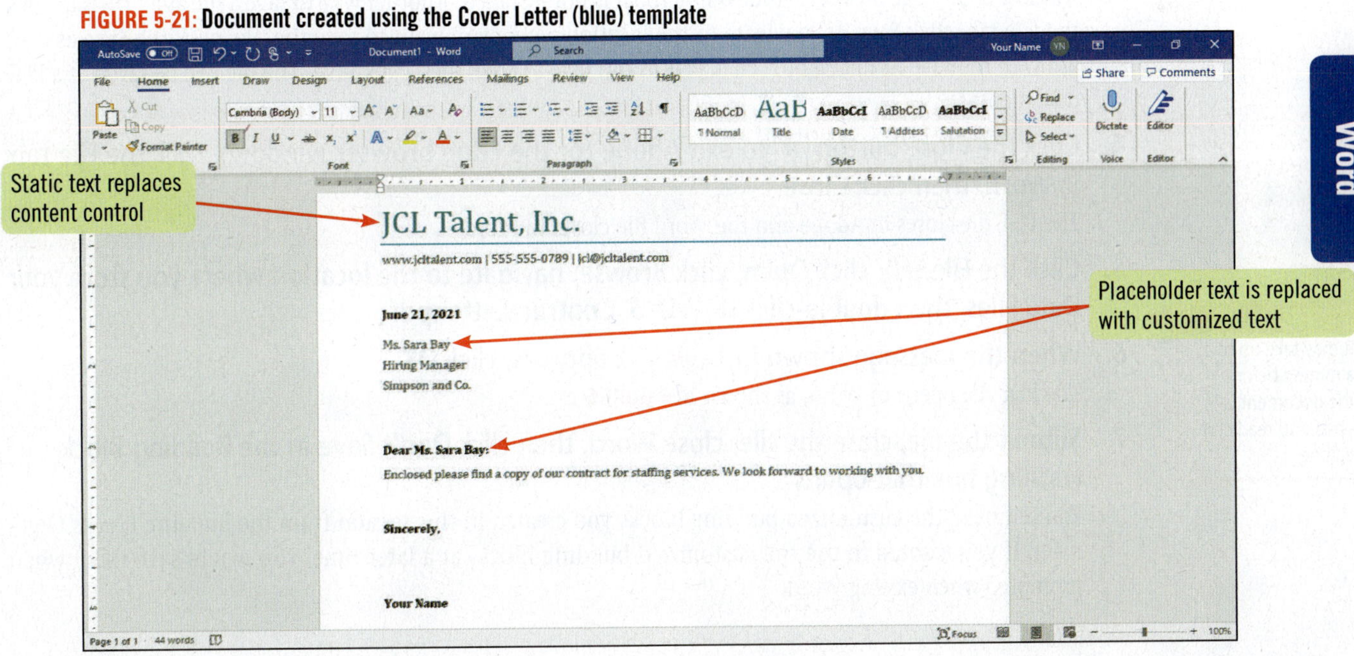

Word
Module 5

Work with PDF Files in Word

Learning Outcomes
- Export a document to PDF
- Open and edit a PDF document

You can save any file you create in Word as a Portable Document Format (PDF) file. In Word, you can also open a file that has been saved as a PDF file and edit the file in Word. If the original PDF document contains only text, the document will look almost identical in Word as it does in the original PDF, although the page to page correspondence may not be exact. If the PDF document includes graphics, some discrepancies between the original and the Word version may appear. **CASE** *You save the letter as a PDF file for distribution to the client. You then open the PDF document to edit it.*

STEPS

1. **Click the Save button on the Quick Access toolbar to save the Word file before saving it as a PDF file**
2. **Click the File tab, click Export, click Create PDF/XPS Document in the list below Export if it is not already selected, then click the Create PDF/XPS button**
   The Publish as PDF or XPS dialog box opens.
3. **Click the Open file after publishing check box if it is not already selected, then click Publish**
   In a few moments, the document is saved as IL_WD_5_ContractLetter.pdf and it opens in an Adobe Acrobat window or an Edge browser window if Acrobat is not installed. Another way to save a file as a PDF is to click the File tab, click Save As, navigate to the location where you want to save the file, click the Save as type arrow in the Save As dialog box, click PDF as the Save as type, then click Save. The file will be saved as a PDF document.
4. **Click the Close button to exit Adobe (or the Edge browser window), click the File tab in Word, then click Close**
   The PDF file closes in Adobe and the Word file closes in Word.
5. **Click the File tab, click Open, click Browse, navigate to the location where you store your Data Files, then double-click IL_WD_5_ContractLetter.pdf**
6. **When the message shown in FIGURE 5-22 appears, click OK**
   The PDF file opens in Word, as shown in FIGURE 5-23.
7. **Submit the file, close the file, close Word, then click Don't Save in the Building Block warning box that opens**
   You removed the customized building blocks you created in this session from the Building Blocks Organizer. If you wanted to use the customized building blocks at a later time, you would save them when prompted when exiting Word.

TROUBLE
It may take up to a minute before the document is open and ready for editing.

FIGURE 5-22: Message box that can appear when opening a PDF file in Word

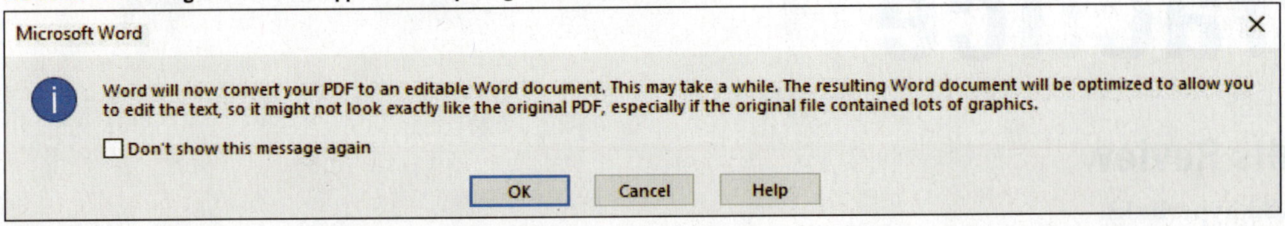

FIGURE 5-23: PDF file open in Word

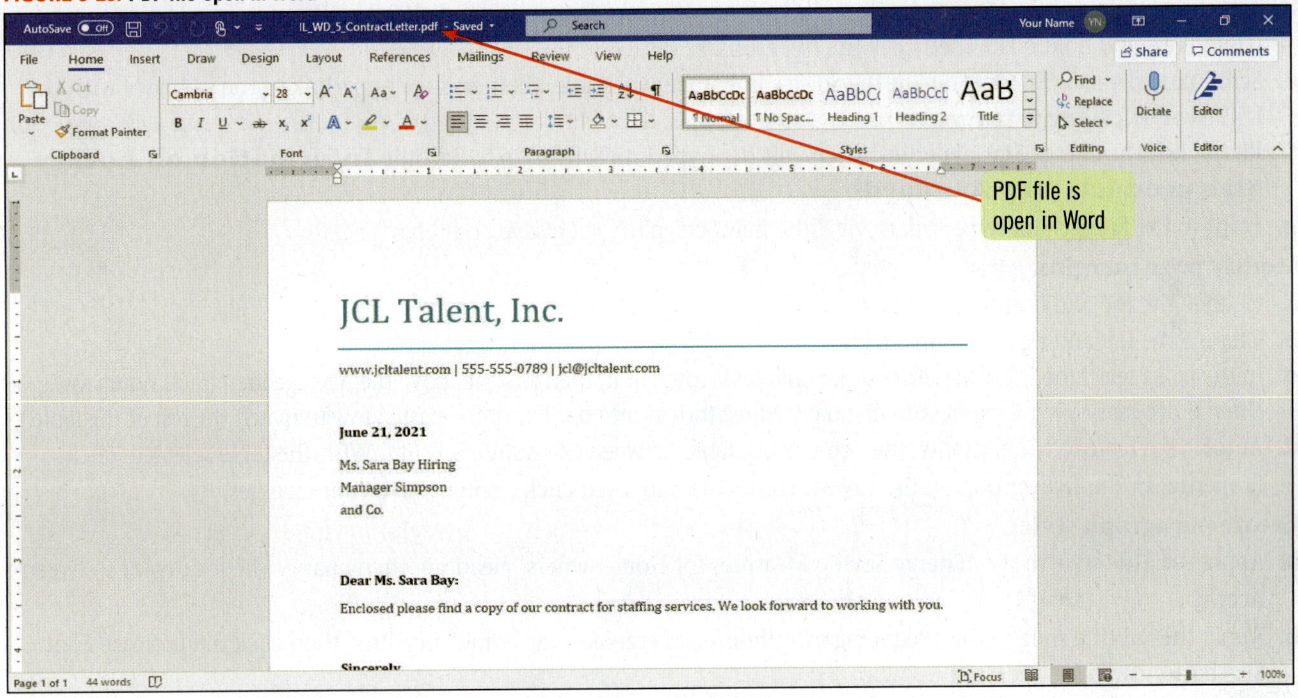

Opening non-native files directly in Word

By default, Microsoft Word saves files in one of its proprietary formats. The saved file is called a native Word file because it is saved in a file format that is native to Word, such as .docx for Word documents and .dotx for Word templates. A Word file may not be recognized by other software programs.

Sometimes you may need to open a file in Word that is a non-native file—that is, a file created with a different software program. Depending on the program used to create the original file, you may not be able to open the non-native file in Word. For example, you will get an error message if you attempt to open an Excel or PowerPoint file in Word.

When you are working with a different program and you want to work with that file in Word, you can save the file as a PDF file, as a txt, or as an rtf file. You can open and work on any of these three non-native file formats in Word. For example, you can save an Excel file as a PDF file, then open and work on the file in Word.

Practice

Skills Review

1. **Add hyperlinks.**
   a. Start Word, open the file IL_WD_5-3.docx from the location where you store your Data Files, then save it as **IL_WD_5_EnergyHome**.
   b. Select the bold text "Contact us" in the fourth paragraph, then open the Insert Hyperlink dialog box.
   c. Create a hyperlink to your email address with the subject **Home Energy Consultation**.
   d. Test the contact us hyperlink, then close the message window that opens and click No if a message window opens. (*Hint*: Press and hold CTRL then click the hyperlink.)
   e. Scroll down, select "Energy Star" in the Source line under the table, then create a hyperlink to the webpage with the URL **www.energystar.gov**.
   f. Right-click the Energy Star hyperlink, then edit the hyperlink ScreenTip to become **Information on Energy Star products and standards**.
   g. Point to the Energy Star hyperlink to view the new ScreenTip, then save your changes.
2. **Modify page margins.**
   a. Change the top and bottom margins to **.75"**.
   b. Change the left and right margins to **.6"**.
   c. In the table, select the Approximate cost per bulb table row, cut it, then paste it above the Average lifespan in hours row. (*Hint*: If necessary, use your mouse to manually adjust the column borders of the pasted row to match the rest of the table.)
   d. AutoFit the table to the contents, then center the table between the margins. (*Hint*: With the table selected, click Properties in the Table group on the Layout contextual tab, then click Center.) Save your changes.
3. **Create paragraph styles.**
   a. Apply the Title style to the "Energy Saving Measures for Homeowners" heading, then change the font color to Green, Accent 6.
   b. Apply the Subtitle style to the "Reducing greenhouse gas emissions at home" heading, then click the Increase Font Size button twice.
   c. Apply the Heading 1 style and Green, Accent 6 font color to the red headings: "Small Steps to Take in Your Home and Yard" and "Use Green Power."
   d. Select the purple heading "Change light bulbs," click the Launcher in the Styles group, then click the New Style button in the Styles pane to open the Create New Style from Formatting dialog box.
   e. Create a new style called **Small Steps** that is based on the Heading 2 style, is italic, and has a Blue, Accent 1 font color.
   f. Apply the Small Steps style to each purple heading.
   g. Open the Reveal Formatting pane, examine the format settings applied to several paragraphs, close all open panes, then save your changes.
4. **Format with themes.**
   a. Change the view to Multiple Pages, then change the Style Set to Basic (Simple). (*Hint*: Use the Style Sets gallery in the Document Formatting group on the Design tab.)
   b. Open the Themes gallery, apply the Slice theme (or any other theme), then zoom in to view each page.
   c. Apply the Metropolitan theme, scroll to see it applied to both pages, zoom out to 50%, then save your changes.
5. **Customize a theme.**
   a. Click the Theme Colors button, then change the theme colors to Marquee.
   b. Click the Theme Colors button again, click Customize Colors, click the Accent 4 arrow, click More Colors, click the Custom tab if it is not the active tab, type **215** in the Red box, type **212** in the Green box, type **71** in the Blue box, then click OK. The Accent 4 color is now yellow green.
   c. Name the palette of new theme colors **Small Steps**, then save it.

Skills Review (continued)

d. Change the theme fonts to Candara, change the theme effects to Smokey Glass, then change the paragraph spacing to Open. (*Hint*: Use the Theme Fonts, Effects, and Paragraph Spacing buttons in the Document Formatting group on the Design tab.)

e. Save the current theme with the name **Small Steps**, then save your changes.

6. Insert Quick Parts.

a. Change the view to 100%, then insert the Retrospect header from the Header gallery.

b. Click the Document Title property control, then type **Small Steps Toward Energy Efficiency**.

c. Press TAB, remove the Date control, insert a Company property control, then type **PKG Consultants**.

d. Insert the Retrospect footer from the Footer gallery, then click the Footer from Bottom down arrow in the Position group on the Header & Footer tab twice.

e. Type your name in the Author property control, close headers and footers, then save your changes.

7. Create Building Blocks.

a. Change the view to Multiple Pages, click the edge of the chart object on page 2 to select it, click the Insert tab, then use the Explore Quick Parts button to save the selection as a Quick Part. (*Note*: Sizing handles and a solid border appear around the chart object when it is selected.)

b. Name the building block **Pie Chart**, assign it to the Quick Parts gallery, create a new category called **Small Steps**, then click OK twice.

c. Zoom in on page 1, turn on the display of paragraph and other formatting marks, select the block of text and table beginning with the heading Change light bulbs through the end of the Energy Star hyperlink, including the paragraph mark after the hyperlink, save the selected block of text and table as a Quick Part, name the building block **Change light bulbs**, assign it to the Quick Parts gallery, assign it to the Small Steps category, then click OK.

d. Open the Header area, click the Table move handle to select the entire header, then save the header to the Header Gallery, using the name **Small Steps header**, creating a **Small Steps category**, then clicking OK twice.

e. Move to the Footer area, click the Table move handle to select the entire footer, then save the footer to the Footer Gallery, using the name **Small Steps footer**, creating a **Small Steps category**, then clicking OK twice.

f. Close the Header and Footer areas, save your changes, submit the document, then close the file without exiting Word. The completed document is shown in FIGURE 5-24.

FIGURE 5-24

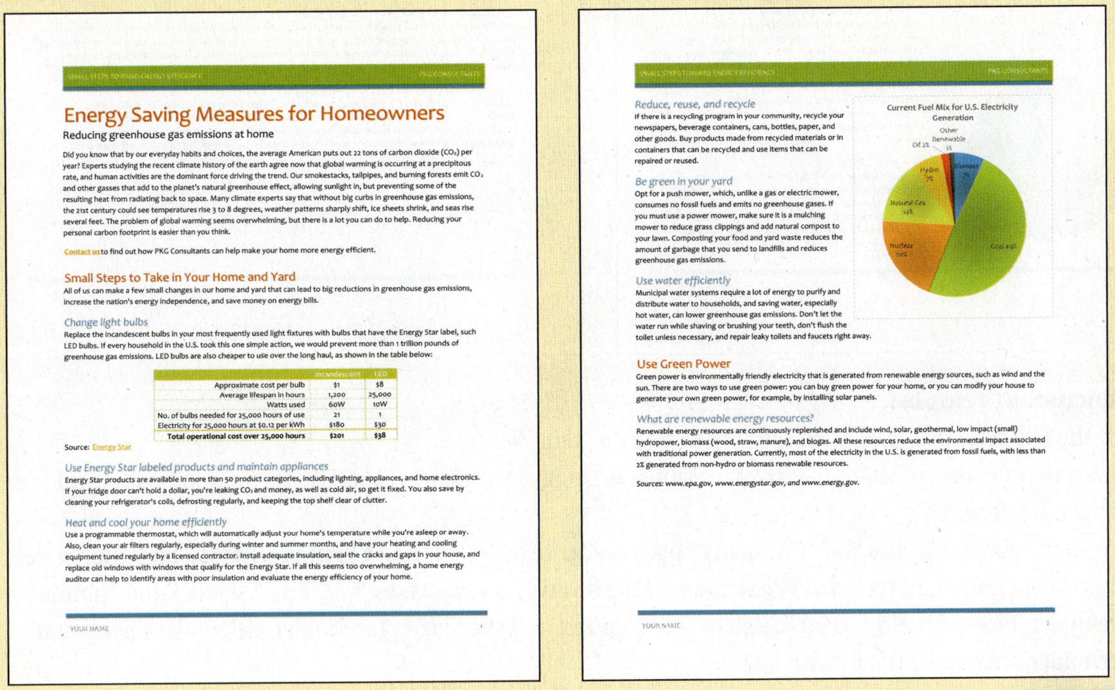

Energy Saving Measures for Homeowners

Reducing greenhouse gas emissions at home

Did you know that by our everyday habits and choices, the average American puts out 22 tons of carbon dioxide (CO_2) per year? Experts studying the recent climate history of the earth agree now that global warming is occurring at a precipitous rate, and human activities are the dominant force driving the trend. Our smokestacks, tailpipes, and burning forests emit CO_2 and other gasses that add to the planet's natural greenhouse effect, allowing sunlight in, but preventing some of the resulting heat from radiating back to space. Many climate experts say that without big curbs in greenhouse gas emissions, the 21st century could see temperatures rise 3 to 8 degrees, weather patterns sharply shift, ice sheets shrink, and seas rise several feet. The problem of global warming seems overwhelming, but there is a lot you can do to help. Reducing your personal carbon footprint is easier than you think.

Contact us to find out how PKG Consultants can help make your home more energy efficient.

Small Steps to Take in Your Home and Yard

All of us can make a few small changes in our home and yard that can lead to big reductions in greenhouse gas emissions, increase the nation's energy independence, and save money on energy bills.

Change light bulbs

Replace the incandescent bulbs in your most frequently used light fixtures with bulbs that have the Energy Star label, such LED bulbs. If every household in the U.S. took this one simple action, we would prevent more than 1 trillion pounds of greenhouse gas emissions. LED bulbs are also cheaper to use over the long haul, as shown in the table below:

	Incandescent	LED
Approximate cost per bulb	$1	$8
Average lifespan in hours	1,200	25,000
Watts used	60W	10W
No. of bulbs needed for 25,000 hours of use	21	1
Electricity for 25,000 hours at $0.12 per kWh	$180	$30
Total operational cost over 25,000 hours	**$201**	**$38**

Source: Energy Star

Use Energy Star labeled products and maintain appliances

Energy Star products are available in more than 50 product categories, including lighting, appliances, and home electronics. If your fridge door can't hold a dollar, you're leaking CO_2 and money, as well as cold air, so get it fixed. You also save by cleaning your refrigerator's coils, defrosting regularly, and keeping the top shelf clear of clutter.

Heat and cool your home efficiently

Use a programmable thermostat, which will automatically adjust your home's temperature while you're asleep or away. Also, clean your air filters regularly, especially during winter and summer months, and have your heating and cooling equipment tuned regularly by a licensed contractor. Install adequate insulation, seal the cracks and gaps in your house, and replace old windows with windows that qualify for the Energy Star. If all this seems too overwhelming, a home energy auditor can help to identify areas with poor insulation and evaluate the energy efficiency of your home.

YOUR NAME 1

Reduce, reuse, and recycle

If there is a recycling program in your community, recycle your newspapers, beverage containers, cans, bottles, paper, and other goods. Buy products made from recycled materials or in containers that can be recycled and use items that can be repaired or reused.

Be green in your yard

Opt for a push mower, which, unlike a gas or electric mower, consumes no fossil fuels and emits no greenhouse gases. If you must use a power mower, make sure it is a mulching mower to reduce grass clippings and add natural compost to your lawn. Composting your food and yard waste reduces the amount of garbage that you send to landfills and reduces greenhouse gas emissions.

Use water efficiently

Municipal water systems require a lot of energy to purify and distribute water to households, and saving water, especially hot water, can lower greenhouse gas emissions. Don't let the water run while shaving or brushing your teeth, don't flush the toilet unless necessary, and repair leaky toilets and faucets right away.

Use Green Power

Green power is environmentally friendly electricity that is generated from renewable energy sources, such as wind and the sun. There are two ways to use green power: you can buy green power for your home, or you can modify your house to generate your own green power, for example, by installing solar panels.

What are renewable energy resources?

Renewable energy resources are continuously replenished and include wind, solar, geothermal, low impact (small) hydropower, biomass (wood, straw, manure), and biogas. All these resources reduce the environmental impact associated with traditional power generation. Currently, most of the electricity in the U.S. is generated from fossil fuels, with less than 2% generated from non-hydro or biomass renewable resources.

Sources: *www.epa.gov, www.energystar.gov, and www.energy.gov.*

YOUR NAME 2

Word

Skills Review (continued)

8. Insert Building Blocks.

a. Open the file IL_WD_5-4.docx from the location where you store your Data Files, save it as **IL_WD_5_EnergyWork**, then apply the Small Steps theme.

b. Insert the Small Steps header from the Small Steps category in the Header gallery.

c. Insert the Small Steps footer from the Small Steps category in the Footer gallery and replace the information in the Author control with your name if necessary.

d. Click the title on page 1, open the Quick Parts gallery, then insert the Pie Chart from the Small Steps category. Select the pie chart object, then position it in bottom left with square text wrapping. (*Hint*: Take care to select only the chart object and not any elements inside the chart object.)

e. Zoom in to page 2, click in front of Manage office equipment… to position the insertion point, then open the Building Blocks Organizer.

f. Click the Category heading to sort the items by category, scroll to locate the items in the Small Steps category, click the Change light bulbs item, then click Insert.

g. Adjust the placement of the items, if necessary, then apply Red, Accent 6 font color to the title "Energy Saving Measures for Workers" and the headings "Small Steps to Take for Commuters" and "Small Steps to Take at Your Office or School."

h. Save your changes, then submit the document. The completed document is shown in **FIGURE 5-25**.

i. Close the file without exiting Word.

FIGURE 5-25

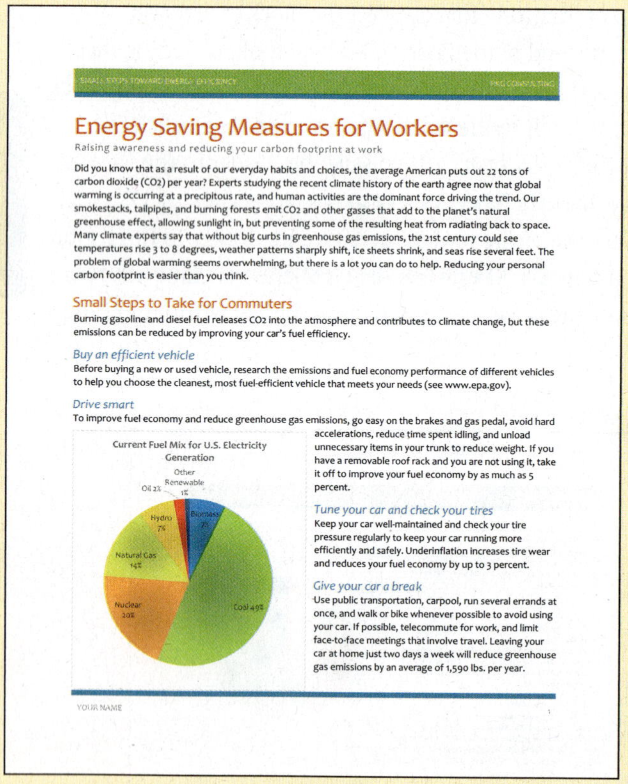

SMALL STEPS TOWARD ENERGY EFFICIENCY PKG CONSULTING

Energy Saving Measures for Workers

Raising awareness and reducing your carbon footprint at work

Did you know that as a result of our everyday habits and choices, the average American puts out 22 tons of carbon dioxide (CO2) per year? Experts studying the recent climate history of the earth agree now that global warming is occurring at a precipitous rate, and human activities are the dominant force driving the trend. Our smokestacks, tailpipes, and burning forests emit CO2 and other gasses that add to the planet's natural greenhouse effect, allowing sunlight in, but preventing some of the resulting heat from radiating back to space. Many climate experts say that without big curbs in greenhouse gas emissions, the 21st century could see temperatures rise 3 to 8 degrees, weather patterns sharply shift, ice sheets shrink, and seas rise several feet. The problem of global warming seems overwhelming, but there is a lot you can do to help. Reducing your personal carbon footprint is easier than you think.

Small Steps to Take for Commuters

Burning gasoline and diesel fuel releases CO2 into the atmosphere and contributes to climate change, but these emissions can be reduced by improving your car's fuel efficiency.

Buy an efficient vehicle

Before buying a new or used vehicle, research the emissions and fuel economy performance of different vehicles to help you choose the cleanest, most fuel-efficient vehicle that meets your needs (see www.epa.gov).

Drive smart

To improve fuel economy and reduce greenhouse gas emissions, go easy on the brakes and gas pedal, avoid hard accelerations, reduce time spent idling, and unload unnecessary items in your trunk to reduce weight. If you have a removable roof rack and you are not using it, take it off to improve your fuel economy by as much as 5 percent.

Tune your car and check your tires

Keep your car well-maintained and check your tire pressure regularly to keep your car running more efficiently and safely. Underinflation increases tire wear and reduces your fuel economy by up to 3 percent.

Give your car a break

Use public transportation, carpool, run several errands at once, and walk or bike whenever possible to avoid using your car. If possible, telecommute for work, and limit face-to-face meetings that involve travel. Leaving your car at home just two days a week will reduce greenhouse gas emissions by an average of 1,590 lbs. per year.

YOUR NAME 1

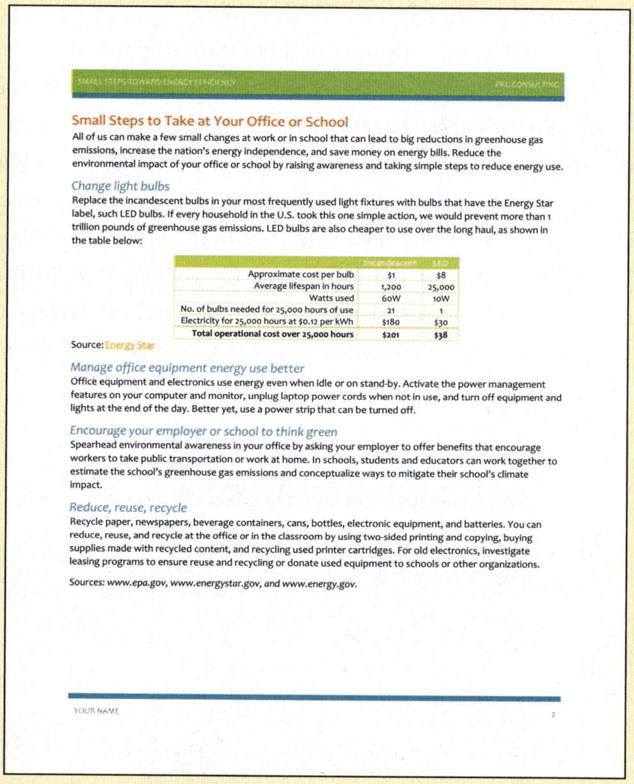

SMALL STEPS TOWARD ENERGY EFFICIENCY PKG CONSULTING

Small Steps to Take at Your Office or School

All of us can make a few small changes at work or in school that can lead to big reductions in greenhouse gas emissions, increase the nation's energy independence, and save money on energy bills. Reduce the environmental impact of your office or school by raising awareness and taking simple steps to reduce energy use.

Change light bulbs

Replace the incandescent bulbs in your most frequently used light fixtures with bulbs that have the Energy Star label, such LED bulbs. If every household in the U.S. took this one simple action, we would prevent more than 1 trillion pounds of greenhouse gas emissions. LED bulbs are also cheaper to use over the long haul, as shown in the table below:

	Incandescent	LED
Approximate cost per bulb	\$1	\$8
Average lifespan in hours	1,200	25,000
Watts used	60W	10W
No. of bulbs needed for 25,000 hours of use	21	1
Electricity for 25,000 hours at \$0.12 per kWh	\$180	\$30
Total operational cost over 25,000 hours	**\$201**	**\$38**

Source: Energy Star

Manage office equipment energy use better

Office equipment and electronics use energy even when idle or on stand-by. Activate the power management features on your computer and monitor, unplug laptop power cords when not in use, and turn off equipment and lights at the end of the day. Better yet, use a power strip that can be turned off.

Encourage your employer or school to think green

Spearhead environmental awareness in your office by asking your employer to offer benefits that encourage workers to take public transportation or work at home. In schools, students and educators can work together to estimate the school's greenhouse gas emissions and conceptualize ways to mitigate their school's climate impact.

Reduce, reuse, recycle

Recycle paper, newspapers, beverage containers, cans, bottles, electronic equipment, and batteries. You can reduce, reuse, and recycle at the office or in the classroom by using two-sided printing and copying, buying supplies made with recycled content, and recycling used printer cartridges. For old electronics, investigate leasing programs to ensure reuse and recycling or donate used equipment to schools or other organizations.

Sources: www.epa.gov, www.energystar.gov, and www.energy.gov.

YOUR NAME 2

9. Use a document template.

a. Click the File tab, click New, then scroll the gallery of templates.

b. Create a new document using the Invoice (Timeless Design) template. (*Hint*: Use the Search box to find the template, if necessary.)

c. Open the header area, click the "Company" placeholder text, type **PKG Consultants**, click the "Street Address…" placeholder, type **45 Westview Highway, Syracuse, NY 13219**, click the "phone" placeholder, type **555-555-0998**, delete the word Fax and the "fax" placeholder, delete the logo graphic placeholder, then close the header area.

Skills Review (continued)

- **d.** After "Invoice No.", type **13**, then replace the Date placeholder with **July 8**, and the current year.
- **e.** Type your name and address in the Bill to section.
- **f.** In the first cell in the Description column, type **Home energy audit, initial assessment**, press TAB twice, then type **$250**.
- **g.** Scroll down, click the "Date" placeholder in the Total due by cell, type **August 8**, press TAB, then type **$250**.
- **h.** Save the document with the filename **IL_WD_5_Invoice13** to the location where you store your Data Files, clicking OK if a warning box opens.

10. Work with PDF files in Word.

- **a.** Click the File tab, click Export, click the Create PDF/XPS button, then click Publish.
- **b.** View the invoice in Adobe or your browser, then click to exit Adobe or your browser.
- **c.** Submit the Word file, click the File tab in Word, then click Close.
- **d.** Click the File tab, click Open, navigate to the location where you store your Data Files, then open **IL_WD_5_Invoice13.pdf**.
- **e.** Submit the PDF file, close the file, do not save changes to the Building Blocks.dotx file if prompted, then exit Word.

Independent Challenge 1

You work in public outreach at the Riverwalk Medical Clinic. You have written the text for a report on annual giving to the Clinic, and now you need to format the report. You'll use styles, themes, and Quick Parts to give the report a cohesive and professional look.

- **a.** Start Word, create a new document using the Report design (blank) template, then save it as **IL_WD_5_RMCGiving**.
- **b.** Insert a Sideline cover page. Type **Riverwalk Medical Clinic Annual Giving** in the Title property control, then type **An Invitation to Donors** in the Subtitle property control.
- **c.** Remove the Company property control, type your name in the Author property control, then remove the Date property control.
- **d.** Scroll to the next page (contains "Title"), select all the body text on the page under the Heading 1 heading (starting with "To get started..."), insert the text file IL_WD_5-5.docx from the location where you store your Data Files. (*Hint*: Click the Object button arrow in the Text group on the Insert tab, click Text from file, then locate and insert the text file.)
- **e.** Scroll up to view the format and content of the report. Press CTRL+HOME, scroll to the second page (contains "Title"), select Title, type **Riverwalk Medical Clinic Annual Giving**, select Heading 1, type **An Invitation to Donors**, then format the following headings in the Heading 1 style: Capital Campaign Exceeds Its Goal, Types of Gifts, and The Cambridge Society.
- **f.** Change the style set of the document to Lines (Stylish), then reduce the font size of the title at the top of the second page of the document (not on the cover page) to 28 points.
- **g.** See how different styles change the look of a document by applying the following heading styles to the Annual Fund Gifts subheading under the Types of Gifts heading: the Heading 1 style, the Heading 2 style, then the Heading 3 style. (*Hint*: Open the Styles pane, click Options, then click All Styles in the Select styles to show box).
- **h.** Apply the Heading 3 style to the following subheadings: Memorial Gifts, Charitable Gifts, Named Endowments.
- **i.** Insert a Next Page section break after the end of the last paragraph above the chart (ends with "...requests for anonymity"), switch to multiple pages view, select the chart object on the last page, open the Page Setup dialog box from the Layout tab, then change the vertical alignment of the page containing the chart to Center.
- **j.** Using the Cover Page command, remove the current cover page, then use the Cover Page command again to insert a different cover page for the report from the Built-in category. Update or remove the content and property controls as necessary. (*Hint*: Scroll as needed to see the Built-in options.)

Independent Challenge 1 (continued)

k. Starting on the first page of the report (contains the text of the report), add a footer to the report that includes a page number and your name. Navigate to the footer on the last page of the report (contains the chart), click the Different First Page check box in the Options group on the Header & Footer ribbon to deselect it, click Page Number in the Header & Footer group, click Format Page Numbers, then click the Continue from previous section option button. Close the footer and verify that the three pages of the report text (not including the cover page) are numbered 1, 2, and 3 similar to the sample report shown in **FIGURE 5-26**.

l. Experiment with different themes, theme colors, theme fonts, theme effects, and paragraph spacing, then use these tools to customize the look of the report.

m. Adjust the elements of the report as necessary to make sure each page has a cohesive and professional look and the text fits comfortably on four pages. Figure 5-26 shows a sample finished report using the Gallery theme, the Facet built-in cover page, and the Integral built-in footer.

n. Save your changes to the document, submit the document to your instructor, close the document, then exit Word.

FIGURE 5-26

Independent Challenge 2

The Education department at the university where you work publishes a blog each month on a different topic in education. The blog is published on the university website and distributed electronically to a mailing list of subscribers. It's your job to format the blog posts and prepare them for electronic distribution. In this exercise you design a layout for a blog post, add hyperlinks to it, then save the document as a PDF file and as a webpage.

a. Start Word, open the file IL_WD_5-6.docx from the location where you store your Data Files, then save it as **IL_WD_5_LiteracyBlog** to the location where you store your Data Files.
b. In the third line of the document, replace YOUR NAME with your name.
c. Replace each instance of green text in the document with a hyperlink to the appropriate website for each source, shown in the table below. Include a ScreenTip in each hyperlink.

Source	Website URL	ScreenTip
UNESCO	www.unesco.org	United Nations Educational, Cultural, and Scientific Organization
ProLiteracy	www.proliteracy.org	Research and data on adult literacy worldwide
National Bureau of Economic Research	www.nber.org	Research and data on public policy
American Journal of Public Health	www.ajph.org	American Public Health Association
American Library Association	www.ala.org/advocacy/literacy	Key resources from the ALA

d. Test each link to make sure it works, then make any necessary adjustments.
e. Apply styles to the document. Format the first three lines of text using styles of your choice, then apply a heading style to each red heading in the document.
f. Apply a style set to the document.
g. Apply a theme to the document. Customize the theme fonts, theme colors, and paragraph spacing to achieve the look you want. FIGURE 5-27 shows a sample layout.
h. Create a new bullet character using a symbol and apply the new symbol bullet to the two bulleted lists in the document.
i. Adjust the margins, alignment, colors, and other formatting so the blog post is readable and the layout is attractive, then save your changes and submit the file.
j. Check the document for compatibility with earlier versions of Word.
k. Save the document as a PDF file, submit the PDF file, then close Adobe or your browser.
l. Save document as a Single File Web Page, view the webpage in Word, submit the webpage file, then save your changes.
m. Close all open files, then exit Word.

FIGURE 5-27

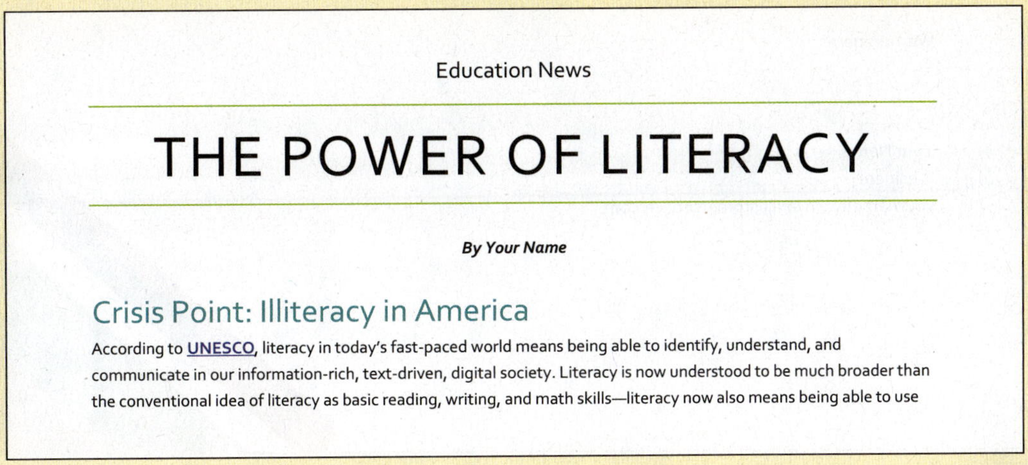
Education News

THE POWER OF LITERACY

By Your Name

Crisis Point: Illiteracy in America

According to UNESCO, literacy in today's fast-paced world means being able to identify, understand, and communicate in our information-rich, text-driven, digital society. Literacy is now understood to be much broader than the conventional idea of literacy as basic reading, writing, and math skills—literacy now also means being able to use

Visual Workshop

Create the letter shown in **FIGURE 5-28**. Start with the Modern Capsules letterhead template. Replace the logo placeholder with an icon. (*Hint*: Right-click the logo placeholder, point to Change Picture, click From Icons, then search for Headset and select the icon shown in the figure.) Resize the icon to be .7" tall and wide. Replace the placeholder text with the text shown in Figure 5-28. For the body of the letter, insert the text file **IL_WD_5-7.docx** from the location where you store your Data Files. (*Hint*: Use the Object arrow on the Insert tab, then click Text from File.) In the address block, remove the space after the paragraphs. Remove any hyperlinks from the letter. Apply the Slice theme and change the theme fonts to Corbel. (*Hint*: If the Slice theme is not available, select a different theme.) Save the document as **IL_WD_5_ArtisanLetter**.

FIGURE 5-28

Artisan Customer Service Agency
1550 East 9th Avenue, Escondido, CA 92025
www.artisancustomerservice.com
Tel: 442-555-0243

August 31, 2021

Ms. Lydia Paulo
Vice President
Cityside Auto Insurance
35 North Tulip Street
Escondido, CA 92029

Dear Ms. Paulo,

Thank you for choosing the Artisan Customer Service Agency to represent Cityside Auto Insurance in your customer service needs. Your business and your customers are in good hands with us.

Our trained customer service representatives are available 24 hours a day to assist your customers in a friendly, efficient, and professional manner. We look forward to working with you to achieve your customer service goals.

Warm regards,

Your Name
President
yourname@artisancustomerservice.com

Merging Word Documents

CASE You need to send a letter to people who signed up for one of the job search workshops offered by the Seattle branch of JCL Talent, Inc. The letter confirms their reservation and receipt of a nonrefundable deposit. You also need to send a general information packet to all the people participating in upcoming JCL Talent workshops. You use mail merge to create a personalized form letter for people who recently signed up for a workshop and mailing labels for the information packet.

Module Objectives

After completing this module, you will be able to:

- Understand mail merge
- Create a main document
- Design a data source
- Enter and edit records
- Add merge fields
- Work with merge rules
- Merge data
- Create labels
- Sort and filter records

Files You Will Need

IL_WD_6-1.docx
Support_WD_6_LabelsData.accdb
IL_WD_6-2.docx
IL_WD_6-3.docx
IL_WD_6-4.docx
Support_WD_6_MuseumData.accdb

Word
Module 6

Understand Mail Merge

Learning Outcomes
- Identify the elements of a mail merge
- State the benefits of performing a mail merge

When you perform a **mail merge**, you merge a standard Word document with a file that contains customized information for many individuals or items. The standard document is called the **main document**. The file with the unique data for individual people or items is called the **data source**. Merging the main document with a data source results in a **merged document** that contains customized versions of the main document, as shown in FIGURE 6-1. The Mail Merge pane steps you through the process of setting up and performing a mail merge. You can also perform a mail merge using the commands on the Mailings tab. **CASE** *You decide to use the Mail Merge pane to create your form letters and the commands on the Mailings tab to create your mailing labels. Before beginning, you explore the steps involved in performing a mail merge.*

DETAILS

- **Create the main document**

  The main document contains the text—often called **boilerplate text**—that appears in every version of the merged document. The main document also includes the merge fields, which indicate where the customized information is inserted when you perform the merge. You insert the merge fields in the main document after you have created or selected the data source. You can create a main document using one of the following: a new blank document, the current document, a template, or an existing document.

- **Create a data source or select an existing data source**

  The data source is a file that contains the unique information for each individual or item, such as a person's name. It provides the information that varies in every version of the merged document. A data source is composed of data fields and data records. A **data field** is a category of information, such as last name, first name, street address, city, or postal code. A **data record** is a complete set of related information for an individual or an item, such as one person's name and address. Think of a data source file as a table: the header row contains the names of the data fields (the **field names**), and each row in the table is an individual data record. You can create a new data source or you can use an existing data source, such as a data source created in Word, an Outlook contact list, an Access database, or an Excel worksheet.

- **Identify the fields to include in the data source and enter the records**

  When you create a new data source, you must first identify the fields to include, such as first name, last name, and street address if you are creating a data source that will include addresses. It is also important to think of and include all the fields you will need (not just the obvious ones) before you begin to enter data. For example, if you are creating a data source that includes names and addresses, you might need to include fields for a person's middle name, title, apartment number, department name, or country, even if some records in the data source will not include that information. Once you have identified the fields and set up your data source, you are ready to enter the data for each record.

- **Add merge fields to the main document**

  A **merge field** is a placeholder that you insert in the main document to indicate where the data from each record should be inserted when you perform the merge. For example, you insert a ZIP Code merge field in the location where you want to insert a ZIP Code. The merge fields in a main document must correspond with the field names in the associated data source. Merge fields must be inserted, not typed, in the main document. The Mail Merge pane and the Mailings tab provide access to the dialog boxes you use to insert merge fields.

- **Merge the data from the data source into the main document**

  Once you have established your data source and inserted the merge fields in the main document, you are ready to perform the merge. You can merge to a new file, which contains a customized version of the main document for each record in the data source, or you can merge directly to a printer or an email message.

FIGURE 6-1: Mail Merge Process

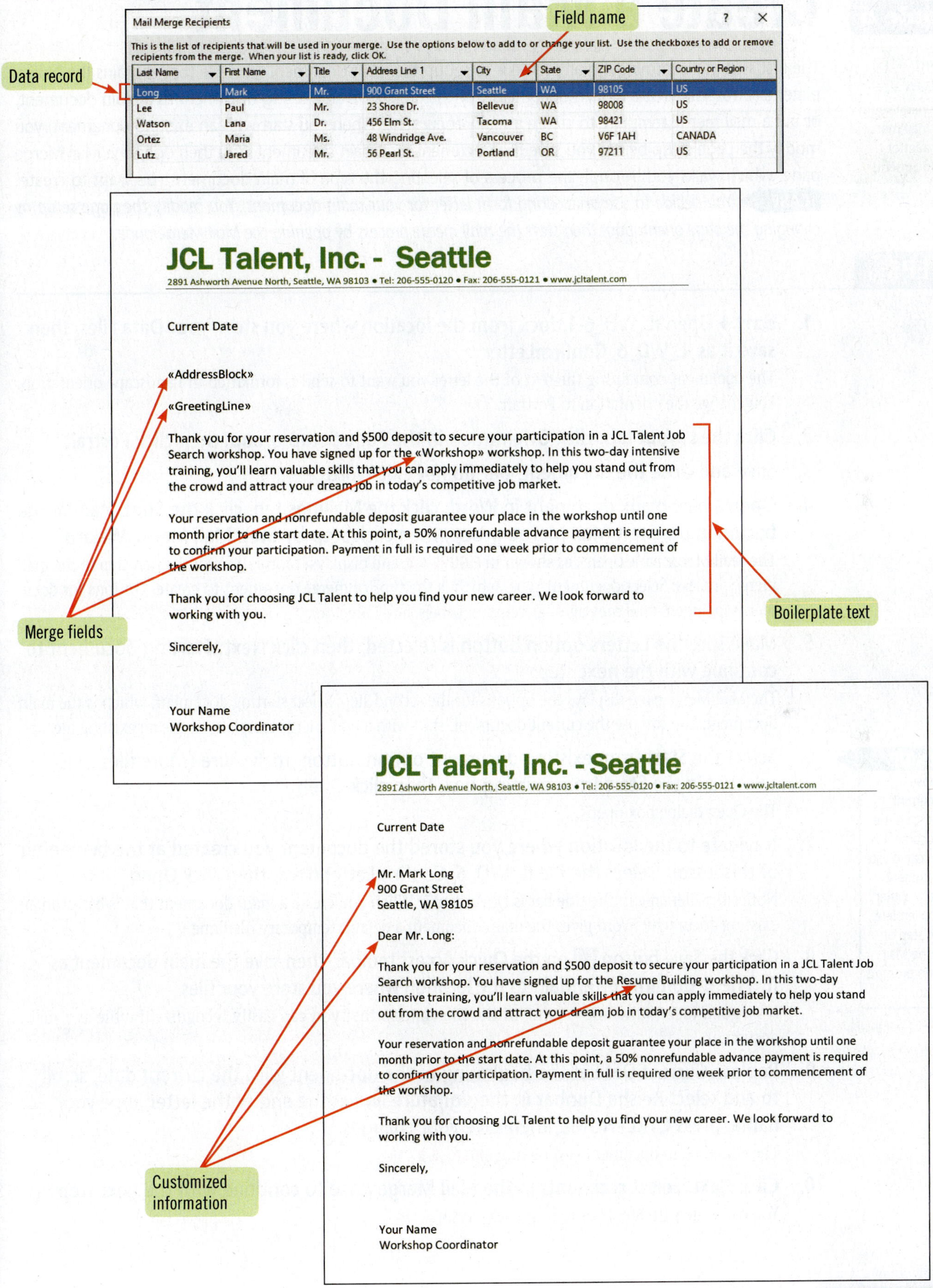

Word

Word
Module 6

Create a Main Document

Learning Outcomes
- Modify page setup
- Start a mail merge
- Create a letter main document

The first step in performing a mail merge is to set up the main document—the file that contains the boilerplate text. You can create a main document from scratch, save an existing document as a main document, or use a mail merge template to create a main document. When you start with an existing document, you modify the page setup before you save the document as a main document. You then open the Mail Merge pane, which walks you through the process of selecting the type of main document you want to create.

CASE *You decide to use an existing form letter for your main document. You modify the page setup by changing the page orientation, then start the mail merge process by opening the Mail Merge pane.*

STEPS

1. **sam Open IL_WD_6-1.docx from the location where you store your Data Files, then save it as IL_WD_6_ConfirmLetter**
   The document containing the text of the letter you want to send is formatted in Landscape orientation. You change the orientation to Portrait.
2. **Click the Layout tab, click Orientation in the Page Setup group, then click Portrait**
3. **Save and close the document, but do not exit Word**
4. **Open a new blank document in Word, click the Mailings tab, click the Start Mail Merge button in the Start Mail Merge group, then click Step-by-Step Mail Merge Wizard**
   The Mail Merge pane opens, as shown in FIGURE 6-2, and displays information for the first step in the mail merge process: Select document type, which is the type of merge document to create. Options for documents include E-mail messages, Envelopes, Labels, and Directory.
5. **Make sure the Letters option button is selected, then click Next: Starting document to continue with the next step**
   The Mail Merge pane displays the options for the second step: Select starting document, which is the main document. You can use the current document, start with a mail merge template, or use an existing file.
6. **Select the Start from existing document option button, make sure (More files...) is selected in the Start from existing box, then click Open**
   The Open dialog box opens.
7. **Navigate to the location where you stored the document you created at the beginning of this lesson, select the file IL_WD_6_ConfirmLetter.docx, then click Open**
   Notice the filename in the title bar is Document1. When you create a main document that is based on an existing document, Word gives the main document a default temporary filename.
8. **Click the Save button on the Quick Access toolbar, then save the main document as IL_WD_6_ConfirmLetterMain to the location where you store your files**
   It's a good idea to include "main" in the filename so that you can easily recognize the file as a main document.
9. **Replace Current Date at the beginning of the document with the current date, scroll to and select Keisha Dunbar in the signature line at the end of the letter, type your name, press CTRL+HOME, then save your changes**
   The edited main document is shown in FIGURE 6-3.
10. **Click Next: Select recipients in the Mail Merge pane to continue with the next step**
    You continue with Step 3 of 6 in the next lesson.

QUICK TIP
If you choose "Use the current document" and the current document is blank, you can create a main document from scratch. Either type the boilerplate text at this step or wait until the Mail Merge pane prompts you to do so.

FIGURE 6-2: Step 1 of 6 Mail Merge pane

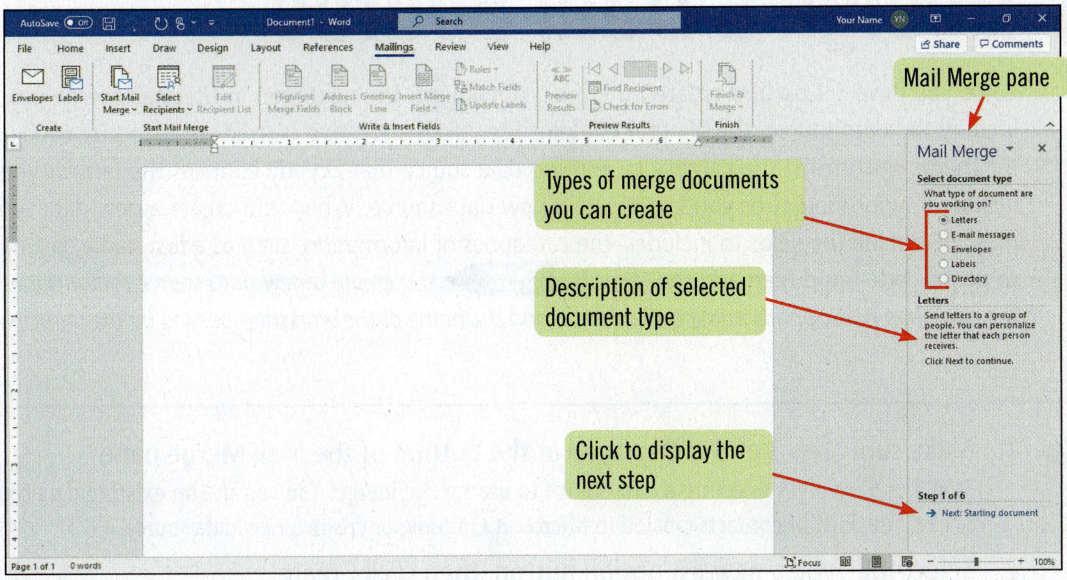

FIGURE 6-3: Main document with Step 2 of 6 Mail Merge pane

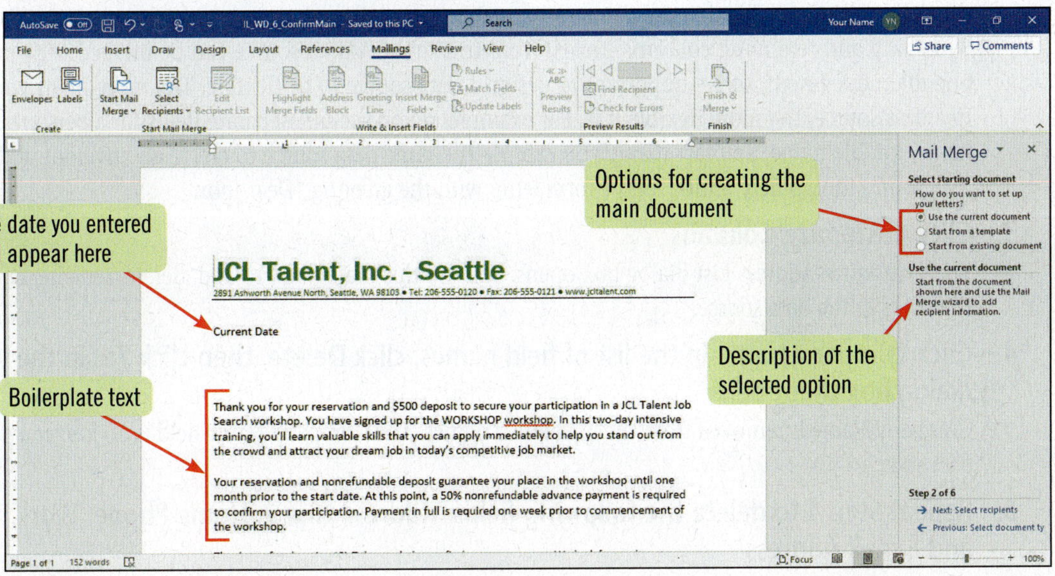

Using a mail merge template

If you are creating letters or faxes, you can use a mail merge template to start your main document. Each template includes placeholder text, which you can replace, and merge fields, which you can match to the field names in your data source. To create a main document that is based on a mail merge template, click the File tab, click New, type "mail merge" in the Search for online templates box, click the Start searching button, select one of the mail merge templates to use as your main document, and then click Create. You can then use the Mail Merge pane or the Ribbon to begin a mail merge using the current document. In the Step 2 of 6 Mail Merge pane, click the Use the current document option button, and then click Next. Once you have created the main document, you can customize the main document with your own information: edit the placeholder text; change the document format; or add, remove, or modify the merge fields.

Before performing the merge, make sure to match the names of the merge fields used in the template with the field names used in your data source. To match the field names, click the Match Fields button in the Write & Insert Fields group on the Mailings tab, and then use the arrows in the Match Fields dialog box to select the field name in your data source that corresponds to each address field component in the main document.

Word

Word
Module 6

Design a Data Source

Learning Outcomes
- Create a data source
- Add and remove fields in a data source

Once you have set up and created the main document, the next step in the mail merge process is to identify the data source, the file that contains the information that is used to customize each version of the merge document. You can use an existing data source that already contains the records you want to include in your merge, or you can create a new data source. When you create a new data source, you must determine the fields to include—the categories of information, such as a first name, last name, city, or postal code—and then add the records. **CASE** *You create a new data source that includes fields for the workshop participant's name and address, and the name of the workshop booked by the participant.*

STEPS

QUICK TIP
Data sources created and saved as an Access database use the .accdb file extension; data sources created and saved in Word as part of the Mail Merge process use the .mdb file extension.

1. **Make sure Step 3 of 6 is displayed at the bottom of the Mail Merge pane**
   Step 3 of 6 involves selecting a data source to use for the merge. You can use an existing data source from Access, use a list of contacts created in Microsoft Outlook, or create a new data source.

2. **Select the Type a new list option button, then click Create**
   The New Address List dialog box opens, as shown in FIGURE 6-4. You use this dialog box both to design your data source and to enter records. The column headings in the Type recipient information... section of the dialog box are fields that are commonly used in form letters, but you can customize your data source by adding and removing columns (fields) from this table. A data source can be merged with more than one main document, so it's important to design a data source to be flexible. The more fields you include in a data source, the more flexible it is. For example, if you include separate fields for a person's title, first name, middle name, and last name, you can use the same data source to create an envelope addressed to "Mr. John Montgomery Smith" and a form letter with the greeting "Dear John".

3. **Click Customize Columns**
   The Customize Address List dialog box opens. You use this dialog box to add, delete, rename, and reorder the fields in the data source.

4. **Click Company Name in the list of field names, click Delete, then click Yes in the warning dialog box that opens**
   Company Name is removed from the list of field names. The Company Name field is no longer a part of the data source.

5. **Repeat Step 4 to delete the following fields: Address Line 2, Home Phone, Work Phone, and E-mail Address**
   The fields are removed from the data source.

6. **Click Add, type Workshop in the Add Field dialog box, then click OK**
   A field called "Workshop", which you will use to indicate the workshop booked by the participant, is added to the data source.

7. **Make sure Workshop is selected in the list of field names, then click Move Up until Workshop is at the top of the list**
   The field name "Workshop" is moved to the top of the list, as shown in FIGURE 6-5. Although the order of field names does not matter in a data source, it's convenient to arrange the field names logically to make it easier to enter and edit records.

8. **Click OK**
   The New Address List dialog box shows the customized list of fields, with the Workshop field first in the list. The next step is to enter each record you want to include in the data source. You add records to the data source in the next lesson.

FIGURE 6-4: New Address List dialog box

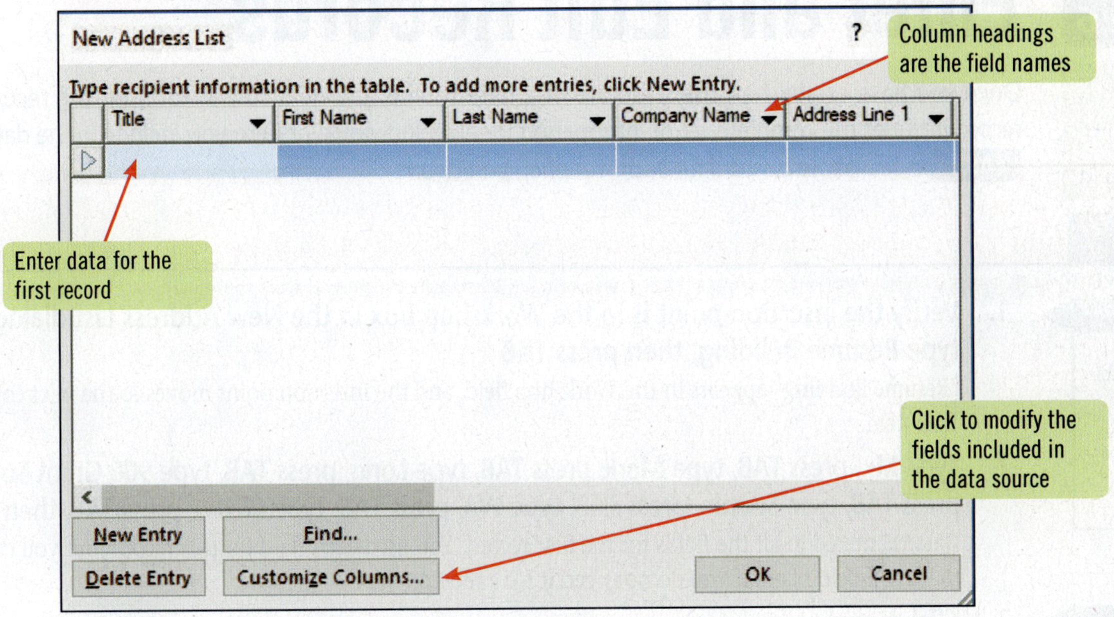

FIGURE 6-5: Customize Address List dialog box

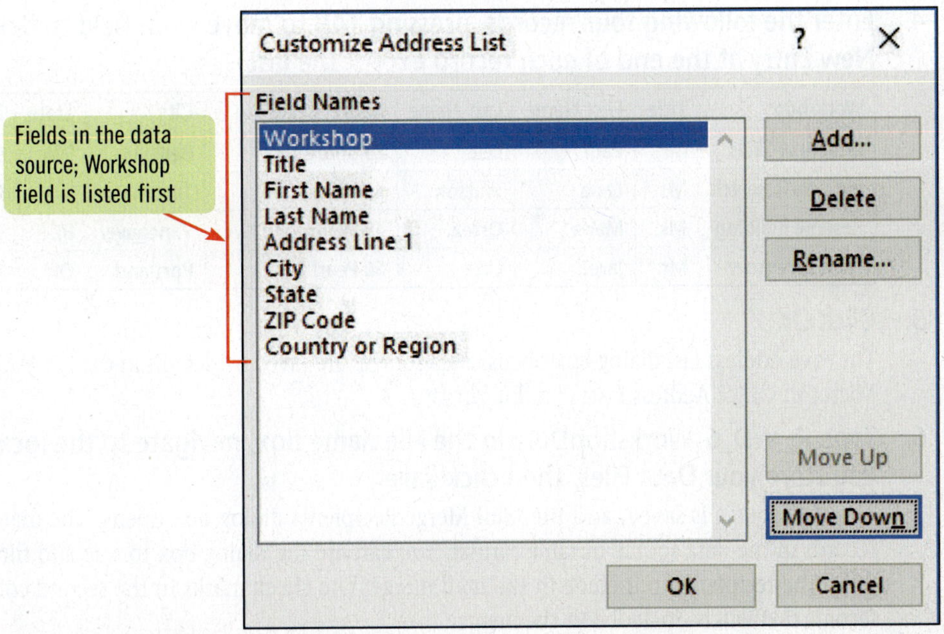

Merging with an Outlook data source

If you maintain lists of contacts in Microsoft Outlook, you can use one of your Outlook contact lists as a data source for a merge. To merge with an Outlook data source, click the Select from Outlook contacts option button in the Step 3 of 6 Mail Merge pane, then click Choose Contacts Folder to open the Choose Profile dialog box. In this dialog box, use the Profile Name arrow to select the profile you want to use, then click OK to open the Select Contacts dialog box. In this dialog box, select the contact list you want to use as the data source, and then click OK. All the contacts included in the selected folder appear in the Mail Merge Recipients dialog box. Here, you can refine the list of recipients to include in the merge by sorting and filtering the records. When you are satisfied, click OK in the Mail Merge Recipients dialog box.

Enter and Edit Records

Learning Outcomes
- Add records
- Edit a recipient list

Once you have established the structure of a data source, the next step is to enter the records. Each record includes the complete set of information for each individual or item you include in the data source.

CASE *You create a record for each workshop participant.*

STEPS

QUICK TIP
Be careful not to add spaces or extra punctuation after an entry in a field, or these will appear when the data is merged.

QUICK TIP
You can also press TAB at the end of the last field to start a new record.

TROUBLE
If a check mark appears in the blank record under Jared Lutz, click the check mark to eliminate the record from the merge.

QUICK TIP
If you want to add new records or modify existing records, click Edit recipient list in the Mail Merge pane.

1. **Verify the insertion point is in the Workshop box in the New Address List dialog box, type Resume Building, then press TAB**

   "Resume Building" appears in the Workshop field, and the insertion point moves to the next column, the Title field.

2. **Type Mr., press TAB, type Mark, press TAB, type Long, press TAB, type 900 Grant Street, press TAB, type Seattle, press TAB, type WA, press TAB, type 98105, press TAB, then type US**

   Data is entered in all the fields for the first record. You used each field for this record, but you can choose to leave a field blank if you do not need it for a record.

3. **Click New Entry**

   The record for Mark Long is added to the data source, and the New Address List dialog box displays empty fields for the next record, as shown in FIGURE 6-6.

4. **Enter the following four records, pressing TAB to move from field to field, and clicking New Entry at the end of each record except the last:**

Workshop	Title	First Name	Last Name	Address Line 1	City	State	ZIP	Country
Interview Skills	Mr.	Paul	Lee	23 Shore Dr.	Bellevue	WA	98008	US
Industry Research	Ms.	Lana	Watson	456 Elm St.	Tacoma	WA	98421	US
Resume Building	Ms.	Maria	Ortez	48 Windridge Ave.	Vancouver	BC	V6F 1AH	CANADA
Skills Inventory	Mr.	Jared	Lutz	56 Pearl St.	Portland	OR	97211	US

5. **Click OK**

   The Save Address List dialog box opens. Data sources are saved by default in the My Data Sources folder in Microsoft Office Address Lists (*.mdb) format.

6. **Type IL_WD_6_WorkshopData in the File name box, navigate to the location where you store your Data Files, then click Save**

   The data source is saved, and the Mail Merge Recipients dialog box opens. The dialog box shows the records in the data source in table format. You can use the dialog box to sort and filter records, and to select the recipients to include in the mail merge. The check marks in the second column indicate the records that will be included in the merge.

7. **Click IL_WD_6_WorkshopData.mdb in the Data Source box at the bottom of the dialog box as shown in FIGURE 6-7**

8. **Click Edit to open the Edit Data Source dialog box**

   You use this dialog box to edit a recipient list, including adding and removing fields, editing field names, adding and removing records, and editing existing records.

9. **Click Ms. in the Title field of the Lana Watson record to select it, then type Dr. as shown in FIGURE 6-8**

10. **Click OK in the Edit Data Source dialog box, click Yes, then click OK in the Mail Merge Recipients dialog box**

    The file type and filename of the data source attached to the main document now appear under Use an existing list heading in the Mail Merge pane.

FIGURE 6-6: Record in New Address List dialog box

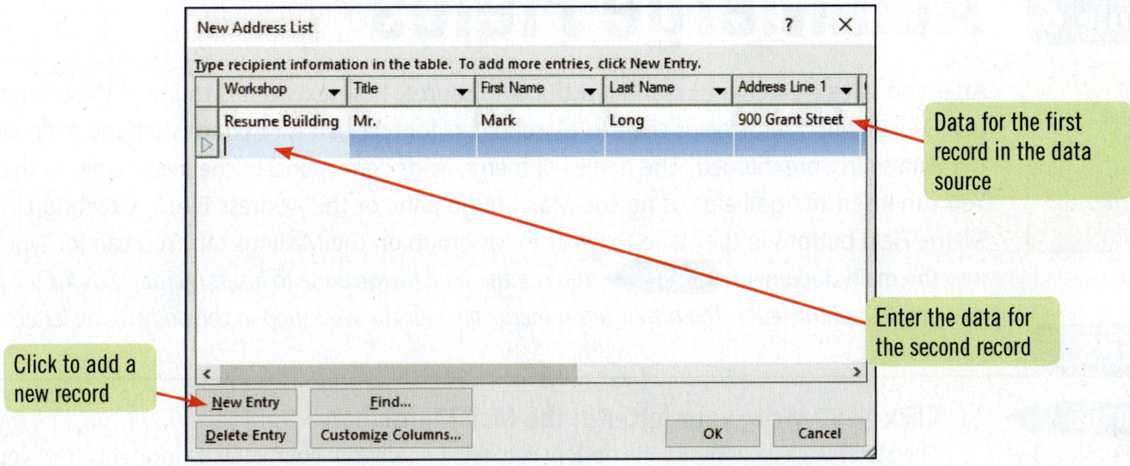

FIGURE 6-7: Data Source selected in the Mail Merge Recipients dialog box

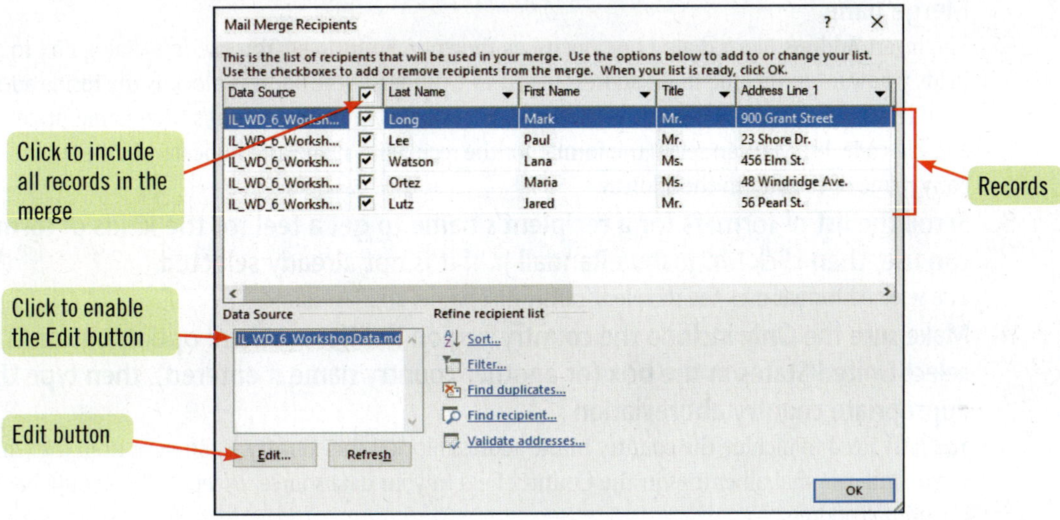

FIGURE 6-8: Edit Data Source dialog box

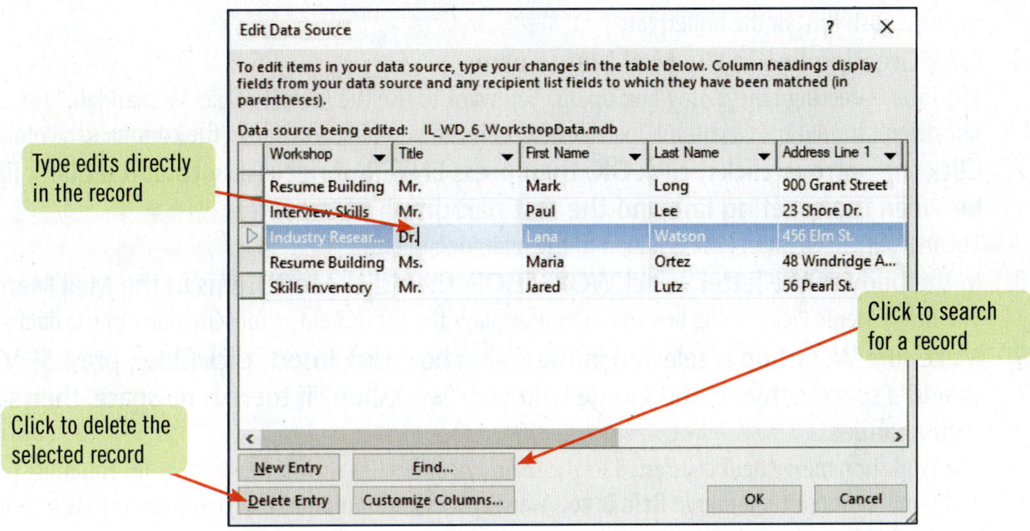

Word

Word
Module 6

Add Merge Fields

Learning Outcomes
- Insert merge fields
- Customize an address block and greeting field

After you have created and identified the data source, the next step is to insert the merge fields in the main document. Merge fields serve as placeholders for text that is inserted when the main document and the data source are merged. The names of merge fields correspond to the field names in the data source. You can insert merge fields using the Mail Merge pane or the Address Block, Greeting Line, and Insert Merge Field buttons in the Write & Insert Fields group on the Mailings tab. You cannot type merge fields into the main document. **CASE** *You use the Mail Merge pane to insert merge fields for the inside address and greeting of the letter. You also insert a merge field for the workshop in the body of the letter.*

STEPS

QUICK TIP
You can also click the Address Block button in the Write & Insert Fields group on the Mailings tab to insert an address block.

QUICK TIP
You cannot simply type chevrons around a field name. You must insert merge fields using the Mail Merge pane or the buttons in the Write & Insert Fields group on the Mailings tab.

QUICK TIP
You can also click the Insert Merge Field button or arrow in the Write & Insert Fields group on the Mailings tab to insert a merge field.

1. **Click Next: Write your letter in the Mail Merge pane**
   The Mail Merge pane shows the options for Step 4 of 6: Write your letter. During this step, you write or edit the boilerplate text and insert the merge fields in the main document. Since your form letter is already written, you are ready to add the merge fields to it.
2. **Click the blank line above the first body paragraph, then click Address block in the Mail Merge pane**
   The Insert Address Block dialog box opens, as shown in FIGURE 6-9. You use this dialog box to specify the fields you want to include in an address block. In this merge, the address block is the inside address of the form letter. An address block automatically includes fields for the recipient's title, name, street, city, state, and ZIP code, but you can select the format for the recipient's name and indicate whether to include a company name or country in the address.
3. **Scroll the list of formats for a recipient's name to get a feel for the kinds of formats you can use, then click Mr. Joshua Randall Jr. if it is not already selected**
   The selected format uses the recipient's title, first name, and last name.
4. **Make sure the Only include the country/region if different than: option button is selected, select United States in the box (or another country name if entered), then type US or the appropriate country abbreviation**
   You only need to include the country in the address block if the country is different from the United States, so you indicate that all entries in the Country field in your data source, except "US", should be included in the printed address.
5. **Deselect the Format address according to the destination country/region check box, click OK, then press ENTER twice**
   The merge field AddressBlock is added to the main document. Chevrons (<< and >>) surround a merge field to distinguish it from the boilerplate text.
6. **Click Greeting line in the Mail Merge pane**
   The Insert Greeting Line dialog box opens. You want to use the format "Dear Mr. Randall:" for a greeting. The default format uses a comma instead of a colon, so you have to change the comma to a colon.
7. **Click the , arrow, click :, click OK, then press ENTER, if necessary to add a blank line between the greeting line and the first paragraph of the letter**
   The merge field GreetingLine is added to the main document.
8. **In the body of the letter select WORKSHOP, then click More items in the Mail Merge pane**
   The Insert Merge Field dialog box opens and displays the list of field names included in the data source.
9. **Make sure Workshop is selected in the dialog box, click Insert, click Close, press SPACEBAR to add a space between the merge field and "workshop" if there is no space, then save your changes**
   The Workshop merge field is inserted in the main document, as shown in FIGURE 6-10. You must type spaces and punctuation after a merge field if you want spaces and punctuation to appear in that location in the merged documents.

FIGURE 6-9: Insert Address Block dialog box

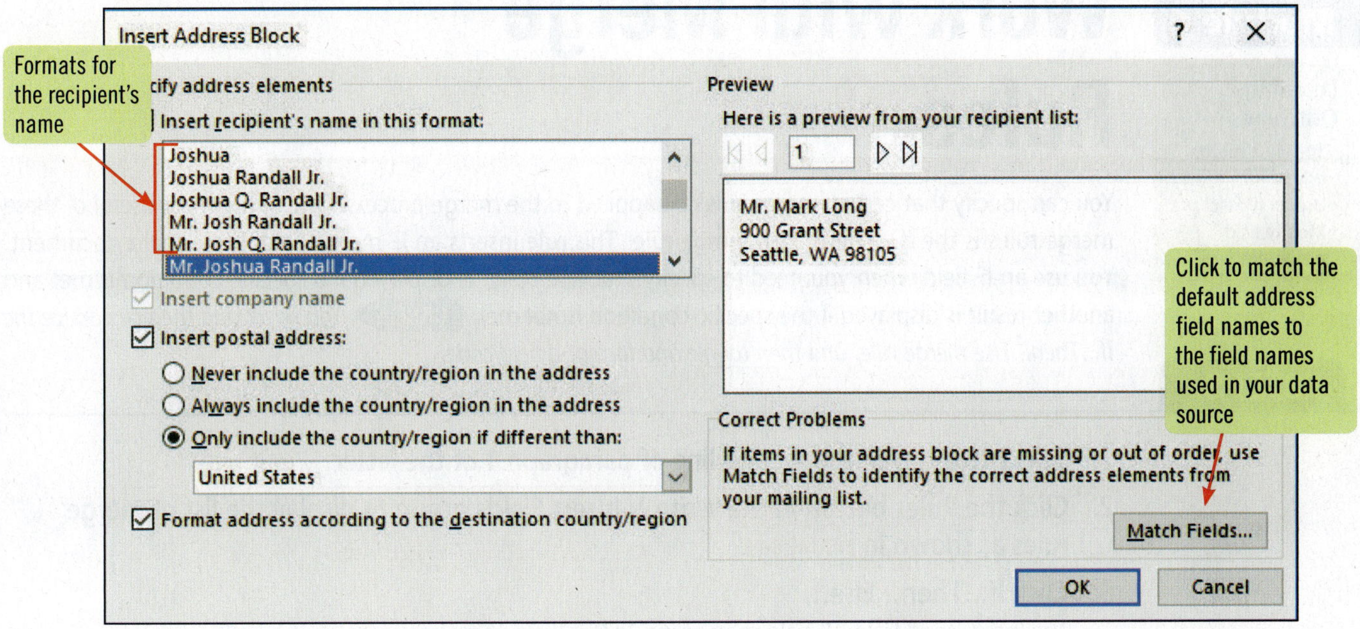

FIGURE 6-10: Merge fields in the main document

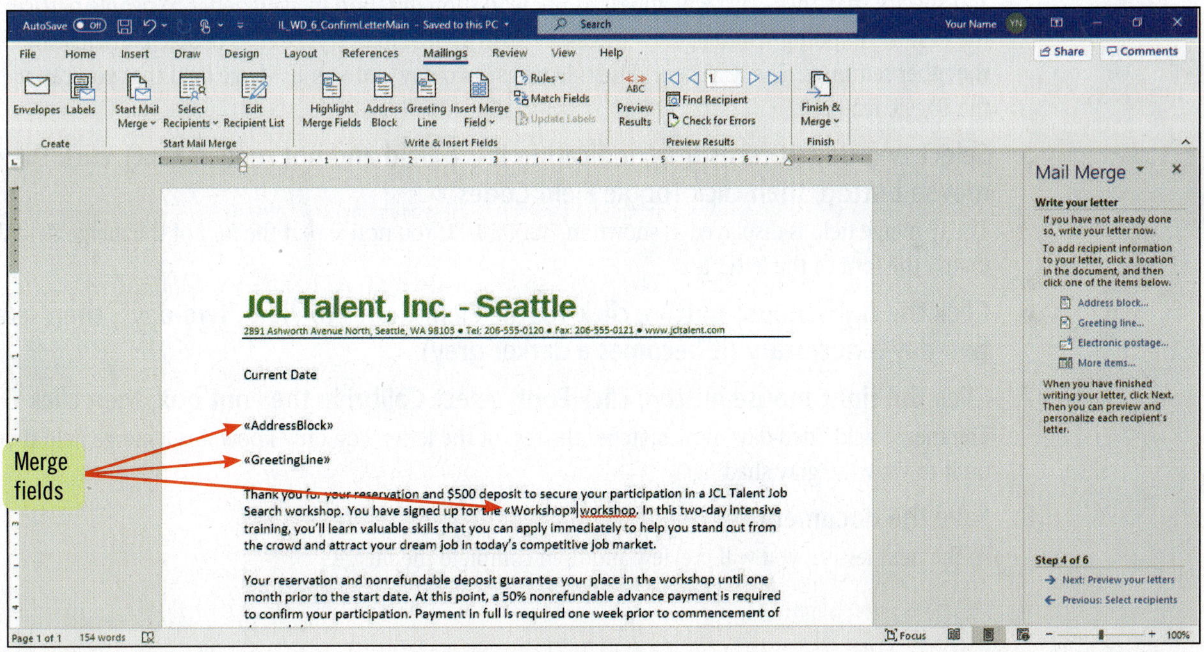

Matching fields

The merge fields you insert in a main document must correspond with the field names in the associated data source. If you are using the Address Block merge field, you must make sure that the default address field names correspond to the field names used in your data source. If the default address field names do not match the field names in your data source, click Match Fields in the Insert Address Block dialog box, then use the arrows in the Match Fields dialog box to select the field name in the data source that corresponds to each default address field name. You can also click the Match Fields button in the Write & Insert Fields group on the Mailings tab to open the Match Fields dialog box.

Work with Merge Rules

Learning Outcomes
- Specify a merge rule
- Use an IF field
- Modify field properties

You can specify that certain merge rules be applied to the merge process. One of the most useful of these merge rules is the If...Then...Else merge rule. This rule inserts an IF merge field into a main document. You use an IF field when you need to specify that one result is displayed if a specific condition is met and another result is displayed if the specific condition is *not* met. CASE *You select and then customize the If...Then...Else merge rule, and then toggle and format a field code.*

STEPS

1. **Select two-day in the second line of paragraph 1 of the letter**
2. **Click the Rules button in the Write & Insert Fields group to display the list of merge rules as shown in FIGURE 6-11**
3. **Click If...Then...Else...**
   The Insert Word Field: IF dialog box opens. In this dialog box, you enter the IF criteria.
4. **Enter criteria for the If...Then...Else rule as shown in FIGURE 6-12, click OK, then press SPACEBAR to add a space between "two-day" and "intensive", if necessary**
   You specify that "two-day" will appear as the workshop duration in every letter to people participating in the Resume Building seminar, and "three-day" will appear in every letter to people participating in any of the other seminars. The If...Then...Else rule turns "two-day" into an IF Merge field that you can view using the Toggle feature.
5. **Select two-day (it turns gray, indicating it is a field and not regular text), click the right mouse button, then click Toggle Field Codes**
   The IF merge field is displayed as shown in FIGURE 6-13. You notice that the font of the merge field does not match the font of the letter text.
6. **Click the right mouse button, click Toggle Field Codes to view "two-day", then select two-day if necessary (it becomes a darker gray)**
7. **Click the right mouse button, click Font, select Calibri in the Font box, then click OK**
   The merge field "two-day" now matches the rest of the letter. You only know it is a merge field if you click on it to view the gray shading.
8. **Save the document**
   In the next lesson, you will preview and then complete the merge.

FIGURE 6-11: List of merge rules

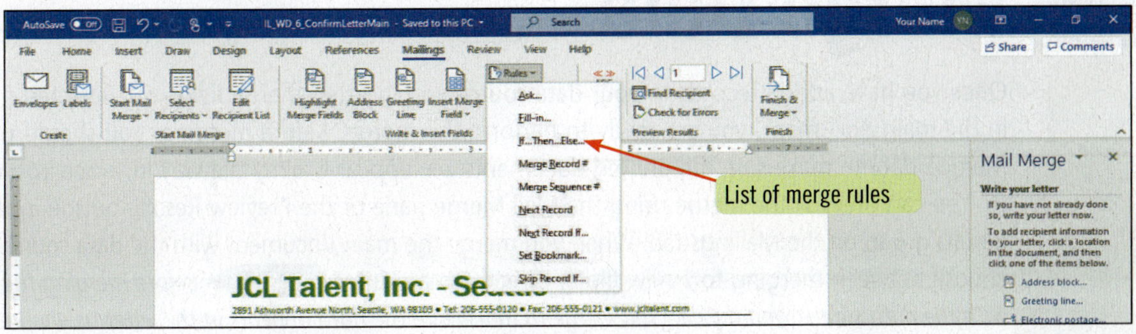

FIGURE 6-12: Insert Word Field: IF dialog box

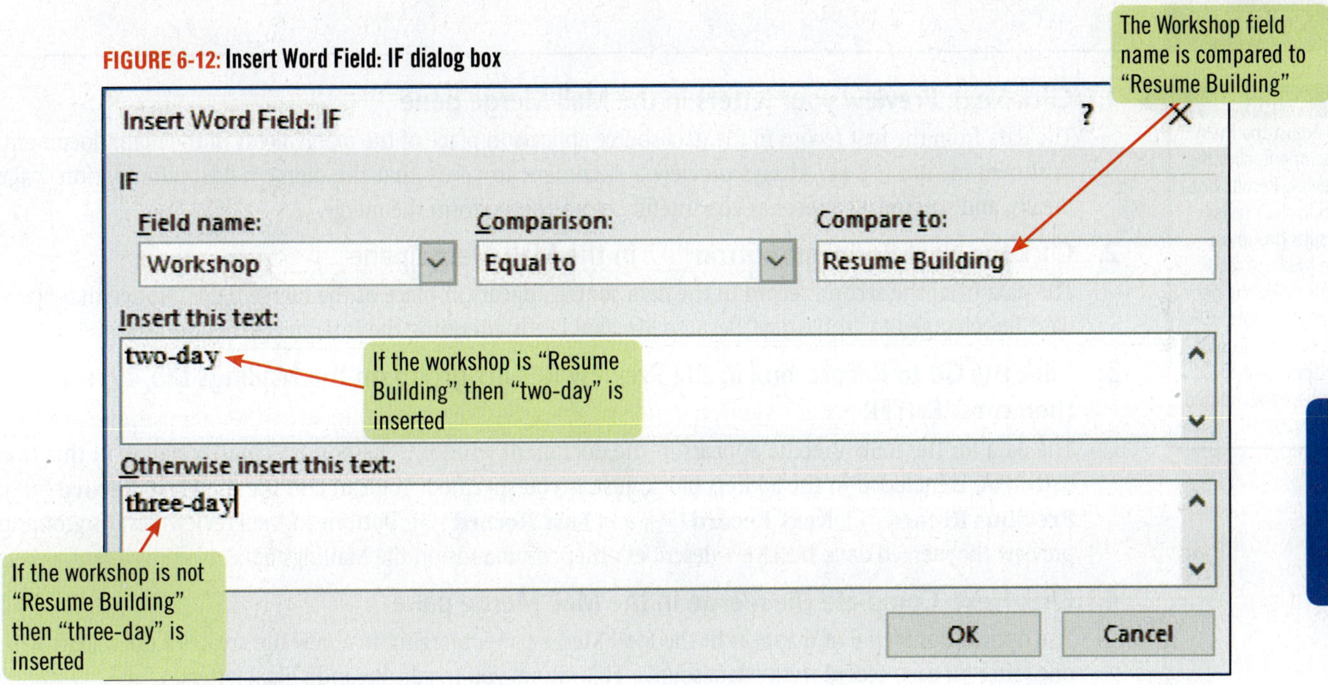

FIGURE 6-13: Toggled IF merge field

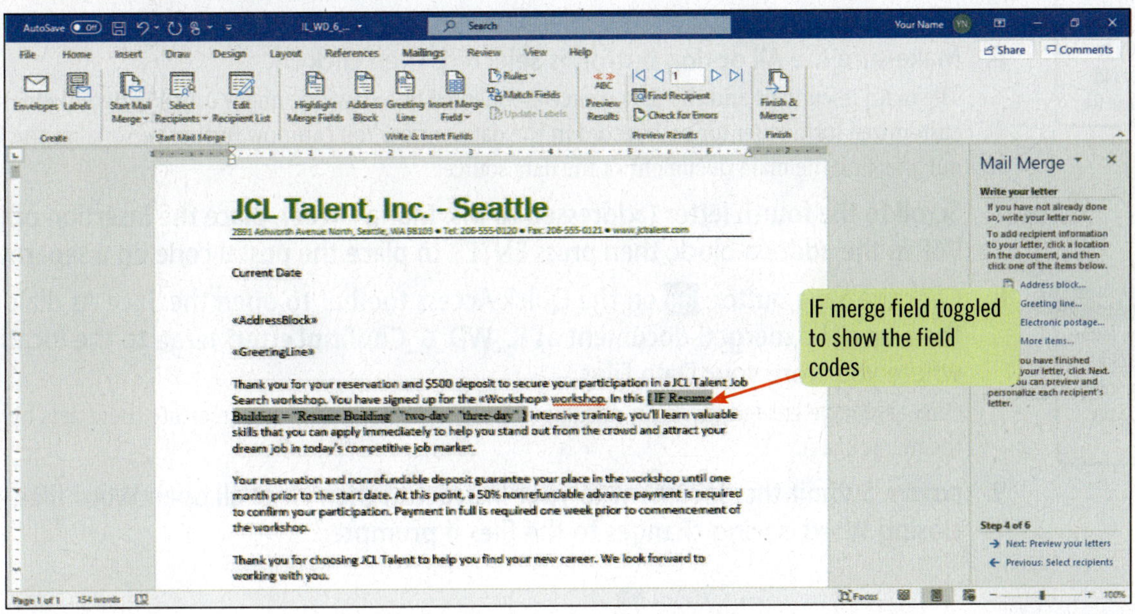

Merge Data

Learning Outcomes
- Preview a merge
- Merge data to a new document
- Customize a merged document

Once you have added records to your data source and inserted merge fields and selected merge rules in the main document, you are ready to perform the merge. Before merging, you should preview the merged data to make sure the printed documents will appear exactly the way in which you want them to. You can preview the merge using the Mail Merge pane or the Preview Results button in the Preview Results group on the Mailings tab. When you merge the main document with the data source, you must choose between merging to a new file or directly to a printer. **CASE** *Before merging the form letter with the data source, you preview the merge to make sure the data appears in the letter as you intended. You then merge the two files to a new document.*

STEPS

QUICK TIP
To adjust the main document, click the Preview Results button in the Preview Results group on the Mailings tab, then make any necessary changes. Click the Preview Results button again to preview the merged data.

1. **Click Next: Preview your letters in the Mail Merge pane**
   The data from the first record in the data source appears in place of the merge fields in the main document, as shown in **FIGURE 6-14**. Always preview a document to verify that the merge fields, punctuation, page breaks, and spacing all appear as you intend before you perform the merge.
2. **Click the Next Recipient button [>>] in the Mail Merge pane**
   The data from the second record in the data source appears in place of the merge fields. Notice that "two-day" has changed to "three-day" because Mr. Paul Lee is attending the Interview Skills workshop.
3. **Click the Go to Record box in the Preview Results group on the Mailings tab, type 4, then press ENTER**
   The data for the fourth record appears in the document window. The non-US country name, in this case CANADA, is included in the address block, just as you specified. You can also use the **First Record** [|◁], **Previous Record** [◁], **Next Record** [▷], and **Last Record** [▷|] buttons in the Preview Results group to preview the merged data. **TABLE 6-1** describes other commands on the Mailings tab.
4. **Click Next: Complete the merge in the Mail Merge pane**
   The options for Step 6 of 6 appear in the Mail Merge pane. Merging to a new file creates a document with one letter for each record in the data source. This allows you to edit the individual letters.

QUICK TIP
If your data source contains many records, you can merge directly to a printer to avoid creating a large file.

5. **Click Edit individual letters to merge the data to a new document**
   The Merge to New Document dialog box opens. You can use this dialog box to specify the records to include in the merge.
6. **Make sure the All option button is selected, then click OK**
   The main document and the data source are merged to a new document called Letters1, which contains a customized form letter for each record in the data source. You can now further personalize the letters without affecting the main document or the data source.
7. **Scroll to the fourth letter (addressed to Ms. Maria Ortez), place the insertion point before V6F in the address block, then press ENTER to place the postal code on a separate line**

QUICK TIP
Print only one letter if you are required to submit a printed document to your instructor.

8. **Click the Save button [💾] on the Quick Access toolbar to open the Save As dialog box, then save the merged document as IL_WD_6_ConfirmLetterMerge to the location where you store your Data Files**
   Once you have created the main document and the data source, you can create the letters by performing the merge again.
9. **sam Submit the document to your instructor, then close all open Word files without closing Word, saving changes to the files if prompted**

FIGURE 6-14: Preview of merged data

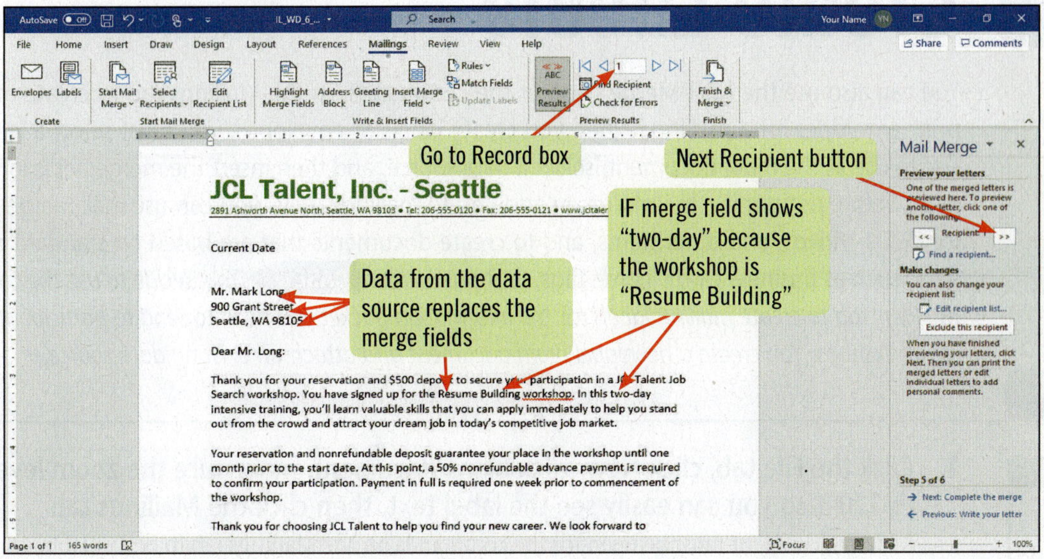

TABLE 6-1: Commands on the Mailings tab

command	use to
Envelopes	Create and print an individual envelope
Labels	Create and print an individual label
Start Mail Merge	Select the type of mail merge document to create and start the mail merge process
Select Recipients	Attach an existing data source to a main document or create a new data source
Edit Recipient List	Edit, sort, and filter the associated data source
Highlight Merge Fields	Highlight the merge fields in the main document
Address Block	Insert an Address Block merge field in the main document
Greeting Line	Insert a Greeting Line merge field in the main document
Insert Merge Field	Insert a merge field from the data source in the main document
Rules	Set rules to control how Word merges the data in the data source with the main document
Match Fields	Match the names of address or greeting fields used in a main document with the field names used in the data source
Update Labels	Update all the labels in a label main document to match the content and formatting of the first label
Preview Results	Switch between viewing the main document with merge fields or with merged data
Find Recipient	Search for a specific record in the merged document
Check for Errors	Check for and report errors in the merge
Finish & Merge	Specify whether to merge to a new document or directly to a printer or to email, then complete the merge

Opening Merge Files

The Word file you have designated as "Main" in the filename is linked to the data source that you attached to it. When you open the Word file, a message appears advising you that "Opening this document will run the following SQL command:". When you click Yes, the data from the data source attached to the merge file will be placed in the document. If you wish to run the merge again, you need to click Yes when this message is displayed.

Word

Word
Module 6

Create Labels

Learning Outcomes
- Create a label main document
- Merge with an existing data source
- Update mailing labels

You can also use the Mail Merge pane or the commands on the Mailings tab to create mailing labels or print envelopes for a mailing. When you create labels or envelopes, you must select a label or envelope size to use as the main document, select a data source, and then insert the merge fields in the main document before performing the merge. In addition to mailing labels, you can use mail merge to create labels for DVDs, videos, and other items, and to create documents that are based on standard or custom label sizes, such as business cards, name tags, and postcards. CASE *You decide to use the commands on the Mailings tab to create mailing labels for the information packet you need to send to participants about upcoming workshops. You create a new label main document and attach an existing data source.*

STEPS

QUICK TIP
To create an envelope mail merge, click Envelopes to open the Envelope Options dialog box, and then select from the options.

QUICK TIP
If your labels do not match FIGURE 6-16, click the Undo button on the Quick Access toolbar, then repeat Step 3, making sure to click the second instance of 30 Per Page.

TROUBLE
Click Enable Content if it appears in a yellow bar in the Access window.

QUICK TIP
To create or change the return address for an envelope mail merge, click the File tab, click Options, click Advanced in the left pane of the Word Options dialog box, then scroll down the right pane and enter the return address in the Mailing address box in the General section.

1. **Click the File tab, click New, click Blank document, make sure the zoom level is set to 120% so you can easily see the label text, then click the Mailings tab**
   A blank document must be open for the commands on the Mailings tab to be available.
2. **Click the Start Mail Merge button in the Start Mail Merge group, click Labels, click the Label vendors arrow in the Label Options dialog box, then click Microsoft if Microsoft is not already displayed**
   The Label Options dialog box opens, as shown in FIGURE 6-15. You use this dialog box to select a label size for your labels and to specify the type of printer you plan to use. The name Microsoft appears in the Label vendors box. You can use the Label vendors arrow to select other brand name label vendors, such as Avery, Staples, or Office Depot. Many standard-sized labels for mailings, business cards, postcards, and other types of labels are listed in the Product number box. The type, height, width, and page size for the selected product are displayed in the Label information section.
3. **Click the second instance of 30 Per Page in the Product number list, click OK, click the Layout contextual tab (to the right of the Table Design tab), click the View Gridlines button in the Table group to turn on the display of gridlines if they are not displayed, then click the Mailings tab**
   A table with gridlines appears in the main document, as shown in FIGURE 6-16. Each table cell is the size of a label for the label product you selected.
4. **Save the label main document with the filename IL_WD_6_WorkshopLabelsMain to the location where you store your Data Files**
   Next, you need to select a data source for the labels. You open a data source in Microsoft Access and resave it with a new name, then attach it to the main document.
5. **Open File Explorer, navigate to the location where you store your Data Files, then double-click Support_WD_6_LabelsData.accdb**
   The data source opens in Access, which is a database program often used to create recipient lists for mail merges.
6. **Click the File tab, click Save As, click the Save As button, navigate to the location where you store your Data Files, change the name of the file to IL_WD_6_LabelsDataSource, click Save, then click the in the top right corner of the Access window to exit Access**
7. **Return to the labels document in Word, click the Select Recipients button in the Start Mail Merge group, then click Use an Existing List**
   The Select Data Source dialog box opens.
8. **Navigate to the location where you store your Data Files, open the file IL_WD_6_LabelsDataSource.accdb, then save your changes**
   The data source file is attached to the label main document, and <<Next Record>> appears in every cell in the table except the first cell, which is blank. In the next lesson, you sort and filter the records before performing the mail merge.

FIGURE 6-15: Label Options dialog box

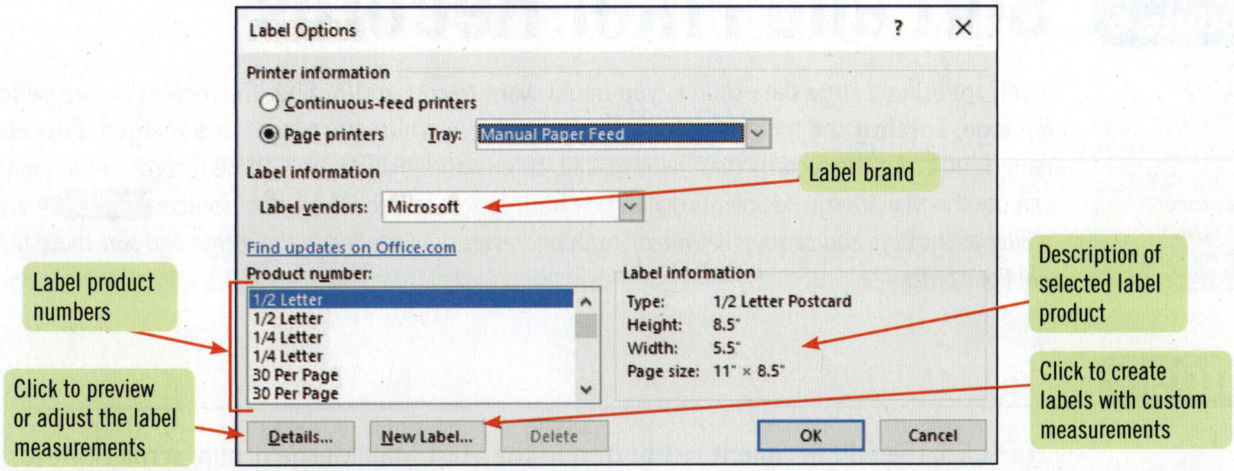

FIGURE 6-16: Label main document

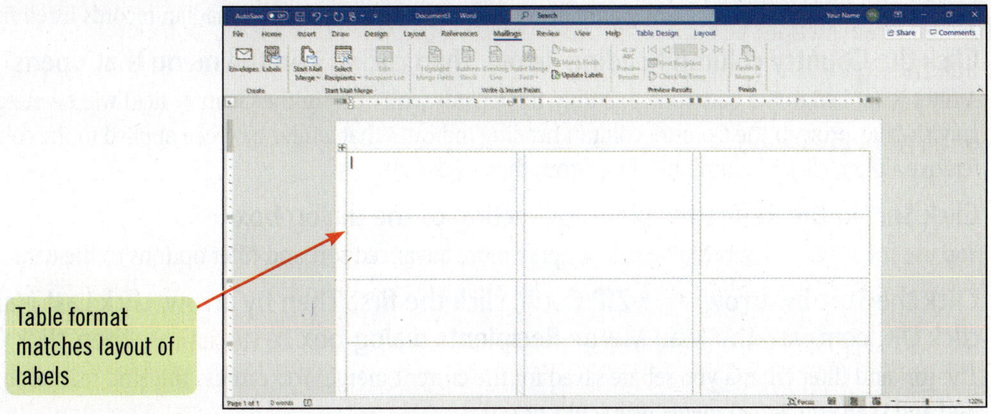

FIGURE 6-17: Envelopes and Labels dialog box

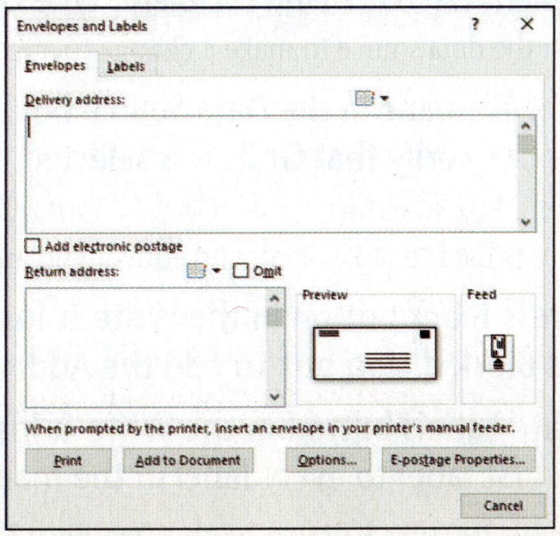

Printing individual envelopes and labels

The Mail Merge feature enables you to easily print envelopes and labels for mass mailings, but you can also quickly format and print individual envelopes and labels using the Envelopes or Labels commands in the Create group on the Mailings tab. Simply click the Envelopes button or Labels button to open the Envelopes and Labels dialog box. On the Envelopes tab, shown in FIGURE 6-17, type the recipient's address in the Delivery address box and the return address in the Return address box. Click Options to open the Envelope Options dialog box, which you use to select the envelope size, change the font and font size of the delivery and return addresses, and change the printing options. When you are ready to print the envelope, click Print in the Envelopes and Labels dialog box. The procedure for printing an individual label is similar to printing an individual envelope: enter the label text in the Address box on the Labels tab, click Options to select a label product number, click OK, and then click Print. Be sure to have envelopes loaded into your printer.

Word
Module 6

Sort and Filter Records

Learning Outcomes
- Filter a data source
- Sort records in a data source
- Find a mail merge recipient

If you are using a large data source, you might want to sort and/or filter the records before performing a merge. **Sorting** the records determines the order in which the records are merged. **Filtering** the records pulls out the records that meet specific criteria and includes only those records in the merge. You can use the Mail Merge Recipients dialog box both to sort and to filter a data source. CASE *You apply a filter to the data source so only United States addresses are included in the merge and sort those records in ZIP Code order.*

STEPS

1. **Click the Edit Recipient List button in the Start Mail Merge group, scroll right to display the Country field, then click the Country column heading**
   The records are sorted in ascending alphabetical order by country, with Canadian records listed first.
2. **Click the Country column heading arrow, then click US on the menu that opens**
   A filter is applied to the data source so only the records with "US" in the Country field will be merged. The grayish-blue arrow in the Country column heading indicates that a filter has been applied to the column. To remove a filter, click a column heading arrow, then click (All).
3. **Click Sort in the Refine recipient list section of the dialog box**
   You use the Filter and Sort dialog box to apply more advanced sort and filter options to the data source.
4. **Click the Sort by arrow, click ZIP Code, click the first Then by arrow, click Last Name, click OK, compare the Mail Merge Recipients dialog box to FIGURE 6-18, then click OK**
   The sort and filter criteria you set are saved for the current merge. You can use the Find feature to quickly find and then edit a mail merge recipient's record.
5. **Click Edit Recipient List, click Find recipient, type Graton, click Find Next, then click Cancel**
   You need to open the data source to make a change to a record.
6. **Double-click the filename in the Data Source box, click Find, type Graton, click Find Next, click Cancel, verify that Graton is selected, type San Francisco, click OK, click Yes, then click OK**
   With your recipients list filtered, sorted, and edited, you are ready to complete the merge.
7. **Click the Address Block button in the Write & Insert Fields group, then click OK in the Insert Address Block dialog box to add the Address Block merge field to the first label**
8. **Click the Update Labels button in the Write & Insert Fields group to copy the merge field from the first label to every label in the main document**
9. **Click the Preview Results button in the Preview Results group**
   A preview of the merged label data appears in the main document, as shown in FIGURE 6-19. Only US addresses are included, and the labels are organized in ZIP Code order, with recipients with the same ZIP Code listed in alphabetical order by Last Name.
10. **Click the Finish & Merge button in the Finish group, click Edit Individual Documents, click OK in the Merge to New Document dialog box, replace Mr. David Friar with your name in the first label, save the document as IL_WD_6_WorkshopLabels_USZipMerge, submit the labels, then save and close all open files and exit Word**

QUICK TIP
Use the options on the Filter Records tab to apply more than one filter to the data source.

QUICK TIP
Sorting and filtering a data source does not alter the records in a data source; it simply reorganizes the records for the current merge only.

QUICK TIP
To change the font or paragraph formatting of merged data, format the merge fields, including the chevrons, before performing a merge.

FIGURE 6-18: US records sorted in zip code order

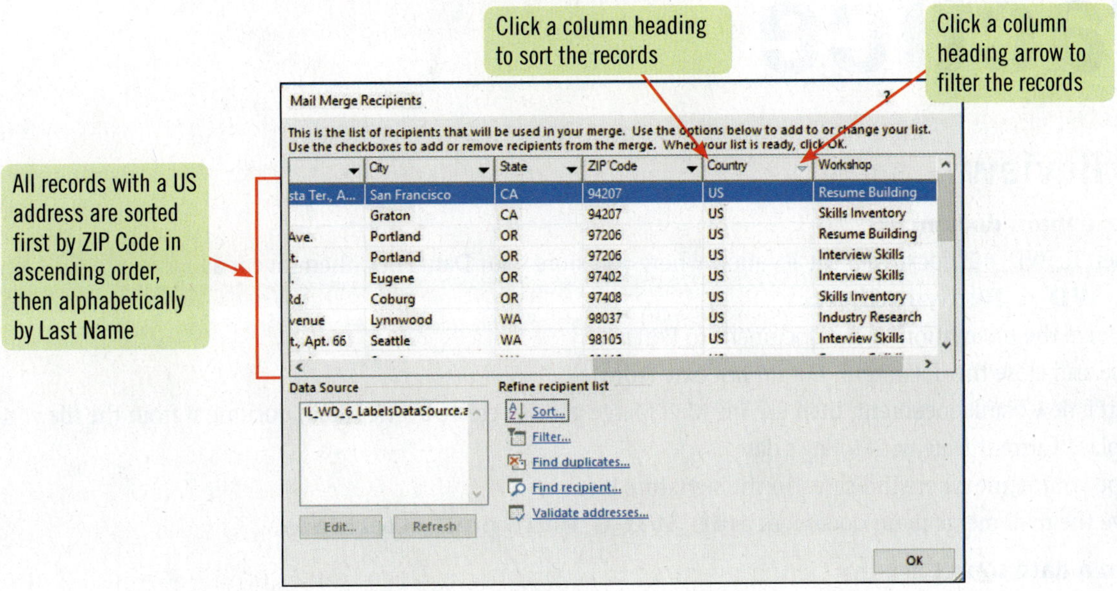

FIGURE 6-19: Merged labels

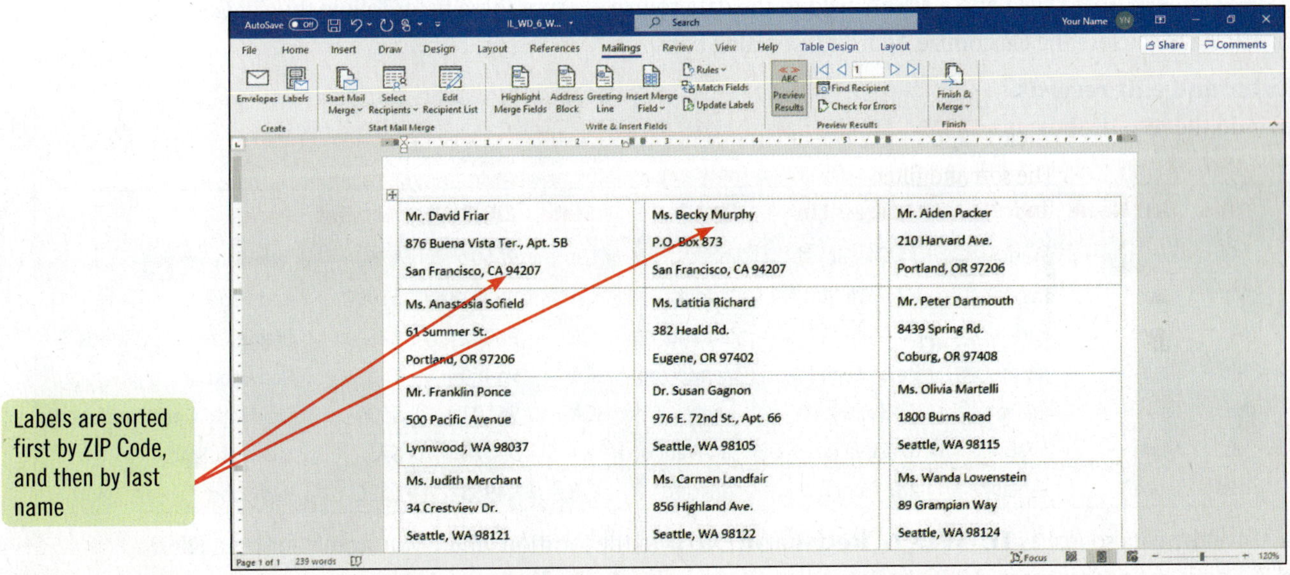

Word

Inserting individual merge fields

You must include proper punctuation, spacing, and blank lines between the merge fields in a main document if you want punctuation, spaces, and blank lines to appear between the data in the merge documents. For example, to create an address line with a city, state, and ZIP Code, you insert the City merge field, type a comma and a space, insert the State merge field, type a space, and then insert the ZIP Code merge field: <<City>>, <<State>> <<ZIP Code>>.

You can insert an individual merge field by clicking the Insert Merge Field arrow in the Write & Insert Fields group and then selecting the field name from the menu that opens. Alternatively, you can click the Insert Merge Field button to open the Insert Merge Field dialog box, which you can use to insert several merge fields at once by clicking a field name in the dialog box, clicking Insert, clicking another field name, clicking Insert, and so on. When you have finished inserting the merge fields, click Close to close the dialog box. You can then add spaces, punctuation, and lines between the merge fields you inserted in the main document.

Practice

Skills Review

1. **Create a main document.**
   a. Open IL_WD_6-2.docx from the location where you store your Data Files, then save it as **IL_WD_6_RedwoodLetter**
   b. Change the orientation of the document to Portrait.
   c. Save and close the document, but do not exit Word.
   d. Start a new blank document, then use the Mail Merge pane to create a letter main document from the file you just saved.
   e. Replace Current Date with today's date.
   f. Type your name where indicated in the signature line.
   g. Save the mail merge main document as **IL_WD_6_RedwoodLetterMain**.
2. **Design a data source.**
   a. Click Next: Select recipients, select the Type a new list option button in the Step 3 of 6... pane, then click Create.
   b. Click Customize Columns in the New Address List dialog box, then remove these fields from the data source: Company Name, Address Line 2, Country or Region, Home Phone, Work Phone, and E-mail Address.
   c. Add an **Amount** field and a **Park** field to the data source. Be sure these fields follow the ZIP Code field.
   d. Click OK to close the Customize Address List dialog box.
3. **Enter and edit records.**
   a. Add the records shown in TABLE 6-2 to the data source.

TABLE 6-2

Title	First Name	Last Name	Address Line 1	City	State	ZIP Code	Amount	Park
Ms.	Jill	Wade	35 Oak St.	Eureka	CA	95501	$250	Jedediah Smith
Mr.	Cary	Poon	223 Elm St.	Redding	CA	96001	$1000	Redwood
Ms.	Grace	Park	62 Main St.	Redding	CA	96002	$25	Prairie Creek Redwoods
Mr.	Paul	Jones	987 Ocean Rd.	Mendocino	CA	95460	$50	Redwood
Ms.	Lin	Juarez	73 Bay Rd.	Eureka	CA	95501	$500	Del Norte Coast Redwoods
Ms.	Maria	Shad	67 Cove Rd.	San Francisco	CA	94121	$75	Jedediah Smith
Ms.	Joyce	Leblanc	287 Concord Rd.	Sausalito	CA	94965	$100	Redwood

   b. Save the data source as **IL_WD_6_RedwoodData** to the location where you store your Data Files.
   c. Change the park for record 2 (Cary Poon) from Redwood to **Jedediah Smith**.
   d. Click OK as needed to close all dialog boxes.
4. **Add merge fields.**
   a. Click Next: Write your letter, then in the blank line between the date and the first body paragraph, insert an Address block merge field, then click OK.
   b. Press ENTER twice, then insert a Greeting Line merge field using the default greeting line format.
   c. In the first body paragraph, replace AMOUNT with the Amount merge field.
   d. In the second body paragraph, replace PARK with the Park merge field. (*Note*: Make sure to insert a space before or after each merge field as needed.) Save your changes to the main document.
5. **Work with merge rules.**
   a. Select National Park at the end of paragraph 2, then select the If...Then...Else merge rule.
   b. Select Park as the field name, then enter criteria for the rule so that when "Redwood" is the record in the Park field, "National Park" is displayed, and if not, then "State Park" is displayed.

Skills Review (continued)

c. Toggle the field codes and verify the code is { IF { MERGEFIELD Park } = "Redwood" "National Park" "State Park" }.
d. Change the font of the field code to Garamond.

6. **Merge data.**
   a. Click Next: Preview your letters to preview the merged data, then use the Next Record button to scroll through each letter, examining it carefully for errors. Check that the merge rule worked.
   b. Click the Preview Results button on the Mailings tab, make any necessary adjustments to the main document, save your changes, then click the Preview Results button to return to the preview of the document.
   c. Click Next: Complete the merge, click Edit individual letters, then merge all the records to a new file.
   d. Save the merged document as **IL_WD_6_RedwoodLetterMerge** to the location where you store your Data Files. The fourth letter is shown in FIGURE 6-20. Submit the file or a copy of the last letter per your instructor's directions, then save and close all open files but not Word.

FIGURE 6-20

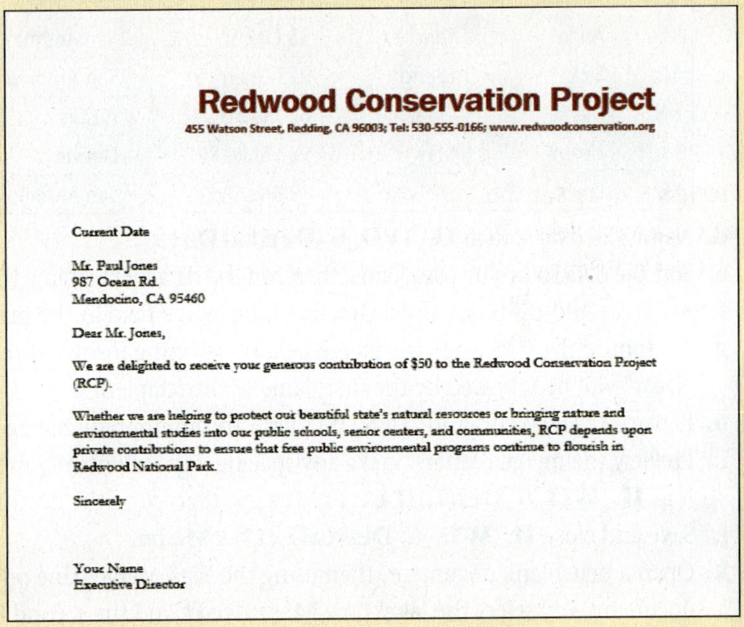
Redwood Conservation Project
455 Watson Street, Redding, CA 96003; Tel: 530-555-0166; www.redwoodconservation.org

Current Date

Mr. Paul Jones
987 Ocean Rd.
Mendocino, CA 95460

Dear Mr. Jones,

We are delighted to receive your generous contribution of $50 to the Redwood Conservation Project (RCP).

Whether we are helping to protect our beautiful state's natural resources or bringing nature and environmental studies into our public schools, senior centers, and communities, RCP depends upon private contributions to ensure that free public environmental programs continue to flourish in Redwood National Park.

Sincerely

Your Name
Executive Director

7. **Create labels.**
   a. Open a new blank document, click the Start Mail Merge button in the Start Mail Merge group on the Mailings tab, then create a Labels main document.
   b. In the Label Options dialog box, select Avery US Letter, select 5160 Address Labels, then click OK.
   c. Click the Select Recipients button, then open the IL_WD_6_RedwoodData.mdb file you created.
   d. Save the label main document as **IL_WD_6_RedwoodLabelsMain** to the location where you store your Data Files.

8. **Sort and filter records.**
   a. Click the Edit Recipient List button, filter the records so that only the records with Redwood in the Park field are included in the merge, sort the records in City order, then click OK as needed to return to the labels document.
   b. Insert an Address Block merge field using the default settings, update the labels, then click the Preview Results button.
   c. Open the Recipient List, find the record for Maria Shad, then change the Park to Redwood.
   d. Verify that Maria's record appears, examine the merged data for errors, then correct any mistakes.
   e. Click the Finish & Merge button, then click the Edit Individual Documents to merge all the records to an individual document, shown in FIGURE 6-21.
   f. Save the merged file as **IL_WD_6_RedwoodLabelsRedwoodOnlyMerge** to the location where you store your Data Files.
   g. In the first label, change Mr. Paul Jones to your name, submit the document to your instructor, save and close all open Word files, then exit Word.

FIGURE 6-21

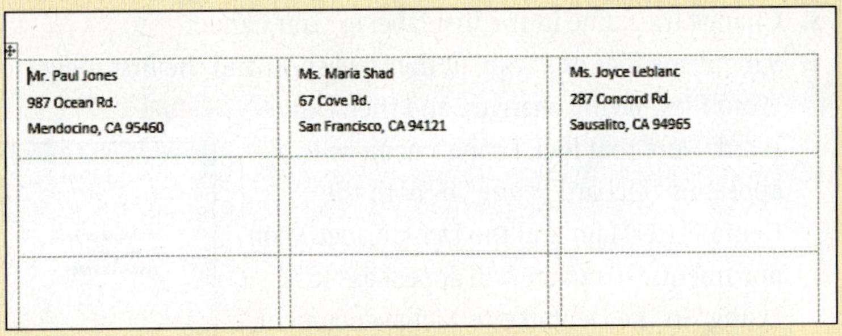

Mr. Paul Jones 987 Ocean Rd. Mendocino, CA 95460	Ms. Maria Shad 67 Cove Rd. San Francisco, CA 94121	Ms. Joyce Leblanc 287 Concord Rd. Sausalito, CA 94965

Word

Independent Challenge 1

As an administrator at Riverwalk Medical Clinic in San Antonio, you handle all the correspondence for the Dental Department, including sending reminders to patients for dental cleaning. You'll use Mail Merge to create the letter and a sheet of labels.

a. Start Word, open IL_WD_6-3.docx from the location where you store your Data Files, save the document as **IL_WD_6_DentalLetter**, change the page orientation to Portrait, add the current date, replace Your Name with your name in the signature block, then save and close the file.

b. Start a new blank document in Word, then using either the Mailings tab or the Mail Merge pane, create a letter main document using the document you just saved. Save the main document as **IL_WD_6_DentalLetterMain**.

c. Create a new recipient list using the data shown below. Remove any field names that are not included.

Title	First Name	Last Name	Address Line 1	City	State	ZIP Code	CHECKUP	DENTIST
Ms.	Anna	Sanchez	35 Oak St.	San Antonio	TX	78215	three-month	Dr. Haven
Mr.	Rick	Leung	223 Cherry St.	San Antonio	TX	78207	annual	Dr. Singh
Ms.	Maria	Ortez	62 Main St.	Austin	TX	78745	six-month	Dr. Singh
Ms.	Helen	May	987 State Rd.	Devine	TX	78016	annual	Dr. Haven
Ms.	Emer	O'Toole	73 River Rd.	San Antonio	TX	78214	three-month	Dr. Singh

d. Name the data source **IL_WD_6_DentalData**.

e. Sort the data source by Last Name, then edit the data by changing the address for Ms. Helen May to **600 County Rd**.

f. Insert an Address Block and a Greeting Line merge field in the main document.

g. Customize the Greeting Line merge field by selecting Joshua as the greeting line format. When the merge is run, "Dear" will be followed by the first name of the recipient.

h. Replace "CHECKUP" and "DENTIST" with the appropriate merge fields.

i. Preview the merged letters, make any spacing adjustments required, merge all the records to a new document, save it as **IL_WD_6_DentalLetterMerge**, then close the document.

j. Save and close **IL_WD_6_DentalLetterMain**.

k. Open a new blank document, then using the Mail Merge pane on the Mailings tab, select Labels as the main document and select the label type **Microsoft** and the second instance of 30 Per Page.

l. Select recipients from the IL_WD_6_DentalData.mdb file you just created.

m. Save the label main document as **IL_WD_6_DentalLabelsMain** to the location where you store your Data Files.

n. Insert an Address Block merge field using the default settings, update the labels, then preview the results.

o. Filter the records so that only the records with Dr. Singh in the Dentist field are included in the merge, then sort the records in City order.

p. In the data source, find the record for Rick Leung, then change "Rick" to **Richard**.

q. Examine the merged data for errors, then correct any mistakes. The three labels should appear as shown in FIGURE 6-22.

r. Merge all the records to an individual document, save the merged file as **IL_WD_6_DentalLabelsSinghOnlyMerge** to the location where you store your Data Files.

s. Change the name in the first label to your name.

t. Submit the files or a copy of the label sheet and the first merge letter per your instructor's directions, close all open Word files, saving changes, and then exit Word. Note that Rick Leung's name will appear as "Richard Leung" in both the DentalLetterMain and the DentalLabelsMain documents. His name will appear as "Rick Leung" in the DentalLetterMerge document because the merged letters are not linked to the data source and so were not updated.

FIGURE 6-22

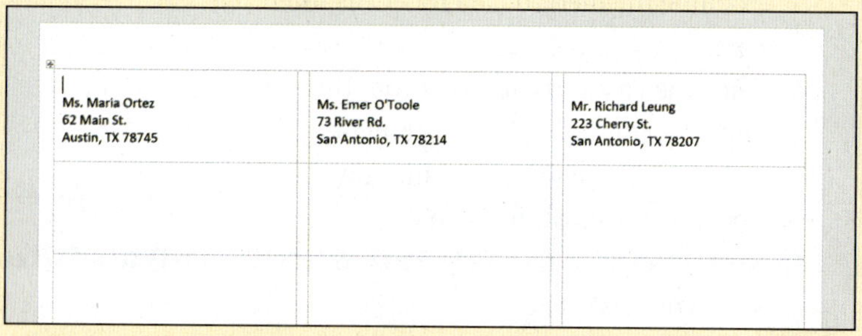

Independent Challenge 2

As the director of the Lake Country Museum in Minnesota, you are hosting an exhibit of old photographs from pioneer times. You want to send a letter to all museum donors with a Minnesota address to advise them of a discount in the museum gift store according to their donation amount and to invite them to the opening of the exhibition. You'll use Mail Merge to create the letter and create an envelope for one letter.

a. Start Word, open a blank document, then using either the Mailings tab or the Mail Merge pane, create a letter main document using the file IL_WD_6-4.docx from the location where you store your Data Files.

b. Replace Current Date with the current date and Your Name with your name in the signature block, then save the main document as **IL_WD_6_MuseumLetterMain**.

c. Use the file **Support_WD_6_MuseumData.accdb** from the location where you store your Data Files as the data source.

d. Sort the data source by Last Name, then filter the data so that only records with MN as the state are included in the merge.

e. Insert an Address Block and a Greeting Line merge field in the main document (separate with a blank line).

f. Replace "AMOUNT" with the Amount merge field.

g. Select 15% discount, then use the If…Then…Else merge rule to change 15% discount to **20% discount** if the Amount field is greater than or equal to "100." (*Hint*: You need to modify the Comparison operator to select Greater Than or Equal To.)

h. Toggle the field code to verify the IF field is correct.

i. Toggle off the field code, select "20% discount," then apply Bold formatting.

j. Preview results, then scroll through the letters to verify that the merge rule worked.

k. Merge all the records to a new document, then save it as **IL_WD_6_MuseumLetterMerge**.

l. Select the recipient address in the first merge letter, then click the Envelopes button in the Create group on the Mailings tab to open the Envelopes and Labels dialog box. (*Note*: You will create one envelope and include it as part of the merge document. If you were doing a mail merge, you would create a separate envelope merge.)

m. On the Envelopes tab in the Envelopes and Labels dialog box, verify that the Omit check box is not selected, then in the Return address box, type your name followed by a comma and **Lake Country Museum**, press ENTER, then type the address **541 Newtown Street, Minneapolis, MN 55404** on one line.

n. Click Options to open the Envelope Options dialog box, click the Envelope Options tab if it is not the active tab, then make sure the Envelope size is set to Size 10.

o. Click the Printing Options tab, select the appropriate Feed method for your printer, then click OK.

p. Click Add to Document, click No if a message box opens asking if you want to save the new return address as the default return address. The dialog box closes without printing the envelope and the envelope is added as the first page of the merge document as shown in FIGURE 6-23.

q. Submit the file or a copy of the envelope and the first merge letter per your instructor's directions, close all open Word files, saving changes, and then exit Word.

FIGURE 6-23

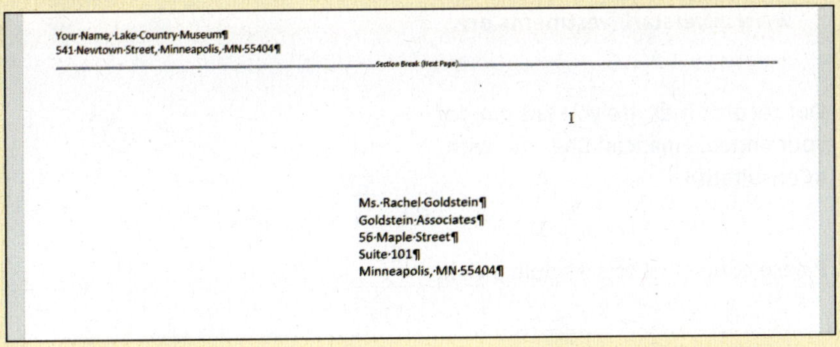

Word

Visual Workshop

Using mail merge, create the data source shown in **FIGURE 6-24** for the postcard main document shown in **FIGURE 6-25**. Use Avery US Letter 3263 Postcards labels for the main document. Save the data source as **IL_WD_6_InvestorData**, save the merge document as **IL_WD_6_InvestorReminderMerge**, and save the main document as **IL_WD_6_InvestorReminderMain**, all to the location where you store your Data Files. Notice that the postcard label main document is formatted as a table. To lay out the postcard, insert a nested table with two columns and one row in the upper-left postcard; add the text and merge field to the nested table; and then remove the outside borders on the nested table. The font is Book Antiqua. Submit a copy of the postcards to your instructor.

FIGURE 6-24

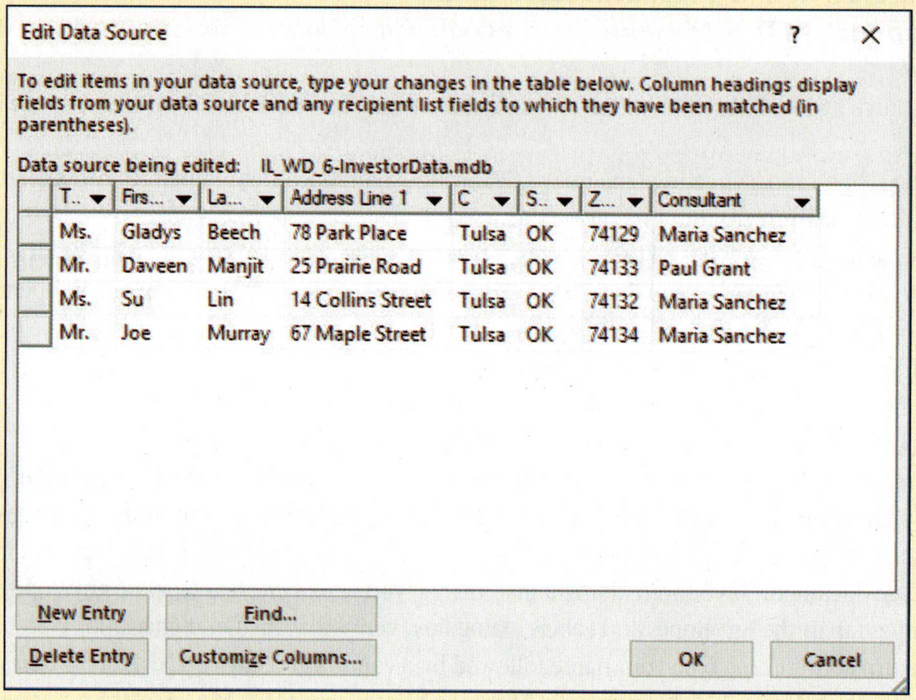

FIGURE 6-25

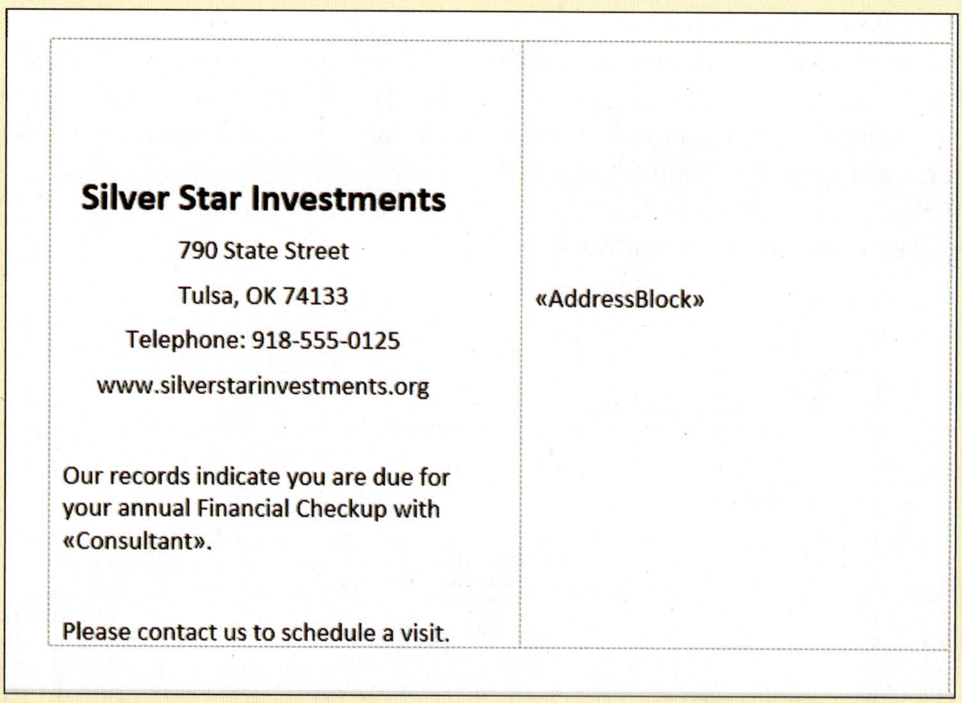

Illustrating Documents with Graphics

CASE You have been asked to edit and finalize a two-page information sheet that will be distributed to clients and job seekers who visit the Vancouver office of JCL Talent, Inc. The information sheet includes short articles about the job market, information about the branch staff, and tips for job seekers.

Module Objectives

After completing this module, you will be able to:

- Use the Office Clipboard
- Create sections and columns
- Create SmartArt graphics
- Modify SmartArt graphics
- Crop and rotate a picture
- Position a graphic
- Create WordArt
- Create a text box
- Insert a Word file

Files You Will Need

IL_WD_7-1.docx
Support_WD_7_References.docx
Support_WD_7_Utilities.jpg
Support_WD_7_Accounts.jpg
Support_WD_7_Interviews.docx
Support_WD_7_Chicago.docx
IL_WD_7-2.docx
Support_WD_7_Risk.docx
Support_WD_7_Quiz.docx
Support_WD_7_Coins.jpg
Support_WD_7_Disaster.jpg
Support_WD_7_RiskReport_WatsonFinancial.docx
IL_WD_7-3.docx
Support_WD_7_Brain.jpg
Support_WD_7_Class.jpg
Support_WD_7_Donations.jpg
Support_WD_7_Education.docx
IL_WD_7-4.docx
Support_WD_7_RemoteWorking.docx
Support_WD_7_DraftReport.docx
IL_WD_7-5.docx

Word Module 7

Use the Office Clipboard

Learning Outcomes
- Copy and cut items to the Clipboard
- Paste items from the Clipboard

You can use the Office Clipboard to collect text and graphics from files created in any Office program and then insert them into your Word documents. The Office Clipboard (the Clipboard) holds up to 24 items at a time. To display the Clipboard, you simply click the launcher in the Clipboard group on the Home tab. You add items to the Clipboard using the Cut and Copy commands. The last item you collect is always added at the top of the Clipboard. **CASE** *You use the Clipboard to store text and a picture that you move within the information sheet.*

STEPS

QUICK TIP You can set the Clipboard pane to open automatically when you cut or copy two items consecutively by clicking Options on the Clipboard pane and then selecting Show Office Clipboard Automatically.

QUICK TIP If you add a 25th item to the Clipboard, the first item you collected is deleted.

QUICK TIP You may see a Preview Not Available icon instead of the picture, depending on the settings.

QUICK TIP To delete an individual item from the Clipboard, click the arrow next to the item, then click Delete.

1. **sam ↓ Start Word, open IL_WD_7-1.docx from the location where you store your Data Files, save it as IL_WD_7_InformationSheet, then click the Launcher in the Clipboard group on the Home tab**

   The Office Clipboard opens in the Clipboard pane. In this pane, each object and text selection you copied or cut in a current Office session is listed. The Clipboard pane will be empty if you have not copied or pasted anything recently.

2. **If items appear in the Clipboard pane, click Clear All, then select the two lines of text at the top of the document from Prepared by Your Name at JCL Talent . . . to the company phone number**

   With the text selected, you can choose to either copy it or cut it. You want to move this text to the document footer, so you need to cut it.

3. **Click the Cut button in the Clipboard group**

   The text is removed from the document and placed in the Clipboard as shown in FIGURE 7-1. The icon next to the item indicates it is cut or copied from a Word document. You can continue to cut or copy additional items to the Clipboard, including objects such as charts and pictures.

4. **Click the picture of the city and mountains, then click the Cut button in the Clipboard group**

   The picture is displayed at the top of the Clipboard pane because it is the most recent item collected. As new items are collected, the existing items move down the Clipboard. Clicking an item on the Clipboard pastes the item in the document at the location of the insertion point. Items remain on the Clipboard until you delete them or close all open Office programs.

5. **Press CTRL+HOME to move to the top of the document, press ENTER two times, press Up Arrow ↑ two times to move to the first line in the document, then click the picture in the Clipboard**

   The picture is inserted at the top of your document.

6. **Click the Insert tab, click the Footer button in the Header & Footer group, click the Blank style, click Prepared by ... in the Clipboard, then press BACKSPACE and DELETE as needed to remove any extra blank lines**

7. **Press CTRL+E to center the text as shown in FIGURE 7-2, replace Your Name with your name, click the Close Header and Footer button in the Close group, then click the Close button on the Clipboard pane**

   The text is pasted into the footer and will appear on both pages of the information sheet.

FIGURE 7-1: Text copied to the Clipboard

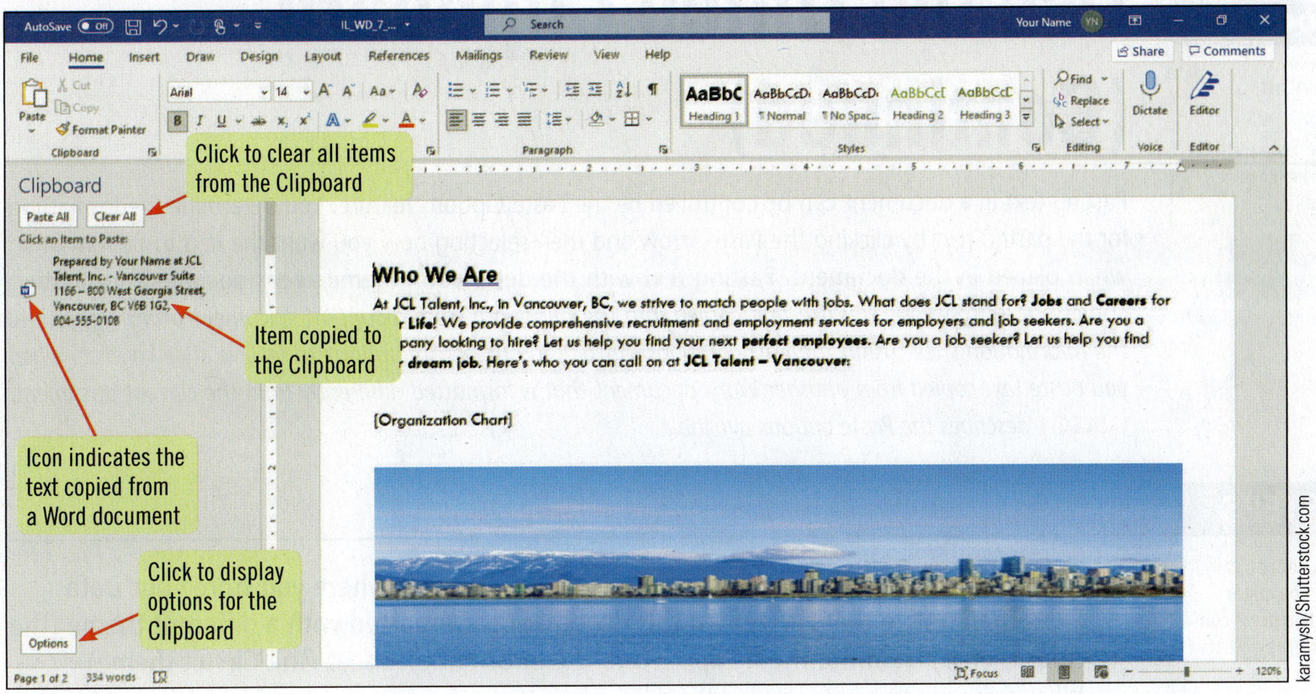

FIGURE 7-2: Footer text copied and formatted

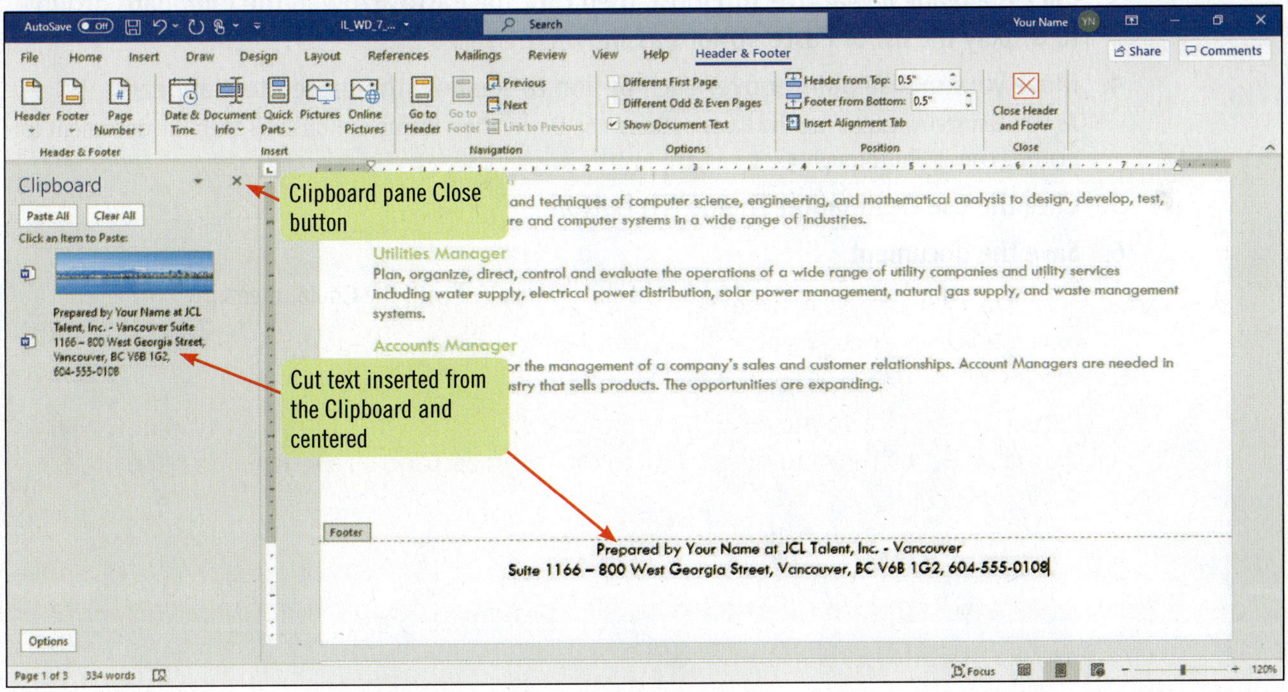

Word

(Continued)

Word
Module 7

Use the Office Clipboard (Continued)

Learning Outcomes
- Use Paste options to resolve style conflicts

Pasting text in a document can be controlled by the Paste Options feature. You determine the formatting for the pasted text by clicking the Paste arrow and then selecting how you want the text to be formatted when placed in the document. Pasting text with the destination theme keeps document formatting consistent. **CASE** *You use text copied into the Clipboard from a support document and paste it into the Information sheet using the Paste Options button. You use paste options to resolve style conflicts when you paste text copied from another Word document that is formatted differently from the current document.* **TABLE 7-1** *describes the Paste options available.*

STEPS

1. **Open Support_WD_7_References.docx from the location where you store your Data Files, then notice that the text in this document is formatted with a different theme (the Atlas theme) from the theme applied to the information sheet (the Circuit theme)**
   When you copy text from another Word document that is formatted with a theme different from the theme of your current document, you use Paste options to choose how you want the pasted text formatted.
2. **Press CTRL+A to select the heading References and the paragraph following, click the Copy button in the Clipboard group, then close the document**
3. **Click the blank line above Top Jobs!, then click the Paste arrow in the Clipboard group to display the list of Paste options as shown in FIGURE 7-3**
4. **Move your mouse pointer over each option to see how the pasted text appears**
   As you can see by exploring the Paste options, the Destination theme options will keep the document formatting consistent throughout.
5. **Click the Use Destination Theme (H) button**
6. **Save the document**
   The text is copied into the current document and is formatted with the Circuit theme.

FIGURE 7-3: Paste options

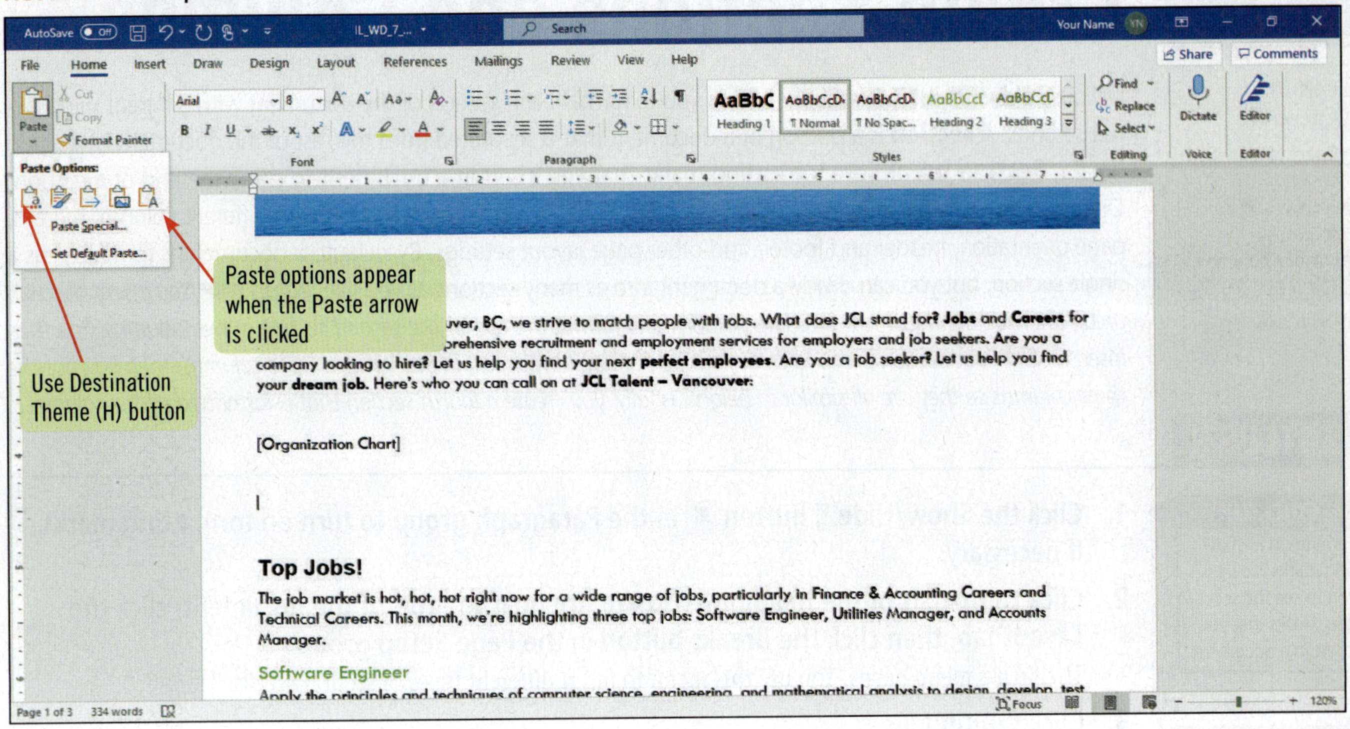

karamysh/Shutterstock.com

TABLE 7-1: Paste options

paste option	description
Use Destination Theme	The formatting applied to text copied from a source file is changed to match the formatting applied to text in the destination file.
Keep Source Formatting	The formatting applied to the copied text in the source file is retained, even if the formatting is different from the formatting applied to text in the destination file.
Merge Formatting	The copied text takes on the style characteristics of the paragraph where it is pasted.
Picture	The copied text is pasted as a picture that you can resize and move like any graphic object.
Keep Text Only	Only the text, with no formatting, is pasted into the destination file.

Create Sections and Columns

Learning Outcomes
- Insert section breaks
- Format text in columns
- Balance columns

Dividing a document into sections allows you to format each section of the document with different page layout settings. A **section** is a portion of a document that is separated from the rest of the document by section breaks. **Section breaks** are formatting marks that you insert in a document to show the end of a section. Once you have divided a document into sections, you can format each section with different column, margin, page orientation, header and footer, and other page layout settings. By default, a document is formatted as a single section, but you can divide a document into as many sections as you like. **CASE** *You insert a section break to divide the document into two sections and format the text in the second section in two columns. You then insert a Next Page section break to create a third section, format text in Section 3 in three columns, then balance the three columns so they are all similar in height. Finally, you create a fourth section that is formatted in one column.*

STEPS

QUICK TIP
Turning on formatting marks allows you to see the section breaks that you insert in a document.

TROUBLE
If you do not see Section 2 in the status bar in the lower-left corner of your screen, right-click the status bar, then click **Section** to add a check mark next to it.

QUICK TIP
When you delete a section break, you delete the section formatting of the text before the break. That text becomes part of the following section and assumes the formatting of that section.

1. **Click the Show/Hide ¶ button ¶ in the Paragraph group to turn on formatting marks, if necessary**
2. **Click to the left of the heading Who We Are near the top of the document, click the Layout tab, then click the Breaks button in the Page Setup group**
   The Breaks menu opens. You use this menu to insert different types of section breaks. See TABLE 7-2.
3. **Click Continuous**
   Word inserts a continuous section break, shown as a dotted double line below the picture and above the "Who We Are" heading. See FIGURE 7-4. When you insert a section break at the beginning of a paragraph, Word inserts the break at the end of the previous paragraph. The section break stores the formatting information for the previous section. The status bar indicates the insertion point is in Section 2.
4. **Click the Columns button in the Page Setup group, then click More Columns**
5. **Select Right in the Presets section, click the Spacing down arrow twice until 0.3" appears, select the Line between check box, compare the dialog box to FIGURE 7-5, then click OK**
   Section 2 is formatted in two unequal columns with .3" of spacing and a vertical line between columns.
6. **Click the View tab, click Multiple Pages to show both pages of the information sheet, click to the left of Top Jobs in column 1, click the Layout tab, click Breaks, then click Next Page**
   Top Jobs and its accompanying text move to the top of page 2 and Section 3 appears on the status bar. Page 2 looks odd at this point, but you'll fix the spacing soon.
7. **Click the Columns button, click More Columns, click Three, change the spacing between columns to .2" and click the Line between check box to deselect it, then click OK**
   All the text and pictures on the page are formatted in three narrow columns.
8. **Return to 100% view, click to the left of the paragraph mark following expanding. at the end of the description of the Accounts Manager position toward the bottom of the first column on page 2, click the Layout tab, click Breaks in the Page Setup group, then click Continuous**
   You inserted a Continuous section break to balance the columns only in the "Top Jobs" section so each column is approximately the same height. Text in the balanced columns flows automatically from the bottom of one column to the top of the next column.
9. **Verify that the insertion point appears to the left of the paragraph mark above the heading Find New Opportunities and below the beginning of the Software Engineer paragraph, click the Columns button in the Page Setup group, click One, then save the document**
   You create another section (Section 4) because you want the remaining information in the document to extend the full width of the page.

FIGURE 7-4: Continuous section break

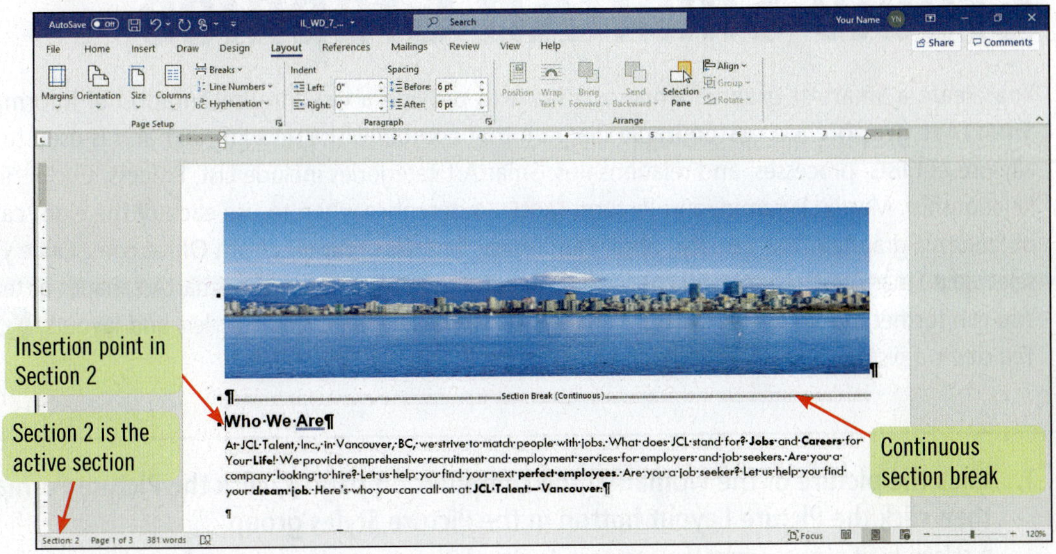

FIGURE 7-5: Columns dialog box

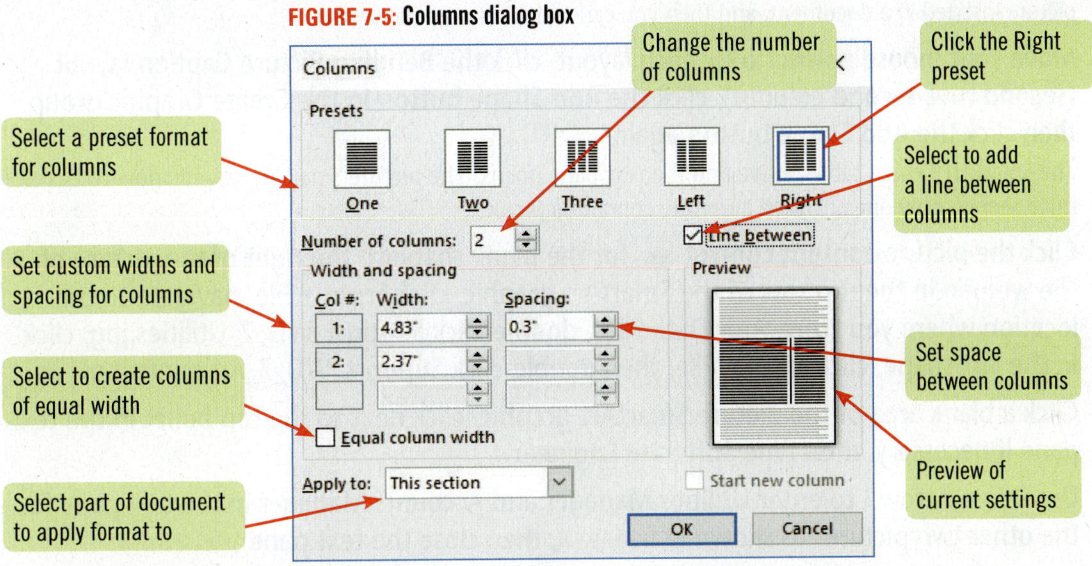

TABLE 7-2: Types of section breaks

section	function
Next page	Begins a new section and moves the text following the break to the top of the next page
Continuous	Begins a new section on the same page
Even page	Begins a new section and moves the text following the break to the top of the next even-numbered page
Odd page	Begins a new section and moves the text following the break to the top of the next odd-numbered page

Changing page layout settings for a section

Dividing a document into sections allows you to vary the layout of a document. In addition to applying different column settings to sections, you can apply different margins, page orientation, paper size, vertical alignment, header and footer, page numbering, footnotes, endnotes, and other page layout settings. To check or change the page layout settings for an individual section, place the insertion point in the section, then open the Page Setup dialog box. Select any options you want to change, click the Apply to arrow, click This section, then click OK. When you select This section in the Apply to box, the settings are applied to the current section only. When you select This point forward, the settings are applied to the current section and all sections that follow it. If you select Whole document in the Apply to box, the settings are applied to all the sections in the document.

Word Module 7

Create SmartArt Graphics

Learning Outcomes
- Create a picture SmartArt Graphic
- Change the SmartArt layout

You create a SmartArt graphic when you want to provide a visual representation of information. A **SmartArt graphic** is a customizable diagram that combines shapes with text and is used to pictorially present lists, processes, and relationships. SmartArt categories include List, Process, Cycle, Hierarchy, Relationship, Matrix, Pyramid, and Picture. TABLE 7-3 describes when to use each of the eight categories of SmartArt graphics. You can also obtain additional SmartArt graphics from Office.com. Once you have selected a SmartArt category, you choose a layout and then type text in the SmartArt shapes or text pane. You can further modify a SmartArt graphic by changing fill colors, shape styles, and layouts. **CASE** *You create a picture SmartArt graphic on page 2 of the information sheet.*

STEPS

QUICK TIP
To insert a new SmartArt graphic, click the Insert tab, then click the SmartArt button in the Illustrations group and select a layout.

TROUBLE
If the text pane does not open, click the **Expand button** on the left side of the SmartArt graphic to open it.

QUICK TIP
You can also click the Text Pane button in the Create Graphic group on the SmartArt Design tab to open and close the text pane.

1. **Click the picture of the woman at the computer on page 2, click the Picture Format tab, then click the Picture Layout button in the Picture Styles group**
   A selection of picture SmartArt layouts is displayed. You can create a picture SmartArt graphic from any picture inserted in a document, and then you can add additional pictures.
2. **Move your mouse pointer over each layout, click the Bending Picture Caption layout (second row, second column), click the Add Shape button in the Create Graphic group, then click the Add Shape button again**
   The SmartArt Design tab is active and the text pane opens. The picture SmartArt graphic now consists of three shapes, only one of which currently contains a picture.
3. **Click the picture content control for the blank shape to the right of the picture of the woman in the top row of the SmartArt graphic, click From a File, navigate to the location where you store your Data Files, double-click Support_WD_7_Utilities.jpg, click in the last shape, click From a File, then double-click Support_WD_7_Accounts.jpg**
4. **Click a blank area of the picture SmartArt graphic, click next to the top bullet in the text pane if necessary, then type Software Engineer**
5. **Use Down Arrow ↓ to enter Utilities Manager and Accounts Manager in the text pane for the other two pictures as shown in FIGURE 7-6, then close the text pane**
6. **Click the More button in the Layouts group on the SmartArt Design tab, then click the Bending Picture Blocks layout (second row, fifth column)**
   You can experiment with how you want the SmartArt graphic to appear by selecting different picture layouts. You set a precise height and width for the SmartArt graphic.
7. **Click the Format tab, click the Size button to show the Height and Width boxes if necessary, select the measurement in the Height box, type 3.8, press TAB to select the measurement in the Width box, type 5.7, then press ENTER**
   You can also format the appearance of each shape in a SmartArt graphic.
8. **Click away from the picture SmartArt graphic to deselect it, click the woman picture, press and hold SHIFT, then click the other two pictures so all three pictures in the picture SmartArt graphic are selected**
9. **Click the Shape Effects button in the Shape Styles group on the Format tab, point to Bevel, click Angle (first column, second row in the Bevel section), click away from the picture SmartArt graphic to deselect it, then save the document**
   The picture SmartArt graphic appears as shown in FIGURE 7-7.

FIGURE 7-6: Data for the picture

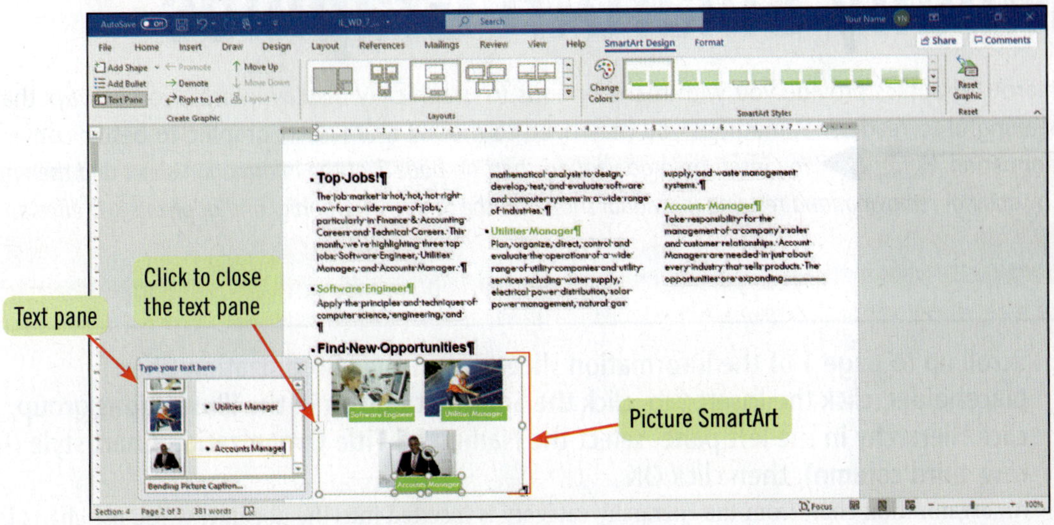

zstock/Shutterstock.com; branislavpudar/Shutterstock.com; Andrey_Popov/Shutterstock.com

FIGURE 7-7: Sized and formatted picture SmartArt graphic

branislavpudar/Shutterstock.com; zstock/Shutterstock.com; zstock/Shutterstock.com; Andrey_Popov/Shutterstock.com

TABLE 7-3: Eight categories of SmartArt graphics

category	when to use
List	To show nonsequential information
Process	To show steps in a process or timeline
Cycle	To show a continual process
Hierarchy	To show an organization chart or decision tree
Relationship	To illustrate connections between the shapes in the graphic
Matrix	To show how parts relate to a whole
Pyramid	To show proportional relationships with the largest component on the bottom
Picture	To use pictures to convey or emphasize visual content

Inserting a picture into a SmartArt shape

You can fill any shape in a SmartArt graphic with a picture, even if the shape does not include a Picture content control. Click the shape, click the Format tab, click the Shape Fill arrow, click Picture, click From a File, navigate to the location of the picture, then click Insert. The picture is inserted into the shape.

Word

Modify SmartArt Graphics

Learning Outcomes
- Create an organization chart
- Modify SmartArt shapes

SmartArt graphics provide you with many options to graphically display information in ways that are meaningful to readers. Sometimes you may need to modify a SmartArt graphic to better convey the information. **CASE** *You insert an organization chart on page 1 of the information sheet and then modify it by adding, removing, and resizing individual shapes in the SmartArt graphic, and applying 3-D effects.*

STEPS

1. **Scroll up to page 1 of the information sheet, select the [Organization Chart] placeholder, click the Insert tab, click the SmartArt button in the Illustrations group, click Hierarchy in the left pane, select the Name and Title Organization Chart style (first row, third column), then click OK**

   An organization chart from the Hierarchy category is inserted into the document. You use charts in the Hierarchy category to show the chain of command within a company or organization.

2. **Close the Text pane if it is open, increase the zoom to 200%, scroll to see the whole graphic, click in the top box, type Sheila Leung, click in the box below Sheila, then type Branch Manager**

   By default, an assistant box is attached to the top box in the Organization chart. Space is limited on the page, so you remove the assistant box and add two subordinates to one of the Level 2 boxes.

> **TROUBLE**
> Click at the far-right edge of the white box to select the box below Sheila and enter text.

3. **Click the edge of the green box below and to the left of Sheila's box, press DELETE, click the SmartArt Design tab if it is not already selected, click the far-left box in the bottom row, click the Add Shape arrow in the Create Graphic group, click Add Shape Below, then click the Add Shape button (not the arrow) to add another shape to the right of the shape you just inserted**

   The Add Shape menu provides options (such as below, after, and above) for adding more shapes to your SmartArt graphic. The new shapes are added based on the currently selected box and the menu selection.

4. **Enter text so the organization chart appears as shown in FIGURE 7-8**

   After entering text in a SmartArt graphic, you sometimes need to modify the text wrapping.

5. **Click the Branch Manager box, then drag the lower-right handle to the right to increase the width of the text box so the text does not wrap**

   You can also rearrange the shapes in a SmartArt graphic.

6. **Click the Anna Ricard box, then click the Move Down button in the Create Graphic group**

   The Move Down command moves the box to the right and on the same level as the other two boxes. The two subordinate boxes attached to Anna's box are also moved. TABLE 7-4 explains the different ways in which you can move shapes in a SmartArt graphic.

> **QUICK TIP**
> Choose from a wide variety of effects to format a SmartArt graphic.

7. **Click the Change Colors button in the SmartArt Styles group, select Colorful – Accent Colors (first selection in the Colorful section), click the More button in the SmartArt Styles group, then click Inset (second selection in the 3-D section)**

8. **Click a blank area of the chart, click the Format tab, click the Size button, type 2.7 in the Height box, type 4.5 in the Width box, then press ENTER**

9. **Click the Jasjit Singh box, press and hold SHIFT, click the remaining four subordinate boxes: Anna Ricard, Gary Ng, Mary Warr, and Phil Banks, release SHIFT, click the Size button, type 1 in the Width box, press ENTER, return to 100% view, click away from the chart, then save the document**

   The width of all the boxes in the Organization chart is decreased to 1" as shown in FIGURE 7-9.

FIGURE 7-8: Text for the organization chart

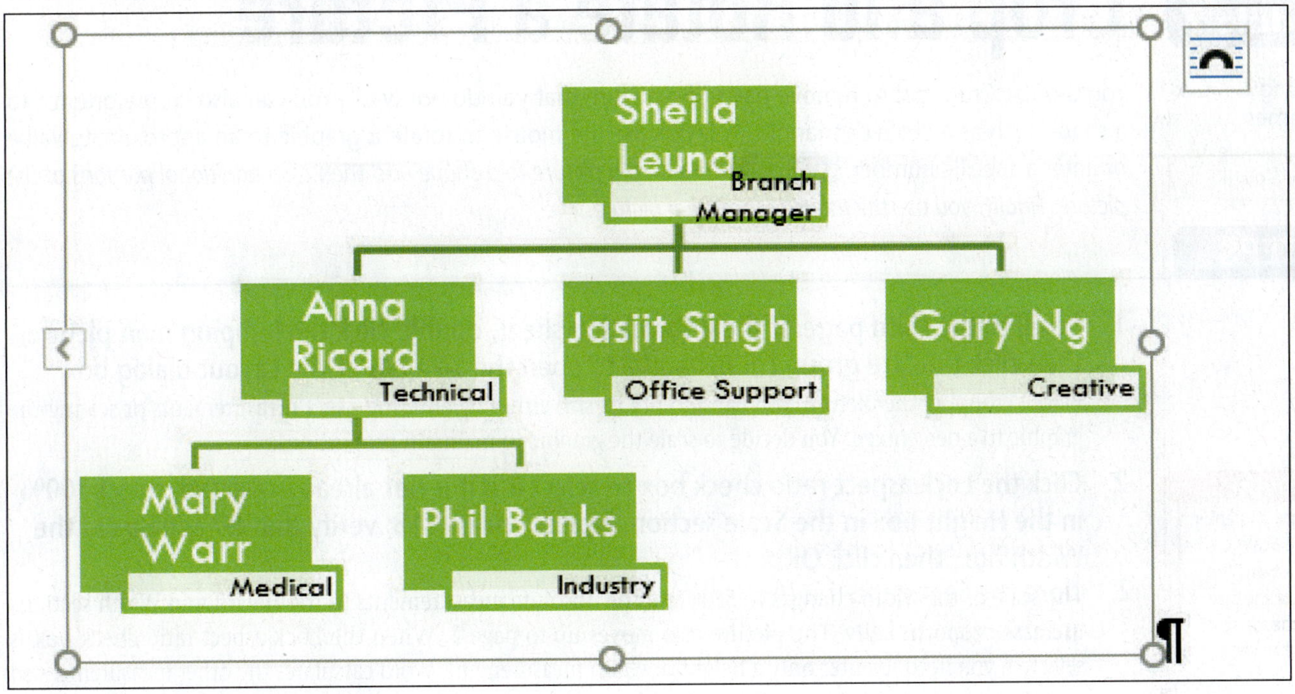

FIGURE 7-9: Completed organization chart

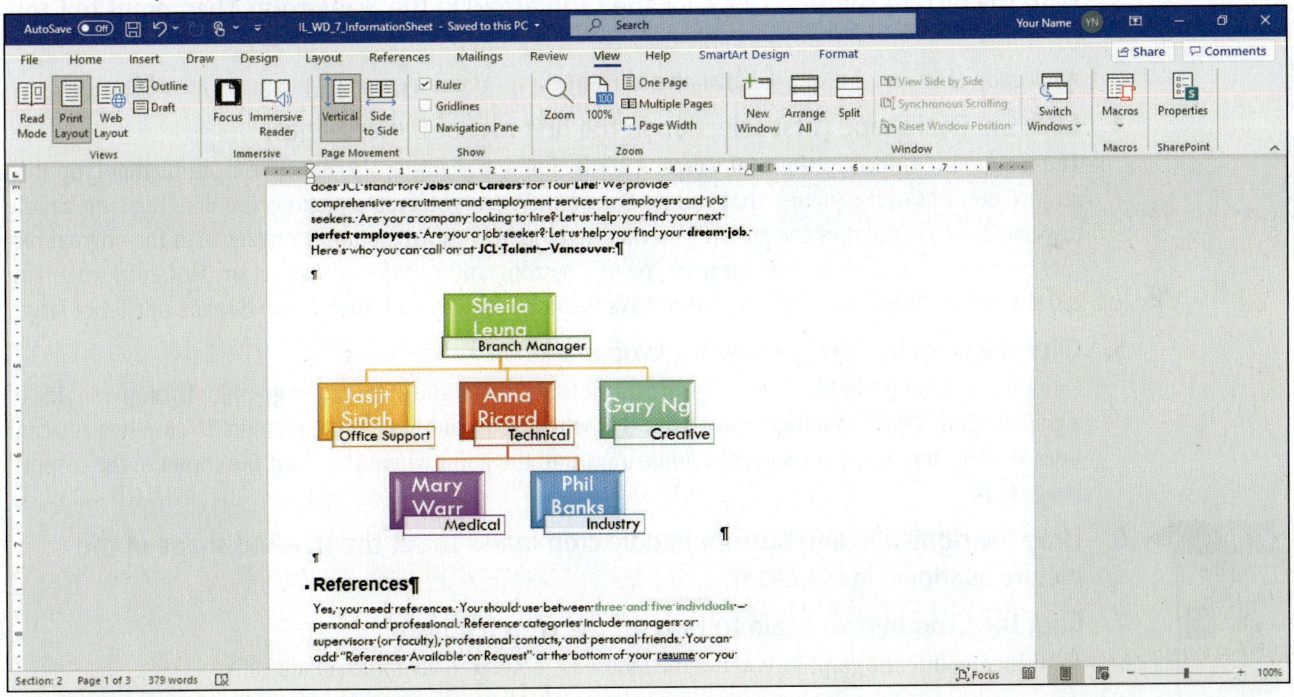

TABLE 7-4: Options for moving shapes in a SmartArt graphic

option	click to move
Promote	a subordinate box up one level
Demote	a subordinate box down one level
Right to Left	a box to the far left or right of the current row of boxes
Move Up	a box to the left of the adjacent box on the current row
Move Down	a box to the right of the adjacent box on the current row

Word
Module 7

Crop and Rotate a Picture

Learning Outcomes
- Crop a picture
- Rotate a picture

You use the Crop tool to remove parts of a picture that you do not want. You can also crop a graphic to a shape such as a circle or triangle. You can use the mouse to rotate a graphic to an approximate value or enter a specific number. **CASE** *You crop a picture to a shape and then crop additional portions of the picture. Finally, you use the mouse to rotate a picture.*

STEPS

1. **Scroll to the third page of the information sheet, double-click the jumping man picture, then click the Size group Launcher to open the Size tab of the Layout dialog box**
   Before cropping the picture, you can modify its size either by entering exact measurements or scaling the graphic to a percentage. You decide to scale the graphic to maintain proportions.

TROUBLE
Make sure you enter 50 in the Scale section toward the bottom of the Size dialog box.

2. **Click the Lock aspect ratio check box to select it if it is not already selected, select 100% in the Height box in the Scale section, type 50, press TAB, verify that 50 appears in the Width box, then click OK**
   The scale of the width changes to 50% and the Absolute measurements in the Height and Width sections increase proportionally. The picture also moves up to page 2. When the Lock aspect ratio check box is selected, you need to enter only a height or width measurement. Word calculates the other measurement so that the resized graphic is proportional.
3. **With the picture still selected, click the Crop arrow in the Size group, then point to Crop to Shape**
   A selection of shapes is displayed as shown in FIGURE 7-10. You can crop any picture to any shape.
4. **Click the Oval shape (first selection in the first row of Basic Shapes)**
   The picture is cropped to the oval shape. After cropping a picture to a shape, you can further crop it to remove portions of the picture that you do not want. When you crop a picture, you drag the crop handle associated with the part of the picture you want to crop. A cropped picture is smaller than the original picture because you take away content from the top, bottom, and/or sides of the picture. However, when you resize a picture, the content of the picture stays the same even though the picture is made smaller or larger.
5. **Click the Crop button to show the crop marks**
   Cropping handles (solid black lines) appear on all four corners and sides of the graphic. To crop one side of a graphic, drag a side cropping handle inward to where you want to trim the graphic. To crop two adjacent sides at once, drag a corner cropping handle inward to the point where you want the corner of the cropped image to be.

QUICK TIP
If you don't like the crop, you can click the Undo button on the Quick Access Toolbar to undo your last crop action.

6. **Drag the right-side and bottom-middle crop marks to set the size and shape of the picture as shown in FIGURE 7-11**
7. **Click the Crop button again to turn off the crop feature**
   To further modify the graphic, you use the mouse to rotate it to an approximate value.
8. **Click the Rotate handle at the top of the picture, drag the mouse to rotate the picture so it appears similar to FIGURE 7-12, click away to deselect the picture, then save the document**

FIGURE 7-10: Shapes for cropping a picture to

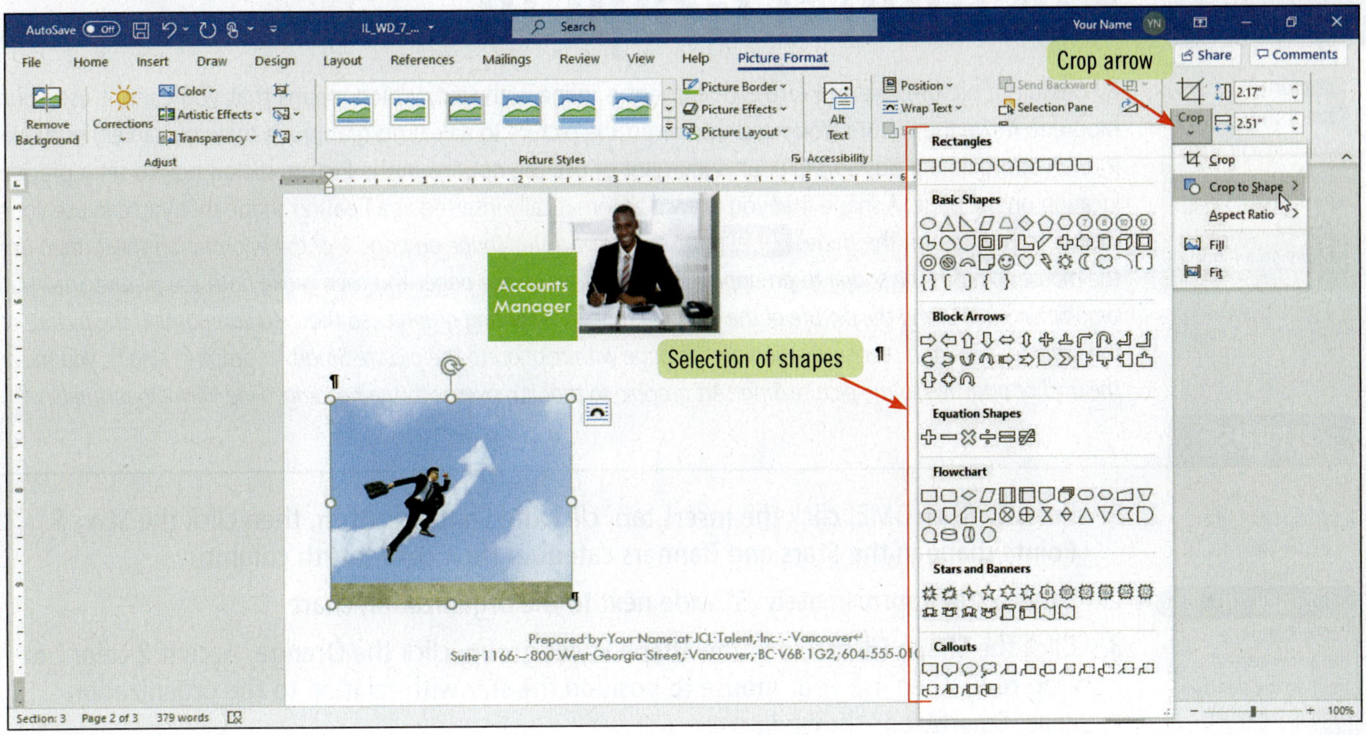

Andrey_Popov/Shutterstock.com; aslysun/Shutterstock.com

FIGURE 7-11: Cropping a picture

aslysun/Shutterstock.com

FIGURE 7-12: Rotating a picture

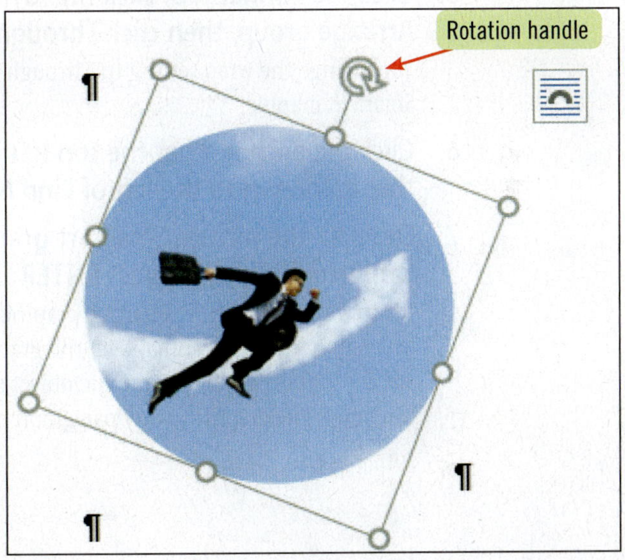

aslysun/Shutterstock.com

Position a Graphic

Learning Outcomes
- Position a floating shape
- Position a floating picture
- Move an anchor

By default, a picture inserted into a document is inline with text, which means that you cannot use your mouse to move the picture. You need to convert the picture to a floating graphic so that you can either move it to an approximate position in your document or use the options in the Picture dialog box to set a precise location on the page. A shape that you draw is automatically inserted as a floating shape that you can use your mouse to position on the page. **CASE** *You draw a star shape on page 1 of the information sheet, then use the mouse to move the shape to an approximate position on the page. You then make both the picture SmartArt graphic on page 2 and the picture of the jumping man into floating graphics so that you can position the picture of the jumping man at a precise location on the page with relation to the picture SmartArt graphic. Finally, you move the anchor attached to the picture SmartArt graphic so that it moves with the heading "Find New Opportunities."*

STEPS

QUICK TIP
You can also use the arrow keys to position the star by moving it in small increments.

1. **Press CTRL+HOME, click the Insert tab, click the Shapes button, then click the Star: 5 Points shape in the Stars and Banners category (first row, fourth column)**
2. **Draw a star approximately .5" wide next to the organization chart**
3. **Click the Shape Fill arrow in the Shape Styles group, click the Orange, Accent 2 color box (top row), then use your mouse to position the star with relation to the organization chart SmartArt as shown in FIGURE 7-13**
4. **Scroll to page 2 of the information sheet, then double-click a white area of the picture SmartArt graphic**
5. **Click the Format tab, click the Arrange button, click the Wrap Text button in the Arrange group, then click Through**

   You change the wrap setting to Through so that you can layer the jumping man picture under the picture SmartArt graphic.
6. **Click the anchor ⚓ at the top left of the picture SmartArt graphic, then drag it up so that it appears to the left of Find New Opportunities as shown in FIGURE 7-14**
7. **Deselect the picture SmartArt graphic, click the first paragraph mark below Find New Opportunities, then press ENTER**

   Notice how the picture SmartArt graphic does not move. Because you moved the anchor up to attach the graphic to the paragraph above, the graphic only moves when you also move its attached paragraph. An anchor is attached to any graphic object such as a picture, SmartArt, or shape that you insert in Word. You can attach the graphic to any paragraph by moving its anchor.

FIGURE 7-13: Star shape filled and positioned

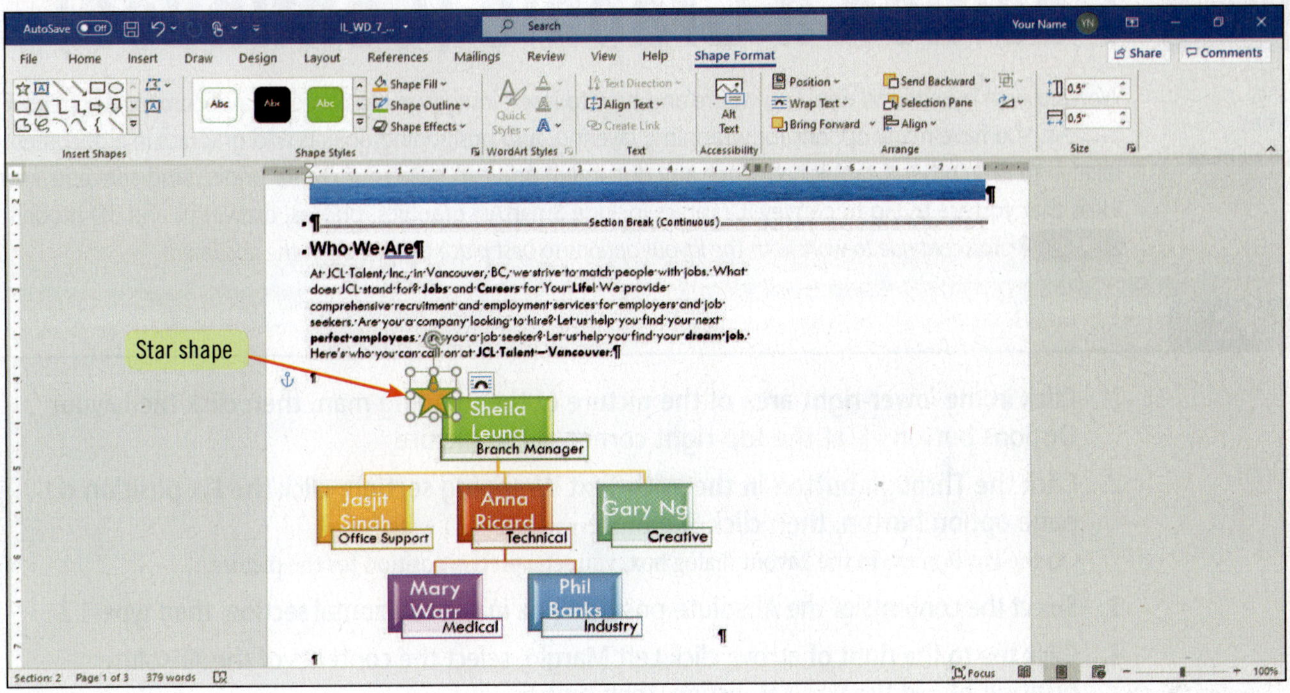

karamysh/Shutterstock.com

FIGURE 7-14: Anchor repositioned

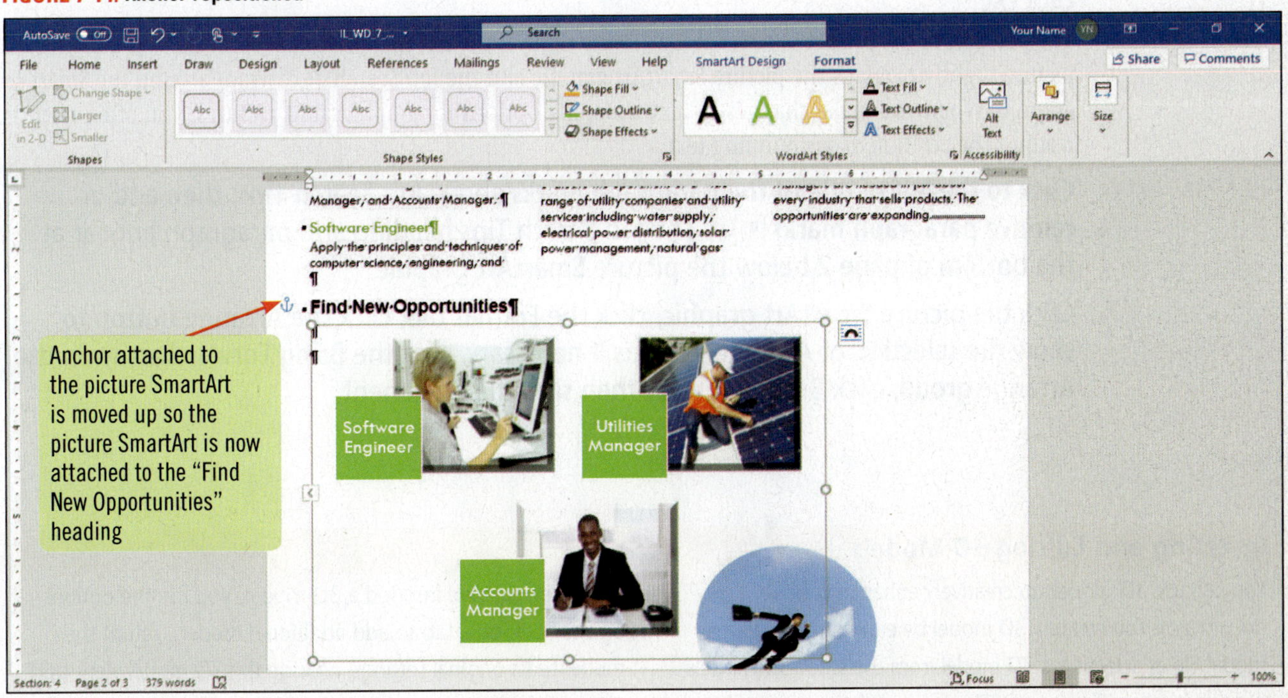

branislavpudar/Shutterstock.com; Andrey_Popov/Shutterstock.com; zstock/Shutterstock.com; aslysun/Shutterstock.com

Word

(Continued)

Position a Graphic (Continued)

Learning Outcomes
- Position a picture
- Insert 3D models

Working with layouts and deciding where and how to insert images and graphics in a document is a creative process. You have many options for wrapping, layering, and positioning objects and graphics in a document relative to each other. Graphics enhance any document and can help your reader understand concepts and ideas that you are trying to convey. Graphics include SmartArt graphics, photos, drawings, and 3D models.

CASE *You continue to work with the layout options to best place the picture in the document.*

STEPS

1. **Click in the lower-right area of the picture of the jumping man, then click the Layout Options button at the top-right corner of the picture**
2. **Click the Through button in the With Text Wrapping section, click the Fix position on page option button, then click See more**

   On the Position tab in the Layout dialog box, you set a precise position for the picture.
3. **Select the contents of the Absolute position box in the Horizontal section, then type 4.2**
4. **Click the to the right of arrow, click Left Margin, select the contents of the Absolute position box in the Vertical section, then type 5**
5. **Click the below arrow, click Top Margin, compare the Layout dialog box to FIGURE 7-15, then click OK**

   The position of the picture is now set 4.2" to the right of the left margin and 5" from the top margin. The picture slightly overlaps the picture SmartArt graphic and the Job Search Text wraps around the SmartArt graphic. When you make changes to text wrapping options for graphics and pictures, you often need to readjust the position of surrounding text.
6. **Click to the left of one of the paragraph marks above Job Search Tips, then add or remove paragraph marks ¶ so the Job Search Tips heading and paragraph appear at the bottom of page 2 below the picture SmartArt graphic**
7. **Click the picture SmartArt graphic, click the Format tab, click the Arrange button to show the selection of Arrange options if necessary, click the Bring Forward arrow in the Arrange group, click Bring to Front, then save the document**

Inserting and Editing 3D Models

You can use 3D models to creatively enhance your documents. You create a 3D model by either inserting a 3D model file or selecting a 3D model from the stock 3D models provided online. To insert a 3D model, click the Insert tab, then click the 3D Models arrow to show two options: This Device and Stock 3D Models. To select a stock 3D model, click Stock 3D Models, click the model category you require, click the model you wish to use, then click Insert. FIGURE 7-16 shows the 3D model of a parrot from the Animals category.

Once you have inserted a 3D model, you use the options on the 3D Model tab to add additional models, return the model to its original settings, change the 3D model view, add Alt text, arrange the position of the 3D model with relation to other objects on the page, and modify the size of the 3D model. FIGURE 7-17 shows how the 3D model of the parrot has been edited.

FIGURE 7-15: Layout dialog box

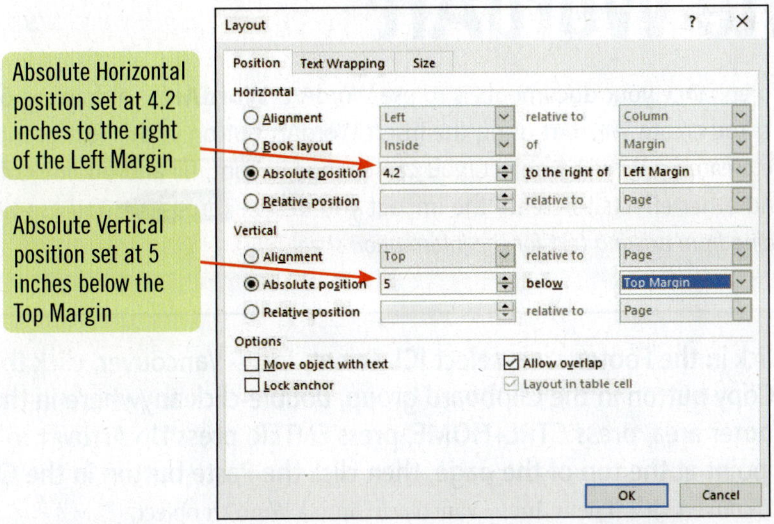

FIGURE 7-16: 3D Model tab

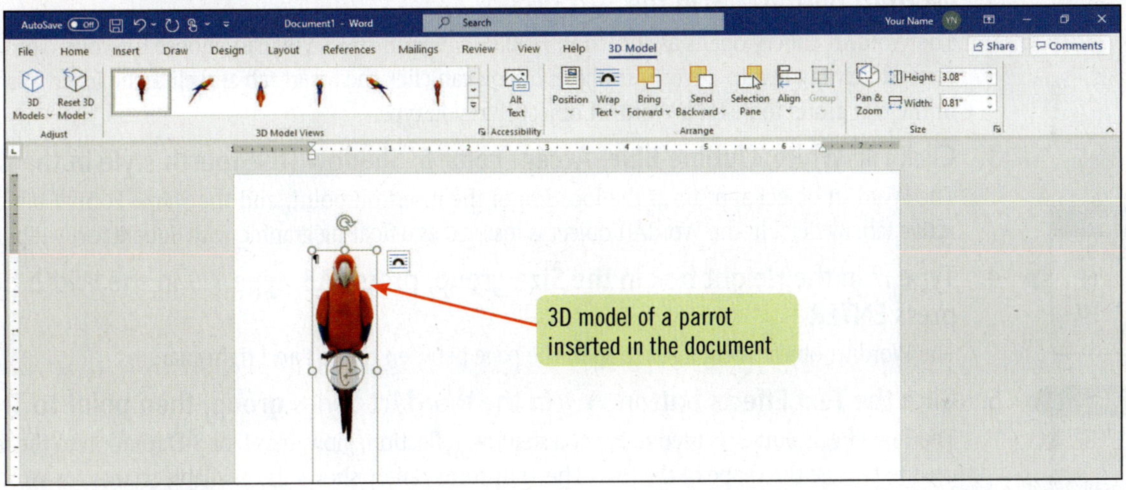

FIGURE 7-17: Editing and enhancing the 3D model

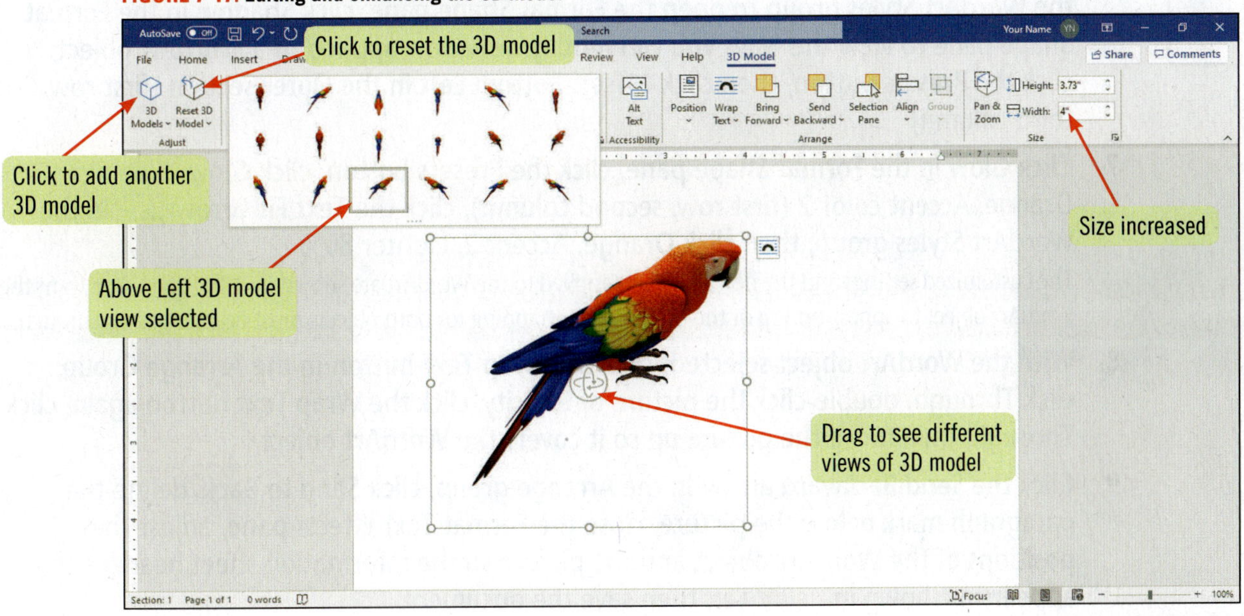

Create WordArt

Learning Outcomes
- Insert WordArt
- Modify WordArt

Another way to enhance your documents is to use WordArt. **WordArt** is a drawing object that contains decorative text. You create WordArt using the Insert WordArt button in the Text group on the Insert tab. Once you have created a WordArt object, you can change its font, fill and outline colors, borders, shadows, shape, and other effects to create the impact you desire. **CASE** *You use WordArt to create an impressive heading from existing text for the information sheet.*

STEPS

1. **Double-click in the Footer area, select JCL Talent, Inc. – Vancouver, click the Home tab, click the Copy button in the Clipboard group, double-click anywhere in the document to exit the footer area, press CTRL+HOME, press ENTER, press Up Arrow ↑ to position the insertion point at the top of the page, then click the Paste button in the Clipboard group**
   You want to convert "JCL Talent, Inc. – Vancouver" into a WordArt object.
2. **Select the text JCL Talent, Inc. – Vancouver, click the Insert tab, then click the Insert WordArt button in the Text group**
   The WordArt gallery opens as shown in FIGURE 7-18 with styles you can choose for your WordArt. You can convert existing text to a WordArt object or you can click the Insert tab and click the Insert WordArt button in the text group to insert a WordArt object that you type.
3. **Click Fill: White; Outline Blue, Accent color 5; Shadow (the fourth style in the first row)**
   The WordArt object appears at the location of the insertion point, and the Shape Format tab becomes the active tab. By default, the WordArt object is inserted as a floating graphic with Square text wrapping.

QUICK TIP
You can change the font or font size of WordArt text using the Mini toolbar.

4. **Type .7 in the Height box in the Size group, press TAB, type 7.5 in the Width box, then press ENTER**
   The WordArt object is enlarged to span the page between the left and right margins.

QUICK TIP
Use the Text Effects and Typography button in the Font group on the Home tab to apply text effects to regular text.

5. **Click the Text Effects button in the WordArt Styles group, then point to Transform**
   The Text Effects button is used to apply a shadow, reflection, glow, bevel, or 3-D rotation to the text. It is also used to change the shape of the text. The Transform gallery shows the available shapes for WordArt text.
6. **Click Warp Up in the Warp section (fourth row, third column), click the Launcher in the WordArt Styles group to open the Format Shape pane, click Shadow in the Format Shape pane to view the ways you can modify a shadow applied to a WordArt object, click the Presets button, then click Offset: Bottom Left in the Outer section (first row, third column)**
7. **Click Glow in the Format Shape pane, click the Presets button, click Glow: 5 point; Orange, Accent color 2 (first row, second column), click the Text Fill arrow in the WordArt Styles group, then click Orange, Accent 2, Lighter 80%**
   The customized settings and the new fill effects applied to the WordArt are shown in FIGURE 7-19. You want the WordArt object to appear on top of the picture. The wrapping for both objects must be changed to Through.
8. **With the WordArt object selected, click the Wrap Text button in the Arrange Group, click Through, double-click the picture of the city, click the Wrap Text button again, click Through, then move the picture up so it covers the WordArt object**
9. **Click the Send Backward arrow in the Arrange group, click Send to Back, delete the paragraph mark below the picture, close the Format Text Effects pane, adjust the positions of the WordArt object and the picture so the information sheet header appears as shown in FIGURE 7-20, then save the document**

FIGURE 7-18: WordArt gallery

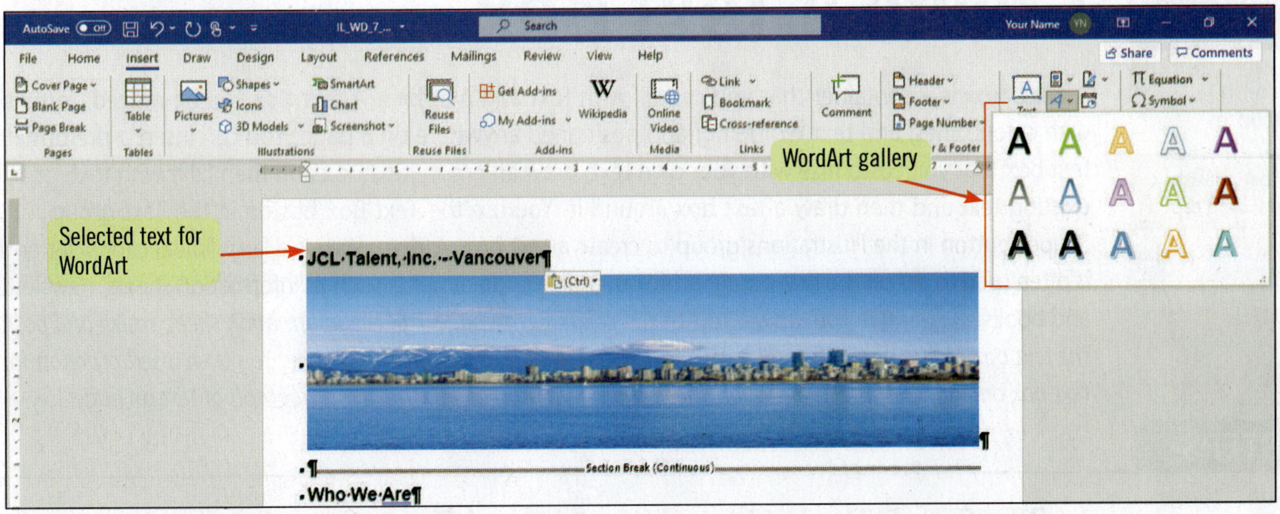

karamysh/Shutterstock.com

FIGURE 7-19: Formatted WordArt object

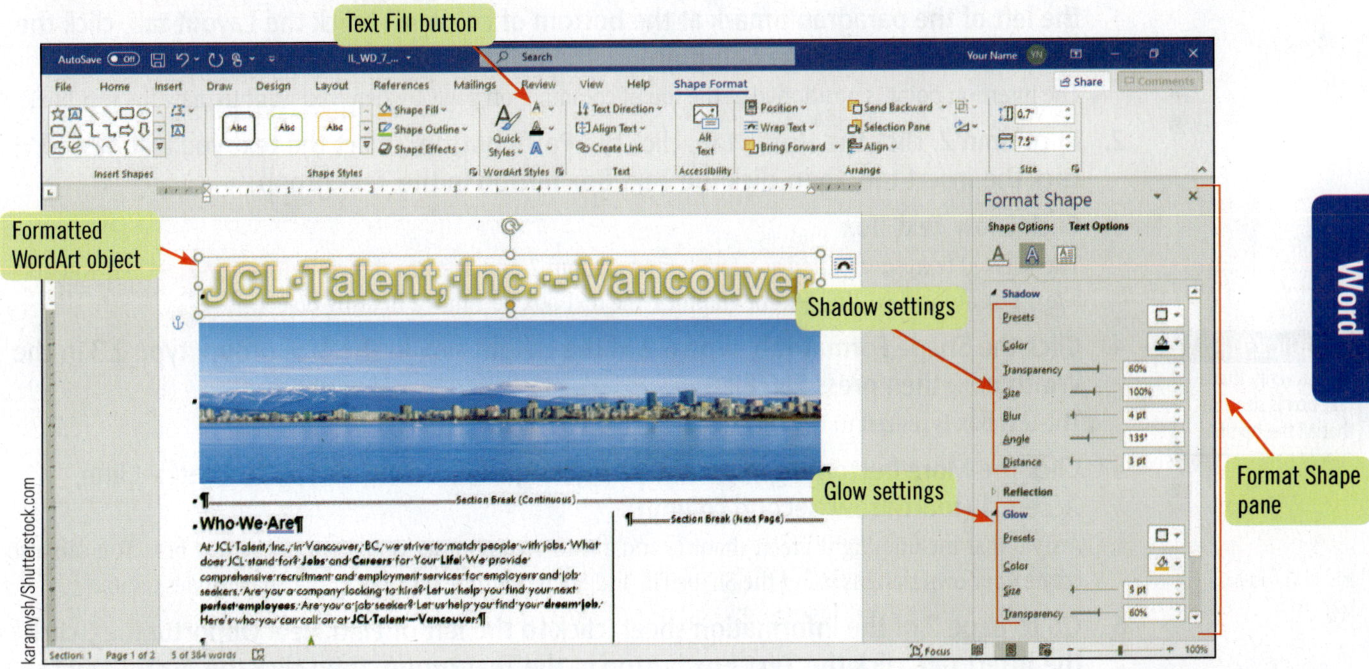

karamysh/Shutterstock.com

FIGURE 7-20: Completed header

karamysh/Shutterstock.com

Create a Text Box

Learning Outcomes
- Draw a text box
- Format a text box
- Add a drop cap

A **text box** is a container that you can fill with text and graphics. A text box can be resized; formatted with colors, lines, and text wrapping; and positioned anywhere on a page. You can insert a preformatted text box that you customize with your own text, draw an empty text box and then fill it with text, or select existing text and then draw a text box around it. You use the Text Box button in the Text group, or the Shapes button in the Illustrations group to create a text box. A **drop cap** is a large initial capital letter that is often used to set off the first paragraph of an article in documents such as information sheets, newsletters, and books. CASE *You draw a text box in column 2 on page 1 of the information sheet, resize and position the text box on the page, then fill it with text and format it using a text box style. You then insert a preformatted text box on page 2 of the information sheet and add a drop cap to the first paragraph of text on page 1.*

STEPS

1. **Press CTRL+END, select the text from Job Search Tips to the end of the document, click the Cut button in the Clipboard group, scroll up to page 1 and click after them. and to the left of the paragraph mark at the bottom of column 1, click the Layout tab, click the Breaks button in the Page Setup group, then click Column**
   The insertion point is positioned at the top of column 2 on page 1 where you want to draw the text box.
2. **In column 2, click the Home tab, click the Paste button, select the text you just pasted, click the Insert tab, then click the Text Box button in the Text group**
3. **Click Draw Text Box**
   The selected text is formatted as a text box in column 2 on page 1 as shown in FIGURE 7-21. When you draw a text box around existing text or graphics, the text box becomes a floating object.

QUICK TIP
Always verify that a text box is sized so that all the text fits.

4. **Click the Shape Format tab, type 6.2 in the Height box in the Size group, type 2.3 in the Width box, then press ENTER**
   The text box is resized to be exactly 6.2" tall and 2.3" wide.
5. **Click the More button in the Shape Styles group, then click Subtle Effect – Lime, Accent 1 (fourth row, second column)**
   A style that includes light green shading and a thin green border is applied to the text box. You can also create your own designs using the Shape Fill and Shape Outline buttons in the Shape Styles group.
6. **Go to page 2 of the information sheet, click to the left of Find New Opportunities, click the Insert tab, click the Text Box button in the Text group, then click the Austin Quote preformatted style (middle selection in the first row)**
7. **Drag the left-middle sizing handle to the right to reduce the width of the text box to approximately 2", move the text box to the right to a blank area, click in the text box, type Contact Anna Ricard or Phil Banks for information about current job opportunities in these sectors., then use your mouse to size and position the text box as shown in FIGURE 7-22**
8. **Click away from the text box, press CTRL+HOME, click in the paragraph below the Who We Are heading in Column 1, click the Insert tab, click the Drop Cap button in the Text group, then click Dropped**
   A drop cap is added to the paragraph. You can modify the size and font of the drop cap.
9. **With the drop cap still selected, click the Drop Cap button, click Drop Cap Options, click the Lines to drop down arrow to show 2, click OK, deselect the drop cap, then save the document**

FIGURE 7-21: Text enclosed in a text box

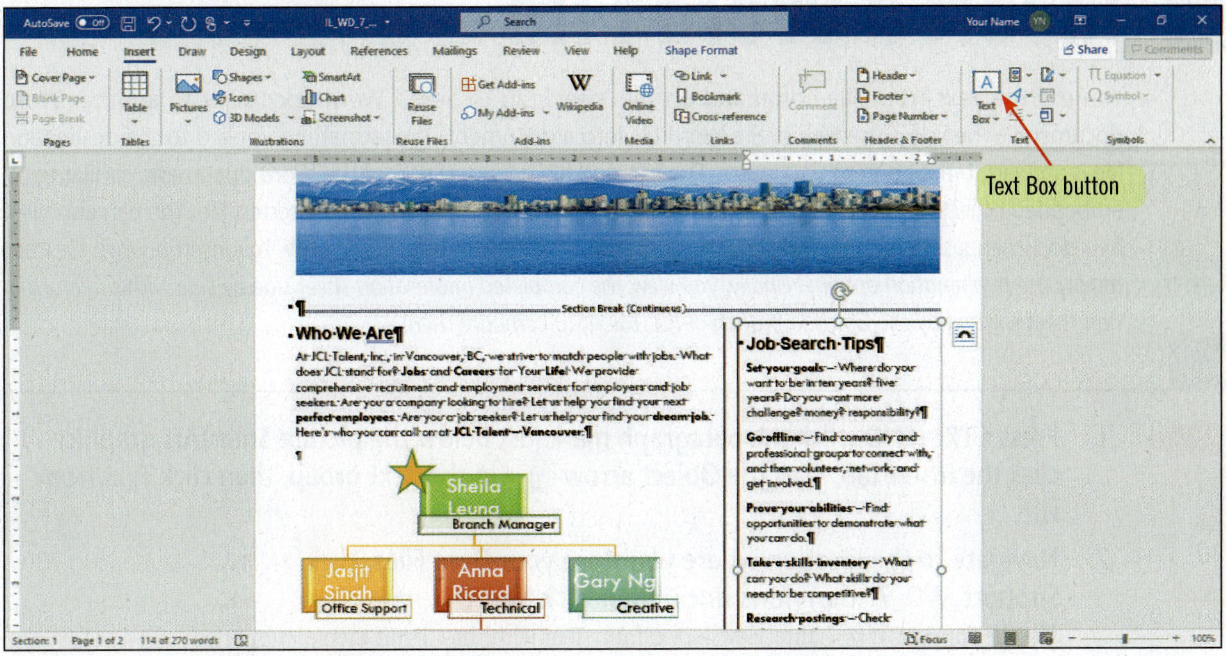

karamysh/Shutterstock.com

FIGURE 7-22: Text box sized and positioned

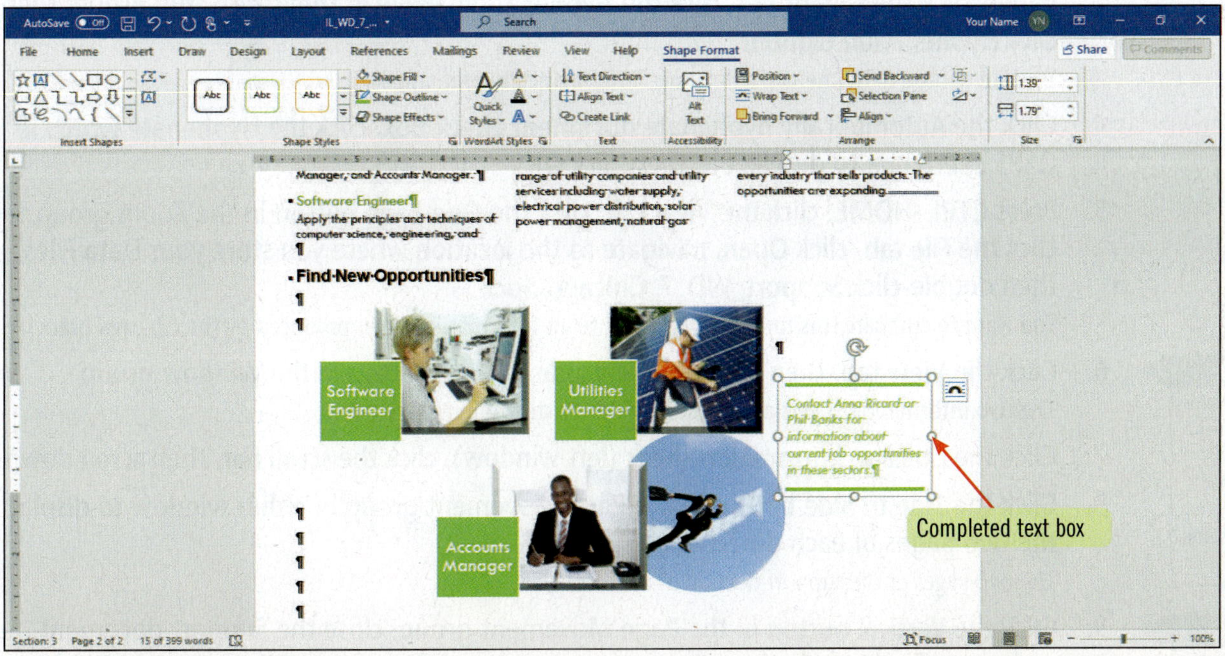

branislavpudar/Shutterstock.com; zstock/Shutterstock.com; aslysun/Shutterstock.com; Andrey_Popov/Shutterstock.com

Word

Linking text boxes

If you are working on a longer document, you might want text to begin in a text box on one page and then continue in a text box on another page. By creating a **link** between two or more text boxes, you can force text to flow automatically from one text box to another, allowing you to size and format the text boxes any way you wish. To link two or more text boxes, you must first create the original text box, fill it with text, and then create a second, empty text box. Then, to create the link, select the first text box, click the Create Link button in the Text group on the Shape Format tab to activate the pointer, and then click the second text box with the pointer. Any overflow text from the first text box flows seamlessly into the second text box. As you resize the first text box, the flow of text adjusts automatically between the two linked text boxes. If you want to break a link between two linked text boxes so that all the text is contained in the original text box, select the original text box, and then click the Break Link button in the Text group.

Word
Module 7

Insert a Word File

Learning Outcomes
- Insert text from a file
- Set hyphenation options
- View documents

You use the Text from File command on the Insert tab to add a Word document to another Word document. When you insert an entire Word file into a document, the formatting applied to the destination file is applied to the content you insert. The inserted file becomes part of the Word document, similar to an embedded object, and you cannot return to the original document from the inserted file. You can also view two documents side by side and scroll through them synchronously. **CASE** *You insert a Word file, then modify the hyphenation options. Finally, you view the completed information sheet side by side with an information sheet created by the Chicago branch of JCL Talent to compare them.*

STEPS

TROUBLE
Do not to select the graphic. If you do, click away from the graphic and try again

1. **Press CTRL+END, click the paragraph mark just below the picture SmartArt graphic, click the Insert tab, click the Object arrow in the Text group, then click Text from File**
2. **Navigate to the location where you store your Data Files, click Support_WD_7_Interviews.docx, then click Insert**

   The file Support_WD_7_Interviews.docx, formatted with the Circuit theme, is inserted.
3. **Delete extra hard returns above and below the text so the document fits on two pages, click the Layout tab, click the Hyphenation arrow in the Page Setup group, then click Hyphenation Options**

   You can choose to hyphenate a document automatically or manually.
4. **Click the Automatically hyphenate document check box, click the Hyphenate words in CAPS check box to deselect it, then click OK**
5. **Press CTRL+HOME, click the View tab, click the One Page button in the Zoom group, click the File tab, click Open, navigate to the location where you store your Data Files, then double-click Support_WD_7_Chicago.docx**

   You want to compare this finished document to an information sheet produced by the Chicago branch.

QUICK TIP
By default, the Vertical page movement option is selected, which means that page 1 of both documents appears side by side.

6. **Click the View tab, then click the View Side by Side button in the Window group**

   The two information sheets appear side by side as shown in FIGURE 7-23.
7. **Click the Chicago information sheet (left window), click the scroll bar, then scroll down**
8. **Click the Side to Side button in the Page Movement group in either window to display the two pages of each document**

   The two pages of the support document are displayed.

QUICK TIP
You need to select the Vertical page movement option to continue working normally in Word.

9. **Click the Vertical button in the Page Movement group, close the Support document, make any spacing adjustments necessary so your document matches FIGURE 7-24, then click the Vertical button in the Page Movement group if necessary**
10. **sam Save your changes, submit a copy to your instructor, then close the file and exit Word**

Configuring line numbers

To add line numbers to selected text, click the Line Numbers button in the Page Setup group on the Layout tab. You can then choose to number lines continuously, restart numbering on each new page or section, or suppress for the current paragraph. You can also choose to display the numbers at intervals. Word counts the number of lines in a document. This is helpful if you want to refer to a specific line in a document such as in a legal contract.

FIGURE 7-23: Two documents viewed side by side

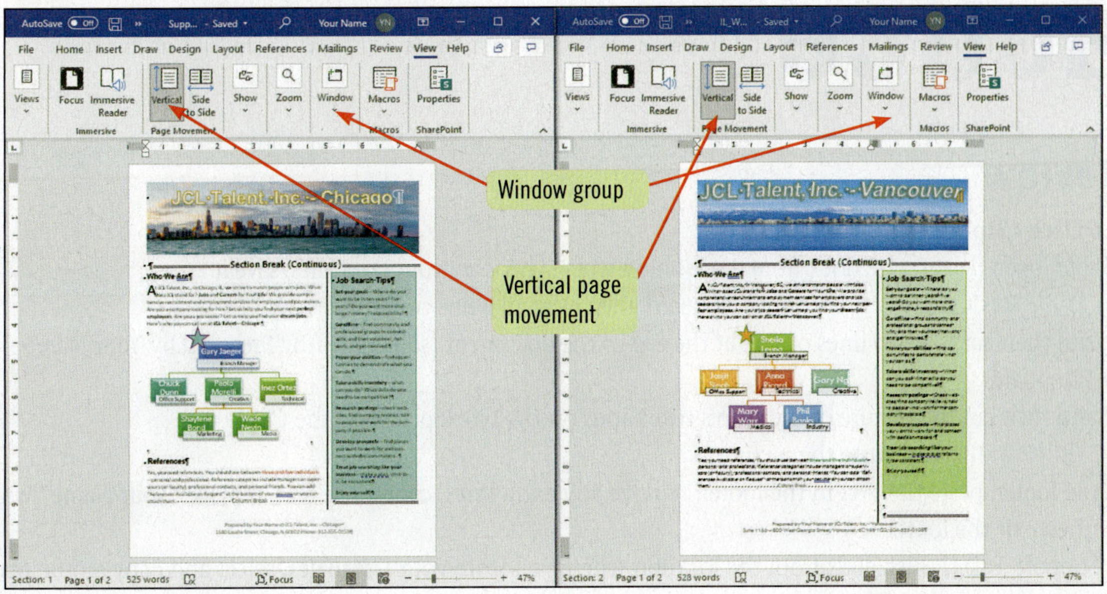

f11photo/Shutterstock.com

karamysh/Shutterstock.com

FIGURE 7-24: Completed information sheet

Who We Are

At JCL Talent, Inc., in Vancouver, BC, we strive to match people with jobs. What does JCL stand for? **Jobs** and **Careers** for Your **Life!** We provide comprehensive recruitment and employment services for employers and job seekers. Are you a company looking to hire? Let us help you find your next **perfect employees.** Are you a job seeker? Let us help you find your **dream job.** Here's who you can call on at **JCL Talent – Vancouver:**

References

Yes, you need references. You should use between three and five individuals – personal and professional. Reference categories include managers or supervisors (or faculty), professional contacts, and personal friends. You can add "References Available on Request" at the bottom of your resume or you can attach them.

Job Search Tips

Set your goals – Where do you want to be in ten years? five years? Do you want more challenge? money? responsibility?

Go offline – Find community and professional groups to connect with, and then volunteer, network, and get involved.

Prove your abilities – Find opportunities to demonstrate what you can do.

Take a skills inventory – What can you do? What skills do you need to be competitive?

Research postings – Check websites, find company reviews, talk to people who work for the company if possible.

Develop prospects – Find places you want to work for and connect with decision-makers.

Treat job searching like your business – Make a plan, stick to it, be consistent.

Enjoy yourself!

Prepared by Your Name at JCL Talent, Inc. - Vancouver
Suite 1166 – 800 West Georgia Street, Vancouver, BC V6B 1G2, 604-555-0108

Top Jobs!

The job market is hot, hot, hot right now for a wide range of jobs, particularly in Finance & Accounting Careers and Technical Careers. This month, we're highlighting three top jobs: Software Engineer, Utilities Manager, and Accounts Manager.

Software Engineer

Apply the principles and techniques of computer science, engineering, and mathematical analysis to design, develop, test, and evaluate software and computer systems in a wide range of industries.

Utilities Manager

Plan, organize, direct, control and evaluate the operations of a wide range of utility companies and utilityservices including water supply, electrical power distribution, solar power management, natural gas supply, and waste management systems.

Accounts Manager

Take responsibility for the management of a company's sales and customer relationships. Account Managers are needed in just about every industry that sells products. The opportunities are expanding.

Find New Opportunities

Contact Anna Ricard or Phil Banks for information about current job opportunities in these sectors.

Top Five Interview Tips

1. Focus on the Interviewer
   You are there to solve a problem for the company not to drone on about your qualifications and experience. How can your skills help them?
2. Clarify the Reasons you want the Job
   Identify your top three to five selling points as a job candidate.
3. Prepare Questions for the Interviewer
   Demonstrate that you've researched the company and are interested in working there. The ideal question is "Can you describe your ideal candidate for this position?"
4. Stay Positive
   Focus on your positive experiences and maintain a cheerful and helpful attitude.
5. Frame Your Weaknesses
   Almost all interviewers ask the question "What are your weaknesses?" Be prepared with an honest answer that emphasizes your willingness to learn and grow.

Prepared by Your Name at JCL Talent, Inc. - Vancouver
Suite 1166 – 800 West Georgia Street, Vancouver, BC V6B 1G2, 604-555-0108

karamysh/Shutterstock.com

zstock/Shutterstock.com; branislavpudar/Shutterstock.com; aslysun/Shutterstock.com; Andrey_Popov/Shutterstock.com

Inserting online videos and online pictures in a document

You can also illustrate your documents with graphics and media that you have found on the web and have permission to use. The Online Video command in the Media group on the Insert tab allows you to insert videos found on the web into your Word documents and play them. Click the Online Video button, type the URL or embed code in the Insert Video dialog box, then click Insert. Use the Pictures button in the Illustrations group to insert images from the web. Click Online Pictures on the Pictures button menu to open the Online Pictures window, type a keyword or phrase in the search box for the image you want to find, then press ENTER. Select an image from the search results, click Insert to add it to the document, then format the item as you would any other graphic object. Videos inserted in a document include a play button that you can click to view the video right in Word.

Practice

Skills Review

1. **Use the Office Clipboard.**
   a. Start Word, open IL_WD_7-2.docx from the location where you store your Data Files, save it as **IL_WD_7_RiskReport**, open the Clipboard, then clear all items currently listed.
   b. Select and then cut the two lines of text at the top of the document (starting with "Prepared by Your Name . . .) to the Clipboard.
   c. Select and then cut the picture of the man's two hands on the block puzzle to the Clipboard.
   d. Press CTRL+HOME, then paste the picture.
   e. Open the footer, paste the text in the footer, remove any extra lines, center the text, replace "Your Name" with your name, then exit the footer.
   f. Open Support_WD_7_Risk.docx from the location where you store your Data Files, select and copy all the text, then close the document.
   g. Click the blank line below the "Organization Chart" placeholder, paste the text using the Use Destination Theme paste option, close the Clipboard, then save the document.
2. **Create sections and columns.**
   a. Turn on formatting marks, if necessary.
   b. Place the insertion point to the left of the heading "Risk Management Team", press ENTER, then insert a continuous section break.
   c. In Section 2, turn on columns with the following settings: Right preset, spacing between set at .4", and the Line between option selected.
   d. In Multiple Pages view, insert a Next Page section break to the left of "Risk Questions".
   e. In Section 3, turn on columns with the following settings: Three, spacing between at .2", and the Line between option deselected.
   f. Return to 100% view, insert a Continuous section break to the left of the paragraph mark following "maintenance?" at the bottom of column 1 to balance the columns containing the Risk Questions text.
   g. Click the paragraph mark above the picture of the blocks in column 1 on page 2, turn on one column (Section 4), then save the document.
3. **Create SmartArt graphics.**
   a. Click the picture of the woman teaching at the bottom of page 2, then create a picture SmartArt graphic using the Bending Picture Blocks layout.
   b. Add two shapes to the picture SmartArt.
   c. Insert **Support_WD_7_Coins.jpg** in the first blank shape, then insert **Support_WD_7_Disaster.jpg** in the second blank shape.
   d. Expand the text pane, if necessary, label the three boxes as follows: **Employee Training, Financial Reserves**, and **Disaster Preparation**, then close the text pane. (*Hint:* Press the down arrow, *not* ENTER, to move to the next bullet. If you press ENTER, click the Undo button.)
   e. Change the layout to Bending Picture Caption (second row, second column).
   f. Set the height of the picture SmartArt graphic to 3.3" and the width to 5.7".
   g. Use SHIFT to select the three pictures in the picture SmartArt graphic, apply the Slant bevel shape effect (first row, fourth column), then save the document.

Skills Review (continued)

4. Modify SmartArt graphics.

a. On page 1 of the Risk Report, select the "Organization Chart" placeholder, then insert a Hierarchy SmartArt graphic using the Name and Title Organization Chart style.

b. Click a white area of the chart, then set the height of the organization chart at 2.8" and the width at 4.7".

c. Add and remove shapes and text so the organization chart appears as shown in FIGURE 7-25.

d. Use the Move Down command to move the box for Edie Quinn so it and its subordinate boxes appear in the middle of row 2.

e. Change the colors of the chart to Colored Fill – Accent 4 (red).

f. Apply the Cartoon SmartArt style from the 3-D section.

FIGURE 7-25

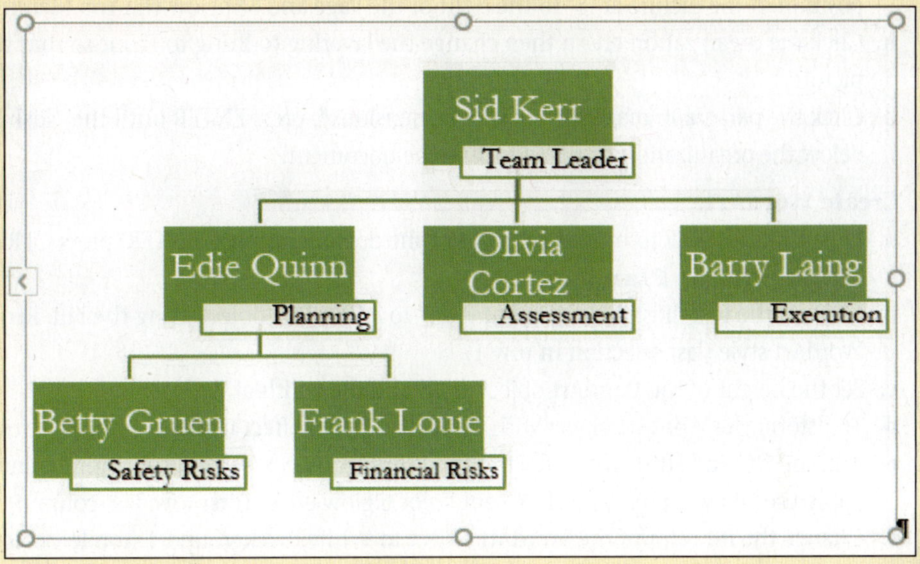

g. Select all five of the subordinate boxes, set the width at 1.1", then save the document.

5. Crop and rotate a picture.

a. Scroll to page 2 of the report, double-click the picture of the three hands and block tower, then scale the picture to 75%. (*Hint:* Remember to verify that the Lock aspect ratio check box is selected so the picture is resized proportionally.)

b. Crop the picture to the Cloud shape (third row, third selection from the right in the Basic Shapes category).

c. See FIGURE 7-26. Further crop the picture and use the mouse to slightly rotate it to the left.

d. Deselect the picture, then save the document.

FIGURE 7-26

Freedomz/Shutterstock.com

6. Position a graphic.

a. Scroll down to view the picture SmartArt graphic, then draw a Lightning Bolt shape that is approximately 1" in height.

b. Fill the lightning bolt with Gold, Accent 6, Lighter 40%.

c. Position the lightning bolt shape in the lower left corner of the picture SmartArt graphic, slightly overlapping the Disaster Preparation box. Refer to the completed document in FIGURE 7-27.

d. On page 1, change the wrapping of the organization chart to Through. Don't worry that text will wrap around it.

Skills Review (continued)

- **e.** Drag the anchor for the chart up so it appears to the left of the paragraph of text that starts "We have embarked upon ...".
- **f.** Scroll down and click the cloud-shaped picture, cut the picture, then paste it at the paragraph mark above the "Risk Dimensions" heading on page 1 of the report.
- **g.** Change the wrapping of the cloud shape to Through, then on the Position tab in the Layout dialog box, set the position of the picture at .5" to the right of the Page and 5" below the Top Margin.
- **h.** Click the organization chart, then change the layering to Bring to Front so that the chart slightly overlaps the cloud picture.
- **i.** Click the paragraph mark above "Risk Dimensions", press ENTER until the "Risk Dimensions" paragraph is moved below the organization chart, then save the document.

7. Create WordArt.

- **a.** Press CTRL+HOME to move to the top of the document, press ENTER, press CTRL+HOME, then type **Risk Management Plan**.
- **b.** Convert the text "Risk Management Plan" to a WordArt object using the Fill: Red, Accent color 4; Soft Bevel WordArt style (last selection in row 1).
- **c.** Set the height of the WordArt object at .9" and the width at 7.5".
- **d.** Transform the WordArt object with the Wave: Down effect (first column, fifth row in the Warp section).
- **e.** Add the Offset: Left shadow effect to the WordArt object (second row, third column in the Outer section), then apply the Glow: 5 point; Gold, Accent color 6 glow effect (first row, last column).
- **f.** Change the fill color of the WordArt object to White, Background 1 (top left color box).
- **g.** Change the wrap setting to Through, then change the wrap setting of the wide picture below to Through.
- **h.** Adjust the WordArt object and picture so the WordArt object appears in front of the picture at the top of the document as shown in the completed report in FIGURE 7-27.
- **i.** Delete the extra paragraph mark below the first picture in the document, then save the document.

8. Create a text box.

- **a.** Scroll to and select the text from "Risk Categories" to the end of the document, then cut it.
- **b.** Scroll up to page 1, click after "monitor it" at the end of the Risk Dimensions paragraph at the bottom of column 1 on page 1, press ENTER, insert a column break, then paste the copied text in the new column.
- **c.** Select the text again, then insert it into a text box using the Draw Text Box option.
- **d.** Set the height of the text box to 7" and the width to 2.2".
- **e.** Apply the Moderate Effect – Red, Accent 4 shape style to the text box.
- **f.** If necessary, remove any extra hard returns following the text box so that page 2 moves up, change the wrapping to Through for the picture SmartArt graphic, then send it behind the lightning bolt.
- **g.** Remove the two paragraph marks above "Be Prepared," then insert a text box using the Austin Quote preformatted text box.
- **h.** Size and position the text box, then type **Contact Betty Gruen for information about company-wide emergency procedures and to obtain emergency kits for each department.** as shown in the completed report in FIGURE 7-27.
- **i.** On page 1 of the report, insert a drop cap that is dropped 2 lines in the paragraph under the "Risk Management Team" heading.
- **j.** Save the document.

Skills Review (continued)

9. Insert a Word file.

- **a.** Double-click below the picture SmartArt graphic on page 2 to position the insertion point, then insert the Word file **Support_WD_7_Quiz.docx** from the location where you store your Data Files.
- **b.** Remove any extra hard returns so that the document fits on two pages.
- **c.** Change the hyphenation options so that the text in the document is automatically hyphenated and words in CAPS are *not* hyphenated.
- **d.** Press CTRL+HOME, then view the document in One Page view.
- **e.** Open Support_WD_7_RiskReport_WatsonFinancial.docx from the location where you store your Data Files.
- **f.** View the two documents side by side, then change the page movement to Side to Side.
- **g.** Return the page movement to Vertical, close the Support document, then make any spacing adjustments necessary so that the two pages of the Risk Management Report appear as shown in FIGURE 7-27.
- **h.** Save the document, submit a copy to your instructor, then close the file and exit Word.

FIGURE 7-27

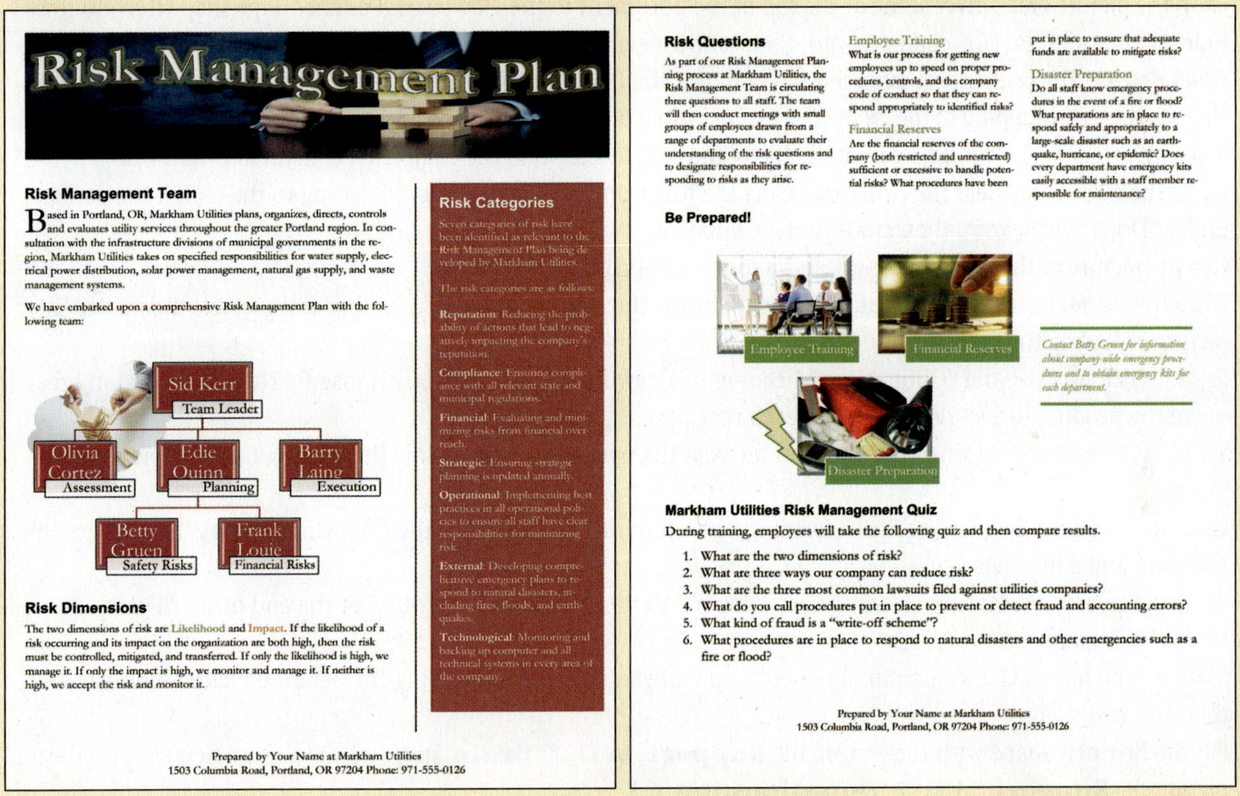

Risk Management Plan

Risk Management Team

Based in Portland, OR, Markham Utilities plans, organizes, directs, controls and evaluates utility services throughout the greater Portland region. In consultation with the infrastructure divisions of municipal governments in the region, Markham Utilities takes on specified responsibilities for water supply, electrical power distribution, solar power management, natural gas supply, and waste management systems.

We have embarked upon a comprehensive Risk Management Plan with the following team:

Risk Dimensions

The two dimensions of risk are Likelihood and Impact. If the likelihood of a risk occurring and its impact on the organization are both high, then the risk must be controlled, mitigated, and transferred. If only the likelihood is high, we manage it. If only the impact is high, we monitor and manage it. If neither is high, we accept the risk and monitor it.

Risk Categories

Seven categories of risk have been identified as relevant to the Risk Management Plan being developed by Markham Utilities.

The risk categories are as follows:

Reputation: Reducing the probability of actions that lead to negatively impacting the company's reputation.

Compliance: Ensuring compliance with all relevant state and municipal regulations.

Financial: Evaluating and minimizing risks from financial overreach.

Strategic: Ensuring strategic planning is updated annually.

Operational: Implementing best practices in all operational policies to ensure all staff have clear responsibilities for minimizing risk.

External: Developing comprehensive emergency plans to respond to natural disasters, including fires, floods, and earthquakes.

Technological: Monitoring and backing up computer and all technical systems in every area of the company.

Prepared by Your Name at Markham Utilities
1503 Columbia Road, Portland, OR 97204 Phone: 971-555-0126

Risk Questions

As part of our Risk Management Planning process at Markham Utilities, the Risk Management Team is circulating three questions to all staff. The team will then conduct meetings with small groups of employees drawn from a range of departments to evaluate their understanding of the risk questions and to designate responsibilities for responding to risks as they arise.

Employee Training

What is our process for getting new employees up to speed on proper procedures, controls, and the company code of conduct so that they can respond appropriately to identified risks?

Financial Reserves

Are the financial reserves of the company (both restricted and unrestricted) sufficient or excessive to handle potential risks? What procedures have been put in place to ensure that adequate funds are available to mitigate risks?

Disaster Preparation

Do all staff know emergency procedures in the event of a fire or flood? What preparations are in place to respond safely and appropriately to a large-scale disaster such as an earthquake, hurricane, or epidemic? Does every department have emergency kits easily accessible with a staff member responsible for maintenance?

Be Prepared!

Contact Betty Gruen for information about company-wide emergency procedures and to obtain emergency kits for each department.

Markham Utilities Risk Management Quiz

During training, employees will take the following quiz and then compare results.

1. What are the two dimensions of risk?
2. What are three ways our company can reduce risk?
3. What are the three most common lawsuits filed against utilities companies?
4. What do you call procedures put in place to prevent or detect fraud and accounting errors?
5. What kind of fraud is a "write-off scheme"?
6. What procedures are in place to respond to natural disasters and other emergencies such as a fire or flood?

Prepared by Your Name at Markham Utilities
1503 Columbia Road, Portland, OR 97204 Phone: 971-555-0126

Jirsak/Shutterstock.com; Mangostar/Shutterstock.com; Singkham/Shutterstock.com; CreativeFireStock/Shutterstock.com

Independent Challenge 1

At Riverwalk Medical Clinic in Cambridge, MA, you've been asked to take over the writing and formatting of the clinic's quarterly news bulletin. The two pages of the bulletin are printed on both sides of one page and distributed to staff. In addition, a PDF of the bulletin can be downloaded from the clinic's website. You open a draft of the Spring bulletin and format it in sections with columns, and then add graphic objects, including text boxes, a picture, a SmartArt graphic, a WordArt object, and a picture cropped to a shape.

- **a.** Start Word, open the file IL_WD_7-3.docx from the location where you store your Data Files, save it as **IL_WD_7_RiverwalkSpringBulletin**, then show formatting marks.
- **b.** Create "Spring Bulletin" as a WordArt object using the Fill: White; Outline: Red, Accent color 2; Hard Shadow: Red, Accent color 2 WordArt style (third row, fourth column).
- **c.** Increase the width of the WordArt object to 5", change the wrapping to Through, then modify the WordArt object using the following settings:
  - Shadow: Offset: Bottom Left in the Outer section
  - Glow: 5 point; Green, Accent color 1
  - Transform: Double Wave: Down-Up (fifth row in the third column in the Warp section)
- **d.** Crop the picture of the river scene at the top of the document to the Flowchart: Punched Tape shape (second row, fourth column in the Flowchart section), then set the height of the cropped picture at 1.3" and the width at 6.5". (*Hint:* deselect the Lock aspect ratio check box in the Size dialog box so the shape is not resized proportionally.)
- **e.** Change the text wrapping of the cropped shape to Through, then use layering and your mouse to position the WordArt object in front of the cropped shape at the top of the page as shown in the completed bulletin in **FIGURE 7-28**.
- **f.** Open the Clipboard, clear the contents, select the text from the "Giving Back" heading to the end of the paragraph under "Donation Hearts", then cut it to the Clipboard.
- **g.** Cut the picture of the women in pink shirts to the Clipboard.
- **h.** Paste the cut text at the second paragraph mark below the "Spring Bulletin" heading and picture, then paste the picture following the text you just pasted.
- **i.** Press ENTER to move the "Clinic News" heading to a new line, if necessary, then insert a Next Page Section break to move the heading to Section 2 at the top of a new page.
- **j.** Scroll up, then insert a Continuous section break at the paragraph mark below the "Spring Bulletin" header and picture.
- **k.** Click to the left of the "Giving Back" heading, then turn on columns with the following settings: Two, .3 spacing between, and a line between.
- **l.** Balance the two columns by inserting a Continuous section break after "$2,000." at the end of the "Donation Hearts" paragraph.
- **m.** Make the picture of the women in pink shirts a picture SmartArt graphic using the Bending Picture Blocks layout, then add two shapes.
- **n.** Fill the first new shape with the picture file **Support_WD_7_Brain.jpg** and the second new shape with the picture file **Support_WD_7_Donations.jpg**.
- **o.** Change the layout of the picture SmartArt graphic to Captioned Pictures, then with the picture SmartArt graphic selected, select One column and modify the width of the picture SmartArt graphic to 6.7" so that it extends in one line of boxes across the bottom of the page as shown in **FIGURE 7-28**. Enter the required captions.
- **p.** On page 2 of the document, make the text "Congratulations" and the paragraph that follows it into a text box formatted with the Subtle Effect – Yellow, Accent 5 shape style.

q. Anchor the text box to the paragraph above it ("New Emergency Room Procedures") by dragging the anchor currently attached to the text box up so it appears to the left of the paragraph above.

r. Add a blank line below the text box, then insert the Word file **Support_WD_7_Education.docx**.

s. Insert the picture **Support_WD_7_Class.jpg**, then format it as follows:
   - Crop the picture to the Oval shape.
   - Further crop the top and bottom of the picture if necessary so it appears as shown in **FIGURE 7-28**.
   - Change the width of the picture to 2.41".
   - Change the text wrapping to Through, then slightly rotate the picture and position it next to the inserted Word file as shown in **FIGURE 7-28**. *(Hint:* Switch to One Page view if necessary so you can see where to position the picture.)

t. View the bulletin in Multiple Pages view, then compare it to **FIGURE 7-28** and make any spacing adjustments.

u. Save your changes, submit a copy to your instructor, close the document, then exit Word.

FIGURE 7-28

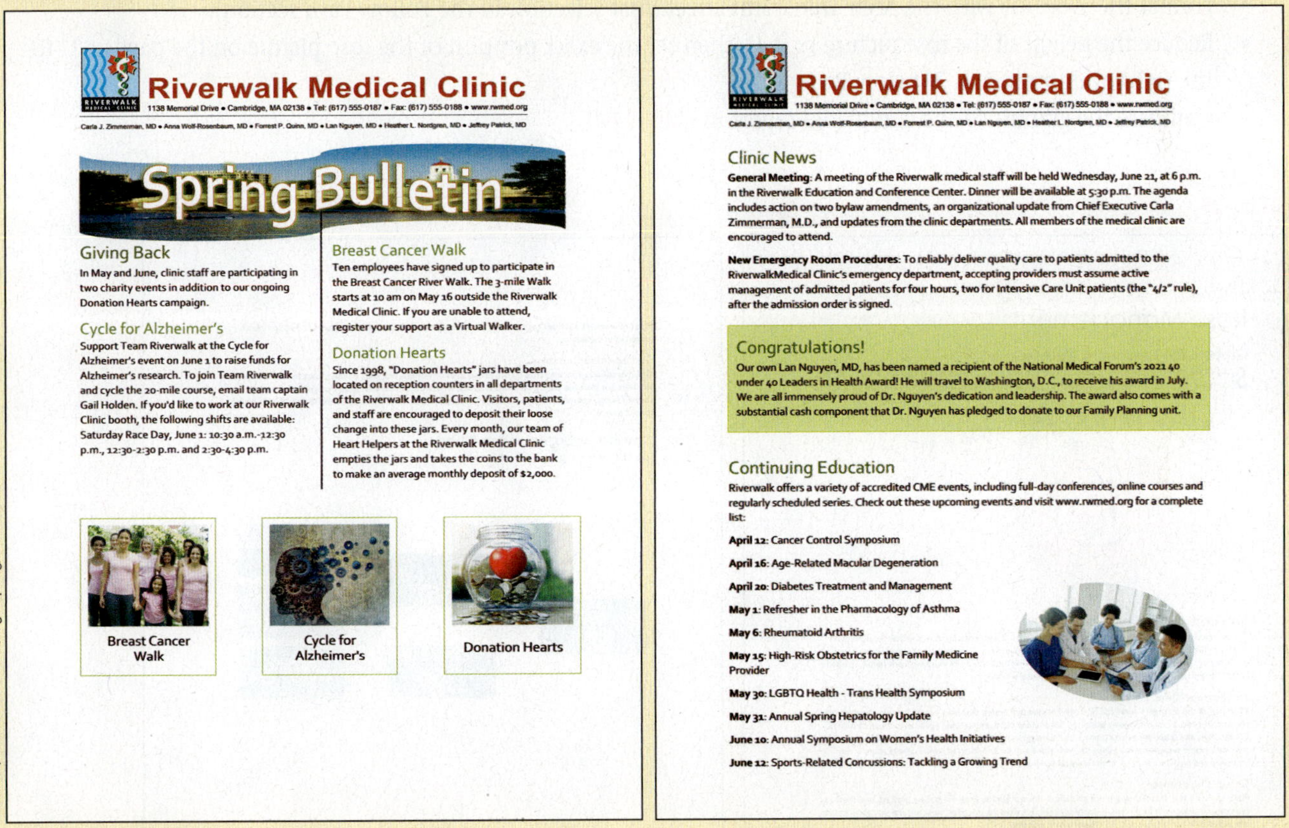

Independent Challenge 2

You have just started working for Rose Management, a management consulting firm created by Margaret Rose and based in Vermont. You've been asked to prepare a short report for distribution at an upcoming meeting of the board of directors. First, you create a graphic for use on the company's revamped website, then you create an organization chart to show the company personnel. Finally, you paste information from another document and format it as a text box that includes drop caps, and then view the document side by side with another report.

a. Start Word, open the file IL_WD_7-4.docx from the drive and folder where you store your Data Files, then save it as **IL_WD_7_RoseManagementReport**.

b. Create a graphic that includes the rose picture and a WordArt object as follows:

- Crop the rose picture to remove as much of the white background as possible so the rose fills the space.
- Change the text wrapping to Through. Press ENTER to move down the text related to the organization chart so you have room to work.
- Type **Rose Management** at the paragraph mark above the rose picture, then create a WordArt object from the text using the Fill: White; Outline: Blue, Accent color 2; Hard Shadow: Blue, Accent color 2 WordArt style (last row, fourth column).
- Format the WordArt with the Arch Transform effect (first selection in the Follow Path section).
- Reduce the height of the rose picture to 2.4", then set the exact position of the rose picture on the page at 1" to the right of Column and 3" below Page.
- Compare the graphic to the completed report in **FIGURE 7-29**.

FIGURE 7-29

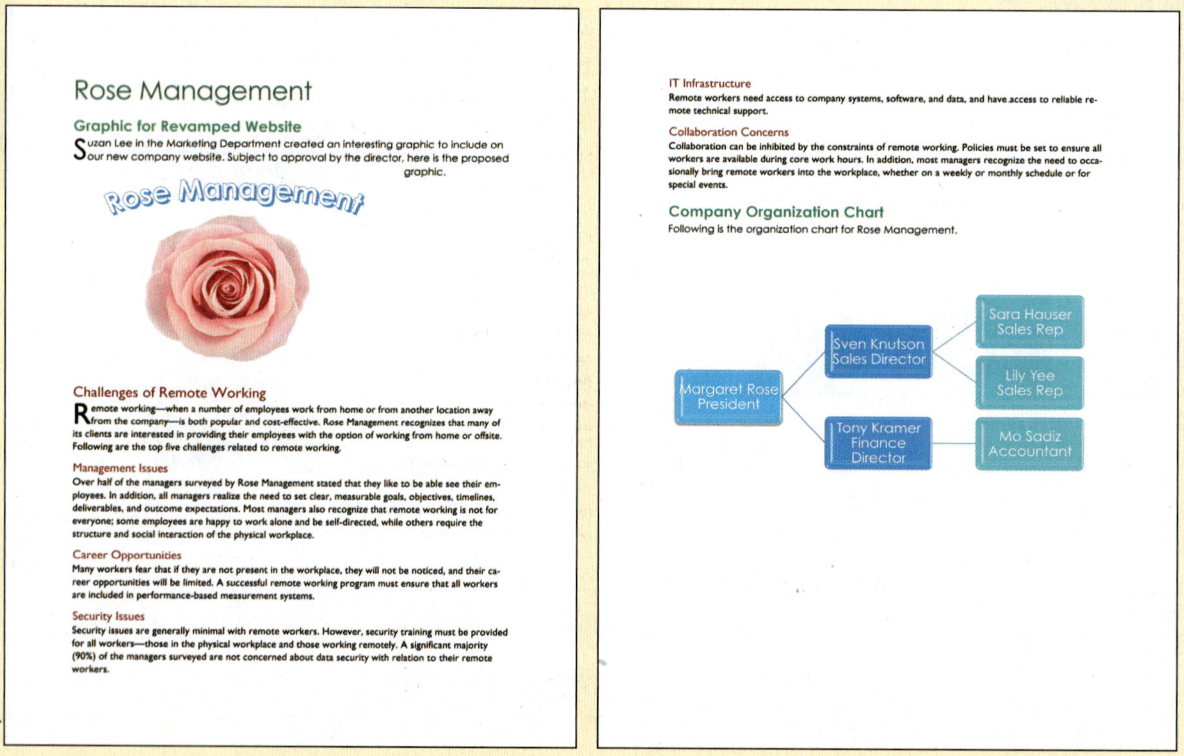
Rose Management

Graphic for Revamped Website

Suzan Lee in the Marketing Department created an interesting graphic to include on our new company website. Subject to approval by the director, here is the proposed graphic.

Rose Management

Challenges of Remote Working

Remote working—when a number of employees work from home or from another location away from the company—is both popular and cost-effective. Rose Management recognizes that many of its clients are interested in providing their employees with the option of working from home or offsite. Following are the top five challenges related to remote working.

Management Issues

Over half of the managers surveyed by Rose Management stated that they like to be able see their employees. In addition, all managers realize the need to set clear, measurable goals, objectives, timelines, deliverables, and outcome expectations. Most managers also recognize that remote working is not for everyone; some employees are happy to work alone and be self-directed, while others require the structure and social interaction of the physical workplace.

Career Opportunities

Many workers fear that if they are not present in the workplace, they will not be noticed, and their career opportunities will be limited. A successful remote working program must ensure that all workers are included in performance-based measurement systems.

Security Issues

Security issues are generally minimal with remote workers. However, security training must be provided for all workers—those in the physical workplace and those working remotely. A significant majority (90%) of the managers surveyed are not concerned about data security with relation to their remote workers.

IT Infrastructure

Remote workers need access to company systems, software, and data, and have access to reliable remote technical support.

Collaboration Concerns

Collaboration can be inhibited by the constraints of remote working. Policies must be set to ensure all workers are available during core work hours. In addition, most managers recognize the need to occasionally bring remote workers into the workplace, whether on a weekly or monthly schedule or for special events.

Company Organization Chart

Following is the organization chart for Rose Management.

Independent Challenge 2 (continued)

- **c.** Scroll down to the Company Organization Chart heading, insert a page break to move the Company Organization Chart heading to the next page, then use the information contained in the table to create a SmartArt graphic organization chart that uses the Horizontal Hierarchy style in the Hierarchy category. (*Hint*: Press SHIFT+ENTER after you type a name so that you can enter the position.)
- **d.** Apply the Polished SmartArt style from the 3-D section of the SmartArt style, then apply the Colorful - Accent Colors color scheme.
- **e.** Apply the Cutout Bevel style to all the boxes in the organization chart.
- **f.** When you have entered the names and positions for the organization chart, delete the table containing the text for the chart.
- **g.** Open Support_WD_7_RemoteWorking.docx, copy all the text, then paste it to the left of the page break on page 1 (below the rose graphic) using the Keep Source Formatting paste option.
- **h.** Delete the page break.
- **i.** Insert a drop cap in paragraph 1 below "Graphic for Revamped Website" and set the dropped to 2, then insert another drop cap with the same settings in the paragraph below "Challenges of Remote Working."
- **j.** Open Support_WD_7_DraftReport.docx, view the draft report side by side with the completed report, scroll the two documents, then close Support_WD_7_DraftReport and return the Page Movement to Vertical.
- **k.** Set the hyphenation options so that text in the document is automatically hyphenated.
- **l.** Type your name in the document footer if requested to do so, save the document, submit the document to your instructor, then close the document and exit Word.

Visual Workshop

Open IL_WD_7-5.docx from the drive and folder where you store your Data Files, then save the document as **IL_WD_7_CommunityTransportationPlan**. Format the text and graphics in the document to match FIGURE 7-30. You will need to move text, create a WordArt object and a picture SmartArt graphic, format selected text in columns, and enclose some of the text in a text box. The WordArt object is formatted with the Fill: Red, Accent color 1; Shadow WordArt style with the Square Transform effect applied and the height of the object reduced to 1". To create the picture SmartArt graphic from the four pictures, create a graphic from the first picture (the walker), add three shapes, then cut and paste each picture into a shape. Select the Bending Picture Semi-Transparent Text layout, a height of 3.7" and a width of 6". Apply the Subtle Effect, Red, Accent 1 style to the text box. Remember you can move the anchor icon attached to a graphic to help you move objects and text on the page. Save the document, submit a copy to your instructor, then close the document and exit Word.

FIGURE 7-30

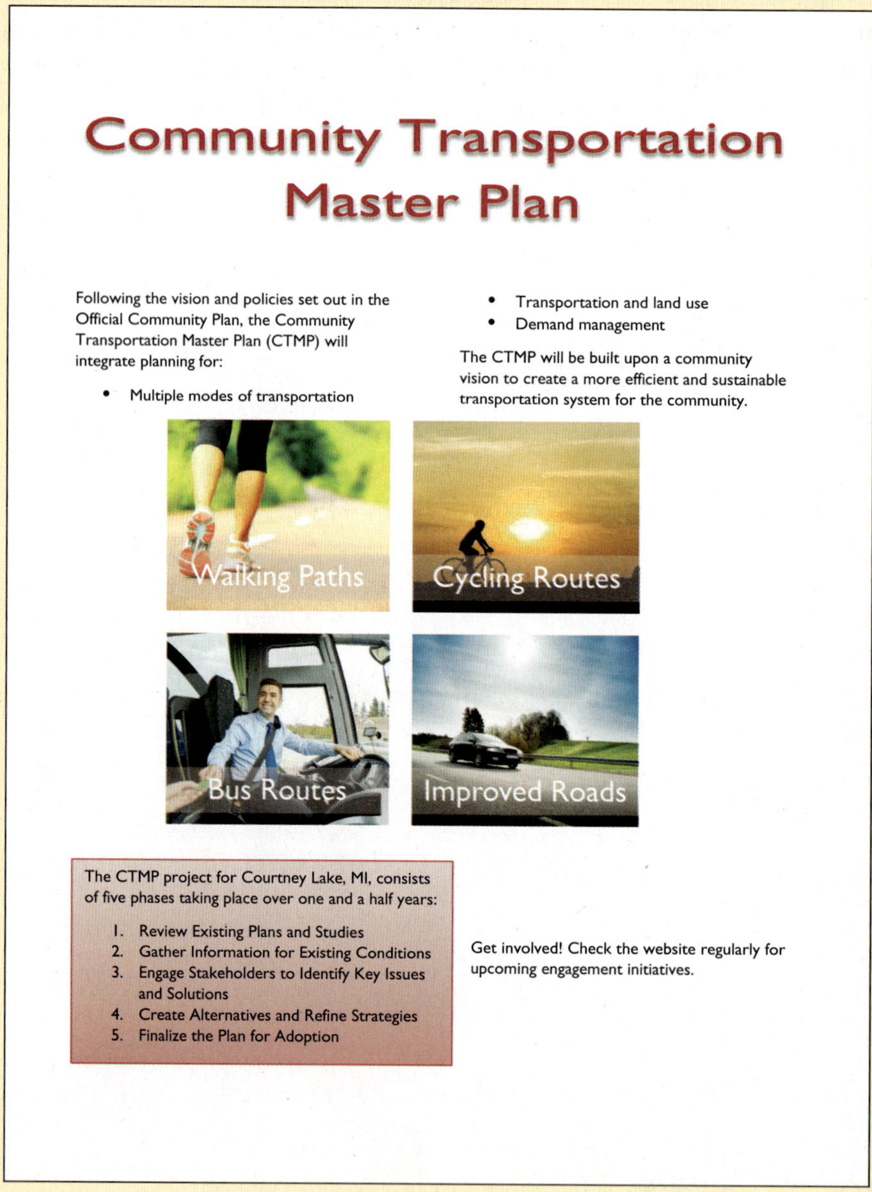
Community Transportation Master Plan

Following the vision and policies set out in the Official Community Plan, the Community Transportation Master Plan (CTMP) will integrate planning for:

- Multiple modes of transportation
- Transportation and land use
- Demand management

The CTMP will be built upon a community vision to create a more efficient and sustainable transportation system for the community.

The CTMP project for Courtney Lake, MI, consists of five phases taking place over one and a half years:

1. Review Existing Plans and Studies
2. Gather Information for Existing Conditions
3. Engage Stakeholders to Identify Key Issues and Solutions
4. Create Alternatives and Refine Strategies
5. Finalize the Plan for Adoption

Get involved! Check the website regularly for upcoming engagement initiatives.

Izf/Shutterstock.com; PhilipYb Studio/Shutterstock.com; LeManna/Shutterstock.com; Syda Productions/Shutterstock.com

Integrating with Other Programs and Collaborating

CASE You've started working for Anthony Martinez, the VP of sales and marketing at the head office of JCL Talent, Inc., in Atlanta. Another colleague has developed content for a report marketing the company's website and has asked you to enhance the report with embedded objects from PowerPoint and Excel, and charts that you create in Word. You then use collaboration tools in Word to edit questions for an online survey aimed at job seekers who visit the JCL Talent website.

Module Objectives

After completing this module, you will be able to:

- Embed an Excel file
- Insert objects from other programs
- Link an Excel chart
- Link a PowerPoint slide
- Manage links
- Create charts
- Format and edit charts
- Track changes
- Work with tracked changes
- Manage reviewers
- Compare documents

Files You Will Need

IL_WD_8-1.docx
Support_WD_8-1.xlsx
Support_WD_8-2.xlsx
Support_WD_8-3.pptx
IL_WD_8-2.docx
IL_WD_8-3.docx
IL_WD_8-4.docx
IL_WD_8-5.docx
Support_WD_8-4.xlsx
Support_WD_8-5.xlsx
Support_WD_8-6.pptx
IL_WD_8-6.docx
IL_WD_8-7.docx
IL_WD_8-8.docx
IL_WD_8-9.docx
Support_WD_8-7.xlsx
Support_WD_8-8.pptx
Support_WD_8-9.xlsx
IL_WD_8-10.docx
IL_WD_8-11.docx
Support_WD_8-10.pptx
Support_WD_8-11.xlsx

Word
Module 8

Embed an Excel File

Learning Outcomes
- Embed an Excel file
- Edit an embedded Excel file

You embed an object, such as an Excel file, in Word when you want to be able to edit the file in Word. You edit the embedded object directly in Word using commands on the Ribbon associated with Excel, the source program. Because the objects are not connected or linked, the edits you make to an embedded object are not made to the object in the source file, and edits you make to the object in the source file are not made to the embedded object. **CASE** *The Marketing Report contains placeholder text to designate where you need to insert objects. You embed an Excel worksheet and then edit the embedded worksheet in Word using Excel tools.*

STEPS

1. **sam Start Word, open the file IL_WD_8-1.docx from the location where you store your Data Files, save it as IL_WD_8_MarketingReport, then click the Show/Hide button ¶ in the Paragraph group to turn on paragraph marks if they are not displayed**
2. **Delete the placeholder text EXCEL WORKSHEET after the "Access Methods" paragraph but not the paragraph mark so a blank line still appears above the page break**
3. **Click the Insert tab, then click the Object button in the Text group**
   The Object dialog box opens. You use the Object dialog box to create a new object using the commands of a program other than Word or to insert an object already created in another program.
4. **Click the Create from File tab, click the Browse button, navigate to the drive and folder where you store your Data Files, click Support_WD_8-1.xlsx, then click Insert**
   The path to the file Support_WD_8-1.xlsx is shown in the File name box. Because you want to create an embedded object, you leave the Link to file check box blank as shown in **FIGURE 8-1**.
5. **Click OK, then double-click the embedded worksheet object**
   The embedded object opens in an Excel object window, and the Excel Ribbon opens in place of the Word Ribbon. The title bar at the top of the window contains the Word filename, indicating that you are still working within a Word file.
6. **Click cell B3, type 250, press ENTER, click cell B8, then click the Bold button B in the Font group on the Excel Ribbon**
   The total number of customers shown in cell B8 increases by 250, from 7955 to 8110. Because you did not select the link option when you embedded the Excel file into the Word document, the changes you make to the embedded file are *not* made in the original Excel source file.
7. **Click the Page Layout tab on the Excel Ribbon, click the Themes button in the Themes group, then select Basis**
   You formatted the embedded Excel file with the same theme (Basis) that has been applied to the Word document. The worksheet object appears in Word as shown in **FIGURE 8-2**.
8. **Click cell A1, then click to the right of the worksheet object to return to Word**
   The Excel Ribbon closes and the Word Ribbon opens. In Word, the embedded object is part of the paragraph and can be formatted as such.
9. **Click the worksheet object to select it, click the Home tab, click the Center button in the Paragraph group, click anywhere in the Word document to deselect the worksheet object, then save the document**

QUICK TIP
Double-click the Excel object when you want to make changes to the data.

TROUBLE
If you are working on more than one screen, Excel may open on a different screen. Close the worksheet in Excel after completing Step 9.

QUICK TIP
Click the Excel object once to select the object and make changes to the object but not the data.

FIGURE 8-1: Create from File tab in the Object dialog box

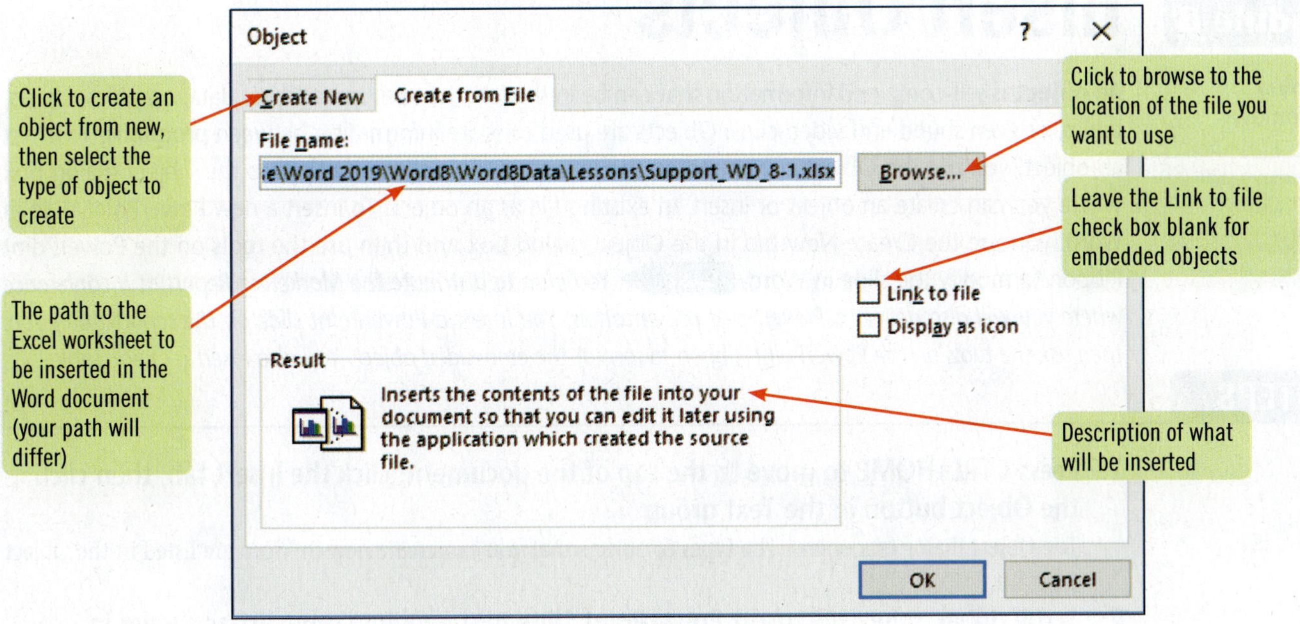

FIGURE 8-2: Excel worksheet embedded in Word document

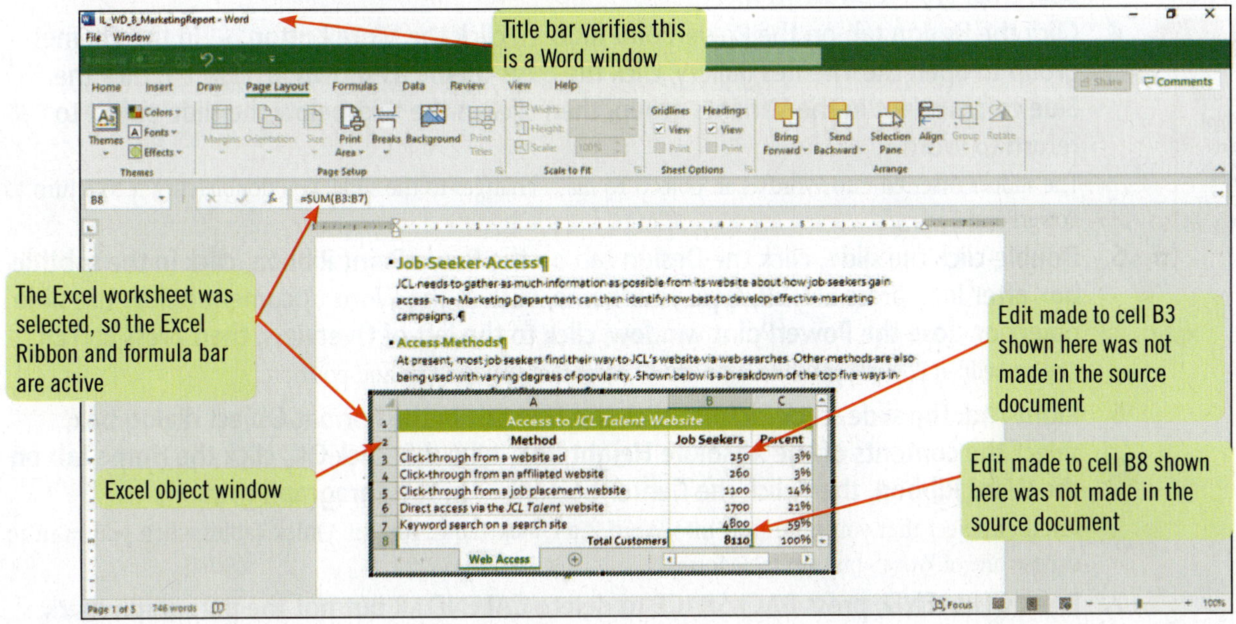

Understanding Object Linking and Embedding

The ability to share information with other programs is called **object linking and embedding (OLE).** Two programs are involved in the OLE process. The **source program** is the program in which information is originally created, and the **destination program** is the program the information is copied to. An embedded object uses the features of another program such as Excel, but it is stored as part of the Word document.

Word

Word
Module 8

Insert Objects

Learning Outcomes
- Insert a PowerPoint slide
- Insert a Quick Table

An **object** is self-contained information that can be in the form of text, spreadsheet data, graphics, charts, tables, or even sound and video clips. Objects are used to share information between programs. To insert an object, you use the Object command on the Insert tab. This command opens the Object dialog box where you can create an object or insert an existing file as an object. To insert a new PowerPoint slide in Word, you use the Create New tab in the Object dialog box and then use the tools on the PowerPoint Ribbon to modify the slide in Word. **CASE** *You plan to distribute the Marketing Report at a conference where you will also deliver a PowerPoint presentation. You insert a PowerPoint slide on the report title page, then use the tools on the PowerPoint Ribbon to format the embedded object. You also insert a Quick Table.*

STEPS

1. **Press CTRL+HOME to move to the top of the document, click the Insert tab, then click the Object button in the Text group**
   The Object dialog box opens. The types of objects that you can create new in Word are listed in the Object type: list.
2. **Scroll down, select Microsoft PowerPoint Slide in the Object type: list as shown in FIGURE 8-3, then click OK**
   A blank PowerPoint slide appears along with the PowerPoint Ribbon.
3. **Click the Click to add title box, type Marketing Report, click the Click to add subtitle box, then type JCL Talent, Inc.**
4. **Click the Design tab on the PowerPoint Ribbon, click the More button in the Themes group to open the Themes gallery, click the Basis theme as shown in FIGURE 8-4, click the Blue color variant in the Variants group, then click in the text below the slide object to return to Word**
   The slide is inserted into Word as an object. To make changes to the slide, you double-click it to return to PowerPoint.
5. **Double-click the slide, click the Design tab on the PowerPoint Ribbon, click in the subtitle box after Inc., press ENTER, type your name, click in the Word document below the slide object or close the PowerPoint window, click to the left of Overview, then press ENTER**
   The embedded PowerPoint slide is a picture object that you can size and position.
6. **Right-click the slide, click Picture, click the Size tab in the Format Object dialog box, select the contents of the Absolute Height box, type 2.5, click OK, click the Home tab on the Word Ribbon, then click the Center button in the Paragraph group**
   Another object that you can insert into Word is a Quick Table. You use Quick Tables when you want to choose one of Word's built-in table forms.
7. **Press CTRL+END, press BACKSPACE to delete CALENDAR but not the paragraph mark, click the Insert tab, click the Table button, point to Quick Tables to display the gallery of built-in tables, then click Calendar 1**
   A table already formatted as a calendar is inserted into the document. You can modify the formatting of the calendar to make it easier to enter data.
8. **Drag the right edge of the table so it is even with the text at the right margin, click the table move handle in the top-left corner of the table to select the entire table, click the Layout tab to the right of the Table Design tab, then click the Distribute Columns button in the Cell Size group**
9. **Click after 5 in the box for December 5, press ENTER, type LAUNCH!, then save the document**
   The Calendar 1 Quick Table appears as shown in FIGURE 8-5.

TROUBLE
If you are working with more than one screen, PowerPoint may open on a different screen. Click the Close button in PowerPoint to return to Word.

FIGURE 8-3: Create New tab in Object dialog box

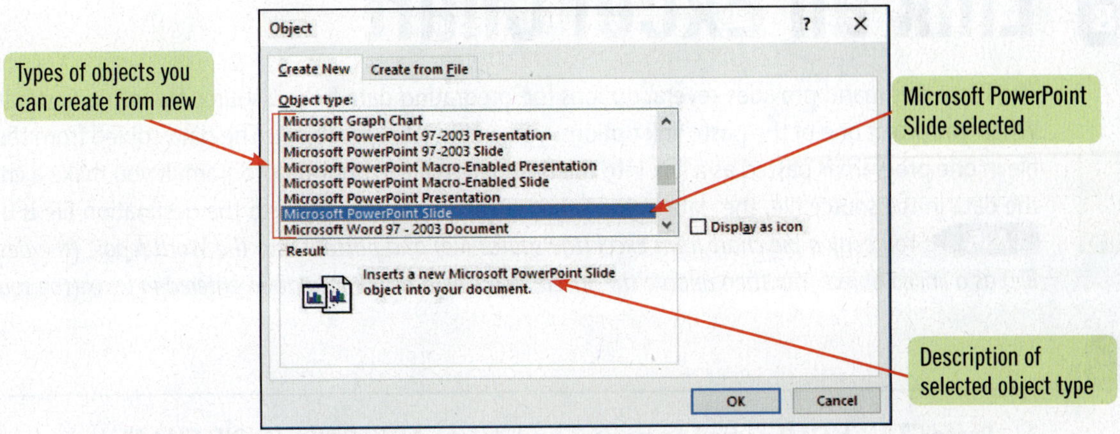

FIGURE 8-4: Basis theme selected

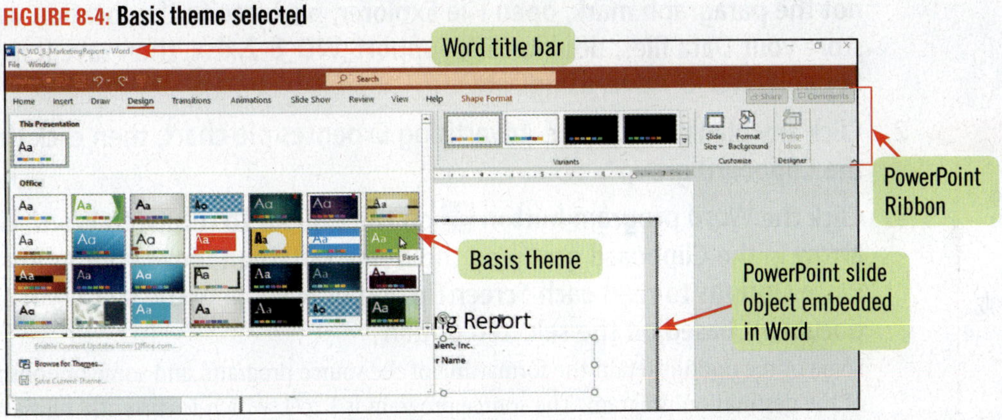

FIGURE 8-5: Calendar 1 Quick Table inserted and formatted

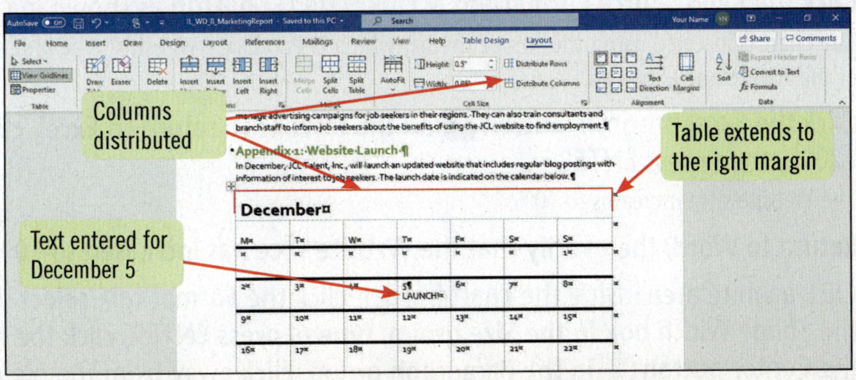

Publishing a blog directly from Word

A blog, which is short for weblog, is an informal journal that is created by an individual or a group and available to the public on the Internet. A blog usually conveys the ideas, comments, and opinions of the blogger and is written using a strong personal voice. The person who creates and maintains a blog, the blogger, typically updates the blog regularly. If you have or want to start a blog, you can configure Word to link to your blog site so that you can write, format, and publish blog entries directly from Word.

To blog directly from Word, you must first obtain a blog account with a blog service provider. Resources, such as the Word Help system and online forums, provide detailed information on obtaining and registering your personal blog account with Word. To create a new blog post, click the File tab, click New, then double-click Blog post (or search for an online template if one does not appear on your New screen) to open a predesigned blog post document that you can customize with your own text, formatting, and images. You can also publish an existing document as a blog post by opening the document, clicking the File tab, clicking Share, and then clicking Post to Blog. In either case, Word prompts you to log onto your personal blog account.

Word Module 8

Link an Excel Chart

Learning Outcomes
- Copy an Excel chart to Word
- Update a linked chart in Word

The Paste command provides several options for integrating data from a source file into a destination file. When you select one of the paste link options, you create a linked object. The data copied from the source file in one program is pasted as a link into the destination file in another program. If you make a change to the data in the source file, the data in the linked object that you copied to the destination file is updated.

CASE *You copy a pie chart from Excel (the source file) and paste it into the Word report (the destination file) as a linked object. You then update the linked object with new information entered in Excel (the source file).*

STEPS

1. **Press CTRL+HOME, scroll to page 2 and delete ADVERTISING PIE CHART, but not the paragraph mark, open File Explorer, navigate to the location where you store your Data files, double-click Support_WD_8-2.xlsx, then save it in Excel as Support_WD_8_AdvertisingData**
2. **Click any blank area of the Advertising Expenses pie chart, then click the Copy button in the Clipboard group**
3. **Click the Word program button on the taskbar to return to Word, click the Paste arrow in the Clipboard group on the Home tab, then move your mouse over each of the Paste Options to read each ScreenTip and preview how the chart will be pasted into the document based on the selected option**

   Some of the options retain the formatting of the source program, and some options adopt the formatting of the destination program. The source program is Excel, which is currently formatted with the Parallax theme. The destination program is Word, which is formatted with the Basis theme.
4. **Click the Keep Source Formatting & Link Data (F) button as shown in FIGURE 8-6**

   The chart is inserted using the source theme, which is Parallax. "Website" (the blue slice) accounts for 6% of the advertising expenses.
5. **Click the Excel program button on the taskbar to return to Excel, click cell B2, type 12000, then press ENTER**

   The Website slice increases to 10%.
6. **Return to Word, then verify that the Website slice has increased to 10%**
7. **Click a white area inside the chart border, click the Format tab, select the contents of the Shape Width box in the Size group, type 6, press ENTER, click the Home tab, click the Center button in the Paragraph group, click away from the pie chart object to deselect it, then compare the pie chart object to FIGURE 8-7**
8. **Click the Excel program button on the taskbar, save and close the workbook, then exit Excel**

   The IL_WD_8_MarketingReport.docx file in Word is again the active document.
9. **Save the document**

TROUBLE
Be sure a solid border with sizing handles surrounds the pie chart and all its related components. If only one component is selected, click outside the chart area, then repeat Step 2.

TROUBLE
If the pie chart did not update, click the chart, click the Chart Design tab, then click the Refresh Data button in the Data group.

TROUBLE
If the Shape Width box is dim and does not accept a value, click to the right of the chart and click the chart border again to be sure the entire chart object is selected.

FIGURE 8-6: Selecting a link paste option

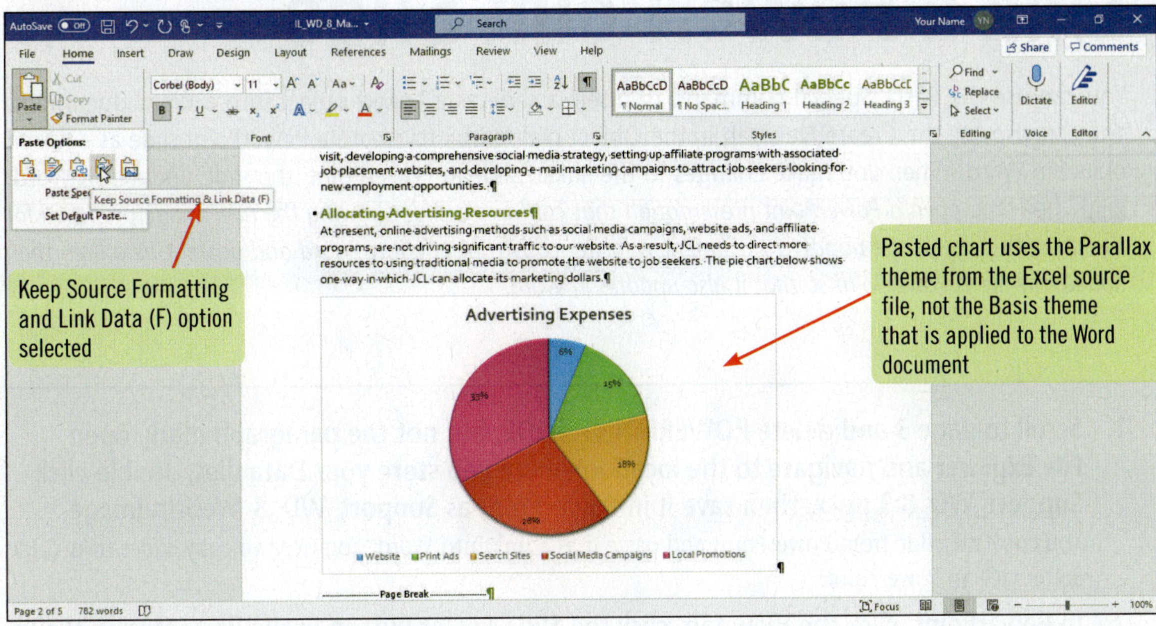

FIGURE 8-7: Linked pie chart updated in Word

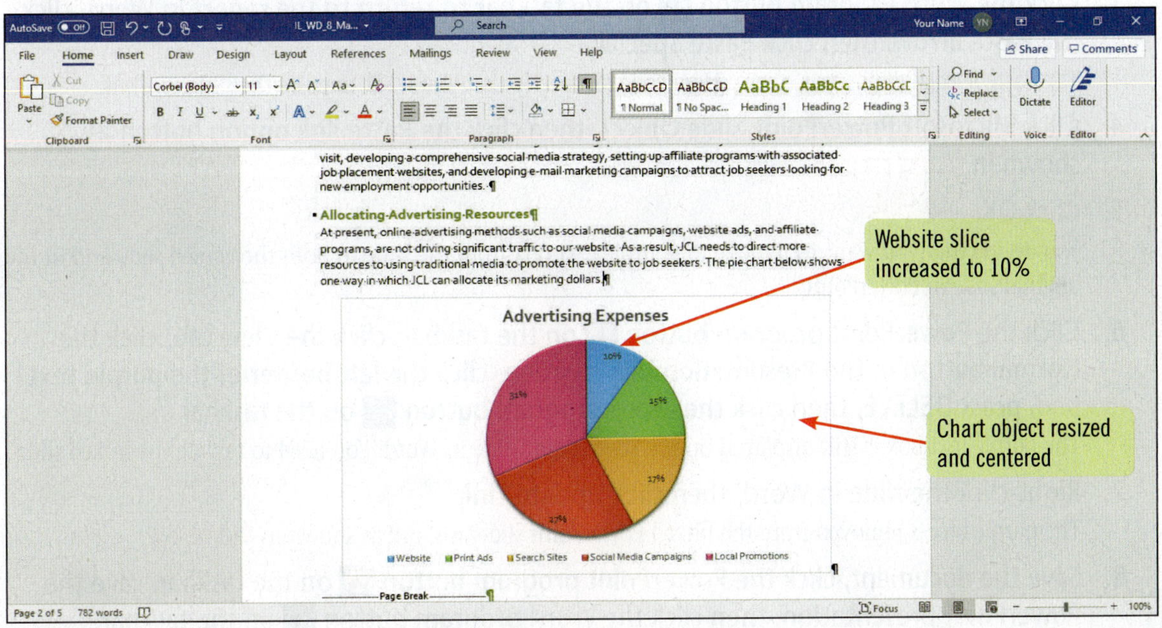

Using the Object dialog box to create a linked file

In addition to using the Paste options, you can create a linked object using the Object dialog box. You open the Object dialog box by clicking Object in the Text group on the Insert tab and then clicking the Create from File tab. You click the Browse button to navigate to and then select the file you want to link, click the Link to file check box to be sure that box is active (has a check mark), and then click OK. The file you select is inserted in the destination file as a linked object.

You create a linked object using one of the options available on the Paste menu when you want to copy only a portion of a file, such as selected cells or a chart in an Excel worksheet. You create a linked object using the Link to file check box in the Object dialog box when you want to insert the entire file, such as the entire worksheet in an Excel file.

Word

Word
Module 8

Link a PowerPoint Slide

Learning Outcome
- Link and update a PowerPoint Slide in Word

You can use the Paste Special command to insert a slide as a linked object into a Word document. You can also use the Create New tab in the Object dialog box to create a PowerPoint slide as a linked object in Word. When you make changes to the linked slide in PowerPoint, the slide updates in Word. **CASE** *You open a PowerPoint presentation that contains a slide showing the new image proposed for the opening page of the updated JCL Talent website, copy the slide into Word and paste it as a link, then update the file in PowerPoint so that it also updates in Word.*

STEPS

1. **Scroll to page 3 and delete POWERPOINT SLIDE, but not the paragraph mark, open File Explorer and navigate to the location where you store your Data files, double-click Support_WD_8-3.pptx, then save it in PowerPoint as Support_WD_8_WebsiteImage**
   You copy the slide from PowerPoint and paste it as a link into Word. You need to copy slides from Slide Sorter view in PowerPoint.
2. **In PowerPoint, click the View tab, click the Slide Sorter button in the Presentation Views group, click the Home tab, then click the Copy button in the Clipboard group**
3. **Click the Word Program button on the taskbar to return to the report in Word, click the Paste arrow, then click Paste Special**
   The Paste Special dialog box opens. Here you can specify that you want to paste the slide as a link.
4. **Click Microsoft PowerPoint Slide Object, then click the Paste link option button as shown in FIGURE 8-8**
5. **Click OK**
   You decide that you want to remove the purple text box from the slide in both the copied slide and in the original slide in PowerPoint.
6. **Click the PowerPoint program button on the taskbar, click the View tab, click the Normal button in the Presentation Views group, click the left border of the purple text box, press DELETE, then click the Word program button on the taskbar**
   The purple text box is still displayed on the PowerPoint slide in Word. You need to update the linked slide.
7. **Right-click the slide in Word, then click Update Link**
   The purple box is removed from the linked PowerPoint slide in Word as shown in FIGURE 8-9.
8. **Save the document, click the PowerPoint program button on the taskbar, save the PowerPoint presentation, then click the Word program button on the taskbar**
   You are returned to the document in Word.

FIGURE 8-8: Paste Special dialog box

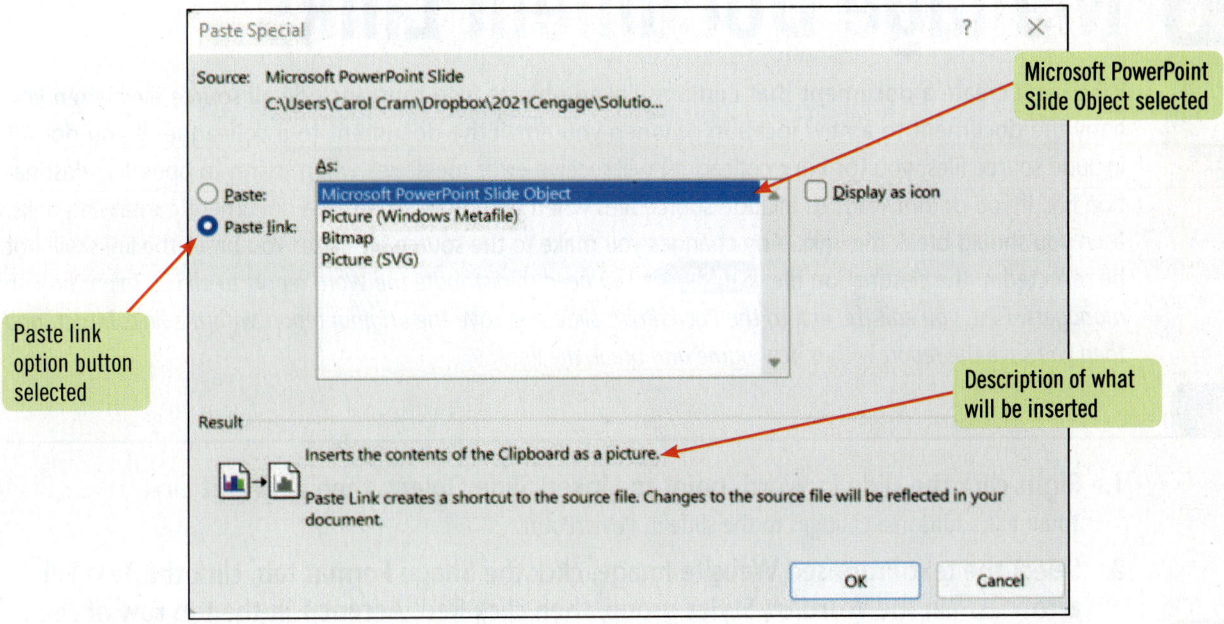

FIGURE 8-9: PowerPoint slide copied into Word as a link

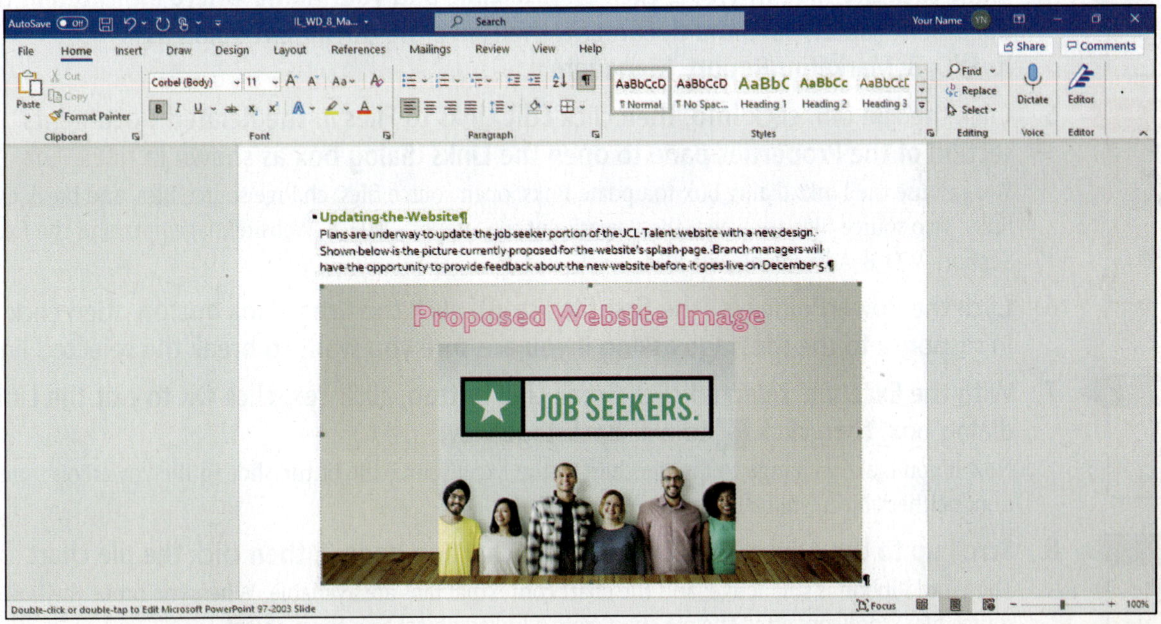

Rawpixel.com/Shutterstock.com

Creating a PowerPoint presentation from a Word outline

When you create a PowerPoint presentation from a Word outline, the Word document is the source file and the PowerPoint document is the destination file. Headings formatted with heading styles in the Word source file are converted to PowerPoint headings in the PowerPoint destination file. For example, each line of text formatted with the Heading 1 style becomes its own slide. To create a PowerPoint presentation from a Word outline, create and then save the outline in Word, close the document, then launch PowerPoint. In PowerPoint, click the New Slide list arrow, click Slides from Outline, navigate to the location where you stored the Word document, then double-click the filename. The Word outline is converted to a PowerPoint presentation, which you can modify in the same way you modify any PowerPoint presentation. Any changes you make to the presentation in PowerPoint are *not* reflected in the original Word document.

Word
Module 8

Manage Document Links

Learning Outcomes
- Edit a link to a file
- Break links

When you create a document that contains linked objects, you must include all source files when you copy the document to a new location or when you email the document to a colleague. If you do not include source files, you (or your colleague) will receive error messages when trying to open the destination file. If you do not want to include source files when you move or email a document containing links, then you should break the links. Any changes you make to the source files after you break the links will not be reflected in the destination file. **CASE** *You need to distribute the Word report to all JCL Talent branch managers. First, you edit the link to the PowerPoint slide and save the original report with the links intact, and then you save the report with a new name and break the links.*

STEPS

1. **Right-click the slide in Word, point to Linked Slide Object, then click Edit Link**
   You make additional changes to the slide in PowerPoint.
2. **Select the text Proposed Website Image, click the Shape Format tab, click the Text Fill arrow in the WordArt Styles group, then click Red, Accent 1 in the top row of the Theme Colors**
3. **Click away from the text, then save the presentation**
4. **Right-click the slide in Word, click Update Link, add your name where indicated in the document footer, save the document, then save the document again as IL_WD_8_MarketingReport_Managers**
5. **Click the File tab, click Info, then click Edit Links to Files in the Related Documents section of the Properties pane to open the Links dialog box as shown in FIGURE 8-10**
   You can use the Links dialog box to update links, open source files, change source files, and break existing links. Two source files are listed: the PowerPoint file Support_WD_8_WebsiteImage.pptx and the Excel file Support_WD_8_AdvertisingData.xlsx.
6. **Click the PowerPoint file (the first file listed), click the Break Link button, then click Yes in response to the message asking if you are sure you want to break the selected link**
7. **With the Excel file selected click Break Link button, click Yes, click OK to exit the Links dialog box, then click to exit Backstage view**
   Now if you make a change to the pie chart in the Excel source file or the slide in the PowerPoint presentation, neither object will be updated in Word.
8. **Scroll up to the Advertising Expenses pie chart on page 2, then click the pie chart**
   The Word Ribbon is still active, and the chart contextual tabs are available. When you broke the link to the source file, Word converted the pie chart from a linked object to a chart object.
9. **Click the Chart Design tab, click the More button in the Chart Styles group, click Style 11 (the second to the last selection), save the document, then compare it to FIGURE 8-11**
   The Style 11 chart style is applied to the chart and the theme is updated to match the theme of the document (Basis).
10. **Click the PowerPoint program button on the taskbar, then exit PowerPoint**

QUICK TIP
After you break links, the Update Links command cannot be used to update information in the destination file.

TROUBLE
You may need to scroll down to see the Edit Links to Files link in the lower-right corner of the screen.

QUICK TIP
An entry remains for the pie chart, but it is no longer linked.

QUICK TIP
You can use commands on the Chart Design and Format tabs to modify the chart object, but you cannot change the content of the pie chart.

FIGURE 8-10: Links dialog box

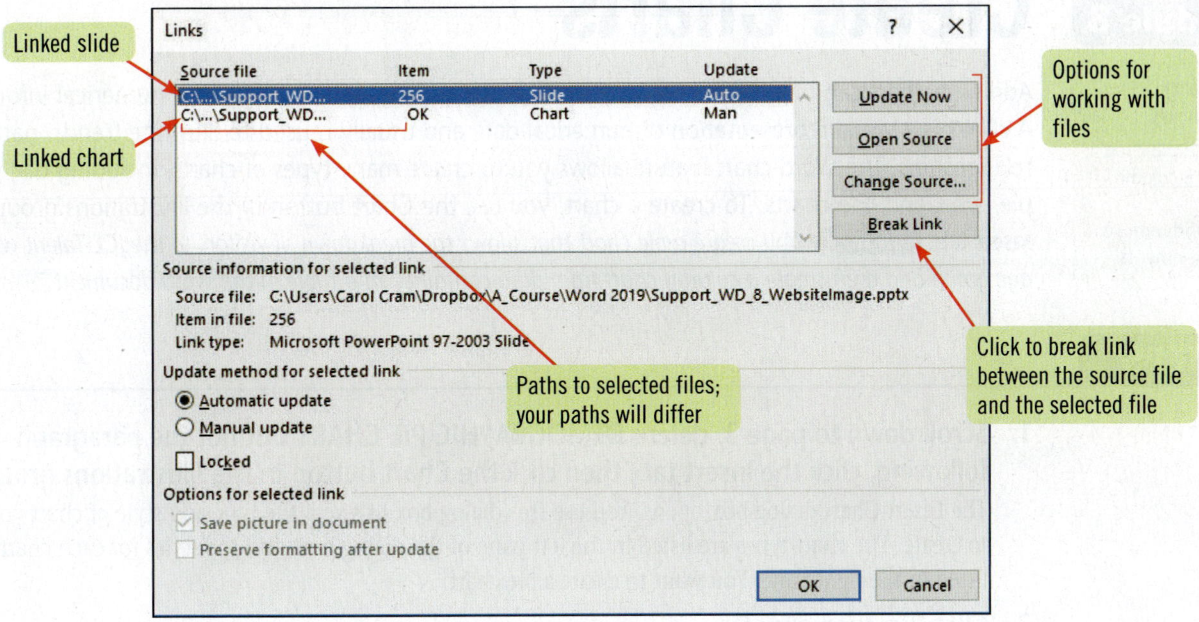

FIGURE 8-11: Formatted pie chart

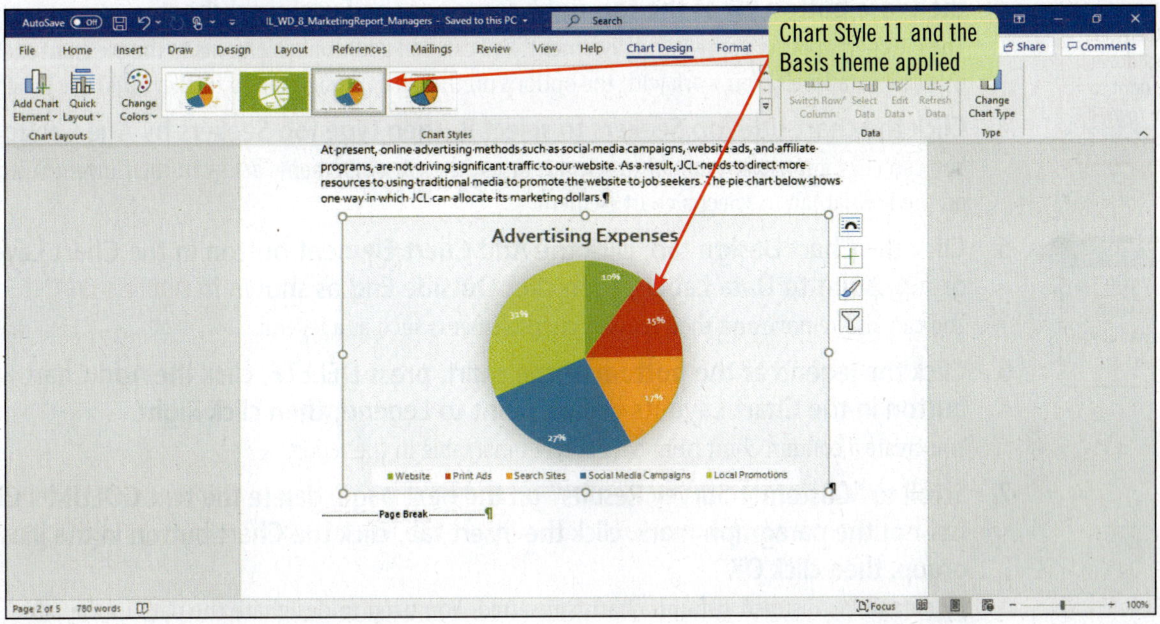

Create Charts

Learning Outcomes
- Insert a pie chart
- Insert a column chart
- Add and remove chart elements

Adding a chart can be an effective way to illustrate a document that includes numerical information. A **chart** is a visual representation of numerical data and usually is used to illustrate trends, patterns, or relationships. The Word chart feature allows you to create many types of charts, including bar, column, pie, area, and line charts. To create a chart, you use the Chart button in the Illustrations group on the Insert tab. **CASE** *You create a pie chart that shows the breakdown of visitors to the JCL Talent website by age group and then create a column chart from data contained in a table in the Word document.*

STEPS

1. **Scroll down to page 3, delete DEMOGRAPHIC PIE CHART but not the paragraph mark following, click the Insert tab, then click the Chart button in the Illustrations group**
   The Insert Chart dialog box opens. You use this dialog box to select the type and style of chart you intend to create. The chart types are listed in the left pane of the dialog box, and the styles for each chart type are listed in the right pane. You want to create a pie chart.
2. **Click Pie, then click OK**
   A worksheet opens in a Chart in Microsoft Word window, and a pie chart appears in the document. The worksheet and the chart contain placeholder data that you replace with your own data. The chart is based on the data in the worksheet. Any change you make to the data is made automatically to the chart.
3. **Click cell A1 in the worksheet, enter the labels and values shown in FIGURE 8-12, then click the Close button ☒ at the top-right corner of the Excel worksheet**
   The pie chart appears in the Word document. You can add additional elements to the pie chart such as a chart title and data labels. You work with the options on the Chart Design tab to further build the pie chart.
4. **Click the chart title Job Seekers to select it, then type Job Seekers by Age Group**
   You can click any chart element to select it or use the Chart Elements arrow in the Current Selection group on the Format tab to select a chart element.
5. **Click the Chart Design tab, click the Add Chart Element button in the Chart Layouts group, point to Data Labels, then click Outside End as shown in FIGURE 8-13**
   You can also remove and then reinsert chart elements such as a legend.
6. **Click the legend at the bottom of the chart, press DELETE, click the Add Chart Element button in the Chart Layouts group, point to Legend, then click Right**
   You create a column chart from data entered in a table in the report.
7. **Scroll to "Customer Survey Results" on the next page, delete the text COLUMN CHART, but not the paragraph mark, click the Insert tab, click the Chart button in the Illustrations group, then click OK**
   By default, a clustered column chart is inserted. You need to designate the data in the table as the data required for the column chart.
8. **Scroll up, click in the table, click the Table move handle ⊞ to select all the text in the table, press CTRL+X to cut the table from the Word document, click cell A1 in the Excel worksheet, then press CTRL+V to paste the chart data into the Excel worksheet**
9. **Close the Excel worksheet, click the chart title, type Educational Levels of Job Seekers, compare the chart to FIGURE 8-14, then save the document**
   In the next lesson, you will further enhance both charts you created in this lesson.

TROUBLE
Drag the lower-right corner of the worksheet object down and to the right to show more rows, if necessary.

QUICK TIP
Point to any part of a chart to see a ScreenTip that identifies the part.

FIGURE 8-12: Data for pie chart

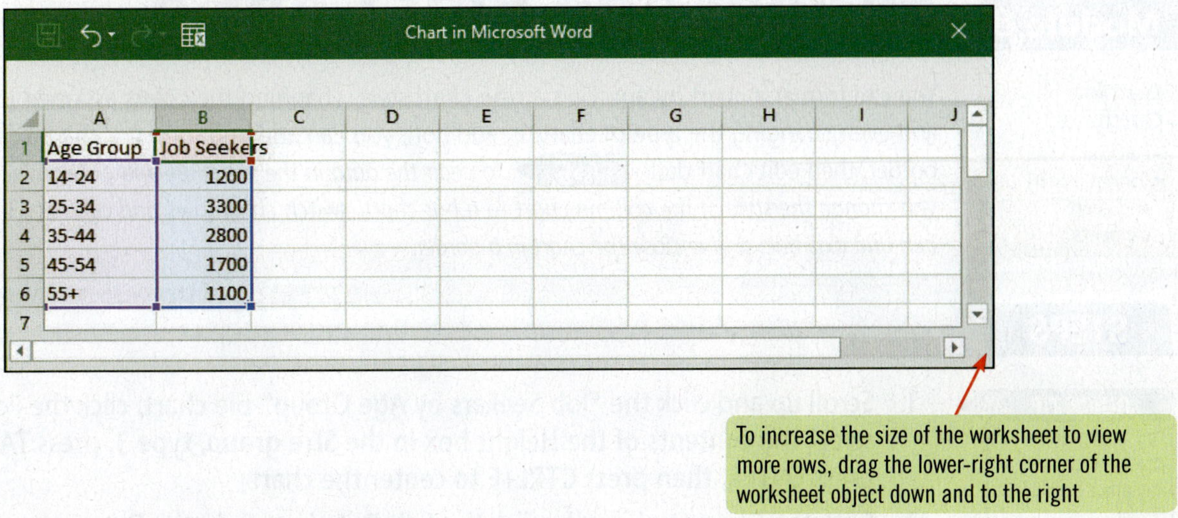

FIGURE 8-13: Adding data labels to a chart

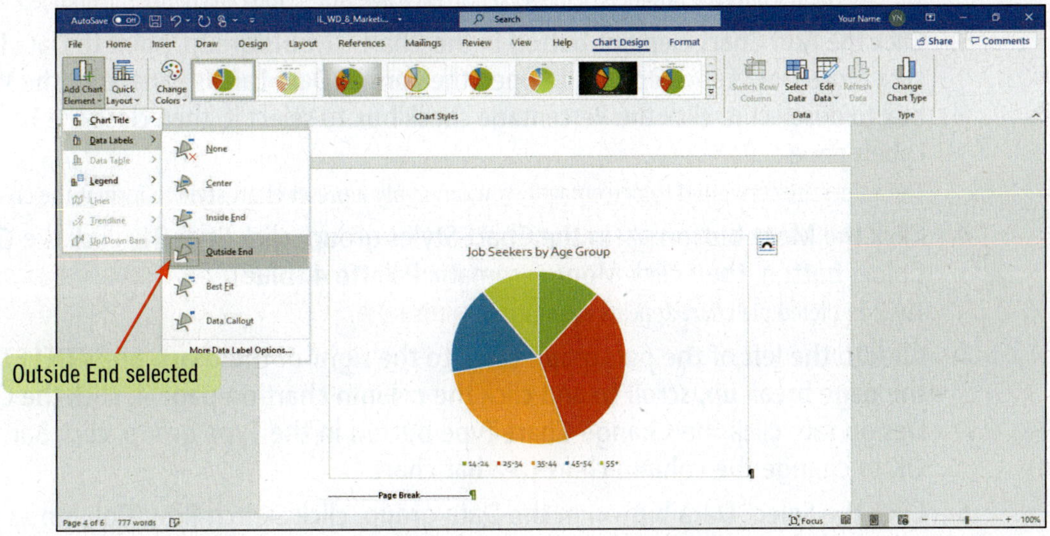

FIGURE 8-14: Column chart created in Word

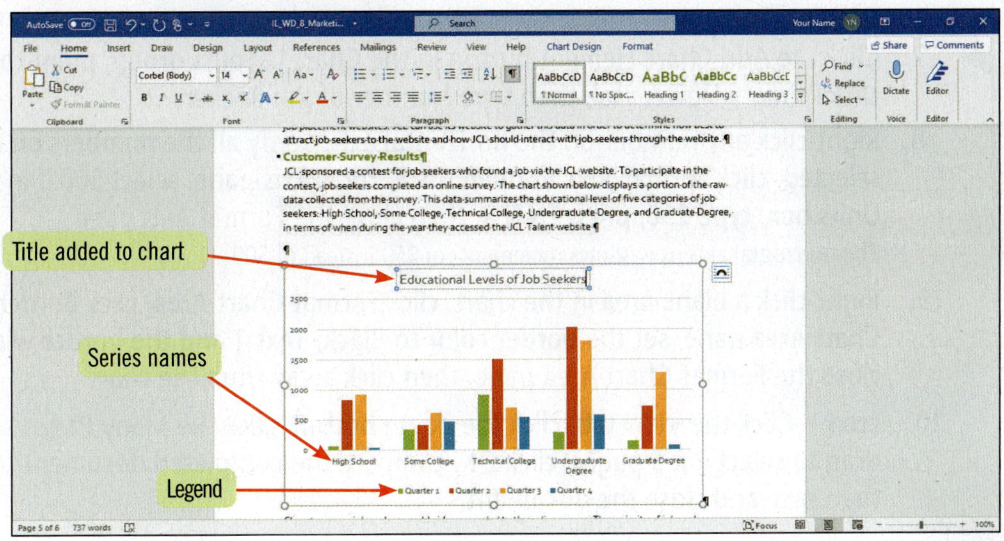

Word Module 8

Format and Edit Charts

Learning Outcomes
- Edit chart data
- Format a chart and chart elements

You can format a chart by applying a new chart style, changing the colors assigned to chart elements, and even changing the type of chart. In addition, you can add and format a chart axis and add a chart border, then edit chart data. **CASE** *You edit the data in the pie chart and change the chart colors, then you change the style of the column chart to a bar chart, switch chart rows and columns, add and format an axis and axis title, and enclose the chart in a border.*

STEPS

QUICK TIP
You can resize a chart in Word like any other graphic object.

1. **Scroll up and click the "Job Seekers by Age Group" pie chart, click the Format tab, select the contents of the Height box in the Size group, type 3, press TAB, type 5, press ENTER, then press CTRL+E to center the chart**
2. **Click the Chart Design tab, click the Edit Data button in the Data group, click cell B5, type 2200, press ENTER, then close the Excel worksheet**
   The chart data shows the numbers of job seekers in each age group. You can change the numbers to percentages.
3. **Click the Add Chart Element button in the Chart Layouts group, point to Data Labels, click More Data Label Options to open the Format Data Labels pane, click the Value check box to deselect it, click the Percentage check box to select it, then close the Format Data Labels pane**
   The values are converted to percentages. You can apply a preset chart style to format the chart.
4. **Click the More button in the Chart Styles group, click Style 12, click the Change Colors button, then click Monochromatic Palette 4 (blue)**
   The completed pie chart appears as shown in FIGURE 8-15.
5. **Click to the left of the paragraph mark to the right of the chart, press DELETE to move the page break up, scroll to and click the column chart on page 4, click the Chart Design tab, click the Change Chart Type button in the Type group, click Bar, then click OK to change the column chart to a bar chart**
6. **Click the Select Data button in the Data group, click Switch Row/Column as shown in FIGURE 8-16, click OK, then close the Excel worksheet**
   When you switch rows and columns, the series data is switched to become labels for the horizontal axis, and data on the horizontal axis is now the series data. In the bar chart, the chart displays "Quarter 1", "Quarter 2", etc. on the vertical axis and the number of job seekers on the horizontal axis.

QUICK TIP
To format any chart element, select it, then click the Format Selection button in the Current Selection group on the Format tab to open the Format pane for that chart element.

7. **Click the Add Chart Element button in the Chart Layouts group, point to Axis Titles, click Primary Horizontal, then type Number of Job Seekers**
8. **Right-click any number on the horizontal axis, verify all the numbers on the axis are selected, click Format Axis to open the Format Axis pane, select 500.0 in the Major Units box, type 250, press ENTER, then close the Format Axis pane**
   The horizontal axis now shows increments of 250 instead of 500.
9. **Right-click a blank area in the chart, click Format Chart Area, click Border in the Format Chart Area pane, set the border color to Black, Text 1 and the border width at 2 pt, close the Format Chart Area pane, then click away from the chart**
10. sam **Click the View tab, click the Zoom button, click the Many Pages option button, drag to select 2 x 3 pages, click OK, compare the completed document to FIGURE 8-17, then save and close the document**

FIGURE 8-15: Edited pie chart

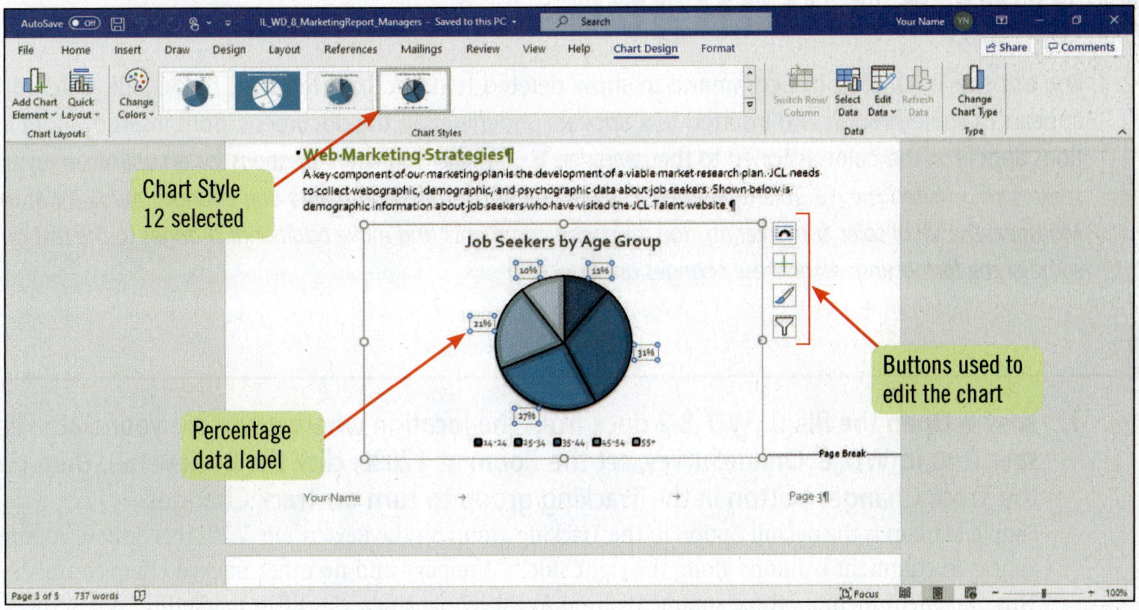

FIGURE 8-16: Select Data Source dialog box

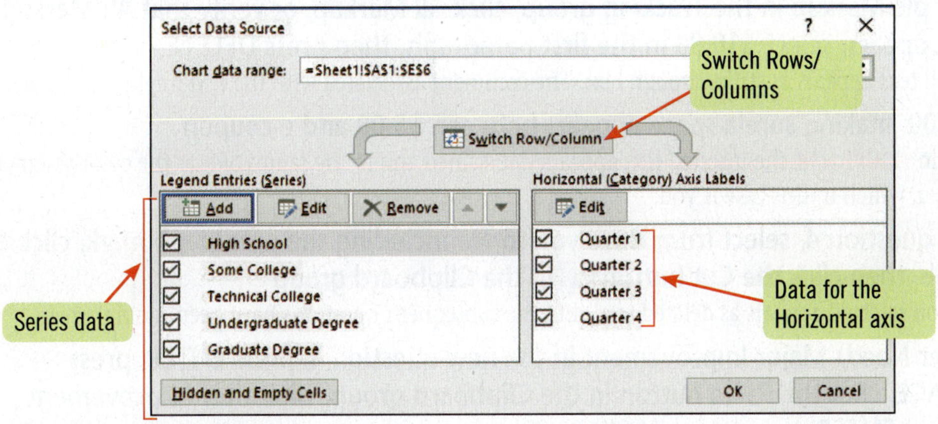

FIGURE 8-17: Completed report

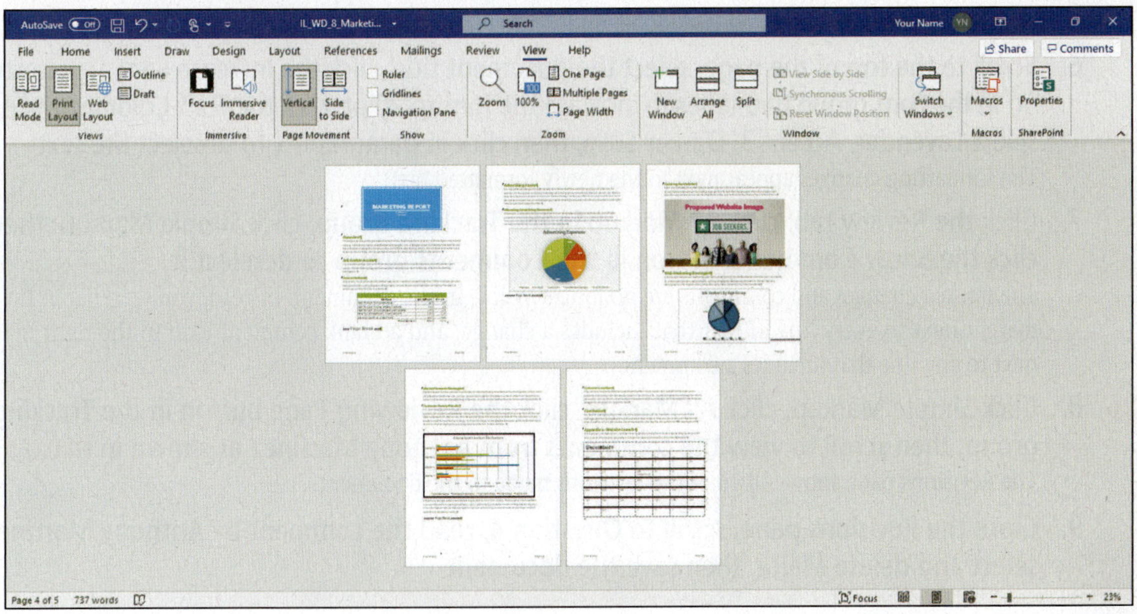

Rawpixel.com/Shutterstock.com

Word

Word
Module 8

Track Changes

Learning Outcomes
- Track insertions and deletions
- Track formatting changes

You use the Track Changes command to show deleted text and inserted text. By default, deleted text appears as ~~strikethrough~~ and inserted text appears underlined in the document. Both insertions and deletions appear in the color assigned to the reviewer. **CASE** *You open questions for an online survey of job seekers who visited the JCL Talent website. The document contains comments and changes made by Anthony Martinez, the VP of sales & marketing. You review his comments and make additional changes to the text and to some of the formatting. All of these changes are tracked.*

STEPS

TROUBLE
A different markup option may be selected if another user was working on the computer before you.

TROUBLE
Use your mouse to completely select "$10.00" so that when you press DELETE, the comment is also deleted. If the comment is not removed when you press DELETE, it will be when you accept the change.

QUICK TIP
You press BACKSPACE to remove a lettered line in a list and to leave a blank line.

TROUBLE
If the comments do not appear in the Revisions pane, click the Show Comments button in the Comments group.

1. **sam Open the file IL_WD_8-2.docx from the location where you store your Data Files, save it as IL_WD_8_OnlineSurvey, set the Zoom at 120%, click the Review tab, then click the Track Changes button in the Tracking group to turn on Track Changes**
   Simple Markup is the default option in the Tracking group on the Review tab. With this option, comments appear in comment balloons along the right side of the page and no other tracked changes are shown. This document includes three comments from Anthony Martinez, the VP of marketing. When the Track Changes button is active, every change you make to the document will appear in colored text.
2. **Click Simple Markup in the Tracking group, click All Markup, or verify that All Markup already appears, select $10.00 in the first paragraph, then press DELETE**
   The deleted text appears as strikethrough text. The comment associated with the text might also be deleted.
3. **Type $5.00, making sure a space appears between $5.00 and e-coupon**
   As shown in FIGURE 8-18, the inserted text appears underlined and in the same color as the color assigned to the reviewer, which in this case is you.
4. **Scroll to question 4, select from Have you to No including the paragraph mark, click the Home tab, then click the Cut button in the Clipboard group**
   The text you selected appears as deleted text, and the subsequent questions have been renumbered.
5. **Click after Needs Major Improvement in the new question 4, press ENTER, press BACKSPACE, click the Paste button in the Clipboard group, click after Improvement (4d.), press ENTER, then press BACKSPACE**
   As shown in FIGURE 8-19, both the cut text and the pasted text appear in a new color and are double-underlined. The new color and the double underlining indicate that the text has been moved.
6. **Scroll to the top of the page, select the document title, click the Increase Font Size button in the Font group two times to increase the font to 20 pt, click the Font Color arrow, select Lavender, Accent 3, Darker 50%, then click in paragraph 1 to deselect the text**
   The formatting changes appear next to the newly formatted text.
7. **Click the Review tab, click All Markup in the Tracking group, click Simple Markup, then click the Show Comments button in the Comments group to deselect it**
   The tracked changes and comments are no longer visible in the document. Instead, you see a bar in the left margin next to every line of text that includes a change, and a blank comment icon in the right margin next to any line that includes a comment.
8. **Click Simple Markup, click All Markup, click the Reviewing Pane button in the Tracking group, then scroll to view the comments from Anthony Martinez as shown in FIGURE 8-20**
   The Revisions pane shows all 16 of the revisions made to the document.
9. **Close the Revisions pane, scroll to Question 4, read the comment by Anthony Martinez, select and delete Major, then save the document**

FIGURE 8-18: Text inserted with Track Changes feature active

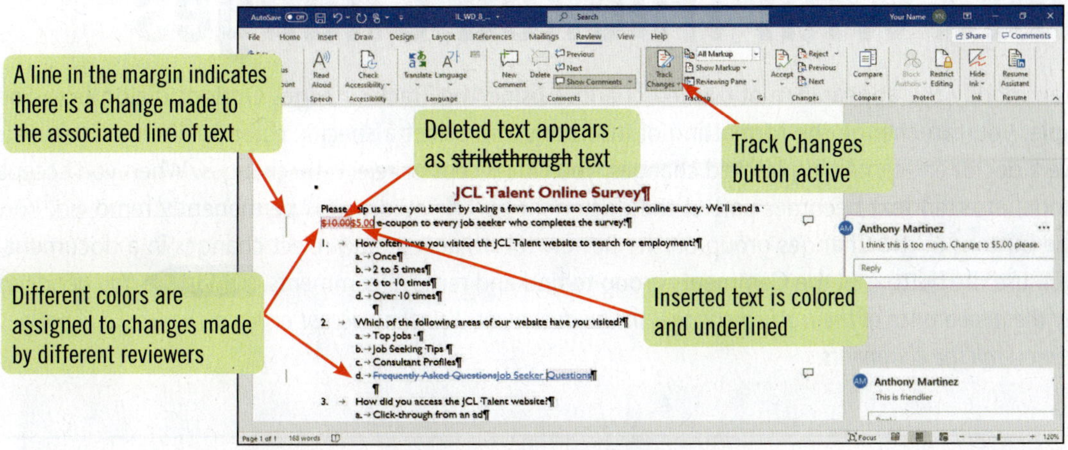

FIGURE 8-19: Tracked changes shows formatting for moved text

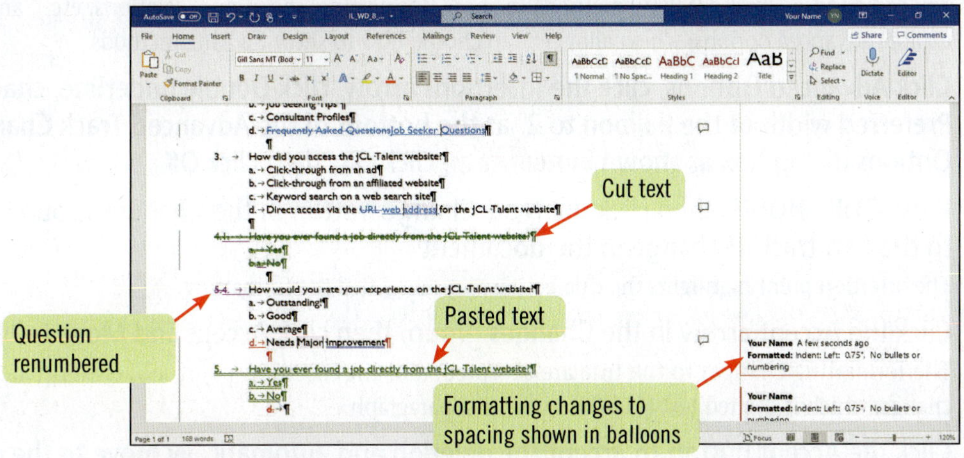

FIGURE 8-20: Document with Revisions pane open

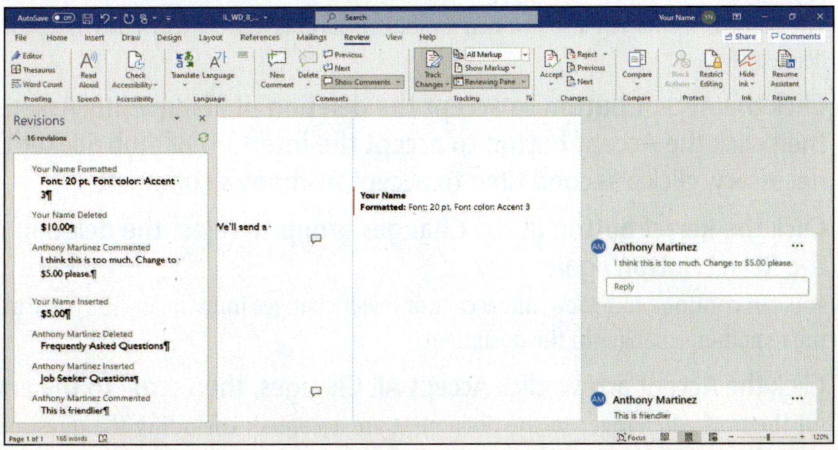

Using Paste and Paste All with tracked changes

If Track Changes is on when you are pasting items from the Clipboard, each item you paste is inserted in the document as a tracked change. If you cut an individual item and then paste it from the Clipboard into a new location, the item is inserted in a new color and with double underlining, which indicates that the item has been moved. If, however, you use the Paste All button on the Clipboard pane to paste all the items on the Clipboard at once, the items are pasted in the document as inserted text at the location of the insertion point. When you use the Paste All button, the items are pasted in the order in which you collected them, from the first item you collected (the item at the bottom of the Clipboard) to the most recent item you collected (the item at the top of the Clipboard).

Word
Module 8

Work with Tracked Changes

Learning Outcomes
- Change track changes options
- Accept and reject changes

You can modify the appearance of tracked changes using the Track Changes Options dialog box. For example, you can change the formatting of insertions and select a specific color for them. When you receive a document containing tracked changes, you can accept or reject the changes. When you accept a change, inserted text becomes part of the document and deleted text is permanently removed. You use the buttons in the Changes group on the Review tab to accept and reject changes in a document, and you use the buttons in the Comments group to find and remove comments. **CASE** *You decide to modify the appearance of the tracked changes in the document. You then accept or reject the tracked changes and remove all the comments.*

STEPS

1. **Click the Launcher in the Tracking group to open the Track Changes Options dialog box**
   You can choose which tracking methods to show (formatting, insertions, deletions, etc.), and you can explore advanced options, which allow you to choose how to show tracking methods.
2. **Click Advanced Options, click the Insertions arrow, click Double underline, change the Preferred width of the balloon to 2" at the bottom of the Advanced Track Changes Options dialog box as shown in FIGURE 8-21, click OK, then click OK**
3. **Press CTRL+HOME, then click the Next Change button in the Changes group to move to the first tracked change in the document**
   The insertion point highlights the title because you modified the formatting.
4. **Click the Accept arrow in the Changes group, then click Accept and Move to Next**
   The formatting changes to the title are accepted, and the insertion point moves to the next tracked change, which is deleted text ($10.00) in the first paragraph.
5. **Click the Accept button to accept the deletion and automatically move to the next change, then click the Accept button again to accept $5.00**
   The $5.00 is formatted as black text to show it has been accepted. The comment was removed with the deleted text.
6. **Click the Accept button to accept the deletion of "Frequently Asked Questions", then click the Accept button to accept the insertion of "Job Seeker Questions" and, if necessary, click a second time to accept Anthony's comment**
7. **Click the Reject button in the Changes group to reject the deletion of "URL", then click the Reject button again**
   You can continue to review and accept or reject changes individually, or you can choose to accept all of the remaining changes in the document.
8. **Click the Accept arrow, click Accept All Changes, then scroll to the end of the document**
   All the tracked changes in the document are accepted, including the question that was moved and renumbered.
9. **Click the Delete arrow in the Comments group, then click Delete All Comments in Document**
   Scroll through the document. Notice that all tracked changes and comments are removed from the document.
10. **sam Scroll to the bottom of the document, click the Track Changes button in the Tracking group to turn off Track Changes, type your name where indicated in the footer, close the footer, show the document in One Page view, compare it to FIGURE 8-22, then save and close the document, but do not exit Word**

QUICK TIP
You should always review all changes and comments before you use any of the Accept All Changes or Delete All Comments commands.

FIGURE 8-21: Advanced Track Changes dialog box

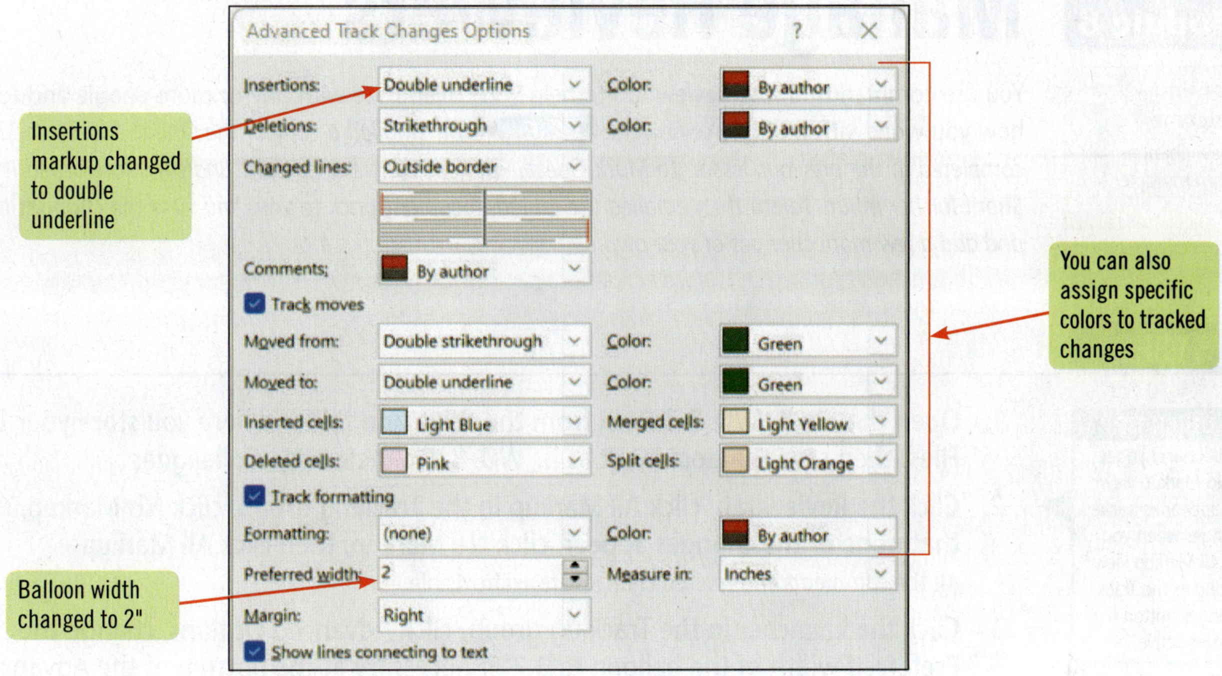

FIGURE 8-22: Completed document with tracked changes accepted and comments deleted

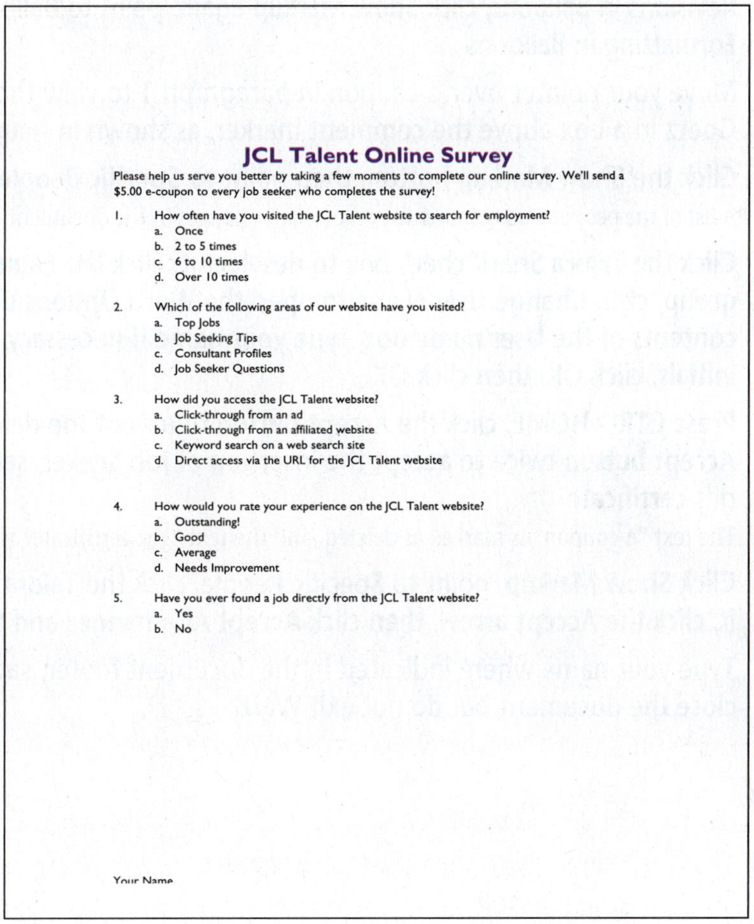

JCL Talent Online Survey

Please help us serve you better by taking a few moments to complete our online survey. We'll send a $5.00 e-coupon to every job seeker who completes the survey!

1. How often have you visited the JCL Talent website to search for employment?
   a. Once
   b. 2 to 5 times
   c. 6 to 10 times
   d. Over 10 times

2. Which of the following areas of our website have you visited?
   a. Top Jobs
   b. Job Seeking Tips
   c. Consultant Profiles
   d. Job Seeker Questions

3. How did you access the JCL Talent website?
   a. Click-through from an ad
   b. Click-through from an affiliated website
   c. Keyword search on a web search site
   d. Direct access via the URL for the JCL Talent website

4. How would you rate your experience on the JCL Talent website?
   a. Outstanding!
   b. Good
   c. Average
   d. Needs Improvement

5. Have you ever found a job directly from the JCL Talent website?
   a. Yes
   b. No

Your Name

Manage Reviewers

Learning Outcome
- View changes from multiple users

You use commands on the Review tab to help you collaborate with one or more people and to manage how you work with multiple reviewers. **CASE** *You emailed a copy of the Online Survey document you completed in the previous lesson to Mark Goetz, who edited the document and then forwarded it to Talora Sharif for her input. Talora then emailed the edited document back to you. You view the changes they made and add a few more changes of your own.*

STEPS

QUICK TIP Additional changes in No Markup view will appear as tracked changes when you use All Markup view as long as the Track Changes button remains active.

TROUBLE The option may be Show Only Comments and Formatting in Balloons.

TROUBLE If mg1 and ts2 appear in square brackets in paragraph 1, point to each set of initials instead.

QUICK TIP You can also change the user name and initials by clicking the File tab, and then clicking Options to open the Word Options dialog box.

QUICK TIP Your name appears as one of the reviewers because you made a tracked change.

1. **Open the file IL_WD_8-3.docx from the drive and folder where you store your Data Files, then save the document as IL_WD_8_OnlineSurvey_Colleagues**
2. **Click the Review tab, click All Markup in the Tracking group, click No Markup, note that none of the changes appear, click No Markup, then click All Markup**
   All the comments and tracked changes are again visible.
3. **Click the Launcher in the Tracking group, click Advanced Options, change the Preferred width of the balloon to 3.7" if necessary at the bottom of the Advanced Changes Options dialog box, click OK, then click OK**
4. **Click the Show Markup button in the Tracking group, point to Balloons, click Show Revisions in Balloons, click Show Markup again, point to Balloons, then click Show Only Formatting in Balloons**
5. **Move your pointer over e-coupon in paragraph 1 to view the comment made by Mark Goetz in a box above the comment marker, as shown in FIGURE 8-23**
6. **Click the Show Markup button, then point to Specific People**
   A list of the people who commented on or made changes to the document appears, as shown in FIGURE 8-24.
7. **Click the Talora Sharif check box to deselect it, click the Launcher in the Tracking group, click Change User Name to open the Word Options dialog box, select the contents of the User name box, type your name if necessary, press TAB, type your initials, click OK, then click OK**
8. **Press CTRL+HOME, click the Accept button to accept the deletion in the title, click the Accept button twice to accept the insertion of Job Seeker, select e-coupon, then type gift certificate**
   The text "e-coupon" is marked as deleted, and the text "gift certificate" is marked as inserted.
9. **Click Show Markup, point to Specific People, click the Talora Sharif check box to select it, click the Accept arrow, then click Accept All Changes and Stop Tracking**
10. **Type your name where indicated in the document footer, save the document, then close the document but do not exit Word**

FIGURE 8-23: Manage reviewers

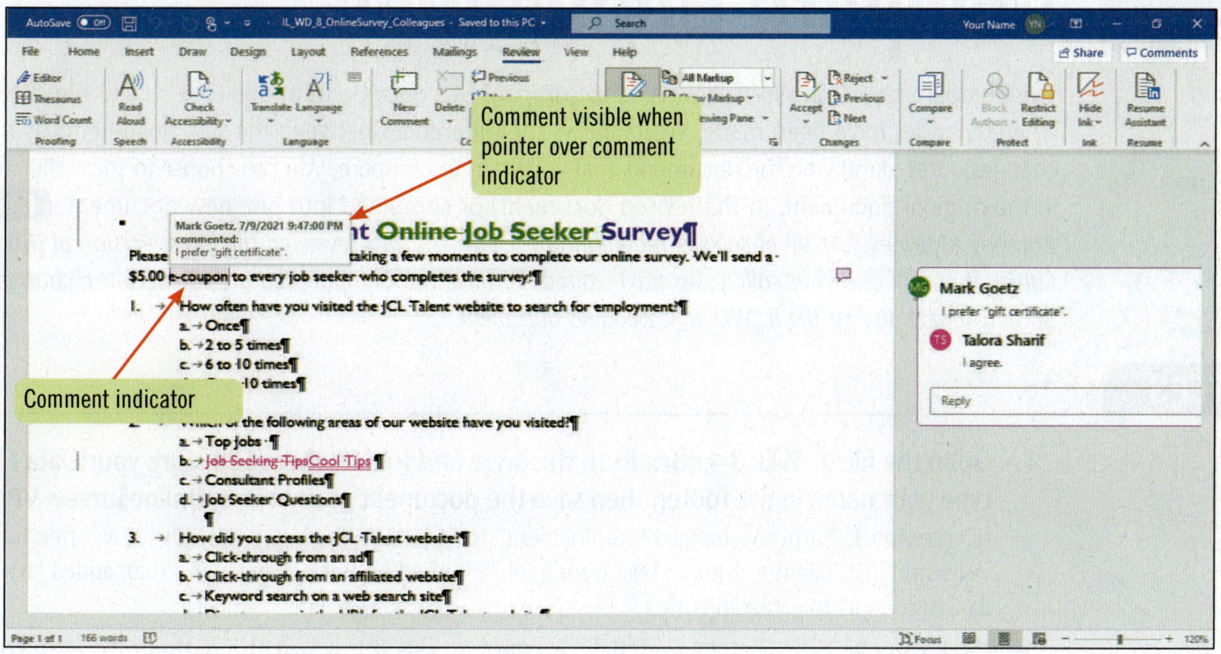

FIGURE 8-24: Showing reviewers

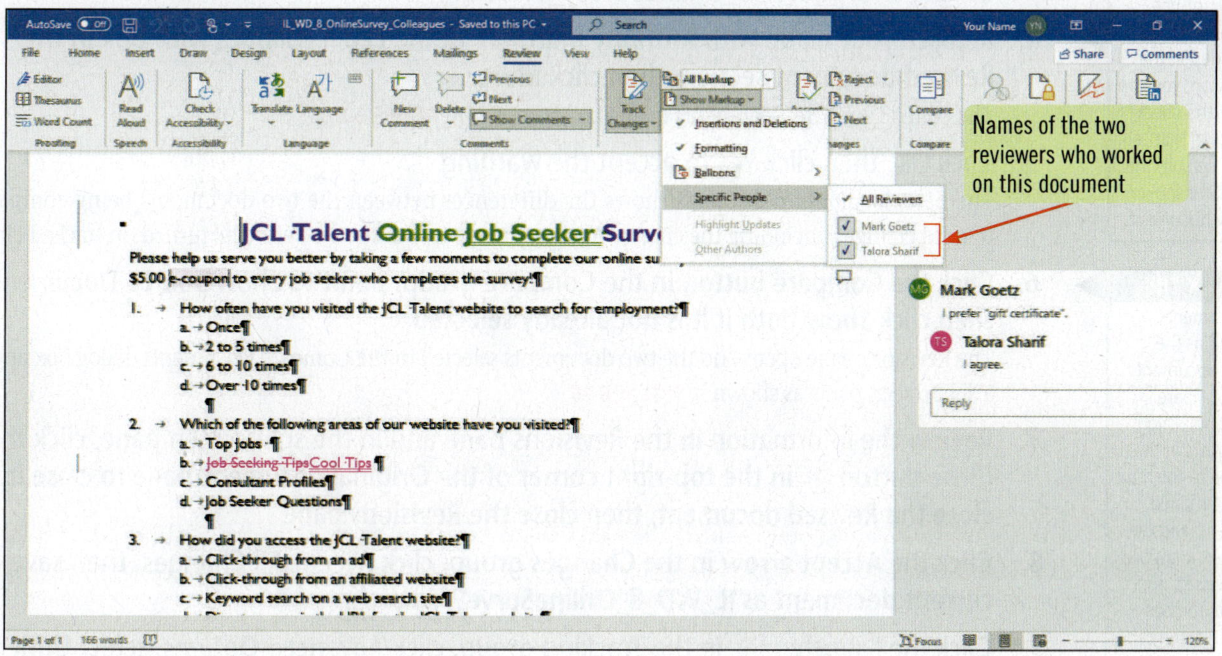

Word **Module 8**

Compare Documents

Learning Outcome
- Identify changes in compared documents

The Compare feature in Word allows you to compare two documents at one time so you can determine where changes have been made. Word shows the differences between the two documents as tracked changes. After identifying the documents that you want to compare, you can choose to show the changes in the original document, in the revised document, or combined into one new document. **CASE** *Anthony Martinez, the VP of sales & marketing at JCL Talent, has reviewed the latest version of the Online Survey that you and your colleagues have edited. You use the Compare feature to check the changes that Anthony made against the IL_WD_8_Colleagues document.*

STEPS

1. **Open the file IL_WD_8-4.docx from the drive and folder where you store your Data Files, type your name in the footer, then save the document as IL_WD_8_OnlineSurvey_VP**
   In Question 1, Anthony changed "employment" to "a job" so the question reads "How often have you visited the JCL Talent website to search for a job?", turned on track changes and then added "within 30 days of receipt" to paragraph one.
2. **Click the File tab, click Close, click the Review tab if it is not the active tab, click the Compare button in the Compare group, then click Compare**
   In the Compare Documents dialog box, you specify which two documents you want to compare.
3. **Click the Browse button in the Original document section, navigate to the location where you save the files for this module, double-click IL_WD_8_OnlineSurvey_Colleagues.docx, click the Browse button in the Revised document section, then double-click IL_WD_8_OnlineSurvey_VP.docx**
4. **Replace your name with Anthony Martinez in the Label changes with box in the Revised document section, then click More**
   The edited Compare Documents dialog box is shown in FIGURE 8-25.
5. **Click OK, then click Yes to accept the warning**
   The new document that opens shows the differences between the two documents being compared as tracked changes, including the change Anthony made to Question 1 before he turned on tracked changes.
6. **Click the Compare button in the Compare group, point to Show Source Documents, then click Show Both if it is not already selected**
   The Revisions pane opens and the two documents selected in the Compare Documents dialog box appear in a split screen pane, as shown in FIGURE 8-26.
7. **Review the information in the Revisions pane and in the split screen pane, click the Close button in the top-right corner of the Original document pane to close it, close the Revised document, then close the Revisions pane**
8. **Click the Accept arrow in the Changes group, click Accept All Changes, then save the current document as IL_WD_8_OnlineSurvey_Final**
9. **Click the Launcher in the Tracking group, click Advanced Options, select Underline for insertions and 3.7" for the balloon width, click OK, click OK, submit all to your instructor, then close all open documents and exit Word**

QUICK TIP
Check marks identify all the document settings that will be compared. If you do not want one of the settings to be included in the comparison, you can uncheck the check box next to that setting. By default, the changes are shown in a new document.

QUICK TIP
The document identified as the original document in the Compare Documents dialog box appears in the top pane to the right of the compared document, and the document identified as the revised document that incorporates Anthony's changes appears in the lower pane.

FIGURE 8-25: Compare Documents dialog box

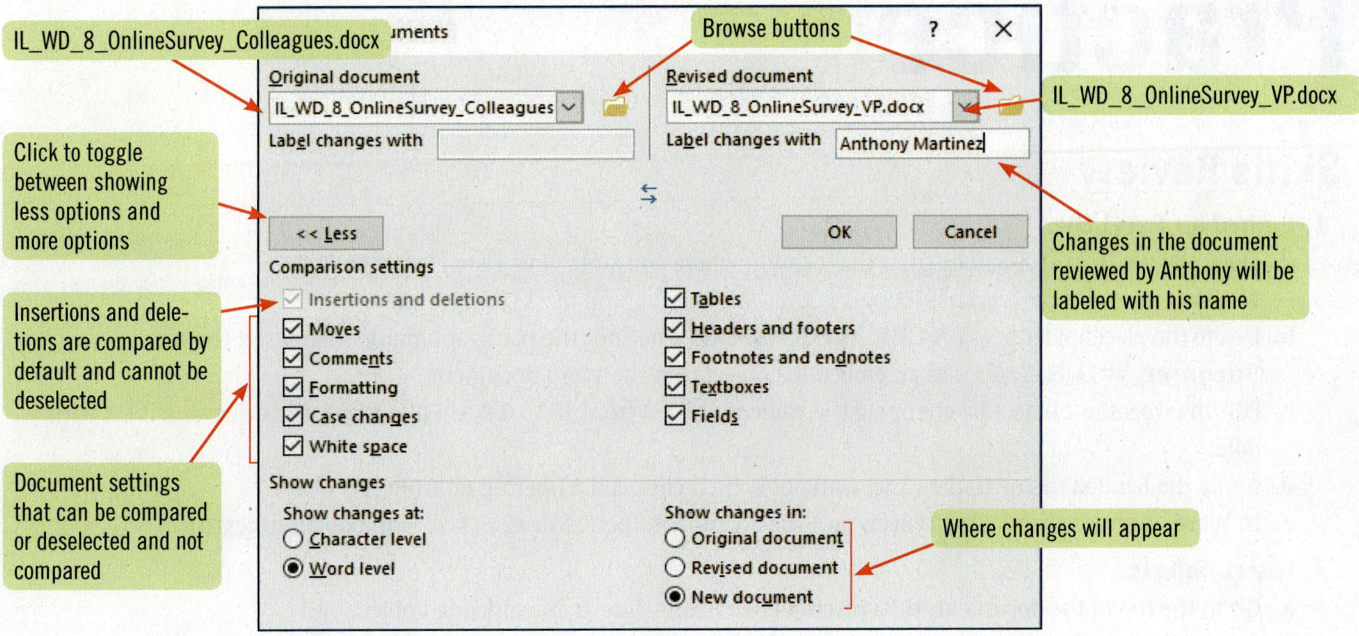

FIGURE 8-26: Comparing documents

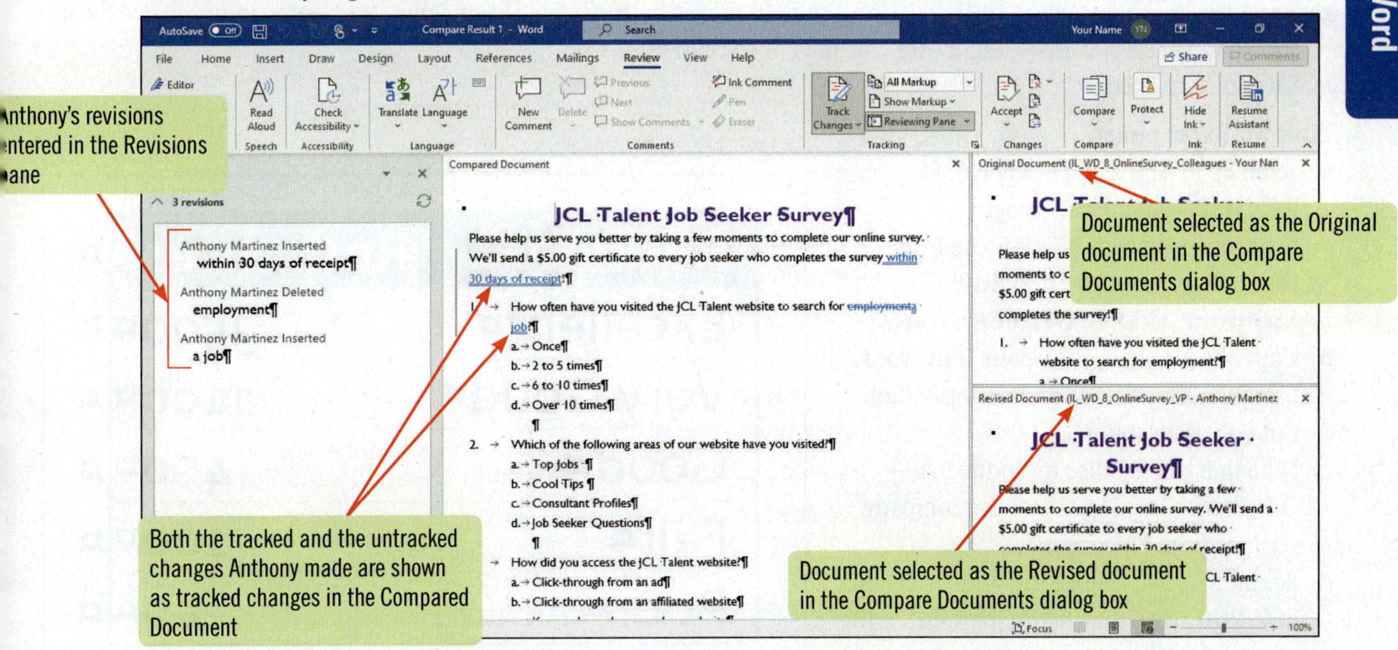

Practice

Skills Review

1. Embed an Excel file.

a. Open the file IL_WD_8-5.docx from the location where you store your Data Files, save it as **IL_WD_8_OfficeRentalsReport**, then show paragraph marks, if necessary.

b. Delete the placeholder text **EXCEL WORKSHEET** but not the paragraph mark, then insert the file **Support_WD_8-4.xlsx** as an embedded object into the Word document.

c. Edit the worksheet object by changing the value in cell C3 from 12 to **14**, then enhance the value in cell D8 with bold.

d. Apply the Banded theme to the Excel workbook, then click cell A1 before returning to Word.

e. In Word, center the worksheet object, save the document, then close the Excel workbook if necessary.

2. Insert objects.

a. Go to the top of the document, then insert a PowerPoint slide as an embedded object.

b. Enter the text **Gleeson Office Solutions** as the slide title, then enter your name as the subtitle.

c. In PowerPoint, apply the Banded theme to the slide object, then return to Word.

d. Double-click the slide object, apply the gray, blue and green variant (far right), click in the text below the slide object to return to Word, then click to the left of "Overview" and press ENTER to add a line break.

e. Reduce the absolute height of the slide object to **2.5"**, then center the slide object.

f. Scroll to page 4, select and delete QUICK TABLE but not the paragraph mark, then insert the Tabular List Quick Table.

g. Select the last three rows in the table, click the right mouse button, click Delete Rows, then enter and format the data shown in FIGURE 8-27. (*Hint*: Right-align the data in column 2.)

h. Save the document.

3. Link an Excel chart.

a. Scroll up to page 2 and delete EXCEL PIE CHART, but not the paragraph mark, open Support_WD_8-5.xlsx from File Explorer, then save it in Excel as **Support_WD_8_OfficeRevenue**.

b. Copy the pie chart, then paste it in Word using the Keep Source Formatting & Link Data (F) paste option.

c. Note that the red slice for Individual Offices accounts for 22% of the company revenue from office rentals.

d. Return to Excel, change the value in cell B2 to **2,200,000**, then verify the value of the Individual Offices slice (33%).

e. Return to Word and verify that the red slice is now 33%.

f. Switch to Excel, then save and close the workbook.

g. In Word, change the width of the pie chart to **5.5"**, then center the pie chart and save the document.

FIGURE 8-27

Rating¤	Responses¤	¤
Excellent¤	3500¤	¤
Very·Good¤	1100¤	¤
Good¤	400¤	¤
Fair¤	100¤	¤
Poor¤	40¤	¤

¶

Skills Review (continued)

4. **Link a PowerPoint slide.**
   a. Scroll to the next page and delete POWERPOINT SLIDE but not the paragraph mark, open **Support_WD_8-6.pptx** from File Explorer, then save it in PowerPoint as **Support_WD_8_OfficeDesign**.
   b. Go to Slide Sorter view in PowerPoint, copy the slide, then paste it in Word as a linked PowerPoint Slide Object.
   c. Return to PowerPoint, view the slide in Normal view, then delete the blue text box.
   d. Switch to Word and update the linked slide to reflect the change.
   e. Save the document, go to PowerPoint, then save the PowerPoint presentation.
5. **Manage document links.**
   a. In Word, right-click the linked slide, then edit the link.
   b. In PowerPoint, select the text "Open Concept Office", then change the fill color of the text to Lime, Accent 2, Lighter 80%.
   c. Update the link in Word, then save the document.
   d. Save and close the PowerPoint presentation.
   e. Save the Word document again as **IL_WD_8_OfficeRentalsReport_Distribution**.
   f. Go to the Links dialog from the File tab, then break the link to the PowerPoint slide.
   g. Break the link to the Excel pie chart.
   h. Exit Backstage view, then scroll up and apply Chart Style 1 to the pie chart.
   i. Save the document.
6. **Create charts.**
   a. Scroll to page 4, use CTRL+C to copy the Ratings Quick Table, then delete CUSTOMER PIE CHART but not the paragraph mark following.
   b. Insert a pie chart.
   c. Click cell A1 in the Worksheet window, then use CTRL+V to paste the table data into the Excel worksheet.
   d. Change the chart title to **Customer Evaluations**.
   e. Add data labels at the Outside End position.
   f. Delete the legend, insert a legend to the right of the pie chart, then close the worksheet.
   g. Scroll up to page 3 and select COLUMN CHART, but not the paragraph mark, then insert a Clustered Column Chart (the default chart type).
   h. Select the table above the chart, use CTRL+X to cut the table, then use CTRL+V to paste the table into cell A1 of the Excel worksheet. Double-click the column header between each column to widen the columns to view the data.
   i. Close the Excel worksheet, enter **Annual Revenue by Location** as the chart title, then save the document.
7. **Format and edit charts.**
   a. Scroll down to the Customer Evaluations pie chart, change the width to **4"** and the height to **3"**, then center the chart.
   b. Edit the chart data by changing 100 to **200** in cell B5.
   c. Format the data labels to show percentages instead of values.
   d. Apply the Style 12 chart style to the pie chart, then change the colors to Monochromatic Palette 3.
   e. Change 100 to **200** in the Quick Table so it matches the chart.
   f. Scroll up to the column chart.
   g. Change the chart type to Bar.
   h. Switch the rows and columns so the city names appear on the Vertical axis. (*Hint:* If the Switch Row/Column button is grayed out, click Select Data to open the Select Data Source dialog box, then click Switch Row/Column. Click OK, then close the Excel worksheet.)
   i. Add an Axis Title to the Primary Horizontal Axis with the text **Revenue**.
   j. Format the Primary Horizontal Axis to show increments of $150,000 in the Major box.
   k. Format the chart area with a Dark Gray, Text 1 border with a weight of 3 points.

Skills Review (continued)

l. Reduce the height of the chart to **2.7"** and the width to **5"**, then center it. The chart should fit on page 3. If not, remove the paragraph mark on the previous page, then remove any extra paragraph marks or page breaks so the report fits on four pages.

m. View the report so that all four pages fit in the document window, compare the completed report to FIGURE 8-28, then save and close the document and exit Excel and PowerPoint if necessary.

FIGURE 8-28

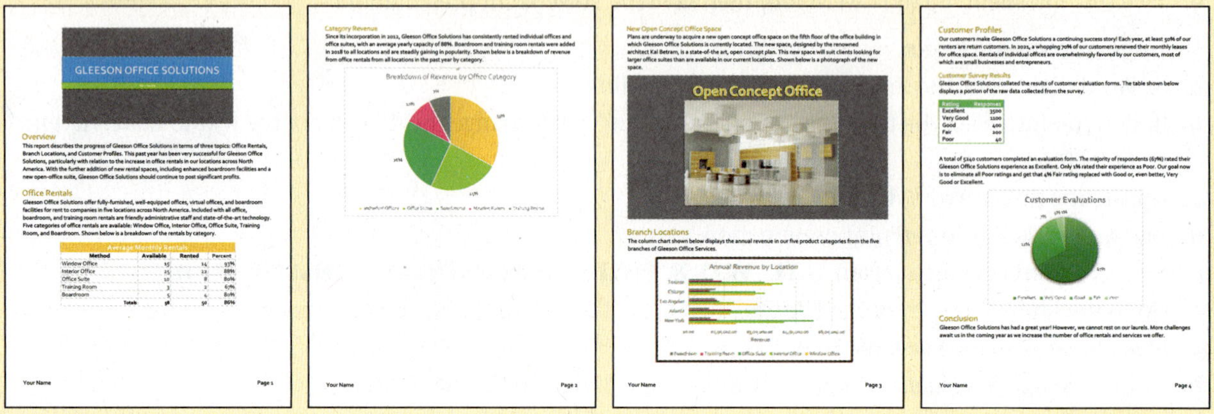

Zastolskiy Victor/Shutterstock.com

8. Track changes.

a. Open the file IL_WD_8-6.docx from the location where you store your Data Files, save it as **IL_WD_8_CompanyDescription**, set Zoom to 100%, then turn on Track Changes from the Review tab if necessary.

b. Select All Markup if necessary, read the comment attached to "friendly" in the first paragraph, then select and delete friendly.

c. Type **welcoming**, adding a space after if necessary.

d. Scroll to the Company Background heading, cut the heading "Company Background" and the paragraph following, then paste them above the "Expansion Plans" heading.

e. Select the document title at the top of the document, decrease the font size to 28 pt, then change the font color to Aqua, Accent 1, Darker 50%.

f. Change the markup view to Simple Markup and show the comments.

g. Return to All Markup, then show the Revisions pane.

h. Close the Revisions pane, scroll to the Company Background paragraph, read the comment by Holly Stewart, delete "incorporated and" along with Holly's comment, then save the document.

9. Work with tracked changes.

a. Open the Advanced Track Changes Options dialog box, show deletions as Double strikethrough, change the width of the balloon to 3", then click OK to exit all open dialog boxes.

b. Go to the beginning of the document, then use the buttons in the Changes group to go to the first change.

c. Accept the change to the title formatting, then accept the changes in the first two body paragraphs.

d. Reject the change from ten to fifteen so the number is again ten.

e. Accept all the remaining changes in the document, then delete all comments.

f. Save and close the document.

10. Manage reviewers.

a. Open the file IL_WD_8-7.docx from the drive and folder where you store your Data Files, then save the document as **IL_WD_8_CompanyDescription_Colleagues**. This document includes changes made by Sara Ramos and Josef Lisowski to the document you just worked on.

b. Show All Markup, if necessary.

Skills Review (continued)

c. Show revisions in balloons, then show formatting in balloons. (*Hint:* The option may be to Show Only Comments and Formatting in Balloons.)

d. Read the comment made by Sara in the first paragraph, then read the comment made by Josef.

e. Show the list of people who worked on the document, then deselect the check box next to Josef Lisowski.

f. Change the user name to your name, if necessary.

g. Go to the beginning of the document, accept the formatting of the title, accept the insertion in the title, accept the deletion of the subtitle, then go to "modern" and change it to **up-to-date**.

h. Show the list of people who worked on the document again, select Josef Lisowski, then delete all the comments and accept all changes and stop tracking.

i. Type your name where indicated in the document footer, save the document, then close the document but do not exit Word.

11. Compare documents.

a. Open the file IL_WD_8-8.docx from the drive and folder where you store your Data Files, type your name in the footer, then save the document as **IL_WD_8_CompanyDescription_Manager**.

b. In the last line of paragraph 1, Holly Stewart, the manager, changed "run" to "operate" before she turned on track changes. After she turned on track changes, she changed "facility" to "service" in the first line of the Company Background paragraph.

c. Close the document, then on the Review tab, click the Compare button and open the Compare Documents dialog box.

d. Open **IL_WD_8_CompanyDescription_Colleagues.docx** as the original document, then open **IL_WD_8_CompanyDescription_Manager.docx** as the revised document.

e. Type **Holly** in the Label changes with box in the Revised document section if necessary.

f. Exit the Compare Documents dialog box, answering Yes when prompted, then show both source documents.

g. Review the information in the Revisions pane and in the split screen pane, close the Original document pane, close the Revised document pane, then close the Revisions pane.

h. Accept all the changes in the document, then save it as **IL_WD_8_CompanyDescription_Final**.

i. Return tracking options to the default settings: Strikethrough for deletions and 3.7" for the balloon width.

j. The completed document with all changes incorporated appears as shown in **FIGURE 8-29**.

k. Submit all the documents you created in this Skills Review to your instructor, then close all open documents and exit Word.

FIGURE 8-29

Gleeson Office Solutions Company Description

Company Overview

Gleeson Office Solutions offers fully-furnished and well-equipped offices, meeting spaces, and training rooms for rent in five locations across North America: New York, Atlanta, Los Angeles, Chicago, and Toronto. Each location is conveniently located in the principal business district and provides welcoming administrative staff and up-to-date technology to help businesses operate smoothly and efficiently.

Company Background

Gleeson Office Solutions was launched in 2003 by Wendy Gleeson who saw a need for a service that provided local businesses with the opportunity to rent office space on a flexible schedule ranging from one hour to one year and beyond. Ms. Gleeson established her first office rentals in Los Angeles. In 2012, she expanded to New York and Chicago, and now manages five locations in the United States and one location in Canada. The company's focus on stellar customer service has won it a loyal clientele and several feature articles in prominent business magazines.

Expansion Plans

Ms. Gleeson is currently investigating opportunities to further expand Gleeson Office Solutions to ten more cities across North America. This plan will require a capital investment of $4.2 million to be repaid within two years.

Target Market

The company's principal competitors are Vista Offices with locations in twenty US cities and Offices For You with branches worldwide. Gleeson Office Solutions differentiates itself from its major competitors by its focus on superior customer service. No request is too small or too large and every office package is customized to each customer's unique needs. Gleeson Office Solutions will continue to build on its reputation for providing excellent personal service at competitive prices.

Word

Independent Challenge 1

At Riverwalk Medical Clinic in Cambridge, Massachusetts, you've been asked to work on a summary of the clinic's charity work that includes results of a survey conducted of the clinic's many volunteers and a summary of the revenue generated through the clinic's charitable work. Almost all of the clinic's 340 volunteers (328 people) took the survey, which was designed to collect data about volunteer ages and their motivations, seasonal variations in volunteer hours, average hours worked, and the clinic programs in which they volunteered. You open the summary and complete it with objects inserted from Excel and PowerPoint, and charts you create in Word.

a. Start Word, open the file IL_WD_8-9.docx from the location where you store your Data Files, then save it as **IL_WD_8_GivingBackSummary**.
b. Insert an embedded PowerPoint slide above "Overview" at the top of the document that includes **Riverwalk Clinic Giving Back Summary** as the title and your name as the subtitle, then format the slide with the Savon theme and the green variant (third variant from the left).
c. Move "Overview" down one line.
d. Select and delete AGE PIE CHART but not the paragraph mark, then cut the table (contains Age Range and Number) and use the data to create a pie chart.
e. Edit the pie chart as follows: Enter **Age Range Distribution** as the chart title, apply the Style 5 chart style, change the colors to Monochromatic Palette 3, then add data labels that show percentages instead of values and with the labels in the Outside End position.
f. Change the position of the legend so it appears to the right of the pie chart, then enclose the pie chart in a black, 1 pt border.
g. Select and delete MOTIVATION TABLE but not the paragraph mark, then insert a Quick Table using the Tabular List format. Enter the data shown in FIGURE 8-30 into the table, change "Number of Volunteers" to **Volunteers**, right-align the data in column 2, then delete any unused rows.
h. Select and delete VOLUNTEER HOURS CHART but not the paragraph mark, open Support_WD_8-7.xlsx from File Explorer, then save it in Excel as **Support_WD_8_VolunteerHours**.
i. Copy the pie chart, then paste it in Word using the Keep Source Formatting & Link Data (F) paste option.
j. Note that the orange slice representing 21 to 30 Hours accounts for 37% of the volunteers who volunteer between 21 and 30 hours a month at the clinic. Return to Excel, change the value in cell B4 to **140**, then verify the value of the 21 to 30 hours slice (40%).
k. Return to Word and verify that the orange slice is now 40%. Change 37% to **40%** in the text above the chart.
l. Scroll to and select the table in the Seasonal Volunteering section, cut the table, then use the data to create a column chart.
m. Change the column chart to a bar chart, then switch the rows and columns.
n. Add **Number of Volunteers** as the horizontal axis title to the chart and change the chart title to **Volunteer Contributions by Season**.
o. Scroll to and delete POWERPOINT SLIDE, but not the paragraph mark, open Support_WD_8-8.pptx from File Explorer, then save it in PowerPoint as **Support_WD_8_Volunteer**.
p. Go to Slide Sorter view in PowerPoint, copy the slide, then paste it in Word as a link.
q. In PowerPoint, delete the orange text box, then switch to Word and update the linked slide to reflect the change.

FIGURE 8-30

Reason	Number of Volunteers
To build skills & experience	102
To meet people	38
To have something to do	19
To contribute to the community	169

Independent Challenge 1 (continued)

r. Delete the placeholder text CHARITIES WORKSHEET but not the paragraph mark, then insert the file **Support_WD_8-9.xlsx** as an embedded object into the Word document.

s. Edit the worksheet object by changing the value in cell C4 from 42 to **52**, apply the Savon theme to the Excel workbook, then click cell A1 before returning to Word.

t. Save the document.

u. Save the document again as **IL_WD_8_GivingBackSummary_Distribution**.

v. Open the Links dialog box, then break the link to the PowerPoint slide and the chart.

w. Scroll through the document, add a page break to the left of "Volunteer Hours" to move it to a new page, change the height of the "Volunteers" pie chart and the "Volunteer Contributions by Season" bar chart to 3.2", then move "Charity Work" to a new page.

x. View the five pages of the document in Multiple Pages view, compare it to **FIGURE 8-31**, then save the document, submit all files to your instructor, close the document, then exit Word and any other open applications.

FIGURE 8-31

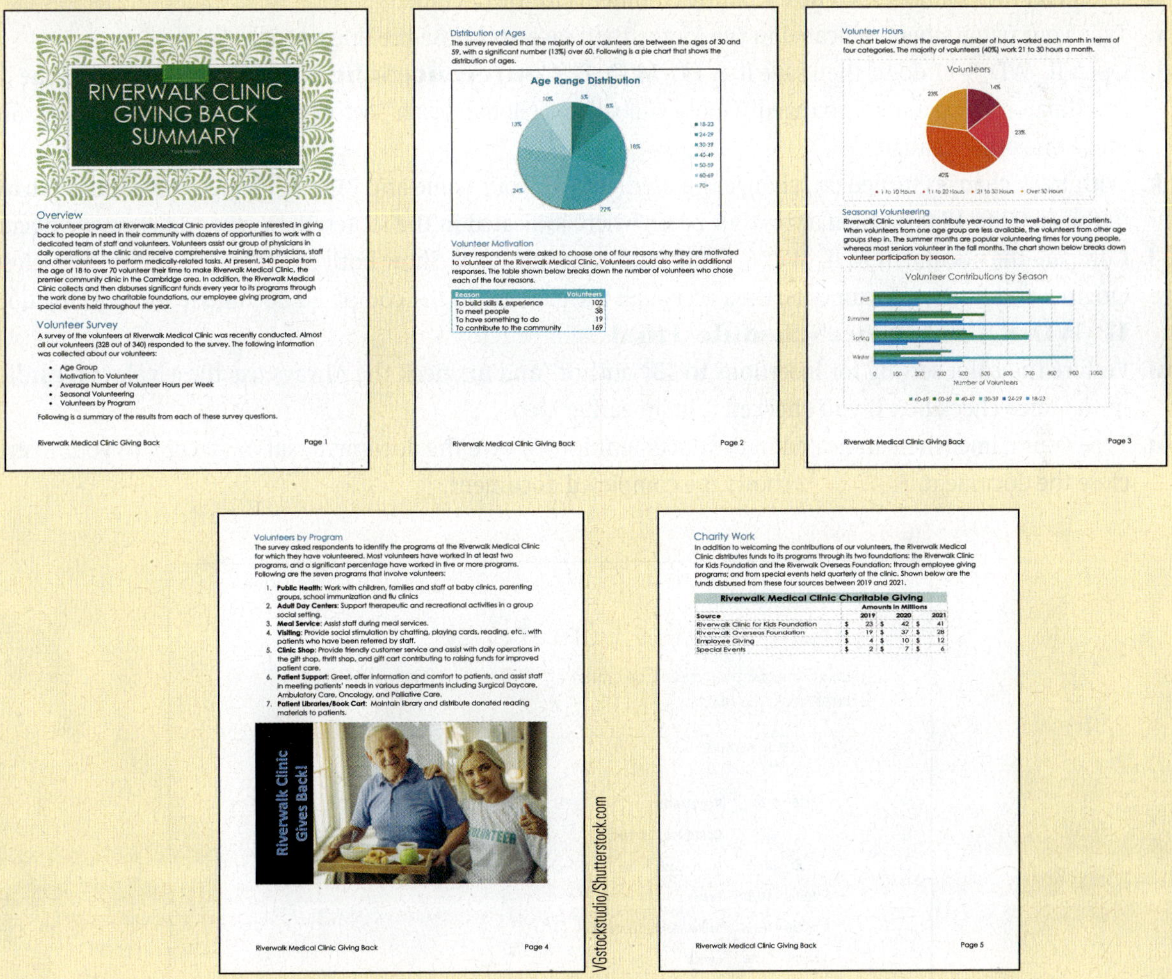

VGstockstudio/Shutterstock.com

Word

Independent Challenge 2

You work for Online Solutions, a large application service provider based in Sydney, Australia. The company is sponsoring a conference called Online Results for local businesses and entrepreneurs interested in enhancing their online presence. Two of your coworkers have been working on a preliminary schedule for the conference. They ask for your input.

a. Start Word, open the file IL_WD_8-10.docx from the drive and folder where you store your Data Files, then save it as **IL_WD_8_ConferenceSchedule**.

b. Scroll through the document to read the comments and view the changes made by Mitzi Borland and Jake Haraki.

c. Change the user name to your name and initials if necessary. (*Hint*: Add a check mark to the Always use these values regardless of sign in to Office check box if you checked this box when you completed the lessons.)

d. Modify tracking options by changing the color of inserted text to Blue.

e. In the 9:00 to 10:00 entry, select "E-Payment Systems: Trends to Watch", then insert a comment with the text **I suggest we change the name of this session to Micro-Cash in the Third Decade.**

f. Be sure the Track Changes feature is active, then apply Bold to the two instances of "Break."

g. Starting with the first comment, make all the suggested changes, including the change you suggested in your comment. Be sure to capitalize "continental" in Continental Breakfast.

h. Accept all the changes, then delete all the comments in the document.

i. Type your name where indicated in the footer, then save and close the document.

j. Open IL_WD_8-11.docx, then save it as **IL_WD_8_ConferenceSchedule_Coordinator**. The conference coordinator, Fiona Marsh, changed "Going Global" to "Global Reach" before turning on track changes. She also made one other change.

k. With track changes turned on, change the user name to your name and initials, change Someone to **Somebody** in the 16:00 to 17:00 session, type your name where indicated in the footer, then save and close the document.

l. Compare the document to IL_WD_8_ConferenceSchedule.docx. Show both of the source documents, close the Original and Revised documents, then accept all the changes in the compared document and save the document as **IL_WD_8_ConferenceSchedule_Final**.

m. Restore the color setting for Insertions to "By author" and uncheck the Always use these values regardless of sign in to Office check box if you checked it in an earlier step.

n. Type your name where indicated in the document footer, save the document, submit a copy to your instructor, then close the document. **FIGURE 8-32** shows the completed document.

FIGURE 8-32

Online Results Conference

LIBRARY BUILDING, UNIVERSITY OF SYDNEY
SYDNEY, NSW, AUSTRALIA

CONFERENCE SCHEDULE

7:30 - 9:30	Registration
	Continental Breakfast
9:00 - 10:00	Micro-Cash in the Third Decade
10:00 - 10:30	**Break**
10:30 - Noon	Social Media Strategies
Noon - 13:30	Lunch
	Keynote Speech: *Global Reach: Australia Sells to the World* Professor Wendy Leung, Professor of Economics, Oxford University
13:30 - 14:30	Copyright Challenges and Solutions
14:30 - 15:00	**Break**
15:00 - 16:00	Backend Integration: Best Practices
16:00 - 17:00	Did Somebody say ROI?

Visual Workshop

Start a new document in Word, select the Celestial theme (or a different theme if the Celestial theme is not available), open the PowerPoint slide Support_WD_8-10.pptx, copy the slide, paste the slide as a Microsoft PowerPoint Object into Word (but *not* as a link), then edit the slide from Word to add your name to the subtitle. Below the slide in Word, add the text **The worksheet and pie chart shown below break down hours billed from September 1 to October 31 by our consulting engineers.** Embed the Excel worksheet from **Support_WD_8-11.xlsx**, then change the hours for Jorge Rosas to **82** and apply the Celestial theme (or the same theme you applied to the Word document). Below the worksheet object, create the pie chart using data from the worksheet. As shown in **FIGURE 8-33**, show the values as percentages with data labels positioned Outside End, then format the chart as shown. You'll need to modify the title, move the legend to the left, and apply Chart Style 12 and the Colorful Palette 2 color scheme. Add a 3 pt border with the color Blue, Accent 2, Darker 25%. Change the height of the chart to 3.2" and the width of the chart to 5.5". Save the document as **IL_WD_8_AtlantisAerospaceConsultants**, submit the file to your instructor, close the document, close the presentation in PowerPoint and the workbook in Excel, then exit all programs.

FIGURE 8-33

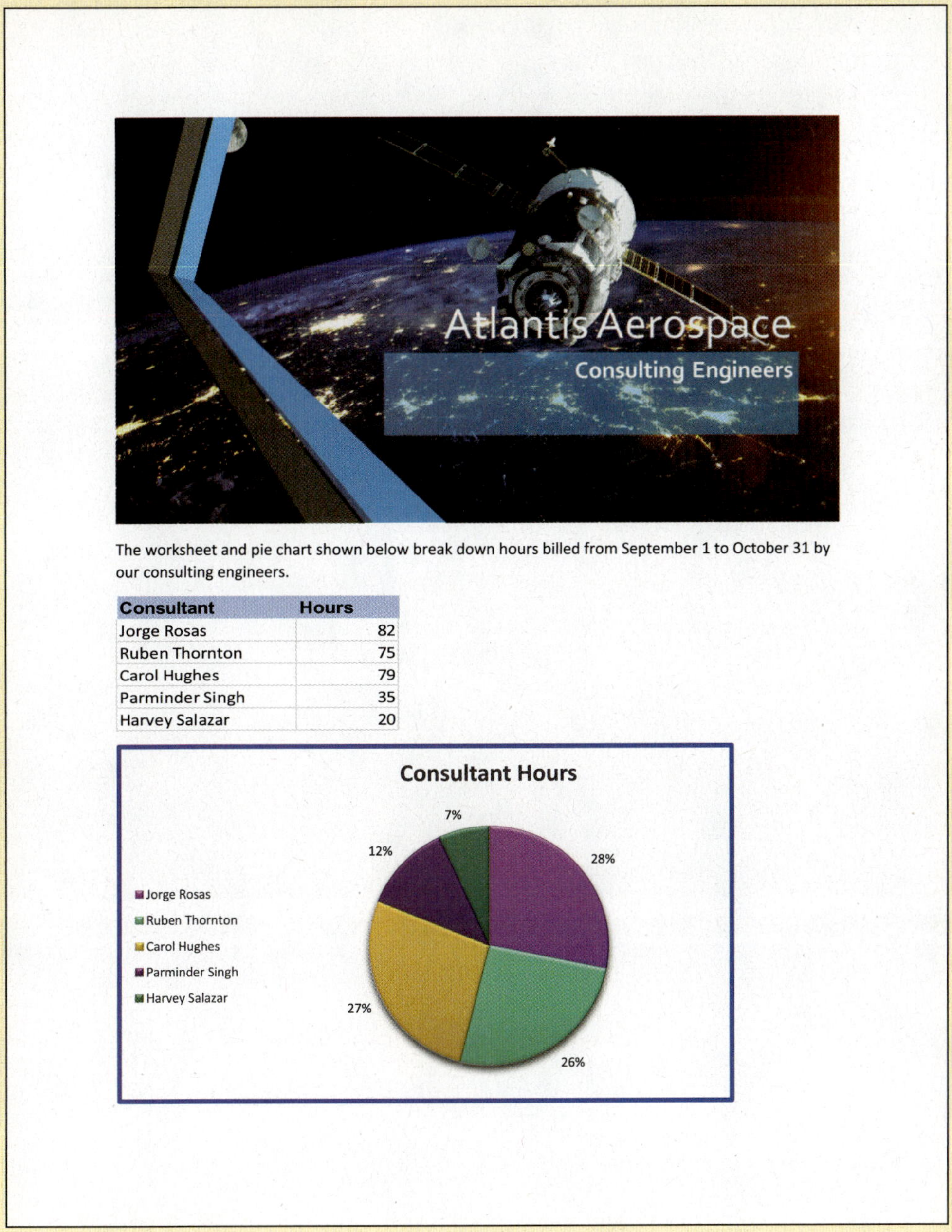

Vadim Sadovski/Shutterstock.com

Word

Developing Multi-Page Documents

CASE As an assistant to Anthony Martinez, the VP of sales & marketing at JCL Talent, Inc., you have been asked to edit and format a set of guidelines to help branch managers sponsor workshops for job seekers. You start by working in Outline view to revise the structure for the guidelines, and then you use several advanced Word features to format the document for publication.

Module Objectives

After completing this module, you will be able to:

- Build a document in Outline view
- Work in Outline view
- Navigate a document
- Create and modify screenshots
- Use advanced find and replace options
- Add and modify captions
- Insert a table of contents
- Mark text for an index
- Generate an index
- Insert footers in multiple sections
- Insert headers in multiple sections
- Finalize a multi-page document
- Work with equations
- Create master documents and subdocuments

Files You Will Need

IL_WD_9-1.docx
Support_WD_9_WorkshopImages.docx
IL_WD_9-2.docx
Support_WD_9_InfoSessions.docx
IL_WD_9-3.docx
IL_WD_9-4.docx
Support_WD_9_CompanyImages.docx
IL_WD_9-5.docx
Support_WD_9_TopTalkPresenters.docx
IL_WD_9-6.docx
IL_WD_9-7.docx
Support_WD_9_MedicalInfoSessions.docx
IL_WD_9-8.docx
Support_WD_9_BusinessProgram.docx
Support_WD_9_CampusLife.docx
Support_WD_9_TheaterProgram.docx
IL_WD_9-9.docx
Support_WD_9_Banking.docx

Word
Module 9

Learning Outcomes
- Open Outline view
- Demote and promote headings

Build a Document in Outline View

You work in Outline view to organize the headings and subheadings that identify topics and subtopics in multi-page documents. In Outline view, each heading is assigned a level from 1 to 9, with Level 1 being the highest level and Level 9 being the lowest level. In addition, you can assign the Body Text level to each paragraph of text that appears below a document heading. Each level is formatted with one of Word's predefined styles. For example, Level 1 is formatted with the Heading 1 style, and the Body Text level is formatted with the Normal style. **CASE** *You work in Outline view to develop the structure of the workshop guidelines.*

STEPS

1. **Start Word, create a new blank document, click the Show/Hide button ¶ in the Paragraph group to show paragraph marks if necessary, click the View tab, then click the Outline button in the Views group**

   In Outline view, the Outlining tab is active. **TABLE 9-1** describes the buttons on the Outlining tab.

TROUBLE
If the headings do not appear blue and bold, click the Show Text Formatting check box in the Outline Tools group to select it.

2. **Type Workshops for Job Seekers**

   FIGURE 9-1 shows the text in Outline view. By default, the text appears at the left margin, is designated as Level 1 and is formatted with the Heading 1 style.

3. **Press ENTER, click the Demote button → in the Outline Tools group to move to Level 2, then type Workshop Requirements**

   The text is indented, designated as Level 2, and formatted with the Heading 2 style.

4. **Press ENTER, then click the Demote to Body Text button ⇥ in the Outline Tools group**

5. **Type the following text: Three activities relate to the organization of a job seeker workshop: gather personnel, advertise the event, and arrange the physical space.**

   The text is indented, designated as Body Text level, and formatted with the Normal style. Notice that both the Level 1 and Level 2 text are preceded by a plus symbol +. This symbol indicates that the heading includes subtext, which could be another subheading or a paragraph of body text.

6. **Press ENTER, then click the Promote to Heading 1 button ⇤ in the Outline Tools group**

   The insertion point returns to the left margin and the Level 1 position.

7. **Type Personnel, press ENTER, then save the document as IL_WD_9_JobSeekerWorkshopsOutline where you store your Data Files**

   When you create a long document, you often enter all the headings and subheadings first to establish the overall structure of your document.

QUICK TIP
Press TAB to move from a higher level to a lower level, and press SHIFT+TAB to move from a lower level to a higher level.

8. **Use the Promote ←, Demote →, and Promote to Heading 1 ⇤ buttons to complete the outline shown in FIGURE 9-2**

9. **Place the insertion point after Workshops for Job Seekers at the top of the page, press ENTER, click ⇥, then type Prepared by followed by your name**

   In addition to Outline view, you can view a document in Draft view.

10. **Click the Close Outline View button in the Close group, click the View tab, click Draft view, then save and close the document**

FIGURE 9-1: Text in Outline view

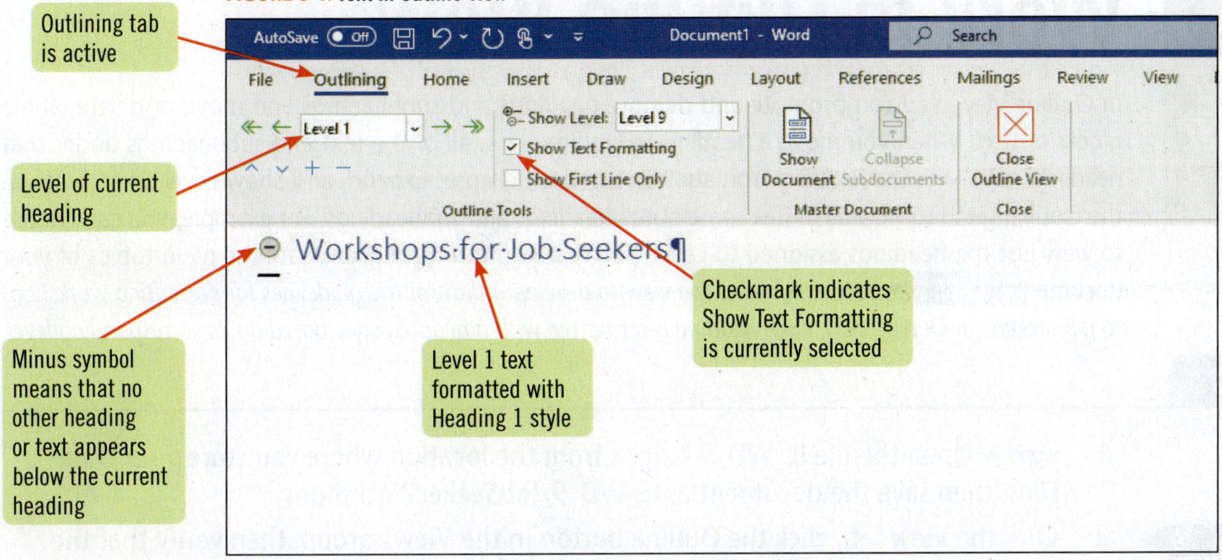

FIGURE 9-2: Completed outline

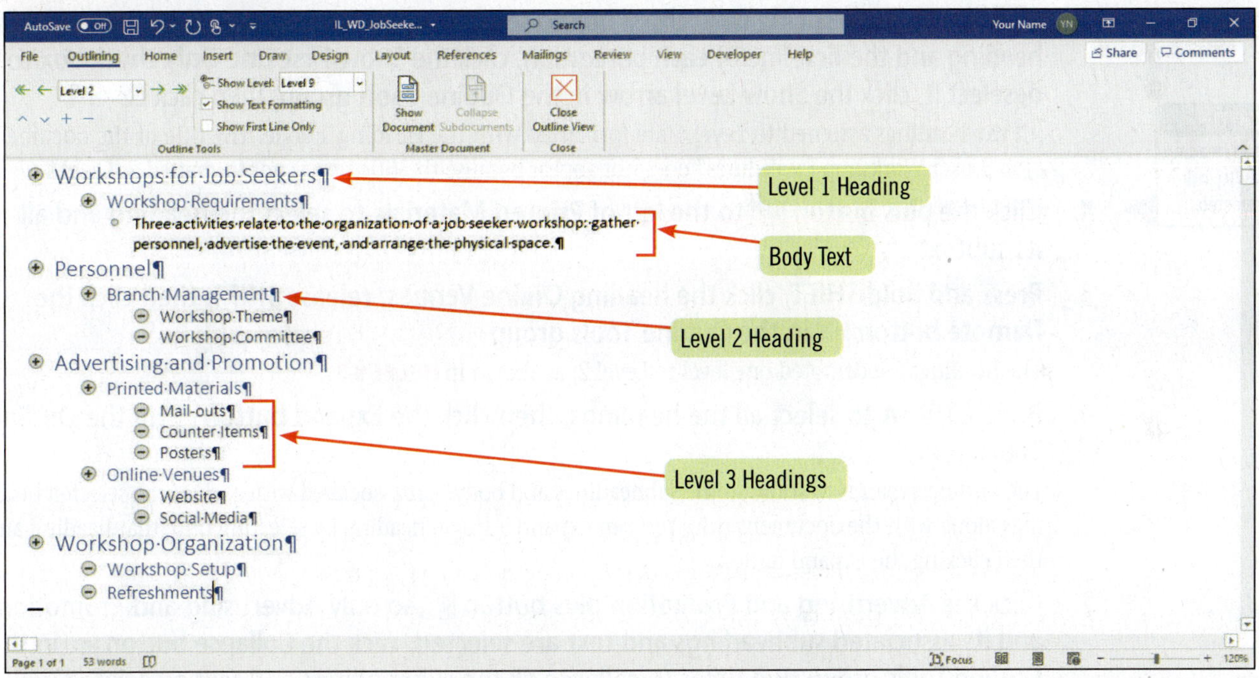

TABLE 9-1: Frequently used buttons in the Outline Tools group on the Outlining tab

button	use to	button	use to
	Promote text to Heading 1		Move a heading and its text up one line
	Promote text one level		Move a heading and its text down one line
	Demote text one level		Expand text
	Demote to body text		Collapse text

Word

Word Module 9

Work in Outline View

Learning Outcomes
- Collapse/expand headings in Outline view
- Move headings and show levels

In Outline view, you can promote and demote headings and subheadings and move or delete whole blocks of text. When you move a heading in Outline view, all of the text and subheadings under that heading move with the heading. You also can use the Collapse, Expand, and Show Level commands on the Outlining tab to view all or just some of the headings and subheadings. For example, you can choose to view just the headings assigned to Level 1 so that you can quickly evaluate the main topics of your document. **CASE** *You work in Outline view to develop a draft of the guidelines for presenting workshops to job seekers. In Outline view, each heading is formatted with a heading style based on its corresponding level.*

STEPS

QUICK TIP
The pictures and the pie chart are not visible in Outline view.

QUICK TIP
The selected heading will be gray to indicate it is selected.

QUICK TIP
A horizontal line appears when you drag the mouse pointer up or down to a new location in the outline.

1. **sam Open the file IL_WD_9-1.docx from the location where you store your Data Files, then save the document as IL_WD_9_JobSeekerWorkshops**
2. **Click the View tab, click the Outline button in the Views group, then verify that the Show Text Formatting check box is selected**
   The document changes to Outline view, and the Outlining tab opens.
3. **Click the Show First Line Only check box to select it, scroll to view every heading and subheading and the first line of each paragraph, click the Show First Line Only check box to deselect it, click the Show Level arrow in the Outline Tools group, then click Level 1**
   All the headings assigned to Level 1 are formatted with the Heading 1 style. The title of the document "Job Seeker Workshop Procedures" does not appear because the title text is not formatted as Level 1.
4. **Click the plus button ⊕ to the left of Printed Materials to select the heading and all its subtext**
5. **Press and hold SHIFT, click the heading Online Venues, release SHIFT, then click the Demote button → in the Outline Tools group**
   The headings are demoted one level to Level 2, as shown in FIGURE 9-3.
6. **Press CTRL+A to select all the headings, then click the Expand button + in the Outline Tools group**
   The outline expands to show all the subheadings and body text associated with each of the selected headings along with the document title. You can expand a single heading by selecting only that heading and then clicking the Expand button.
7. **Click the Advertising and Promotion plus button ⊕ so only Advertising and Promotion and its associated subheadings and text are selected, click the Collapse button − in the Outline Tools group two times to collapse all the subheadings and text associated with each subheading, click the Personnel plus button ⊕, then click the Collapse button −**
8. **Click the Move Up button ^ in the Outline Tools group once, then click the Personnel plus button ⊕ three times**
   When you move a heading in Outline view, all subheadings and their associated text also move.
9. **Click the Show Level arrow, click Level 3, double-click the Printed Materials plus button ⊕, click the Counter Items plus button ⊕, press DELETE, then compare the revised outline to FIGURE 9-4**
10. **Click the Close Outline View button in the Close group, then save the document**

FIGURE 9-3: Headings demoted to Level 2

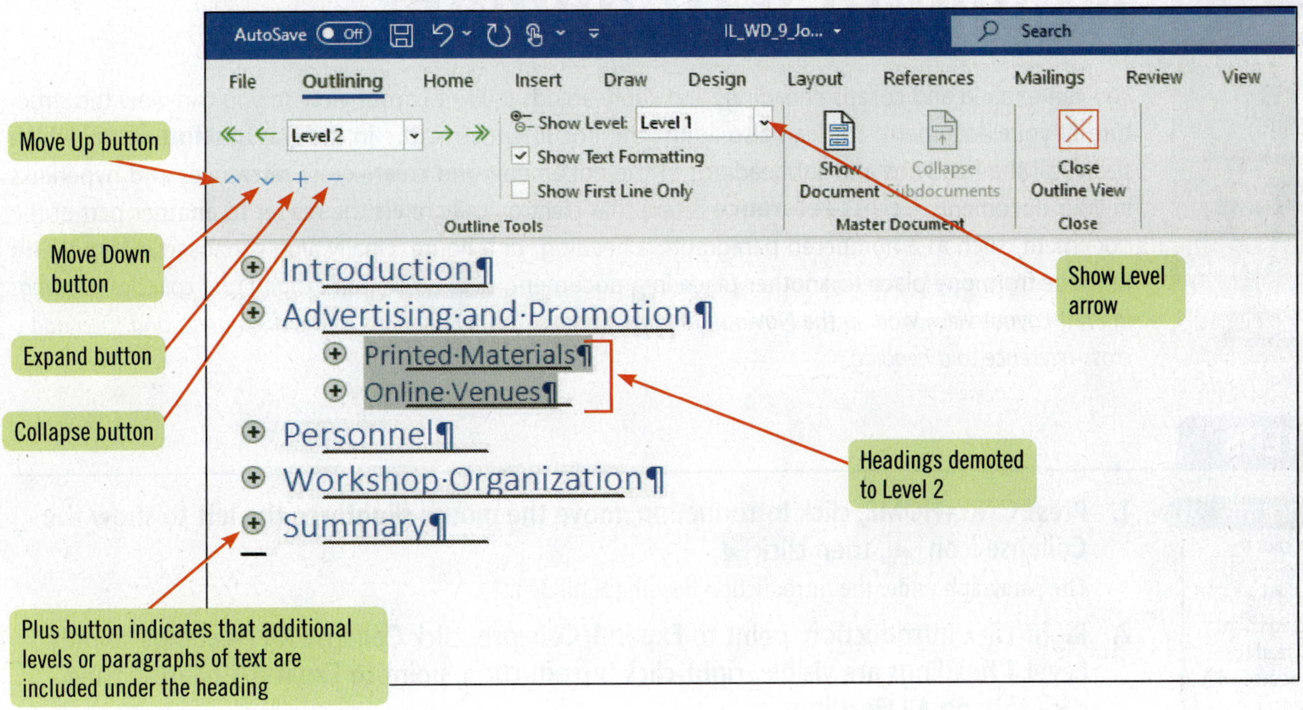

FIGURE 9-4: Revised outline

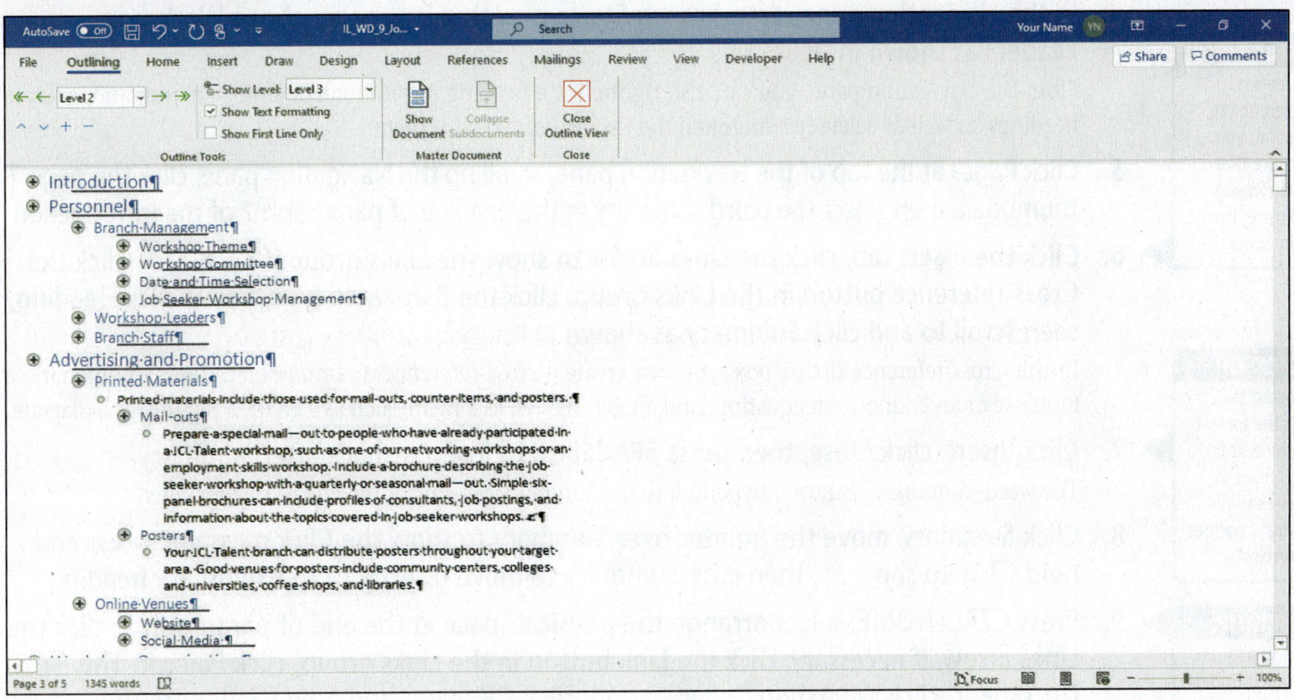

Word

Word Module 9

Navigate a Document

Learning Outcomes
- Collapse/expand headings
- Move headings in the Navigation pane
- Create a hyperlink and cross-reference

You can expand and collapse headings and subheadings in Print Layout view so you can view the structure of your document. You can also adjust the document structure in the **Navigation pane**, which shows all the headings and subheadings in the document, and create cross-references and hyperlinks in your document. A **cross-reference** is text that electronically refers the reader to another part of the document, such as a numbered paragraph, a heading, or a figure. Finally, you can insert a **hyperlink** to move from one place to another place in a document. **CASE** *You expand and collapse headings in Print Layout view, work in the Navigation pane to make further changes to the document, and then add a cross-reference to a heading.*

STEPS

QUICK TIP
You can click the Expand arrow ▷ to expand the heading again so you can read the text associated with that heading.

1. **Press CTRL+HOME, click Introduction, move the mouse slightly to the left to show the Collapse icon ◢, then click ◢**
   The paragraph under the Introduction heading is hidden.
2. **Right-click Introduction, point to Expand/Collapse, click Collapse All Headings so only Level 1 headings are visible, right-click Introduction, point to Expand/Collapse, then click Expand All Headings**
   All headings and their associated text are visible again.
3. **Click the View tab, click the Navigation Pane check box in the Show group, click Headings at the top of the Navigation pane if it is not already selected, then click Branch Staff in the Navigation pane**
   The Branch Staff subheading is selected in the Navigation pane, and the insertion point moves to the Branch Staff subheading in the document.
4. **In the Navigation pane, drag Branch Staff up so that it appears above Workshop Leaders as shown in FIGURE 9-5**
   From the Navigation pane, you can also right-click a heading to promote, demote, expand, and collapse headings, as well as delete headings and the text associated with them.

QUICK TIP
If you create a cross-reference to an equation, you must ensure that the equation was created using the Equation Editor.

5. **Click Pages at the top of the Navigation pane, scroll up the Navigation pane, click the page 1 thumbnail, then select the word summary in the first line of paragraph 2 of the Introduction**
6. **Click the Insert tab, click the Links arrow to show the Links group if necessary, click the Cross-reference button in the Links group, click the Reference type arrow, click Heading, then scroll to and click Summary as shown in FIGURE 9-6**
   In the Cross-reference dialog box, you can create a cross-reference to a numbered item, a bookmark, a footnote or an endnote, an equation, and a table, as well as a figure such as a chart, a picture, or a diagram.

QUICK TIP
The selected text takes on the formatting of the text it is being linked to, so in this example "summary" changes to "Summary".

7. **Click Insert, click Close, then press SPACEBAR to insert a space after Summary**
   The word "Summary" is now a hyperlink to the Summary heading at the end of the document.
8. **Click Summary, move the pointer over Summary to show the Click message, press and hold CTRL to show 👆, then click Summary to move directly to the Summary heading**

QUICK TIP
Text you specify as a hyperlink is underlined and shown in a different color.

9. **Press CTRL+HOME, select arrange the physical space at the end of paragraph 1, click the Links arrow, if necessary, click the Link button in the Links group, click Place in This Document, click Workshop Organization, click OK, press and hold CTRL, click the underlined text arrange the physical space, then save the document**
   The insertion point goes directly to the "Workshop Organization" heading in the document.

FIGURE 9-5: Changing the order of a subheading in the Navigation pane

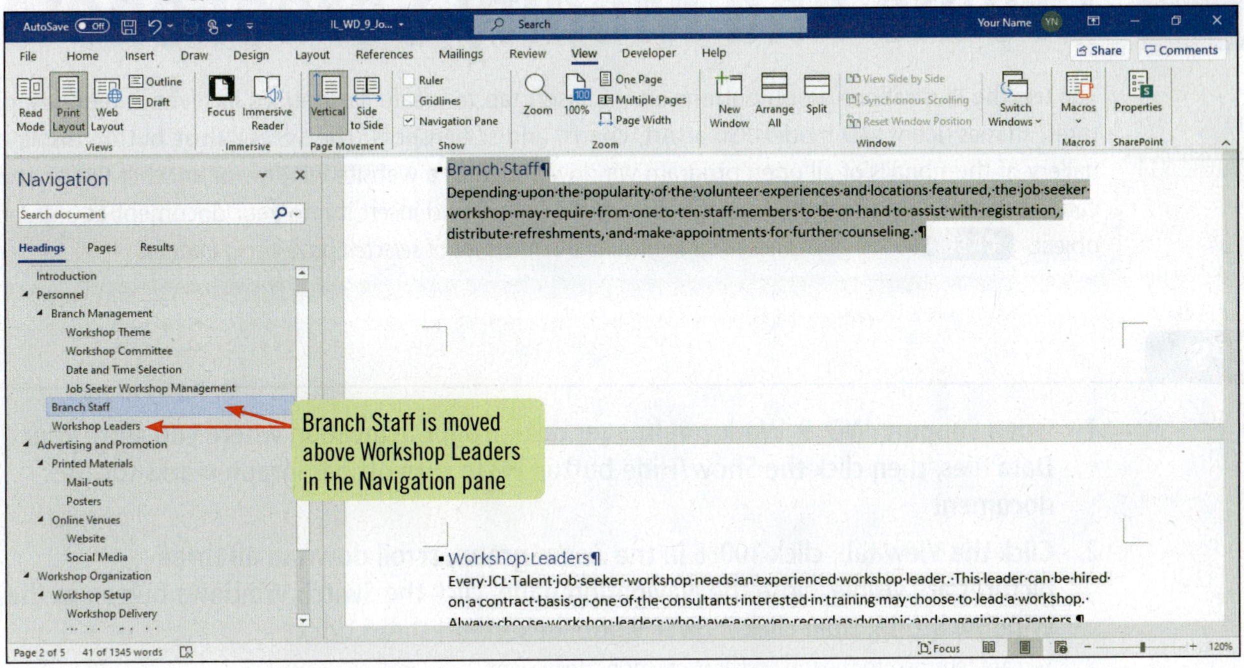

FIGURE 9-6: Cross-reference dialog box

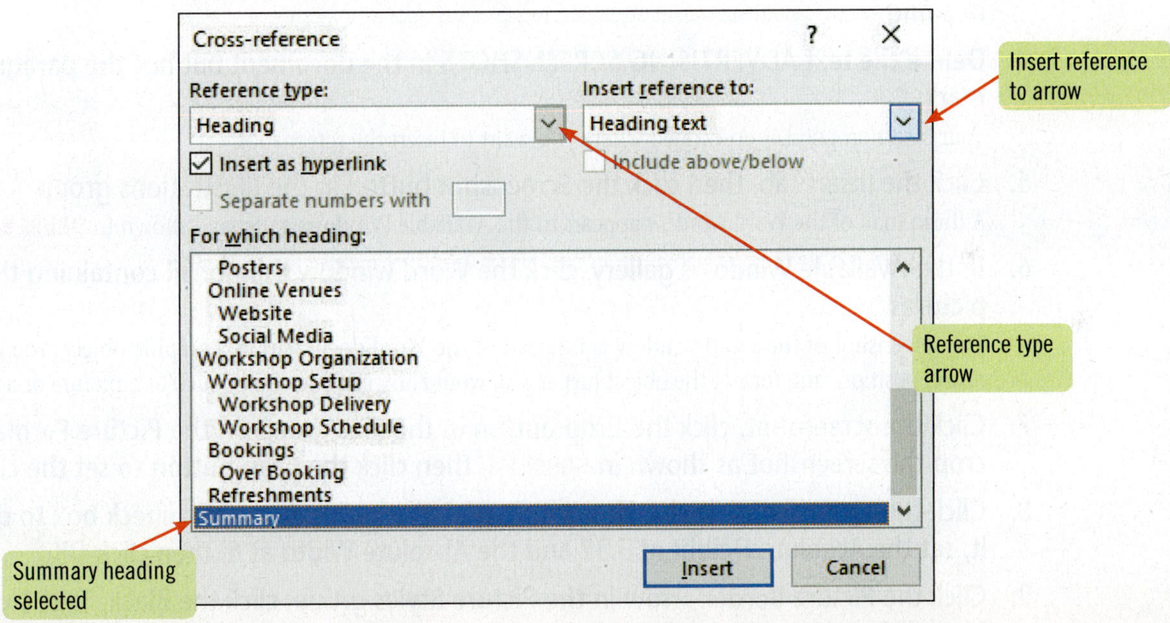

Using bookmarks

A **bookmark** identifies a location or a selection of text in a document. To create a bookmark, you first move the insertion point to the location in the text that you want to reference. This location can be a word, the beginning of a paragraph, or a heading. Click the Insert tab, then click the Bookmark button in the Links group to open the Bookmark dialog box. In this dialog box, you type a name (which cannot contain spaces) for the bookmark, then click Add. To find a bookmark, press CTRL+G to open the Find and Replace dialog box with the Go To tab active, click Bookmark in the Go to what box, click the Enter bookmark name arrow to see the list of bookmarks in the document, select the bookmark you want to go to, click Go To, then close the Find and Replace dialog box. To delete a bookmark you no longer need, click the Bookmark in the Links group, click the bookmark button you want to remove, then click Delete in the Bookmark dialog box. You can also create a hyperlink to a bookmark. Click the Insert tab, click the Link button in the Links group, click Place in This Document, click Bookmarks, click the bookmark you want the hyperlink to go to, then click OK.

Word
Module 9

Create and Modify Screenshots

Learning Outcome
- Insert a screenshot

You use the Illustrations group buttons on the Insert tab to create illustrations in seven categories: pictures, shapes, icons, 3D models, SmartArt, charts, and screenshots. The **Screenshot** button displays a gallery of thumbnails of all open program windows, such as a website window or another Office application window. You select the screenshot from the gallery and insert it into your document as a graphic object. **CASE** *The guidelines need to include a screenshot of selected advertising images.*

STEPS

1. **Open Support_WD_9_WorkshopImages.docx from the location where you store your Data files, then click the Show/Hide button ¶ to turn off paragraph marks for this document**
2. **Click the View tab, click 100% in the Zoom group, scroll down so all three pictures are visible, close the Navigation pane, click the Switch Windows button in the Window group, then click IL_WD_9_JobSeekerWorkshops.docx**
   You are returned to the Job Seeker Workshops document.
3. **Click Headings in the Navigation pane, then click the Advertising and Promotion heading**
4. **Delete the text ADVERTISING SCREENSHOTS in the document but not the paragraph mark**
   Your insertion point is positioned where you want to insert the screenshot.
5. **Click the Insert tab, then click the Screenshot button in the Illustrations group**
   A thumbnail of the Word window appears in the Available Windows gallery, as shown in FIGURE 9-7.
6. **In the Available Windows gallery, click the Word window thumbnail containing the pictures**
   The screenshot of the Word window is inserted in the Word document as a graphic object. You can crop, resize, position, and format the object just as you would any graphic object, such as a picture or a chart.
7. **Click the screenshot, click the Crop button in the Size group on the Picture Format tab, crop the screenshot as shown in FIGURE 9-8, then click the Crop button to set the crop**
8. **Click the Launcher in the Size group, click the Lock aspect ratio check box to deselect it, set the Absolute Height at 3.37 and the Absolute Width at 5, then click OK**
9. **Click the Picture Border arrow in the Picture Styles group, click the Black, Text 1 color box, click the Home tab, click the Center button in the Paragraph group, click away from the screenshot to deselect it, then continue to the next lesson to add a screen clipping**

FIGURE 9-7: Thumbnail of a window available for screenshot

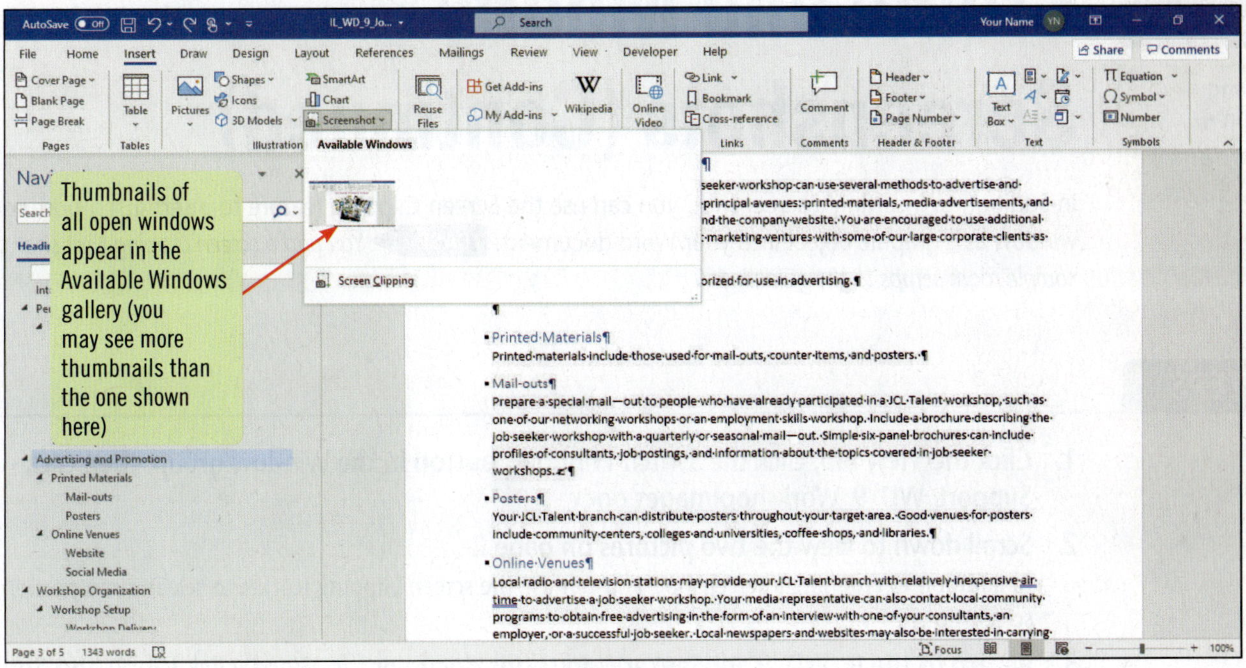

FIGURE 9-8: Screenshot cropped

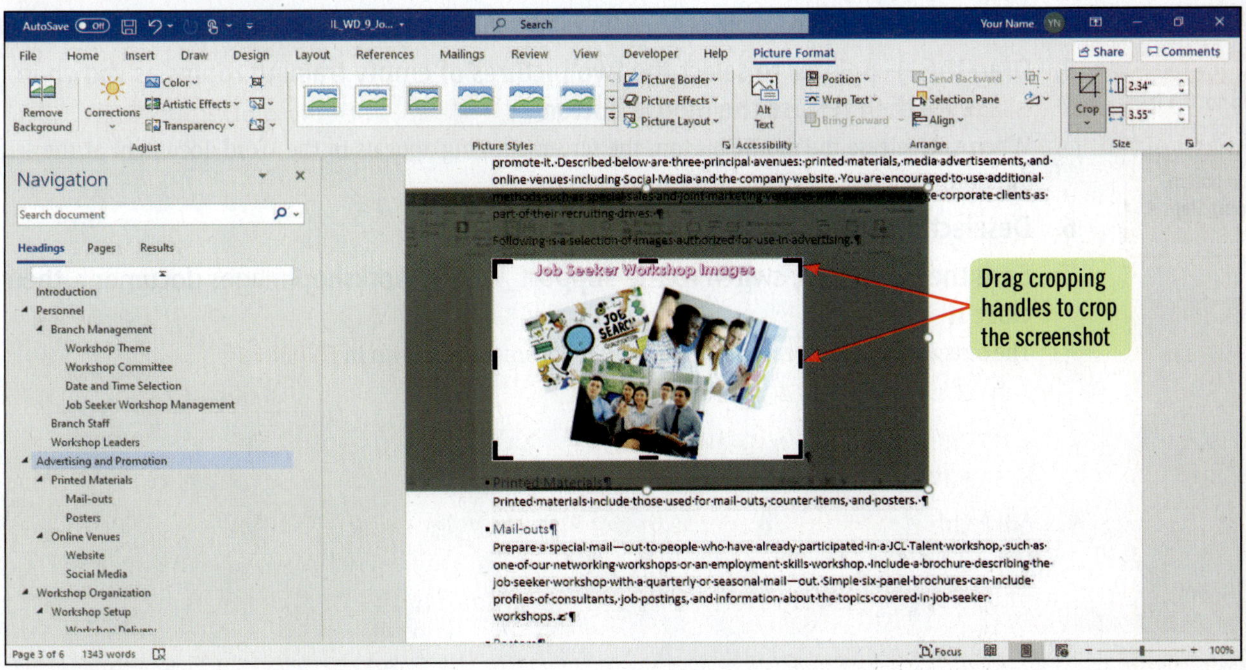

Word

tsyhun/Shutterstock.com; Rawpixel.com/Shutterstock.com; Dragon Images/Shutterstock.com

(Continued)

Word
Module 9

Learning Outcome
- Create a screen clipping

Create and Modify Screenshots (Continued)

In addition to inserting a screenshot, you can use the Screen Clipping feature to insert just a portion of a window as a graphic object into your Word document. **CASE** *You add a screen clipping that shows two sample room setups to the guidelines.*

STEPS

TROUBLE

If you do not like the appearance of the clipped screen, click the Undo button, then repeat Steps 4 and 5.

1. **Click the View tab, click the Switch Windows button in the Window group, then click Support_WD_9_WorkshopImages.docx**
2. **Scroll down to view the two pictures on page 2**

   In addition to cropping a screenshot, you can use the screen clipping feature to select just a portion of a screenshot.
3. **Return to the IL_WD_9_JobSeekerWorkshops document in Word, click Workshop Setup in the Navigation pane, then delete SETUP SCREENSHOT but not the paragraph mark**
4. **Click the Insert tab, click the Screenshot button in the Illustrations group, then click Screen Clipping**

   The Support_WD_9_WorkshopImages Word window fills the screen and is dimmed as shown in FIGURE 9-9.
5. **Drag the + pointer to select the two pictures of empty training rooms as shown in FIGURE 9-9, then release the mouse button**

   When you release the mouse button, the screen clipping appears in the Word document at the selected location.
6. **Deselect the image**
7. **Save the document, switch to the Support_WD_9_WorkshopImages document, then close it**

   The screen clipping appears in the guidelines document as shown in FIGURE 9-10.

FIGURE 9-9: Selecting a screen clipping

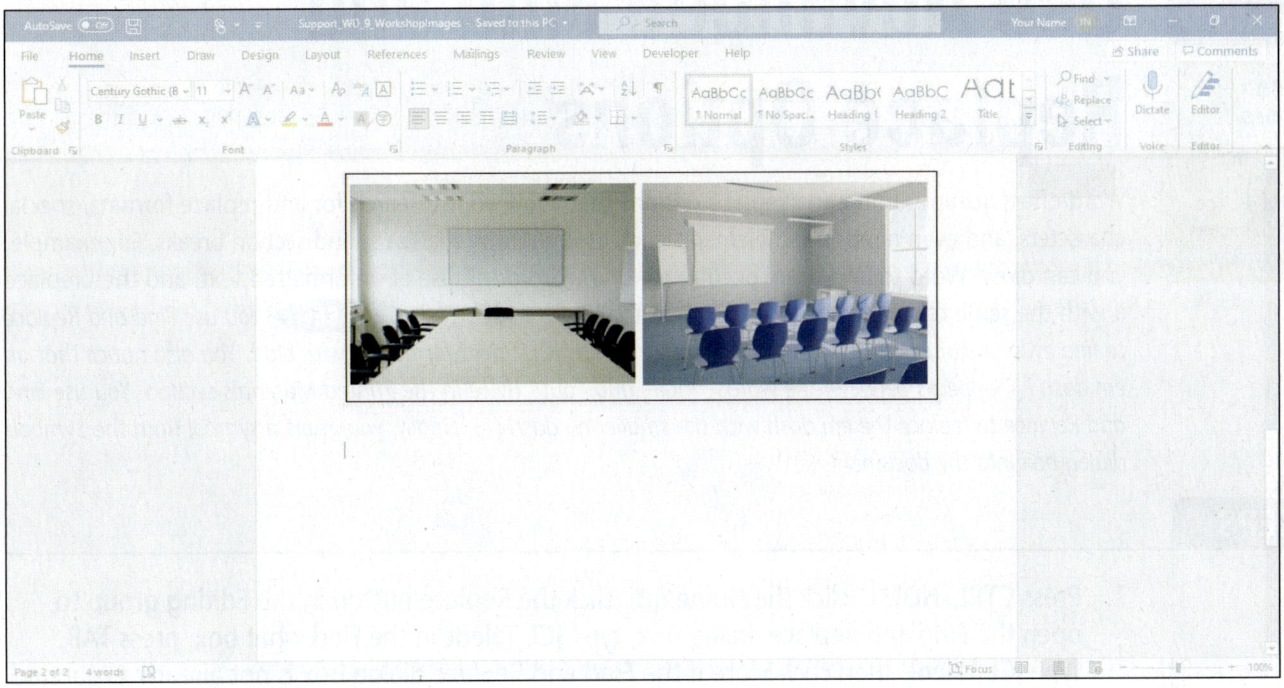

Robert Kneschke/Shutterstock.com

FIGURE 9-10: Screen clipping inserted in the document

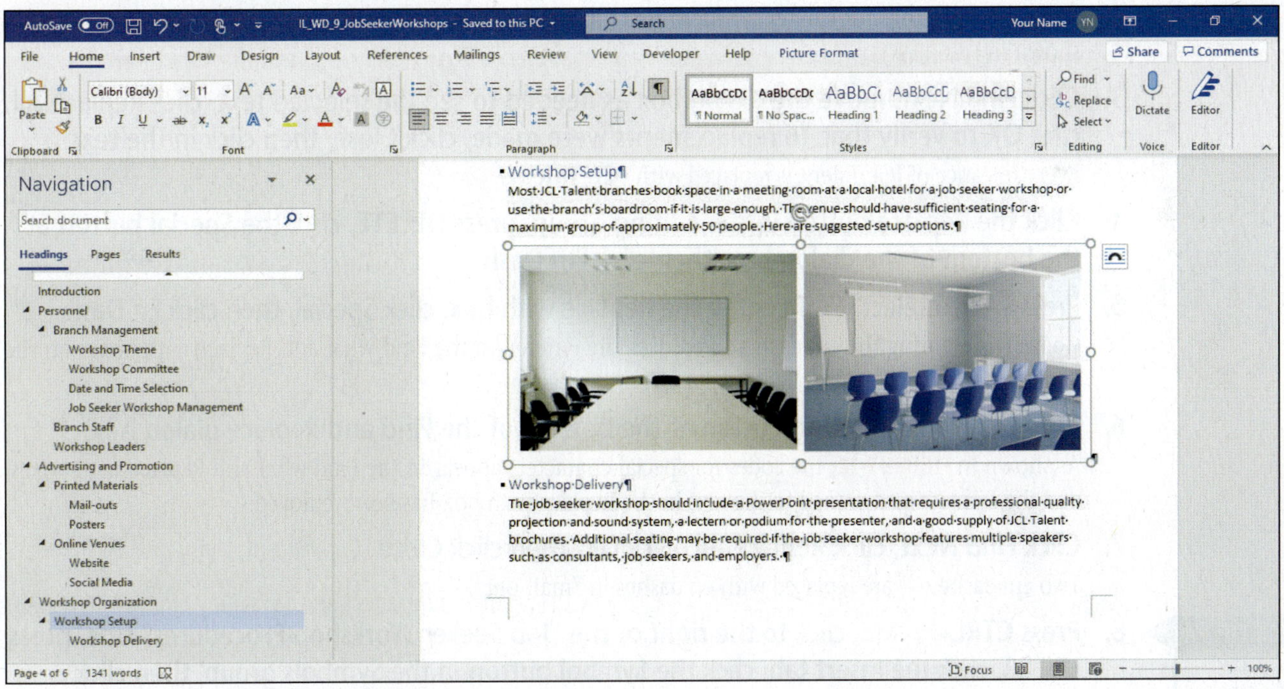

Robert Kneschke/Shutterstock.com

Word

Word
Module 9

Learning Outcomes
- Find and replace formatting
- Find and replace special characters
- Insert a symbol

Use Advanced Find and Replace Options

Word offers advanced find and replace options that allow you to search for and replace formats, special characters, and even nonprinting elements such as paragraph marks (¶) and section breaks. For example, you can direct Word to find every occurrence of a word or phrase of unformatted text, and then replace it with the same text formatted in a different font style and font size. **CASE** *You use Find and Replace to find every instance of JCL Talent, then replace it with JCL Talent formatted with bold. You also notice that an em dash (–) appears between the words "mail" and "out" twice in the Printed Materials section. You use Find and Replace to replace the em dash with the smaller en dash (–). Finally, you insert a symbol from the Symbols dialog box into the document.*

STEPS

1. **Press CTRL+HOME, click the Home tab, click the Replace button in the Editing group to open the Find and Replace dialog box, type JCL Talent in the Find what box, press TAB, type JCL Talent, then click More if the Find and Replace dialog box is not already expanded**
   The Find and Replace dialog box expands, and a selection of Search Options appears.
2. **Click the Format button at the bottom of the Find and Replace dialog box, click Font to open the Replace Font dialog box, click Bold in the Font style list, then click OK**
   The format settings for the replacement text "JCL Talent" appear in the Find and Replace dialog box, as shown in FIGURE 9-11.
3. **Click Find Next, move the dialog box as needed to see the selected text, click Replace All, click OK to verify that 16 replacements were made, click Close, then click in the text**
   Every instance of JCL Talent is replaced with **JCL Talent**.
4. **Click the Replace button in the Editing group, press DELETE, click the Special button at the bottom of the dialog box, then click Em Dash**
5. **Press TAB to select JCL Talent in the Replace with box, click Special, then click En Dash**
   Codes representing the em dash and en dash are entered in the Find what and Replace with boxes on the Replace tab in the Find and Replace dialog box.
6. **Click the No Formatting button at the bottom of the Find and Replace dialog box**
   As shown in FIGURE 9-12, the codes for special characters appear in the Find what and Replace with boxes, and the formatting assigned to the text in the Replace with box has been removed.
7. **Click Find Next, click Replace All, click OK, then click Close**
   Two em dashes (–) are replaced with en dashes in "mail-out".

QUICK TIP
Special characters are called symbols.

8. **Press CTRL+HOME, click to the right of the "Job Seeker Workshop Procedures" title, press ENTER, click the Insert tab, click the Symbol button in the Symbols group, then click More Symbols**
   In the Symbol dialog box, you can select from hundreds of symbols in numerous fonts. Some of the symbols are like small pictures.
9. **Click the Font arrow, scroll the alphabetical list of fonts to Wingdings, click Wingdings, click the happy face symbol shown in FIGURE 9-13, click Insert, click Insert two more times, click Close, then save the document**
   Three happy face symbols are inserted below the document title.

FIGURE 9-11: Find and Replace dialog box

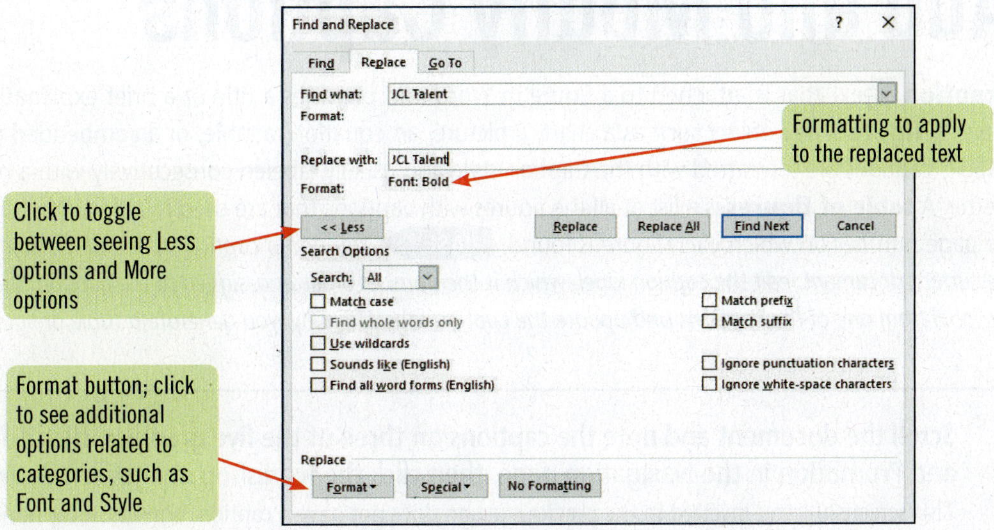

FIGURE 9-12: Find and Replace dialog box

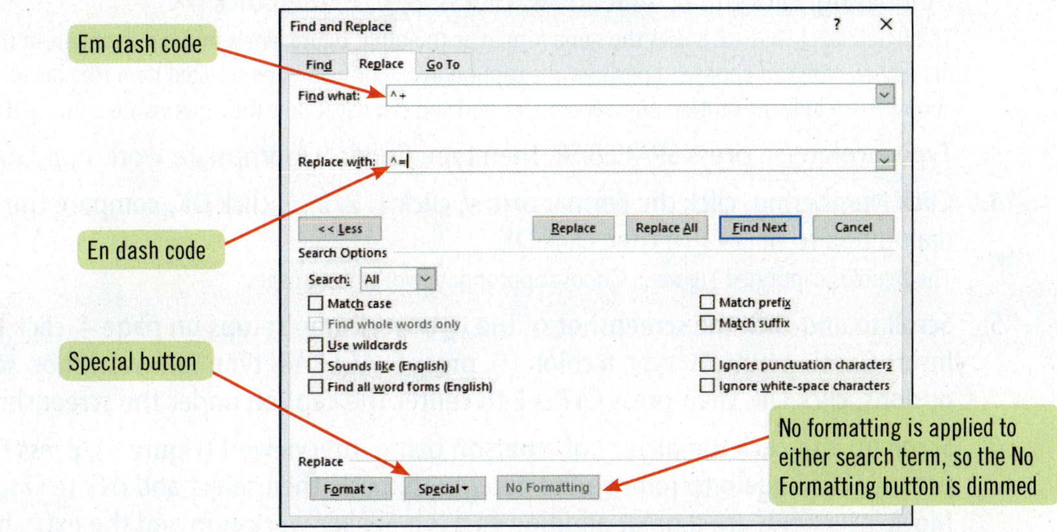

FIGURE 9-13: Symbol selected in the Symbol dialog box

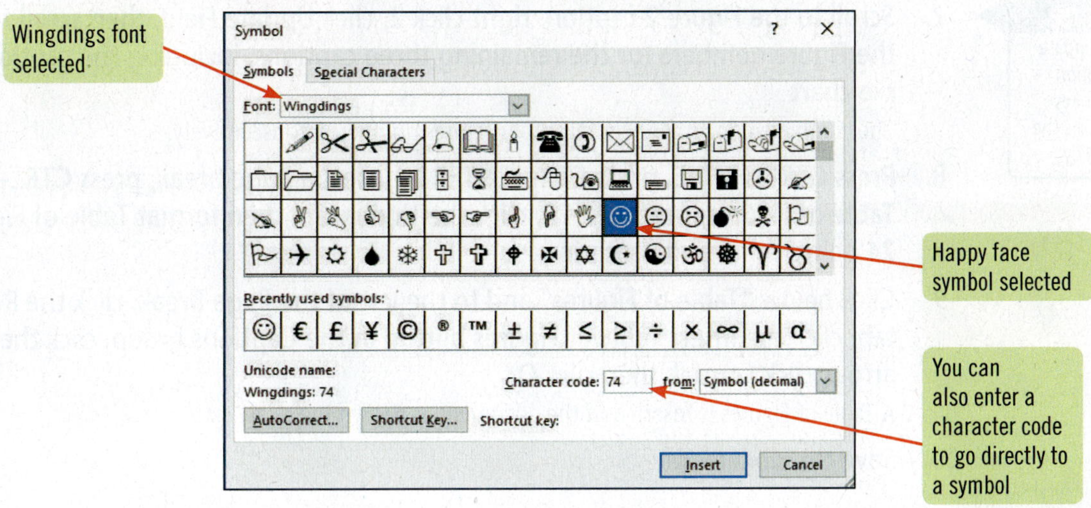

Add and Modify Captions

Learning Outcomes
- Insert and update captions
- Insert a table of figures

A **caption** is text that is attached to a figure in Word and provides a title or a brief explanation of the figure. A **figure** is any object such as a chart, a picture, an equation, a table, or an embedded object. By default, captions are formatted with the Caption style and usually labeled consecutively with a number or a letter. A **table of figures** is a list of all the figures with captions that are used in a document along with the page number on which each figure is found. **CASE** *You add a caption to one of the screenshots in the current document, edit the caption label, which is the number or letter assigned to the caption, then remove the label from one of the captions and update the caption labels. Finally, you generate a table of figures.*

STEPS

QUICK TIP
The figures are labeled using letters, FIGURE A, FIGURE B, and so on.

1. **Scroll the document and note the captions on three of the five graphics, click Advertising and Promotion in the Navigation pane, then click the workshop images screenshot**
   This screenshot you inserted in the previous lesson does not have a caption. You insert captions from the References tab.
2. **Click the References tab, click the Insert Caption button in the Captions group, click Numbering, click the Format arrow, click A, B, C,..., then click OK**
   The figure label FIGURE B uses the same format as the other figure labels in the document. In the Caption dialog box, you can choose to position the caption above or below the selected item (the default). You can choose to exclude the caption number or letter, and you can select how the captions are numbered or lettered.
3. **Type a colon (:), press SPACEBAR, then type Choose appropriate workshop images**
4. **Click Numbering, click the Format arrow, click 1, 2, 3,..., click OK, compare the Caption dialog box to FIGURE 9-14, then click OK**
   The figure is captioned Figure 2: Choose appropriate workshop images.
5. **Scroll to and click the screenshot of the two workshop setups on page 4, click the Insert Caption button, type a colon (:), press SPACEBAR, type Two workshop setup options, click OK, then press CTRL+E to center the caption under the screenshot**
6. **Scroll up and click the picture of a person being interviewed (Figure 1), press DELETE, press DELETE again to remove the paragraph mark, then select and delete Figure 1: Mock interviews are a great addition to a Job Seeker workshop and the extra blank line between the paragraphs**
   After you delete a caption, you need to update the numbering of the remaining captions.

QUICK TIP
Press F9 to update selected caption labels if your keyboard supports the F9 function key.

7. **Scroll to the Figure 2 caption, right click 2, click Update Field, then scroll to and update the Figure numbers for the remaining three captions, including the caption under the pie chart**
   The completed document contains four figures numbered consecutively.
8. **Press CTRL+HOME, press CTRL+ENTER to insert a page break, press CTRL+HOME, type Table of Figures, press ENTER, click the Home tab, then format Table of Figures using 24 point, bold, and centering**
9. **Click below "Table of Figures" and to the left of the Page Break, click the References tab, click the Insert Table of Figures button in the Captions group, click the Formats arrow, click Formal, then click OK**
   A Table of Figures is inserted in the document as shown in FIGURE 9-15.
10. **Save the document**

FIGURE 9-14: Caption dialog box

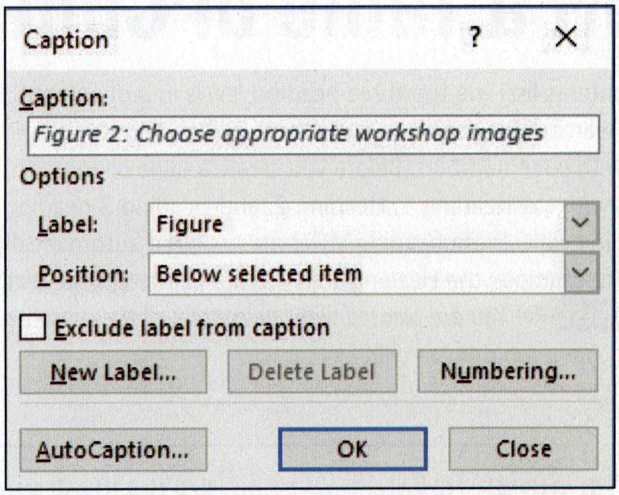

FIGURE 9-15: Table of figures

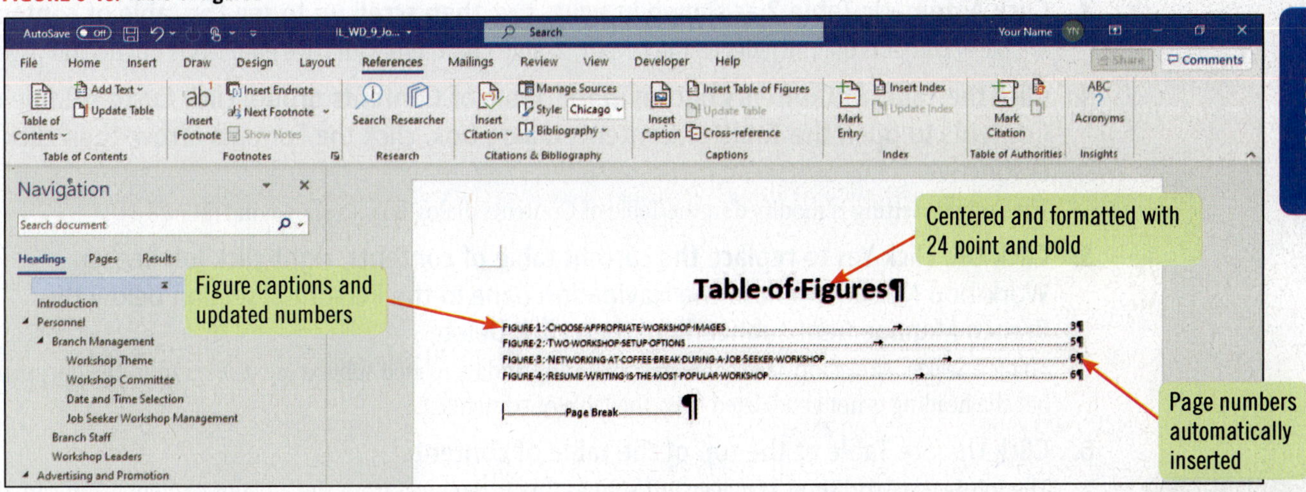

Table of Authorities

A table of authorities lists all the cases, statutes, rules, and other legal references included in a legal document, along with the page on which each reference appears. To create a table of authorities, click the References tab, go to the first reference (called a citation) that you wish to include in the table of authorities, then click the Mark Citation button in the Table of Authorities group. After you have marked all the citations in the document, click the Insert Table of Authorities button in the Table of Authorities group to build the table of authorities. Word organizes and then displays each citation you marked by category.

Insert a Table of Contents

Learning Outcomes
- Insert a table of contents
- Update a table of contents

A table of contents lists the top three heading levels in a document. When you generate a table of contents, Word searches for headings, sorts them by heading levels, and then displays the completed table of contents with page numbers. Before you create a table of contents, you must format the headings and subheadings with the Heading 1, Heading 2, and Heading 3 heading styles. When you organize a document in Outline view, these heading styles are assigned automatically to text based on the outline level of the text. For example, the Heading 1 style is applied to Level 1 text, the Heading 2 style to level 2 text, and so on. **CASE** *You are pleased with the content of the document and are now ready to create a new page that includes a table of contents.*

STEPS

1. **Press CTRL+HOME, click the Insert tab, click the Blank Page button in the Pages group, press CTRL+HOME, click the Home tab, then click the Clear All Formatting button in the Font group**
   The insertion point is positioned at the left margin where the table of contents will begin.
2. **Click the References tab, then click the Table of Contents button in the Table of Contents group**
   A gallery of predefined styles for a table of contents opens.
3. **Click Automatic Table 2 as shown in FIGURE 9-16, then scroll up to see the table of contents**
   A table of contents that includes all the Level 1, 2, and 3 headings with page numbers is inserted on page 1.
4. **Click the Table of Contents button in the Table of Contents group, click Custom Table of Contents to open the Table of Contents dialog box, click the Formats arrow, then click Distinctive**
   The Formats setting is modified in the Table of Contents dialog box, as shown in FIGURE 9-17.
5. **Click OK, click Yes to replace the current table of contents, right-click Job Seeker Workshop Management in the Navigation pane in the Personnel section below the Branch Management subheading, then click Delete**
   The Job Seeker Workshop Management subheading and its related subtext are deleted from the document, but the heading is not yet deleted from the table of contents.
6. **Click Update Table at the top of the table of contents**
   The Job Seeker Workshop Management subheading is removed from the table of contents. You can also change the appearance of the table of contents.
7. **Click the Table of Contents button in the Table of Contents group, click Custom Table of Contents, click the Tab leader arrow, click the dotted line tab leader style (top selection), click OK, click Yes, then scroll up to view "Table of Contents"**
   The Table of Contents is updated as shown in FIGURE 9-18.
8. **Move the pointer over the heading Online Venues in the Table of Contents, press and hold CTRL, then click Online Venues**
   The insertion point moves to the Online Venues heading in the document.
9. **Save the document**

QUICK TIP
To remove a table of contents, click the table of contents in the document, click the References tab, click the Table of Contents button in the Table of Contents group, then click Remove Table of Contents.

FIGURE 9-16: Inserting an automatic table of contents

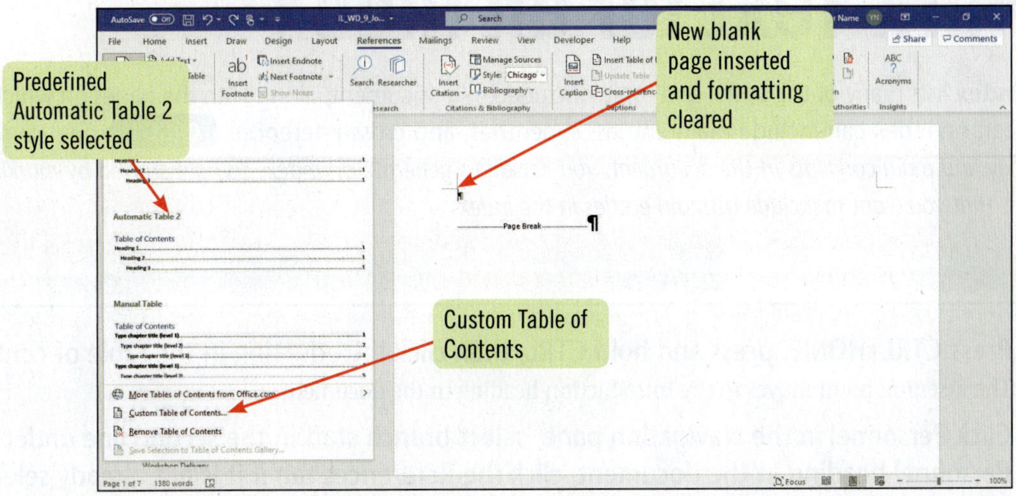

FIGURE 9-17: Table of Contents dialog box

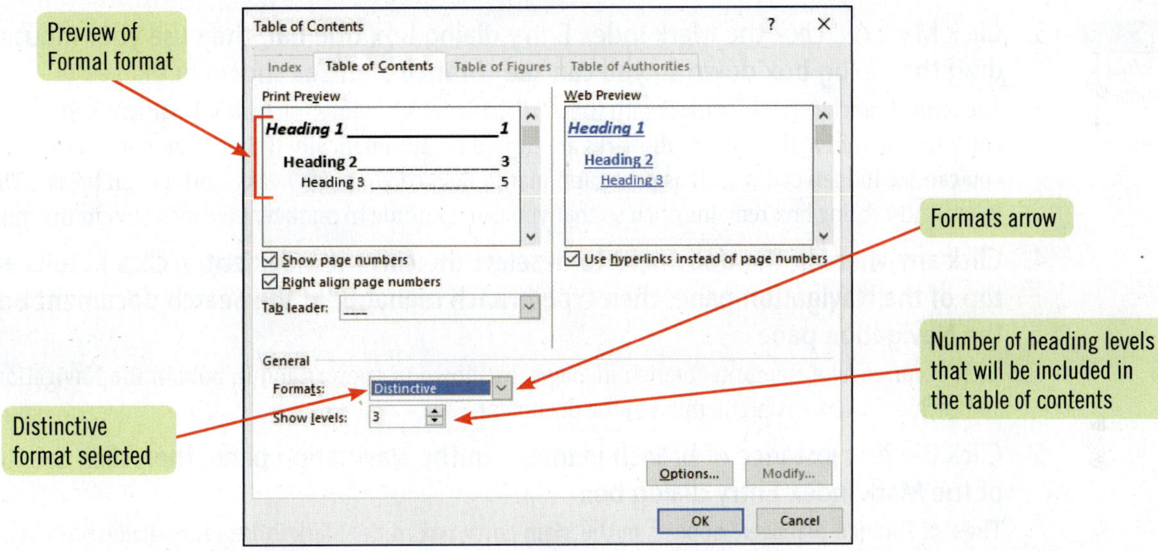

FIGURE 9-18: Formatted and updated table of contents

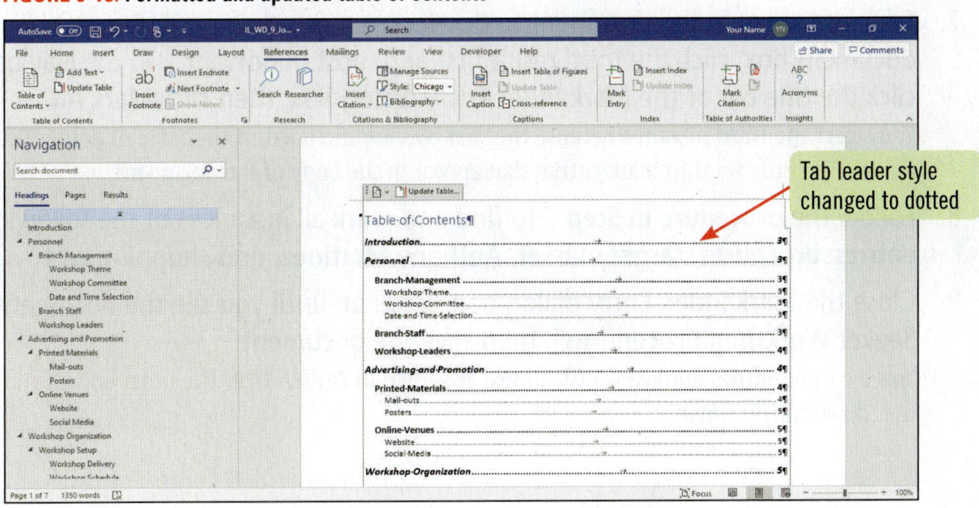

Word
Module 9

Mark Text for an Index

Learning Outcomes
- Mark index entries
- Search for text to index

An **index** lists many of the terms and topics included in a document, along with the pages on which they appear. An index can include main entries, subentries, and cross-references. CASE *To help readers quickly find main concepts in the document, you decide to generate an index. You get started by marking the terms that you want to include as main entries in the index.*

STEPS

1. **Press CTRL+HOME, press and hold CTRL, then click Introduction in the table of contents**
   The insertion point moves to the Introduction heading in the document.
2. **Click Personnel in the Navigation pane, select branch staff in the second line under the Personnel heading in the document, click the References tab if it is not already selected, then click the Mark Entry button in the Index group**
   The Mark Index Entry dialog box opens. By default, the selected text is entered in the Main entry box and is treated as a main entry in the index.
3. **Click Mark All, click the Mark Index Entry dialog box title bar, then use your mouse to drag the dialog box down so you can see "branch staff" as shown in FIGURE 9-19**
   The term "branch staff" is marked with the XE field code. **XE** stands for **Index Entry**. When you mark an entry for the index, the paragraph marks are turned on automatically if they were not already on so that you can see hidden codes such as paragraph marks, field codes, page breaks, and section breaks. The Mark Index Entry dialog box remains open so that you can continue to mark text for inclusion in the index.

   QUICK TIP
   Hidden codes do not appear in the printed document.
4. **Click anywhere in the document to deselect the current index entry, click Results at the top of the Navigation pane, then type branch manager in the Search document box in the Navigation pane**
   Each occurrence of the term "branch manager" is shown in context and in bold in the Navigation pane, and each occurrence is highlighted in the document.
5. **Click the first instance of branch manager in the Navigation pane, then click the title bar of the Mark Index Entry dialog box**
   The text "branch manager" appears in the Main entry box in the Mark Index Entry dialog box.
6. **Click Mark All**
   All instances of "branch manager" in the document are marked for inclusion in the index.
7. **Click anywhere in the document to deselect "branch manager", type theme in the Search document box, click the third result first and most important... in the Navigation pane, click the title bar of the Mark Index Entry dialog box, then click Mark All**
   You select the third instance because the first two are included in the table of contents and the table of figures. You only want to mark entries that appear in the body of the document.
8. **Follow the procedure in Step 7 to find and mark all instances of the following main entries: brochures, target market, Anthony Martinez, and shopping cart**

   QUICK TIP
   Make sure you click in the document to deselect the currently selected text before you enter another search term.
9. **Close the Mark Index Entry dialog box, scroll up until you see the document title "Job Seeker Workshop Procedures", then save the document**
   You see three entries marked for the index, as shown in FIGURE 9-20. The other entries you marked are further down the document.

FIGURE 9-19: Selected text in the Mark Index Entry dialog box

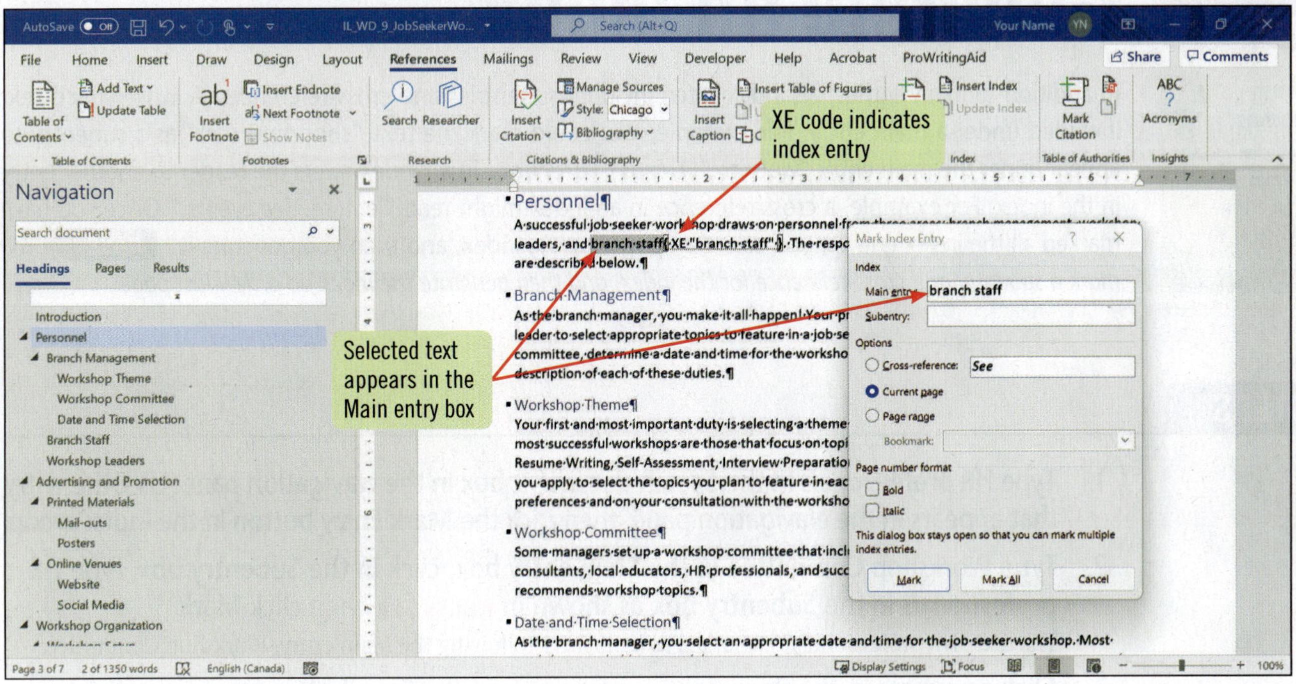

FIGURE 9-20: Index entries on the first page of the document

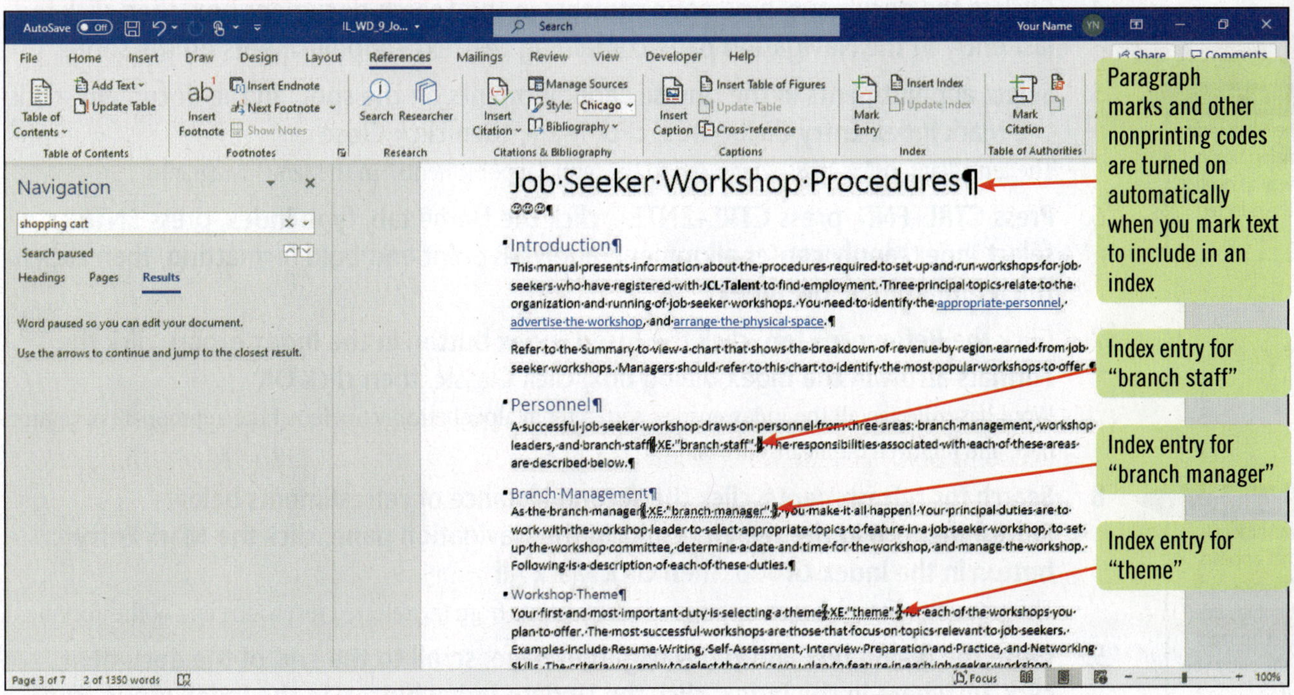

Word
Module 9

Generate an Index

Learning Outcomes
- Mark index subentries
- Insert a cross-reference in an index
- Generate an index

In addition to main entries, an index often includes subentries and cross-references. A **subentry** is text included under a main entry. For example, you could mark the text "shopping cart" as a subentry to appear under the main entry "website." A **cross-reference** in an index refers the reader to another entry in the index. For example, a cross-reference in an index might read "lecture. *See* events." Once you have marked all the index entries, you select a design for the index, and then you generate it. **CASE** *You mark a subentry and cross-reference for the index, and then generate the index on a new last page.*

STEPS

1. **Type HR professionals in the Search document box in the Navigation pane, click the entry that appears in the Navigation pane, then click the Mark Entry button in the Index group**
2. **Type Workshop Committee in the Main entry box, click in the Subentry box, type HR professionals in the Subentry box as shown in FIGURE 9-21, then click Mark**
   The text "HR professionals" is marked as a subentry following the Main entry, Workshop Committee.
3. **Click anywhere in the document, type laptops in the Search document box, click the Cross-reference option button in the Mark Index Entry dialog box, click after See, type appointments as shown in FIGURE 9-22, then click Mark**
   You also need to mark "appointments" so the Index lists the page number for "appointments."
4. **Click in the document, type appointments in the Search document box, then click the last entry in the Navigation pane containing the text "appointments on the spot"**
5. **Select appointments in the phrase "appointments on the spot" in the document, click the Mark Index Entry dialog box, click Mark, then click Close**
   The term "laptops" is cross-referenced to the term "appointments" in the same paragraph.
6. **Press CTRL+END, press CTRL+ENTER, click the Home tab, type Index, press ENTER, select Index, apply center alignment, apply 18 point and bold formatting, then click at the left margin below Index**
7. **Click the References tab, click the Insert Index button in the Index group, click the Formats arrow in the Index dialog box, click Classic, then click OK**
   Word has collected all the index entries, sorted them alphabetically, included the appropriate page numbers, and removed duplicate entries.
8. **Search for refreshments, click the second instance of refreshments below Refreshments 6 in the search results in the Navigation pane, click the Mark Entry button in the Index Group, then click Mark All**
   The index now includes each instance of refreshments from the selected text to the end of the document.
9. **Close the dialog box and the Navigation pane, scroll to the end of the document, click anywhere in the index, click the Update Index button in the Index group, click the Insert Index button in the Index group, click the Formats arrow, scroll to and click Formal, click OK, click OK to replace the index, then compare the index to FIGURE 9-23**
10. **sam Save and close the document**

QUICK TIP
Drag the Mark Index Entry dialog box out of the way as needed to see the selected phrase.

QUICK TIP
The refreshments entry that appears in the table of contents is not included because it appears before the entry you selected.

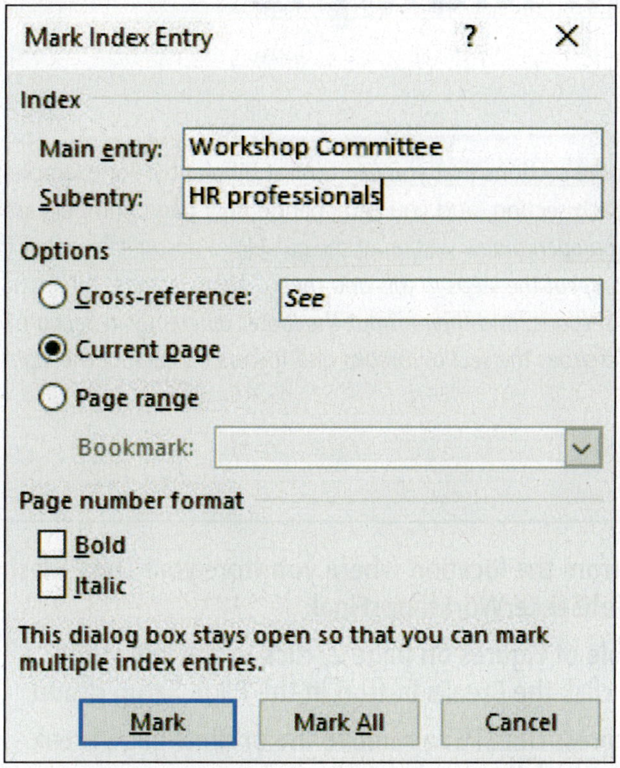

FIGURE 9-21: Subentry in the Mark Index entry dialog box

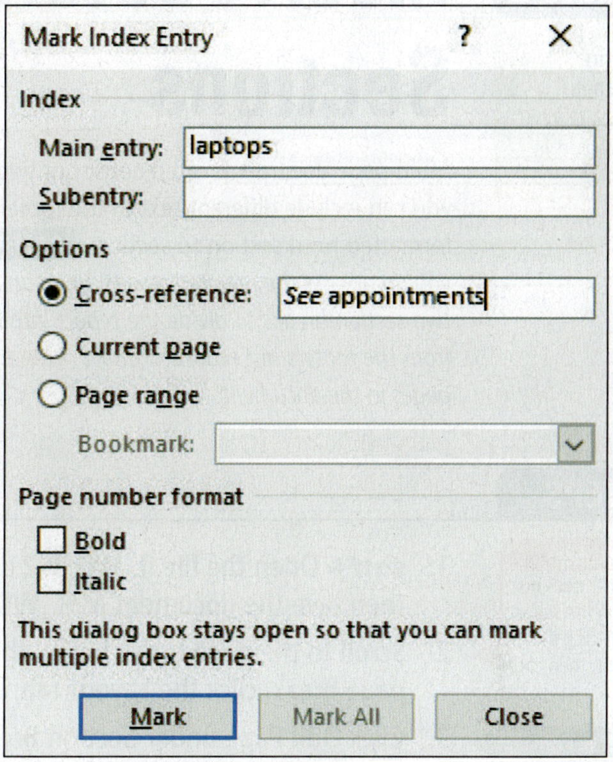

FIGURE 9-22: Cross-reference in the Mark Index entry dialog box

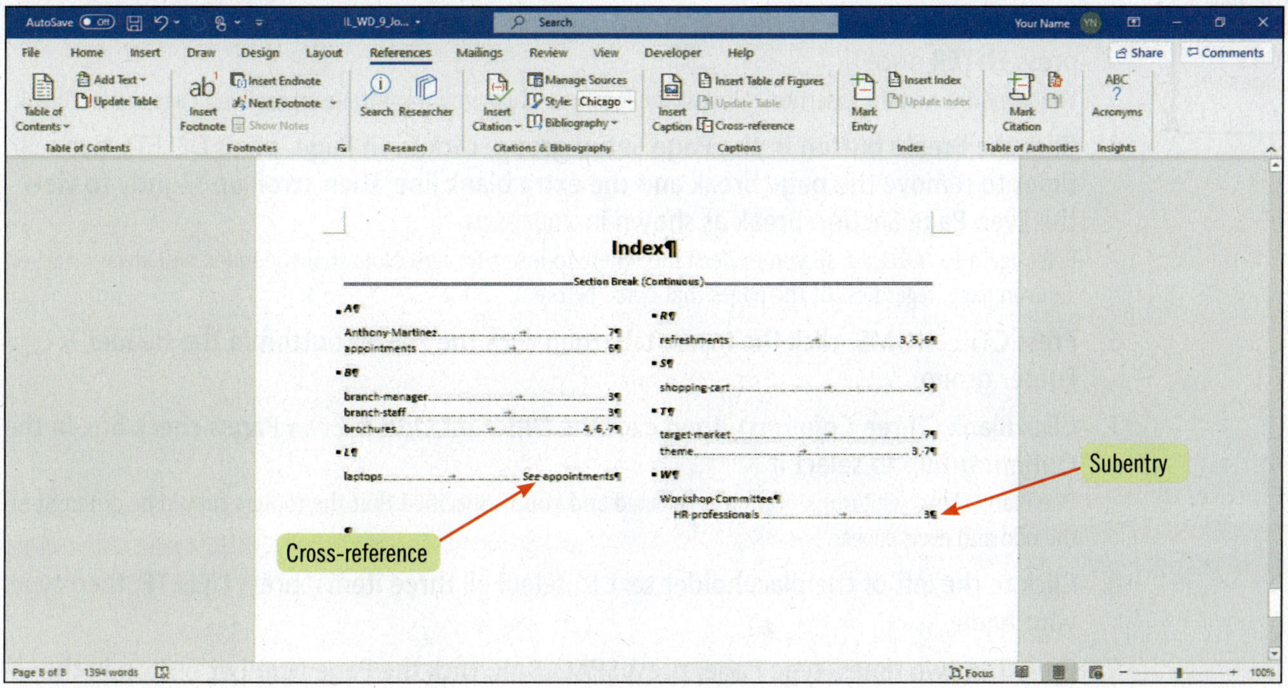

FIGURE 9-23: Completed index

Word
Module 9

Insert Footers in Multiple Sections

Learning Outcomes
- Insert sections
- Insert footers in sections

Multi-page documents often consist of two or more sections that you can format differently. For example, you can include different text in the footer for each section, and you can change how page numbers are formatted from section to section. **CASE** *You open a new version of the guidelines document so that if you do not get the required results, you can easily repeat the steps in this and the following lessons. You insert two section breaks to divide the report into three sections, and then format the footer differently in Section 1 from the footers in Sections 2 and 3.* **TABLE 9-2** *describes the section breaks and footers on each of the eight pages in the document.*

STEPS

TROUBLE

If Section 1 does not appear on the status bar, right-click the **status bar**, then click **Section**.

QUICK TIP

If Section 1 contained 3 pages, Word would insert a blank page and start the Introduction in Section 2 on the fifth page of the document because that is the first odd page after Section 1.

1. **sam Open the file IL_WD_9-2.docx from the location where you store your Data Files, then save the document as IL_WD_9_JobSeekerWorkshopsFinal**
2. **Scroll to the page break below the Table of Figures on page 2, click to the left of the page break, click the Layout tab, then click the Breaks button in the Page Setup group**
3. **Click Odd Page under Section Breaks, press DELETE to remove the original page break, then press DELETE to remove the extra blank line**

   By inserting an Odd Page section break, you guarantee that page 1 of the document always starts on an odd number, regardless of what page comes before it. Section 1 contains the Table of Contents and the Table of Figures and Section 2 contains the body of the document and the index.
4. **Scroll to page 7, click to the left of the page break on page 7 (below the pie chart), then press ENTER once**

   You've positioned the insertion point at the location where you want to insert an Even Page section break.
5. **Click the Breaks button in the Page Setup group, click Even Page, press DELETE two times to remove the page break and the extra blank line, then scroll up slightly to view the Even Page Section Break as shown in FIGURE 9-24**

   Refer again to TABLE 9-2 so you understand where to insert footers. Note that the index will always start on an even page, regardless of the pages that come before it.
6. **Press CTRL+HOME, click the Insert tab, then click the Footer button in the Header & Footer group**
7. **Click Blank (Three Columns), then click the Different Odd & Even Pages check box in the Options group to select it**

   The Blank (Three Columns) format is selected and you've specified that the footers should be different on the odd and even pages.
8. **Click to the left of the placeholder text to select all three items, press DELETE, then type your name**
9. **Press TAB two times, type Page, press SPACEBAR, click the Page Number button in the Header & Footer group, point to Current Position, click Plain Number, then continue to the next lesson to finish inserting footers**

   The Odd Page Footer for the entire document contains your name at the left margin and the page number at the right margin.

FIGURE 9-24: Even page section break on page 7

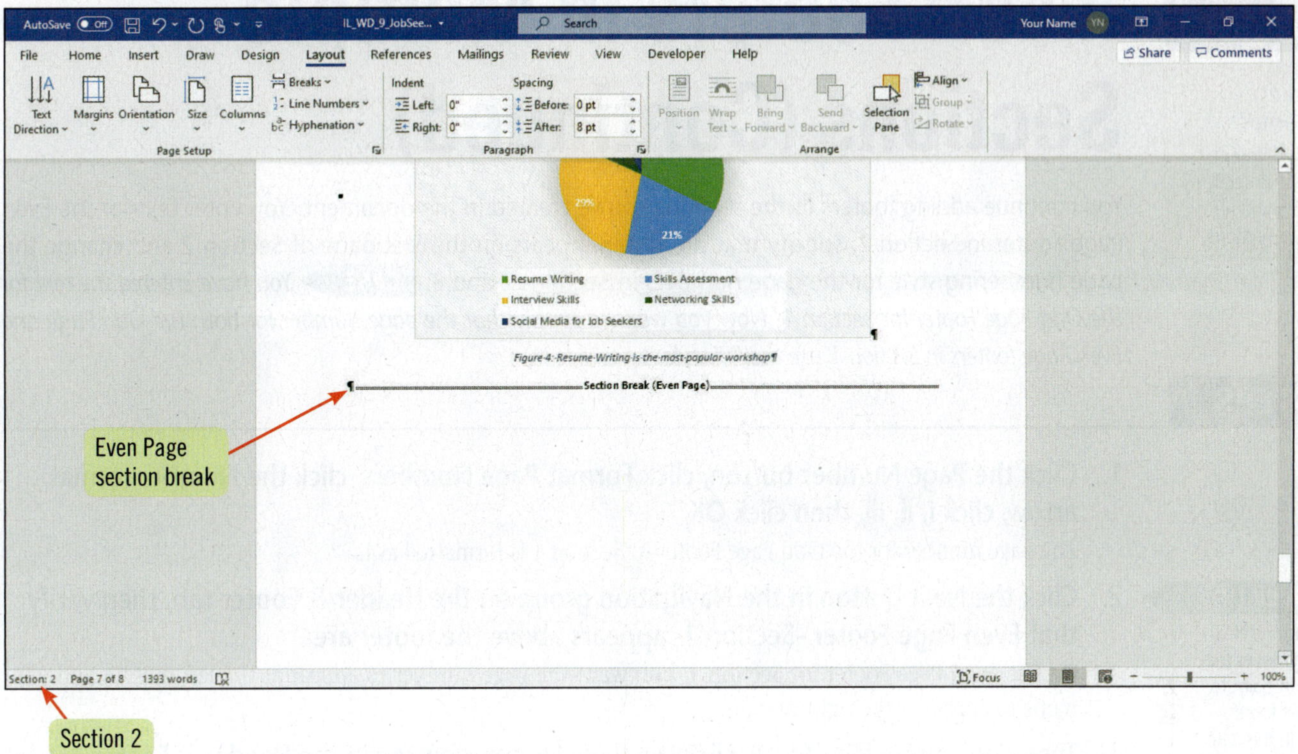

TABLE 9-2: Description of document sections and footers

Section	Page	Footer
Section 1	Table of Contents – page i	Odd page footer with Your Name at the left margin and the "i" style page number at the right margin
Section 1	Table of Figures – Page ii	Even page footer with the "i" style page number at the left margin and Your Name at the right margin
Section 2 – Must start on an Odd Page	First page of the document ("Introduction")	No footer: specified that the first page footer for Section 2 is different from the other footers
Section 2	Second page of the document	Even page footer with the "1" style page number at the left margin and Your Name at the right margin
Section 2	Third page of the document	Odd page footer with Your Name at the left margin and the "1" style page number at the right margin
Section 2	Fourth page of the document	Even page footer
Section 2	Fifth page of the document	Odd page footer
Section 3 – Must start on an even page	Sixth page of the document	Even page footer

(Continued)

Word
Module 9

Learning Outcomes
- Insert different footers in sections
- Insert page numbers in sections

Insert Footers in Multiple Sections (Continued)

You continue adding footers to the sections you've created in the document. You enter text for the Even Page Footer in Section 2, specify that no footer appears on the first page of Section 2 and change the page numbering style for the page numbers in Sections 2 and 3. **CASE** *You have entered the text for the Odd Page Footer for Section 1. Now you want to specify that the page number for both the Odd Page and Even Page footers in Section 1 use the "i" style.*

STEPS

QUICK TIP

Clicking the Next button moves the insertion point to the next footer, which in this case is the even page footer for Section 1 as indicated by the section number in the status bar and on the Footer tab.

1. **Click the Page Number button, click Format Page Numbers, click the Number format arrow, click i, ii, iii, then click OK**
   The page number for the Odd Page Footer in Section 1 is formatted as i.
2. **Click the Next button in the Navigation group on the Header & Footer tab, then verify that Even Page Footer -Section 1- appears above the footer area**
   On the Even Page Footer for Section 1, you want the page number to appear at the left margin and your name to appear at the right margin.
3. **Type Page, press SPACEBAR, click the Page Number button in the Header & Footer group, point to Current Position, click Plain Number, press TAB two times, then type your name**
4. **Click the Next button in the Navigation group to go to the Odd Page Footer for Section 2, then click the Different First Page check box in the Options group to select it**
5. **Click the Link to Previous button in the Navigation group to deselect it**
   The Link to Previous button is deselected when it is no longer shaded gray. Deselecting the Link to Previous button is a crucial step when you want to make sure that the contents of the current footer (in this case, no text) is different from the contents in the previous footer, which includes your name and a page number.
6. **Click the Page Number button in the Header & Footer group, click Format Page Numbers, click the Start At option button, verify that 1 appears, then click OK**
7. **Click the Next button in the Navigation group, verify that Page 2 appears at the left margin and your name at the right margin as shown in FIGURE 9-25, click the Next button, verify that your name appears at the left margin and Page 3 appears at the right margin, then click the Next button to go to Section 3, which is Page 6 (the Index page)**
   You do not need to deselect Link to Previous for the Even Page Footer for Section 3 because you want it to display the page number and your name the same way as for the other pages of the document.
8. **Click the Close Header and Footer button, verify you are returned to page i, the Table of Contents page, then save the document**

FIGURE 9-25: Even Page footer in Section 2

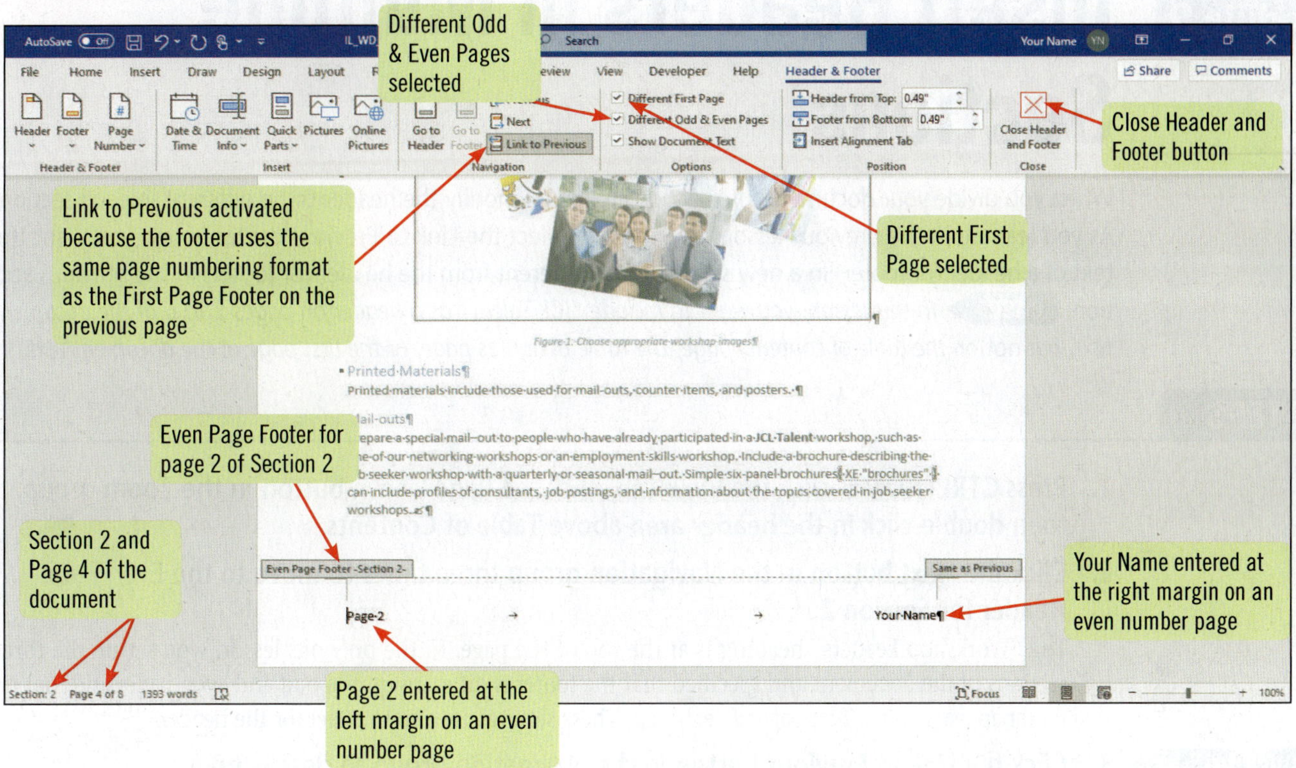

Using text flow options

You adjust text flow options to control how text in a multi-page document breaks across pages. To change text flow options, you use the Paragraph dialog box. To open the Paragraph dialog box, click the Launcher in the Paragraph group on the Home tab, and then select the Line and Page Breaks tab. In the Pagination section, you can choose to select or deselect four text flow options. For example, you select the Widow/Orphan control option to prevent the last line of a paragraph from printing at the top of a page (a widow) or the first line of a paragraph from printing at the bottom of a page (an orphan). By default, Widow/Orphan control is active. You can also select the Keep lines together check box to keep a paragraph from breaking across two pages.

Word
Module 9

Learning Outcome
- Insert headers in sections

Insert Headers in Multiple Sections

When you divide your document into sections, you can modify the header to be different in each section. As you learned in the previous lesson, you must deselect the Link to Previous button when you want the text of a header (or footer) in a new section to be different from the header (or footer) in the previous section. **CASE** *In this lesson, you want to include "JCL Talent" as a header on pages 2 to 6 of the document text, but* not *on the table of contents page, the table of figures page, or the first page of the document text.*

STEPS

1. **Press CTRL+HOME, click the View tab, click the Page Width button in the Zoom group, then double-click in the header area above Table of Contents**
2. **Click the Next button in the Navigation group three times to move to the Even Page Header for Section 2**
   The "Workshop Leaders" heading is at the top of the page. In the previous lesson, you set up the three sections of the document and specified that the footer is different on the odd and even pages and that no footer appears on the first page of Section 2. These settings are also in effect for the header.
3. **Click the Link to Previous button in the Navigation group to deselect it**
   You deselect the Link to Previous button because you don't want the header text to appear on the even page header in Section 1 of the document.
4. **Type JCL Talent, select the text JCL Talent including the paragraph mark, click the Home tab, increase the font size to 14 point, apply bold, then center the text as shown in FIGURE 9-26**
5. **Click the Copy button in the Clipboard group**
6. **Click the Header & Footer tab, then click the Next button in the Navigation group**
   The insertion point moves to the left margin of the Odd Page Header for Section 2.
7. **Click the Link to Previous button to deselect it so the header doesn't appear on page i of Section 1 (the Table of Contents page), press CTRL+V to paste the text, click the Close Header and Footer button in the Close group, press CTRL+HOME, then scroll through the document to verify the headers and footers are inserted correctly**
   No header text appears on the Table of Contents and Table of Figures pages in Section 1. No header and no footer appear on the first page of Section 2 (the first page of the document text). The text ("JCL Talent") appears in both the odd and even headers for Sections 2 and 3. The status bar displays the total number of pages in the document. The page numbers reflect the pagination you specified in the footers.
8. **Press CTRL+HOME, change the Zoom to 100%, update the entire table of contents, compare the updated table of contents to FIGURE 9-27, save the document, then continue to the next lesson to adjust the page layout**

QUICK TIP
You *must* click the Link to Previous button *before* you add text to a header when you don't want the text to appear in the header in the previous section.

TROUBLE
If the headers and footers do not appear as described, close the document, then return to the lesson "Inserting Footers in Multiple Sections" and repeat the steps.

FIGURE 9-26: Header text entered on the Even Page Header for Section 2

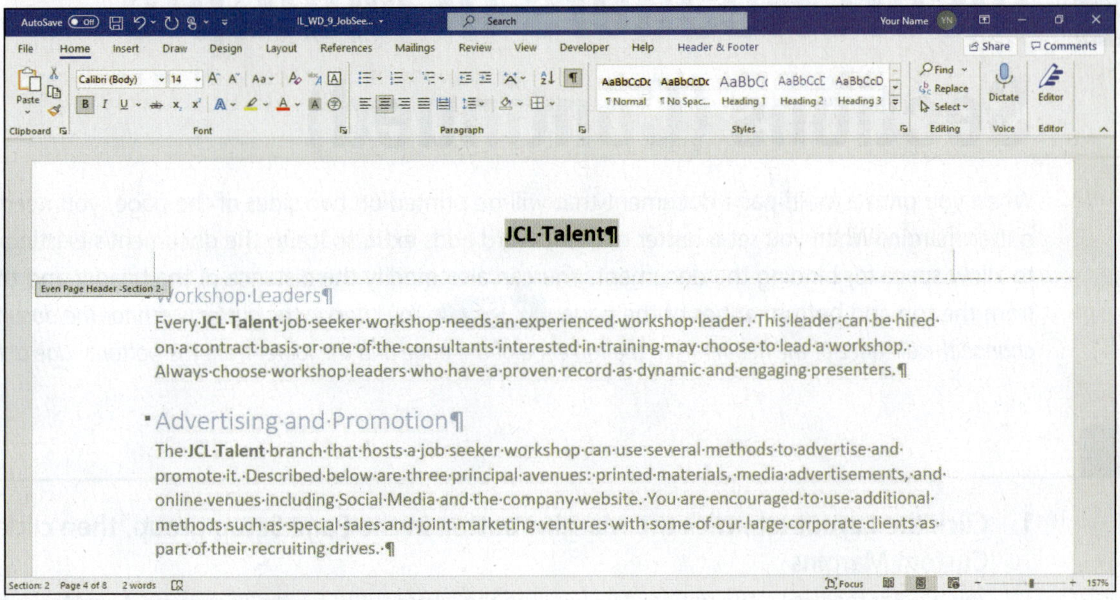

FIGURE 9-27: Updated table of contents

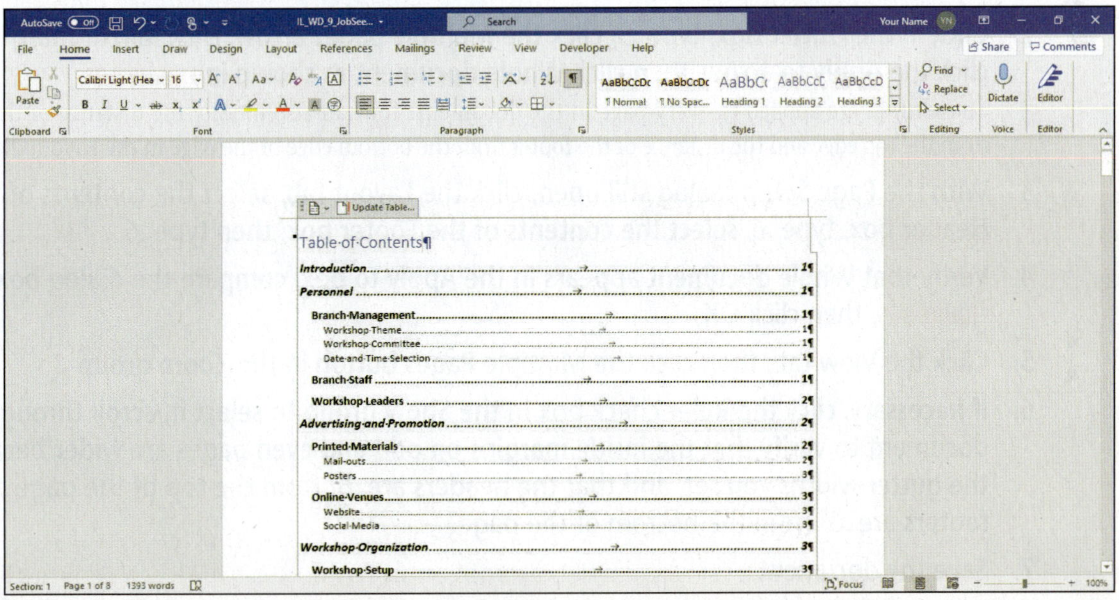

Word

Understanding headers, footers, and sections

One reason you divide a document into sections is so that you can modify the page layout and the headers and footers differently in different sections. You can even modify the header and footer within a section because each section consists of two parts. The first part of a section is the first page, and the second part of the section is the remaining pages in the section. This section structure allows you to omit the header and footer on the first page of a section, and then include the header and footer on all subsequent pages in the same section. To do this, place the insertion point in the section you want to modify, then click the Different First Page check box in the Options group to specify that you wish to include a different header and/or footer (or no header and footer at all) on the first page of a section. In addition, you can also choose to format odd and even pages in a document in different ways by clicking the Different Odd & Even Pages check box in the Options group. For example, you can choose to right-align the document title on odd-numbered pages and left-align the chapter indicator on even-numbered pages.

(Continued)

Word
Module 9

Learning Outcome
- Set a gutter margin

Insert Headers in Multiple Sections (Continued)

When you print a multi-page document that will be printed on two sides of the page, you need to set a gutter margin. When you set a gutter margin, Word adds extra space to the document's existing margins to allow space for binding the document. You can also modify the distance of the header and the footer from the top and bottom edges of the page. **CASE** *You change the gutter width for the document and change the distance of the header from the top edge of the page and the footer from the bottom edge of the page.*

STEPS

1. **Click the Layout tab, click the Margins button in the Page Setup group, then click Custom Margins**
   You modify the page setup options by changing the gutter width for the document. A **gutter** is the blank space on the inside of each page, where the pages are bound together. You generally want to set a gutter width that adds to the inside margin and is wider than the outside margin to allow room for binding.
2. **Click in the Gutter box, type .5, click the Multiple pages arrow, click Mirror margins, click the Apply to arrow, then click Whole document as shown in FIGURE 9-28**
   The settings are applied to every page in the document. You can also modify the distance of the header from the top edge and the distance of the footer from the bottom edge of the page in the Layout dialog box.
3. **With the Page Setup dialog still open, click the Layout tab, select the contents of the Header box, type .6, select the contents of the Footer box, then type .6**
4. **Verify that Whole document appears in the Apply to box, compare the dialog box to FIGURE 9-29, then click OK**
5. **Click the View tab, then click the Multiple Pages button in the Zoom group**
6. **If necessary, click the Ruler check box in the Show group to select it, scroll through the document to verify that the inside margins on odd and even pages are wider because of the gutter widths you set, and that the headers are .6" from the top of the page and the footers are .6" from the bottom of the page.**
7. **Save the document**

FIGURE 9-28: Setting the gutter width in the Page Setup dialog box

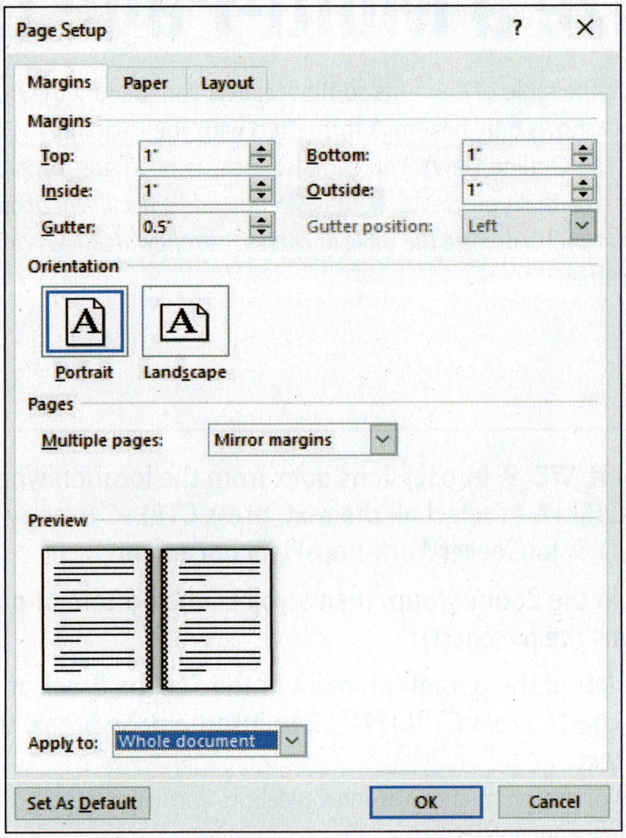

FIGURE 9-29: Setting the header and footer margin

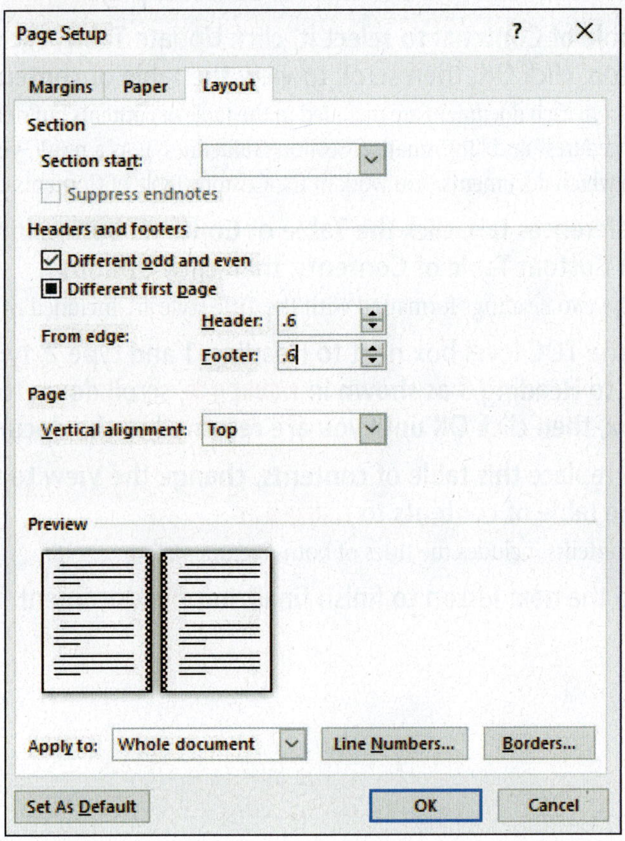

Word

Word
Module 9

Finalize a Multi-Page Document

Learning Outcome
- Customize a table of contents

You can customize the table of contents so that readers can identify the document structure. By default, a table of contents shows only headings formatted with the Heading 1, Heading 2, or Heading 3 styles (Levels 1, 2, and 3 in Outline view). You can also include headings formatted with other styles, such as the Title style or a style that you create. **CASE** *You add a document about planning information sessions to the current document, customize the table of contents to show four levels instead of three, then change the spacing between entries.*

STEPS

1. **Open Support_WD_9_InfoSessions.docx from the location where you store your data files, press CTRL+A to select all the text, press CTRL+C to copy all the text, then switch to the IL_WD_9_JobSeekerWorkshopsFinal document**
2. **Click 100% in the Zoom group, then scroll to the bottom of page 5 of the document text (contains the pie chart)**
3. **Click to the left of the paragraph mark of the Section Break at the bottom of page 5 (below the chart), press CTRL+ENTER to insert a page break, then press CTRL+V to paste the copied text**

   The two pages of the Information Session Guidelines document are inserted into Section 2 and the document should now contain 10 pages.
4. **Verify that Page 7 appears in the footer on the second page of the Information Sessions Guidelines, then scroll up to the table of contents page**
5. **Click the Table of Contents to select it, click Update Table, click the Update entire table option button, click OK, then scroll to view the table of contents**

   The headings from each document are included in the table of contents but not the document titles ("Job Seeker Workshop Procedures" and "Information Session Guidelines"). As a result, you cannot easily see which headings belong to which documents. You work in the Custom Table of Contents dialog box to fix this problem.
6. **Click the References tab, click the Table of Contents button in the Table of Contents group, click Custom Table of Contents, then click Options**

   Specify that the two headings formatted with the Title style are included in the table of contents.
7. **Select 1 in the TOC level box next to Heading 1 and type 2, type 3 next to Heading 2, type 4 next to Heading 3 as shown in FIGURE 9-30, scroll down to the Title box, type 1 in the Title box, then click OK until you are returned to the document**
8. **Click Yes to replace this table of contents, change the View to One Page, scroll up, then compare the table of contents to FIGURE 9-31**

   The table of contents includes the titles of both documents.
9. **Continue to the next lesson to finish finalizing the document**

FIGURE 9-30: Table of Contents Options dialog box

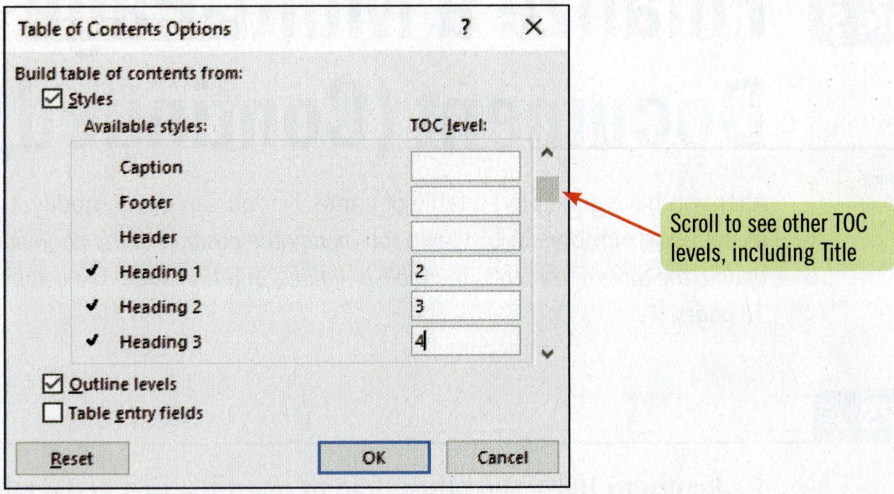

FIGURE 9-31: Revised table of contents

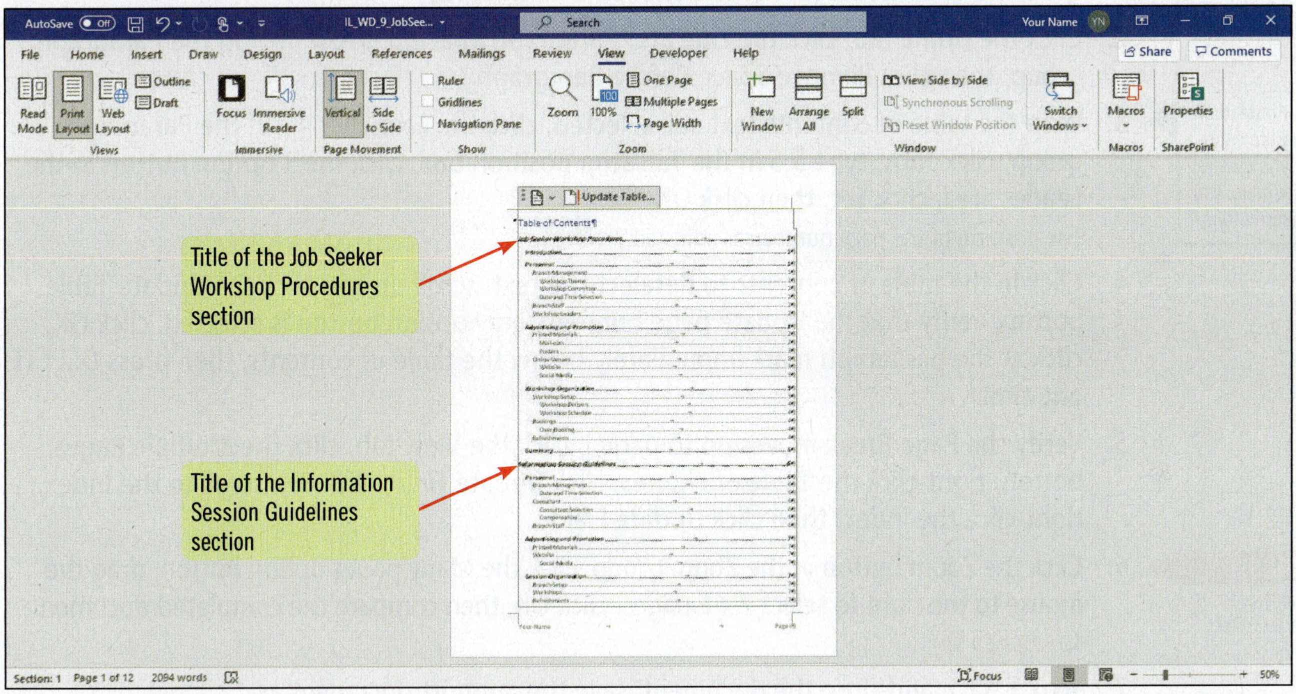

Word

(*Continued*)

Finalize a Multi-Page Document (Continued)

Learning Outcome
- Modify table of contents page numbers

After you have generated a table of contents, you can easily modify its format and change the position of the page numbers. **CASE** *You modify the position of the page number in the table of contents, then update the table of contents, the table of figures, and the index. The completed document consists of a total of 10 pages.*

STEPS

QUICK TIP
After you modify the formatting of a table of contents, you update page numbers only instead of updating the entire table. If you update the entire table, you lose the formatting.

TROUBLE
If you can't select 2 x 5 pages, select 2 x 4 pages.

1. **Return to 100% view, then drag to select the text in the table of contents from Job Seeker Workshop Procedures to the page number following Summary at the end of the table of contents (the text is shaded a darker gray)**
2. **Click the Home tab, click the Line and Paragraph Spacing arrow in the Paragraph group, then click Remove Space Before Paragraph**
3. **With the table of contents text still selected, click the Launcher in the Paragraph group, click Tabs, type 5.5 in the Tab stop position box, click the 3 option button in the Leader area, click Set, then click OK**
   The position of the page numbers is adjusted.
4. **Click in the table of contents to deselect the text, scroll up and click the Update Table button, verify that the Update page numbers only option button is selected, click OK, click at the paragraph mark immediately below the table of contents, then press DELETE one time**
5. **Verify the Page Break moves up to page i, click the View tab, click the Multiple Pages button, right-click the Table of Figures, click Update Field, click OK, scroll to the Index, right-click the Index, then click Update Field**
6. **Click the Zoom button in the Zoom group, click the Many pages option button, drag the mouse to the right to select 2 x 5 pages, click OK, then compare the completed document to FIGURE 9-32**
7. **sam Save and close the document, save the Support document as Support_WD_9_InfoSessions2 to the location where you store your files, then close the document but do not exit Word**

FIGURE 9-32: The 10 pages of the completed document

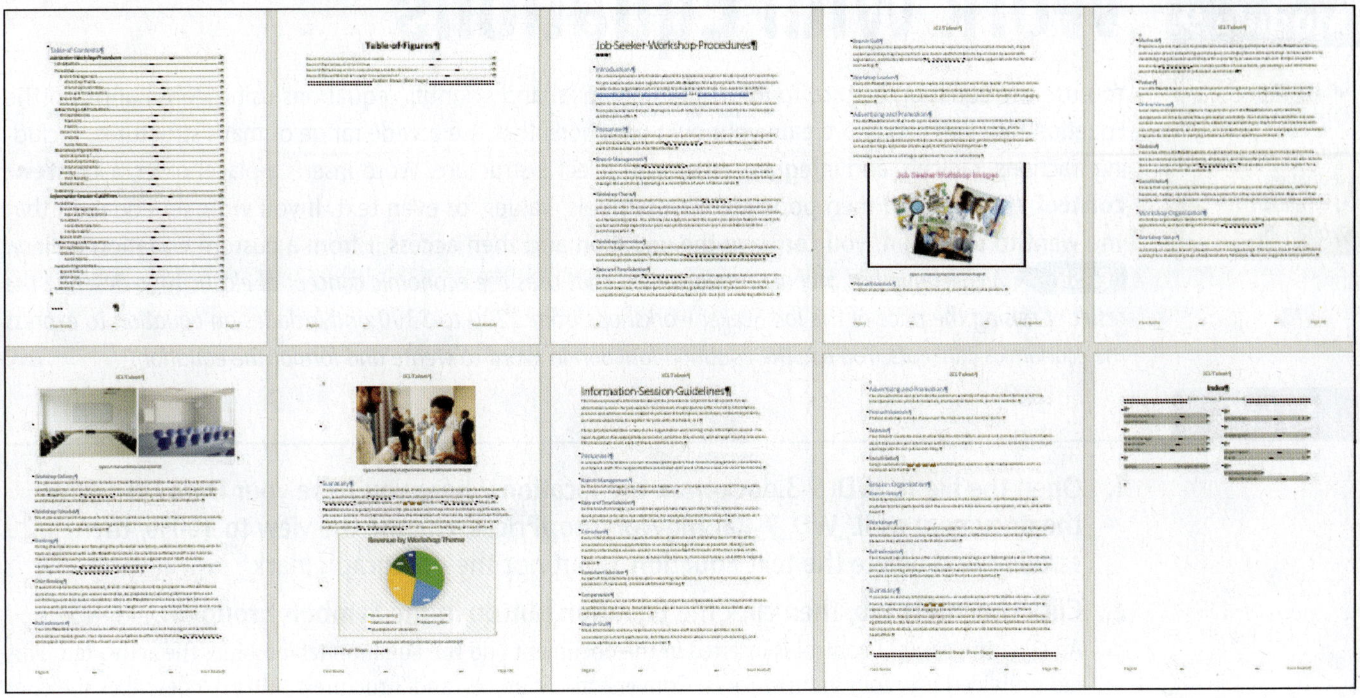

Syda Productions/Shutterstock.com; Robert Kneschke/Shutterstock.com

Rawpixel.com/Shutterstock.com; tsyhun/Shutterstock.com; Dragon Images/Shutterstock.com

Word

Using Advanced Print Options

With Word, you can scale a document to fit a different paper size, and you can choose to print pages from specific sections or a series of sections, even when the page numbering restarts in each section. To scale a document, click the File tab, click Print, click the 1 Page Per Sheet arrow, then point to Scale to Paper Size and view the list of paper sizes available. You can also choose to print a multiple-page document on fewer sheets; for example, you can print the document on two pages per sheet up to 16 pages per sheet. In the Print screen, you can also specify how to print the pages of a multiple-section document that uses different page numbering in each section. You need to enter both the page number and the section number for the range of pages you wish to print. The syntax required is: PageNumberSectionNumber-PageNumberSectionNumber, which is shortened to p#s#-p#s#. For example, if you want to print from page 1 of Section 1 to page 4 of Section 3, you enter p1s1-p4s3 in the Pages box in the Settings area, and then click Print.

Word
Module 9

Work with Equations

Learning Outcomes
- Create an equation
- Format an equation

You use the Equation feature to insert mathematical and scientific equations using commands on the Equation tab. You can also create your own equations that use a wide range of math structures, including fractions, radicals, and integrals. When you select a structure, Word inserts a placeholder, a **content control**, that you can then populate with symbols, values, or even text. If you write an equation that you want to use again, you can save the equation and then access it from a custom equation gallery.

CASE *A colleague has prepared a document that uses the economic concept of elasticity to describe the result of raising the price of the Job Seeker workshops from $200 to $300 and includes an equation to express the economics concepts. You use the equation function in Word to create and format the equation.*

STEPS

1. **Open the file IL_WD_9-3.docx from the location where you store your Data Files, save the document as IL_WD_9_RaisingWorkshopPrices, change the view to 100%, then scroll to and delete the text Equation 1, but not the paragraph mark**
2. **Click the Insert tab, then click the Equation button in the Symbols group**
   An equation content control is inserted in the document and the Equation tab becomes the active tab. This tab is divided into four groups: Tools, Conversions, Symbols, and Structures. TABLE 9-3 describes the content of each group.
3. **Click the Fraction button in the Structures group to show a selection of fraction structures, click the Stacked Fraction structure (the first structure in the top row), then increase the zoom to 180%**
   Increasing the zoom helps you see the components of the equation.
4. **Click in the top half of the fraction (the numerator)**
   The box is shaded to indicate it is selected.
5. **Click the More button in the Symbols group to expand the Symbols gallery, click the Basic Math arrow on the title bar, click Greek Letters, then click the Delta symbol (Δ) as shown in FIGURE 9-33**
   You can select commonly used math symbols from eight galleries as follows: Basic Math, Greek Letters, Letter-Like Symbols, Operators, Arrows, Negated Relations, Scripts, and Geometry.
6. **Type Q, press DOWN ARROW to move to the bottom half of the fraction (the denominator), type Q, press RIGHT ARROW, type an equal sign (=), then complete the equation as shown in FIGURE 9-34, making sure to insert fraction structures as needed**
7. **Click the selection handle (a portion of the equation is shaded), click the Home tab, change the Font size to 14 point, click the Shading arrow in the Paragraph group, click the Green, Accent 6, Lighter 80% color box, then click away from the equation**
8. **Save and close the document, but do not exit Word**

TROUBLE
Follow Step 3 to insert the fraction structure each time; use the keyboard arrow keys to move to different parts of the equation. If your insertion point moves outside the equation, click in the equation again.

More equation options

From the Equation tab, you can click the Ink Equation button to write an equation using a digital pen or other pointing device. Word converts the written symbols into typed symbols.

From the Shapes button menu on the Insert tab, you can select one of the six equation shapes shown in FIGURE 9-35. You modify these shapes in the same way you modify any drawing shape.

FIGURE 9-35:

FIGURE 9-33: Selecting a symbol

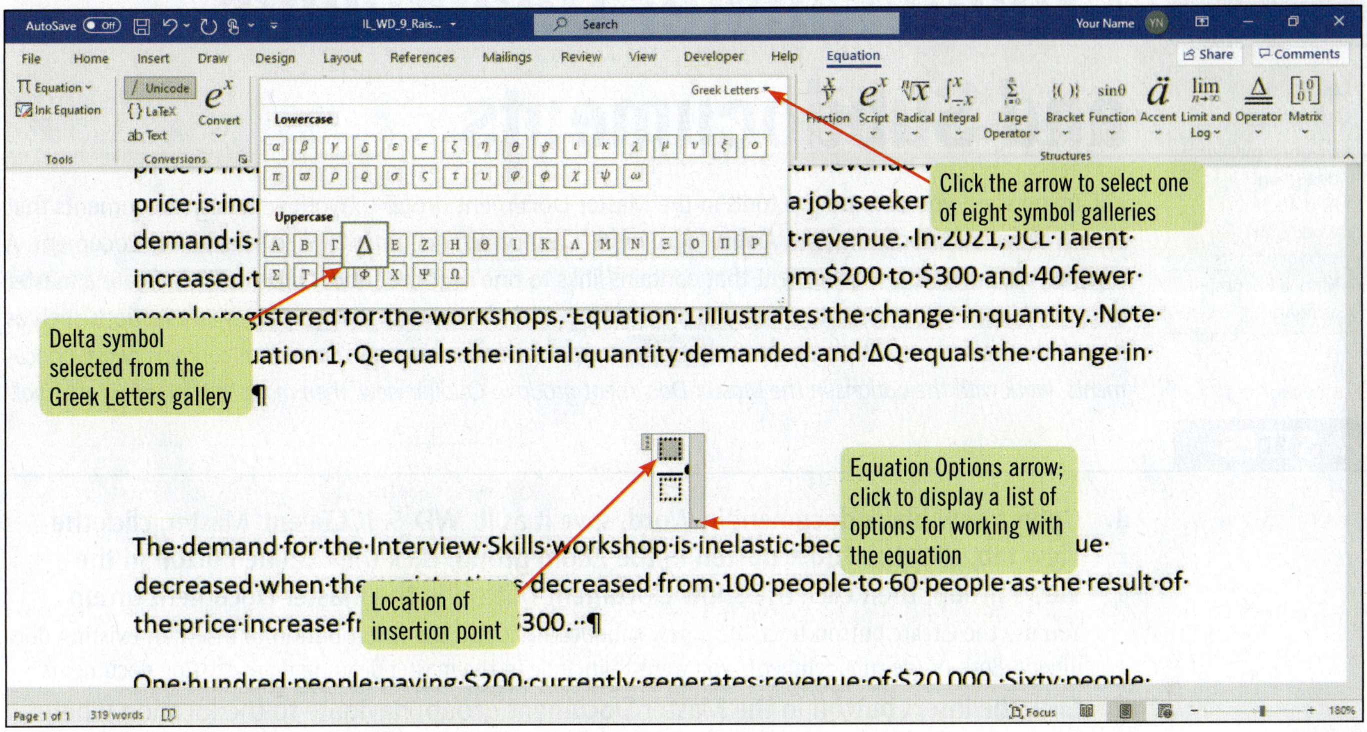

FIGURE 9-34: Completed Equation 1

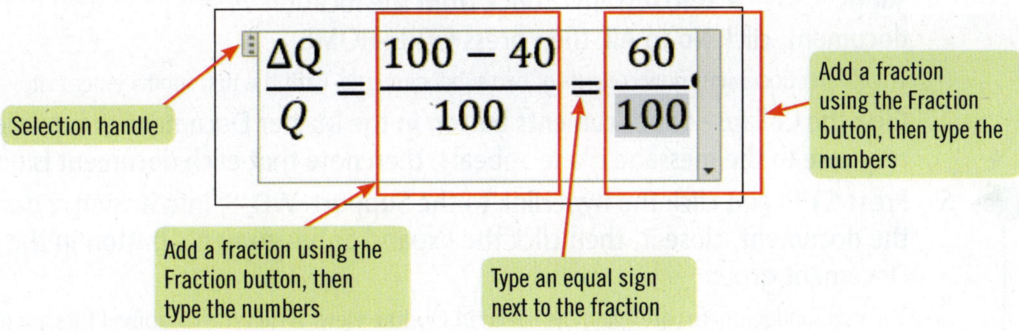

TABLE 9-3: Contents of the Equation tab

Tools	• Use the Equation button to select a built-in equation • Select the equation style: Professional, Linear, or Normal Text
Conversions	• Convert equations to various formats; for example, you can convert an existing equation to a linear format • Click the Launcher to access the Equation Options dialog box where you can specify equation settings and access the Math AutoCorrect list of symbols
Symbols	• Select commonly used mathematical symbols such as (±) and (∞) • Click the More button to show a gallery of symbols • Click the arrow in the gallery to select the group for which you would like to see symbols
Structures	• Select common math structures, such as fractions and radicals • Click a structure button (such as the Fraction button) to select a specific format to insert in the equation for that structure

Create Master Documents and Subdocuments

Learning Outcomes
- Create a master document
- Add and work with subdocuments
- Mark a document as final

In Outline view, you can use the tools in the Master Document group to work with large documents that consist of several subdocuments. A **subdocument** is a separate document linked to a master document. A **master document** is a document that contains links to one or more subdocuments. You create a master document and subdocuments when you are working with documents that contain many sections such as a book that includes multiple chapters. **CASE** *You create a master document that contains two subdocuments, work with the options in the Master Document group in Outline view, then mark the document as Final.*

STEPS

1. **Open a new blank document in Word, save it as IL_WD_9_JCLTalent_Master, click the View tab, click the 100% button in the Zoom group, click the Outline button in the Views group, then click the Show Document button in the Master Document group**
   You use the Create button to create a new subdocument and the Insert button to insert an existing document. Both of the subdocuments you want to include in the master document are existing documents.
2. **Click the Insert button in the Master Document group, navigate to the location where you saved the document IL_WD_9_RaisingWorkshopPrices, double-click IL_WD_9_RaisingWorkshopPrices, then click No to All**
3. **Click the Insert button in the Master Document group, insert Support_WD_9_InfoSessions2.docx from the location where you saved the document, click No to All, then press CTRL+HOME**
   The master document now consists of two subdocuments, with the first subdocument shown in FIGURE 9-36.
4. **Click the Collapse Subdocuments button in the Master Document group, click OK in response to the message if one appears, then note that each document is now a hyperlink**
5. **Press CTRL and click the hyperlink to the Support_WD_9_InfoSessions2 document, view the document, close it, then click the Expand Subdocuments button in the Master Document group**
   The two subdocuments are again displayed in Outline view. When the combined files are not large, you can choose to unlink the subdocuments so they become part of the master document.

QUICK TIP
You keep subdocuments as links to a master document when you want to reduce the file size of a master document.

6. **Scroll to the Information Session Guidelines document and click the Selection button to the left of the document, as shown in FIGURE 9-37 to select the entire subdocument, then click Unlink button in the Master Document group**
   The Information Session Guidelines document is no longer a subdocument and cannot be collapsed to a link.
7. **Scroll up and click the Increasing Workshop Prices document Selection button, click the Lock Document button in the Master Document group, double click any word in the document, then try to type text**
   The subdocument is locked; you cannot make any changes. You can also protect the entire document from changes.
8. **Click the File tab, click Info, click Protect Document in the Info pane, view the protection options available, click Mark as Final, click OK, then click OK**
   When you open a document that has been marked as Final, a message appears telling you that the document was marked as final to discourage editing. If you wish to edit the document, click Edit Anyway.
9. **Click , close the document, submit the files to your instructor, then exit Word**

FIGURE 9-36: Subdocuments inserted in Outline view

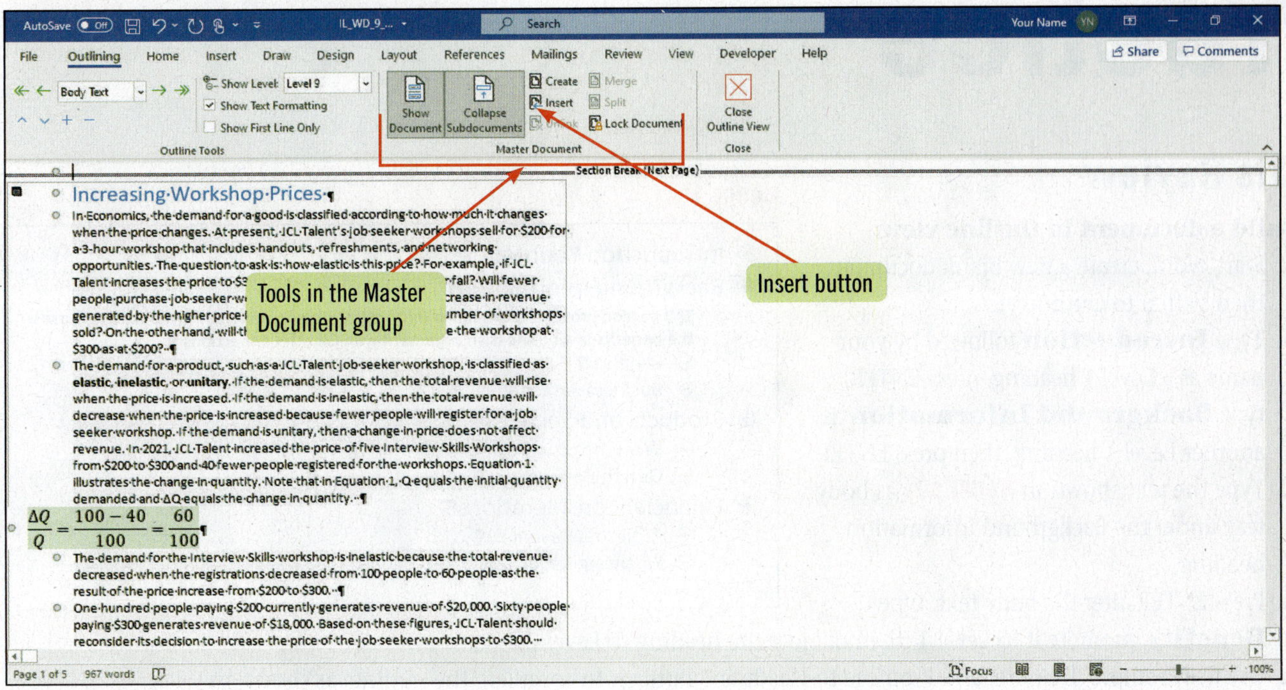

FIGURE 9-37: Subdocument selected in Outline view

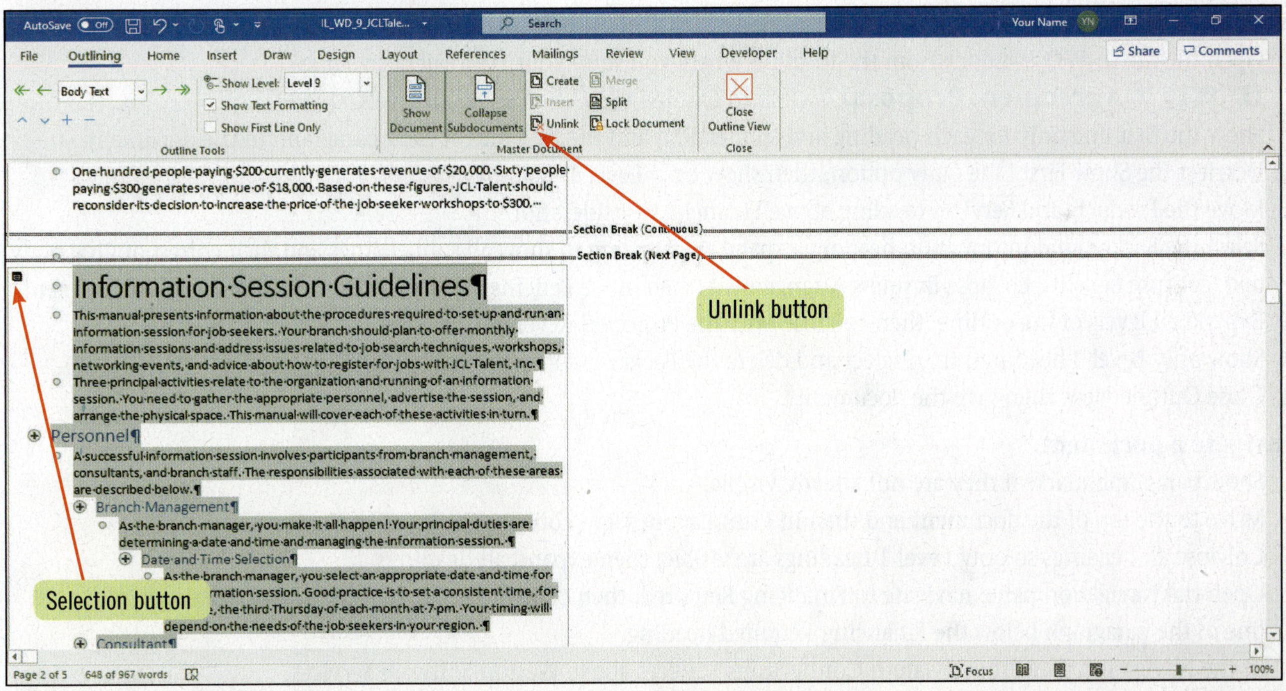

Inserting endnotes

Click the Insert Endnote button in the Footnotes group on the References tab to insert a note reference mark for an endnote. When you click the Insert Endnote button, the insertion point moves to the end of your document so that you can enter text for the endnote in the same way you enter text for a footnote. You click above the endnote separator to return to the text of your document. You work in the Footnote and Endnote dialog box to modify options for endnotes.

Practice

Skills Review

1. Build a document in Outline view.

- **a.** Start Word, create a new blank document, then switch to Outline view.
- **b.** Type **Introduction** followed by your name as a Level 1 heading, press ENTER, type **Background Information** as another Level 1 heading, then press ENTER.
- **c.** Type the text shown in FIGURE 9-38 as body text under the Background Information heading.
- **d.** Press ENTER after the body text, type **Benefits**, promote it to Level 1, then demote the heading to Level 2.
- **e.** Use the Promote, Demote, and Promote to Heading 1 buttons to complete the outline, as shown in FIGURE 9-38.
- **f.** Save the document as **IL_WD_9_AgreementOutline** to the location where you store your Data Files, then close the document.

FIGURE 9-38

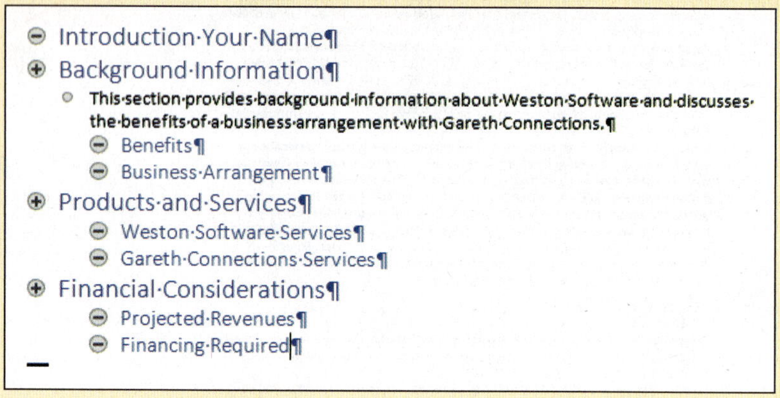

2. Work in Outline view.

- **a.** Open the file IL_WD_9-4.docx from the location where you store your Data Files, save it as **IL_WD_9_AgreementProposal**, switch to Outline view, then show all levels.
- **b.** Show the first line only for each heading and subheading and the first line of each paragraph in the document.
- **c.** Deselect the Show First Line Only option, then show only Level 1 headings.
- **d.** Move the Products and Services heading above Financial Considerations.
- **e.** Select the Background Information heading, expand the heading to show all subheadings and their corresponding body text, collapse Benefits, collapse Business Arrangement, then move Benefits and its subtext below Business Arrangement.
- **f.** Expand all levels of the outline, then collapse only the Projected Revenues heading.
- **g.** Show only Level 3 headings, then select and delete the Package Opportunities heading.
- **h.** Close Outline view, then save the document.

3. Navigate a document.

- **a.** Show paragraph marks if they are not already visible.
- **b.** Move to the top of the document and then in Print Layout view, collapse the Introduction heading.
- **c.** Collapse all headings so only Level 1 headings are visible, then expand all headings.
- **d.** Open the Navigation pane, navigate to Financing Required, then change "eight months" to **two years** in the last line of the paragraph below the Financing Required heading.
- **e.** In the Navigation pane, move Gareth Connections Services above Weston Software Services.
- **f.** View the thumbnails of the document pages in the Navigation pane, click the first page, scroll to the Benefits heading on page 2 of the document, then select the text "Projected Revenues" at the end of the paragraph.
- **g.** Create a cross-reference from the text "Projected Revenues" to the Projected Revenues heading.
- **h.** Test the cross-reference.
- **i.** Go to the top of the document, create a hyperlink from the text "Products and Services" in the list of factors (the other two factors are already hyperlinks) in the middle of paragraph 1 under "Introduction," to the Products and Services heading, then test the hyperlink.
- **j.** Save the document and keep the Navigation pane open.

Skills Review (continued)

4. Create and modify screenshots.

- **a.** Open **Support_WD_9_CompanyImages.docx** from the location where you save your Data files, turn off paragraph marks, then ensure the View is 100%.
- **b.** Switch to the IL_WD_9_AgreementProposal document.
- **c.** Scroll to and delete the text SEATTLE SCREENSHOT in the Background Information section on page 1, but not the paragraph mark.
- **d.** Insert a screenshot of the Word window containing the support document showing the two pictures of Seattle.
- **e.** Crop the screenshot to the edges of the document containing the "Awesome Seattle" heading and the two pictures.
- **f.** Change the width of the cropped screenshot to 5", apply a picture border using the Black, Text 1 color, then center the screenshot.
- **g.** Switch back to the Support_WD_9_CompanyImages document, then scroll to view the three pictures on page 2 of the document.
- **h.** Return to the main document in Word, navigate to the Gareth Connections Services heading, delete SERVICES PICTURES but not the paragraph mark, then create a screen clipping that includes only the three pictures and the heading on page 2 of the Support document.
- **i.** Change the width of the screen clipping to 5", apply a picture border using the Black, Text 1 color, then center the screenshot.
- **j.** Save the document, switch to the Support document, then close it.

5. Use advanced find and replace options.

- **a.** Go to the top of the document, then use Advanced Find and Replace to find every instance of **Gareth Connections** and replace it with **Gareth Connections** formatted in bold.
- **b.** In the Find and Replace dialog box, delete the text in the Find what and Replace what text boxes and remove the formatting.
- **c.** Use the list of Special characters from the Replace dialog box to find every instance of an em dash and replace it with an en dash. You will make two replacements.
- **d.** Search for **SQL skills**, then click after the period.
- **e.** Insert three computer symbols (Character Code 58) from the Wingdings font.
- **f.** Save the document.

6. Add and modify captions.

- **a.** Scroll through the document and note the captions on three of the five graphics, then navigate to the Background Information heading and click the screenshot of the Seattle images.
- **b.** Insert a caption on the picture using the A, B, C, numbering style.
- **c.** Type a colon (:), press SPACEBAR then type **Most clients are based in Seattle** as the caption text.
- **d.** Change the numbering style to 1, 2, 3,..., then exit the Captions dialog box.
- **e.** Scroll to and click the screenshot of the three services images, then insert a caption with that includes a colon (:) and the text **Gareth Connections uses these images to promote its services**.
- **f.** Scroll up and then delete the picture and the caption of the people clapping.
- **g.** Update the numbering for all the remaining captions in the document.
- **h.** Go to the top of the document, insert a manual page break, press CTRL+HOME, then enter the text **Table of Figures** followed by a hard return at the top of the new blank page.
- **i.** Center the text and format it with 24 point and bold.
- **j.** Click after "Figures," press ENTER, then clear the formatting (*Hint*: Clear the Clear All Formatting button in the Font group on the Home tab).
- **k.** Generate a table of figures using the Distinctive format.
- **l.** Save the document.

Skills Review (continued)

7. **Insert a table of contents.**
   a. Go to the top of the document.
   b. Insert a page break, then return to the top of the document and clear all the formatting.
   c. Insert a table of contents using the Automatic Table 2 predefined style.
   d. Replace the table of contents with a custom table of contents using the Distinctive format.
   e. Use CTRL+click from the table of contents to navigate to Business Arrangement in the document, view the document headings in the Navigation pane, then right-click and delete the Eastways Communications heading from the Navigation pane.
   f. Update the table of contents, then save the document.
8. **Mark text for an index.**
   a. Show the Results section of the Navigation pane, find the words **computer labs**, then mark all occurrences for inclusion in the index.
   b. Find and mark only the first instance of each of the following main entries: **website design**, **networking**, **software training**, and **PowerPoint**. (*Hint*: Click Mark instead of Mark All.)
   c. Save the document.
9. **Generate an index.**
   a. Find **social media**, click in the Mark Index Entry dialog box, select social media in the Main entry box, type **Gareth Connections Services** as the Main entry and **social media** as the Subentry, then click Mark All.
   b. Repeat the process to insert **business writing seminars** as a subentry of Gareth Connections Services.
   c. Find the first instance of the text **courses**, then create a cross-reference in the Mark Index Entry dialog box to **software training**. Note that you already have an index entry for software training.
   d. Close the Mark Index Entry dialog box.
   e. Insert a new page at the end of the document, type **Index** at the top of the page, center the text and format it with bold and 24 point.
   f. Double-click below the index, clear any formatting and press BACKSPACE if necessary so the insertion point appears at the left margin, then insert an index using the Modern format.
   g. Find the text **Seattle**, click the second entry in the Navigation pane, open the Mark Index Entry dialog box and click Mark All, then close the Mark Index Entry dialog box and the Navigation pane.
   h. Scroll to the index page, update the index so it includes the new entry, then save and close the document.
10. **Insert footers in multiple sections.**
   a. Open the file IL_WD_9-5.docx from the location where you store your Data Files, then save it as **IL_WD_9_AgreementProposalFinal**.
   b. At the top of the document, check that Section 1 appears on the status bar and that the document contains 7 pages.
   c. Scroll to the page break below the Table of Figures on page 2, click to the left of the page break, then insert an Odd Page section break.
   d. Press DELETE to remove the original page break, then press DELETE again to remove the extra blank line.
   e. Scroll to the Index page, scroll up and click to the left of the page break on page 6, insert an Even Page section break, then delete the original page break and the extra blank line.
   f. On the table of contents page, insert a footer using the Blank (Three Columns) format.
   g. Select the Different Odd & Even Pages check box.
   h. Click to the left of the placeholder text to select all three items, press DELETE, type your name, press TAB two times, type **Page**, press SPACEBAR, then insert a page number at the current position of the insertion point using the Plain Number page number.
   i. Format the page numbers with the i, ii, iii style.
   j. Press Next in the Navigation group to go to the Even Page Footer for Section 1, type **Page**, press SPACEBAR, insert a Plain Number page number at the current position of the insertion point, press TAB two times, then type your name.

Skills Review (continued)

k. Click Next in the Navigation group, select the Different First Page check box, then click the Link to Previous button to deselect it (the button is no longer gray).

l. Change the format of the page numbers to start at 1.

m. Click Next to go to the next footer (Even Page Footer -Section 2-), verify that Page 2 appears at the left margin and your name at the right margin, click Next, verify that your name appears at the left margin and Page 3 at the right margin, then click Next to go to Section 3, which is Page 6 (the Index page) and the Even Page Footer for Section 3. Note that Page 8 of 8 appears in the status bar because the entire document, including the table of contents and table of figures pages (Section 1) contains 8 pages.

n. Exit the footer area, then scroll through the document to verify that the footers appear correctly. Note that your name and Page i appears on the Table of Contents page, Page ii and your name appears on the Table of Figures page, no footer appears on the first page of the document text, Page 2 and your name appears on page 2 of the document text and your name and Page 3 appears on page 3 of the document text and so on to the end of the document.

o. Save the document.

11. Insert headers in multiple sections.

a. Press CTRL+HOME to go to the top of the document, change the View to Page Width, close the Navigation pane if necessary, insert a header using the blank format, then move to the Even Page Header for Section 2. Verify that Even Page Header -Section 2- appears, *not* First Page Header -Section 2-.

b. Deselect the Link to Previous button, then enter **Business Arrangement** as the header text.

c. Format the header text with a font size to 14 point, apply bold, center the text, then copy the header text, including the paragraph mark.

d. Move to the Odd Page Header -Section 2-, deselect the Link to Previous button, paste the "Business Arrangement" header text, then, if necessary, remove a paragraph mark so only one blank line appears between "Business Arrangement" and the document text.

e. Exit the header area, then return to the top of the document.

f. Scroll through the document to verify that no header text appears on the first three pages of the document. The header text appears only on pages 2 to 8 of the document text.

g. In the Page Setup dialog box, set the Gutter width for the whole document to .5, then mirror the margins.

h. Set the distance of the Header and Footer from the top and bottom of the page to .3 for the whole document.

i. View the entire document in Multiple Pages view, verify the headers and footers are correct, then save the document.

12. Finalize a multi-page document.

a. Open **Support_WD_9_TopTalkPresenters.docx** from the location where you store your data files, select and copy all the text.

b. Switch to the IL_WD_9_AgreementProposalFinal document, return to Page Width, scroll to the bottom of page 4 (contains the Conclusion), click to the left of the section break, then insert a page break.

c. Paste the copied text.

d. Update the entire table of contents.

e. Modify the table of contents options so that Heading 1 corresponds to TOC level 2 text, Heading 2 corresponds to TOC level 3 text, Heading 3 corresponds to TOC level 4 text, and Title text corresponds to TOC level 1 text.

f. Verify that the updated table of contents includes the titles of the two documents, select all the text in the table of contents, then remove the Before Paragraph spacing.

g. Open the Tabs dialog from the Paragraph dialog box, then set a tab of 5.5 with the 2 Leader style.

h. Update the Table of Figures, then update the Index.

i. View 2 × 5 pages in the Zoom dialog box, then compare the completed document to FIGURE 9-39. If you can't view 2 × 5 pages, view 2 × 4 pages.

j. Save and close the document, close the Support document, but do not exit Word.

Skills Review (continued)

FIGURE 9-39

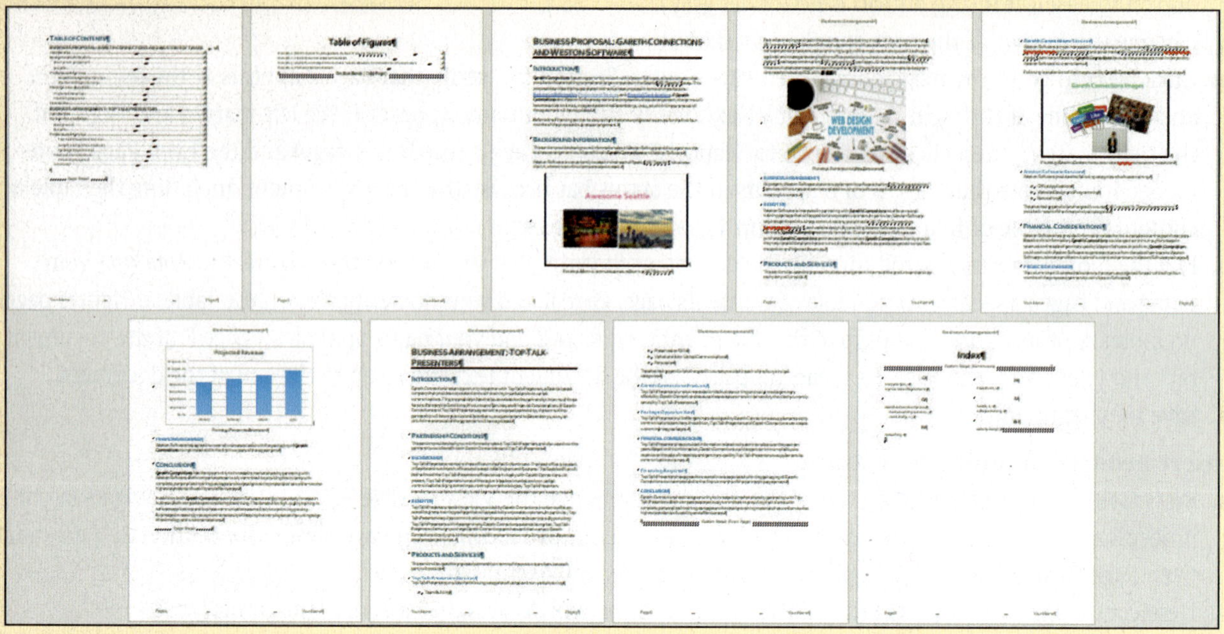

MCarter/Shutterstock.com; stoatphoto/Shutterstock.com; Matej Kastelic/Shutterstock.com; Oleksiy Mark/Shutterstock.com; Dean Drobot/Shutterstock.com; TomKli/Shutterstock.com

13. Work with equations

a. Open the file IL_WD_9-6.docx from the location where you store your Data Files, then save the document as **IL_WD_9_SeminarPrice**.

b. Go to the [Equation1] placeholder, then replace it with an equation content control.

c. Increase the zoom to 180%, then create the equation shown in FIGURE 9-40.

d. Format the new equation by increasing its font size to 16 point, then shade it with Blue, Accent 5, Lighter 80%. (*Hint*: Remember to select the equation content control before applying the shading).

e. Save and close the document, but do not exit Word.

FIGURE 9-40

$$\frac{\Delta Q}{Q} = \frac{100 - 30}{100} = \frac{70}{100}$$

14. Create master documents and subdocuments.

a. Open a new blank document in Word, save the document as **IL_WD_9_GarethConnections_Master**, then switch to Outline view.

b. Insert the document **IL_WD_9_SeminarPrice.docx** you saved in the previous activity, clicking No to All if prompted.

c. Insert **Support_WD_9_TopTalkPresenters.docx** from the location where you store your Data Files for this book, answering No to All if prompted.

d. Collapse the subdocuments, answering OK when prompted, click the hyperlink to the Support_WD_9_TopTalkPresenters.docx file, view the document, then close it.

e. Expand the subdocuments.

f. Select and then unlink the IL_WD_9_SeminarPrice.docx subdocument.

g. Collapse the Support_WD_9_TopTalkPresenters.docx subdocument, then use the Lock Document button to lock it.

h. Exit Outline view, then mark the entire document as final.

i. Close the document, submit all the files you have created in this Skills Review to your instructor, then exit Word.

Independent Challenge 1

Tony Sanchez, RN, the office manager at Riverwalk Medical Clinic, asks you to help him develop guidelines related to office management, filing procedures, and receptionist duties at the clinic. Tony plans to use these documents as the basis for a Procedures Manual for the clinic.

a. Start Word, open the file IL_WD_9-7.docx from the drive and folder where you store your Data Files, save it as **IL_WD_9_MedicalOfficeGuidelines**, then switch to Outline view.

b. Show only Level 1 headings, select the Applications and Manual Content headings, then demote them to Level 2.

c. Select and expand all the headings, collapse both the Creating a Procedures Manual and the Designating Staff Positions headings, then move the Designating Staff Positions heading above the Creating a Procedures Manual heading.

d. Show only Level 3 headings, select and delete the heading Managing Suppliers and its associated subtext, then close Outline view.

e. Move to the top of the document, collapse the Introduction heading, collapse all headings, expand all headings, show the headings in the Navigation pane, then drag the Administrative Meetings heading up so it appears above Staff Meetings.

f. View the thumbnails in the Navigation pane, scroll to and click the page 1 thumbnail, position the insertion point after "summary" in the last sentence in the paragraph below the Office Manager heading (fourth line), insert a cross-reference to the chart (Figure 1), then select Above/below in the Insert reference to list.

g. Ensure a space appears before and after "below", then test that the cross-reference goes to the figure caption for the chart.

h. Move to the top of the document, insert a blank page, move to the top of the document again, press ENTER, press the Up arrow, insert a table of contents using the Automatic Table 2 option, then replace the table of contents with a custom table of contents using the Formal format.

i. Use the Navigation pane to navigate to the Manual Format subheading, delete the subheading and its associated text, then update the table of contents.

j. Show Results in the Navigation pane, search for **Office Manager**, click the second instance in the Navigation pane, open the Mark Entry dialog box, then mark all instances of "Office Manager" for inclusion in the index.

k. Find and mark all instances of the following main entries: **Medical Office Assistant**, **equipment**, **orientation, budget**, **inventory**, **medications**, and **biologics**.

l. Search for **stock control**, then enter **inventory** in the Main entry box and **stock control** in the Subentry box. Mark the one instance.

m. Search for **office supplies**, then create a cross-reference for office supplies to inventory.

n. Go to the end of the document, insert an index using the Formal format, search for **support staff**, mark it for inclusion in the index, then update the index.

o. Move to the top of the document, scroll to the page break below the table of contents, replace the page break with an Odd Page section break, then remove the page break and the extra hard return.

p. Move to the page break above the index, replace the page with an Even Page section break, then remove the page break and the extra hard return.

q. On page 1 of the document (Section 1), insert a footer using the Blank (Three Columns) format, then select Different Odd and Even pages.

r. Delete the placeholder text, type **Page** at the left margin followed by a space and a plain page number, press TAB two times, type your name at the right margin, then change the page number format to i, ii, iii.

s. Go to Odd Page Footer -Section 2-, then click the Link to Previous button to deselect it. Format the page numbers to start at 1.

Word

Independent Challenge 1 (continued)

t. Go to the Even Page Footer -Section 2-, enter your name at the left margin, press TAB twice to move to the right margin, type **Page** followed by the plain page number, then verify the page number format is 1, 2, 3.

u. Exit the footer area, save the document, then scroll to the chart, click after areas at the end of the caption for the chart, then add a page break to the left of the current Even Page section break.

FIGURE 9-41

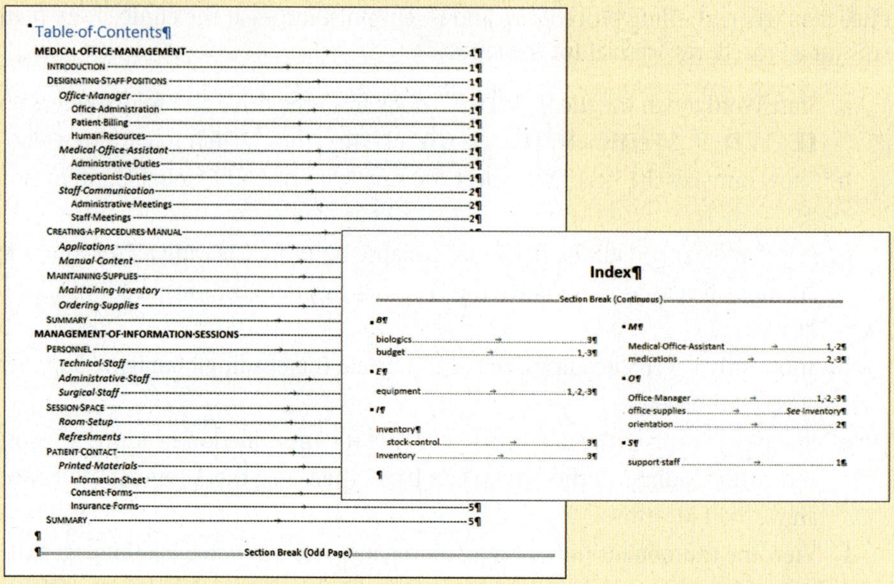

v. Open **Support_WD_9_MedicalInfoSessions.docx**, select and then copy all the text, switch to the document IL_WD_9_MedicalOfficeGuidelines, then paste the copied text.

w. Scroll up to the table of contents, update the table of contents, open the Custom Table of Contents Options dialog box, then designate heading levels as follows: Heading 1: 2, Heading 2: 3, Heading 3: 4 and Title: 1.

x. Select all the text in the table of contents, change the Before and After Spacing to 0, set the right tab at 5.5", then select the 3 tab leader style.

y. Scroll to and update the index, then compare the revised table of contents and updated index to FIGURE 9-41.

z. Save the document, submit the file to your instructor, then close all documents.

Independent Challenge 2

As the program assistant at Hansen College in Denver, Colorado, you are responsible for creating and formatting reports about programs at the college. You modify an existing report, then make the report a master document and insert two subdocuments that each contain information about a different college program.

a. Open IL_WD_9-8.docx, save it as **IL_WD_9_HansenCollegePrograms**, open **Support_WD_9_CampusLife.docx**, then turn off paragraph marks if they are showing. Set the view at 100%, then switch back to IL_WD_9_HansenCollegePrograms.

b. Select and delete STUDYING SCREEN CLIPPING but leave a blank line, then insert a screen clipping of the picture of students studying.

c. Clip the picture so only the oval picture is selected. Change the width of the screen clipping to 4", then center it.

d. In the Support_WD_9_CampusLife file, scroll to the second page, return to the main document, select and delete CAMPUS FUN SCREENSHOT, then insert a screenshot of the Word window containing the pictures of the students on campus.

e. Crop the screenshot in the main document so that only the pictures and heading are visible. Enclose the screen shot in a black border, center it, then change its width to 3.5".

f. Go to the top of the document, then use Advanced Find and Replace to find a section break and replace it with a manual page break.

g. Scroll to the page break, then if necessary delete any extra blank lines so the "Elementary Education" heading starts on page 2.

Independent Challenge 2 (continued)

h. Go to the top of the document, then use Advanced Find and Replace to find every instance of **Hansen College** and replace it with **Hansen College** formatted in bold and italic.

i. On the blank line below the document title "Hansen College", insert three symbols of a hand writing from Wingdings (symbol 63). Increase the font size of the three symbols to 18 point, then center them below the title.

j. Insert a caption on the oval picture with the text: **Students enjoy studying at Hansen College** using the a, b, c, style, then change the numbering style to the 1, 2, 3 style.

k. Insert a caption on the picture of the students on campus with the text: **The campus at Hansen College is a welcoming place**.

l. Scroll to the picture of the girl reading on page 2, update the caption number, then scroll to the next picture of children and update the caption number. (*Hint*: If a caption is not updated, select the entire caption, click the Insert Caption button, then click OK.)

m. Scroll up slightly, then delete EQUATION 1 but not the paragraph mark.

n. Insert the equation shown in FIGURE 9-42, typing X for the multiplication sign.

o. Format the equation by changing the font size to 16 point and applying the Purple, Accent 1, Lighter 80% shading.

p. Go to the top of the document, insert a Next Page section break, then return to the top of the page, type **Table of Figures**, clear the formatting, format it with 16 point and bold, center it, then add a blank line following the title.

q. Insert a table of figures using the Formal format.

r. Insert a header in Section 1 using the Blank (Three Columns) format, delete the placeholder text, go to Section 2, deselect the Link to Previous button, type the text **Hansen College Programs** at the left margin, press TAB two times to move to the right margin, enter your name at the right margin, then exit the header area.

s. Go to the end of the document, switch to Outline view, then click the Show Document button in the Master Document group.

t. Open the file Support_WD_9_BusinessProgram.docx from the location where you store your Data Files, save it as **Support_WD_9_BusinessProgram2**, close it, then insert it as a subdocument, answering No to All if prompted.

u. Open the file Support_WD_9_TheaterProgram.docx from the location where you store your Data Files, save it as **Support_WD_9_TheaterProgram2**, close it, then insert it as a subdocument, answering No to All if prompted.

v. Collapse the subdocuments, click OK in response to any message, scroll down as needed to verify that the two subdocuments are now hyperlinks, press and hold CTRL and click the hyperlink to the Support_WD_9_TheaterProgram2.docx file, view the document, then close it.

w. Expand all the Subdocuments, close Outline view, navigate to the picture of the young woman in the Theater Program document, verify that the figure is updated to Figure 5 or update it if necessary.

x. In the Master document, set the gutter width at .5" for the whole document and select Mirror Margins.

y. Update the table of figures, then compare it to FIGURE 9-43.

z. Save the document, close it, then submit your files to your instructor.

FIGURE 9-42

$$\frac{1}{2}X\frac{1}{2}=\frac{1}{4}$$

FIGURE 9-43

Table·of·Figures¶

FIGURE·1:·STUDENTS·ENJOY·STUDYING·AT·HANSEN·COLLEGE .... 2¶
FIGURE·2:·THE·CAMPUS·AT·HANSEN·COLLEGE·IS·A·WELCOMING·PLACE. .... 2¶
FIGURE·3:·TEACHING·CHILDREN·TO·LOVE·READING·IS·A·HIGH·PRIORITY .... 3¶
FIGURE·4:·CHILDREN·ARE·FASCINATED·BY·SCIENCE .... 4¶
FIGURE·5:·LIGHTING·DESIGN·IS·AN·INTEGRAL·PART·OF·THE·THEATRICAL·DESIGN·AND·PRODUCTION·PROGRAM .... 6¶
¶
¶ Section Break (Next Page)

Visual Workshop

Open the file IL_WD_9-9.docx from the drive and folder where you store your Data Files, then save it as **IL_WD_9_SeaviewBankMarketingPlan**. Switch to Outline view, then modify the outline so that it appears as shown in FIGURE 9-44. You need to change the order of two sections and demote two subheadings. Exit Outline view, add a Next Page section break at the beginning of the document, then on the new blank page, generate a custom table of contents using the Fancy format with four levels showing. (*Hint*: Click the Show levels arrow in the Table of Contents dialog box, then click 4.) Insert a page break before Promotion in the text, then create a footer in Section 2 (remember to deselect Link to Previous *before* you type text) with your name at the left margin and a page number that starts with 1 at the right margin. Make sure no text appears in the footer in section 1. In Print Layout view, insert and crop the screen clipping included in the file Support_WD_9_Banking.docx to the left of the page break. Refer to FIGURE 9-45. Change the width to 2.5", then add the caption **Online Banking: The Future is Here**. Update the table of contents. Save and close the document, then submit the file to your instructor.

FIGURE 9-44

FIGURE 9-45

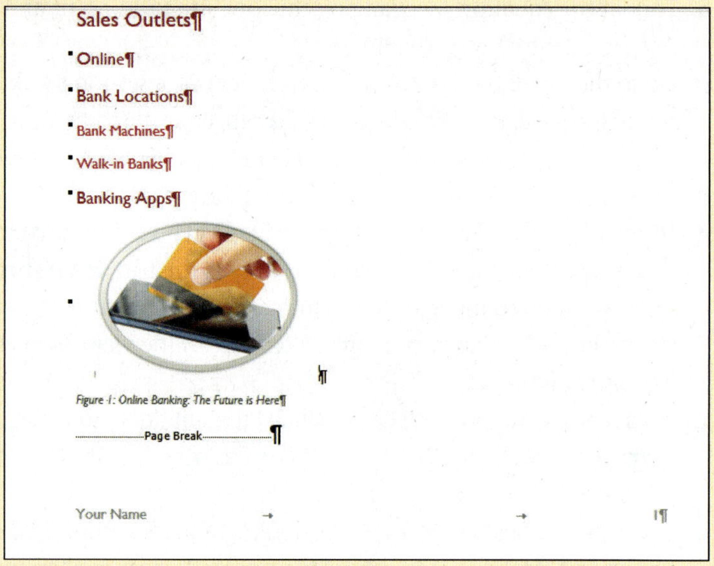

Sinisa Botas/Shutterstock.com

Building Forms

CASE You work with Anthony Martinez, the VP of sales & marketing at JCL Talent, Inc., to create a form to survey branch managers about their experiences delivering workshops for job seekers. You start by creating the form template, then you add content controls, format and protect the form, and fill it in as a user.

Module Objectives

After completing this module, you will be able to:

- Convert tables and text
- Construct a form template
- Add Text content controls
- Add Date Picker and Picture content controls
- Add Repeating Section and Check Box content controls
- Add Building Block content controls
- Add Drop-Down content controls
- Insert Legacy Tools controls
- Format and Protect a form
- Edit a form
- Fill in a form as a user

Files You Will Need

IL_WD_10-1.docx
Support_WD_10_Trainer1.jpg
Support_WD_10_Trainer2.jpg
IL_WD_10-2.docx
Support_WD_10_Instructor.jpg
IL_WD_10-3.docx
Support_WD_10_Peru.jpg
IL_WD_10-4.docx
Support_WD_10_SolarEnergy.jpg

Word
Module 10

Convert Tables and Text

Learning Outcomes
- Change the paper size
- Convert text to a table
- Convert a table to text

You can convert text that is separated by a tab, a comma, or another separator character, into a table. For example, to create a two-column table of last and first names, you could type the names as a list with a comma separating the last and first name in each line, and then convert the text to a table. The separator character—a comma in this example—indicates where you want to divide the table into columns, and a paragraph mark indicates where you want to begin a new row. Conversely, you can convert a table to text that is separated by tabs, commas, or some other character. **CASE** *You open a document containing much of the text needed for your form and convert a table containing the company's contact information into text and then convert the text required for the form into a table. You start by changing the page size.*

STEPS

1. **sam Start Word, open the file IL_WD_10-1.docx from the location where you store your Data Files, save the document as IL_WD_10_WorkshopSurveySetup, then click the Show/Hide button ¶ in the Paragraph group to show paragraph marks, if necessary**
2. **Click the Layout tab, then click the Size button in the Page Setup group**
   A selection of page sizes appears. The Executive page size is currently selected.
3. **Click Letter**
4. **Click anywhere in the table under JCL Talent, Inc., then click the table move handle**
   You select the table so that you can then convert the table into a line of text.
5. **Click the Layout contextual tab for tables, then click the Convert to Text button in the Data group**
   When you convert a table into text, you can choose various ways in which you want to separate the text contained in each table cell. For this table, you want the text separated with the | symbol.
6. **As shown in FIGURE 10-1, click the Other option button, type |, then click OK**
   The company contact information appears as a line of text with the sections separated by the | symbol.
7. **Select the text from Name to Top Workshops**
   Notice the TAB characters between the text. You want each TAB character to convert into a table cell.
8. **Click the Insert tab, click the Table button in the Tables group, then click Convert Text to Table**
   The Convert Text to Table dialog box opens. In this dialog box, 4 is entered as the number of columns based on the number of TAB characters in the selected text, as shown in FIGURE 10-2.
9. **Click OK, click below the table to deselect it, then save the document**
   Word converts the TAB characters and text into a table containing four columns. The Word document appears as shown in FIGURE 10-3.

QUICK TIP
To enter the | symbol, press **SHIFT** and then the backslash (\) key.

FIGURE 10-1: Convert Table to Text dialog box

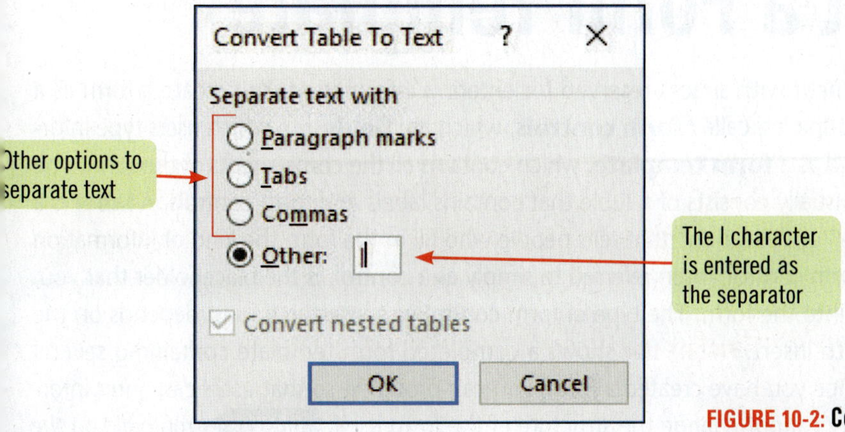

FIGURE 10-2: Convert Text to Table dialog box

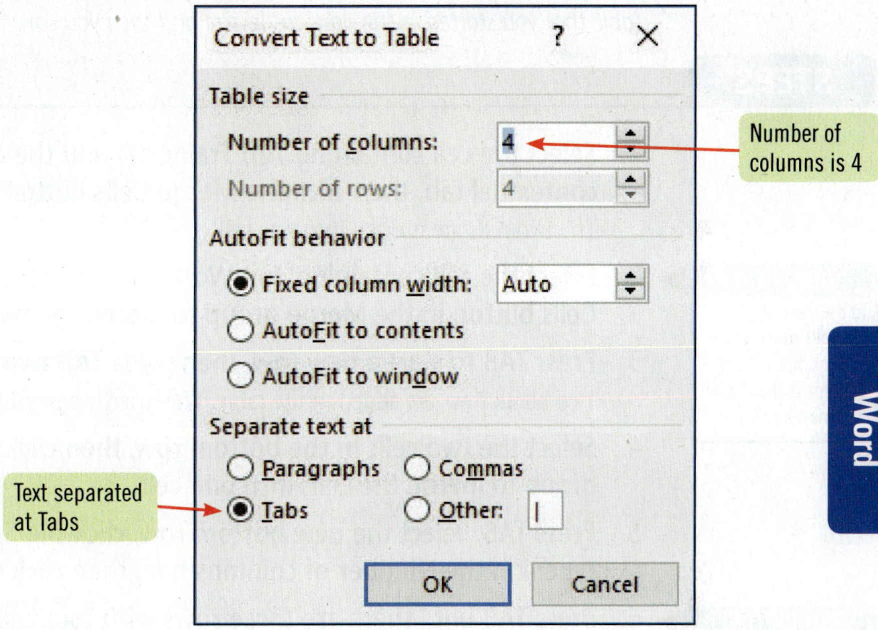

FIGURE 10-3: Table for the form

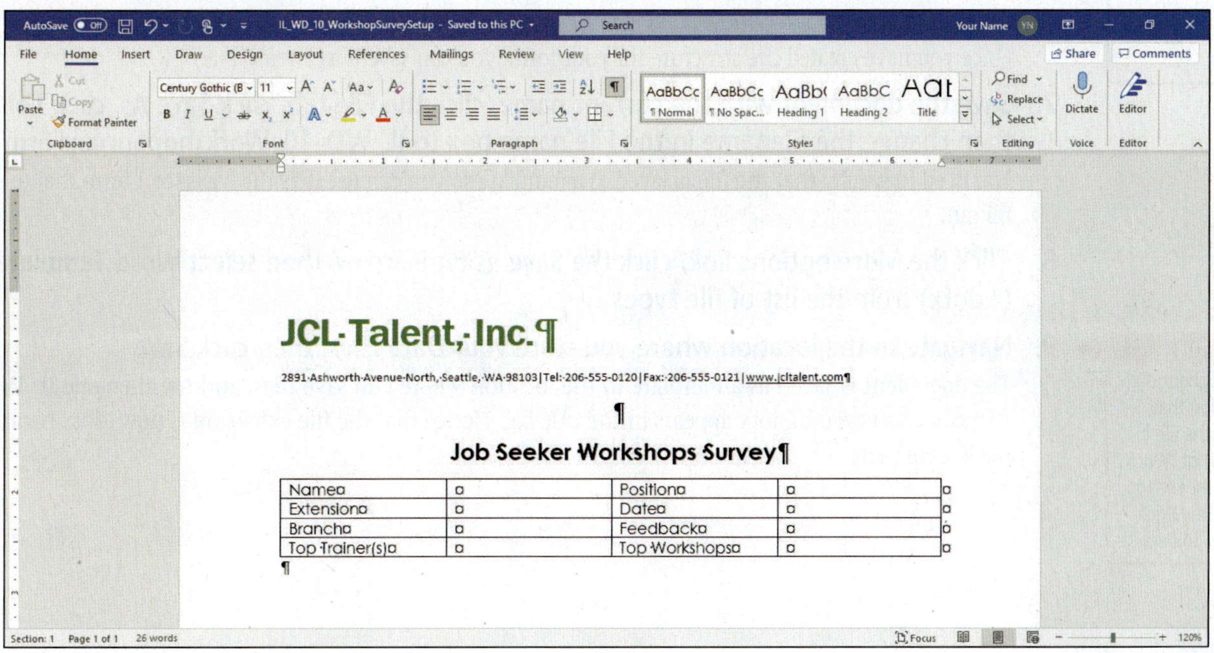

Word

Word
Module 10

Construct a Form Template

Learning Outcome
- Save a form as a template

A **form** is a structured document with spaces reserved for entering information. You create a form as a template that includes labeled spaces, called **form controls**, which are **fields** into which users type information. A Word form is created as a **form template**, which contains all the components of the form. The structure of a form template usually consists of a table that contains labels and form controls. A **label** is a word or phrase such as "Date" or "Location" that tells people who fill in the form the kind of information required for a given field. A form control, often referred to simply as a control, is the placeholder that you, as the form developer, insert into the form. The type of form control you insert in a form depends on the type of data you want users to insert. FIGURE 10-4 shows a completed form template containing several different types of controls. Once you have created a form, you can protect it so that users can enter information into the form, but they cannot change the structure of the form itself. **CASE** *You build on the table that you started in the previous lesson and then you save the document as a template.*

STEPS

QUICK TIP
To merge cells, the cells must be contiguous, that is, they must share a common border.

QUICK TIP
Press TAB to move from cell to cell when entering text in a table.

TROUBLE
You *must* change the location that you save the file to. If you do not, Word will save the file to the Custom Office Templates folder.

1. **Select the cell containing Top Trainer(s) and the cell to the right, click the Layout contextual tab, then click the Merge Cells button in the Merge group**
   The two cells are merged into one cell.
2. **Select the cell containing Top Workshops and the cell to its right, then click the Merge Cells button in the Merge group to merge the two cells into one cell**
3. **Press TAB to start a new row, then press TAB two more times**
   Two blank rows are added to the table. The insertion point is in the first cell of the bottom row.
4. **Select the two cells in the bottom row, then click the Merge Cells button in the Merge group to merge the cells into one cell**
5. **Press TAB, select the new bottom row, click the Split Cells button in the Merge group, type 4 in the Number of columns box, then click OK**
6. **Press TAB until there are three rows with four cells in each row at the bottom of the table, merge the last three cells in the last row, then enter text in the table as shown in FIGURE 10-5**
   Once you have created the structure for your form, you can save it as a template.
7. **Save the document with the current name, click the File tab, click Save As, click This PC, then change the filename in the File name box to IL_WD_10_WorkshopSurveyForm**
   You need to specify that the file is saved as a template so you can use it as the basis for a form that users will fill out.
8. **Click the More options link, click the Save as type arrow, then select Word Template (*.dotx) from the list of file types**
9. **Navigate to the location where you store your Data Files, then click Save**
   The document is saved as a template to the location where you save files, and the filename IL_WD_10_WorkshopSurveyForm.dotx appears in the title bar. Notice that the file extension is now .dotx because the file is a template.

FIGURE 10-4: Form construction

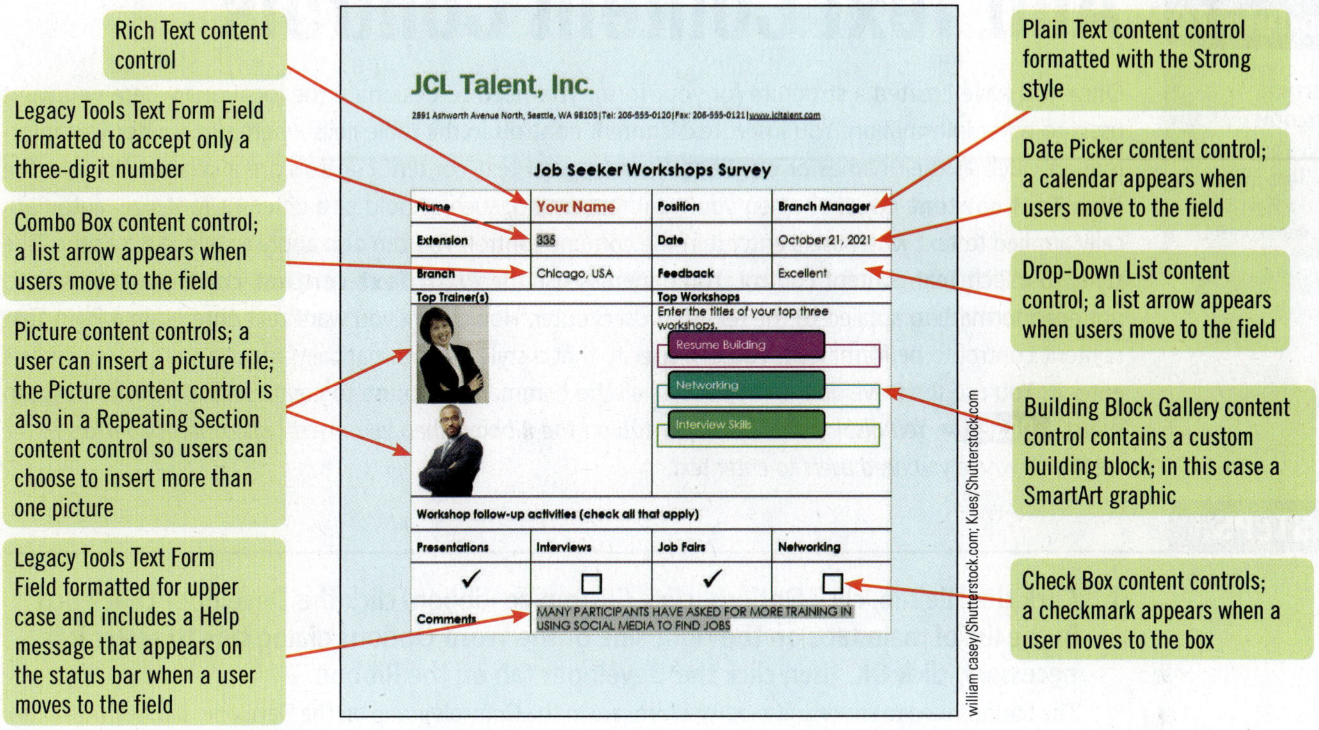

FIGURE 10-5: Table form with labels and merged cells

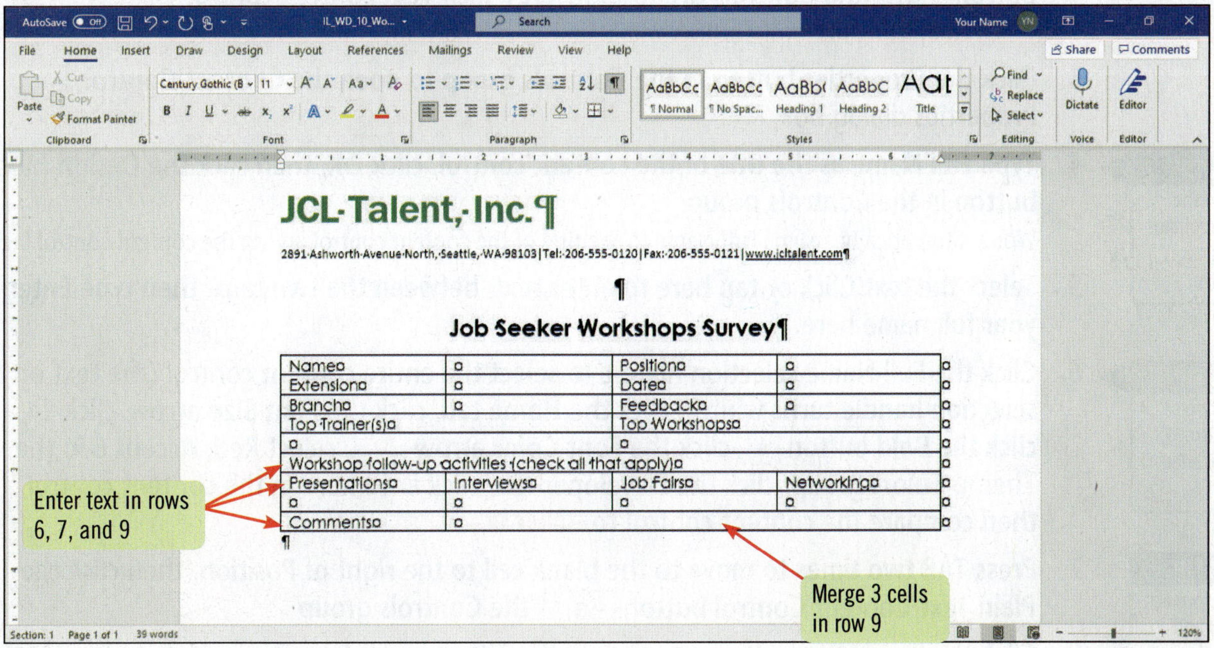

Editing a Template

A template is not the same as a document. You need to use a specific set of steps to open a template when you want to edit it. If you choose not to complete all the lessons in this module at one sitting, you will need to use the following procedure to open the template file so you can continue working. Click the File tab, click Open, click Browse, navigate to the location where you store your files for this book, click IL_WD_10_WorkshopSurveyForm.dotx, then click Open. If you double-click the file, a new document opens. Close this document and use the procedure described to open the template file so that you can continue working with it.

Add Text Content Controls

Learning Outcomes
- Add a Rich Text content control
- Add a Plain Text content control

Once you have created a structure for your form, you need to designate the locations where you want users to enter information. You insert text content controls in the table cells where users enter text information, such as their names or positions. Two types of text content controls are available. You use the **Rich Text content control** when you want formatting, such as bold or a different font size, automatically applied to text when users enter it in the content control. You can also apply a style, such as the Title style, to a Rich Text content control. You generally use the **Plain Text content control** when you do not need formatting applied to the text that users enter. However, if you want text entered in a Plain Text content control to be formatted, you can specify that a style be automatically applied to text when users enter it. You use the Developer tab to access all the commands you use to create and work with forms in Word. **CASE** *You display the Developer tab on the Ribbon, then you insert text content controls in the table cells where you need users to enter text.*

STEPS

1. **Click the File tab, click Options, click Customize Ribbon, click the Developer check box in the list of main tabs on the right side of the Word Options dialog box to select it if necessary, click OK, then click the Developer tab on the Ribbon**
   The buttons used to create and modify a form are in the Controls group on the Developer tab; see TABLE 10-1.
2. **Click in the blank cell to the right of Name, then click the Rich Text Content Control button [Aa] in the Controls group to insert a Rich Text content control**
   When completing the form, the user will be able to enter text into this content control.
3. **Click the Properties button in the Controls group to open the Content Control Properties dialog box**
4. **Type Full Name as the title of the content control, click OK, then click the Design Mode button in the Controls group**
   Word automatically assigns Full Name to the title of the content control and to the content control tags.
5. **Select the text Click or tap here to enter text. between the two tags, then type Enter your full name here.**
6. **Click the Full Name selection handle to select the entire content control (the text on the selection handle turns white), click the Home tab, click the Font Size arrow, click 14, click the Bold button [B], click the Font Color arrow [A], select Red, Accent 6 in the Theme Colors group, click the Developer tab, click anywhere in the content control, then compare the content control to FIGURE 10-6**
7. **Press TAB two times to move to the blank cell to the right of Position, then click the Plain Text Content Control button [Aa] in the Controls group**
8. **Click the Properties button, type Job in the Title box, click the Use a style to format text typed into the empty control check box, click the Style arrow, select Strong as shown in FIGURE 10-7, then click OK**
   If you want text entered in a Plain Text content control to appear formatted when the user fills in the form, you must apply a paragraph style. The Strong paragraph style that you applied to the Plain Text content control will show when you fill in the form as a user.
9. **Select the Click or tap here to enter text. text between the two Job tags, type Enter your job title here., click outside the table, then click the Save button [Save] on the Quick Access toolbar to save the template**

QUICK TIP
You can view the content control tags only when Design Mode is active.

QUICK TIP
When the content control is selected, the control is shaded gray.

QUICK TIP
If you apply formats, such as bold and font size, to the Plain Text content control, the formatting will be lost when the form is opened and filled in by a user. You can format both Rich Text and Plain Text content controls with a paragraph style.

FIGURE 10-6: Rich Text content control

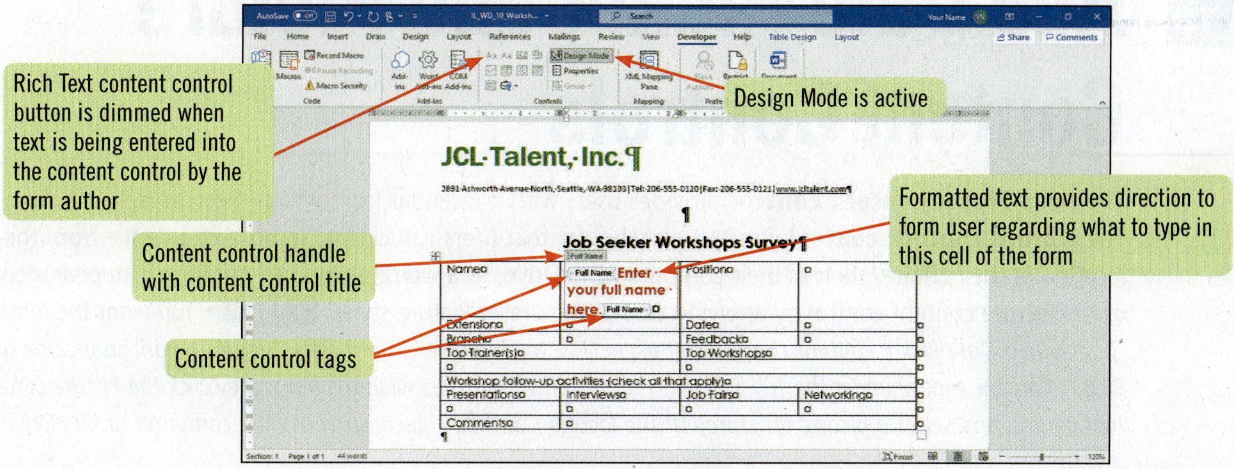

FIGURE 10-7: Content Control Properties dialog box

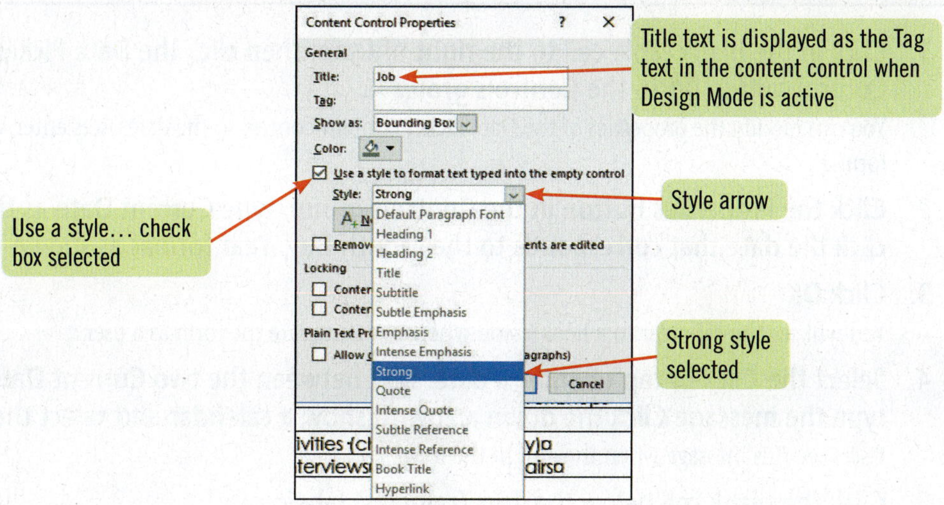

TABLE 10-1: Buttons in the Controls group

button	use to insert a
Aa	Rich Text content control when you want to apply formatting, such as bold, to text users type
Aa	Plain Text content control when you want the text that users type to display as plain, unformatted text
	Picture content control when you want users to be able to insert a picture file
	Building Block Gallery content control when you want to insert a custom building block, such as a cover page
	Check Box content control when you want to insert a check box that users can click to indicate a selection
	Combo Box content control when you want users to select from a list or be able to add a new item
	Drop-Down List content control when you want to provide users with a list of restricted choices
	Date Picker content control when you want to include a calendar control that users can use to select a specific date
	Repeating Section content control when you want to repeat content, including other content controls
	Control from the Legacy Tools options when you want additional control over the content that can be entered into a control; if you have programming experience, you can insert ActiveX Controls into forms using the Legacy Tools button

Learning Outcomes
- Add a Date Picker content control
- Add a Picture content control

Add Date Picker and Picture Content Controls

The **Date Picker content control** provides users with a calendar from which they can select a date. The **Picture content control** inserts a placeholder that users can click to insert a picture file from the location of their choice, such as their computer, OneDrive, or a website. You can modify the appearance of the Picture content control by applying one of the preset Picture styles. **CASE** *You want the form to include a Date Picker content control that users click to enter the current date. You also want to include a Picture content control under the Top Trainer(s) table cell. When users fill in the form, they click the Picture content control and select a picture file stored at the location of their choice, such as their computer or OneDrive account.*

STEPS

1. **Click in the blank table cell to the right of Date, then click the Date Picker Content Control button in the Controls group**
   You can modify the properties of the Date Picker content control so the date users enter appears in a specific format.
2. **Click the Properties button in the Controls group, type Current Date as the title, then click the date that corresponds to the Month Day, Year format as shown in FIGURE 10-8**
3. **Click OK**
   You will see the calendar in a later lesson when you complete the form as a user.
4. **Select the Click or tap to enter a date. text between the two Current Date tags, then type the message Click the down arrow to show a calendar and select the current date.**
   Users see this message when they fill in the form.
5. **Click the blank cell below the Top Trainer(s) label**
6. **Click the Picture Content Control button in the Controls group**
   A Picture content control is inserted in the table cell. When users fill in the form, they click the picture icon to insert a picture file from a location of their choice, such as their computer's hard drive, their OneDrive account, or a website.
7. **Click the Properties button, type Insert up to three pictures as the title, then click OK**
   The title text advises users that they will be able to insert more than one picture.
8. **Click the Design Mode button in the Controls group to toggle out of Design mode, compare the table form to FIGURE 10-9, then save the template**
   You need to toggle out of Design mode so you can work with the Repeating Section content control in the next lesson.

FIGURE 10-8: Selecting a date format

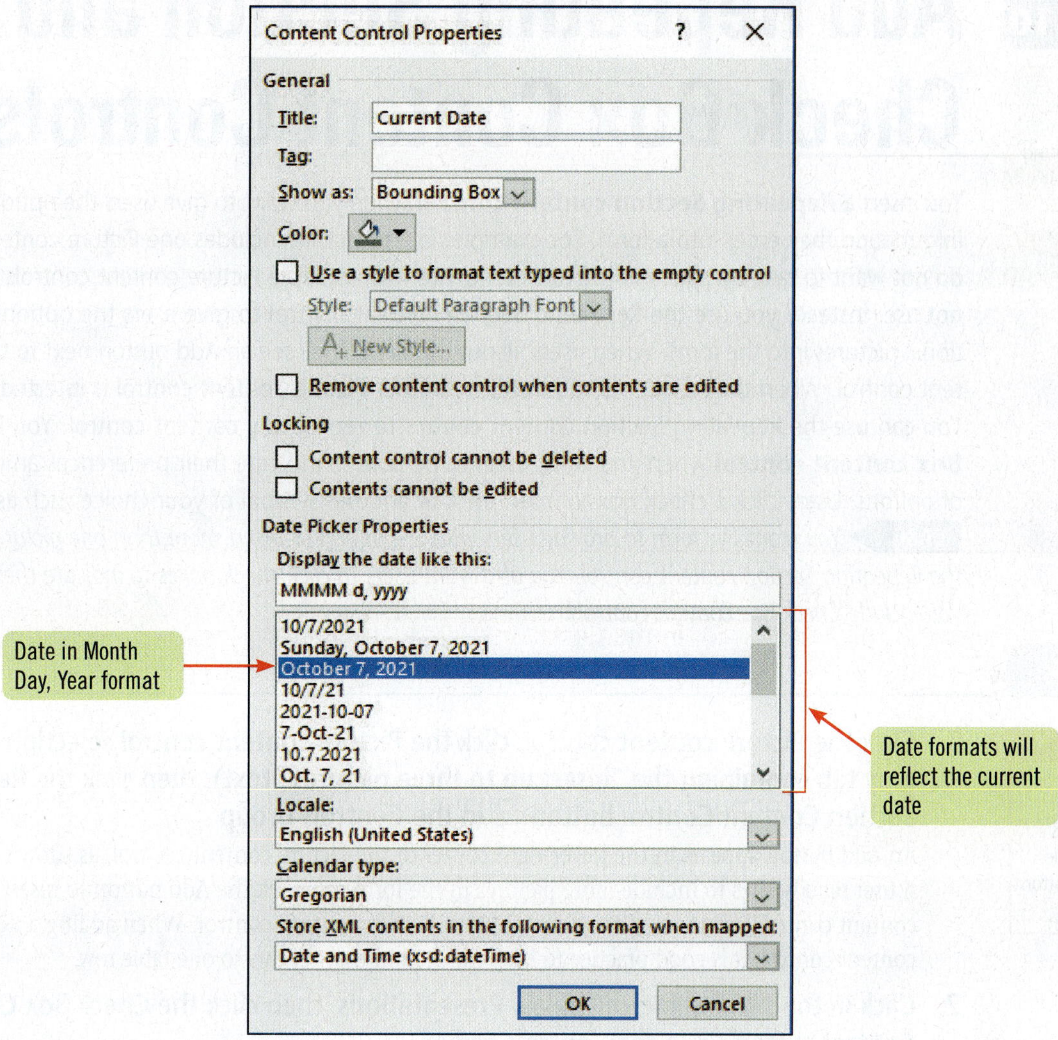

FIGURE 10-9: Picture content control

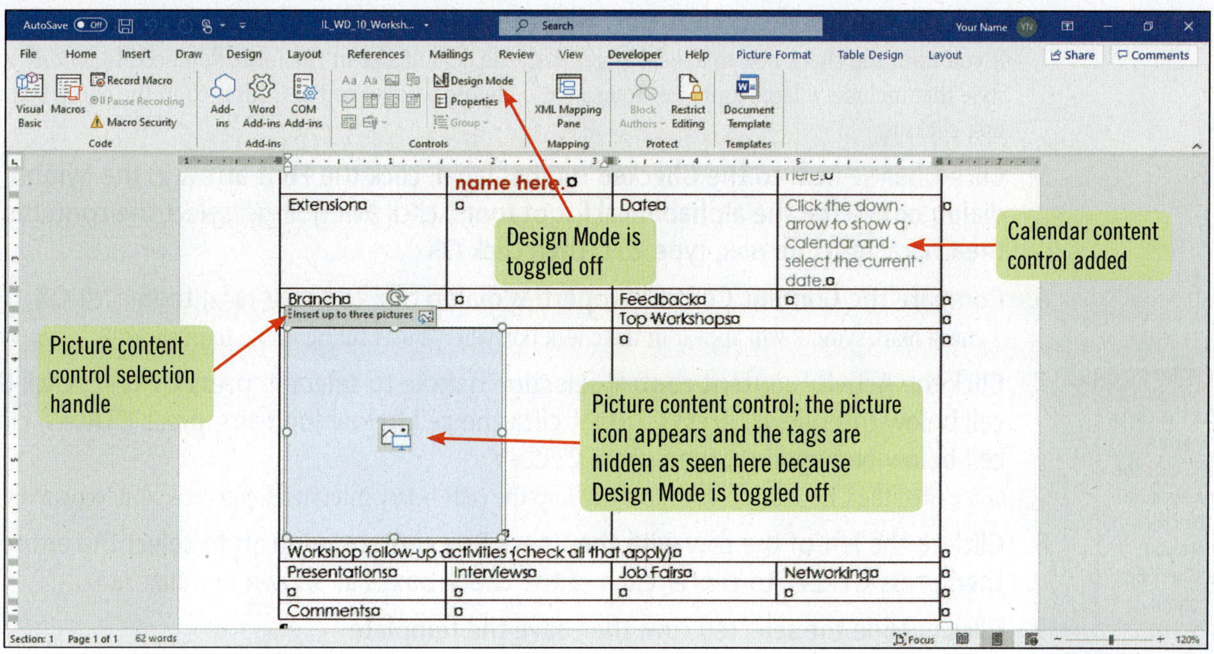

Add Repeating Section and Check Box Content Controls

Learning Outcomes
- Use the Repeating Section content control
- Add Check Box content controls

You insert a **Repeating Section content control** when you want to give users the option to add to the information they enter into a form. For example, in a form that includes one Picture content control, you do not want to take up space in the form template with multiple Picture content controls that users may not use. Instead, you use the Repeating Section content control to give users the option to insert additional pictures into the form. When users fill out the form, they see an Add button next to the Picture content control. When they click the Add button, another Picture content control is inserted into the form. You can use the Repeating Section content control to repeat any content control. You insert a **Check Box content control** when you want users to be able to indicate their preferences among a selection of options. Users click a check box to insert an X or another symbol of your choice such as a check mark. **CASE** *You want the form to provide users with the option to insert more than one picture so you include the Repeating Section content control. You also want users to click check boxes to indicate their preferences so you include Check Box content controls.*

STEPS

TROUBLE
If the Repeating Section Content Control button is dimmed, click the Design Mode button to toggle it off.

1. **Click the Picture content control, click the Picture content control selection handle (the gray tab containing the "Insert up to three pictures" text), then click the Repeating Section Content Control button in the Controls group**

   An Add button appears in the lower-right corner of the Picture content control, as shown in FIGURE 10-10. A user who wishes to include more pictures in the form can click the Add button to insert another Picture content control and then add a picture to that Picture content control. When adding a Repeating Section content control, it is good practice to keep the section that repeats to one table row.

2. **Click in the blank table cell below Presentations, then click the Check Box Content Control button in the Controls group**

3. **Click the Properties button, then type Activity**

4. **Click the Use a style... check box, click the Style arrow, then click Title**

   If you want the check box to appear larger than the default size in the form, you need to modify it with a style that includes a large font size. You can also choose which symbol is inserted in the check box when a user clicks it.

5. **Click Change next to the Checked symbol label, click the Font arrow in the Symbol dialog box, scroll the alphabetical list of fonts, click Wingdings, select the contents of the Character code box, type 252, then click OK**

6. **Compare the Content Control Properties dialog box to FIGURE 10-11, then click OK**

   A check mark symbol will appear in the check box when a user filling in the form clicks it.

TROUBLE
If you click the check box and insert a checkmark, click the check box again to remove the checkmark before you copy the Check Box content control.

7. **Click the Activity content control selection handle to select it, press CTRL+C, click the cell below Interviews, press CTRL+V, click the cell below Job Fairs, press CTRL+V, click the cell below Networking, then press CTRL+V**

   You pasted the Check Box content control into the cells below Interviews, Job Fairs, and Networking.

8. **Click to the left of the row with the Check Box content controls to select the entire row, then press CTRL+E to center each of the check boxes as shown in FIGURE 10-12**

9. **Click outside the selected row, then save the template**

FIGURE 10-10: Add button for the Repeating Section content control

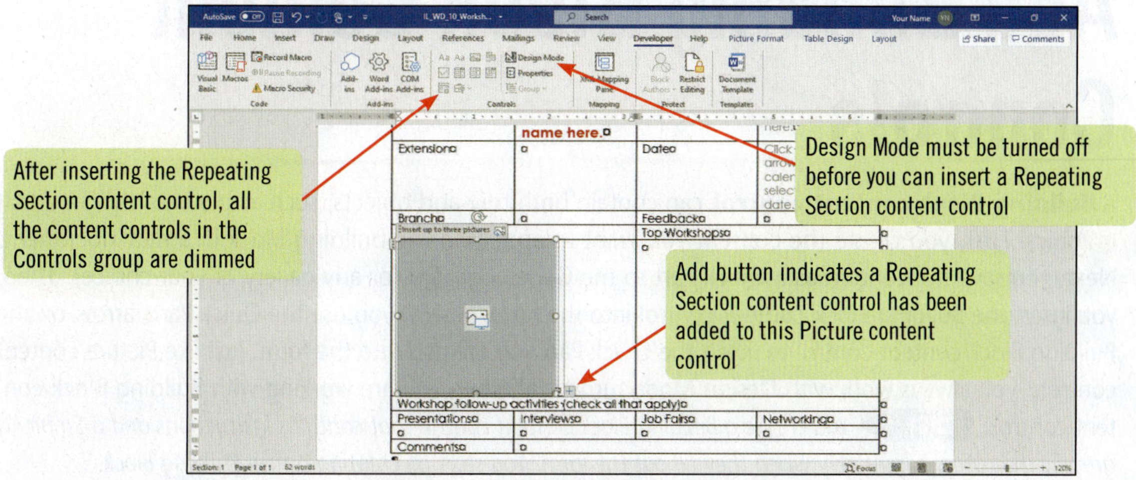

FIGURE 10-11: Check Box content control properties

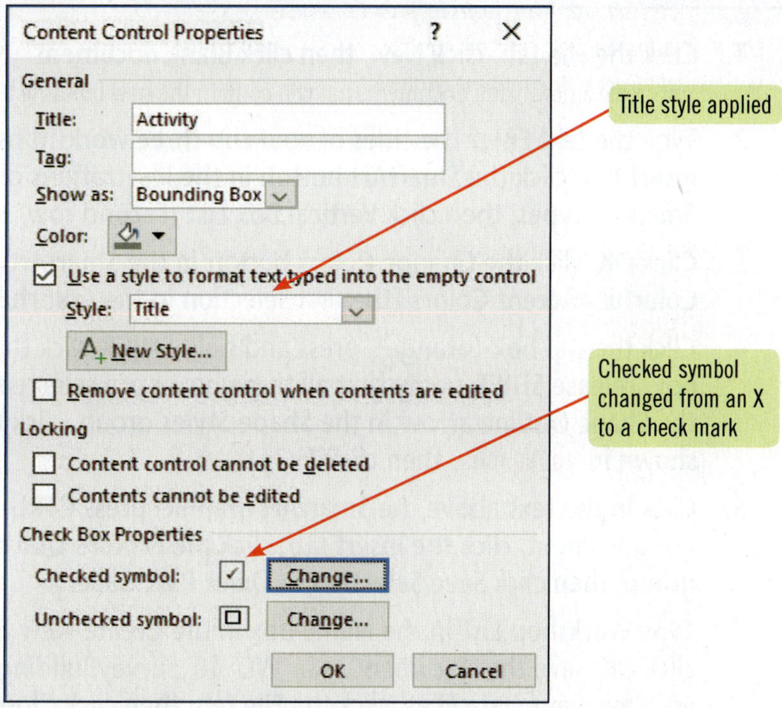

FIGURE 10-12: Table form with the Check Box content controls added

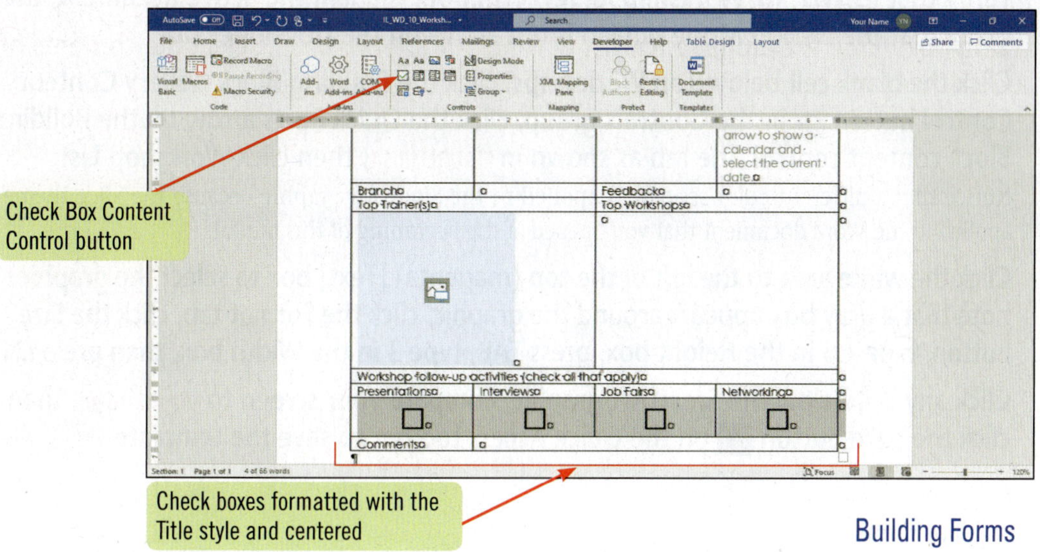

Word Module 10

Add Building Block Content Controls

Learning Outcomes
- Create a Quick Part
- Add a Building Block content control

A **Building Block content control** can contain both text and objects, such as pictures and SmartArt graphics. First, you create the content you want to appear in the building block in a new document. Next, you save the content as a Quick Part to the General gallery (or any gallery of your choice). Then, you insert the Building Block content control into the form. Finally, you use the Quick Parts arrow on the Building Block content control to insert the Quick Part you created into the form. Just like Picture content controls, you always work with Design Mode turned off when you are working with Building Block content controls. CASE *You create a Building Block content control that contains instructions and a SmartArt graphic that users can modify when they fill out the form. You start by creating a new Building Block.*

STEPS

1. **Click the File tab, click New, then click Blank document**
   You create a new blank document that will contain the new building block you want to appear in the form.
2. **Type the text Enter the titles of your top three workshops., press ENTER, click the Insert tab, click the SmartArt button in the Illustrations group, click List in the list of SmartArt types, then click Vertical Box List (second row, second column)**
3. **Click OK, click the Change Colors button in the SmartArt Styles group, then click Colorful - Accent Colors (the first selection in the Colorful section)**
4. **Click the top box (orange), press and hold SHIFT, click the gray box, click the yellow box, release SHIFT, verify that all three boxes are selected, click the Format tab, click the Shape Outline arrow in the Shape Styles group, click Weight, point to 1½ pt as shown in FIGURE 10-13, then click 1½ pt**
5. **Click in the text above the SmartArt graphic, press CTRL+A to select the contents of the document, click the Insert tab, click the Explore Quick Parts button in the Text group, then click Save Selection to Quick Part Gallery**
6. **Type Workshop List in the Name box in the Create New Building Block dialog box, click OK, save the document as IL_WD_10_SurveyBuildingBlock to the location where you save your Data Files, click the File tab, then click Close**
7. **Verify that IL_WD_10_WorkshopSurveyForm.dotx is again the active document, then verify that the Design Mode button is not active on the Developer tab**
8. **Click the blank cell below Top Workshops, click the Building Block Gallery Content Control button in the Controls group, click the Quick Parts arrow on the Building Block content control title tab as shown in FIGURE 10-14, then click Workshop List**
   Notice that a different color scheme is applied to the SmartArt graphic because the Slice theme was applied to the Word document that you opened at the beginning of this module.
9. **Click the white area to the left of the top (magenta) [Text] box to select the graphic, note that a gray box appears around the graphic, click the Format tab, click the Size button, type 1.6 in the Height box, press TAB, type 3 in the Width box, then press ENTER**
10. **Click any cell below the SmartArt graphic, compare your screen to FIGURE 10-15, then click the Save button on the Quick Access toolbar to save the template**

QUICK TIP
The default Office theme was applied when you created the SmartArt graphic in a new document.

FIGURE 10-13: Shape Outline weight selected

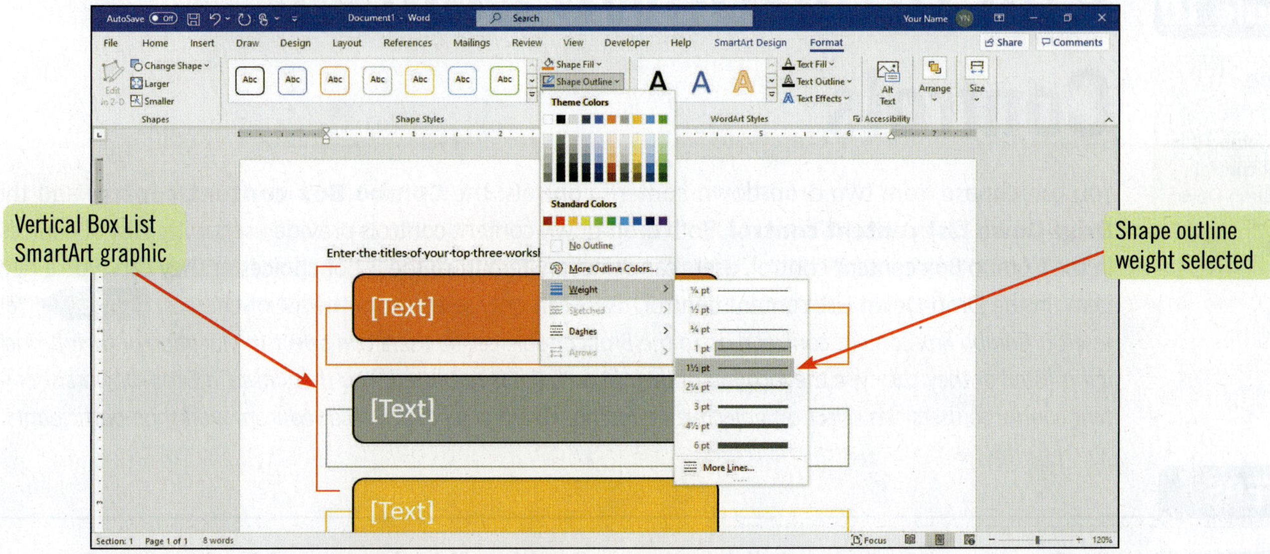

FIGURE 10-14: Inserting a Building Block content control

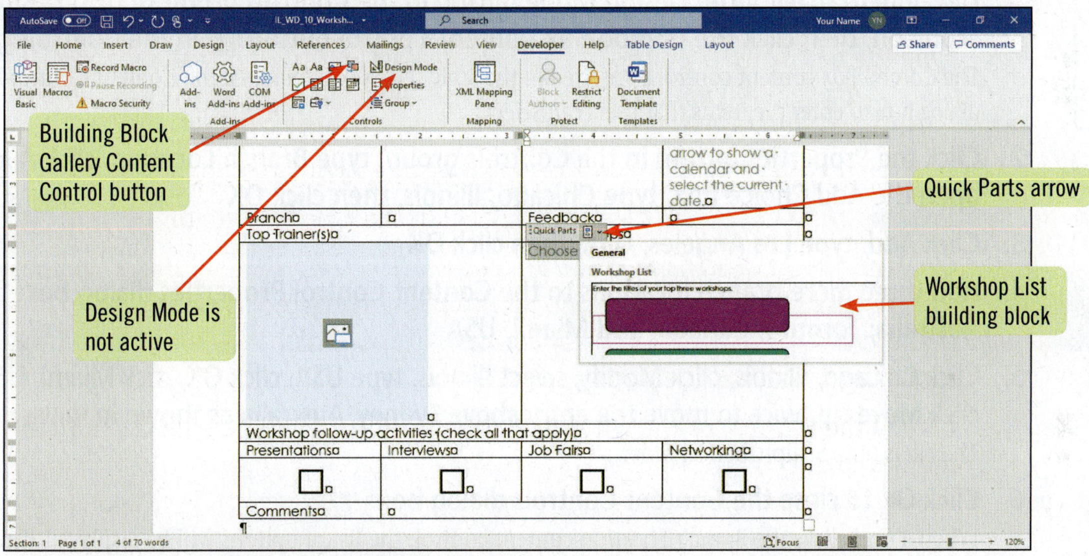

FIGURE 10-15: Completed Building Block content control

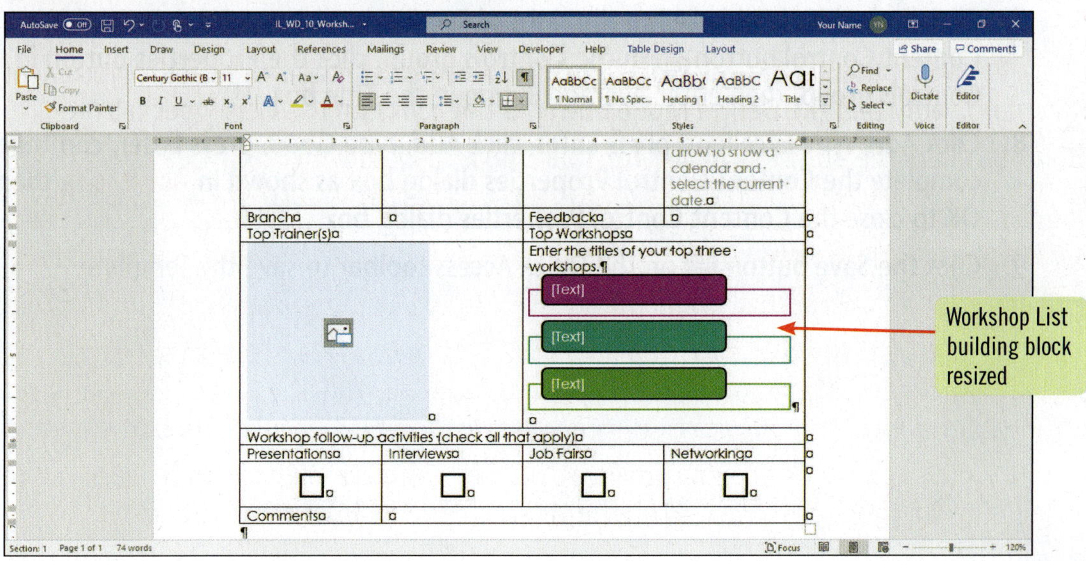

Word

Add Drop-Down Content Controls

Learning Outcomes
- Add a Combo Box content control
- Add a Drop-Down List content control

You can choose from two drop-down content controls: the **Combo Box content control** and the **Drop-Down List content control**. Both drop-down content controls provide users with a list of choices. In the Combo Box content control, users can select an item from the list of choices or they can type a new item. In the Drop-Down List content control, users can only select from the list of choices. CASE *You insert a Combo Box content control next to the Branch table cell so users can select the location of their branch if it is listed or they can type the location of their branch if it is not listed. You then insert a Drop-Down List content control so users can select an adjective to describe average feedback received from workshop participants.*

STEPS

QUICK TIP
With Design Mode on, you can see the tags associated with each content control.

1. **Scroll up as needed and click in the blank table cell to the right of Branch, click the Developer tab, click the Design Mode button in the Controls group to turn Design Mode on, then click the Combo Box Content Control button in the Controls group**
   The Combo Box content control is inserted in the table cell. Next, you open the Content Control Properties dialog box to enter the items that users can select.
2. **Click the Properties button in the Controls group, type Branch Location, click Add to open the Add Choice box, type Chicago, Illinois, then click OK**
3. **Click Add, type Los Angeles, USA, then click OK**
4. **Add three more branch locations to the Content Control Properties dialog box: Sydney, Australia; Toronto, Canada; and Miami, USA**
5. **Click Chicago, Illinois, click Modify, select Illinois, type USA, click OK, click Miami, USA, then click Move Up twice to move the entry above Sydney, Australia as shown in FIGURE 10-16**
   The list is now in alphabetical order.
6. **Click OK to close the Content Controls dialog box**
   When a user clicks the Branch Location content control, the list of options will be displayed. The user can select one of the options or type a branch location in the box.
7. **Click in the blank table cell to the right of Feedback, click the Drop-Down List Content Control button in the Controls group, click the Properties button in the Controls group, then enter Average Rating in the Title box**
8. **Click Add, type Excellent, press Enter, click Add, type Good, press Enter, continue to complete the Content Control Properties dialog box as shown in FIGURE 10-17, then click OK to close the Content Control Properties dialog box**
9. **Click the Save button on the Quick Access toolbar to save the template**

FIGURE 10-16: Entries for the Combo Box content control

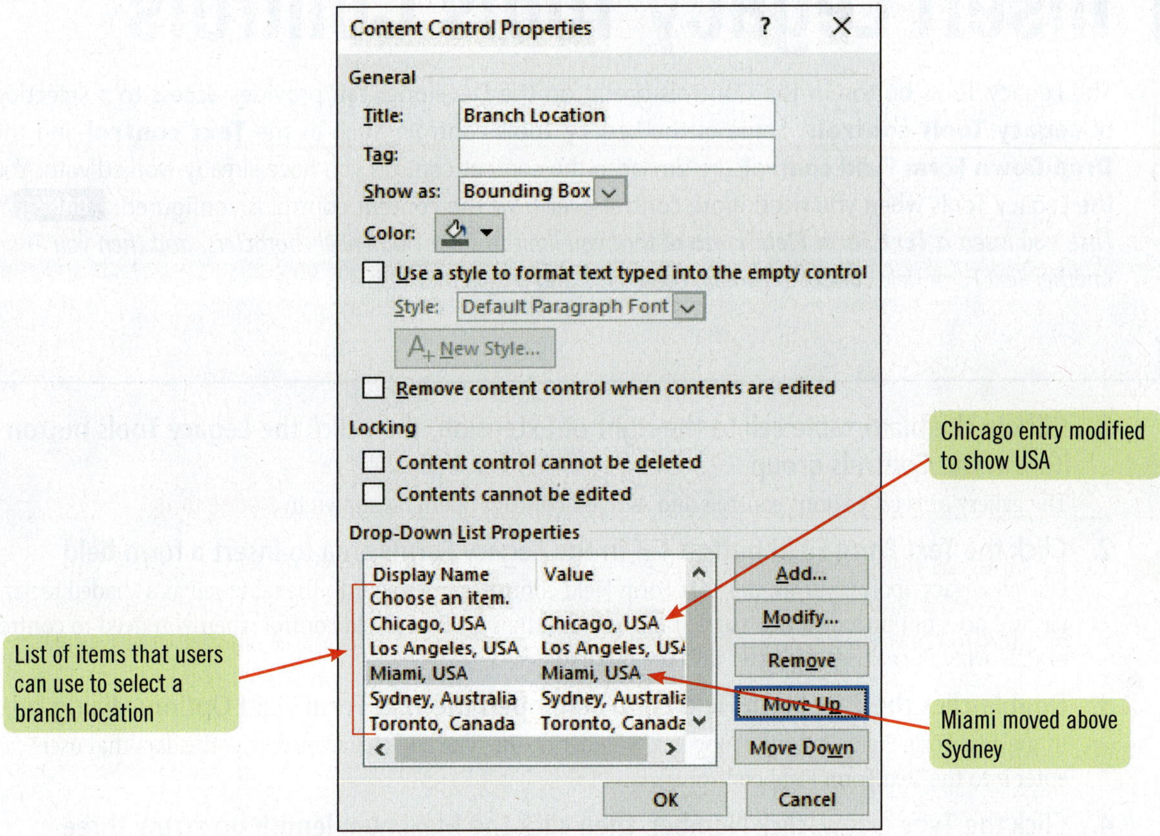

FIGURE 10-17: Entries for the Drop-Down List content control

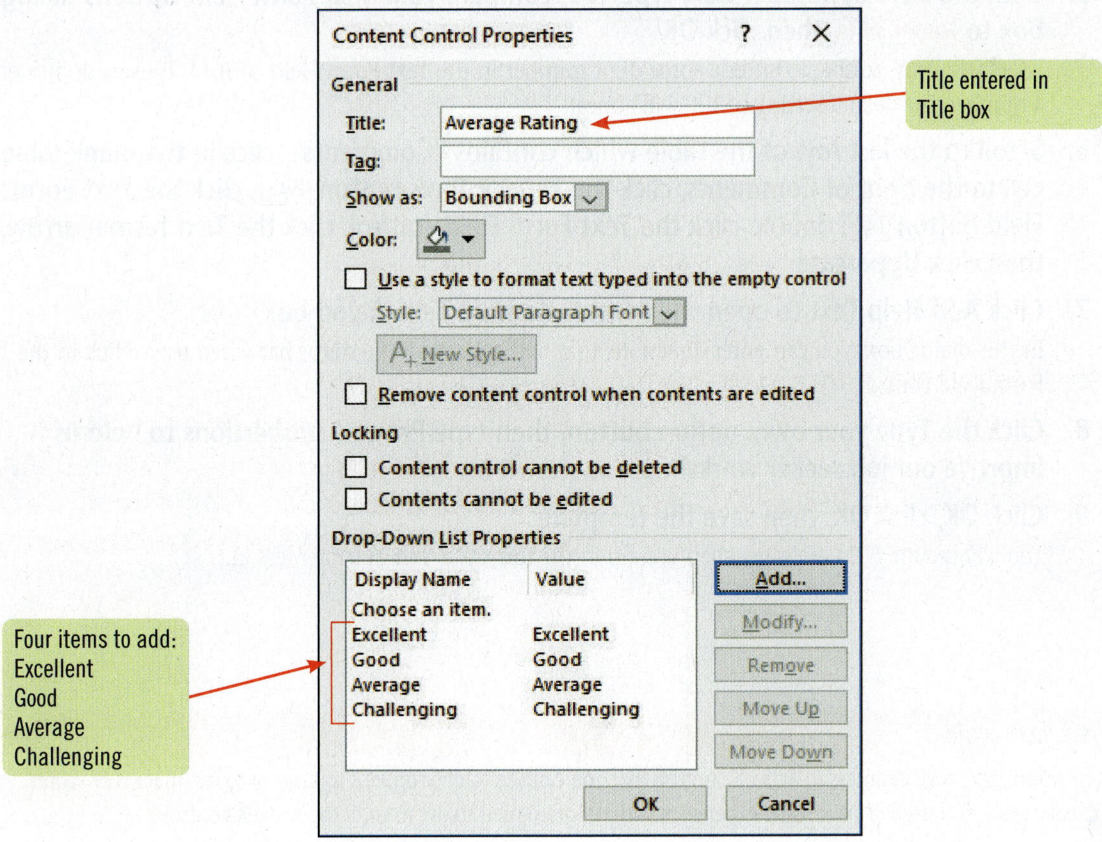

Word
Module 10

Insert Legacy Tools Controls

Learning Outcomes
- Insert a Text form field
- Add Help text

The Legacy Tools button in the Controls group on the Developer tab provides access to a selection of **Legacy Tools controls**. Some of the Legacy Tools controls, such as the **Text control** and the **Drop-Down Form Field control**, are similar to the content controls you have already worked with. You use Legacy Tools when you need more control over how the content control is configured. CASE *First, you insert a* ***Text Form Field control*** *that you limit to three numerical characters, and then you insert another Text Form Field control to contain comments and a Help message.*

STEPS

1. **Click in the blank table cell to the right of Extension, then click the Legacy Tools button in the Controls group**
   The gallery of Legacy Forms controls and ActiveX controls opens, as shown in FIGURE 10-18.
2. **Click the Text Form Field button in the Legacy Forms area to insert a form field**
   Like all Legacy Tools controls, the Text Form Field control is inserted into the table cell as a shaded rectangle and does not include a title bar or tags. You use the Text Form Field control when you need to control exactly what data a user can enter into the placeholder.
3. **Double-click the Text Form Field control to open the Text Form Field Options dialog box**
   In the Text Form Field Options dialog box, you define the type and characteristics of the data that users can enter into the Text Form Field control.
4. **Click the Type arrow, click Number, then click the Maximum length up arrow three times to set the maximum length of the entry at 3**
5. **Click the Default number box, type 100, compare your Text Form Field Options dialog box to FIGURE 10-19, then click OK**
   Users will only be able to enter a three-digit number in the Text Form Field control. If users do not enter a number, the default setting of 100 will appear.
6. **Scroll to the last row of the table which contains "Comments", click in the blank table cell to the right of Comments, click the Legacy Tools button, click the Text Form Field button, double-click the Text Form Field control, click the Text format arrow, then click Uppercase**
7. **Click Add Help Text to open the Form Field Help Text dialog box**
   In this dialog box, you can enter directions that will appear on the status bar when users click in the Text Form Field control.
8. **Click the Type your own: option button, then type Provide suggestions to help us improve our job seeker workshops. as shown in FIGURE 10-20**
9. **Click OK, click OK, then save the template**
   You will see the Help message when you fill in the form as a user in a later lesson.

Using ActiveX controls

The Legacy Tools button also provides access to ActiveX controls that you can use to offer options to users or to run macros or scripts that automate specific tasks. You need to have some experience with programming to use most of the ActiveX controls.

FIGURE 10-18: Inserting a Text Form Field control

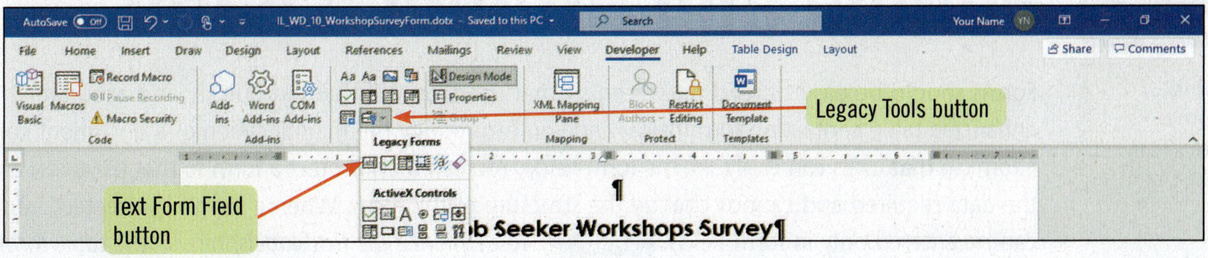

FIGURE 10-19: Text Form Field Options dialog box

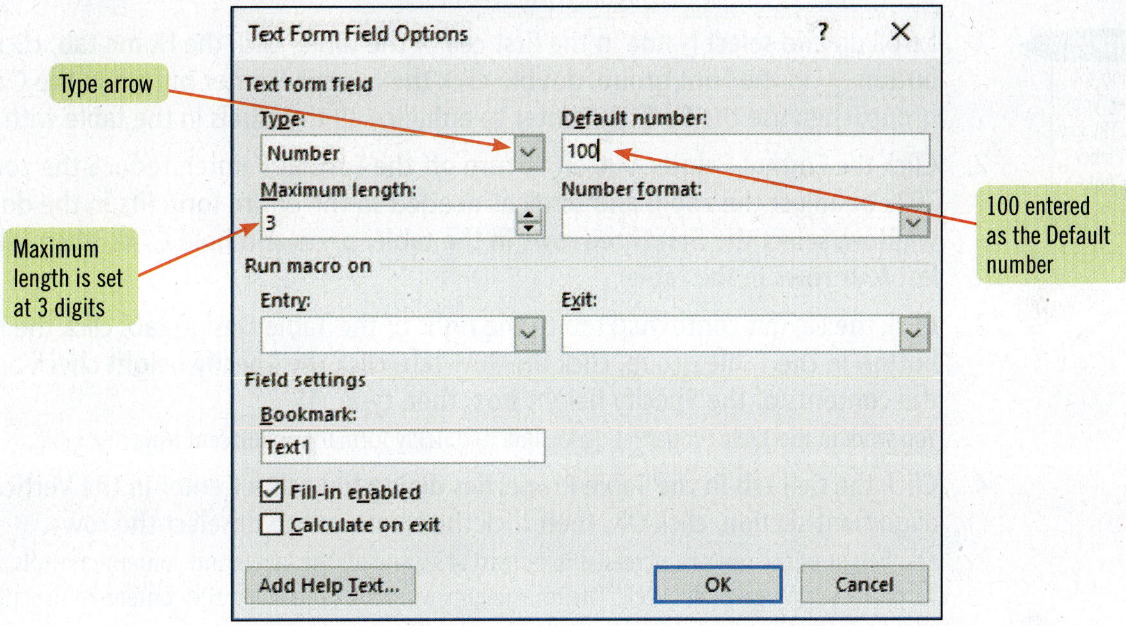

FIGURE 10-20: Adding Help text

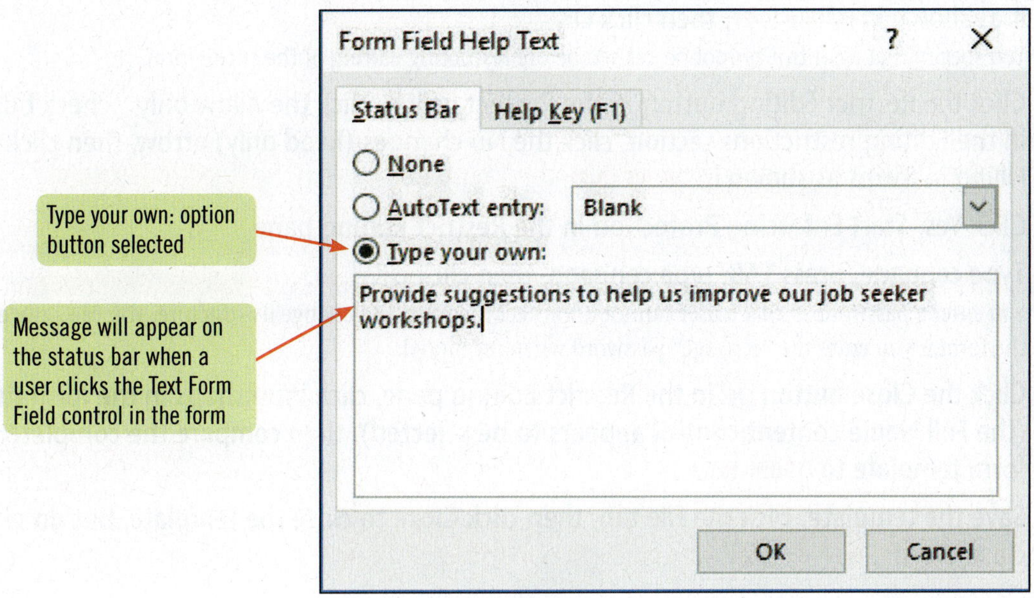

Word

Format and Protect a Form

Learning Outcomes
- Format a form
- Protect a form

Forms should be easy to read on-screen so that users can fill them in quickly and accurately. You can enhance a table containing form fields, and you can modify the magnification of a document containing a form so that users can easily see the form fields. You can then protect a form so that users can enter only the data required and cannot change the structure of the form. When a form is protected, information can be entered only in form fields. **CASE** *You enhance the field labels, modify the table form, specify that the Name content control cannot be deleted, and then protect and save the template.*

STEPS

QUICK TIP Instead of using the Format Painter, you can use the CTRL key to select each label, then click the Bold button.

1. **Scroll up and select Name in the first cell of the table, click the Home tab, click the Bold button [B] in the Font group, double-click the Format Painter button in the Clipboard group, then use the Format Painter to enhance all the labels in the table with bold**
2. **Click the Format Painter button to turn off the Format Painter, reduce the zoom to 70% or adjust the zoom and scroll as needed so the entire form fits in the document window, select the first three rows in the table, press and hold CTRL, then select the last four rows in the table**
3. **Click the Layout contextual tab to the right of the Table Design tab, click the Properties button in the Table group, click the Row tab, click the Specify height check box, select the contents of the Specify height box, then type .45**

   You work in the Table Properties dialog box to quickly format nonadjacent rows in a table.
4. **Click the Cell tab in the Table Properties dialog box, click Center in the Vertical alignment section, click OK, then click the Name cell to deselect the rows**

   The height of the rows is increased to at least .45", and all the labels and content controls are centered vertically within each table cell. The row heights will look even when the content control directions are removed after the user enters information.

QUICK TIP Before you protect a document, you must be sure Design Mode is turned off.

5. **Click the Developer tab, verify that Design Mode is not active, click the Position content control in the top row, rightmost cell of the form, click the Properties button in the Controls group, click the Content Control cannot be deleted check box to select it as shown in FIGURE 10-21, then click OK**

   You specify that a control cannot be deleted before restricting editing of the entire form.
6. **Click the Restrict Editing button in the Protect group, click the Allow only...check box in the Editing restrictions section, click the No changes (Read only) arrow, then click Filling in forms as shown in FIGURE 10-22**

TROUBLE If the passwords don't match, you will be prompted to reenter the password.

7. **Click Yes, Start Enforcing Protection in the Restrict Editing pane**
8. **Type cengage, press TAB, type cengage, then click OK**

   You enter a password so that a user cannot unprotect the form and change its structure. You can only edit the form if you enter the "cengage" password when prompted.
9. **Click the Close button [×] in the Restrict Editing pane, click Workshops in the form title (the Full Name content control appears to be selected), then compare the completed form template to FIGURE 10-23**
10. **Save the template, click the File tab, then click Close to close the template, but do not close Word**

FIGURE 10-21: Locking a content control

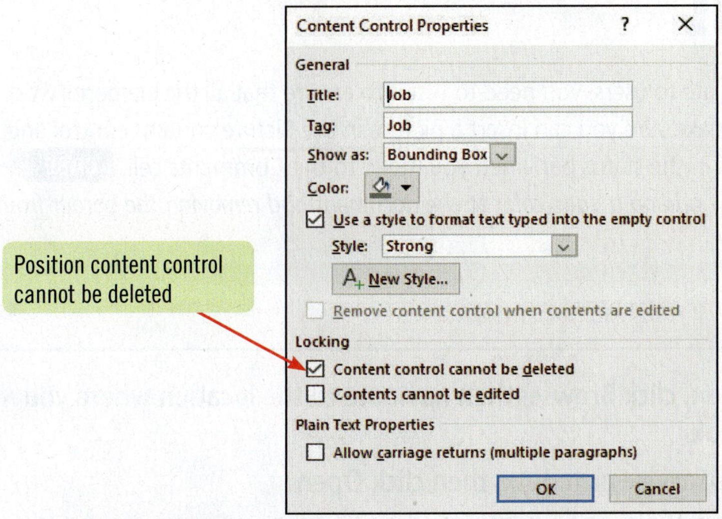

FIGURE 10-22: Protecting a form

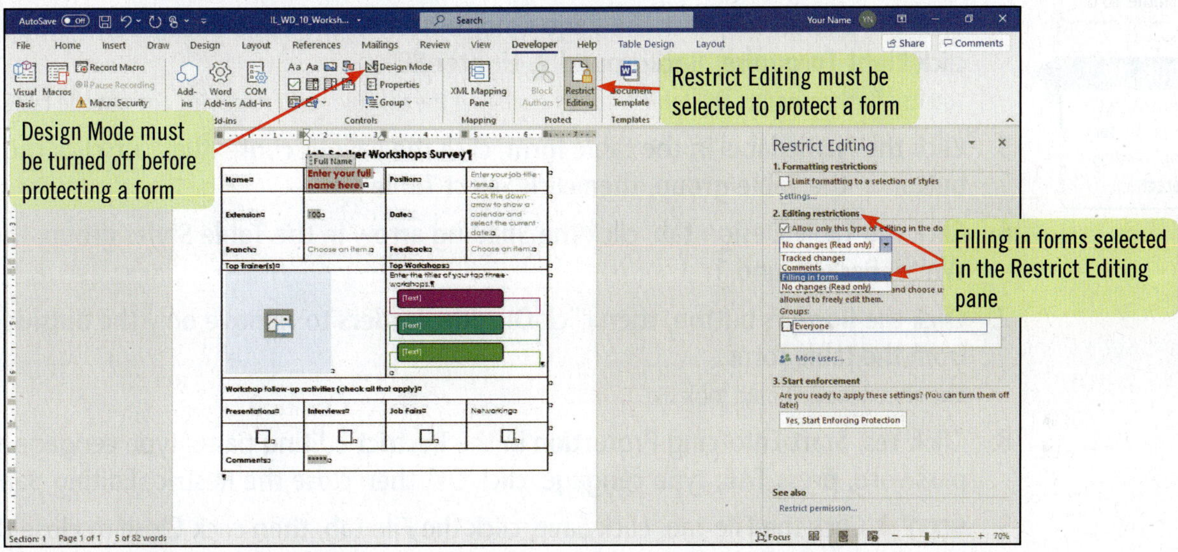

FIGURE 10-23: Completed form template

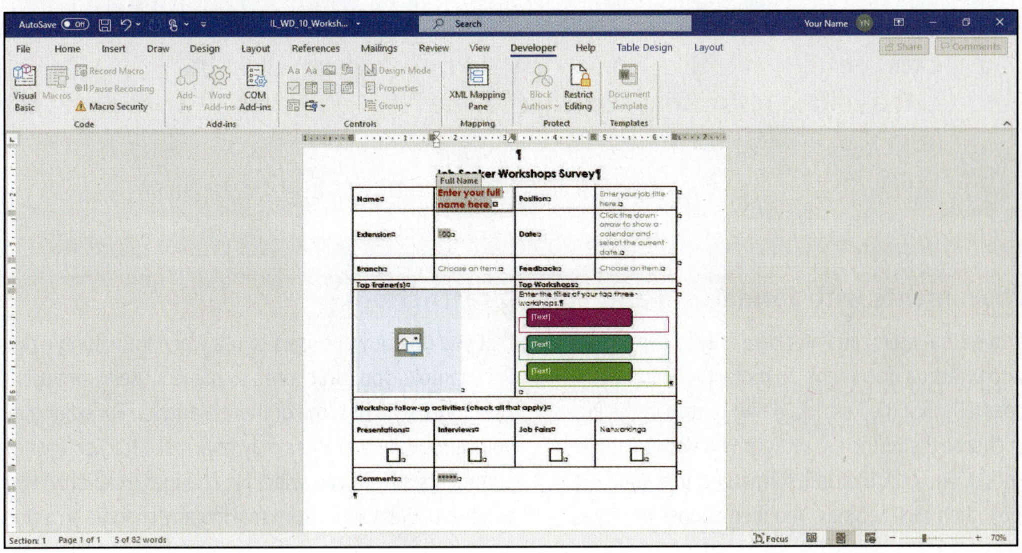

Edit a Form

Learning Outcomes
- Change the page color
- Edit a form

Before you distribute a form template to users, you need to test it to ensure that all the elements work correctly. For example, you want to make sure you can insert a picture in the Picture content control and that the Help text you entered appears in the status bar when you move to the Comments cell. **CASE** *You open and edit the form template by adding a page color to the document and removing the border from the table form.*

STEPS

TROUBLE
Do *not* double-click the filename to open it. You must use the File, Open method to open the template file so that you can make changes to it.

QUICK TIP
Before you can edit any part of the template, you need to stop protection.

1. **Click the File tab, click Open, click Browse, then navigate to the location where you store your files for this book**
2. **Click IL_WD_10_WorkshopSurveyForm.dotx, then click Open**
3. **Click the Developer tab, click the Restrict Editing button in the Protect group, click Stop Protection in the Restrict Editing pane, type cengage as shown in FIGURE 10-24, then click OK**
4. **Click the Design tab, click the Page Color button in the Page Background group, then click Light Turquoise, Background 2, Lighter 80%**
   You can further modify the table form by changing the fill color and removing the outside table border.
5. **Click the Name label in the table form, click the Layout contextual tab, click the Select button in the Table group, then click Select Table**
6. **Click the Table Design tab, click the Shading arrow in the Table Styles group, then click White, Background 1**
7. **Click the Borders button, then click Outside Borders to remove only the outside border from the table form**
   The edited form should look like FIGURE 10-25.
8. **Click Yes, Start Enforcing Protection in the Restrict Editing pane, type cengage as the password, press TAB, type cengage, click OK, then close the Restrict Editing pane**
9. **sam Click the File tab, click Save, click the File tab, then click Close to close the template but do not exit Word**
   You saved and closed the template but did not exit Word.

Protecting documents with formatting and editing restrictions

You protect a form so that users can enter data only in designated areas. You can also protect a document. To protect a document, click the Developer tab, click the Restrict Editing button in the Protect group, then choose the restriction settings you wish to apply. To restrict formatting, you click the Limit formatting to a selection of styles check box, then click Settings. You then choose the styles that you do not want users to use when formatting a document. For example, you can choose to prevent users from using the Heading 1 style or some of the table styles. For editing restrictions, you can specify that users may only make tracked changes or insert comments, or you can select No changes (read only) when you want to prevent users from making any changes to a document.

FIGURE 10-24: Unprotecting the form

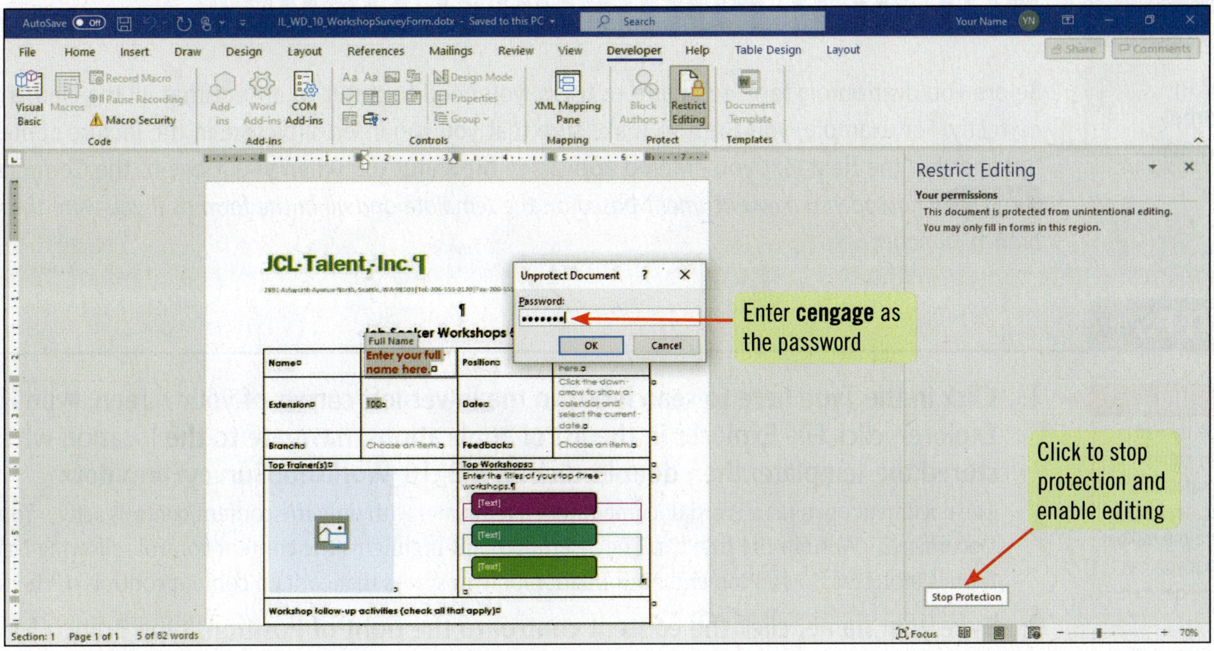

FIGURE 10-25: Formatted form

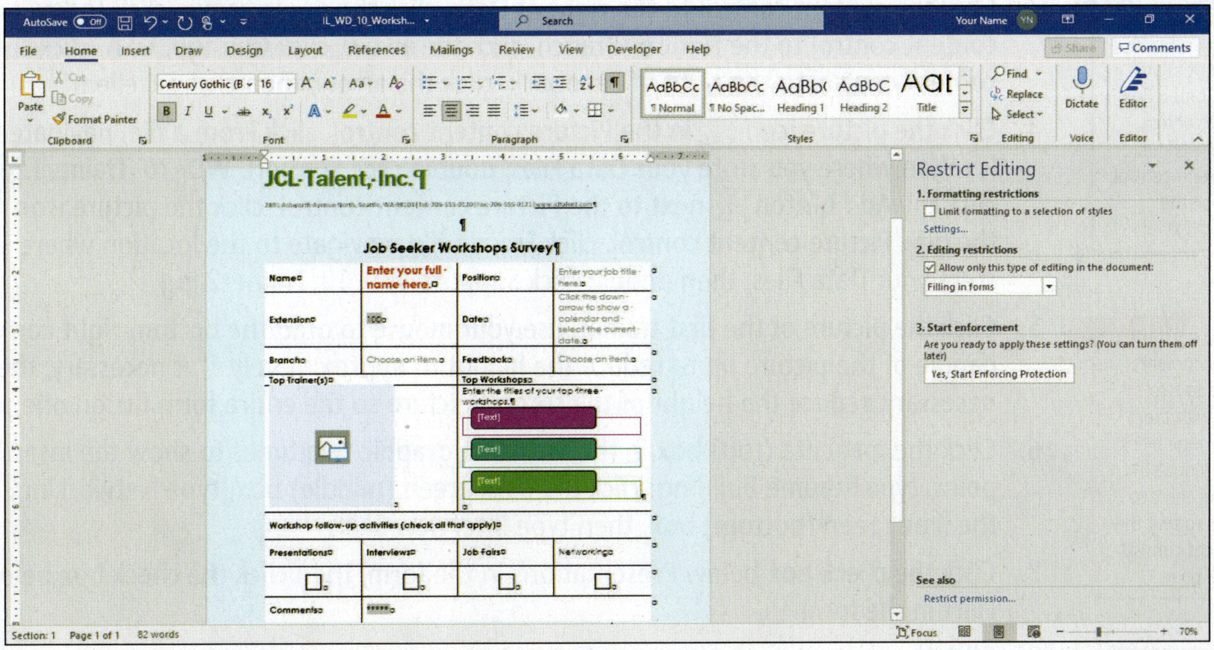

Word

Word
Module 10

Fill in a Form as a User

Learning Outcome
- Fill in a form

Before you distribute a form template to users, you need to test it to ensure that all the elements work correctly. For example, you want to make sure that you can insert a picture in the Picture content control and that the Help text you entered appears in the status bar when you move to the Comments cell. **CASE** *You open a new document based on the template and fill in the form as if you were the Chicago branch manager.*

STEPS

TROUBLE
The Type here to search box might be in a different location, depending on where the taskbar is docked.

1. **Click in the Type here to search box in the lower-left corner of your screen, type File Explorer, click File Explorer in the list of applications, navigate to the location where you stored the template, then double-click IL_WD_10_WorkshopSurveyForm.dotx**
   The document opens as a Word document (not a template) with only the content controls active. You will see Document2 - Word in the title bar. The insertion point highlights the content control following Name. The form is protected, so you can enter information only in spaces that contain content controls or check boxes.
2. **Type your name, click the content control to the right of Position, type Branch Manager, double-click 100 next to Extension, then type 335**
   Notice how Branch Manager appears bold because you applied the Strong style when you inserted the Plain Text content control.

QUICK TIP
To enter a choice that is not listed in the Combo Box content control, select the text in the content control, then type the required text.

3. **Click the content control to the right of Date, click the down arrow, click Today, click the content control to the right of Branch, click the arrow, click Chicago, USA, click the content control to the right of Feedback, click the arrow, then click Excellent**
4. **Click the picture icon in the Picture content control, click From a file, navigate to the location where you store your Data Files, double-click Support_WD_10_Trainer1.jpg, click the Add button next to the Picture content control, click the picture icon in the new Picture content control, click From a file, navigate to the location where you store your Data Files, then double-click Support_WD_10_Trainer2.jpg**

TROUBLE
If the document extends to two pages (with the second page blank), further reduce the height of the two pictures so that the document consists of just one page.

5. **Click the picture of the first trainer, use your mouse to drag the bottom-right corner handle of the picture up to reduce the height to approximately 1" if necessary, then, if necessary, reduce the height of the second picture so the entire form fits on one page**
6. **Click the magenta (top) box in the SmartArt graphic two times to show the insertion point, type Resume Building, click the dark green (middle) box, type Networking, click the lime green (bottom) box, then type Interview Skills**
7. **Click the check box below Presentations in the form, then click the check box below Job Fairs in the form**
8. **Click the content control next to Comments, note the message that appears on the status bar, then type the comment text shown in FIGURE 10-26, noting that it will appear in sentence case as you type**

TROUBLE
A form template that you open and fill as a user and then save as a Word document will open in Read Mode. To fill in the form with additional information or to edit it, click View on the Ribbon, then click Edit Document.

9. **Press TAB, scroll down, note that the text appears in uppercase, increase the zoom to 120%, compare the completed form to FIGURE 10-27, save the document as a Word document with the name IL_WD_10_WorkshopSurvey_Completed to the location where you store your Data Files, don't save the Building Blocks.dotx file if asked, submit all files to your instructor, then close the document and exit Word**

FIGURE 10-26: Comment entry

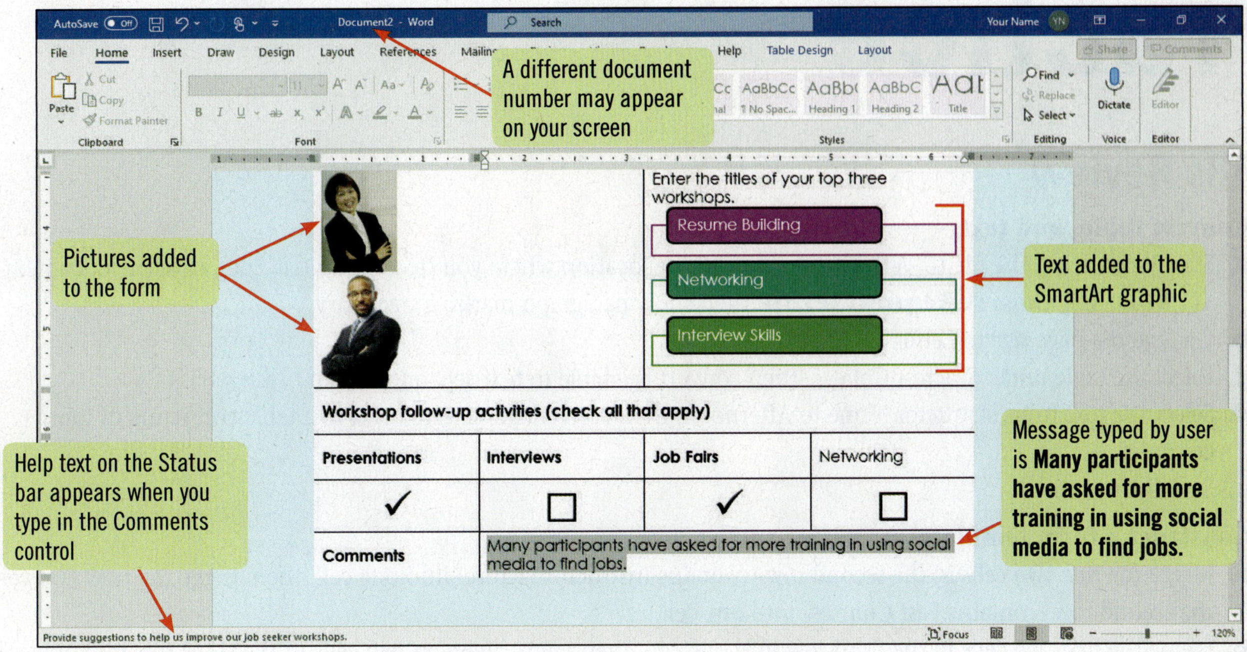

william casey/Shutterstock.com; Kues/Shutterstock.com

FIGURE 10-27: Completed form

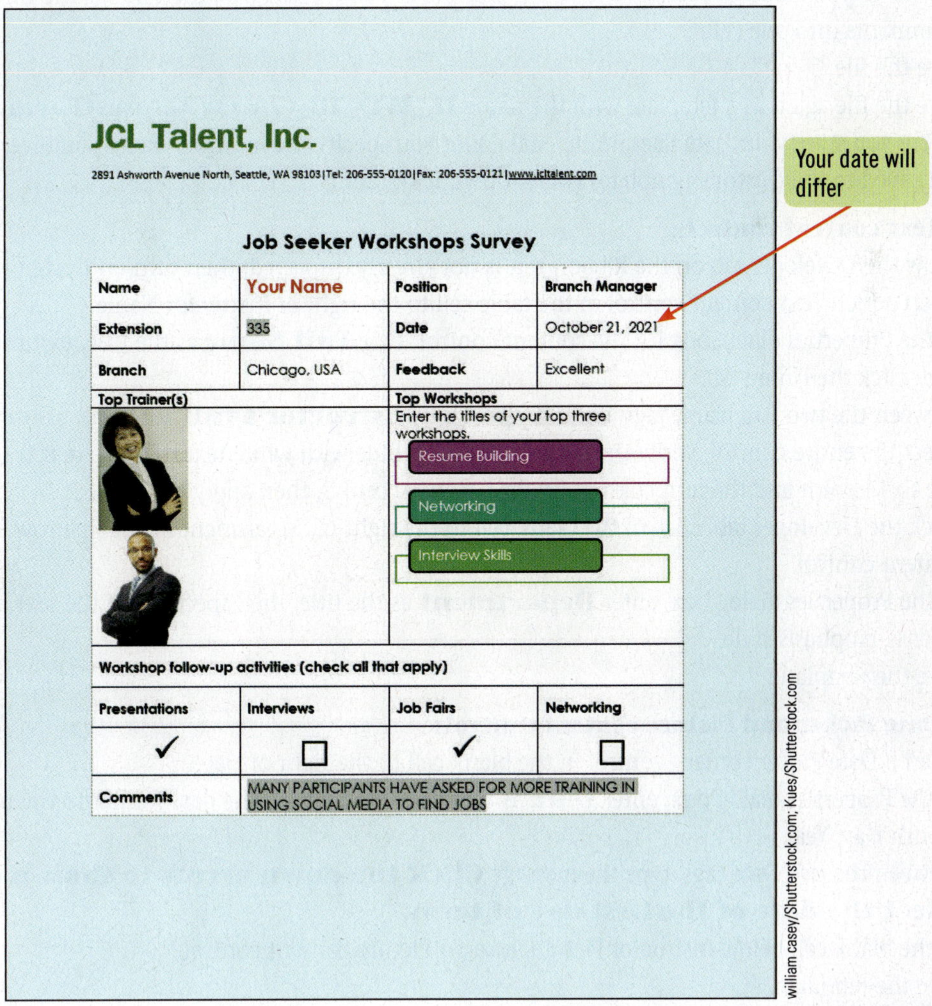

william casey/Shutterstock.com; Kues/Shutterstock.com

Practice

Skills Review

1. **Convert tables and text.**
   a. Start Word, open the file IL_WD_10-2.docx from the location where you store your Data Files, save the document as **IL_WD_10_CourseRequestSetup**, then show paragraph marks, if necessary.
   b. Change the page size to Letter.
   c. Select the table under Seacrest College, then convert the table to text separated by an * (asterisk).
   d. Select the text from Instructor Name to Afternoon, then convert the selected text to a table consisting of four columns.
   e. Save the document.
2. **Construct a form template.**
   a. Merge the first two cells in the second row (contains Instructor Picture) into one cell, then merge the next two cells in the second row (contains Past Courses) into one cell.
   b. Merge the first two cells in the third row into one cell, then merge the next two cells in the third row into one cell so row 3 matches row 2.
   c. Press TAB from the cell containing Afternoon to start a new row, press TAB another four times to start another new row, type **Comments** in the first cell of the last row, press TAB, then merge the three cells to the right of Comments into one cell.
   d. Save the file.
   e. Save the file again as a template with the name **IL_WD_10_CourseRequestForm.dotx** to the location where you store your Data Files. (*Note:* Make sure you specify the location where you save the template so that it is not saved to the Custom Templates Folder on your system.)
3. **Add Text content controls.**
   a. Show the Developer tab on the Ribbon if it is not already displayed, then turn on Design Mode.
   b. Insert a Rich Text content control in the table cell to the right of Instructor Name.
   c. In the Properties dialog box for the content control, type **Full Name** as the title, exit the Properties dialog box, then click the Home tab.
   d. Between the two Full Name tags, enter **Type the instructor's full name.**
   e. Select the entire control, verify the control handle is blue with white text to indicate it is selected, change the font size to 14 point and the font color to Bright Green, Accent 5, then apply bold.
   f. Click the Developer tab, click in the blank cell to the right of Department in the first row, then insert a Plain Text content control.
   g. In the Properties dialog box, enter **Department** as the title, then specify that the text be formatted with the Intense Emphasis style.
   h. Save the template.
4. **Add Date Picker and Picture content controls.**
   a. Insert a Date Picker content control in the blank cell to the right of Date.
   b. In the Properties dialog box, enter **Date** as the title, then change the date format to the format that corresponds to Month Day, Year.
   c. Between the two Date tags, type the message **Click the down arrow to show a calendar, then select the date of the first day of term.**
   d. In the blank cell below Instructor Picture, insert a Picture content control.
   e. Save the template.

Skills Review (continued)

5. Add Repeating Section and Check Box content controls.

a. Select the blank row below the Course Name, Course Number, Morning, and Afternoon labels, insert a Repeating Section content control, then turn off Design Mode to view the Add button. You will add controls to this row in a later step.

b. Turn on Design Mode, then insert a Check Box content control in the cell below Morning.

c. In the Content Control Properties dialog box, apply the Heading 2 style to the Check Box content control, then change the Checked symbol to Character code **251** (a stylized x) from the Wingdings font.

d. Select the Check Box content control, copy it, then paste it in the cell below Afternoon.

e. Save the template.

6. Add Building Blocks content controls.

a. Start a new blank document, then type the text **Enter up to three of your most recent courses.**

b. Press ENTER, then insert a SmartArt graphic using the Basic Block List type in the List category.

c. Click the border of the left box in the row of two boxes to select it, press DELETE, then delete another box so only three boxes are included in the SmartArt graphic.

d. Apply Colorful Range - Accent Colors 4 to 5 to the SmartArt graphic, change the weight of the shape outline of all the boxes to 2¼ pt, then click away from the graphic to deselect it.

e. Press CTRL+A to select the contents of the document, then save the selection to the Quick Part Gallery using the name **Course List** as the building block name.

f. Save the document as **IL_WD_10_CourseRequestBuildingBlock** to the location where you store your Data Files, then close the document.

g. Verify that IL_WD_10_CourseRequestForm.dotx is again the active document, then verify that the Design Mode button on the Developer tab is not active.

h. Click the blank cell below Past Courses, then insert the Course List building block content control by clicking the Building Block Gallery Content Control button in the Controls group.

i. Select the graphic, then change the height to **1.3"** and the width to **3"**.

j. Save the template.

7. Add Drop-Down content controls.

a. Click in the cell below Course Name, then insert a Combo Box content control.

b. In the Content Control Properties dialog box, enter **Course Name** as the title.

c. Add the following entries: **Blogging for Business**, **Networking**, **Social Media Marketing**, and **Planning**.

d. Change Planning to **Event Planning**, then move Event Planning up so it appears immediately after Blogging for Business.

e. Click in the cell below Course Number, then insert a Drop-Down List content control.

f. In the Content Control Properties dialog box, enter **Course Number** as the title, then add the following entries: **100**, **150**, **200**, **220**, **300**.

g. Save the template.

8. Insert Legacy Tools controls.

a. Insert a Text Form Field control from the Legacy Tools gallery in the blank cell to the right of Office Local.

b. Double-click the control to open the Text Form Field Options dialog box, change the Type to Number, change the Maximum length to **4**, then enter **1234** as the default.

c. Insert a Text Form Field control from the Legacy Tools gallery in the blank cell to the right of Comments.

d. Specify that the text format should be uppercase, add the help text: **Provide additional details if necessary**, then save the template.

Skills Review (continued)

9. **Format and protect a form.**
   a. Verify that Design Mode is off, then apply bold to all the labels in the form template.
   b. Change the view to 90%, select the table, then change the row height to at least **.3"**.
   c. Vertically center align the text in all the cells. (*Hint*: Use the Cell tab in the Table Properties dialog box.)
   d. Protect the document for users filling in forms using the password **skills**, then save and close the template but do not exit Word. (*Note*: If you turned Design Mode on, it must be turned off to protect the document.)
10. **Edit a form.**
    a. From Word, open the template IL_WD_CourseRequestForm.dotx (remember *not* to double-click it to open it), then stop protection using the **skills** password.
    b. Change the page color to Gold, Accent 3, Lighter 80%.
    c. Fill the table form with the White, Background 1 shading color.
    d. Remove only the outside border from the table form.
    e. Click below the table, press ENTER, then type your name.
    f. Protect the form again using the **skills** password.
    g. Save and close the template but do not exit Word.
11. **Fill in a form as a user.**
    a. Open File Explorer, navigate to the Course Request template, then double-click it to start a new document.
    b. Refer to FIGURE 10-28 to complete the form. Insert Support_WD_10_Instructor.jpg in the Picture content control and **3455** for the Office Local.
    c. Select the current date, select the information for the first course (Blogging for Business), then click the Repeating Section content control and enter the information for the second course (Event Planning). The comment text is: **My experience creating the college blog has given me a good insight into the process.**
    d. Save the document as **IL_WD_10_CourseRequestForm_Completed** to the location where you store your Data Files, answer no to save the Building Blocks.dotx file, submit the file to your instructor, then close the document and exit Word.

FIGURE 10-28

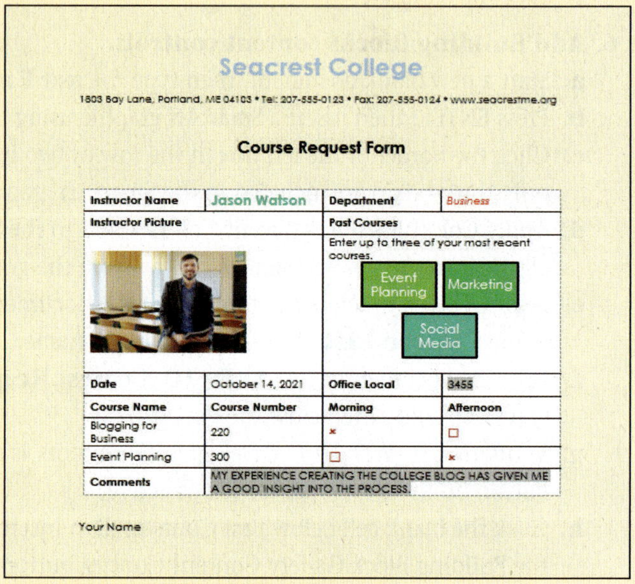

Seacrest College

1803 Bay Lane, Portland, ME 04103 • Tel: 207-555-0123 • Fax: 207-555-0124 • www.seacrestme.org

Course Request Form

Instructor Name	Jason Watson	Department	Business
Instructor Picture		Past Courses	
		Enter up to three of your most recent courses. Event Planning Marketing Social Media	
Date	October 14, 2021	Office Local	3455
Course Name	Course Number	Morning	Afternoon
Blogging for Business	220	☒	☐
Event Planning	300	☐	☒
Comments	MY EXPERIENCE CREATING THE COLLEGE BLOG HAS GIVEN ME A GOOD INSIGHT INTO THE PROCESS.		

Your Name

Africa Studio/Shutterstock.com

Independent Challenge 1

You work in the Administration Department at Riverwalk Medical Clinic in Cambridge, MA. Several clinic administrators and senior medical staff take trips to hospitals and medical facilities around the world to investigate innovative programs in a variety of medical areas. Your supervisor asks you to create an itinerary form that staff can complete online to help them keep track of their travel details.

a. Start Word and open the file IL_WD_10-3.docx from the drive and folder where you store your Data Files. Save it as **IL_WD_10_ItineraryFormSetup**.
b. Turn on paragraph marks, if necessary, then convert the table containing the contact information for Riverwalk Medical Clinic into text separated by the | character. Center the line of text.
c. Select the text from Name to the paragraph mark following Picture of Location, then convert the selected text into a table consisting of four columns and rows.
d. Merge the three cells to the right of Purpose of Travel into one cell, then merge the three cells to the right of Picture of Location into one cell.
e. Add two new rows with four cells in each. In the first new row, enter the following four labels: **Date**, **Location**, **Category**, **Details**.

Independent Challenge 1 (continued)

f. From the Developer tab, make the Design Mode active, then insert a Rich Text content control in the blank cell to the right of the Name label. Enter **Full Name** as the title, then format the control with 14 pt and bold.

g. Insert a Date Picker control in the blank cell to the right of Report Date. Enter **Date** as the title, then select the date format that corresponds with 17-Dec-24.

h. Insert a Drop-Down List content control in the blank cell to the right of Department. Enter **Department** as the title, then add **Surgical**, **Research**, and **Human Resources**, and put the entries in alphabetical order.

i. Insert a Text Form Field control from the Legacy Tools gallery in the blank cell to the right of Extension. Specify the type as Number, a Maximum length of **3**, and **200** as the Default number.

j. Insert a Plain Text content control in the cell to the right of Purpose of Travel. Enter **Travel Purpose** for the title, then apply the Emphasis style.

k. Copy the Date Picker content control you inserted next to Report Date, then paste it in the cell below Date.

l. Insert a Combo Box content control in the cell below Location. Enter **Location** as the title, then add three selections: **Hong Kong**, **London**, **New York**. Enter the text **Select a location or type your own.** between the two tags.

m. Insert a Drop-Down List Box content control in the cell below Category. Enter **Category** as the title, then add three selections: **Transportation**, **Accommodation**, and **Meeting** and put them in alphabetical order.

n. Insert a Rich Text content control in the cell below Details. Enter the text **Click the Add button for more rows.** between the tags, then open the Content Control Properties dialog box, enter **Details** as the title, and select the Orange color for the control.

o. Select the last row in the form (contains four content controls), then click the Repeating Section Content Control button. If the plus sign is not visible, turn off Design Mode. When users fill in the form, they can click the plus sign to add more rows to supply more itinerary details.

p. Insert a Picture content control in the blank cell to the right of Picture of Location. Click the Picture content control, then drag the middle-right sizing handle to the right to increase the width of the control so it almost fills the table cell.

q. Apply bold to all the form labels.

r. Save the document.

s. Save the document again as a template with the name **IL_WD_10_ItineraryForm.dotx** to the location where you store your Data Files.

t. Protect the form using the Filling in forms selection, enter **ic1** as the password, then save and close the template but do not exit Word.

u. Start a new document by double-clicking the IL_WD_10_ItineraryForm.dotx template file in File Explorer (verify that Document1 or another number appears in the title bar), enter your name and the current date in row 1, then enter **Research** as the Department, **239** as the Extension, and **To attend a conference for medical researchers in Peru.** as the Purpose of Travel.

v. Insert Support_WD_10_Peru.jpg in the Picture content control.

w. Enter itinerary information as shown in TABLE 10-2, clicking the Add button after you've entered data for each row for a total of four rows. Note that you will need to type the Location information ("Lima" and "Machu Picchu") in the Combo Box control.

TABLE 10-2

date	location	category	details
5-Apr-21	Lima	Transportation	AA Flight 240 to Lima
6-Apr-21	Lima	Accommodation	Lima Ritz
7-Apr-21	Machu Picchu	Meeting	Day Trip to Clinic
8-Apr-21	Lima	Meeting	Presentation

x. Save the completed form as **IL_WD_10_Itinerary_Peru**, submit a copy to your instructor, then close the document and exit Word.

Independent Challenge 2

You work for a government agency that provides business skills workshops to the employees of companies and organizations in the San Diego area. Clients complete a feedback form after they participate in a workshop. You create a Word form to email clients.

a. Start Word and open the file IL_WD_10-4.docx from the location where your Data Files are located. Save it as a template with the name **IL_WD_10_EvaluationForm** to the location where you store your Data Files.

b. Change the page size to Executive.

c. From the Developer tab, switch to Design Mode, then insert and format controls as described in TABLE 10-3:

TABLE 10-3

location	content Control	title	properties
Name	Rich Text content control	**Full Name**	Format with Heading 1
Workshop Date	Date Picker content control	**Date**	Format with the 10.10.2021 date format.
Instructor	Drop-Down List content control	**Instructor**	Add the names of four instructors: **Oliver Greer, Tamsin Quinn, Kat Martin,** and **Jasjit Singh** and put them in alphabetical order by first name.
Subject	Combo Box content control	**Subject**	Add entries for three subjects in alphabetical order: **Social Media, Negotiating Skills,** and **Leadership Development;** type the text **Select a subject or enter a new subject.** between the form tags as a direction to users.
Workshop Element	Text Form Field control from Legacy Tools		Enter the Help text **Click the Add button to insert up to four more elements.**
Rankings	Check Box content control in each of the 4 blank cells for the ranking of a course element	**Rank**	Format with the Wingdings **254** check mark character (*Hint:* Insert and modify the first check box content control, then copy and paste it to the remaining table cells.)

d. Select the row containing the Text Form Field and Check Box content controls and make the row a Repeating Section. Turn off Design Mode and verify that the Add button appears to the right of the last cell in the row.

e. Save the template, then create a new blank document.

f. Turn on bold, then type the text: **Type three words that summarize your experience at the workshop you attended**.

g. Press ENTER, then insert the Converging Radial SmartArt graphic from the Relationship category.

h. Type **Feedback** in the circle shape, then apply the Color Range – Accent Colors 5 to 6 color scheme.

i. Select all the text and the SmartArt graphic, then save it as a building block with the name **Feedback** in the Quick Parts gallery.

j. Save the document as **IL_WD_10_FeedbackBuildingBlock** to the location where you store your Data Files, then close it.

k. In the form template, verify that Design Mode is off, then insert the Feedback building block into the last row of the table. Resize the size of the graphic to 2" high and 4" wide so the entire form fits on one page.

l. Click away from the table, then change the page color for the document to Light Green, Accent 2, Lighter 80%.

m. Protect the form for filling in forms, click OK to bypass password protection when prompted, then save and close the template but do not exit Word.

n. Open the template IL_WD_10_EvaluationForm.dotx and unprotect it, then remove Kat Martin from the list of the instructors in the Drop-Down List content control so the list includes only three instructors.

o. Protect the form again, then save and close the template but do not exit Word.

Independent Challenge 2 (continued)

p. Start a new document by double-clicking IL_WD_10_EvaluationForm.dotx in File Explorer, enter your name in the Name cell and the current date in the Workshop Date cell, select Jasjit Singh as the instructor, then type **Finance** in the Combo Box content control to the right of Subject.

q. In the content control below Workshop Element, type **Workshop Materials**, then click the 2 check box.

r. Use the Add button to add another row. (*Note:* Workshop Materials is entered, but you can type over it.) Enter **Instructor** as the course element and 4 as the rank, then add another row and enter **Location** as the course element and 3 as the rank.

s. Type these three words in the three boxes of the SmartArt graphic: **Informative**, **Helpful**, **Fun**.

t. Save the document as **IL_WD_10_EvaluationForm_Completed** to the location where you store the files for this book, don't save the Building Blocks.dotx file, submit the form document to your instructor, then close the document and exit Word.

Visual Workshop

You work for Exhibitor Assist, a company that provides event planning, conference organization, and related business services to companies in the Vancouver area. You are organizing a Green Technology conference and need to create a form for exhibitors to complete in Word. Work in Design Mode to create and enhance the form template shown in FIGURE 10-29. The Organic theme is applied to the document, the Title heading is applied to "Green Technology Conference," and the Heading 1 style is applied to "Exhibitor Form." You do not need to include titles and tags on the controls for this exercise. Use the Rich Text content control for Company Name formatted with Bold and 14 pt; use the Plain Text content controls for Mailing Address and Email Address; use these entries for a Combo Box content control for Category: **Fuel Products**, **Building Materials**, **Engineering**, **Renewable Energy** and put them in alphabetical order. Format the Check Box content control with Heading 1 and symbol 252. Resize the Picture content control so it is **1.7"** in height (the width will adjust automatically). Save the template as **IL_WD_10_ConferenceForm.dotx** to the location where you store your Data Files. Protect the form, but do not password protect it, close the template, then open a new document based on the template. Complete the form as shown in FIGURE 10-30, using the picture file Support_WD_10_SolarEnergy.jpg. Save the completed form as **IL_WD_10_ConferenceForm_Completed** to the location where you store your Data Files, submit a copy to your instructor, then close the document.

FIGURE 10-29

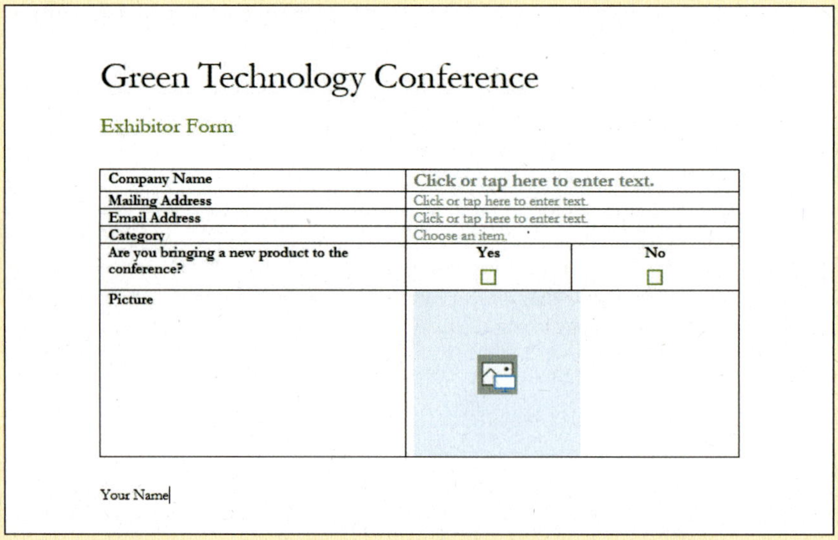
Green Technology Conference

Exhibitor Form

Company Name	Click or tap here to enter text.	
Mailing Address	Click or tap here to enter text.	
Email Address	Click or tap here to enter text.	
Category	Choose an item.	
Are you bringing a new product to the conference?	Yes ☐	No ☐
Picture		

Your Name

FIGURE 10-30

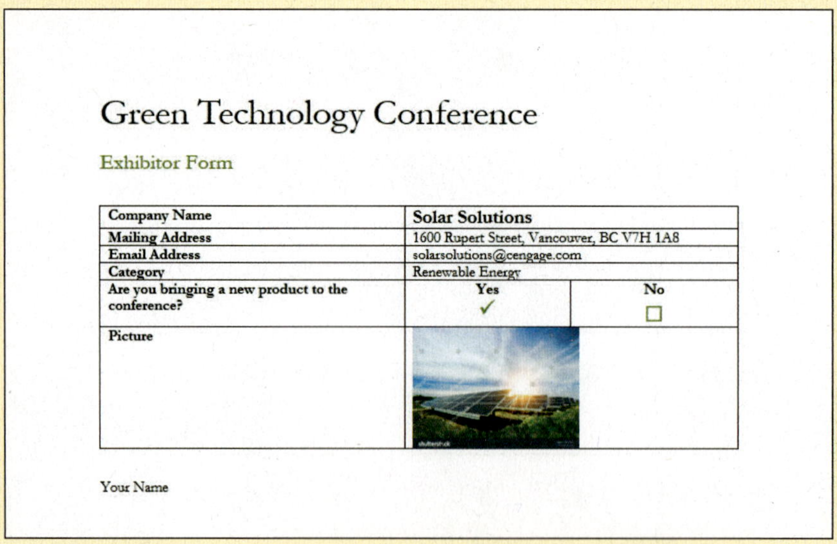
Green Technology Conference

Exhibitor Form

Company Name	Solar Solutions	
Mailing Address	1600 Rupert Street, Vancouver, BC V7H 1A8	
Email Address	solarsolutions@cengage.com	
Category	Renewable Energy	
Are you bringing a new product to the conference?	Yes ✓	No ☐
Picture		

Your Name

Diyana Dimitrova/Shutterstock.com

Word **Module 11**

Automating and Customizing Word

CASE As part of your duties in the sales and marketing department at JCL Talent, Inc., you have been asked to produce profiles of two of JCL Talent's top trainers who deliver workshops for job seekers. You also need to format a series of excerpts from employment journals created by successful job seekers. You start by formatting paragraphs and graphics and creating styles for a profile of top trainer Shaleen Dixon. You then create a macro to automate formatting tasks for the journal excerpts and you customize Word options. To finish up, you add a digital signature to the document.

Module Objectives

After completing this module, you will be able to:

- Manage pages
- Edit pictures
- Use layering options
- Arrange and compress graphics
- Create character styles
- Manage styles
- Plan a macro
- Record macro steps
- Run a macro
- Edit a macro in Visual Basic
- Customize Word
- Sign a document digitally

Files You Will Need:

IL_WD_11-1.docx
Support_WD_11_Shaleen.jpg
IL_WD_11-2.docx
IL_WD_11-3.docx
IL_WD_11-4.docx
IL_WD_11-5.docx
Support_WD_11_Solar.jpg
IL_WD_11-6.docx
IL_WD_11-7.docx
IL_WD_11-8.docx
IL_WD_11-9.docx
Support_WD_11_Clinic.jpg
Support_WD_11_SpringBulletin.docx
IL_WD_11-10.docx
IL_WD_11-11.docx
IL_WD_11-12.docx

Word
Module 11

Manage Pages

Learning Outcomes
- Set paragraph pagination options
- Format text as hidden

You apply pagination settings to control the flow of text between pages or between columns in a document. These settings specify where Word positions automatic page breaks. Choose the Keep with next option when you want a paragraph to appear together with the next paragraph on the same page. Choose the Keep lines together option to keep all the lines in a selected paragraph together on a page. To add an automatic page break before a specific paragraph, choose the Page break before option. You can set Widow/Orphan control options to control the number of lines appearing at the top or bottom of a page. Turned on by default, **Widow/Orphan control** ensures that at least two lines of a paragraph appear at the top and bottom of every page or column. You can also designate selected text in a document as hidden text. **CASE** *You open a document containing text needed for a two-page description of top trainer Shaleen Dixon, modify how the paragraphs break across pages, then designate selected text as hidden.*

STEPS

TROUBLE
Click the **Show/Hide button** ¶ in the Paragraph group to show paragraph marks, if necessary.

1. **sam Start Word, open the file IL_WD_11-1.docx from the location where you store your Data Files, verify paragraph marks are showing, then save the document as IL_WD_11_ShaleenDixonProfile**
2. **Scroll down and click in the Research the Employer heading, click the Launcher in the Paragraph group, then click the Line and Page Breaks tab**
   The Line and Page Breaks tab in the Paragraph dialog box opens as shown in **FIGURE 11-1**. By default, the Heading 1 style applied to the heading includes three settings: Widow/Orphan control, Keep with next, and Keep lines together.
3. **Click OK, click in the line that starts with Knowledge is power, click the Launcher in the Paragraph group, click the Keep lines together check box, then click OK**
   The three lines of the paragraph along with the heading move to the top of page 2.
4. **Scroll back up to page 1, click in the heading Top Tips for Job Interview Success, click the Launcher in the Paragraph group, click the Page break before check box, then click OK**
5. **Scroll to the top of page 3**
   The last word in the paragraph appears alone at the top of the page. This line is a widow. A **widow** is the last line of a paragraph appearing along at the top of a page. An **orphan** is the first line of a paragraph appearing alone at the bottom of a page.
6. **Scroll back up to page 2, click in the paragraph under the Send a Thank-You Note or Email, click the Launcher in the Paragraph group, click the Widow/Orphan control check box, then click OK**
   The last two lines of the paragraph move to the top of page 3.

TROUBLE
If you select the paragraph mark and then hide the text, the blank line between the two paragraphs will be removed when the document is printed.

7. **Press CTRL+HOME, then select the sentence that begins From a very young age, but *not* the paragraph mark in the Early Life paragraph, as shown in FIGURE 11-2**
8. **Click the Launcher in the Font group, click the Hidden check box as shown in FIGURE 11-3, click OK, then click away from the selected text**
   A dotted line appears under the text. This text will not appear in the printed document.
9. **Click the File tab, click Print, note that the sentence does not appear in the Early Life section in the Print Preview screen, click the Back button to return to the document, then save the document**

FIGURE 11-1: Paragraph dialog box

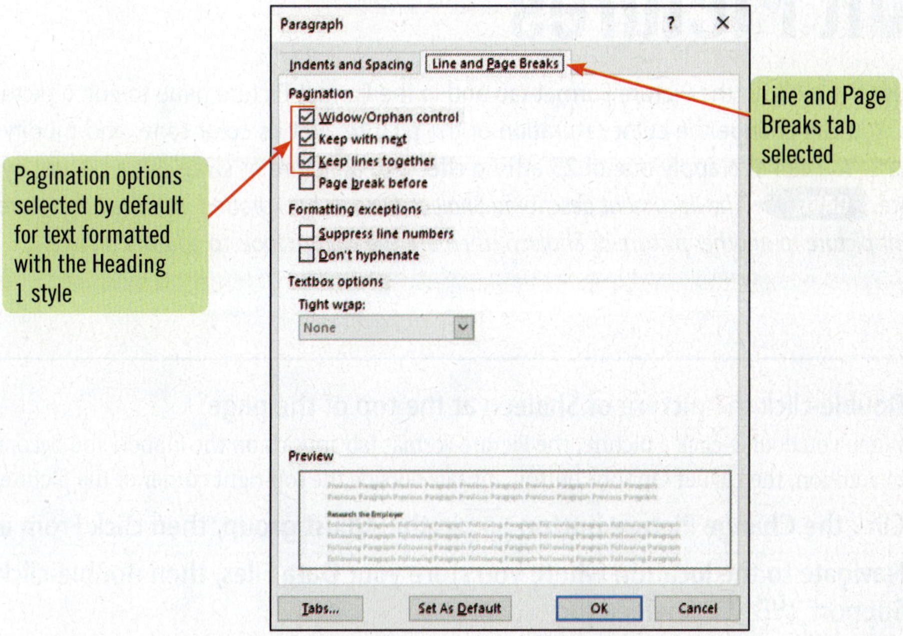

FIGURE 11-2: Text selected to make hidden

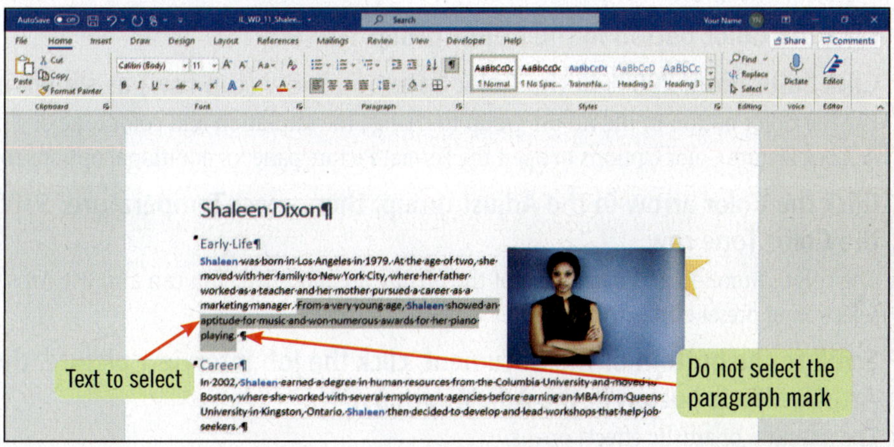

NakoPhotography/Shutterstock.com

FIGURE 11-3: Hidden effect selected

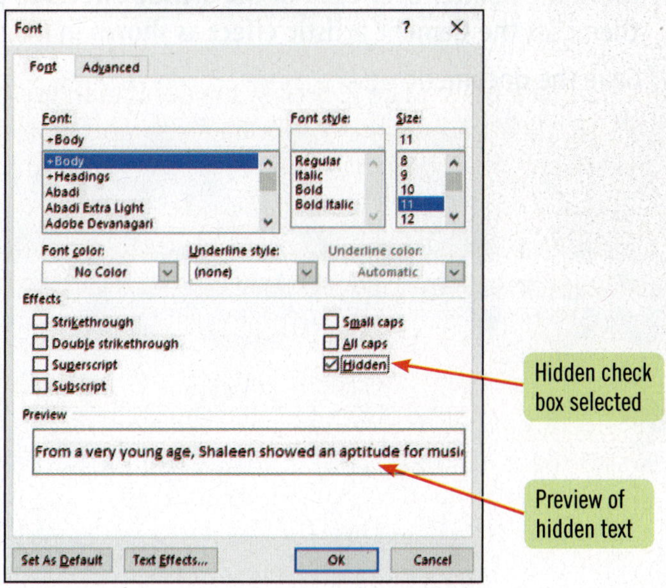

Word

Word
Module 11

Edit Pictures

Learning Outcome
- Apply artistic and picture effects

You use the tools on the Picture Format tab and in the Format Picture pane to edit a picture in a variety of ways. You can change the color saturation of the picture, edit its color tone, and modify its sharpness or softness. You can also apply one of 23 artistic effects to a picture or swap out a picture by selecting a new picture. **CASE** *The document describing Shaleen Dixon's background includes her picture. You change the current picture to another picture of Shaleen, then use the picture tools to edit the picture.*

STEPS

1. **Double-click the picture of Shaleen at the top of the page**
   When you double-click a picture, the Picture Format tab appears on the Ribbon and becomes the active tab. In addition, the Layout Options button appears outside the top-right corner of the picture.
2. **Click the Change Picture button in the Adjust group, then click From a File**
3. **Navigate to the location where you store your Data Files, then double-click Support_WD_11_Shaleen.jpg**
   A different picture of Shaleen is inserted. You also make adjustments to the appearance of the picture using the Adjust group on the Picture Format tab.
4. **Click the Color button in the Adjust group**
5. **Click Saturation: 200% in the Color Saturation row (top row) as shown in FIGURE 11-4**
   Use the Color button in the Adjust group to change the saturation and color tone of a picture, or to recolor it. Click Picture Color Options to open the Format Picture pane for additional options to modify the picture.
6. **Click the Color arrow in the Adjust group, then select Temperature: 5300 K color tone in the Color Tone row**
   The color saturation and color tone of the picture are modified. You can also use Artistic Effects to apply a selection of preset effects to a picture.
7. **Scroll to the bottom of the document, click the Job Interview picture, then click the Artistic Effects button in the Adjust group**
   The selection of artistic effects opens.
8. **Move the pointer over each of the artistic effects to preview how the picture changes, then click the Cement artistic effect as shown in FIGURE 11-5**
9. **Save the document**

QUICK TIP
ScreenTips appear to help you select the correct saturation or color tone effects.

QUICK TIP
To change the sharpness and contrast of a picture, click the Corrections button in the Adjust group.

FIGURE 11-4: Selecting color saturation

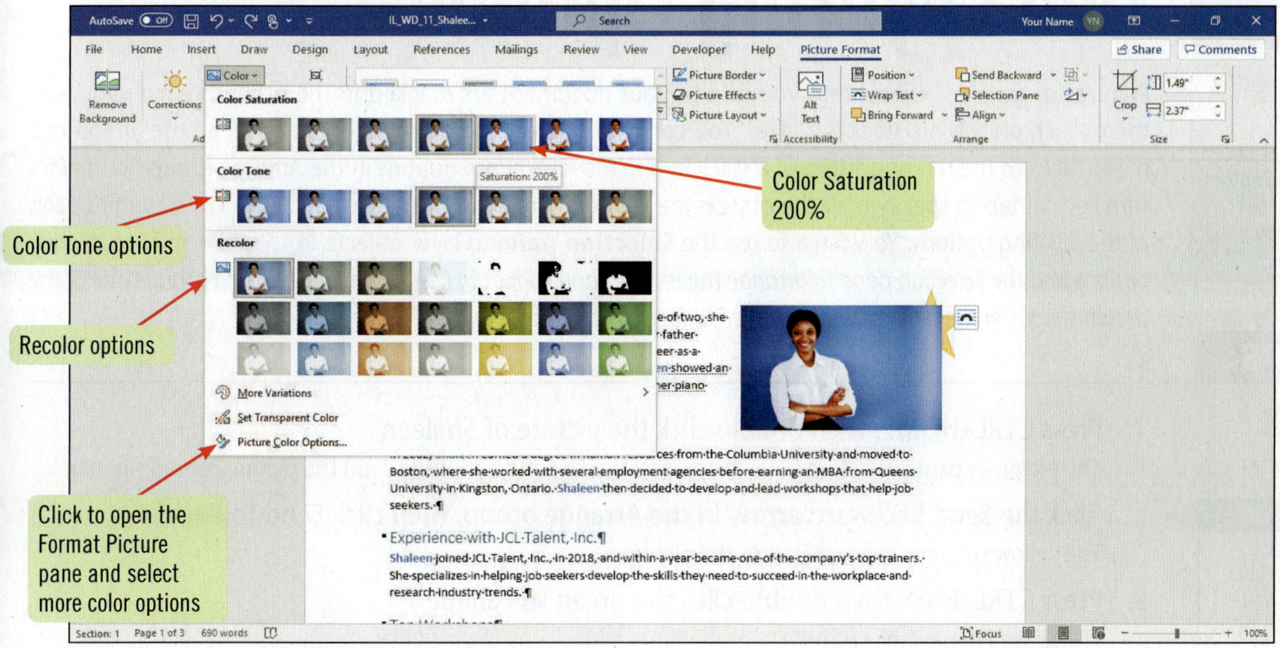

NakoPhotography/Shutterstock.com

FIGURE 11-5: Applying an artistic effect to a picture

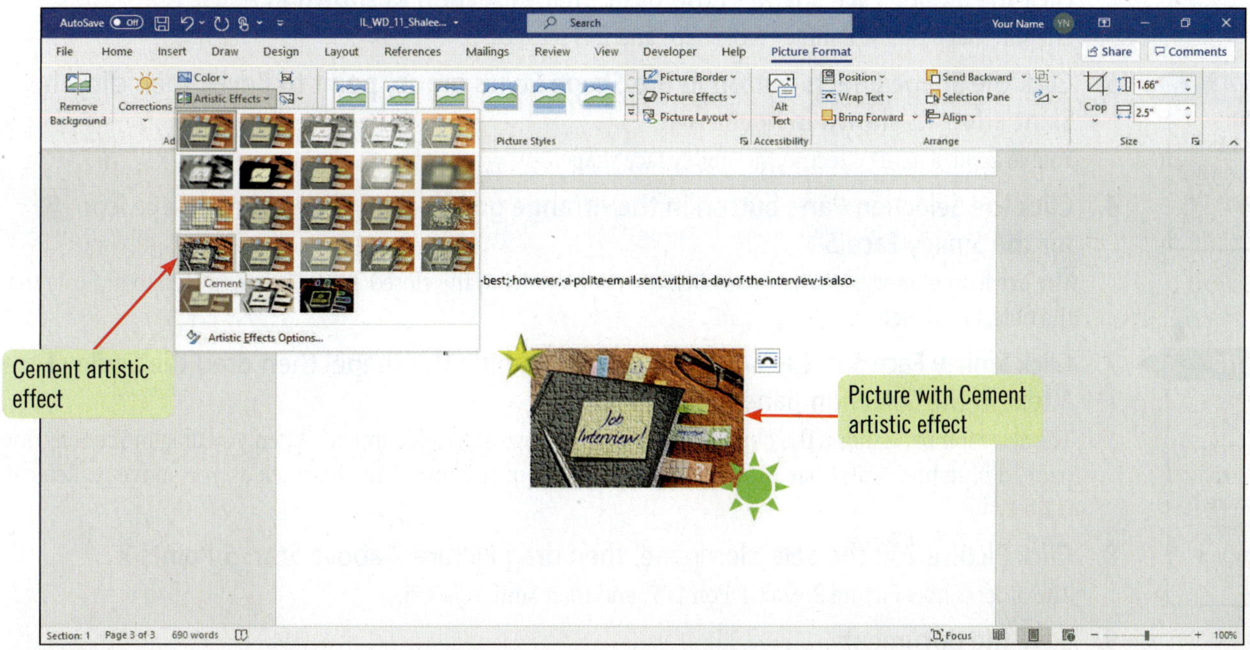

Zerbor/Shutterstock.com

Applying 3-D and 3-D Rotation effects to a picture

You can enhance a picture with a variety of picture effects including reflection, shadow, glow, soft edges, and bevel. The bevel picture effect applies a 3-D effect to the selected picture. To add a 3-D bevel effect, click the Picture Effects button on the Picture Format tab, point to Bevel, then select a preset bevel effect. To further modify a bevel effect, click 3-D Options below the selection of bevel effects to open the 3-D Format section of the Format Picture pane. Here, you can specify the width and height of the top and bottom bevels, and specify a color, depth, contour, material, and lighting for the 3-D effect. You can achieve a wide variety of interesting 3-D effects by selecting different options in the Format Picture pane. Another 3-D effect you can apply to a picture is a 3-D Rotation effect. Click Picture Effects in the Picture Styles group, point to 3-D Rotation, then select a 3-D rotation effect from one of three categories: Parallel, Perspective, and Oblique.

Word
Module 11

Use Layering Options

Learning Outcomes
- Arrange objects around each other
- Format shapes
- Use the Selection pane

Pictures or graphic objects that you add to your document are stacked in the order in which you add them. Each object in a stack is a layer. You can move objects up or down one layer at a time or you can move them to the top or bottom of a stack in one move. You use options in the Arrange group on the Picture Format tab to specify how the objects are stacked in relation to each other. TABLE 11-1 describes each of the layering options. You can also use the **Selection pane** to layer objects. **CASE** *You use layering options and the Selection pane to arrange the pictures and shapes in the document. You also change one of the drawn shapes in the document to another shape and enhance it with a 3-D effect.*

STEPS

1. **Press CTRL+HOME, then double-click the picture of Shaleen**
   The picture is partially hiding a star shape. You use layering options to send the picture behind the star.
2. **Click the Send Backward arrow in the Arrange group, then click Send to Back**
   The yellow star now overlaps part of the picture.
3. **Press CTRL+END, then double-click the green sun shape**
   The Shape Format tab is active.
4. **Click the Edit Shape button in the Insert Shapes group, point to Change Shape, then click the Smiley Face shape in the Basic Shapes section as shown in FIGURE 11-6**
   The sun shape is now a smiley face shape and it is selected.
5. **Click the Shape Effects button in the Shape Styles group, point to Bevel, then click the Slant effect as shown in FIGURE 11-7**
   You've applied a 3-D effect to the smiley face shape.
6. **Click the Selection Pane button in the Arrange group, then click the open eye icon for the Smiley Face 5**
   The eye icon is a toggle. When you click the open eye icon, the closed eye icon is activated to indicate that the object is hidden.
7. **Click Smiley Face 5 in the Selection pane to unhide the shape, then drag the Smiley Face 5 text in the Selection pane below Picture 2**
   The Selection pane shows the objects on the current page of the document. When you drag in the Selection pane, a blue horizontal bar shows you the location of the object in the stack as you move it. Refer to FIGURE 11-8.
8. **Click Picture 2 in the Selection pane, then drag Picture 2 above Star: 5 Points 7**
   The order is now Picture 2, Star: 5 Points 7, and then Smiley Face 5.
9. **Save the document**
   You keep the Selection pane open so that you can next group the two shapes and the picture into one object.

QUICK TIP
When you are working with just two objects, you have only two layers so you can also click Send Backward to move one object behind the other.

QUICK TIP
You can further enhance the 3-D effect by clicking 3-D Options to open the Format pane.

QUICK TIP
To rename an object in the Selection pane, such as "Interview Photo" instead of Picture 2, double-click the name, then type a new name.

TABLE 11-1: Layering Options

layering option	to move an object	layering option	to move an object
Bring Forward	up one layer	Send Backward	down one layer
Bring to Front	to the top of a stack of objects	Send to Back	to the bottom of a stack of objects
Bring in Front of Text	in front of text	Send Behind Text	behind text

FIGURE 11-6: Changing a shape to another shape

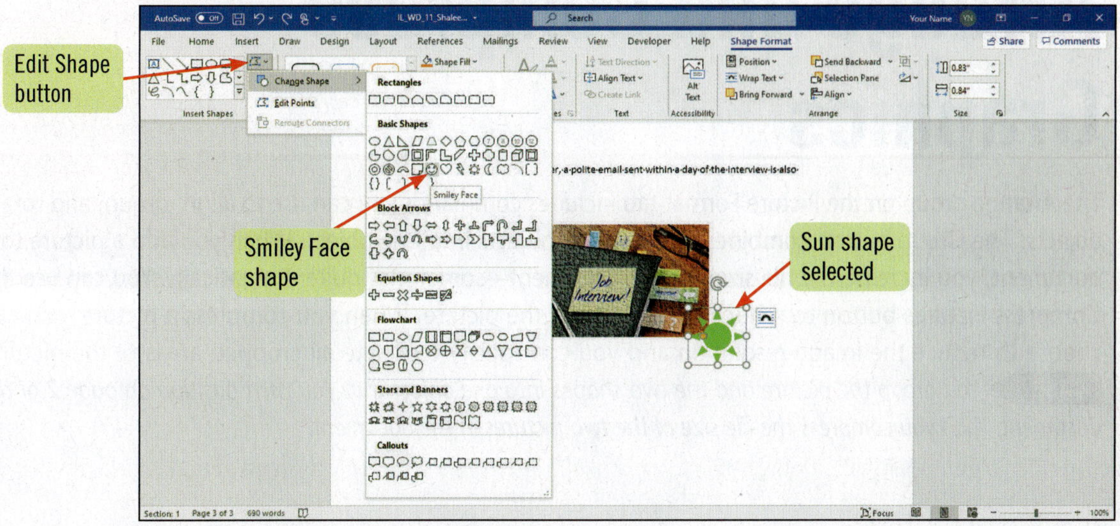

Zerbor/Shutterstock.com

FIGURE 11-7: Applying a Bevel 3-D effect

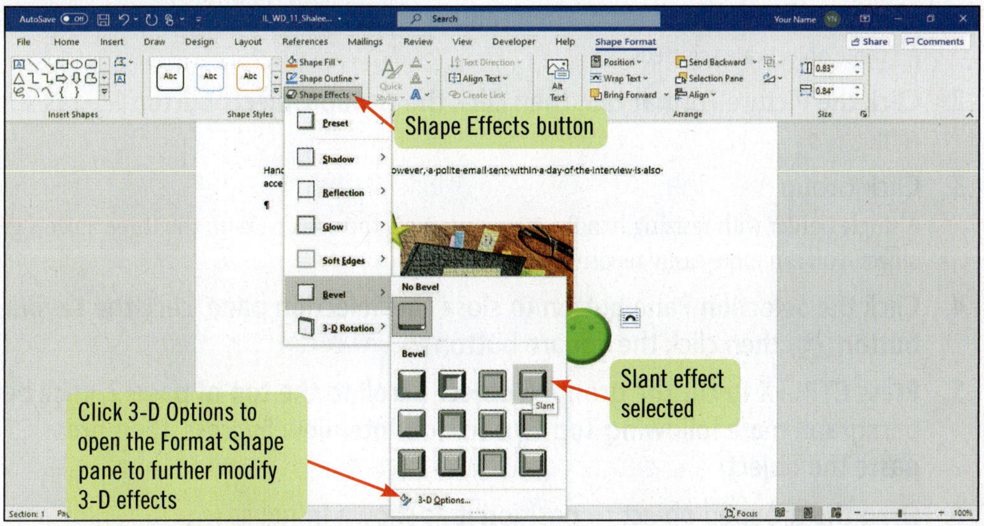

Zerbor/Shutterstock.com

FIGURE 11-8: Moving an object in the Selection pane

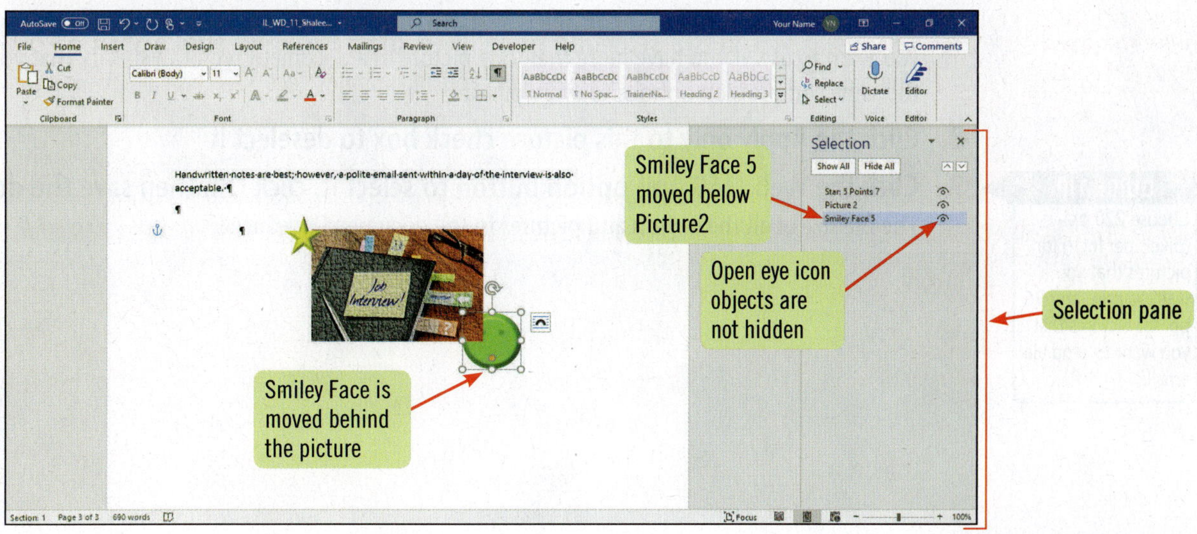

Zerbor/Shutterstock.com

Word

Word
Module 11

Learning Outcomes
- Group objects
- Compress pictures

Arrange and Compress Graphics

The Arrange group on the Picture Format tab includes commands you can use to align, group, and rotate objects. The Group button combines two or more objects into one object. When you add a picture to a document, you increase the file size of your document—sometimes quite dramatically. You can use the Compress Pictures button to reduce the file size of the picture. When you compress a picture, you can choose to reduce the image resolution and you can specify to delete all cropped areas of the picture. **CASE** *You group the picture and the two shapes into one object that you then position on page 2 of the document, then you compress the file size of the two pictures in the document.*

STEPS

1. **In the Selection pane, verify that Picture 2 is selected, press and hold CTRL, click Star: 5 Points 7, click Smiley Face 5, then release CTRL**
   All three objects are selected.

> **QUICK TIP**
> In the Selection pane, the three objects are listed under Group 3 to show they are all included in one group.

2. **Click the Picture Format tab, then click the Group Objects button as shown in FIGURE 11-9**
3. **Click Group**
   A single border with resizing handles now surrounds the objects. With the three objects grouped into one object, you can more easily reposition it.

> **QUICK TIP**
> To ungroup the object, click the Group Objects button, then click Ungroup.

4. **Click the Selection Pane button to close the Selection pane, click the Layout Options button, then click the Square button**
5. **Press CTRL+X to cut the grouped object, scroll to the top of page 2, click before the paragraph mark following Top Tips for Job Interview Success, then press CTRL+V to paste the object**
6. **Drag the grouped object to position it as shown in FIGURE 11-10**
7. **With the grouped object still selected, click the Picture Format tab, then click the Compress Pictures button in the Adjust group**
   The Compress Pictures dialog box opens as shown in FIGURE 11-11. Here, you can specify the resolution that you want to use. If you have more than one picture in a document, you can specify that you wish to apply the same compression options to every picture.
8. **Click the Apply only to this picture check box to deselect it**

> **QUICK TIP**
> Choose 220 ppi (pixels per inch) for pictures that you want to print and 96 ppi for pictures that you want to send via email.

9. **Click the Web (150 ppi) option button to select it, click OK, then save the document**
   The file size of all the objects and pictures in the document is reduced.

FIGURE 11-9: Grouping objects

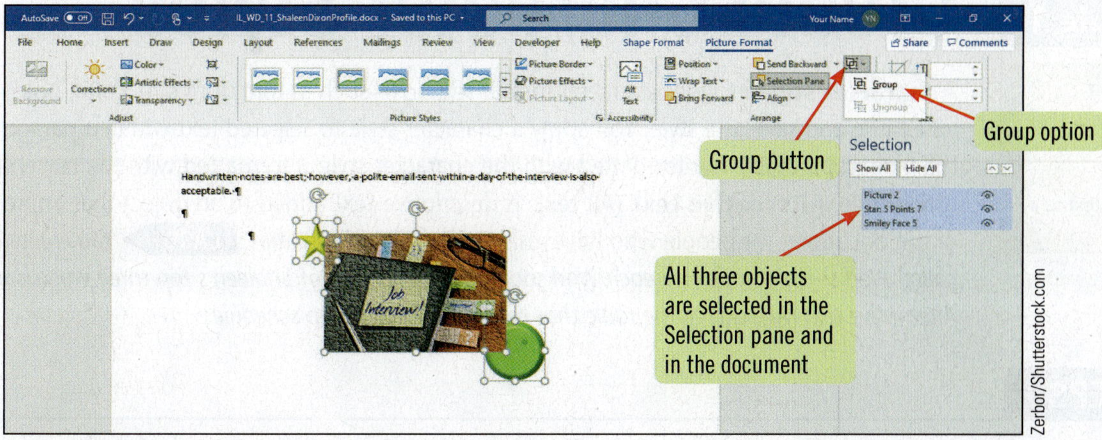

Zerbor/Shutterstock.com

FIGURE 11-10: Positioning the grouped object

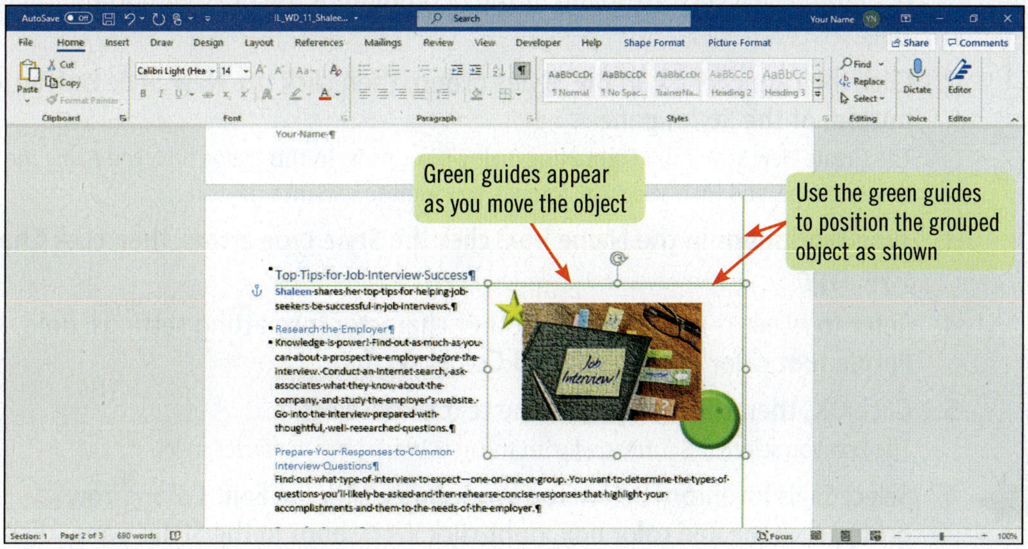

Zerbor/Shutterstock.com

FIGURE 11-11: Compress Pictures dialog box

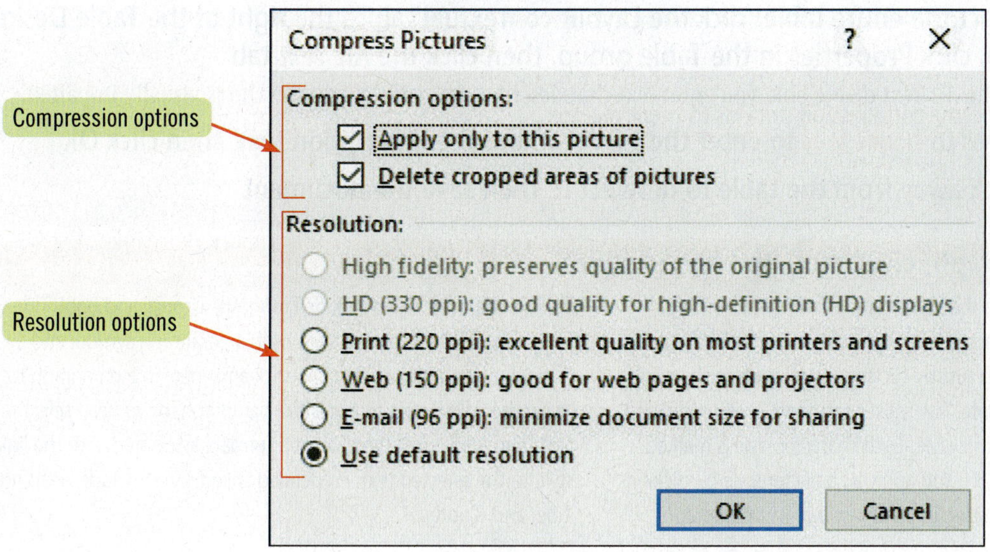

Word Module 11

Create Character Styles

Learning Outcomes
- Create a character style
- Add Alt text to a table

A **character style** includes character format settings—such as font, font size, color, bold, and italic—that you name and save as a style. You apply a character style to selected text within a paragraph. Any text in the paragraph that is not formatted with the character style is formatted with the currently applied paragraph style. **Alternative text** (Alt text) is descriptive text added to an object that improves accessibility of the document for people who have vision or reading disabilities. **CASE** *You create a character style called Workshops to apply to each Workshop name in the list of Shaleen's top three workshops. You also add Alternative text (Alt text) to the table that lists the Fall workshop schedule.*

STEPS

QUICK TIP
You use CTRL to select all the noncontiguous text you wish to format with a new style.

1. **Scroll up to page 1, select Skills Inventory in the first line below the Top Workshops heading, press and hold CTRL, select Industry Research at the beginning of the next paragraph, select Networking at the beginning of the next paragraph, then release CTRL**
   Three sets of text are selected.
2. **Click the Launcher in the Styles group, then click the New Style button at the bottom of the Styles pane**
   The Create New Style from Formatting dialog box opens. In this dialog box, you name the new style, select the style type, and then select the formats you want to enhance the text.
3. **Type Workshops in the Name box, click the Style type arrow, then click Character as the style type**
4. **Refer to FIGURE 11-12 to select the other character formatting settings: Bold, Italic, and the Purple font color in the Standard Colors section**
5. **Click OK, then click away from the text to deselect it**
   The text you selected is formatted with the new Workshops character style.

QUICK TIP
You can modify an existing character style.

6. **Select Skills Inventory below Top Workshops, click the Font Color arrow in the Font group, click the Red color box, right-click Workshops in the Styles pane, click Update Workshops to Match Selection as shown in FIGURE 11-13, then close the Styles pane**
   The three phrases formatted with the Workshops character style are updated with the red font color.
7. **Click anywhere in the Fall Workshop Schedule table, click the table select icon to select the entire table, click the Layout contextual tab to the right of the Table Design tab, click Properties in the Table group, then click the Alt Text tab**
   In the Alt Text dialog box, you enter text that describes the table for a user who is visually impaired.
8. **Refer to FIGURE 11-14 to enter the title text and the description text, then click OK**
9. **Click away from the table to deselect it, then save the document**

Identifying paragraph, character, and linked styles

Style types are identified in the Styles pane by different symbols. Each paragraph style is marked with a paragraph symbol: ¶. You can apply a paragraph style just by clicking in any paragraph or line of text and selecting the style. The most commonly used predefined paragraph style is the Normal style. Each character style is marked with a character symbol: a. You apply a character style by clicking anywhere in a word or by selecting a phrase within a paragraph. Built-in character styles include Emphasis, Strong, and Book Title. Each linked style is marked with both a paragraph symbol and a character symbol: ¶a. You can click anywhere in a paragraph to apply the linked style to the entire paragraph, or you can select text and then apply only the character formats associated with the linked style to the selected text. Predefined linked styles include Heading 1, Title, and Quote.

FIGURE 11-12: Create New Style From Formatting dialog box

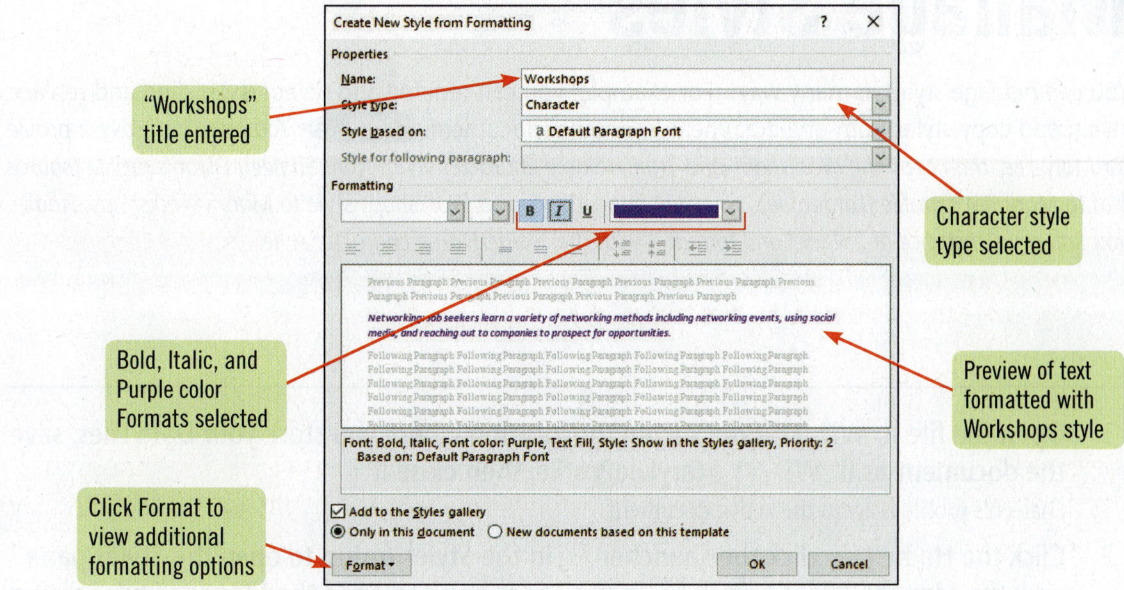

FIGURE 11-13: Updating the Workshops character style

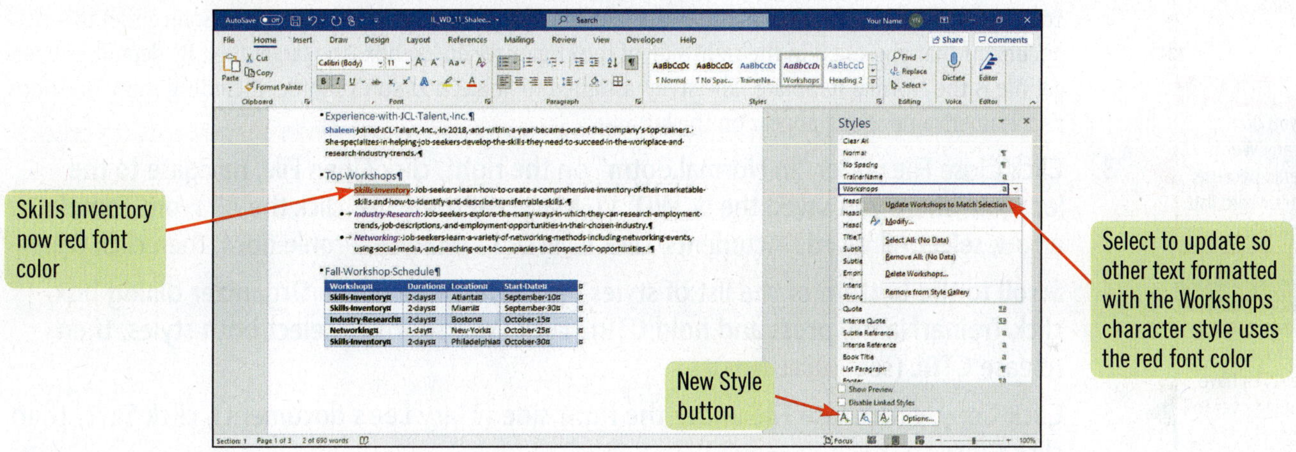

FIGURE 11-14: Adding Alt Text

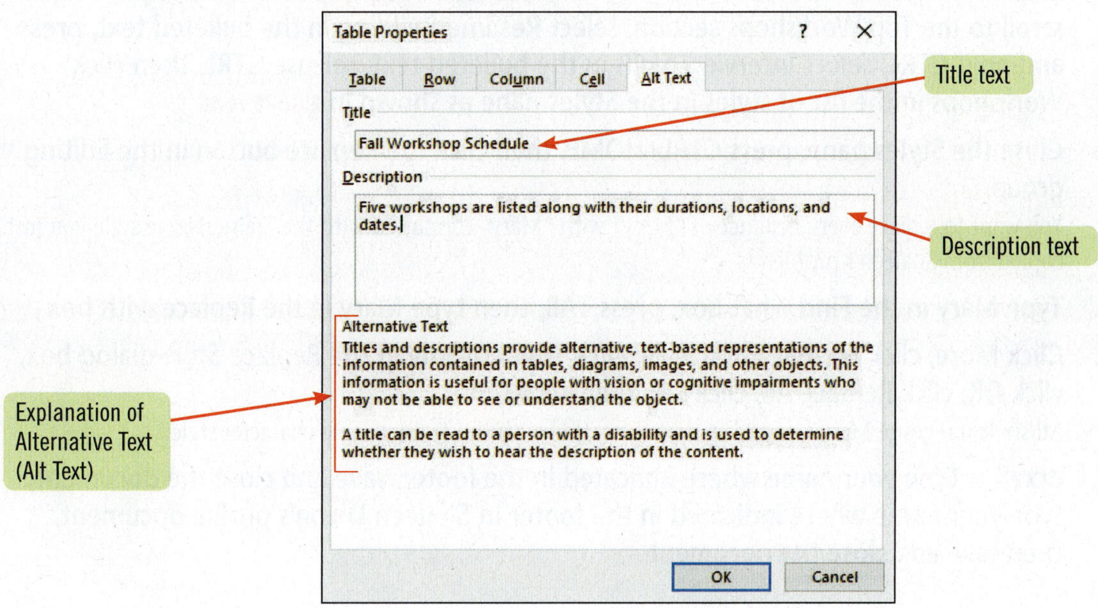

Word

Manage Styles

Learning Outcomes
- Copy styles between documents
- Find and replace styles

You can manage styles in many ways. For example, you can rename and delete styles, find and replace styles, and copy styles from one document to another document. **CASE** *You open and save a profile for Mary Lee, then copy the Workshops and TrainerName character styles from Shaleen Dixon's profile (source file) to Mary Lee's profile (target file). You then apply the copied Workshops style to Mary's workshops. Finally, you find every instance of "Mary" and format it with the TrainerName character style.*

STEPS

1. **Open the file IL_WD_11-2.docx from the location where you store your Data Files, save the document as IL_WD_11_MaryLeeProfile, then close it**
   Shaleen's profile is again the active document.
2. **Click the Home tab, click the Launcher in the Styles group to open the Styles pane, click the Manage Styles button in the Styles pane to open the Manage Styles dialog box, then click Import/Export**
   You copy styles from the document in the left side of the Organizer dialog box (the source file) to a new document that you open in the right side of the Organizer dialog box (the target file). By default, the target file is the Normal template. The styles assigned to Shaleen Dixon's profile, including the Workshops and TrainerName styles, appear on the left side.

TROUBLE
At first you do not see any Word documents because, by default, Word lists only templates.

3. **Click Close File under "in Normal.dotm" on the right, click Open File, navigate to the location where you saved the IL_WD_11_MaryLeeProfile file, click the All Word Templates arrow, select All Word Documents, click IL_WD_11_MaryLeeProfile.docx, then click Open**
4. **Scroll to the bottom of the list of styles on the left side of the Organizer dialog box, click TrainerName, press and hold CTRL, click Workshops to select both styles, then release CTRL (see FIGURE 11-15)**

QUICK TIP
Scroll down the right list to verify that the styles have been copied over to that file.

5. **Click Copy, click Close File under the right side (Mary Lee's document), click Save, then click Close**

TROUBLE
Do not select the text in the table.

6. **Click File, click Open, click IL_WD_11_MaryLeeProfile.docx, open the Styles pane again, scroll to the Top Workshops section, select Resume Building in the bulleted text, press and hold CTRL, select Interview Skills in the bulleted text, release CTRL, then click Workshops in the list of styles in the Styles pane as shown in FIGURE 11-16**
7. **Close the Styles pane, press CTRL+HOME, then click the Replace button in the Editing group**
   You want to replace every instance of "Mary" with "Mary" formatted with the TrainerName style you just copied from Shaleen's profile.
8. **Type Mary in the Find what box, press TAB, then type Mary in the Replace with box**
9. **Click More, click Format, click Style, click TrainerName in the Replace Style dialog box, click OK, click Replace All, click OK, then click Close**
   All six instances of Mary's name are now formatted with the TrainerName character style.
10. **sam Type your name where indicated in the footer, save and close the document, type your name where indicated in the footer in Shaleen Dixon's profile document, then save and close the document**

FIGURE 11-15: Managing styles using the Organizer dialog box

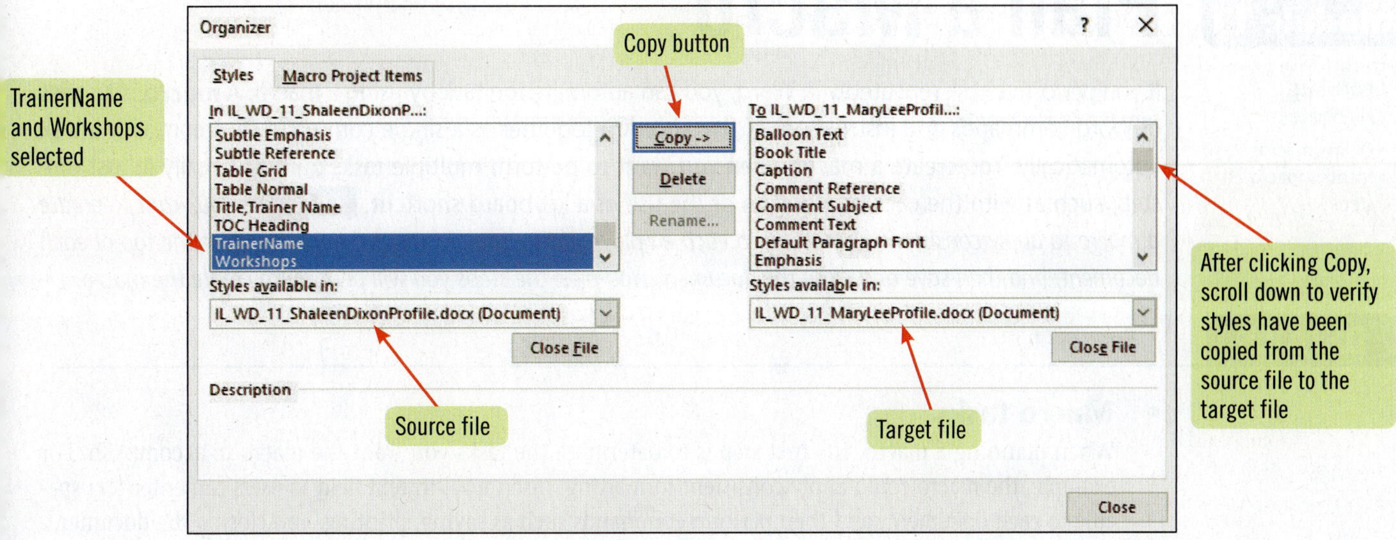

FIGURE 11-16: Applying the Workshops style

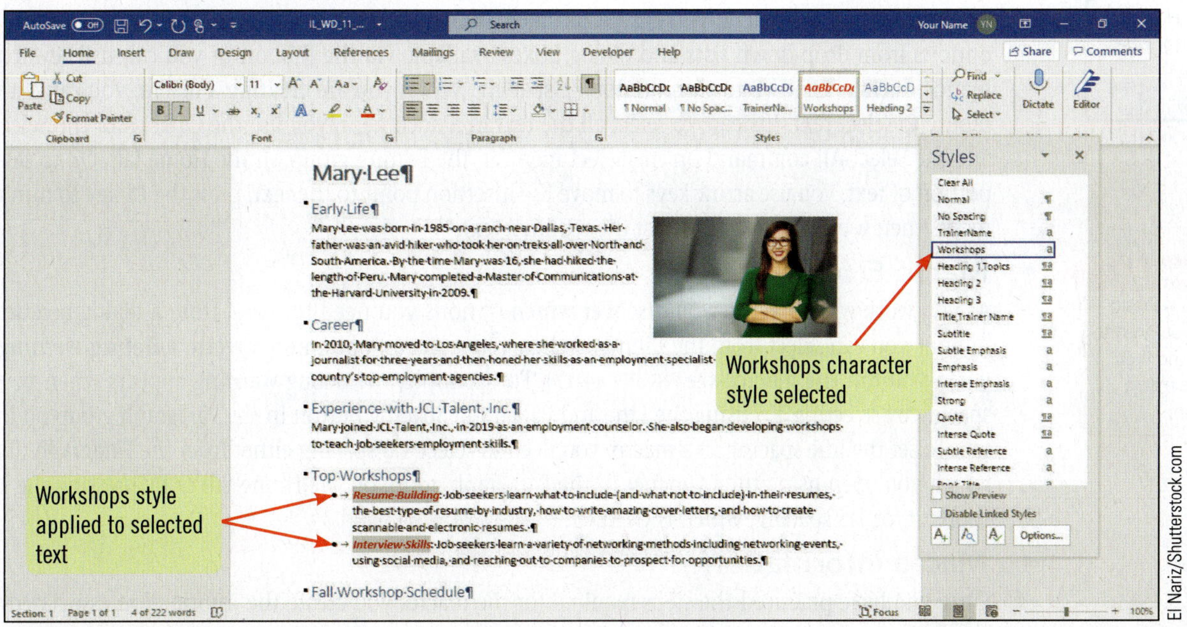

More ways to manage styles

To rename a style, right-click it in the Styles pane, click Modify, type a new name, then press ENTER. To delete a style, right-click the style, then click Delete [Style name]. The style is deleted from the Styles pane, but it is not deleted from your computer. Click the Manage Styles button at the bottom of the Styles pane, select the style to delete, click Delete, then click OK to close the Manage Styles dialog box.

Plan a Macro

Learning Outcomes
- Define macros
- Identify macro steps

If you perform a task repeatedly in Word, you can automate the task by using a macro. A **macro** is a series of Word commands and instructions that you group together as a single command to accomplish a task automatically. You create a macro when you want to perform multiple tasks quickly, usually in just one step, such as with the click of a button or the use of a keyboard shortcut. **CASE** *You want to create a macro to apply consistent formatting to each employment journal document, enter a title at the top of each document, and then save and close the document. You plan the steps you will perform to create the macro.*

DETAILS

- **Macro tasks**

  When planning a macro, the first step is to determine the tasks you want the macro to accomplish. For example, the macro could apply consistent formatting, insert a fill-in text field so users can enter text specific to each document, and then perform commands such as saving, printing, and closing the document. TABLE 11-2 lists all the tasks that you want your macro to perform.

QUICK TIP
You plan and practice the macro steps before you create a macro so you can perform the steps without error when you create the macro.

- **Macro steps**

  TABLE 11-2 also lists all the steps required to accomplish each task in the macro. If you make an error while recording the steps in the macro, you usually need to stop recording and start over because the recorded macro will include not only the correct steps but also the errors. By rehearsing the steps required before recording the macro, you ensure accuracy. While recording a macro, you can use the mouse to select options from drop-down lists and dialog boxes available via the Ribbon or you can use keystroke commands, such as CTRL+2 to turn on double spacing. When you are creating a macro, you cannot use your mouse to select text. Instead, to select all the text in a document, you use the CTRL+A or the Select button and the Select All command on the Select menu in the Editing group on the Home tab. Or, to select just a portion of text, you use arrow keys to move the insertion point to the text, press the F8 key to turn on select mode, then use arrow keys to select the required text.

TROUBLE
If a debug warning appears, you need to click End and then record the macro steps again.

- **Macro Errors**

  As you work with macros, you discover which options you need to select from a dialog box and which options you can select from the Ribbon. When you select an option incorrectly, a **debug** warning appears when you run the macro (see FIGURE 11-17). For example, the debug warning appears when you set line spacing by selecting 1.5 using the Line and Paragraph Spacing button in the Paragraph group on the Home tab. To set the line spacing in a macro, you need to select 1.5 spacing either from the Paragraph dialog box, which you open using the Launcher in the Paragraph group on the Home tab or by pressing the keyboard shortcut for 1.5 spacing, which is CTRL+5.

- **Macro information**

  Once you have practiced the steps required for the macro, you create the information associated with the macro. You open the Record Macro dialog box and then you name the macro and enter a short description of the macro. This description is usually a summary of the tasks the macro will perform. You also use this dialog box to assign the location where the macro should be stored. The default location is in the Normal template so that the macro is accessible in all documents that use the Normal template.

- **Record macro procedure**

  When you click OK after completing the Record Macro dialog box, the Macro Recorder pointer is the active pointer, indicating that you are ready to start recording the macro. In addition, the Stop Recording button and the Pause Recording button appear in the Code group on the Developer tab as shown in FIGURE 11-18. These buttons are toggle buttons. You click the Pause Recording button if, for example, you want to pause recording to perform steps not included in the macro. For example, you may need to pause to check information in another document or even attend to an email. You click the Stop Recording button when you have completed all the steps required for the macro, or when you have made a mistake and want to start over.

FIGURE 11-17: "Debug" warning that appears when the macro does not recognize a step

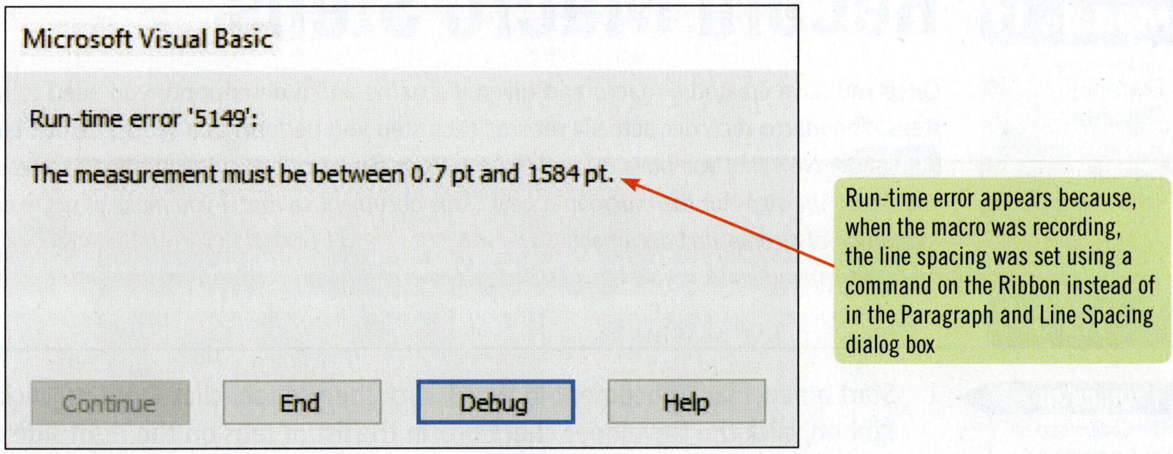

FIGURE 11-18: Recording a macro

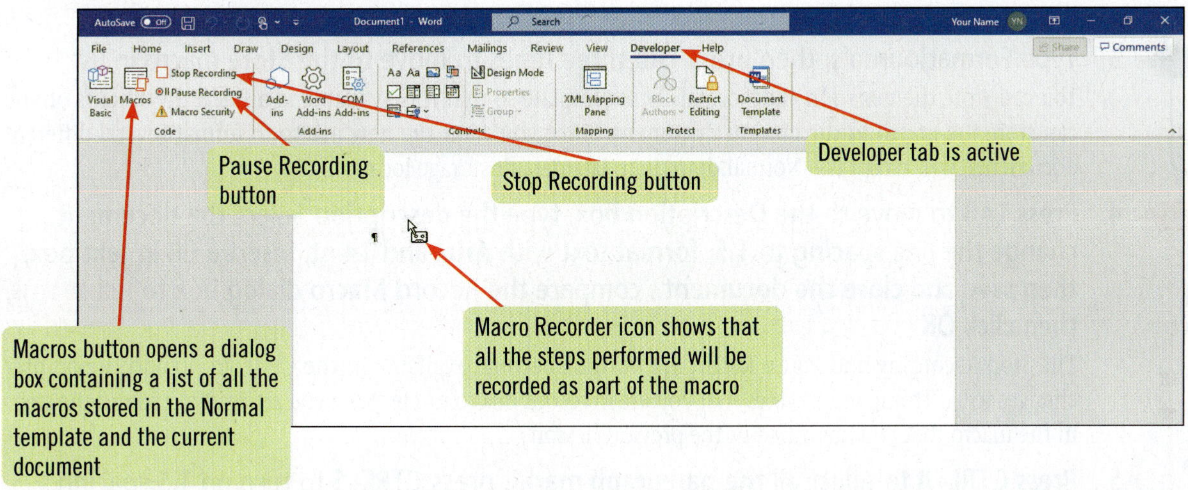

TABLE 11-2: Macro tasks and steps to complete the tasks

task to complete	steps to create macro
Select all the text	Press **CTRL+A**
Change the line spacing to 1.5	Press **CTRL+5**
Select the Arial font	Click the **Font arrow** in the Font group, then click **Arial**
Select 14 pt	Click the **Font Size arrow**, then click **14**
Insert a fill-in field text box	Press [↑] once to deselect the text and move to the top of the document, click the **Insert tab**, click the **Quick Parts button**, click **Field**, scroll down the list of Field names, click **Fill-in**, click **OK**, then click **OK**
Add a blank line	Press **ENTER**
Save the document	Click the **Save button** on the Quick Access toolbar
Close the document	Click the **File tab**, then click **Close**

Word Module 11

Record Macro Steps

Learning Outcomes
- Create and record a macro
- Add a custom field

Once you have created a macro and given it a name and a description, you need to record the macro steps. The macro recorder actually records each step you perform as a sequence of **Visual Basic** codes. **CASE** *Now that you have created the macro, as described previously in* TABLE 11-2*, you record the steps. You record the steps for the macro in a new blank document so that if you make errors, you do not affect the formatting of a completed document.*

STEPS

QUICK TIP
The Code group on the Developer tab contains the buttons you use to create and modify a macro.

1. **Start a new blank document in Word, click the File tab, click Options, click Customize Ribbon, click the Developer check box in the list of tabs on the right side of the Word Options dialog box if the box is not checked, click OK, then click the Developer tab**
2. **Save the blank document as IL_WD_11_JournalsMacroSetup to the location where you store your Data Files, press ENTER three times, then click the Record Macro button in the Code group**

   The Record Macro dialog box opens where you enter the macro name, the location where you want to store the macro, and a description.

QUICK TIP
A macro name cannot contain any spaces.

3. **Type FormatJournals, then press TAB three times to move to the Store macro in list**

   You can store the macro in the Normal.dotm template so that it is available to all new documents or you can store the macro in the current document. Since you want the new macro to format several different documents, you accept the Normal.dotm template default storage location.

TROUBLE
DO NOT press any keys or click any other options except those specified in the steps. If you make a mistake, stop recording the macro and create the macro again, answering Yes to replace it.

4. **Press TAB to move to the Description box, type the description Select the document, change the line spacing to 1.5, format text with Arial and 14 pt, insert a fill-in text box, then save and close the document., compare the Record Macro dialog box to FIGURE 11-19, then click OK**

   The Stop Recording and Pause Recording buttons become available in the Code group and the pointer changes to the record macro pointer. This icon indicates that you are in record macro mode. Now you are ready to record the steps in the macro that you identified in the previous lesson.
5. **Press CTRL+A to select all the paragraph marks, press CTRL+5 to turn on 1.5 spacing, click the Home tab, click the Font arrow in the Font group, scroll to and click Arial, click the Font Size arrow in the Font group, then click 14**

QUICK TIP
When you are recording a macro, you must use keystrokes to move around a document. You cannot use the mouse to position the insertion point.

6. **Press UP ARROW once to move to the top of the document, click the Insert tab, click the Explore Quick Parts button in the Text group, click Field, scroll down and click Fill-in from the list of Field names as shown in FIGURE 11-20, then click OK**

   When you run the macro, you will enter text in the fill-in field text box as shown in FIGURE 11-21.
7. **Click OK, press ENTER, click the Save button on the Quick Access toolbar, click the File tab, then click Close**
8. **Click the Developer tab, then click the Stop Recording button in the Code group**

   The file is saved and closed. The macro steps are completed, the Stop Recording button no longer appears in the Code group, and the Pause Recording button is dimmed.
9. **Click File, click Open, click IL_WD_11_JournalsMacroSetup to open this file, type your name on the first line, then save and close the document**

FIGURE 11-19: Record Macro dialog box

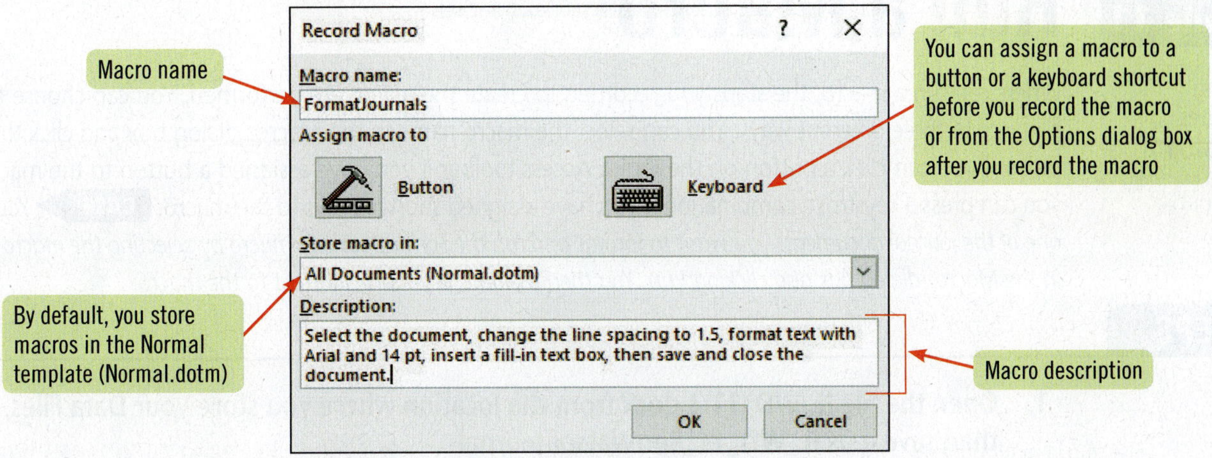

FIGURE 11-20: Field dialog box

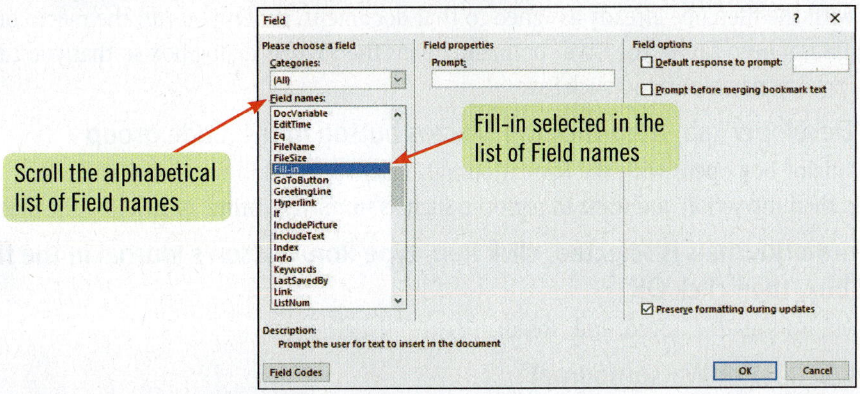

FIGURE 11-21: Inserting the Fill-in text box

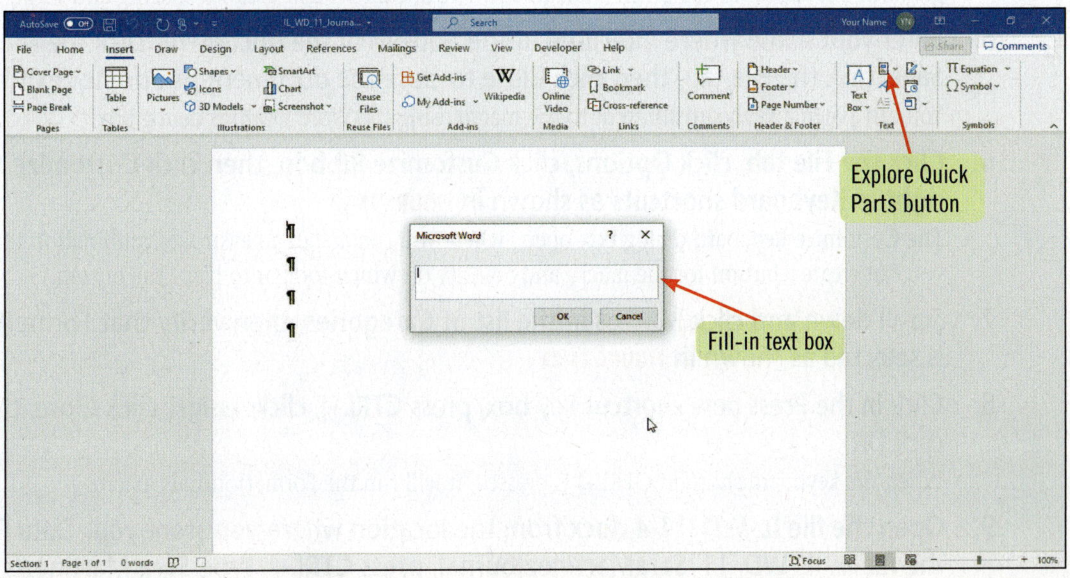

Pausing when recording a macro

If you need to interrupt the macro recording to perform other work such as checking an email or working on a different Word document, you can pause the recording. Click the Pause Recording button in the Code group on the Developer tab. When you want to resume recording the macro steps, press the Pause Recording button again.

Run a Macro

Learning Outcomes
- Run a macro
- Assign a keyboard shortcut to a macro

When you run a macro, the steps you recorded to create the macro are performed. You can choose to run a macro in three different ways. You can select the macro name in the Macros dialog box and click the Run button, you can click a button on the Quick Access toolbar if you have assigned a button to the macro, or you can press a keystroke combination if you have assigned shortcut keys to the macro. **CASE** *You open one of the journal documents you want to format and run the FormatJournals macro by selecting the macro name in the Macros dialog box and clicking Run. You then assign a keyboard shortcut to the macro.*

STEPS

1. **Open the file IL_WD_11-3.docx from the location where you store your Data Files, then save it as IL_WD_11_RonWatsonJournal**
   The file contains a journal entry made by Ron Watson after he participated in three of the JCL Talent, Inc., workshops. When you run the macro on a document that you open, the Save command saves the document with the filename already assigned to that document. When you run the macro on a document that has not been saved, the Save command opens the Save As dialog box so that you can enter a filename in the File name box and click Save.
2. **Click the Developer tab, then click the Macros button in the Code group**
   The Macros dialog box opens with the FormatJournals macro selected in the Macro name box. You select a macro and then the action you want to perform, such as running, editing, or deleting the macro.
3. **Be sure FormatJournals is selected, click Run, type Ron Watson's Journal in the fill-in field text box, then click OK**
   The document is formatted, saved, and closed.
4. **Open IL_WD_11_RonWatsonJournal**
   The text you entered in the fill-in field text box appears at the top of the page highlighted in gray. The gray will not appear in the printed document. The document text uses 1.5 spacing and 14 pt, Arial text.
5. **Enter your name where indicated at the bottom of the document, click the File tab, click Save, click the File tab, then click Close to close the document but do not exit Word**
   You can assign a keyboard shortcut to the macro using the Word Options dialog box.
6. **Click the File tab, click Options, click Customize Ribbon, then click Customize to the right of Keyboard shortcuts as shown in FIGURE 11-22**
   The Customize Keyboard dialog box opens where you can assign a keystroke combination to a macro or you can create a button for the macro and identify on which toolbar to place the button.
7. **Scroll down and click Macros in the list of Categories, then verify that FormatJournals is selected as shown in FIGURE 11-23**
8. **Click in the Press new shortcut key box, press CTRL+J, click Assign, click Close, then click OK**
   When the keyboard shortcut CTRL+J is pressed, it will run the FormatJournals macro.
9. **Open the file IL_WD_11-4.docx from the location where you store your Data Files, save the file as IL_WD_11_SaraMartinezJournal, press CTRL+J, type Sara Martinez's Journal in the fill-in field text box, then click OK**
   The macro formats, saves, and closes the document.
10. **Open the file IL_WD_11_SaraMartinezJournal.docx to verify that the macro has been applied, then close the file but do not exit Word**

TROUBLE
If a run-time error appears when you run the macro, delete the macro, and repeat the previous lesson to record the macro again.

FIGURE 11-22: Word Options dialog box

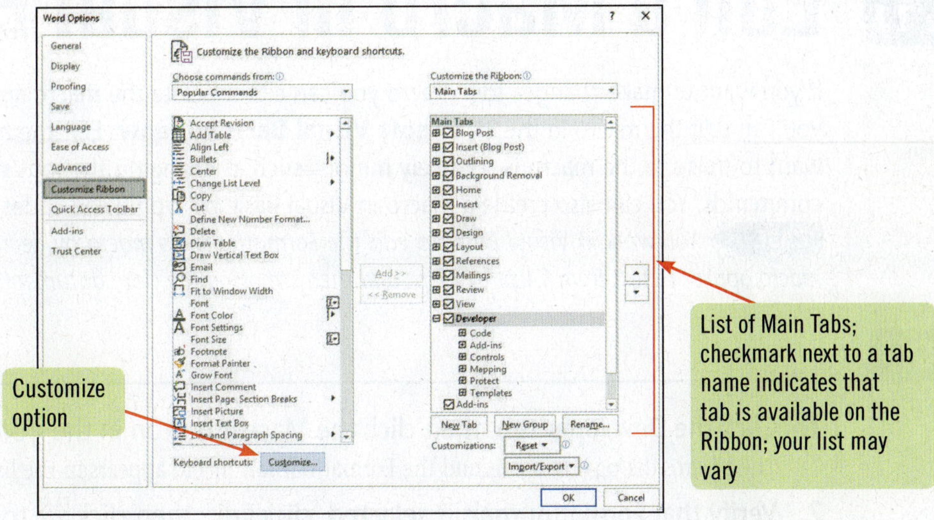

FIGURE 11-23: Customize Keyboard dialog box

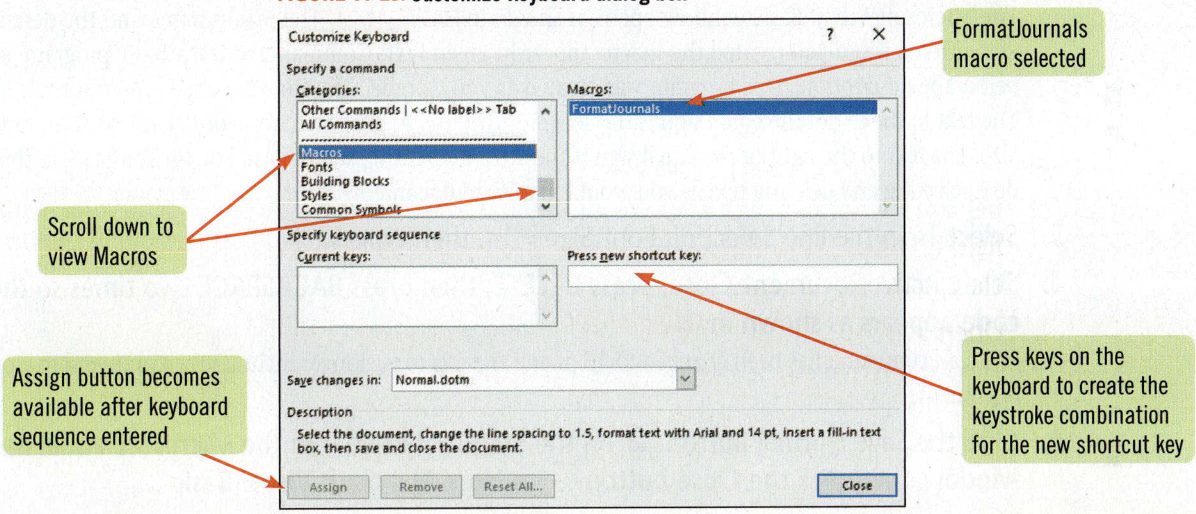

Finding keyboard shortcuts

Word includes hundreds of keyboard shortcuts that you can use to streamline document formatting tasks and to help you work efficiently in Word. You access the list of Word's keyboard shortcuts from Help. Click in the Search box on the title bar, type "keyboard shortcuts", then click "keyboard shortcuts" in the Get Help on section of the menu that opens. In the Help pane that opens, click links to articles to read more about keyboard shortcuts. You can also create your own keyboard shortcuts for procedures you use frequently. **TABLE 11-3** shows some common keyboard shortcuts.

TABLE 11-3: Some common keyboard shortcuts

function	keyboard shortcut	function	keyboard shortcut
Bold text	CTRL+B	Print a document	CTRL+P
Center text	CTRL+E	Redo or repeat an action	CTRL+Y
Copy text	CTRL+C	Save a document	CTRL+S
Cut text	CTRL+X	Select all text	CTRL+A
Open a document	CTRL+O	Turn on double spacing	CTRL+2
Paste text	CTRL+V	Undo an action	CTRL+Z

Word
Module 11

Edit a Macro in Visual Basic

Learning Outcome
- Edit a macro in Visual Basic

If you want to make changes to a macro you can either delete the macro and record the steps again, or you can edit the macro in the **Microsoft Visual Basic window**. Edit the macro when the change you want to make to the macro is relatively minor—such as changing the font style or removing one of the commands. You can also create a macro in Visual Basic by typing the codes in the Visual Basic window. **CASE** *You work in Visual Basic to edit the FormatJournals macro by decreasing the font size that the macro applies to text from 14 pt to 12 pt and then removing the close document command.*

STEPS

1. **Click the Developer tab, then click the Macros button in the Code group**
   The Macros dialog box opens and the FormatJournals macro appears in the list of available macros.
2. **Verify that FormatJournals is selected, click Edit, then click ☐ to maximize the Microsoft Visual Basic window, if necessary**
   The Microsoft Visual Basic window opens as shown in FIGURE 11-24. The macro name and the description you entered when you created the macro appear in green text. Command codes, a Basic program, appear below the description. This program was created as you recorded the steps for the FormatJournals macro. The text to the left of the equal sign is the specific attribute, such as Selection.Font.Name or Selection.Font. Size. The text to the right of the equal sign is the attribute setting, such as Arial or 14. You work in this window selecting and deleting text as you would in a Word document.
3. **Select 14 in the line Selection.Font.Size = 14, then type 12**
4. **Select ActiveDocument.Close, press DELETE, then press BACKSPACE two times so the code appears as shown in FIGURE 11-25**
   The font command has been changed to 12 pt and the macro no longer includes the command to close the document.
5. **Click the Save Normal button on the Standard toolbar in the Microsoft Visual Basic window, then click the Close button ☒ to close Microsoft Visual Basic**
6. **Open the file IL_WD_11_SaraMartinezJournal.docx from the location where you store your Data Files, press CTRL+J to run the macro, then click Cancel to close the fill-in field text box**
   The second time you run the macro you don't need to enter a title in the fill-in field text box. The font size of the document is reduced to 12 pt and the document is saved but not closed.
7. **Type your name where indicated at the bottom of the document, then save the document**
8. **Click the Developer tab, click the Visual Basic button in the Code group, press CTRL+A to select all the FormatJournals macro code in the Visual Basic window, press CTRL+C to copy the code to the Clipboard, then close the Microsoft Visual Basic window**
9. **Press CTRL+N to open a new blank Word document, press CTRL+V, press ENTER, type Created by followed by your name, save the document as IL_WD_11_MacroCodes, then close the document**
   The journal for Sara Martinez is again the active document.

QUICK TIP
You save a copy of your macro code so you have a reference to verify the macro steps you performed.

FIGURE 11-24: Visual Basic window

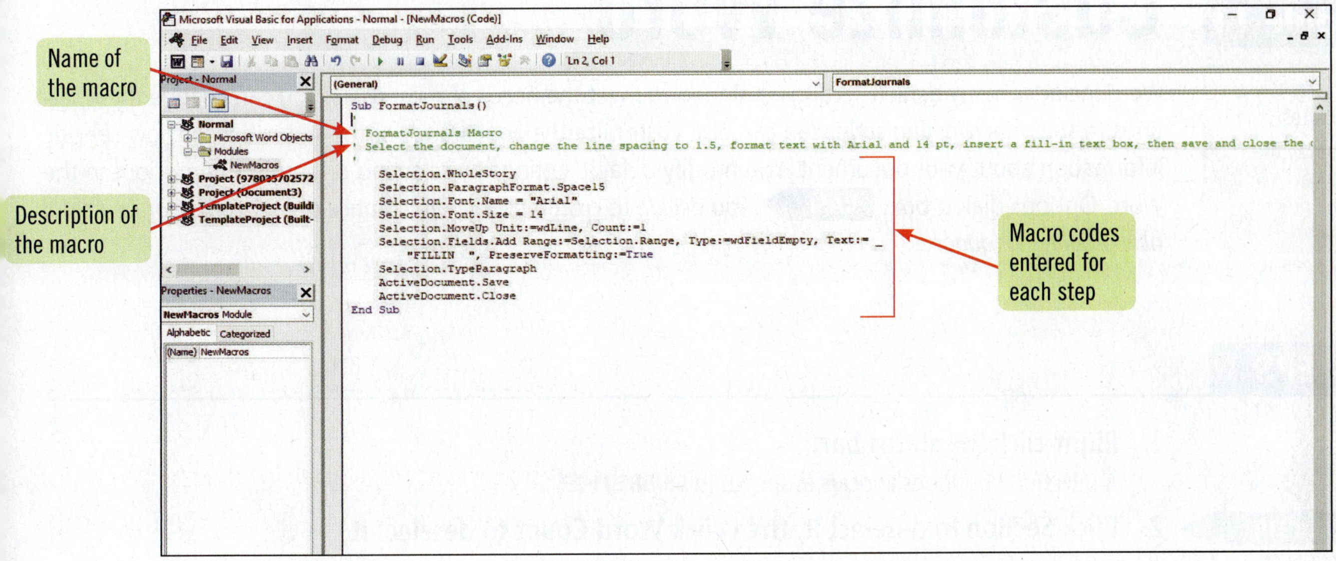

FIGURE 11-25: Edited macro

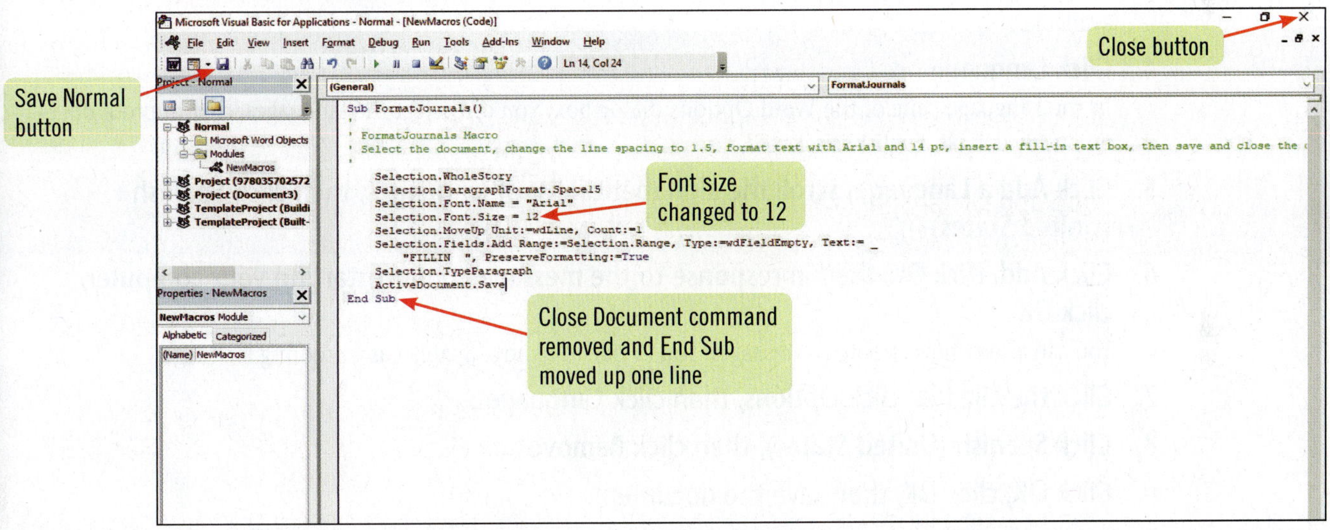

Creating a Macro in Visual Basic

You can create a macro by entering codes into Visual Basic. From the Developer tab, click the Macros button in the Code group, type a macro name, select the template or document in which to store the macro, then click Create to open the Visual Basic Editor. You can paste code from an existing macro or you can enter codes for the macro. To find a list of codes and information about working with Visual Basic, press F1 to open the Microsoft Visual Basic Help menu or click Help on the menu bar, then click Microsoft Visual Basic for Applications Help.

Word
Module 11

Customize Word

Learning Outcomes
- Customize the status bar
- Set the proofing language

Word includes many default settings designed to meet the needs of most users. You can change these settings to suit your working style. You can also customize the appearance of the status bar to show specific information about your document. You modify default settings by selecting or deselecting options in the Word Options dialog box. **CASE** *You decide to customize the appearance of the status bar and set a new proofing language.*

STEPS

QUICK TIP
To restore items, right-click the status bar, then click the items again.

1. **Right-click the status bar**
   A selection of options appears as shown in FIGURE 11-26
2. **Click Section to deselect it, then click Word Count to deselect it**
   These two options are now removed from the status bar.
3. **Click the File tab, scroll down, if necessary, then click Options**
   From the Word Options dialog box you can customize the Ribbon and the Quick Access toolbar. You can also access nine other categories that you can modify to meet your needs. TABLE 11-4 lists the categories available.
4. **Click Language**
   In the Language pane of the Word Options dialog box, you can select the languages used to proof documents. By default, English is selected.
5. **Click Add a Language, scroll the alphabetical list of languages, then click Spanish (United States)**
6. **Click Add, click OK, then in response to the message about restarting your computer, click OK**
   You can also remove proofing languages. You decide to remove Spanish as a proofing language.
7. **Click the File tab, click Options, then click Language**
8. **Click Spanish (United States), then click Remove**
9. **Click OK, click OK, then save the document**

Copying a Macro to Another Document

You can copy a macro that you saved in a document instead of in the Normal template to another document. You use the same procedure to copy a macro from one document to another document as you used to copy a style or selection of styles from one document to another document. Click the Launcher in the Styles group on the Home tab, click the Manage Styles button at the bottom of the Styles pane, then click Import/Export. In the Organizer dialog box, click the Macro Projects Items tab, open the file containing the macro you want to copy (the source file), open the file you want to copy the macro to (the destination file), select the macro in the source file, then click Copy.

FIGURE 11-26: Customize the status bar options

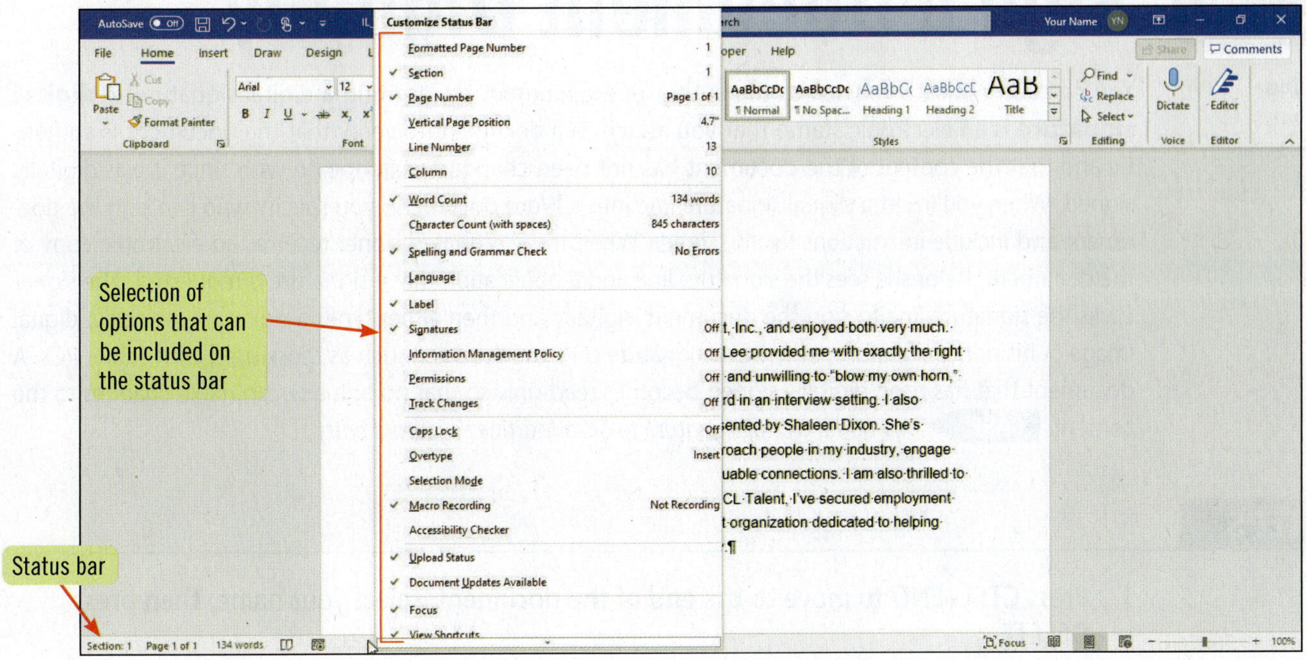

TABLE 11-4: Categories in the Word Options dialog box

category	description
General	Options include those used to modify the user interface, personalize Office, and modify collaboration options
Display	Change the page display, formatting options, and printing options
Proofing	Modify AutoCorrect and spelling and grammar options and exceptions
Save	Modify options related to saving documents and editing them offline
Language	Select editing, display and Help languages
Ease of Access	Select feedback options, application and document display options, and automatic alt text
Advanced	Modify options related to editing, images, document display, saving, and printing, layout, and document compatibility
Add-ins	Includes the list of programs included with or added to Word
Trust Center	Access security options and the Microsoft Word Trust Center

Word
Module 11

Sign a Document Digitally

Learning Outcome
- Add a digital signature

You can authenticate yourself as the author of a document by inserting a digital signature. A **digital signature** is an electronic stamp that you attach to a document to verify that the document is authentic and that the content of the document has not been changed or tampered with since it was digitally signed. When you insert a digital signature line into a Word document, you specify who can sign the document and include instructions for the signer. When the designated signer receives an electronic copy of the document, he or she sees the signature line and a notification that a signature is requested. The signer clicks the signature line to sign the document digitally and then either types a signature, selects a digital image of his or her signature, or writes a signature on a touch screen such as those used with Tablet PCs. A document that has been digitally signed becomes read-only so that no one else can make changes to the content. **CASE** *You add a digital signature to Sara Martinez's journal entry.*

STEPS

1. **Press CTRL+END to move to the end of the document, select your name, then press DELETE**
2. **Press ENTER to position the insertion point where want to add the signature line**
3. **Click the Insert tab, then click the Add a Signature Line button in the Text group**
   The Signature Setup dialog box opens. You enter information about the person who can sign the document in this dialog box.
4. **Type your name in the Suggested signer box in the Signature Setup dialog box as shown in FIGURE 11-27**
5. **Click OK**
   A space for your signature, with an X and your name below a horizontal line appears in the footer at the position of the insertion point.
6. **Double-click the signature line, read the message that appears, then click No**
   If you click in the line and then click Yes, you are taken to a page on the Microsoft website that lists Microsoft partners that supply digital IDs. Once you have obtained a Digital ID, you can enter it in the signature line. However, you will not be obtaining a Digital ID, so the signature line will remain blank.
7. **Click in the document, then save the document**
8. **Submit a copy of all the files you created in this module to your instructor, then exit Word**

TROUBLE
If you do not see the message after double-clicking the signature line, type your name, click Sign, read the message that appears, then click No. In Step 7, Click Cancel, then save the document.

FIGURE 11-27: Signature Setup dialog box

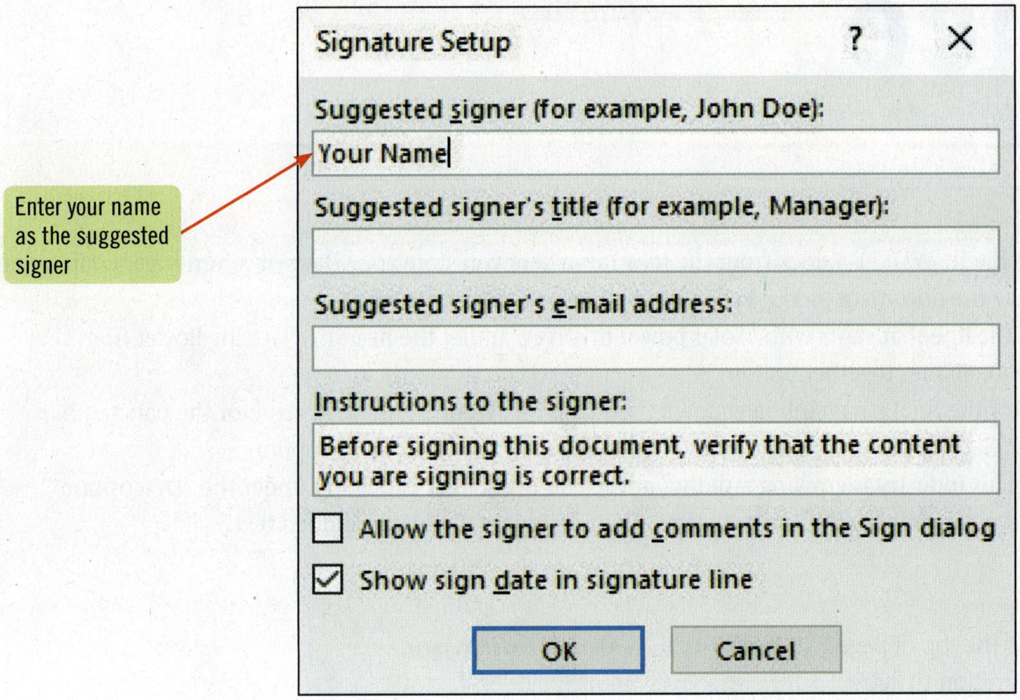

Customizing the Quick Access toolbar

To customize the Quick Access toolbar, click the File tab, click Options, then click Quick Access Toolbar. The buttons included by default on the Quick Access toolbar appear in the list on the right. These buttons are AutoSave, Save, Undo, and Redo. To add a new command to the Quick Access toolbar, select the command from the list on the left, then click Add. To remove a button from the Quick Access toolbar, select the command in the list on the right, then click Remove.

Acquiring a Digital ID

You acquire a **digital ID** by purchasing one from a Microsoft partner. When you click Yes to acquire a digital ID, you are taken to a page with links to Microsoft partners. You can click on one of the links and purchase a digital ID. Other people can use the digital ID to verify that your digital signature is authentic. The Microsoft partner that issues the digital ID ensures the authenticity of the person or organization that acquires the digital ID.

Practice

Skills Review

1. **Manage pages.**
   a. Start Word, open the file IL_WD_11-5.docx from the location where you store your Data Files, verify paragraph marks are showing, then save the document as **IL_WD_11_SolarIndustryProfile**.
   b. Scroll down, click in the line that starts with "Solar power involves" under the heading "Getting Power from the Sun", then apply the Keep lines together option.
   c. Scroll to the last line of the final paragraph (a widow), then turn on Widow/Orphan control for the paragraph.
   d. Click in the heading "Getting Power from the Sun", then apply the Page break before option.
   e. Select the sentence "This industry is growing rapidly." at the end of the first paragraph under the "Description" heading, verify that the paragraph mark is not selected, then designate the text as hidden text.
   f. Save the document.
2. **Edit pictures.**
   a. Change the picture at the top of page 1 to **Support_WD_11_Solar.jpg**.
   b. Change the color saturation to 300%.
   c. Change the color tone to Temperature: 8800 K.
   d. Scroll to the bottom of the document, click the picture, then apply the Glow Diffused artistic effect.
   e. Save the document.
3. **Use layering options.**
   a. Go to the top of page 1, then send the picture of the solar panels behind the lightning bolt shape.
   b. Go to the end of the document, then change the yellow cloud shape to a sun shape.
   c. Apply the Round Convex bevel effect to the sun shape.
   d. Open the Selection pane, hide the picture of the sun shape, then show the picture again.
   e. Drag the picture of the sun shape below Picture 2 in the Selection pane.
   f. Drag Picture 2 above Star: 10 Points 7 in the Selection pane.
   g. Save the document.
4. **Arrange and compress graphics.**
   a. In the Selection pane, verify that Picture 2 is selected, then use CTRL to select the other two objects so all three objects in the Selection pane are selected.
   b. Group the three objects into one object.
   c. Change the wrapping of the grouped object to Square.
   d. Cut the grouped object, paste it at the top of page 2, then position it to the right of the "Getting Power from the Sun" heading as shown in the completed document in FIGURE 11-28.
   e. Compress all the pictures in the document using the Web (150 ppi) option.
   f. Save the document and close the Selection pane.
5. **Create character styles.**
   a. On page 1, select the text "PV Power" in the first bulleted point below the Technologies heading, then use CTRL to select "CS Power" so both phrases are selected.
   b. Create a new style called **Technology**, then designate it as a Character style.
   c. Select these character formatting settings: a font size of 14 pt, Bold, and the Dark Red font color (first selection in the Standard Colors section).
   d. Deselect the text.

Skills Review (continued)

- **e.** Select just "PV Power", change the font color to Green in the Standard Colors section, then update the Technology character style to match the selection.
- **f.** Close the Styles pane.
- **g.** Select the table below the "Geographic Segmentation" heading, then add the following Alt text: Title: **Locations of Solar Industry** and the Description: **Four geographic areas are listed along with their percent share of the solar power industry.**
- **h.** Save the document.

6. Manage styles.

- **a.** Open the file **IL_WD_11-6.docx** from the location where you store your Data Files, save the document as **IL_WD_11_WindIndustryProfile**, then close it.
- **b.** Open the Organizer dialog box from the Styles pane.
- **c.** Verify that the source file is IL_WD_11_SolarIndustryProfile.docx.
- **d.** Open IL_WD_11_WindIndustryProfile.docx as the destination file. Remember to select All Word Documents to view the Word document.
- **e.** Copy the styles **Energy** and **Technology** from the source file to the destination file.
- **f.** Close and save the destination file, then close the Organizer dialog box.
- **g.** Open IL_WD_11_WindIndustryProfile.docx, use CTRL to select the two configurations "Horizontal axis turbine" and "Vertical axis turbine", then apply the Technology character style.
- **h.** Go to the top of the document, then use the Replace feature to find every instance of **wind** and replace it with "wind" formatted with the Energy character style you just copied from the Solar Energy document.
- **i.** Type your name where indicated in the footer, save and close the document, type your name where indicated in the footer in the Solar Energy document, then save and close the document. The completed Solar Energy document appears as shown in **FIGURE 11-28**.

FIGURE 11-28

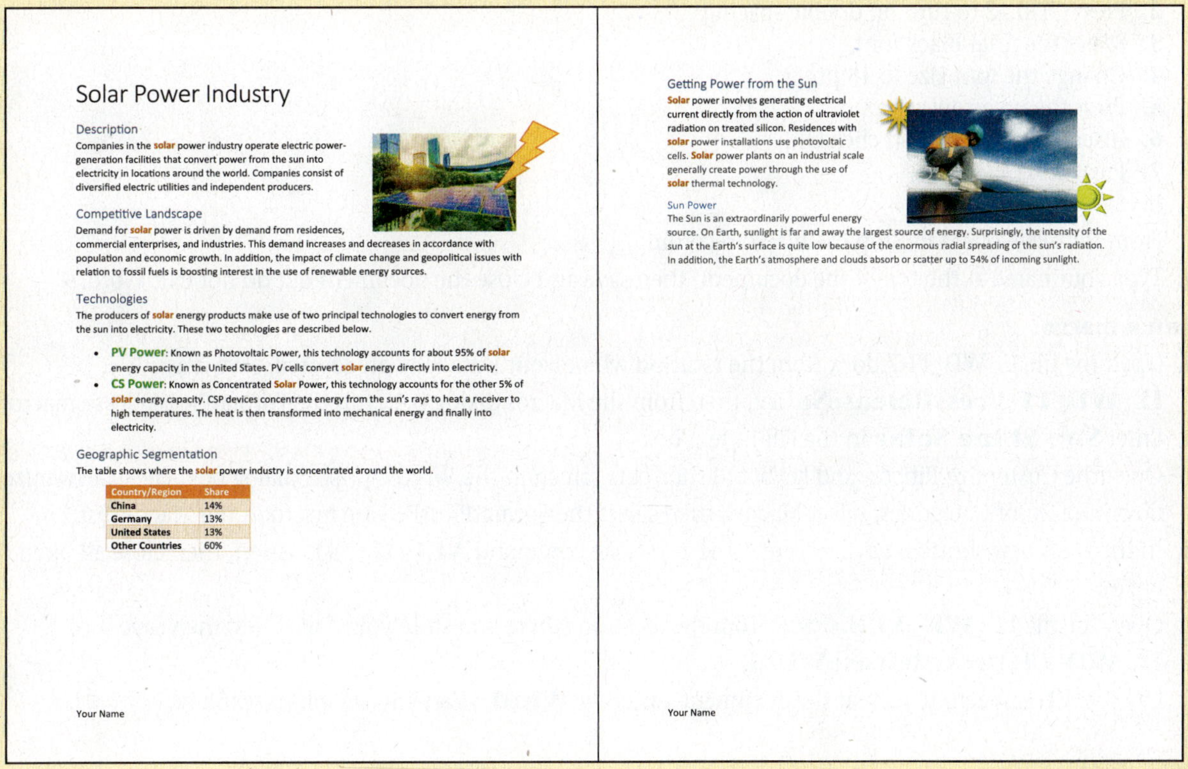

Solar Power Industry

Description

Companies in the solar power industry operate electric power-generation facilities that convert power from the sun into electricity in locations around the world. Companies consist of diversified electric utilities and independent producers.

Competitive Landscape

Demand for solar power is driven by demand from residences, commercial enterprises, and industries. This demand increases and decreases in accordance with population and economic growth. In addition, the impact of climate change and geopolitical issues with relation to fossil fuels is boosting interest in the use of renewable energy sources.

Technologies

The producers of solar energy products make use of two principal technologies to convert energy from the sun into electricity. These two technologies are described below.

- PV Power: Known as Photovoltaic Power, this technology accounts for about 95% of solar energy capacity in the United States. PV cells convert solar energy directly into electricity.
- CS Power: Known as Concentrated Solar Power, this technology accounts for the other 5% of solar energy capacity. CSP devices concentrate energy from the sun's rays to heat a receiver to high temperatures. The heat is then transformed into mechanical energy and finally into electricity.

Geographic Segmentation

The table shows where the solar power industry is concentrated around the world.

Country/Region	Share
China	14%
Germany	13%
United States	13%
Other Countries	60%

Your Name

Getting Power from the Sun

Solar power involves generating electrical current directly from the action of ultraviolet radiation on treated silicon. Residences with solar power installations use photovoltaic cells. Solar power plants on an industrial scale generally create power through the use of solar thermal technology.

Sun Power

The Sun is an extraordinarily powerful energy source. On Earth, sunlight is far and away the largest source of energy. Surprisingly, the intensity of the sun at the Earth's surface is quite low because of the enormous radial spreading of the sun's radiation. In addition, the Earth's atmosphere and clouds absorb or scatter up to 54% of incoming sunlight.

Your Name

asharkyu/Shutterstock.com

Federico Rostagno/Shutterstock.com

Skills Review (continued)

7. Plan a macro.

a. Refer to TABLE 11-5 to review the steps required for the macro you will create in the next step:

TABLE 11-5: **Macro tasks plan**

Macro tasks	steps to complete the tasks
Select all the text	Press **CTRL+A**
Change the line spacing to double	Press **CTRL+2**
Select the Arial Black font	Click the **Font arrow** in the Font group, then click **Arial Black**
Select 18 pt	Click the **Font Size arrow**, then click **18**
Insert a fill-in field text box	Press the up arrow once to deselect the text and move to the top of the document, click the **Insert tab**, click the **Explore Quick Parts button**, click **Field**, scroll down the list of Field names, click **Fill-in**, click **OK**, then click **OK**
Add a blank line	Press **ENTER**
Save the document	Click the **Save button** on the Quick Access toolbar

8. Record macro steps.

a. Start a new blank document, then show the Developer tab if it is not already displayed on the Ribbon.

b. Press ENTER three times, then save the blank document as **IL_WD_11_PressReleaseMacroSetup**.

c. Make the Developer tab the active tab, open the Record Macro dialog box, then type **FormatPressRelease** as the macro name.

d. Enter the following description in the Description box: **Select all the text, change the line spacing to double, change the font to Arial Black and 18 pt, insert a fill-in text box, then save the document.**

e. Exit the Record Macro dialog box, then perform the macro steps as follows:

1. Press CTRL+A to select all the text.
2. Press CTRL+2 to turn on double spacing.
3. Select the Arial Black font.
4. Change the font size to 18 pt.
5. Press the up arrow once.
6. Insert a Fill-in box and click OK.
7. Press ENTER.
8. Save the document.

f. From the Developer tab, stop the macro recording.

g. Type your name at the top of the document, then save and close the document but do not exit Word.

9. Run a macro.

a. Open the file IL_WD_11-7.docx from the location where your Data Files are located, save it as **IL_WD_11_PressReleaseSolar**, then from the Macros dialog box, run the FormatPressRelease macro.

b. Enter **Sun Shine Solar** in the Fill-in text box.

c. Open the Customize Ribbon and keyboard shortcuts screen in the Word Options dialog box, click Customize, scroll down the list of Categories, select Macros, then select the FormatPressRelease macro in the Macros list.

d. In the Press new shortcut key box, enter the keystroke command **ALT+H**, click Assign, then close all open dialog boxes.

e. Open the file **IL_WD_11-8.docx** from the location where you store your Data Files, then save it as **IL_WD_11_PressReleaseWind**.

f. Use the Alt+H macro to format the document, entering **Wind Ways** in the fill-in text box.

Skills Review (continued)

10. Edit a macro in Visual Basic.

- **a.** Open the Macros dialog box, select the FormatPressRelease macro, then click Edit. (*Note*: Two macros are listed—the FormatJournals macro you created in the lessons and the FormatPressRelease macro you just created. In the steps that follow, you make corrections to the FormatPressRelease macro.)
- **b.** Find Selection.Font.Name = "Arial Black", change the font to **Calibri** and keep the quotation marks around Calibri, then change Selection.Font.Size = 18 to **14**.
- **c.** Save the macro, select all the components of the FormatPressRelease macro in the Visual Basic window, copy them, close the Visual Basic window, press CTRL+N to open a new blank Word document, paste the code into the blank document, type **Created by** followed by your name below the last line, save the document as **IL_WD_11_PressReleaseMacroCodes** to the location where you store your files for this book, then close it.
- **d.** Verify that IL_WD_11_PressReleaseWind is the active document, then use the ALT+H keystrokes to run the revised macro. Remember to press Cancel to bypass the Fill-in box.
- **e.** Verify that the font style of the document title is now Calibri and the font size is 14 pt, type your name where indicated at the end of the document, then save the document.

11. Customize Word.

- **a.** Customize the status bar so that Section and Word Count are both selected.
- **b.** In the Language section of the Options dialog box, Add French (Canada) as a proofing language.
- **c.** Remove French (Canada) as a proofing language, then save the document.

12. Sign a document digitally.

- **a.** Delete your name in the current document, then press Enter to position the insertion point where you want to add a signature line.
- **b.** Insert a signature line that includes your name.
- **c.** Save and close the document, then save and close all files.
- **d.** Submit a copy of all the files you created in this module to your instructor, then exit Word.

Independent Challenge 1

One of your duties in the administration department at Riverwalk Medical Clinic in Cambridge, MA, is to write and format the clinic's quarterly news bulletin. You open a draft of the Fall bulletin and set paragraph pagination options, edit pictures, and create and then modify a character style. Finally, you copy a character style from the Spring bulletin to the Fall bulletin and apply it to selected text.

- **a.** Start Word, open the file IL_WD_11-9.docx from the location where you store your Data Files, save it as **IL_WD_11_RiverwalkFallBulletin**, then show formatting marks if necessary.
- **b.** Apply the Keep with next option to the heading "Share Your Ideas".
- **c.** Format the text "One of our schedulers will find a time that works best for you." at the end of the "Physical Exams" paragraph on page 1 as hidden.
- **d.** Change the picture on page 1 to the picture **Support_WD_11_Clinic.jpg**.
- **e.** Apply the Texturizer artistic effect to the picture, then set the color saturation at 200% and the color tone at 7200 K.
- **f.** Use the Selection pane to move the picture below the red cross shape, then modify the red cross shape so it uses the Divot bevel effect.
- **g.** Group the red cross shape and the picture into one object.
- **h.** Select the phrases "Health Hijinks" and "Silent Auction" in the bulleted list, then create a character style called **Event** that uses the following formats: Bold, Italic, and the Blue font color (in the Standard Colors section.)

Independent Challenge 1 (continued)

i. Select "Health Hijinks" and remove italics, then update the Event character style to match the selection.

j. Select the table on page 2, then add Alt text. Enter **Statistics** as the title, then in the description box type **Two-column table showing patient and volunteer statistics from August 1 to September 30.**

k. Save the document, then close it.

l. From a blank Word document, open the Organizer dialog box from the Styles pane. Close the file on the left (the current blank document), then open the file **Support_WD_11_SpringBulletin.docx** from the location where you save your files. This is the source file.

m. Close the file on the right, then open the file **IL_WD_11_RiverwalkFallBulletin.docx**. This is the destination file.

n. Copy the Clinic character style from the Spring Bulletin document on the left to the Fall Bulletin document on the right.

o. Close and save the Riverwalk Fall Bulletin, then close the Organizer dialog box.

p. Open **IL_WD_11_RiverwalkFallBulletin** and use Find and Replace to find every instance of "Riverwalk" and replaced it with **Riverwalk** formatted with the Clinic style.

q. Type your name where shown in the footer on the second page, save the document, then close it and any other open documents. The completed document appears as shown in **FIGURE 11-29**.

FIGURE 11-29

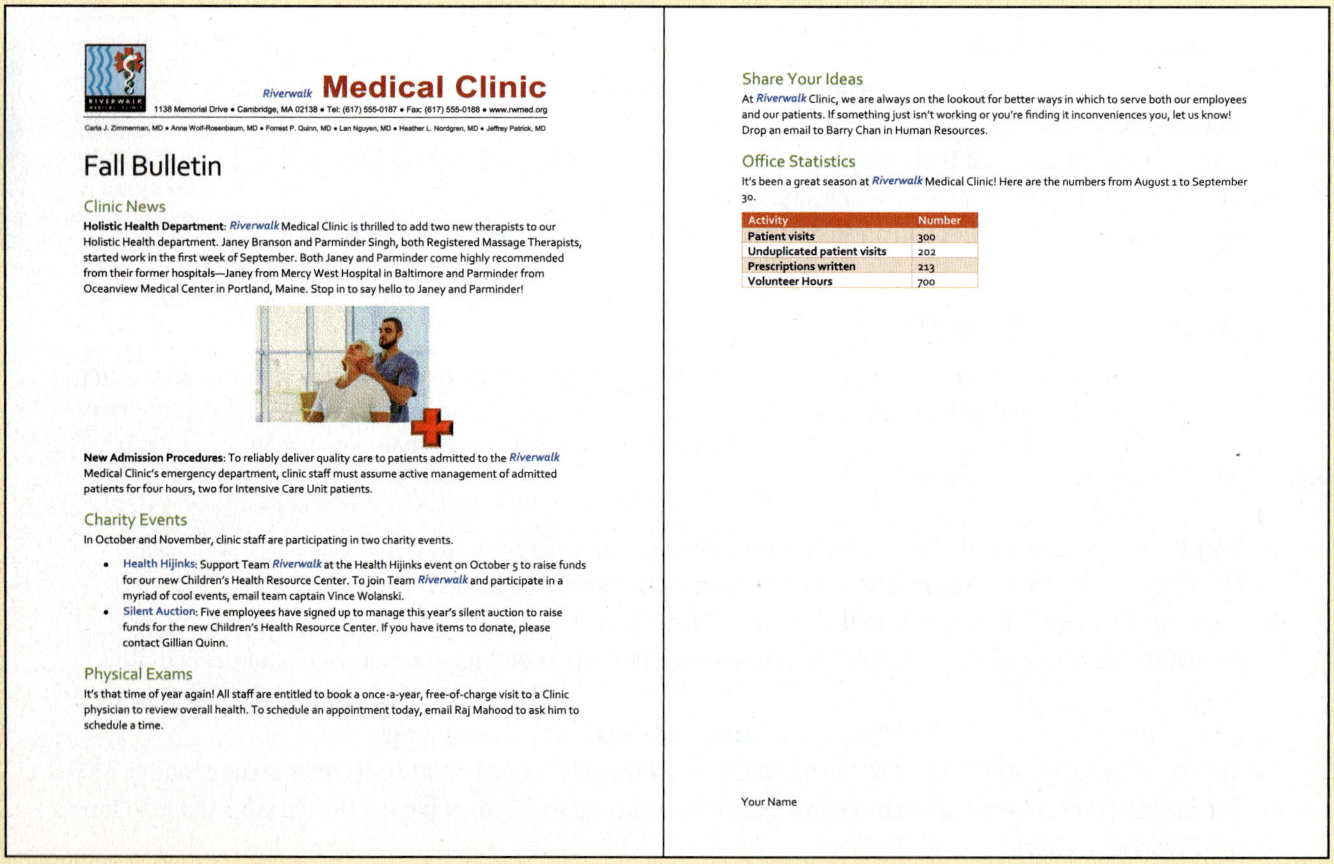

Riverwalk **Medical Clinic**

1138 Memorial Drive • Cambridge, MA 02138 • Tel: (617) 555-0187 • Fax: (617) 555-0188 • www.rwmed.org

Carla J. Zimmerman, MD • Anna Wolf-Rosenbaum, MD • Forrest P. Quinn, MD • Lan Nguyen, MD • Heather L. Nordgren, MD • Jeffrey Patrick, MD

Fall Bulletin

Clinic News

Holistic Health Department: *Riverwalk* Medical Clinic is thrilled to add two new therapists to our Holistic Health department. Janey Branson and Parminder Singh, both Registered Massage Therapists, started work in the first week of September. Both Janey and Parminder come highly recommended from their former hospitals—Janey from Mercy West Hospital in Baltimore and Parminder from Oceanview Medical Center in Portland, Maine. Stop in to say hello to Janey and Parminder!

New Admission Procedures: To reliably deliver quality care to patients admitted to the *Riverwalk* Medical Clinic's emergency department, clinic staff must assume active management of admitted patients for four hours, two for Intensive Care Unit patients.

Charity Events

In October and November, clinic staff are participating in two charity events.

- Health Hijinks: Support Team *Riverwalk* at the Health Hijinks event on October 5 to raise funds for our new Children's Health Resource Center. To join Team *Riverwalk* and participate in a myriad of cool events, email team captain Vince Wolanski.
- Silent Auction: Five employees have signed up to manage this year's silent auction to raise funds for the new Children's Health Resource Center. If you have items to donate, please contact Gillian Quinn.

Physical Exams

It's that time of year again! All staff are entitled to book a once-a-year, free-of-charge visit to a Clinic physician to review overall health. To schedule an appointment today, email Raj Mahood to ask him to schedule a time.

Share Your Ideas

At *Riverwalk* Clinic, we are always on the lookout for better ways in which to serve both our employees and our patients. If something just isn't working or you're finding it inconveniences you, let us know! Drop an email to Barry Chan in Human Resources.

Office Statistics

It's been a great season at *Riverwalk* Medical Clinic! Here are the numbers from August 1 to September 30.

Activity	Number
Patient visits	300
Unduplicated patient visits	202
Prescriptions written	213
Volunteer Hours	700

Your Name

Africa Studio/Shutterstock.com

Independent Challenge 2

You work for Hilltown Marketing in San Francisco. Over the years, clients have provided testimonials about their experiences with Hilltown Marketing. You create a macro that standardizes the formatting and then you apply it to format two testimonials.

a. Start a new blank document, show the Developer tab if it is not already displayed on the Ribbon, press ENTER three times, then save the blank document as **IL_WD_11_TestimonialMacroSetup**.

b. Open the Record Macro dialog box, then enter **Testimonial** as the macro name.

c. Enter the following description in the Description box: **Select all the text, change the line spacing to single, change the font to Times New Roman and 12 pt, apply italics, insert a fill-in text box, then save the document.**

d. Exit the Record Macro dialog box, then perform the macro steps as follows:
   1. Press CTRL+A to select all the text.
   2. Press CTRL+1 to turn on single spacing.
   3. Select the Times New Roman font.
   4. Change the font size to 12 pt.
   5. Press Ctrl+I to apply italics.
   6. Press the up arrow once.
   7. Insert a Fill-in text box and click OK.
   8. Press ENTER.
   9. Save the document.

e. From the Developer tab, stop the macro recording.

f. Type your name at the top of the document, then save and close the document but do not exit Word.

g. Open the file **IL_WD_11-10.docx**, then save it as **IL_WD_11_Testimonial1**.

h. From the Macros dialog box, run the Testimonial macro, entering **Bayside Financing** in the Fill-in text box.

i. Open the Customize the Ribbon and keyboard shortcuts screen in the Word Options dialog box, click Customize, scroll down the list of Categories, select Macros, then select the Testimonials macro in the Macros list.

j. In the Press new shortcut key box, enter the command ALT+T, click Assign, then close all dialog boxes.

k. Open the file **IL_WD_11-11.docx** from the location where you store your Data Files, then save it as **IL_WD_11_Testimonial2**.

l. Use the Alt+T macro to format the document, entering **Ace Architects** in the fill-in text box.

m. Open the Macros dialog box, select the Testimonial macro, then click Edit.

n. Find Selection.Font.Name = "Times New Roman", change the font to **Arial** and keep the quotation marks around Arial, then change Selection.Font.Size = 12 to **13**.

o. Save the macro, select all the components of the Testimonial macro in the Visual Basic window, copy them, close the Visual Basic window, press CTRL+N to open a new blank Word document, paste the code into the blank document, type **Created by** followed by your name below the last line, save the document as **IL_WD_11_TestimonialMacroCodes**, then close it.

p. Verify that IL_WD_11_Testimonial2 is the active document, then use the ALT+T keystrokes to run the revised macro. Remember to press Cancel to bypass the Fill-in text box.

q. Verify that the font style of the document title is now Arial and the font size is 13 pt, then type your name where indicated at the end of the document.

r. Customize the status bar so that the language is selected.

s. In the Language section of the Options dialog box, add English (Canada) as a proofing language, if necessary.

t. Delete Your Name in the current document, press Enter then insert a signature line that includes your name. Do not sign the document.

u. Save and close the document, then save and close the Testimonial1 document. Remove English (Canada) as a proofing language.

v. Submit a copy of all the files you created for Independent Challenge 2 to your instructor, then exit Word.

Visual Workshop

You work for Gregson Financials in Chicago. Each year, the company awards a trip to the top sales manager. You've been asked to create a poster to distribute around the company to celebrate this year's winner. Open IL_WD_11-12.docx from the location where you store your Data Files, then save it as **IL_WD_11_GregsonFinancialsPoster**. Select Kate Epstein (but not the paragraph mark following), then create a character style called **Winner** that uses these formats: Bold, Italic, 18 pt, and the Light Blue font color. Apply the Winner character style to **Tuscany**. Modify the character style by changing the font size to 14 pt and the color to Red. Format, arrange, and group the three graphic objects so the completed poster appears as shown in **FIGURE 11-30**. You will need to apply the Convex bevel effect to the sun shape and the Pastels Smooth artistic effect and 8800 K color tone to the oval picture of the Tuscany landscape. Compress all the pictures in the document to 150 ppi. Enter your name where indicated in the footer, save the document, submit a copy to your instructor, then close the document.

FIGURE 11-30

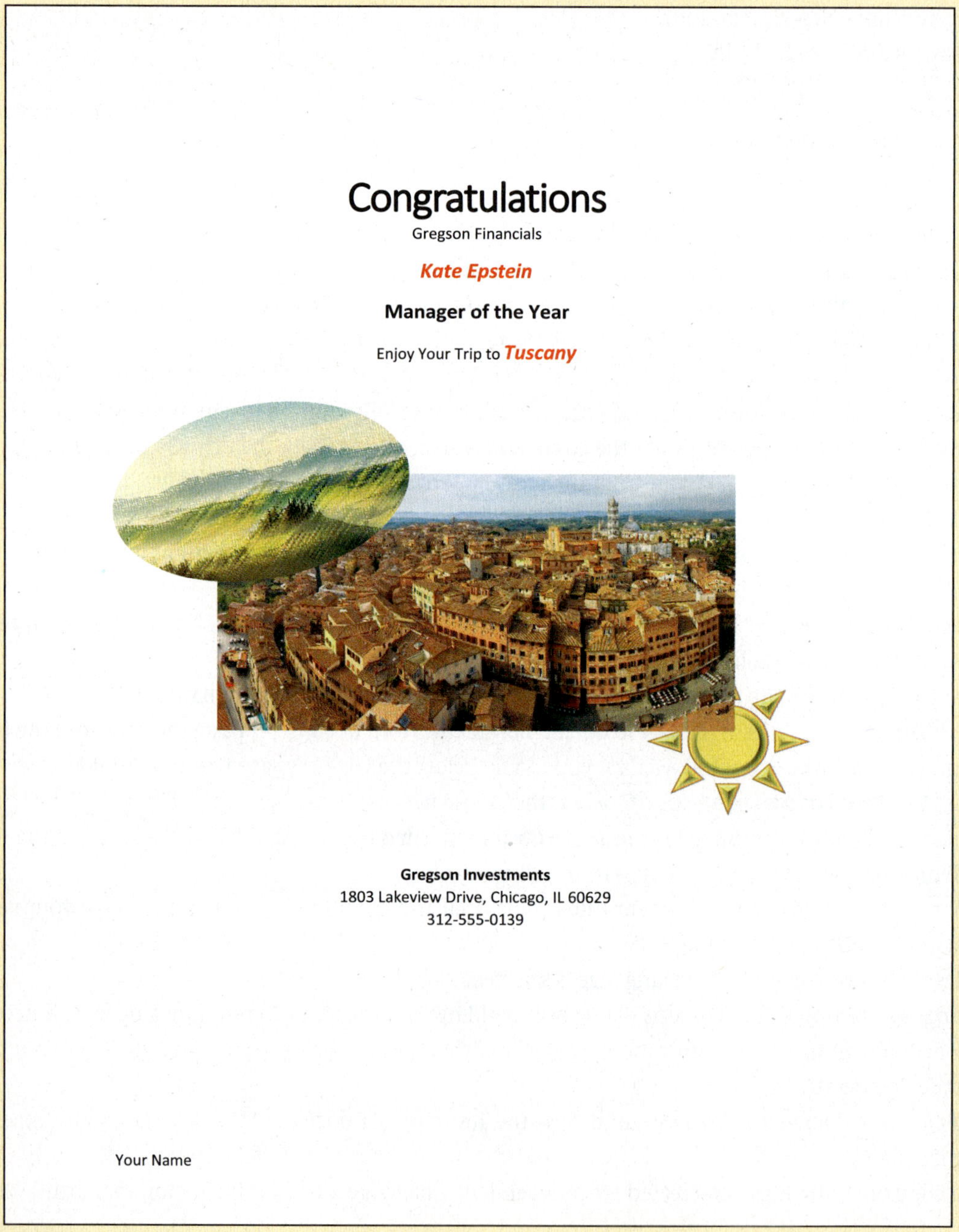

S.Borisov/Shutterstock.com; kavalenkava/Shutterstock.com

Index

A

Accessibility Checker, WD 3-19
ActiveX controls, WD 10-16
adding
Building Block content control, WD 10-12–10-13
captions, WD 9-14–9-15
Check Box content control, WD 10-10–10-11
custom header/footer to gallery, WD 4-9
Date Picker content control, WD 10-8
Drop-Down List content control, WD 10-13–10-14
hyperlink(s), WD 5-2–5-3
merge fields, WD 6-10–6-11
merge fields to main document, WD 6-2
Picture content control, WD 10-8, WD 10-9
Repeating Section content control, WD 10-10–10-11
text content control, WD 10-6–10-7
Add-ins, WD 2-11
Address Block dialog box, WD 6-11
advanced find and replace options
using, WD 9-12–9-13
Advanced Print Options, WD 9-33
Advanced Track Changes dialog box, WD 8-19
alignment
vertical, of documents, WD 5-5
Alternative text. *See* **Alt text**
Alt text, WD 11-10
adding, WD 11-11
command, WD 3-19
anchored, WD 3-14
arranging
graphics, WD 11-8–11-9
Artistic Effects command, WD 3-18
ascending order, WD 4-14
AutoComplete, WD 1-6, WD 1-7
AutoCorrect, WD 1-6, WD 1-7, WD 2-9
inserting text, WD 2-9
automatic page break, WD 2-16
automating
Word, WD 11-1–11-25

B

Back button, WD 1-9
Backstage view, WD 1-4
bar tab, WD 3-5
Basis theme, WD 5-9
bibliography, WD 2-24
creating, WD 2-24–2-25
bitmap graphics, WD 1-26
blank table, WD 3-9
blog
defined, WD 8-5
publishing directly from Word, WD 8-5
boilerplate text, WD 6-2
bookmarks
defined, WD 9-7
using, WD 9-7
borders, WD 3-6–3-7, WD 3-8
brightness, WD 3-18
Building Block content control, WD 10-12–10-13
building blocks, WD 4-9
creating, WD 5-14–5-17
defined, WD 5-14
editing properties, WD 5-17
inserting, WD 5-18–5-19
organizer, WD 5-17, WD 5-19
renaming, WD 5-17
bullet characters
customized, WD 5-12
bulleted list, WD 4-5
bullets, WD 1-24
adding, WD 1-24–1-25
applied to list, WD 1-25
buttons
Comment, WD 1-4
Controls group, WD 10-7
Save As dialog box, WD 1-9

C

captions
adding, WD 9-14–9-15
defined, WD 9-14
modifying, WD 9-14–9-15
cell, defined, WD 3-8
cell reference, WD 4-18
cells, tables
changing margins, WD 4-16
merge, WD 4-16–4-17
split, WD 4-16–4-17
split into three rows, WD 4-17
center tab, WD 3-5
Change your view button, WD 1-9
character(s)
customized bullet, WD 5-12
identifying, WD 11-10
separator, WD 10-2
character spacing
defined, WD 4-2
modifying, WD 4-2–4-3
character styles, WD 11-10
creating, WD 11-10–11-11
chart(s)
adding data labels, WD 8-13
creating, WD 8-12–8-13
defined, WD 8-12
editing, WD 8-14–8-15
formatting, WD 8-14–8-15
Check Box content control, WD 10-10
adding table form with, WD 10-11
properties, WD 10-11
Check for Issues, WD 2-27
Choose Profile dialog box, WD 6-7
citation, WD 2-22–2-23
citation dialog box, WD 2-23
Clear All Formatting, WD 3-3
Click and Type pointers, WD 1-5
Clip art, WD 3-14
Clipboard, WD 1-16
Color command, WD 3-18
color saturation, WD 3-18
color tone, WD 3-18
column(s)
copying, WD 4-10
creating, WD 7-6–7-7
deleting, WD 3-10–3-11
inserting, WD 3-10–3-11
modifying, WD 4-12–4-13
moving, WD 4-10

column(s) (*continued*)
resized, WD 4-13
selecting, WD 4-11
column break, WD 2-17
Combo Box content control, WD 10-13
entries, WD 10-14
commands on the Mailings tab, WD 6-2, WD 6-15
comment, WD 2-2
inking, WD 2-5
inserting, WD 2-2–2-5
Comment button, WD 1-4
comment entry, WD 10-23
Company property control, WD 5-13
Compare Documents dialog box, WD 8-23
Compare feature in Word, WD 8-22–8-23
compressing
graphics, WD 11-8–11-9
Compress Pictures dialog box, WD 11-9
content control, WD 2-18, WD 9-34
locking, WD 10-19
Content Control Properties dialog box, WD 10-7
contrast, WD 3-18
converting
tables, WD 10-2–10-3
text, WD 10-2–10-3
Convert Table to Text dialog box, WD 10-3
Convert Text to Table command, WD 3-9
Convert Text to Table dialog box, WD 10-3
copy, WD 1-18
copying, WD 1-18–1-19
columns in tables, WD 4-10
rows in tables, WD 4-10
Corrections command, WD 3-18
cover page
inserting, WD 4-24–4-25
Create New Building Block dialog box, WD 5-15
Create New Theme Colors dialog box, WD 5-11
Create New Theme Fonts dialog box, WD 5-11
creating
bibliography, WD 2-24–2-25
building blocks, WD 5-14–5-17
character styles, WD 11-10–11-11
charts, WD 8-12–8-13
column(s), WD 7-6–7-7
data source, WD 6-2
labels, WD 6-16–6-17
macro in Visual Basic, WD 11-21
main document, WD 6-2, WD 6-4–6-5
master documents, WD 9-36–9-37
paragraph style, WD 5-6–5-7
PowerPoint presentation from a Word outline, WD 8-9
report source, WD 2-23
screenshots, WD 9-8–9-11
section, WD 7-6–7-7
SmartArt graphic, WD 7-8–7-9
subdocuments, WD 9-36–9-37
text box, WD 7-20–7-21
WordArt, WD 7-18–7-19
cropping
picture, WD 7-12–7-13
Crop tool, WD 7-12–7-13
cross-reference, WD 9-20
defined, WD 9-6
custom footer, WD 4-9
custom header, WD 4-9
Customize Address List dialog box, WD 6-7
Customize Keyboard dialog box, WD 11-19
customizing. *See also* **modifying**
bullet characters, WD 5-12
Quick Access toolbar, WD 11-25
table format, WD 4-22–4-23
themes, WD 5-10–5-11
Word, WD 11-22–11-23
cut and paste, WD 1-15–1-16
cut text, WD 1-16

D

data
field, WD 6-2
merging, WD 6-14–6-15
merging from data source into main documents, WD 6-2
record, WD 6-2
sorting table, WD 4-14–4-15
data source
creating, WD 6-2
defined, WD 6-2
designing, WD 6-6–6-7
identifying fields to include, WD 6-2
selecting existing, WD 6-2
date format selection, WD 10-9
Date Picker content control, WD 10-8
debug, WD 11-14
decimal tab, WD 3-5
default themes, WD 5-9
Define New Bullet dialog box, WD 5-12
deleting
rows and columns, WD 3-10–3-11
demoted items list, WD 4-5
descending order, WD 4-14
designing
data source, WD 6-6–6-7
destination program, WD 8-3
digital ID
acquiring, WD 11-25
digital signature, WD 11-24
document(s), WD 1-2
applying themes to, WD 5-8–5-11
bibliography field, WD 2-25
borders and shading, WD 3-7
building in Outline view, WD 9-2–9-3
checking compatibility, WD 5-3
cloud shapes, WD 3-21
comparing, WD 8-22–8-23
copying and moving items between, WD 1-19
copying macro to another, WD 11-22
created using the Cover Letter (blue) template, WD 5-21
edited memo text, WD 1-7
formatted, WD 2-27
formatting, WD 4-1–4-25
header and footer, WD 2-19
highlighting in text, WD 1-13
inserting icons, WD 5-15
inserting online pictures, WD 7-23
inserting online videos, WD 7-23
inspecting, WD 2-26–2-27
links, WD 8-10–8-11
manual page break, WD 2-17
memo text, WD 1-7
merged, WD 6-2
modifying page margins, WD 5-4–5-5
navigating, WD 9-6–9-7
navigating using Navigation pane and Go to command, WD 2-7
new comment, WD 2-3
page number, WD 2-17
planning, WD 1-3
protecting with formatting and editing restrictions, WD 10-20
renumbered footnotes, WD 2-21
resolved comment, WD 2-5
results after inspecting, WD 2-27
saving, WD 1-8–1-9
saving as webpage, WD 5-7
screen clipping inserted, WD 9-11
setting margins, WD 1-22–1-23
shape, WD 3-19
sharing, from Word, WD 5-3

signing digitally, WD 11-24–11-25
with smaller margins, WD 5-5
splitting to copy and move items in long document, WD 1-18
starting, WD 1-6–1-7
text highlighted in, WD 2-7
using template, WD 5-20–5-21
vertical alignment, WD 5-5
viewing and navigating, WD 1-14–1-15
document properties, WD 1-14
Backstage view, WD 1-15
document window, WD 1-4
Draft view, WD 1-15
drag and drop, WD 1-16
drawing canvas, WD 3-23
drawing shapes, WD 3-18–3-21
Draw Table command, WD 3-9
Draw Table feature, WD 4-23
drop cap, WD 7-20
Drop-Down Form Field control, WD 10-16
Drop-Down List content control
adding, WD 10-13–10-14
entries, WD 10-14

E

Edit Data Source dialog box, WD 6-9
editing
charts, WD 8-14–8-15
forms, WD 10-20–10-21
macro in Visual Basic, WD 11-20–11-21
pictures, WD 11-4–11-5
properties of building blocks, WD 5-17
records, WD 6-8–6-9
template, WD 10-5
3D models, WD 7-16–7-17
Editor pane, WD 2-9
Effects command, WD 3-21
embedding
Excel file in Word file, WD 8-2–8-3
endnote(s), WD 2-20–2-21
inserting, WD 9-37
entering
records, WD 6-8–6-9
envelopes
printing, WD 6-17
Envelopes and Labels dialog box, WD 6-17
Equation Tools Design tab, WD 9-34
contents, WD 9-35
equation(s)
working, WD 9-34–9-35
Excel
chart, link/linking in Word file, WD 8-6–8-7
file, embedding in Word file, WD 8-2–8-3
Excel Spreadsheet command, WD 3-9

F

Field dialog box, WD 11-17
field names, WD 6-2
fields, WD 2-16, WD 4-15, WD 10-4
figure, defined, WD 9-14
file, WD 1-8
filename, WD 1-8
File tab, WD 1-4
filling in form as user, WD 10-22–10-23
filtering
defined, WD 6-18
records, WD 6-18–6-19
finalizing
multi-page documents, WD 9-30–9-33
Find and Replace dialog box, WD 2-7
Find and Replace text, WD 2-6–2-7
first line indent, WD 2-13
floating graphic, WD 1-26, WD 1-27
font, WD 1-20
document formatted, WD 1-20–1-21
list, WD 1-21
size, WD 1-20
footer(s), WD 2-18, WD 9-27
adding, WD 2-18–2-19
custom, WD 4-9
inserting, in multiple sections, WD 9-22–9-25
footnotes, WD 2-20–2-21
Format Painter, WD 3-2–3-3
formatting
charts, WD 8-14–8-15
clear, from text, WD 3-3
with fonts, WD 1-20–1-21
forms, WD 10-18–10-19, WD 10-21
shapes, WD 3-18–3-21
tables and documents, WD 4-1–4-25
text using Mini toolbar and ribbon, WD 1-12–1-13
with themes, WD 5-8–5-9
formatting marks, WD 1-10
form controls, WD 10-4
form contruction, WD 10-5
form(s)
ActiveX controls, WD 10-16
building, WD 10-3–10-23
Building Block content control, WD 10-12–10-13
Check Box content control, WD 10-10, WD 10-11
Combo Box content control, WD 10-13
completed, WD 10-23
Date Picker content control, WD 10-8
defined, WD 10-4
Drop-Down Form Field control, WD 10-16
Drop-Down List content control, WD 10-13–10-14
editing, WD 10-20–10-21
fields, WD 10-4
filling in as user, WD 10-22–10-23
formatting, WD 10-18–10-19, WD 10-21
Legacy Tools controls, WD 10-16
Picture content control, WD 10-8, WD 10-9
Plain Text content control, WD 10-6
protecting, WD 10-18–10-19
Repeating Section content control, WD 10-10
Rich Text content control, WD 10-6, WD 10-7
table, WD 10-3
Text control, WD 10-16
Text Form Field control, WD 10-16
unprotecting, WD 10-21
form template, WD 10-19
constructing, WD 10-4–10-5
defined, WD 10-4
Formula command, WD 4-19
Formula dialog box, WD 4-19
formulas, WD 4-19
Forward button, WD 1-9

G

generating, index, WD 9-20–9-21
Go to command, WD 2-7
graphic(s)
arranging, WD 11-8–11-9
arranging objects, WD 3-22–3-23
bitmap, WD 1-26
compressing, WD 11-8–11-9
floating, WD 1-26, WD 1-27
inline, WD 1-26
inserting, WD 1-26–1-27
objects enhancement with style and effects, WD 3-21
positioning, WD 7-14–7-17
sizing and scaling, WD 3-16–3-17
SmartArt, WD 3-24–3-25

gridlines, WD 4-17
groups, WD 1-4
gutter, WD 9-28

H

Hand pointer, WD 1-5
hanging indent, WD 2-13
header(s), WD 2-18, WD 9-27
  adding, WD 2-18–2-19
  inserting, in multiple sections, WD 9-26–9-29
header row, WD 4-14
Hide white space pointer, WD 1-5
Highlighting, WD 1-13
horizontal ruler, WD 1-4
horizontal scroll bars, WD 1-4
hyperlink(s), WD 1-10, WD 9-6
  adding, WD 5-2–5-3
  defined, WD 5-2
  in documents, WD 5-3

I

I-beam pointer, WD 1-5
icons
  inserting, in documents, WD 5–15
IF dialog box, WD 6-13
indent markers, WD 2-12
indents, WD 2-12
  changing, WD 2-12–2-13
  types, WD 2-13
  working, WD 4-4–4-5
index
  completed, WD 9-21
  cross-reference, WD 9-20
  defined, WD 9-18
  generating, WD 9-20–9-21
  marking text, WD 9-18–9-19
  subentry, WD 9-20
Index Entry, WD 9-18
individual merge fields, inserting, WD 6-19
inline graphic, WD 1-26, WD 1-27, WD 3-15
Insert Address Block dialog box, WD 6-11
Insert Hyperlink dialog box, WD 5-3
inserting
  Building Block content control, WD 10-13
  building blocks, WD 5-18–5-19
  citations, WD 2-22–2-23
  comment, WD 2-2–2-5
  cover page, WD 4-24–4-25
  endnotes, WD 9-37
  footers in multiple sections, WD 9-22–9-25
  graphic, WD 1-26–1-27
  headers in multiple sections, WD 9-26–9-29
  icons in documents, WD 5-15
  individual merge fields, WD 6-19
  Legacy Tools controls, WD 10-16–10-17
  object, WD 8-4–8-5
  Object dialog box, WD 8-7
  online pictures, WD 3-14–3-15
  online pictures, in documents, WD 7-23
  online videos, WD 7-23
  page numbers and page breaks, WD 2-16–2-17
  Quick Parts, WD 5-12–5-13
  rows and columns, WD 3-10–3-11
  section break, WD 4-6–4-9
  table, WD 3-8–3-9
  table of contents, WD 9-16–9-17
  Text Form Field control, WD 10-17
  3D models, WD 7-16–7-17
  Word file, WD 7-22–7-23
insertion point, WD 1-4
Insert Table command, WD 3-9
integral header, WD 4-9

J

job roles
  researching, WD 4-3

K

kerning, WD 4-2
keyboard shortcuts, WD 1-17
  common, WD 11-19
  finding, WD 11-19
keyword, WD 3-14

L

labels, WD 10-4
  creating, WD 6-16–6-17
  printing, WD 6-17
landscape orientation, WD 1-22
layering options, using, WD 11-6–11-7
Layout dialog box, WD 7-17
left indent, WD 2-13
left tab, WD 3-5
Legacy Tools controls, WD 10-16
line numbers
  configuring, WD 7-22
line spacings, WD 2-12–2-13
linked styles, identifying, WD 11-10
link/linking
  defined, WD 7-21
  document links, WD 8-10–8-11
  Excel chart in Word file, WD 8-6–8-7
  PowerPoint slide to Word, WD 8-8–8-9
  text boxes, WD 7-21
Links dialog box, WD 8-11
list(s)
  bulleted, WD 4-5
  demoted items, WD 4-5
  multilevel, WD 4-5
  Outlook contact, WD 6-7
  sorting, WD 4-15
locking content control, WD 10-19

M

macro
  copying to another document, WD 11-22
  creating in Visual Basic, WD 11-21
  defined, WD 11-14
  editing in Visual Basic, WD 11-20–11-21
  errors, WD 11-14
  information, WD 11-14
  pausing when recording, WD 11-17
  planning, WD 11-14–11-15
  recording procedure, WD 11-14
  recording steps, WD 11-16–11-17
  running, WD 11-18–11-19
  steps, WD 11-14
macro tasks, WD 11-14, WD 11-15
  steps to complete, WD 11-15
mail merge
  defined, WD 6-2
  process, WD 6-3
  understanding, WD 6-2–6-3
Mail Merge pane, WD 6-2
mail merge template
  using, WD 6-5
main documents
  adding merge fields, WD 6-2
  creating, WD 6-2, WD 6-4–6-5
  defined, WD 6-2
  merging data from data source into, WD 6-2
Manage Document, WD 2-27
managing
  pages, WD 11-2–11-3
  styles, WD 11-12–11-13
manual page break, WD 2-16
margins, WD 1-22
  mirror, WD 1-23
  setting document, WD 1-22–1-23

Margins tab, WD 5-5
master documents
creating, WD 9-36–9-37
defined, WD 9-36
Match Fields dialog box, WD 6-5
matching fields, WD 6-11
merge cells, WD 4-16–4-17
merge data, WD 6-14–6-15
merged document, defined, WD 6-2
Merge Field dialog box, WD 6-19
merge fields
adding, WD 6-10–6-11
adding to main document, WD 6-2
defined, WD 6-2
inserting individual, WD 6-19
merge files
opening, WD 6-15
merge rules, WD 6-12–6-13
merging, data from data source into main document, WD 6-2
Microsoft Visual Basic window, WD 11-20
Microsoft Word 2019. *See also* **document(s)**
adding bullets or numbering, WD 1-24–1-25
adding footnotes and endnotes, WD 2-20–2-21
adding headers and footers, WD 2-18–2-19
applying style to text, WD 2-14–2-15
applying table style, WD 3-12–3-13
applying theme, WD 1-28–1-29
borders, WD 3-6–3-7
copying and pasting text, WD 1-18–1-19
creating bibliography, WD 2-24–2-25
creating SmartArt graphic, WD 3-24–3-25
cut and paste text, WD 1-16–1-17
drawing and formatting shapes, WD 3-18–3-21
exploring window, WD 1-4–1-5
Find and Replace text, WD 2-6–2-7
formatting text using Mini toolbar and ribbon, WD 1-12–1-13
formatting with fonts, WD 1-20–1-21
graphics objects, WD 3-22–3-23
inserting and deleting rows and columns, WD 3-10–3-11
inserting citations, WD 2-22–2-23
inserting comment, WD 2-2–2-5
inserting graphics, WD 1-26–1-27
inserting Online Pictures, WD 3-14–3-15
inserting page numbers and page breaks, WD 2-16–2-17
inserting table, WD 3-8–3-9
inspecting document, WD 2-26–2-27
line spacings and indents, WD 2-12–2-13
mouse pointers, WD 1-5
Read Aloud feature, WD 2-10
report created using, WD 1-3
research information, WD 2-10–2-11
saving document, WD 1-8–1-9
selecting text, WD 1-10–1-11
setting document margins, WD 1-22–1-23
shading, WD 3-6–3-7
sizing and scaling graphics, WD 3-16–3-17
Spelling and Grammar, WD 2-8–2-9
starting document, WD 1-6–1-7
tabs, WD 3-4–3-5
using, WD 1-2
using Format Painter, WD 3-2–3-3
viewing and navigating document, WD 1-14–1-15
Mini toolbar, WD 1-12
buttons, WD 1-13
mirror margins, WD 1-23
Modify Building Block dialog box, WD 5-17
modifying
captions, WD 9-14–9-15
character spacing, WD 4-2–4-3
page margins, WD 5-4–5-5
rows and columns, WD 4-12–4-13
screenshots, WD 9-8–9-11
SmartArt graphic, WD 7-10–7-11
table, WD 4-10–4-11
table style options, WD 4-20–4-21
mouse pointers, WD 1-5
moving
columns in tables, WD 4-10
rows in tables, WD 4-10
multilevel list, WD 4-5
creating, WD 4-4
multi-page documents
adding captions, WD 9-14–9-15
building in Outline view, WD 9-2–9-3
creating and modifying screenshots, WD 9-8–9-11
creating master documents, WD 9-36–9-37
creating subdocuments, WD 9-36–9-37
finalizing, WD 9-30–9-33
generating an index, WD 9-20–9-21
insert footers in multiple sections, WD 9-22–9-25
inserting headers in multiple sections, WD 9-26–9-29
inserting table of contents, WD 9-16–9-17
marking text for an index, WD 9-18–9-19
modifying captions, WD 9-14–9-15
navigating, WD 9-6–9-7
using advanced find and replace options, WD 9-12–9-13
working in Outline view, WD 9-4–9-5
working with equations, WD 9-34–9-35

N

navigating
document, WD 1-14–1-15
multi-page documents, WD 9-6–9-7
Navigation pane, WD 2-7, WD 9-6
changing order of subheading, WD 9-7
negative indent, WD 2-13
nested tables, WD 4-17
New Address List dialog box, WD 6-6–6-7, WD 6-9
New folder button, WD 1-9
non-native files, WD 5-23
Normal style, WD 1-6
note reference mark, WD 2-20
numbered library, WD 1-25
numbered list, WD 1-25
numbering
adding, WD 1-24–1-25

O

object
defined, WD 8-4
inserting, WD 8-4–8-5
Object dialog box, WD 8-3, WD 8-5
for creating linked file, WD 8-7
object linking and embedding (OLE), WD 8-3. *See also* link/linking
Office Clipboard, WD 1-16
paste options, WD 7-5
using, WD 7-2–7-5
online pictures
inserting, 3-14–3-15
inserting, in documents, WD 7-23
online videos
inserting, in documents, WD 7-23
Options command, WD 3-21
Organize button, WD 1-9
Organizer dialog box, WD 11-13, WD 11-22
orphan, defined, WD 11-2
outdent, WD 2-13
Outline view, WD 1-15
building document, WD 9-2–9-3
multi-page documents, WD 9-4–9-5

Outline view, *(continued)*
subdocument selected, WD 9-37
subdocuments inserted, WD 9-37
text, WD 9-3
working, WD 9-4–9-5
Outlook contact lists, WD 6-7
Outlook data source, WD 6-7

P

page break, WD 2-17
automatic, WD 2-16
inserting, WD 2-16–2-17
manual, WD 2-16
page layout settings
changing, for section, WD 7-7
page margins
modifying, WD 5-4–5-5
page numbers, inserting, WD 2-16–2-17
Page Setup dialog box, WD 5-5
Page Setup options, WD 5-4
pages, managing, WD 11-2–11-3
paragraph(s)
identifying, WD 11-10
sorting, WD 4-15
paragraph style
creating, WD 5-6–5-7
defined, WD 5-6
style set, WD 5-8
Paragraph group, WD 4-4
Paste All button, WD 8-17
Paste options, WD 8-7
Paste Options feature, WD 7-4–7-5
Paste Special dialog box, WD 8-9
paste, text, WD 1-16, WD 1-18–1-19
picture(s)
applying 3-D and 3-D rotation effects, WD 11-5
applying an artistic effect, WD 11-5
cropping, WD 7-12–7-13
editing, WD 11-4–11-5
rotating, WD 7-12–7-13
Picture content control, WD 10-8, WD 10-9
Picture dialog box, WD 7-14
Picture Tools Format tab, WD 11-4–11-6, WD 11-8
Plain Text content control, WD 10-6
planning
documents, WD 1-3
macro, WD 11-14–11-15
point, WD 1-20
Portable Document Format (PDF) file
open in Word, WD 5-23
working with, in Word, WD 5-22–5-23
portrait orientation, WD 1-22
positioning
graphic(s), WD 7-14–7-17
PowerPoint
link/linking slide, to Word, WD 8-8–8-9
presentation from a Word outline, WD 8-9
printing
individual envelopes, WD 6-17
labels, WD 6-17
Print Layout view, WD 1-15
property control, WD 4-8, WD 5-12
Protect Document, WD 2-27
protecting
documents with formatting and editing restrictions, WD 10-20
forms, WD 10-18–10-19

Q

Quick Access toolbar, WD 1-4
customizing, WD 11-25
Quick Parts feature, WD 5-12–5-13
Quick Parts gallery, WD 5-17
Quick Tables command, WD 3-9

R

Read Aloud feature, WD 2-10
Read Mode view, WD 1-15
recording
macro procedure, WD 11-14
macro steps, WD 11-16–11-17
Record Macro dialog box, WD 11-14, WD 11-17
records
editing, WD 6-8–6-9
entering, WD 6-8–6-9
filtering, WD 6-18–6-19
identifying fields to enter, WD 6-2
sorting, WD 6-18–6-19
Redo command, WD 1-11
renaming
building blocks, WD 5-17
Repeat command, WD 1-11
Repeating Section content control, WD 10-10
adding button, WD 10-11
report source, creating, WD 2-23
researching job roles, WD 4-3
resizing
columns in tables, WD 4-13
rows in tables, WD 4-13
Restrict Editing button, WD 10-20
Resume Assistant, WD 4-3
Reveal Formatting pane, WD 5-7
reviewers, managing, WD 8-20–8-21
Review tab, WD 8-20–8-21
ribbon
formatting text using, WD 1-12–1-13
Ribbon Display Options button, WD 1-4
Rich Text content control, WD 10-6, WD 10-7
right indent, WD 2-13
Right-pointing arrow pointer, WD 1-5
right tab, WD 3-5
rotate handle, WD 1-26
rotating
picture, WD 7-12–7-13
rows
deleting, WD 3-10–3-11
inserting, WD 3-10–3-11
rows, tables
copying, WD 4-10
modifying, WD 4-12–4-13
moving, WD 4-10
running
macro, WD 11-18–11-19

S

save, WD 1-8
documents, WD 1-8–1-9
Save As command, WD 1-14
Save As dialog box, WD 1-9
Save command, WD 1-14
scale, WD 3-16
screen clipping
inserted in the document, WD 9-11
selecting, WD 9-11
Screenshot button, WD 9-8
screenshots
creating, WD 9-8–9-11
cropped, WD 9-9
modifying, WD 9-8–9-11
thumbnail of window available for, WD 9-9
ScreenTip, WD 1-4
scroll, WD 1-14
scroll arrows, WD 1-4
scroll boxes, WD 1-4
Search box, WD 1-4
section(s), WD 9-27
changing page layout settings, WD 7-7
creating, WD 7-6–7-7
defined, WD 4-6, WD 7-6
varying layout of document, WD 4-7
section breaks, WD 7-6
continuous, WD 7-7
defined, WD 4-6

inserting, WD 4-6–4-9
Next Page, WD 4-7
types of, WD 7-7
select, WD 1-10
Selection pane, WD 11-6
moving an object, WD 11-7
Selection pointer, WD 1-5
separator character, WD 10-2
shading, WD 3-6–3-7
shapes
drawing, WD 3-18–3-21
formatting, WD 3-18–3-21
Share button, WD 1-4
shortcut key, WD 1-8, WD 1-17
Show white space pointer, WD 1-5
sidebar, WD 5-2
Signature Setup dialog box, WD 11-25
signing
document digitally, WD 11-24–11-25
sizing handles, WD 1-26
SmartArt graphic, WD 3-24–3-25, WD 7-8
categories, WD 7-9
creating, WD 7-8–7-9
inserting picture, WD 7-9
modifying, WD 7-10–7-11
options for moving shapes, WD 7-11
sized and formatted picture, WD 7-9
Sort dialog box, WD 4-15
Sorted table, WD 4-15
sorting
defined, WD 4-14, WD 6-18
lists, WD 4-15
paragraphs, WD 4-15
records, WD 6-18–6-19
table data, WD 4-14–4-15
Source Manager dialog box, WD 2-25
source program, WD 8-3
Spelling and Grammar, WD 1-7, WD 2-8–2-9
split cells, WD 4-16–4-17
Split Cells dialog box, WD 4-17
status bar, WD 1-4
customize, WD 11-23
Style gallery, WD 5-7
styles, WD 2-14
applying to text, WD 2-14–2-15
linked, WD 11-10
managing, WD 11-12–11-13
more ways to manage, WD 11-13
style sets, WD 2-14, WD 5–8
changing, WD 2-15
subdocuments
creating, WD 9-36–9-37
defined, WD 9-36
inserted in Outline view, WD 9-37
selected in Outline view, WD 9-37
subentry, WD 9-20
SUM function, WD 4–19
symbol gallery, WD 3-3

T

tab, WD 1-4
types, WD 3-5
working, WD 3-4–3-5
table of authorities, WD 9-15
table of contents
formatted, WD 9-17
inserting, WD 9-16–9-17
inserting automatic, WD 9-17
revised, WD 9-31
updated, WD 9-17, WD 9-27
table of figures
defined, WD 9-14
table(s), WD 3-8
blank, WD 3-9
cell references, WD 4-19
completed, WD 4-23
customizing format, WD 4-22–4-23
difference calculated, WD 4-19
formatting, WD 4-1–4-25
Gallery of shading colors from Green theme, WD 4-23
inserting, WD 3-8–3-9
menu commands, WD 3-9
modifying, WD 4-10–4-11
new row, WD 3-9, WD 4-11
performing calculations, WD 4-18–4-19
text, WD 3-9
tab leaders, WD 3-4, WD 3-5
table style, WD 3-12–3-13
table style options
modifying, WD 4-20–4-21
tab stop, WD 3-4–3-5
Tell Me what you want to do box, WD 1-4
template
defined, WD 5–20
editing, WD 10-5
using document, WD 5-20–5-21
text
applying shadows, WD 1-21
applying text effects, WD 1-21
apply styles, WD 2-14–2-15
boilerplate, WD 6-2
clear formatting, WD 3-3
copying and pasting, WD 1-18–1-19
cut and paste, WD 1-16–1-17
dragging and dropping, WD 1-16, WD 1-17
Find and Replace, WD 2-6–2-7
formatting using Mini toolbar and ribbon, WD 1-12–1-13
marking for an index, WD 9-18–9-19
methods for selecting, WD 1-11
moving with Paste option, WD 1-17
Outline view, WD 9-3
selecting, WD 1-10–1-11
underlining, WD 3-6
text box
creating, WD 7-20–7-21
linking, WD 7-21
sized and positioned, WD 7-21
text enclosed, WD 7-21
text content control
adding, WD 10-6–10-7
Plain Text content control, WD 10-6
Rich Text content control, WD 10-6–10-7
types, WD 10-6
Text control, WD 10-16
text flow options, WD 9-25
Text Form Field control
defined, WD 10-16
inserting, WD 10-17
Text Form Field Options dialog box, WD 10-17
text selection, WD 1-10–1-11
methods, WD 1-11
text wrapping, WD 2-17
theme(s), WD 1-20, WD 1-28–1-29
applying, to documents, WD 5-8–5-11
changing default, WD 5-9
customizing, WD 5-10–5-11
formatting, WD 5-8–5-9
Thesaurus pane, WD 2-11
3D models
editing, WD 7-16–7-17
inserting, WD 7-16–7-17
3-D rotation effects
applying to picture, WD 11-5
title bar, WD 1-4
Title property control, WD 5-13
toggle button, WD 1-10
track changes, WD 8-16–8-17
using paste, WD 8-17
using Paste All button, WD 8-17
work, WD 8-18–8-19
Track Changes command, WD 8-16–8-17

U

Undo command, WD 1-11
Up to button, WD 1-9

V

vertical alignment of documents, WD 5-5
vertical buttons, WD 1-4
vertical ruler, WD 1-4
view buttons, WD 1-4
viewing
document, WD 1-14–1-15
Visual Basic
creating macro, WD 11-21
editing macro, WD 11-20–11-21
Visual Basic codes, WD 11-16

W

watermark, WD 4-24
Web Layout view, WD 1-15
webpage
saving documents, WD 5-7
Web publication source, WD 2-23
widow, defined, WD 11-2
Widow/Orphan control, WD 11-2
Word
automating, WD 11-1–11-25
checking compatibility of documents, WD 5-3
column chart created, WD 8-13
Compare feature, WD 8-22–8-23
customizing, WD 11-22–11-23
inserting icons in documents, WD 5-15
linking PowerPoint slide, WD 8-8–8-9
opening non-native files directly, WD 5-23
outline, and PowerPoint presentation, WD 8-9
publishing a blog directly, WD 8-5
Quick Parts feature, WD 5-12–5-13
sharing documents, WD 5-3
working with Portable Document Format (PDF) file, WD 5-22–5-23
WordArt, WD 1-21
creating, WD 7-18–7-19
defined, WD 7-18
formatted, WD 7-19
gallery, WD 7-19
Word Count dialog box, WD 2-11
Word file
embedding Excel file, WD 8-2–8-3
inserting, WD 7-22–7-23
link/linking Excel chart, WD 8-6–8-7
Word Options dialog box, WD 11-19
categories, WD 11-23
word processing program, WD 1-2
Word program window, WD 1-4–1-5
Word Researcher tool, WD 2-25
word wrap, WD 1-6
works cited, WD 2-24

X

XE field code, WD 9-18

Z

ZIP Code, WD 6-2, WD 6-19
Zoom level button, WD 1-4
Zoom slider, WD 1-4, WD 1-15